PowerPoint 2000
A PROFESSIONAL APPROACH

Sharon Fisher-Larson
Elgin Community College
Elgin, IL

Margaret Marple
MMPC
West Wardsboro, VT

Glencoe
McGraw-Hill

New York, New York   Columbus, Ohio   Woodland Hills, California   Peoria, Illinois

This program has been prepared with the assistance of Gleason Group, Inc., Norwalk, CT.

Editorial Director: Pamela Ross

Developmental Editors: Pamela Ross, Rose Anderson, Terry Hicks

Copy Editor: Malinda McCain, Vickie West, Beth Conover

Composition: PDS Associates, Creative Ink, Inc.

Screens were captured using FullShot 97 For Windows from Inbit Incorporated, Mountain View, CA.

Glencoe/McGraw-Hill

A Division of The **McGraw·Hill** *Companies*

PowerPoint 2000: A Professional Approach
Student Edition
ISBN 0-02-805599-3

4   5   6   7   8   9   10   071   04   03   02   01

Contents

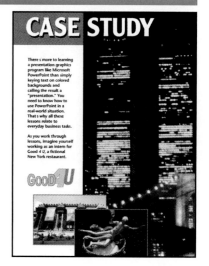

UNIT 2

Developing a Presentation

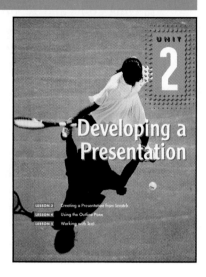

UNIT 3

Customizing a Presentation

UNIT 4

Advanced Techniques   303

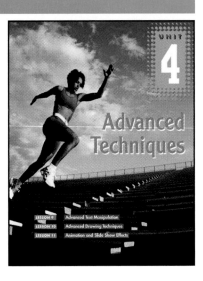

UNIT 5

Charts and Tables   405

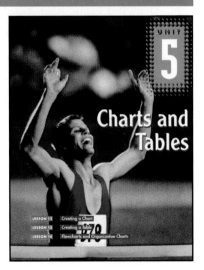

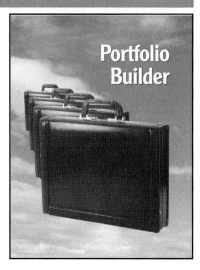

Appendices A-1

Appendices

A Windows Tutorial
B Using the Mouse
C Using Menus and Dialog Boxes
D File Management
E Proofreaders Marks
F MOUS Certification
G Advanced Presentation Delivery Options

Preface

PowerPoint 2000 is written to help you master Microsoft PowerPoint for Windows. The text takes you step-by-step through the PowerPoint features that you're likely to use in both your personal and business life.

Case Study

Learning about the features of PowerPoint is one thing, but applying what you learn is another. That's why a *Case Study* runs through the text. The Case Study offers the opportunity to learn PowerPoint in a realistic business context. Take the time to read the Case Study about Good 4 U, a fictional restaurant set in New York City. All the presentations for this course involve Good 4 U.

Organization of the Text

The text includes six *units*. Each unit is divided into smaller *lessons*. There are 15 lessons, each building on previously learned procedures. This building block approach, together with the Case Study and the features listed below, enable you to maximize the learning process.

Features of the Text

- ☑ *Objectives* are listed for each lesson
- ☑ Required skills for the *Microsoft Office User Specialist (MOUS) Certification Program* are listed for each lesson
- ☑ The *estimated time* required to complete each lesson (up to the Concepts Review) is stated
- ☑ Within a lesson, each *heading* corresponds to an objective
- ☑ Easy-to-follow *Exercises* emphasize "learning by doing"
- ☑ *Key terms* are italicized and defined as they are encountered
- ☑ Extensive *graphics* display screen contents
- ☑ *Toolbar buttons* and *keyboard keys* are shown in the text when they are used
- ☑ *Large toolbar buttons in the margins* provide easy-to-see references
- ☑ Lessons contain important *Notes* and useful *Tips*
- ☑ A *Command Summary* lists the commands learned in the lesson
- ☑ *Using Help* introduces you to a Help topic related to the content of the lesson
- ☑ *Concepts Review* includes true/false, short answer, and critical thinking questions that focus on lesson content
- ☑ *Skills Review* provides skill reinforcement for each lesson

  ☑ *Lesson Applications* ask you to apply your skills in a more challenging way

  ☑ *Unit Applications* give you the opportunity to use the skills you learn in a unit

  ☑ Appendices

  ☑ Glossary

  ☑ Index

Microsoft Office User Specialist (MOUS) Certification Program

The Microsoft Office User Specialist (MOUS) certification program offers certification at two skill levels—"Core" and "Expert." This certification can be a valuable asset in any job search. For more information about this Microsoft program, go to www.mous.net. For a complete listing of the MOUS skills for the PowerPoint 2000 certification exam (and a correlation to the lessons in the text), see Appendix F: "MOUS Certification."

Conventions Used in the Text

This text uses a number of conventions to help you learn the program and save your work.

- Text that you're asked to key appears either in **boldface** or as a separate figure.

- Filenames appear in **boldface**.

- You're asked to save each presentation with your initials, followed by the exercise name. For example, an exercise may end with the instruction: "Save the presentation as *[your initials]*5-12.ppt." Presentations are saved in folders for each lesson after the first lesson.

- Menu letters you can key to activate a command are shown as they appear on screen, with the letter underlined (for example, "Choose Print from the File menu"). Dialog box options are also shown this way, and they appear in title case to increase readability (for example, in the Header and Footer dialog box, "Date and Time" rather than "Date and time").

If You Are Unfamiliar with Windows

If you're unfamiliar with Windows 98, you'll want to work through *Appendix A: "Windows Tutorial"* before beginning Lesson 1. You may also need to review *Appendix B: "Using the Mouse," Appendix C: "Using Menus and Dialog Boxes,"* and *Appendix D: "File Management"* if you've never used a mouse or any version of Windows before.

Screen Differences

As you read about and practice each concept, illustrations of the screens help you follow the instructions. Don't worry if your screen is different from the illustration. These differences are due to variations in system and computer configurations.

Acknowledgments

We want to thank the reviewers of this text and the students and teachers who used this book in the past for their valuable assistance. We would particularly like to thank the following reviewers: Mary Davey, Computer Learning Network, Camp Hill, PA; and Pamela Wiese, Hartnell College, San Jose, CA.

Installation Requirements

You'll need Microsoft PowerPoint 2000 (from Microsoft Office 2000) to work through this textbook. PowerPoint needs to be installed on the computer's hard drive (or on a network). Use the following checklist to evaluate installation requirements.

Hardware

- ☑ Pentium computer with 32 MB or more of RAM
- ☑ 3.5-inch high-density disk drive and CD-ROM drive
- ☑ 200 MB or more of hard disk space for a "Typical" Office installation
- ☑ VGA or higher-resolution video monitor
- ☑ Printer (laser or ink-jet recommended)
- ☑ Mouse
- ☑ *Optional:* Modem

Software

- ☑ PowerPoint 2000 (from Microsoft Office 2000)
- ☑ Windows 95 (or later) or Microsoft Windows NT Workstation 4.0 with Service Pack 3.0 installed
- ☑ *Optional:* Browser (and Internet Service Provider)

Installing New Features

Some Lessons take advantage of PowerPoint or Office features that are not installed during a "Typical" installation. The following table lists those features, explains their use, and indicates where you can find the features in the Setup program. The procedure after the table explains how to install a feature.

Non-"Typical" Features Used in Lessons

LESSON	FEATURE	USE	LOCATION IN SETUP PROGRAM
Lesson 2	Company Meeting wizard	Required to complete Exercise 2–18	Microsoft PowerPoint for Windows; Content Templates; Additional Content Templates
Lesson 3	Design templates	Install to provide more variety. Used throughout course.	Microsoft PowerPoint for Windows; Content Templates; Additional Design Templates
Lesson 4	Import an outline from Word	Required to complete Exercises 4–9 and 4–15	Microsoft Office; Converters and Filters
Lesson 5	Picture bullets	Install to provide more variety. Not required.	Office Tools; Clip Gallery; Clip Files
Lesson 6	Clip art	Install to provide more variety. Used throughout course.	Office Tools; Clip Gallery
Lesson 11	Sound clips and movie clips	Install to provide more variety. Used from this point forward in the course.	Office Tools; Clip Gallery
Lesson 14	Organization chart	Required to complete the Lesson.	Office Tools; Organization Chart
Lesson 15	Pack and Go	Required to complete the Lesson.	Microsoft PowerPoint for Windows; Pack and Go Wizard

To install a feature:

1. Close all programs.
2. Click the Windows Start button, point to Settings, and click Control Panel.
3. Double-click the Add/Remove Programs icon.
4. Display the Install/Uninstall tab, if necessary.
5. If you installed PowerPoint using the Office Setup program, choose Microsoft Office from the list of programs and click Add/Remove. If you installed PowerPoint individually, choose Microsoft PowerPoint from the list and click Add/Remove.
6. Click the plus sign to the left of an Office feature to expand the options. Click the down arrow to the right of a feature you want to add and choose Run All From My Computer. When you're done choosing features, click Update Now. Follow the onscreen instructions (which include loading the Office CD-ROM).

CASE STUDY

There's more to learning a presentation graphics program like Microsoft PowerPoint than simply keying text on colored backgrounds and calling the result a "presentation." You need to know how to use PowerPoint in a real-world situation. That's why all these lessons relate to everyday business tasks.

As you work through lessons, imagine yourself working as an intern for Good *4 U*, a fictional New York restaurant.

Good 4 U

900 Central Park South
New York, NY 10019
(212) 555-4663

Good *4 U* has been in business for only a little over three years—but it's been a success from the time it served its first veggie burger. The restaurant—which features healthy food and has a theme based on the "everyday active life"—seems to have found an award-winning recipe for success.

The food at Good *4 U* is all low-fat. The menu features lots of vegetables (all organic, of course!), as well as fish and chicken. The restaurant doesn't serve alcohol, instead offering fruit juices and sparkling water.

Good *4 U*'s theme of "everyday active life" is reflected on the restaurant's walls with running, tennis, and bicycling memorabilia. (The pictures opening each unit in the text depict some of the sports activities enjoyed by regular customers.)

Working As an Intern

You'll be working as an intern at Good *4 U*. This position gives you a chance to experience working with most of the company's departments. Good *4 U* management stresses that this experience is your "trial period" in which you have an opportunity to demonstrate your skills.

Good *4 U* expects that any incoming employee will have a solid foundation of skills.*

• Basic Skills
Reading, writing, arithmetic/mathematics, listening, and speaking

• Thinking Skills
Creative thinking, decision making, problem solving, being able to visualize problems and solutions, knowing how to learn, and reasoning

• Personal Qualities
Responsibility, self-esteem, sociability, self-management, and integrity/honesty

In addition, Good 4 U believes that the five competencies identified below are the keys to job-performance.

Keys to Successful Job-Performance*

1. **Resources: Identifies, organizes, plans, and allocates resources**
   A. *Time*—Selects goal-relevant activities, ranks them, allocates time, and prepares and follows schedules.
   B. *Money*—Uses or prepares budgets, makes forecasts, keeps records, and makes adjustments to meet objectives.
   C. *Material and Facilities*—Acquires, stores, allocates, and uses materials or space efficiently.
   D. *Human Resources*—Assesses skills and distributes work accordingly, evaluates performance and provides feedback.

2. **Interpersonal: Works with others**
   A. *Participates as a Member of a Team*—Contributes to the group effort.
   B. *Teaches Others New Skills*
   C. *Serves Clients/Customers*—Works to satisfy customers' expectations.
   D. *Exercises Leadership*—Communicates ideas to justify a position, persuades and convinces others, responsibly challenges existing procedures and policies.
   E. *Negotiates*—Works toward agreements involving exchanges of resources, resolves differing interests.
   F. *Works with Diversity*—Works well with men and women from diverse backgrounds.

3. **Information: Acquires and uses information**
   A. *Acquires and Evaluates Information*
   B. *Organizes and Maintains Information*
   C. *Interprets and Communicates Information*
   D. *Uses Computers to Process Information*

4. **Systems: Understands complex relationships**
   A. *Understands Systems*—knows how social, organizational, and technological systems work and operates effectively with them.
   B. *Monitors and Corrects Performance*—Distinguishes trends, predicts impacts on system operations, diagnoses systems' performance and corrects malfunctions.
   C. *Improves or Designs Systems*—Suggests modifications to existing systems and develops new or alternative systems to improve performance.

5. **Technology: Works with a variety of technologies**
   A. *Selects Technology*—Chooses procedures, tools or equipment including computers and related technologies
   B. *Applies Technology to Task*—Understands overall intent and proper procedures for setup and operation of equipment.
   C. *Maintains and Troubleshoots Equipment*—Prevents, identifies, or solves problems with equipment, including computers and other technologies.

* These skills and competencies were identified by the Secretary of Labor and the Secretary's Commission on Achieving Necessary Skills (SCANS). They are included in the report *What Work Requires of Schools: A SCANS Report for America 2000*, published in June, 1991, by the U.S. Department of Labor.

Key People at GooD4U

In your work as an intern, you'll have a chance to meet many of the people who work at Good *4 U*. You will certainly interact with the four key people profiled here. In fact, you'll be doing most of your work for Roy Olafsen, the Marketing Manager.

Gus Irvinelli
Co-owner

Gus Irvinelli was formerly a New York real-estate developer. He's an avid tennis player and was selected for the U.S. Amateur team. When he's not working at the restaurant or playing tennis, Gus runs an adoption program for greyhounds that have been retired from dog tracks. He can often be seen running in Central Park with one of his three greyhounds.

Julie Wolfe
Co-owner

Julie Wolfe led the New York Flash to two Women's Professional Basketball Association championships in her ten years with the team. When she retired, she started Good *4 U*, explaining that "it was the sort of restaurant that I wanted to go to, but could never find." Today Julie keeps active by running in marathons. She's run in the New York City Marathon every year since she retired from basketball.

Roy Olafsen
Marketing Manager

Two years ago, Roy Olafsen was a marketing manager for a large hotel chain. He was overweight and out-of-shape. In the same week that his doctor told him to eat better and exercise regularly, Roy received a job offer from Good *4 U*. "It was too good to pass up," he says. "It was my chance to combine work and a healthy life style." On weekends or weeknights, Roy can be seen with his family skating in the park.

Michele Jenkins
Head Chef

Michele started her cooking career at the Culinary Institute of America in Hyde Park, New York. After working for five years in an upscale restaurant in New York, she quit to take a position in a small restaurant in the Provence region of France. While in France, Michele began long-distance bicycling. Now, she rides ten miles every day in and around Central Park.

In your first meeting with Roy Olafsen, he gave you the following tips for designing presentations. These tips can be applied to any presentation, but can be modified, as needed.

Tips for Designing Presentations

✔ Every presentation should have a title slide. Make sure the title relates to the presentation content.

✔ Maintain a consistent color scheme throughout the presentation.

✔ Keep the background simple, making sure the text can be seen clearly.

✔ Avoid long lines of text. Avoid too many lines of text. No line should consist of more than seven words; no slide should consist of more than seven lines.

✔ Avoid small text. Text on slides should be no smaller than 24 points, text for overheads should be no smaller than 18 points.

✔ For bulleted text, avoid using a single bullet or more than five bullets per slide. Don't use more than two levels of bullets.

✔ Use consistent wording in bulleted text.

✔ Use clip art that relates to the content and doesn't distract from the message. Avoid the temptation to "jazz up" a slide show with too much clip art.

✔ Keep charts simple. The most effective charts are pie charts with three or four slices and column charts with three or four columns.

✔ Provide some form of handout so your audience can keep track of the presentation.

✔ Your final slide should provide a recommendation or summary.

Sample PowerPoint Presentation

This is a sample presentation to be delivered onscreen (on a computer) in a conference room. The audience includes Good *4 U* sales and marketing staff and the restaurant owners.

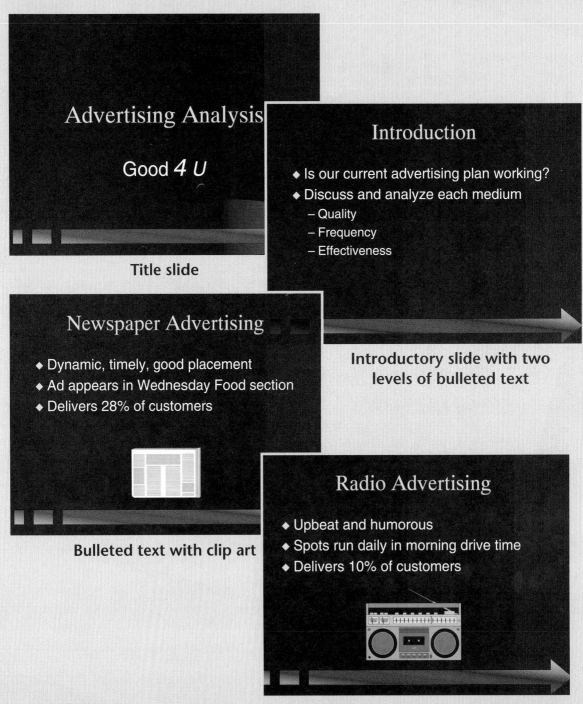

Title slide

Introductory slide with two levels of bulleted text

Bulleted text with clip art

Bulleted text with clip art

Mailers

◆ Two-for-one lunch coupons
◆ Mailers sent six times a year
◆ Delivers 12% of customers

Bulleted text with clip art

Yellow Pages

◆ Attractive display, prominent placement
◆ Ad appears in all metro editions
◆ Delivers 6% of customers

Bulleted text with clip art

Advertising Analysis

	% Customers Delivered	% Total Revenue
Newspaper	28%	30%
Radio	10%	5%
Mailers	12%	18%
Yellow Pages	6%	12%

Slide with a table

Advertising Budget

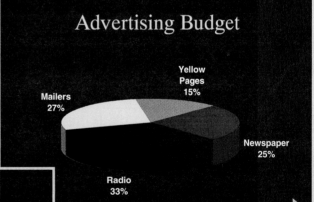

Yellow Pages 15%
Mailers 27%
Newspaper 25%
Radio 33%

Slide with a pie chart

Next Steps

◆ Evaluate current ad design/copy
◆ Meet with account executives
◆ Distribute customer questionnaire
◆ Submit media plan by next month

Closing slide

Preview

As you learn Microsoft PowerPoint, you'll produce professional presentations and handouts for Good *4 U*. You'll learn about important PowerPoint features, from keying slide text and working with fills and colors to using templates and clip art.

You'll display your presentations with an array of dazzling slide show effects. By "working" as an intern at Good *4 U*, you'll gain experience that you can apply to real-world business.

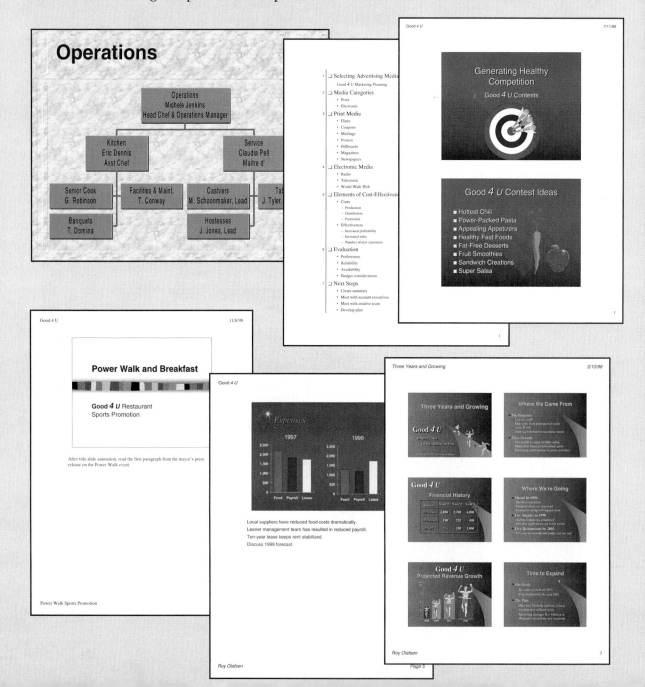

Basic Skills

What is PowerPoint?

After completing this lesson, you will be able to:

1. Start PowerPoint.
2. Navigate in PowerPoint.
3. Key text on a slide.
4. Use PowerPoint views.
5. Run a presentation as a slide show.
6. Name and save a presentation.
7. Print slides and handouts.
8. Close a presentation and exit PowerPoint.

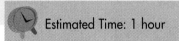

Estimated Time: 1 hour

MOUS
ACTIVITIES
In this lesson:
PP2000 **1.4**
PP2000 **3.3**
PP2000 **6.3**
PP2000 **7.1**
PP2000 **7.2**
PP2000 **7.4**
PP2000 **8.1**
PP2000 **8.2**
PP2000 **8.3**
PP2000 **8.4**

See Appendix F.

Microsoft PowerPoint is a powerful but easy-to-use presentation graphics program you can use to create professional-quality slide presentations. This lesson begins with an overview of many PowerPoint features and provides a road map of the five PowerPoint screen views.

Starting PowerPoint

There are several ways to start PowerPoint, depending on your system set-up and your personal preferences. For example, you can use the Start button on the Windows taskbar or double-click a PowerPoint shortcut icon that may appear on your Windows desktop.

EXERCISE 1-1 Start PowerPoint

1. Turn on your computer to load Windows.
2. Click the Start button on the Windows taskbar and point to Programs.

FIGURE 1-1
Starting
PowerPoint from
the Windows
taskbar

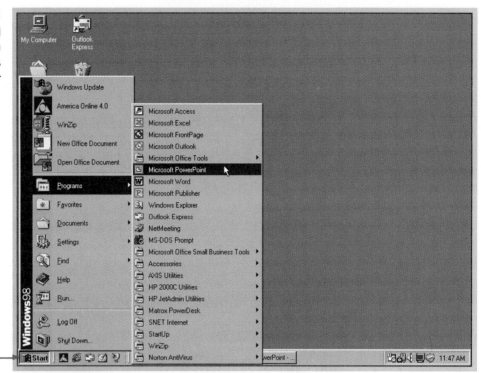

Start button

FIGURE 1-2
PowerPoint
opening dialog
box

NOTE: Windows provides many ways to start applications. If you have problems, ask your instructor for help.

3. On the Programs submenu, click Microsoft PowerPoint. A dialog box opens in the PowerPoint window, prompting you to create a new presentation or open an existing one.

EXERCISE 1-2 Open an Existing Presentation

1. In the PowerPoint opening dialog box, choose <u>O</u>pen an Existing Presentation (next to the yellow file folder icon). Click OK. The Open dialog box appears.

2. Click the down arrow to the right of the Look <u>I</u>n box to choose the appropriate drive and folder for the student files used in this text. Your instructor will advise you as to which drive and folder to use.

NOTE: If you were working at home and opening files on your computer's hard drive, you might use the *Places bar* on the left side of the Open dialog box. For example, "My Documents" and "Web Folders" are folders created by Windows to help you organize your files. "History" lists the most recently used files and folders. "Favorites" contains shortcuts to files or folders you add to this category for easy access. See Table 1-1.

FIGURE 1-3
Files listed in the
Open dialog box

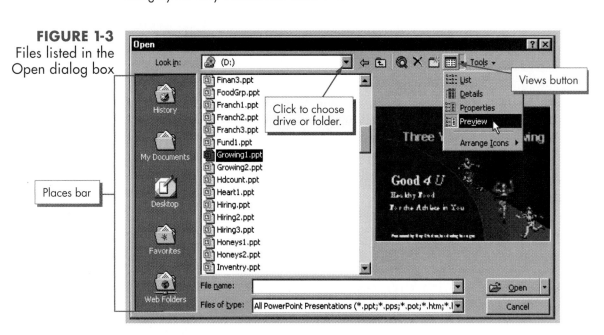

3. Once you locate the student files, click the arrow next to the Views button in the Open dialog box to display a menu of view options.

4. Choose <u>L</u>ist to list all files by filename, if necessary.

5. Locate the filename **Growing1.ppt** and click it once to select the file. Click the Views button and choose Pre<u>v</u>iew to get a quick look at the presentation's first slide before opening it.

6. Click <u>O</u>pen. (You can also double-click the filename to open the file.) PowerPoint opens the file and displays it in Normal view.

TABLE 1-1   Places Bar Folders in the Open Dialog Box

BUTTON	NAME	PURPOSE
	History	Lists the most recently used files and folders.
	My Documents	Opens a folder that Windows provides to help you organize your document files.
	Desktop	Lists items on your computer's desktop.
	Favorites	Lists folders that have been designated as "favorites" by using the Add to Favorites command on the Tools menu.
	Web Folders	Opens a folder that Windows provides to help you organize your HTML files.

TABLE 1-2   Toolbar Buttons in the Open Dialog Box

BUTTON	NAME	PURPOSE
	Up One Level	Moves up one level in the hierarchy of folders or drives on your computer or on computers connected to your computer.
	Search the Web	Opens the Search page of your Internet browser so you can search the Web for information.
	Delete	Deletes a file or folder.
	Create New Folder	Allows you to create a new folder to organize your files.
	Views	Opens a menu of view options for displaying files and file icons.
	Tools	Opens a menu of other file utilities, such as finding a file, renaming a file, and adding a file or folder to the Favorites folder.

Navigating in PowerPoint

If you are already familiar with other Microsoft Office programs, you'll feel right at home with PowerPoint. Although a number of new buttons appear in the PowerPoint screen, it's easy to recognize similarities to Microsoft Word and Microsoft Excel.

FIGURE 1-4
PowerPoint screen

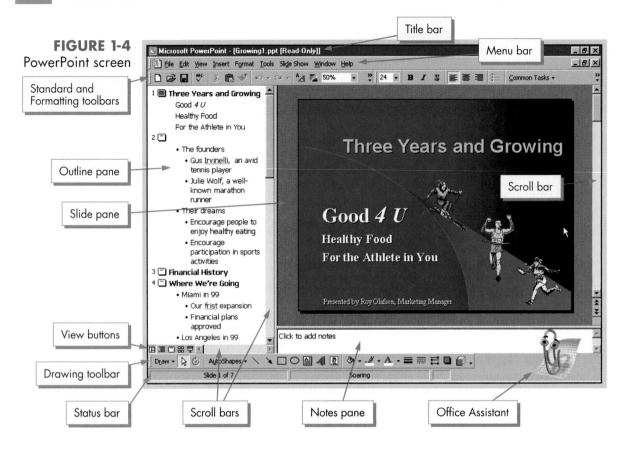

TABLE 1-3   Parts of the PowerPoint Screen

PART	PURPOSE
Title bar	Contains the name of the presentation.
Menu bar	Displays the names of menus you use to perform various tasks. You can open menus by using the mouse or the keyboard.
Toolbars	Rows of buttons that give instant access to a wide range of commands. Each button is represented by an icon and accessed by using the mouse. PowerPoint opens with the Standard and Formatting toolbars displayed in abbreviated form on one line at the top of the screen and the Drawing toolbar at the bottom of the screen.
Slide pane	The area where you create, edit, and display presentation slides.

continues

TABLE 1-3   Parts of the PowerPoint Screen   *continued*

PART	PURPOSE
Outline pane	The area that displays just the presentation text.
Notes pane	The area where you can add presentation notes for either the presenter or the audience.
Scroll bars	Used with the mouse to move a slide view or outline text right or left and up or down. You can also use the vertical scroll bar to move from slide to slide.
View buttons	Five buttons located on the left side of the horizontal scroll bar. You use these buttons to change the way you view a PowerPoint presentation.
Status bar	Displays information about the presentation you're working on.
Office Assistant	Provides tips as you work and suggests Help topics related to the work you're doing.

EXERCISE   1-3   Identify Parts of the Screen

The first step to getting familiar with PowerPoint is to identify the parts of the screen you'll be working with in this course, such as menus, toolbars, and panes.

In Normal view, PowerPoint displays three panes:

- Slide pane—shows how your text and graphics look on each slide
- Outline pane—used to organize and develop the content of your presentation
- Notes pane—used to add notes for presentation delivery

1. Use the mouse to point to the Normal View button in the lower left corner of the screen. PowerPoint displays a *ScreenTip*, a box under the button that contains the button name. If this button is not already pressed, click it with the left mouse button.

FIGURE 1-5
Identifying a
button

2. Point to other buttons on the screen to identify them by name.

3. If the Office Assistant is displayed, click it with the right mouse button to display a shortcut menu. Choose Hide on the shortcut menu.

TIP: If you'd prefer to display the Office Assistant, click Help on the menu bar and choose Show the Office Assistant. Once the Office Assistant is displayed, you can also right-click it and use the shortcut menu to choose another animated character.

Work with Menus and Toolbars

You access PowerPoint commands by choosing menu items or toolbar buttons.

1. Move the pointer to View on the menu bar. Click the left mouse button to open the menu. PowerPoint displays a short version of the view menu with the most commonly used View menu commands.

2. Expand the menu by either keeping it open for a few seconds or by pointing to the arrows at the bottom of the menu. Notice the additional commands on the expanded menu.

NOTE: PowerPoint's short menus are adaptive—they change as you work, listing the commands you use most frequently.

FIGURE 1-6
Displaying menu
options

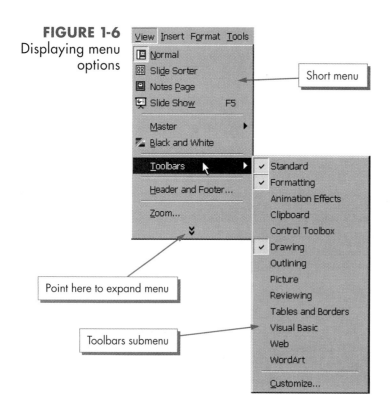

Point here to expand menu

Toolbars submenu

3. To close the menu, click View or a blank area of the screen, or press Esc.

4. Open the View menu again and point to Toolbars. On the Toolbars submenu, three toolbars should be checked: Standard, Formatting, and Drawing. If one of these is not checked, click it on the Toolbars submenu to check it.

5. Close the View menu. Open the Tools menu and expand it. Without clicking the mouse button, move the pointer left to Format on the menu bar. Continue moving the pointer left on the menu bar until you display the File menu. Close the File menu.

TIP: The menu shows which commands have corresponding toolbar buttons or keyboard shortcuts. For example, you can save a document by choosing <u>S</u>ave from the <u>F</u>ile menu, by clicking the Save button on the Standard toolbar, or by pressing Ctrl+S.

6. Point to buttons on the Standard toolbar to identify them by name.

7. Click the More Buttons button at the end of the Standard toolbar to see the rest of this toolbar's buttons. Move the mouse pointer over any button to identify it.

FIGURE 1-7
Side-by-side
toolbars

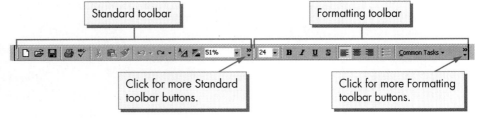

8. Click More Buttons at the end of the Formatting toolbar to see additional toolbar buttons. Press Esc to hide the additional buttons.

 NOTE: When you click and use one of these "hidden" toolbar buttons, the button will move off the More Buttons list and onto the regular toolbar. PowerPoint's toolbars are adaptive—they change as you work, displaying the buttons you use most frequently.

9. Click the <u>C</u>ommon Tasks button on the Formatting toolbar. This opens the Common Tasks menu, which contains frequently used PowerPoint commands.

10. Point to the gray bar at the top of the Common Tasks menu. The bar changes to blue and a ScreenTip tell you that you can drag the menu to "float" it.

FIGURE 1-8
Floating a menu

11. Hold down the left mouse button and drag the menu by its blue bar, away from the toolbar. The Common Tasks menu now floats on your screen. You can position it wherever it's convenient for you.

 NOTE: You can also float toolbars, such as the Formatting or Standard toolbar, by dragging them to another location on the screen. Another option is to display both of these toolbars on separate lines so more buttons are visible. Ask your instructor for information about how to customize toolbars.

12. Close the Common Tasks floating menu by clicking its Close button.

EXERCISE 1-5 Move from Slide to Slide

PowerPoint provides several ways to move from slide to slide in a presentation, using the mouse or the keyboard.

1. Drag the vertical scroll box to the bottom of the scroll bar. Notice the boxes that display slide numbers and slide titles as you drag.

FIGURE 1-9
Dragging the vertical scroll box to move to another slide

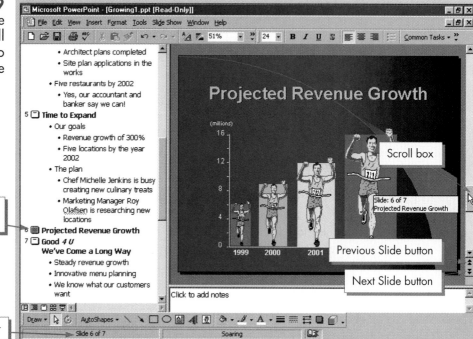

Highlighted slide icon shows current slide

Slide number indicator

When you release the mouse button at the bottom of the scroll bar, slide 7 appears on your screen. Notice that the text in the outline pane scrolls to correspond with the slide currently displayed.

2. Drag the scroll box up to display slide 7. Notice that the slide number is indicated on the left side of the status bar.

3. At the bottom of the vertical scroll bar, click the Previous Slide ⬆ button several times to move back in the presentation. Use the Next Slide ⬇ button to move forward.

4. As an alternative to clicking ⬇ and ⬆, press `PgDn` and `PgUp` several times. Use this method to move to slide 2. Check the status bar for the slide number.

Keying Text on a Slide

Editing text in PowerPoint is just like editing text in a word processor. You click to position the insertion point where you want to key new text and drag the pointer to select existing text. The keys Enter, Delete, and Backspace also work the same way. You can edit presentation text by using the slide pane or the outline pane.

EXERCISE　1-6　Edit Text on a Slide

1. With slide 2 displayed, click anywhere on the line of text that begins "Gus Irvinelli" in the slide pane. Notice the box that surrounds the text. All PowerPoint text is contained in *text boxes*. The wide border made up of tiny diagonal lines indicates the text box is activated and in edit mode, meaning you can edit and insert text.

2. Without clicking, move the mouse pointer outside the text box to the right and then back inside the text box. Notice the changes in the pointer shape: it's an arrow outside a text box ⍋, an arrow with a four-headed arrow on top of the text box border ⍖, and an I-beam I inside the text box.

3. Drag the I-beam across the text "an avid" to select it. (Click to the left of "an avid," hold down the left mouse button and drag the I-beam across the two words, and then release the mouse button.)

FIGURE 1-10
Selecting text to
edit it

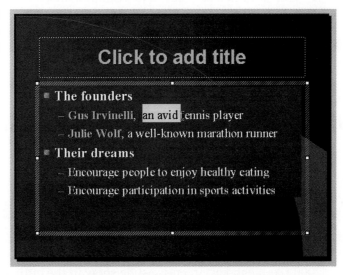

4. Key **a professional** to replace the selected text. (You don't need to delete text before keying new text.) Notice that the new text also appears in the outline pane.

5. To insert a new line, click the insertion point to the right of the words "healthy eating" near the bottom of the slide and press ⌷Enter⌷. Notice that a new bullet appears at the beginning of the new line.

> **NOTE:** Bulleted text lists the points in a slide presentation. This presentation has bulleted text that starts with either a square "bullet" or a hyphen-shaped "bullet." You learn about changing bullet shapes in Lesson 5: "Working with Text."

6. On the new blank bullet line, key **Make their financial investment grow**

7. Instead of a title, slide 2 contains a *placeholder*—a dotted box that is holding a place for the title. Click the placeholder text ("Click to add title") to activate the placeholder. Then key the title **Where We Came From**

8. Click a blank part of the slide area to deactivate the text box. To make sure you're clicking a blank area, click when the pointer is a simple arrow, not an I-beam.

Using the PowerPoint Views

PowerPoint provides different views to help you work on a presentation. The most common views are Normal view, which you've been working in, and Slide Sorter view. You can also create a presentation by using Outline view and Slide view.

EXERCISE 1-7 **Use PowerPoint Views**

1. Click the Outline View button ▤ in the lower left corner of the screen (the left side of the horizontal scroll bar). Outline view changes the proportions of the panes you saw in Normal view, focusing on the text portion of the presentation with smaller slide and notes panes.

2. Scroll down in the outline pane until you see the text for slide 4. (See Figure 1-11 on the next page.)

3. Using normal text-editing methods, change "Miami in 99" to read "Miami in 1999." Change "99" in the next bulleted item (Los Angeles) to read "2000." You can key an entire slide show in the outline pane if that's the way you like to work. Notice that the slide pane shows you a miniature of the slide as you enter or edit text.

FIGURE 1-11
Working in
Outline view

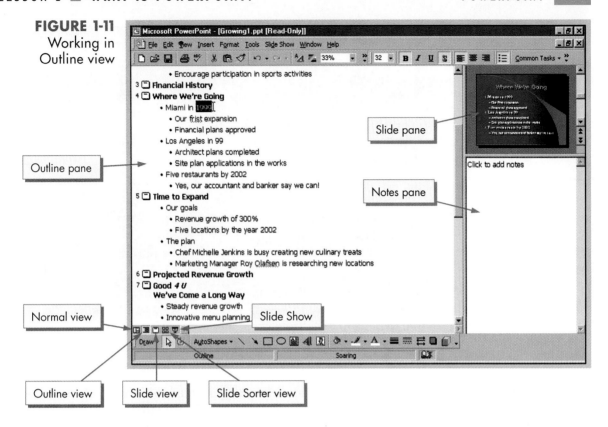

NOTE: You learn to create a presentation in Outline view and use the Outlining toolbar in Lesson 4 "Using the Outline Pane."

4. For a better view of the slide text you edited, click the Slide View button ▣. Slide view focuses on the actual slide. There is no notes pane and, where the outline pane was, only the slide icons remain. You can click an icon to display a particular slide.

5. Notice the wavy red underline beneath the word "frist." Like Word, PowerPoint checks your spelling as you work and uses the same red underline to indicate mistakes. Position the I-beam over the word "frist," click the right mouse button, and choose "first" from the shortcut menu. (See Figure 1-12 on the next page.)

6. Click the slide icon for slide 1 to display the first slide.

TIP: Instead of switching to Outline view to see more of the outline or Slide view to see more of the slide, you can manually adjust the size of the outline or slide pane in Normal view. For example, position the pointer on the outline pane's right border. When you see a double-headed arrow, drag to the right to make the outline pane larger or drag to the left to make the slide pane larger. Likewise, you can enlarge the Notes pane by dragging its top border up.

FIGURE 1-12
Working in
Slide view

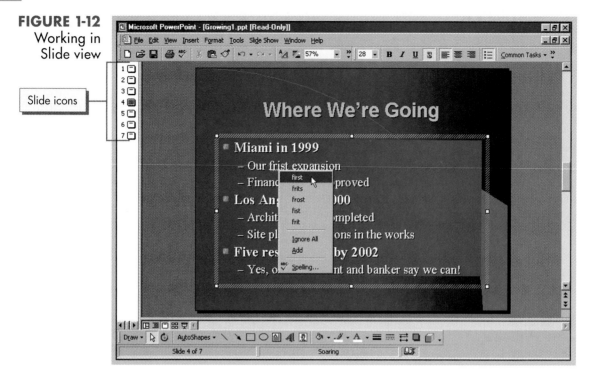

7. Click the Slide Sorter View button , located to the right of the Slide
View button. You can now see several slide miniatures on the screen. In
this view you can rearrange your slides or apply special slide show effects.

FIGURE 1-13
Slide Sorter view

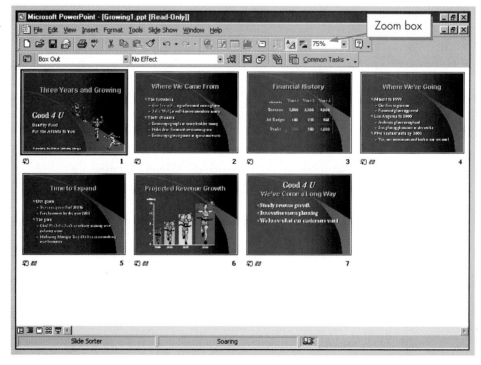

8. On the Standard toolbar, click the down arrow next to the Zoom box and choose 66% or another percentage from the drop-down list so you can see all seven slides in this presentation at the same time.

> **NOTE:** Experiment with the zoom percentage. Depending on your screen resolution, any setting from 50% to 100% could be the right percentage for your computer.

9. Double-click slide 1 to look at it in the last view you were working in, Slide view.

Running a Slide Show

The goal of creating a PowerPoint presentation is to present it as a slide show. Once you begin running a slide show, PowerPoint provides navigation tools to move from slide to slide.

EXERCISE 1-8 Run a Slide Show

1. Click the Slide Show button 🖥 at the bottom left of the screen. After a few seconds, the first slide in the presentation fills the screen.

2. Click the left mouse button to move to slide 2. The left mouse button is one of many ways to move forward in a slide presentation.

3. Press N on the keyboard to move to the next slide, slide 3.

> **TIP:** As an alternative to clicking the left mouse button, you can press N to move forward through the slides. N means "Next" and P means "Previous." You can also use the right and left arrow keys and PgUp and PgDn to move backward and forward in a slide show.

4. Press N again to move to slide 4, which is titled "Where We're Going."

5. Using the left mouse button, click anywhere to see a sample of a PowerPoint text animation. Click twice more to see the remaining text on this slide.

6. Press Esc to end the slide show.

EXERCISE 1-9 Start a Slide Show from Any Slide

If you had to interrupt a slide show, or you only want to show specific slides, you can begin a slide show from any slide.

1. Display slide 5 in Slide view.

2. Click the Slide Show button to resume the slide show from slide 5.

3. Click the left mouse button twice to display the text animations on this slide.

EXERCISE   **1-10**   **Use Onscreen Navigation Tools and the Pen during a Presentation**

During a slide show, you can navigate from slide to slide or to a specific slide by using a shortcut menu. You can also highlight points to your audience by using a pen pointer that allows you to write or draw right on the screen.

1. With slide 5 still displayed, right-click anywhere on the screen to display the shortcut menu, which provides a variety of options related to the slide show. Notice that you can click <u>N</u>ext or <u>P</u>revious to move forward or backward in the slide show.

FIGURE 1-14
Slide Show
shortcut menu

 TIP: You can also click the button at the bottom left corner of the slide show screen to open the shortcut menu.

2. Point to <u>G</u>o on the shortcut menu. Notice the additional options for navigating within the slide show. Point to By <u>T</u>itle to go to a specific slide in the presentation. Click "3 Financial History" to go to slide 3.

3. Click the left mouse button repeatedly to advance through slide 4 ("Where We're Going"), slide 5 ("Time to Expand"), and slide 6 ("Projected Revenue Growth"), displaying each slide and all the animated slide text and objects.

4. When all four graphic objects of slide 6 are displayed, click the menu button in the bottom left corner of the screen.

5. Choose Pointer Options, Pen from the shortcut menu. This activates the pen pointer and allows you to write or draw on the slide.

6. Using the pen pointer, draw a circle around the "16" at the top left of the chart. Draw a circle around "2002" at the bottom right of the chart. (Don't try to draw a perfect circle—the pen is not a precision tool. The aim is to simply point out this information to an audience.)

FIGURE 1-15
Using the pen during a slide show

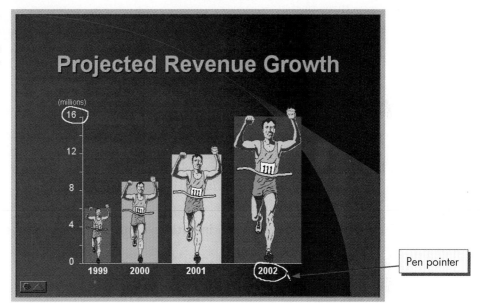

TIP: You can erase your pen marks by opening the shortcut menu and choosing Screen, Erase Pen. You can also change the pen color by choosing Pointer Options, Pen Color from the shortcut menu. Pen marks are not permanent—they disappear when you advance the slide.

7. Open the shortcut menu again and choose Pointer Options, Arrow to restore the arrow pointer.

8. Advance through the last slide. When you reach the end of the presentation, click to exit.

NOTE: If your computer is equipped for sound, you'll hear the audio effects contained on slides 6 and 7.

Naming and Saving a Presentation

In PowerPoint, presentations are saved as files. When you create a new presentation or make changes to an existing one, you must save the presentation to make your changes permanent. Until your changes are saved, they can be lost if there's a power failure or a computer problem.

The first step in saving a document is to give it a *filename*. Filenames can be up to 255 characters long and are followed by a period and a three-character extension. Filename extensions distinguish different types of files. For example, PowerPoint presentations have the extension .ppt and Word documents have the extension .doc.

Throughout the exercises in this book, your document filenames will consist of three parts:

- *[Your initials]*, which may be your initials or an identifier that your instructor asks you to use, such as **rst**
- The number of the exercise, such as **3-1**
- The **.ppt** extension that PowerPoint uses automatically for presentations. An example of a filename is **rst3-1.ppt**

Before you save a new presentation, you must decide where you want to save it. Unless you specify otherwise, PowerPoint saves the presentation in the current drive and folder. For example, to save a presentation to a diskette, you need to change to the appropriate drive.

 NOTE: Your instructor will advise you of the proper drive to use in this course.

 When you're working with an existing file, choosing the <u>S</u>ave command (or clicking the Save button ▣ on the Standard toolbar) replaces the file on the disk with the file on which you're working. After saving, the old version of the file no longer exists and the new version contains all your changes.

When you give an existing presentation a new name by using the Save <u>A</u>s command, the original presentation remains on the disk unchanged and a second presentation is saved on the disk as well.

EXERCISE 1-11 **Name and Save a Presentation**

1. Click <u>F</u>ile to open the <u>F</u>ile menu and choose Save <u>A</u>s. The Save As dialog box appears.

FIGURE 1-16
Save As
dialog box

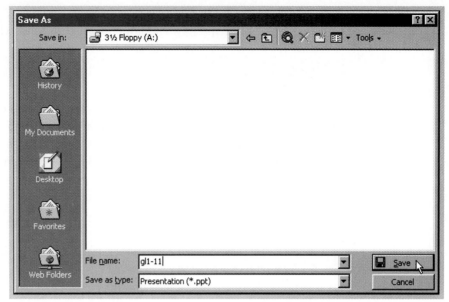

2. In the File <u>N</u>ame text box, key *[your initials]***1-11**. You don't have to key the filename extension, .ppt. PowerPoint adds it automatically.

> **NOTE:** To name files, you can use uppercase letters, lowercase letters, or a combination of both. Filenames can also include spaces. For example, you can use "Good 4 U Sales Report" as a filename.

3. If necessary, change the drive to your data disk by clicking the down arrow in the Save <u>I</u>n drop-down list box and choosing the appropriate drive. If you are saving the file on a diskette, make sure a formatted disk is in the drive.

4. Click <u>S</u>ave and your document is saved and named for future use. Notice that the title bar displays the new filename.

EXERCISE   1-12   Save in HTML File Format

When you save a presentation as a presentation-type file (with the .ppt extension), you need PowerPoint to open and read the file. However, when you save a file using the HTML (*Hypertext Markup Language*) file format, anyone can open and view the presentation by using a *browser* such as Internet Explorer. This means anyone with a browser can read a PowerPoint presentation, a Word document, or an Excel spreadsheet saved using the HTML file format, without opening PowerPoint, Word, or Excel.

Files saved in the HTML file format are used to create Web pages.

1. Click <u>F</u>ile to open the File menu and choose Save as Web Page. In the File <u>N</u>ame box, notice the new filename extension .htm (which is short for HTML).

2. Choose the appropriate location in the Save <u>I</u>n box.

> **NOTE:** PowerPoint creates a folder of supporting files when you save in HTML format. This folder is saved in the same location as the HTML file and is necessary to display the HTML file in a browser. If you move the HTML file to another location, you need to move the supporting file folder along with it.

3. Click <u>S</u>ave. The file is saved in HTML format. It can now be read in the browser Microsoft Internet Explorer 4.0 or a later version.

> **NOTE:** To save the presentation for use in an earlier version of Microsoft Internet Explorer or in another browser, click <u>P</u>ublish in the Save As dialog box instead of clicking <u>S</u>ave. In the Publish as Web Page dialog box, under Browser Support, choose the appropriate option. Click <u>P</u>ublish. Open the file in your browser and view the presentation.

4. Try previewing the presentation in your Web browser by choosing We<u>b</u> Page Preview from the <u>F</u>ile menu. (You may have to expand the menu to locate this command.) The presentation appears in your browser window.

5. Close the browser window by clicking the window's Close button ▣.

Printing Slides and Handouts

Although the primary way of viewing a presentation will usually be as a slide show, you can also print PowerPoint slides, just as you print Word documents or Excel spreadsheets. PowerPoint provides a variety of print options, including printing each slide on a separate page or printing several slides on the same page. You can start printing in one of three ways:

- Choose <u>P</u>rint from the <u>F</u>ile menu.
- Press [Ctrl]+[P].
- Click the Print button 🖨.

The first two methods open the Print dialog box, where you can choose printing options. The Print button 🖨 prints a presentation with the most recently used print options (or print options as set in the Options dialog box, Print tab).

Throughout this book you usually print handouts instead of full-size slides. *Handouts* contain several scaled-down slide images on each page (2, 3, 4, 6, or 9 to a page), and they are often given to an audience during a presentation. Printing handouts saves both paper and printing time.

EXERCISE 1-13 Print a Slide

1. To print the first slide in your presentation, display slide 1 and choose <u>P</u>rint from the <u>F</u>ile menu. The Print dialog box displays PowerPoint's default settings and indicates the designated printer.

FIGURE 1-17
Print dialog box

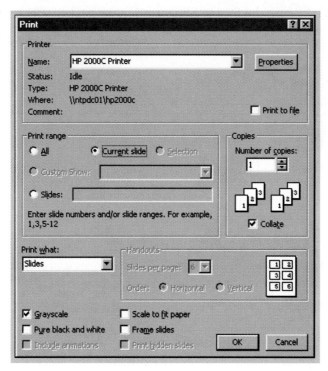

2. In the Print range option box, choose Curr<u>e</u>nt Slide.

3. From the Print <u>W</u>hat drop-down list box, choose Slides.

4. Check the <u>G</u>rayscale box, if necessary. This setting optimizes color slides for a black and white printer. If you have a color printer, clear this check box to print your presentation in color.

5. Click OK to start printing. As the print job proceeds, you see the animated printer icon on the PowerPoint status bar. You may also see a printer icon on the far right side of the Windows taskbar.

EXERCISE 1-14 Print a Presentation Handout

Printing several slides on a single page is a handy way to review your work and to create audience handouts. It's also a convenient way to print class assignments.

1. Press Ctrl+P to open the Print dialog box.

2. Choose All as the Print range option.

3. From the Print What drop-down list box, choose Handouts. Handouts are set to six slides per page, by default.

4. Choose Horizontal, if necessary, so the slides are ordered in three rows, from left to right, instead of in two columns, from top to bottom.

5. Make sure the Frame Slides option is checked. Click OK. PowerPoint prints the entire presentation on two pages (six framed slide images on the first page and one on the second page).

Closing Presentations and Exiting PowerPoint

After you finish working on a presentation and save it, you can close it and open another file or you can exit the program.

To close a presentation and exit PowerPoint, you can:

- Use the File menu.
- Use keyboard shortcuts. Ctrl+W closes a presentation and Alt+F4 exits PowerPoint.
- Use the Close button ✖ in the upper right corner of the window.

EXERCISE `1-15` **Close a Presentation and Exit PowerPoint**

1. Choose Close from the File menu to close the presentation.

2. Click Yes to save the presentation again. (After printing a presentation, you are prompted to save it before closing.)

 3. Click the Close button ✖ in the upper right corner of the screen to close PowerPoint and display the Windows desktop.

COMMAND SUMMARY

FEATURE	BUTTON	MENU	KEYBOARD
Next Slide	⬇		PgDn
Previous Slide	⬆		PgUp
Zoom	75% ▼	View, Zoom	

FEATURE	BUTTON	MENU	KEYBOARD
Normal view	▣	View, Normal	
Slide Sorter view	▦	View, Slide Sorter	
Slide Show	▣	View, Slide Show	F5
Next (Slide Show)	Left mouse button	Right-click, Next	N
Previous (Slide Show)		Right-click, Previous	P
End a slide show		Right-click, End Show	Esc
Save	▣	File, Save	Ctrl + S
Save As		File, Save As	
Print	▣	File, Print	Ctrl + P
Close a presentation	▣	File, Close	Ctrl + W or Ctrl + F4
Exit PowerPoint	▣	File, Exit	Alt + F4

USING HELP

The Office Assistant is your guide to PowerPoint online Help. The Office Assistant provides tips based on the kind of work you're doing and directs you to relevant Help topics. It may also amuse you with its animated movements. If you find the Office Assistant annoying, you can hide it or choose another character.

Get acquainted with the Office Assistant:

1. Start PowerPoint, if necessary. Click Cancel in the opening PowerPoint dialog box.

2. Click the Office Assistant. If the Office Assistant is not displayed, open the Help menu and choose Show the Office Assistant. The Office Assistant appears with a balloon with the question "What would you like to do?"

3. Key **use the Office Assistant** in the text box and click Search (or press Enter). The Office Assistant locates Help topics related to your question.

4. Review the displayed topics and click the topic "Ways to get assistance while you work." A PowerPoint Help window with the same topic name is displayed alongside the PowerPoint window, which is reduced in size.

FIGURE 1-18
Using PowerPoint
Help

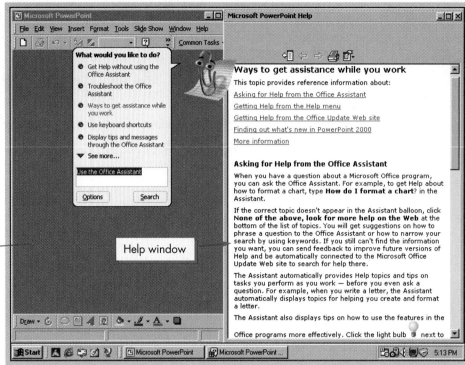

5. Scroll the Help window to review its contents. Click the window's Close button to close Help.

6. Hide the Office Assistant by choosing Hide the Office Assistant from the Help menu.

Concepts Review

Each of the following statements is either true or false. Indicate your choice by circling T or F.

T F **1.** When you start PowerPoint, it automatically displays a blank presentation.

T F **2.** Slide view contains an outline pane, a slide pane, and a notes pane.

T F **3.** You can edit text in Normal view or Slide view.

T F **4.** You can display multiple slides in miniature in Slide Sorter view.

T F **5.** Editing text in PowerPoint is similar to editing text in a word processor.

T F **6.** When viewing a slide show, pressing the plus sign moves to the next slide.

T F **7.** A handout is a page with more than one slide printed on it.

T F **8.** If you click the Print button 🖨, you can choose exactly which items to print.

Write the correct answer in the space provided.

1. Where on the PowerPoint screen are the view buttons located?

_____

2. Name one method for moving to the previous slide during a slide show by using the keyboard.

_____

3. What are the names of the five view buttons?

_____

4. What shape does the mouse pointer have when you move it over a text box?

_____

5. Which key do you press to stop a slide show?

_____

6. When you use the Save as Web Page command, what file type is created?

_____

7. What is the maximum number of slides you can print on a handout page?

_____

8. Which menu and menu option would you use to save a copy of your presentation under a new filename?

_____

_____

CRITICAL THINKING

Answer these questions on a separate page. There are no right or wrong answers. Support your answers with examples from your own experience, if possible.

1. PowerPoint and other Microsoft Office applications for Windows allow filenames that can be 255 characters in length. In previous versions of Microsoft Office applications, only 8 characters were allowed. Some people think the 8-character system is better because it forces you to create a set of rules for naming files. What do you think?

2. You can produce screen shows, printouts, overhead transparencies, 35mm slides, and other presentation media with PowerPoint. How might you choose among these options for any particular presentation? Why would you choose one medium over another? What factors would influence your decision?

Skills Review

EXERCISE 1-16

Open a file; identify parts of the PowerPoint screen; key text; save, print, and close the file.

1. If PowerPoint is already open, skip to Step 2. Otherwise, start PowerPoint by following these steps:
   a. Click the Start button [🔠 Start] on the Windows taskbar.
   b. Point to Programs, point to Microsoft PowerPoint, and click it.
   c. Click Cancel to close the PowerPoint dialog box if it appears.

2. Open a presentation by following these steps:

    a. Click the Open button 🖼 on the Standard toolbar.

    b. Choose the appropriate drive and folder, if necessary.

    c. Double-click the file **Buttons.ppt**.

3. Click anywhere on the text "Click to add subtitle" and key your full name.

4. Select the two question marks in the text "Exercise 1-??" by dragging the I-beam across them. Key the number of this exercise.

5. To move to slide 2, click the Next Slide button 🔽 at the bottom of the vertical scroll bar.

6. Key the answers to the questions on slide 2 by following these steps:

    a. Click to position the insertion point after the word "Answer:" and press [Spacebar].

    b. Key the answer.

    c. Key the answers to the next two questions. Remember, to identify a toolbar button by name, point to the button. If necessary, click More Buttons 🔹 to locate the button.

7. Save the presentation as *[your initials]*1-16.ppt by following these steps:

    a. Choose Save As from the File menu to open the Save As dialog box.

    b. Choose the appropriate drive and folder, if necessary.

    c. Key the filename *[your initials]*1-16 in the File name text box. (Remember, you don't have to key the filename extension, .ppt.)

    d. Click Save.

8. Print the presentation by following these steps:

    a. Choose Print from the File menu.

    b. Choose All in the Print Range option box, if necessary.

    c. Choose Handouts from the Print What drop-down list.

    d. Since this is a two-slide presentation, change the Slides Per Page setting to 2.

    e. Make sure the options Grayscale and Frame Slides are selected. Click OK.

9. Close the presentation by clicking the lower Close button ❎ in the upper right corner of the window.

EXERCISE 1-17

Edit text on a slide, run a slide show, and save and print.

1. Open the file **Menu1.ppt**.

2. Notice on the status bar that this is a three-slide presentation (slide 1 of 3 now appears). Move to slide 3 by dragging the vertical scroll box.

3. Make the corrections as shown in Figure 1-19 (on the next page).

FIGURE 1-19

4. Run the presentation as a slide show by following these steps:

   a. Display slide 1. Click the Slide Show button 🖳.

   b. After slide 1 appears, click the left mouse button to advance to the next slide.

   c. Click the left mouse button again and then return to Normal view.

5. Save the presentation as *[your initials]*1-17.ppt.

6. Print the presentation as handouts, 3 slides per page, grayscale, framed.

7. Close the presentation.

EXERCISE 1-18

Change the view of a presentation, edit a presentation in Slide view, run a slide show, and save and print.

   1. Open the file **Codes1.ppt**.

   2. Click 🔳 to view the presentation in Outline view.

   3. Click 🔲 to view the presentation in Slide view.

   4. Click 🔠 to view the presentation in Slide Sorter view.

   5. Double-click slide 1 in Slide Sorter view to change back to Slide view.

   6. Click the I-beam to the right of "Training Session" on slide 1 and press Enter to start a new line. Key your name. Press Enter again and key today's date.

7. Run a slide show and navigate within the show by following these steps:

   a. Click the Slide Show button 🖳.

   b. After slide 1 appears, click the right mouse button to open the shortcut menu. Point to <u>G</u>o and point to By <u>T</u>itle to see all slides listed by title. Move the pointer back to the main shortcut menu and click <u>N</u>ext to display slide 2.

   c. Advance through the rest of the presentation by pressing [PgDn]. Return to Slide view.

8. Save the presentation as *[your initials]*1-18.ppt.

9. Print the presentation as handouts, 4 slides per page, grayscale, framed.

10. Close the presentation.

EXERCISE 1-19

Key text on a slide, save the file in HTML format, and print.

1. Open the file **Events1.ppt**.

2. Display slide 2.

3. Insert a new line of bulleted text by following these steps:

   a. Click the I-beam to the right of the word "team" at the end of the line "National In-Line Skate demo team."

   b. Press [Enter] to start a new line with an automatic bullet.

   c. Key **Autograph session with Marsha Miles**

4. Edit the text you keyed by following these steps:

   a. Click the I-beam between the words "with" and "Marsha" to position the insertion point.

   b. Key **aerobic video star** and insert any necessary spaces.

5. Save the presentation as an HTML file by following these steps:

   a. Choose Save as Web Page from the <u>F</u>ile menu.

   b. In the File <u>N</u>ame box, key *[your initials]*1-19.

   c. Choose the appropriate location in the Save <u>I</u>n box.

   d. Click Save.

NOTE: If possible, preview the presentation in your Web browser by choosing We<u>b</u> Page Preview from the <u>F</u>ile menu. Close the browser window by clicking the window's Close button ☒.

6. Print the slides full-size by following these steps:

   a. Choose <u>P</u>rint from the <u>F</u>ile menu.

   b. Choose Slides from the Print <u>W</u>hat drop-down list box, if necessary.

   c. Click OK.

7. Close the presentation.

Lesson Applications

Edit text; change presentation views; save, print, and close a presentation.

1. Open the file **Newyr1.ppt**.
2. Using Normal view, make the changes to slides 2 and 3 as shown in Figure 1-20:

FIGURE 1-20

Entertainment

- Audition bands
  - Charlie's Dingbats
  - The Electrolytes
  - ~~Wired Rabbits~~ *Pure Power*
- Contact Marsha Miles
  - Is she willing to lead *dance-style* aerobics?
  - Is she available New Year's Eve?

Slide 2

Menu

- Michelle needs suggestions by November 1
- Staff *tasting* party to be held December 2 / *5*
- Menu printing deadline is December 10

Slide 3

3. View the presentation in Slide view.
4. Save the presentation as *[your initials]*1-20.ppt.
5. Print the presentation as handouts, 6 slides per page, grayscale, framed.
6. Close the presentation.

EXERCISE 1-21

Edit text in Normal view and Slide view; run a slide show; save, print, and close a presentation.

1. Open the file **July4-1.ppt**.
2. Working in Normal view, display slide 2. Change "am" in the first and second bullets to **a.m.** Change the date in the last bullet to **June 25th**
3. Switch to Slide view and display slide 3. In the second bulleted item, change the age from 21 to 18.
4. Display slide 1. Run a slide show of the presentation, clicking to display each new slide and text animation.
5. Save the presentation as *[your initials]*1-21.ppt.
6. Print the presentation as handouts, 6 slides per page, grayscale, framed.
7. Close the presentation.

EXERCISE 1-22

Edit text; change presentation views; save, print, and close a presentation.

1. Open the file **Codes2.ppt**.
2. On slide 1, key the word **Personnel** to the left of "Training" so the title reads "Personnel Training Session."
3. Locate the last line of text on slide 2 (which begins "Under no circumstances"). Position the insertion point at the end of that line and key **while on the job**
4. Locate the last line of text on slide 3. Position the insertion point between "Good 4 U" and "test" and key **proficiency** (the phrase should read "Good 4 U proficiency test").
5. Change to Slide view and move to slide 4. Delete the periods at the end of the two sentences that begin "Guests."
6. Below the third bullet, change "Shirts are" to **T-shirts will be**
7. Save the presentation as *[your initials]*1-22.ppt.
8. Print the presentation as handouts, 6 slides per page, grayscale, framed.
9. Close the presentation.

EXERCISE 1-23 *Challenge Yourself*

Edit text, save a file in HTML format, print a slide and handouts, and close a presentation.

1. Open the file **Prerace.ppt**.

2. Using whichever view you choose, edit slide 2 as shown in Figure 1-21.

FIGURE 1-21

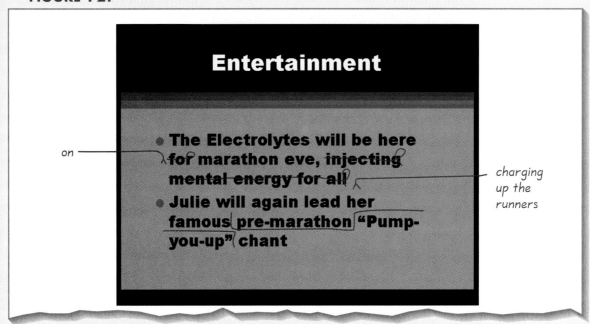

3. Edit slide 3 as shown in the outline pane of Figure 1-22.

FIGURE 1-22

4. View the presentation in Slide Sorter view.

5. Run a slide show of the presentation, beginning with slide 1.

6. Save the presentation in HTML format as *[your initials]***1-23.htm**.

7. View the presentation in your Web browser (<u>F</u>ile, We<u>b</u> Page Preview), if possible and then close the browser window.

8. Print all slides in grayscale.

9. Print the presentation as handouts, 4 slides per page, grayscale, framed.

10. Close the presentation.

Basic Presentation Tools

OBJECTIVES

MOUS
ACTIVITIES
In this lesson:
PP2000 **1.1**
PP2000 **1.3**
PP2000 **1.6**
PP2000 **1.7**
PP2000 **1.9**
PP2000 **2.1**
PP2000 **2.2**
PP2000 **3.1**
PP2000 **3.8**
PP2000 **6.2**
PP2000 **7.3**

See Appendix F.

After completing this lesson, you will be able to:

1. Use the AutoContent Wizard.
2. Change sample text.
3. Use the spelling checker and style checker.
4. Use the Find and Replace features.
5. Rearrange slides; use Cut, Copy, and Paste; and delete slides.
6. Add headers and footers.
7. Choose printing options.

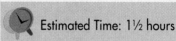 Estimated Time: 1½ hours

This lesson introduces you to basic presentation tools, starting with the AutoContent Wizard. A *wizard* is an online guide that helps you complete a task. The AutoContent Wizard provides step-by-step help for creating a presentation.

After creating the presentation, you learn how to check for spelling errors and style inconsistencies, how to find and replace text, and how to edit a presentation by using the Cut, Copy, and Paste commands. You apply slide and handout headers and footers and learn about more print options.

Using the AutoContent Wizard

The quickest way to create a presentation is with the AutoContent Wizard. It asks a series of questions and uses your answers to develop the framework for a new presentation.

EXERCISE **2-1** **Use the AutoContent Wizard**

---

1. Start PowerPoint.

2. In the PowerPoint opening dialog box, choose <u>A</u>utoContent Wizard and click OK. The AutoContent Wizard opening dialog box appears.

 NOTE: If PowerPoint was already open when you started this lesson, choose <u>N</u>ew from the <u>F</u>ile menu. On the General tab, choose AutoContent Wizard and click OK.

FIGURE 2-1
AutoContent
Wizard opening
screen

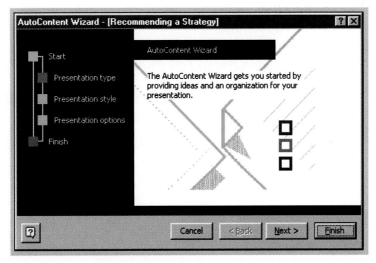

3. In the AutoContent Wizard opening dialog box, click <u>N</u>ext. Notice the "road map" on the left side of the dialog box. As you move from one dialog box to the next, a green square indicates where you are in the process. You move forward and backward by clicking the <u>N</u>ext and <u>B</u>ack buttons or by clicking the gray boxes.

4. In the Presentation Type dialog box, the wizard asks what kind of presentation you want to give and shows a list of presentation types on the right side of the dialog box. You can click one of the buttons to the left of the list to show only specific types of presentations.

FIGURE 2-2
Presentation Type
dialog box

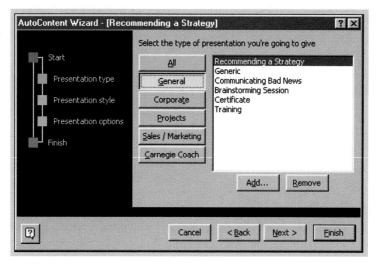

5. Click Sales and Marketing to view the type of presentations in this category.

6. Click General and choose Recommending a Strategy from the list. Click Next. The green square moves to Presentation style options.

7. In the Presentation Style dialog box, you tell the wizard how you plan to use this presentation. Choose On-screen Presentation and click Next.

8. In the Presentation Options dialog box, key **Good 4 U Restaurant** in the Presentation Title text box. Press Tab to move to the next text box and key

FIGURE 2-3
Presentation
created using the
AutoContent
Wizard (see Step 9)

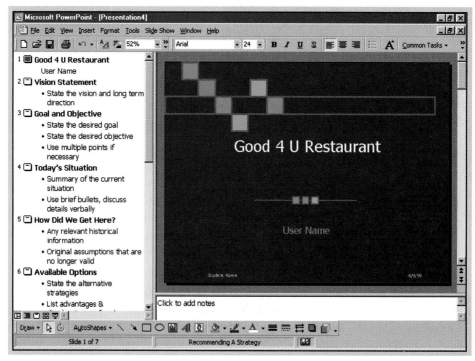

your name as the footer. Clear the check box for <u>S</u>lide Number by clicking the check box. The footer will include your name and the date.

9. Click <u>N</u>ext to move to the last dialog box. Click <u>F</u>inish. PowerPoint creates a seven-slide strategy presentation for you and displays it in Normal view. Notice the presentation design and the sample text. (See Figure 2-3 on the previous page.)

Changing Sample Text

The AutoContent Wizard creates a presentation based on a suggested outline, with sample text. You can replace the sample text with your own content by using basic editing techniques. As you learned in Lesson 1, editing presentation text is much the same as editing text in a word processor.

EXERCISE 2-2 Edit Sample Text in a Title Placeholder

Each slide in the sales presentation contains a title placeholder with sample text. For example, slide 2 is titled "Vision Statement" and slide 3 is named "Goal and Objective." You can select and then edit these sample text objects.

1. In the slide pane, click at the bottom of the vertical scroll bar to view slide 2. Notice the sample text for the title and bulleted list. As you examine each slide, note how the sample text suggests the content for a sales presentation.

2. Display slide 4. (Remember, you can drag the scroll box, click ▼, or press `PgDn`.)

3. In slide 4, move the pointer over the title ("Today's Situation") until it becomes an I-beam. Click the I-beam to activate the title placeholder.

4. Drag the I-beam over the sample title text to select it. Key the new title **Good 4 U Provides** in place of the selected text.

5. Click outside the title placeholder to deactivate it.

> **NOTE:** After you edit placeholder text, deactivate the placeholder by clicking elsewhere on the screen. Be sure you see the white arrow pointer when you click.

6. Return to slide 1. Below the title is the subtitle text box. If it is empty, click it and key the subtitle **Planning a Strategy**. If there is an existing subtitle (such as the name of your computer or school), select the text and then key the new text.

EXERCISE   2-3   Edit Sample Text in a Text Placeholder

In this presentation, all the slides contain sample text, some in title placeholders and some in bulleted text placeholders. You can edit sample text in bulleted text placeholders and add additional bullets.

1. Return to slide 3 (titled "Goal and Objective"). With the I-beam pointer, click the bulleted list to activate the text placeholder.

2. At the right of the first bullet, drag to select the text "State the desired goal" and key **Encourage corporations to use Good 4 U for special events** in its place. Notice that the text wraps to a new line.

3. Press Enter to add a new bullet and key **Provide healthy food that tastes good**

4. Triple-click within the text "State the desired objective" to select the entire line. Press Delete to remove it.

 NOTE: When you select bulleted text, the bullet character is not highlighted.

TABLE 2-1   Selecting Text

METHOD	RESULT
Click and drag	Selects text with the mouse
Double-click a word	Selects the entire word
Ctrl +click text	Selects the sentence
Triple-click text	Selects the paragraph or bulleted item

5. Select the last bullet line on slide 3 by clicking the bullet at the beginning of the line. Key **Provide "something different"** (include the quotation marks).

6. Press Enter to create another bulleted item and key **Accommodate large groups** (See Figure 2-4 on the next page.)

7. In slide 4, select and delete both bulleted items. Key the following four bulleted items, pressing Enter to start each new item:

   - **Low-fat, natural foods**
   - **Innovative menu**
   - **Three stars from the New York Times**
   - **Private dining for 25 to 500 people**

FIGURE 2-4
Editing sample text
on slide 3

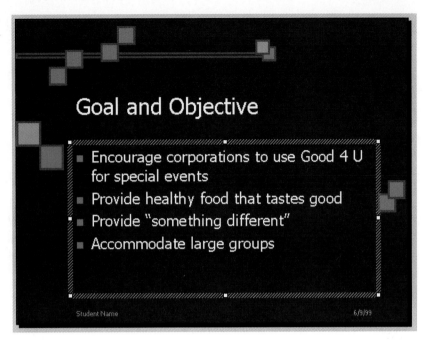

TABLE 2-2   **Editing Text**

METHOD	RESULT
Arrow key	Moves the insertion point right, left, up, or down within the text
Ctrl + Arrow key	Moves the insertion point to the next word or paragraph (bulleted item)
Backspace	Deletes characters to the left of the insertion point
Ctrl + Backspace	Deletes the word to the left of the insertion point
Delete	Deletes characters to the right of the insertion point
Ctrl + Delete	Deletes the word to the right of the insertion point

8. Choose Save As from the File menu. You're going to save the presentation in a new folder that will contain all the files you create in this Lesson.

9. Choose the folder location from the Save In drop-down list. (For example, to save your files to a floppy disk, put a disk in the drive and make sure Save In indicates drive A:.)

 NOTE: Check with your instructor about where to save the new folder.

10. Click the Create New Folder button and key the folder name *[your initials]*Lesson 2.

11. Enter the filename *[your initials]*2-3 and click Save. Leave the presentation open.

Using the Spelling Checker and Style Checker

PowerPoint provides three tools to improve your spelling and the overall appearance of your presentation:

- A spelling checker, which corrects spelling by comparing words to an internal dictionary file

- AutoCorrect, which corrects common spelling and capitalization errors automatically as you key text

- A style checker, which automatically checks a presentation for visual clarity and consistency of case and punctuation

EXERCISE 2-4 **Use the Spelling Checker**

The spelling checker in PowerPoint works much the same as it does in other Microsoft Office applications. As you type, it flags misspelled words with a red wavy underline. It can also check an entire presentation at once.

1. Without closing the current presentation, open the file **July4-2.ppt**. (You'll need to navigate from your Lesson 2 folder to the folder that stores the files for this course.)

2. On slide 1, a word in the title has a wavy underline indicating a spelling error. Right-click the word in either the outline or slide pane. Choose the correct spelling ("Celebration") from the shortcut menu.

3. Notice the spelling of "Forth" in the title. This is an example of a word that is correctly spelled but incorrectly used. Spelling checker can't help you with this kind of mistake. Change the spelling to **Fourth**.

4. To run the spelling checker for the entire presentation, click the Spelling button on the Standard toolbar or press F7. PowerPoint highlights "Registraton," the first word it doesn't find in its dictionary. It displays the word in the Spelling dialog box and suggests a corrected spelling. (See Figure 2-5 on the next page.)

NOTE: PowerPoint also displays a light bulb on slide 2, indicating a style inconsistency. Ignore the light bulb for the moment.

FIGURE 2-5
Using the
spelling checker

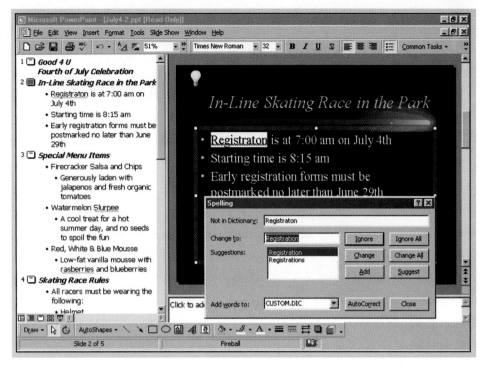

5. Click <u>C</u>hange to apply the correct spelling of "Registration."

6. When the spelling checker locates "Slurpee," click <u>I</u>gnore because this word is spelled correctly.

 NOTE: If the Spelling dialog box is hiding a misspelled word, move the dialog box to a different position by dragging its title bar.

7. At the next spelling error, click <u>C</u>hange to apply the corrected spelling of "raspberries."

8. At the next spelling error, click <u>C</u>hange to apply the first suggested spelling, "guardian." Click OK when the spelling check is complete.

EXERCISE 2-5 **Use AutoCorrect**

If you key "teh" instead of "the," or "can;t" instead of "can't," AutoCorrect corrects the word automatically as you key. The correction takes place after you press Spacebar or Enter or enter punctuation, such as a period or comma.

1. Display slide 3 of the active presentation (**July4-2.ppt**).

2. Choose <u>A</u>utoCorrect from the <u>T</u>ools menu (you may need to expand the menu). If necessary, turn on the AutoCorrect feature by checking Replace <u>T</u>ext as You Type.

FIGURE 2-6
AutoCorrect
dialog box

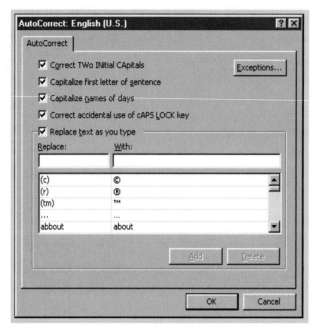

3. In the AutoCorrect dialog box, scroll through the list to see the changes AutoCorrect will make automatically. Click OK.

4. Under the first bulleted item on slide 3, select the text "Generously laden with." Key **Amde from** (including the misspelling). "Amde" is automatically corrected to "Made." Leave the file open for the next Exercise.

TIP: You can customize AutoCorrect to catch your own common typos or to expand abbreviations. Just key the error or abbreviation (for example, **asap**) in the <u>R</u>eplace box and then key the correction (for example, **as soon as possible**) in the <u>W</u>ith box. Next, click <u>A</u>dd to put your entry on the list. For example, you could create an entry to replace your company's initials with its full name. To delete a <u>R</u>eplace entry, select it in the list and click <u>D</u>elete.

EXERCISE   **2-6**   **Use the Style Checker**

The style checker automatically looks for consistency, balance, and overall readability of your presentation. For example, if your presentation has a bulleted item that ends with a period or a title that is uppercase when all other titles are in title case, it will mark the problem with a light bulb. You click the light bulb and then choose an appropriate option.

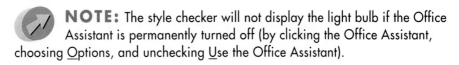 **NOTE:** The style checker will not display the light bulb if the Office Assistant is permanently turned off (by clicking the Office Assistant, choosing Options, and unchecking Use the Office Assistant).

1. Choose Show the Office Assistant from the Help menu, if necessary.

2. In the active presentation (**July4-2.ppt**), display slide 2.

3. Click the light bulb. The style checker detects a capitalization problem and provides options.

NOTE: The style checker is questioning the uppercase "L" in "In-Line." Slide titles use title case, in which only the first letter of each word (except articles such as "in," "the," and so on) is capitalized. In a sentence, a hyphenated word such as "in-line" would be lowercase, but in a heading or name, it is correct as "In-Line."

4. Click OK because you don't want to change to title case, ignore the rule, or change style checker options.

5. Display slide 5. Click the light bulb and notice another capitalization problem. This is the only slide in the presentation with an all-uppercase title.

6. Click the first option to change the text to title case. The title text "ENTERTAINMENT" becomes "Entertainment."

7. Return to slide 1.

Using Find and Replace

When you create presentations, especially long presentations, you often need to review or change text. In PowerPoint, you can do this quickly by using the Find and Replace commands.

The Find command locates specified text in a presentation. The Replace command finds the text and replaces it with a specified alternative.

EXERCISE   2-7   Find and Replace Text

1. With slide 1 displayed in the presentation **July4-2.ppt**, choose Find from the Edit menu to open the Find dialog box.

FIGURE 2-7
Find dialog box

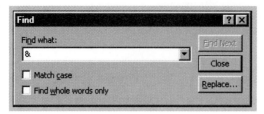

2. Key **&** in the Find What text box.

3. Click Find Next. PowerPoint locates and selects the text.

4. Close the Find dialog box. Key **and** in place of "&" to be consistent with the first bulleted item on this slide.

5. Choose Replace from the Edit menu. You're going to replace all occurrences of "am" with "a.m."

6. In the Find What text box, key **am**. In the Replace With text box, key **a.m.**

7. Check Match Case and Find Whole Words Only to ensure that you find only the lowercase text "am" and not words that contain these letters (such as "America" or "ramp").

FIGURE 2-8
Replace dialog box

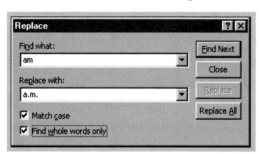

8. Click Find Next. PowerPoint finds the first occurrence of "am." Click Replace. Click Replace again at the next occurrence. Click OK in the Office Assistant balloon when PowerPoint finishes the search. Close the dialog box.

 TIP: If you're certain about what you're looking for, you can use the Replace All command to replace all occurrences of text in one step.

9. Click the light bulb now displayed on slide 2. The style checker thinks that the second bulleted item has ending punctuation (a period) because of the change from "am" to "a.m." Click the option to ignore this rule for this presentation.

10. Save the presentation as *[your initials]***2-7.ppt** in your Lesson 2 folder. Leave the presentation open for the next Exercise.

Making Changes in Slide Sorter View

Slide Sorter view provides an overview of your entire presentation by displaying a miniature version of the slides in the order they appear. You can change the order of slides by dragging them. You can also rearrange slides by using the Cut, Copy, and Paste commands, and you can delete slides.

EXERCISE 2-8   Change the Order of Slides by Dragging

1. Display the presentation *[your initials]*2-7.ppt in Slide Sorter view.
2. Click slide 3 to select it. Notice the border around the selected slide.
3. Position the arrow pointer within the selected slide's borders, press the left mouse button, and drag the pointer between the first and second slides. Notice the vertical line and the drag-and-drop pointer as you drag.

FIGURE 2-9
Moving a slide in
Slide Sorter view

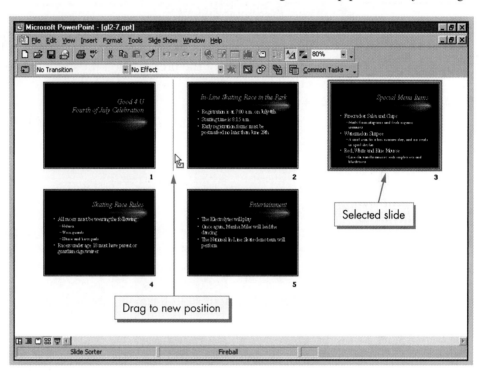

4. Release the mouse button. Slide 3, titled "Special Menu Items," becomes slide 2.

EXERCISE 2-9   Cut, Copy, and Paste Slides

Using the Cut, Copy, and Paste commands, you can rearrange slides within a presentation or from one presentation to another in Slide Sorter view.

Each item you cut or copy is stored temporarily on the Windows *Clipboard*.

 NOTE: You'll learn more about another clipboard, the Office Clipboard, in the next Exercise.

1. With *[your initials]*2-7.ppt still in Slide Sorter view, select slide 5 ("Entertainment").

2. Click the Cut button ✗ on the Standard toolbar. This deletes the slide and stores it on the Clipboard.

3. Click to the right of slide 2.

4. Click the Paste button 🖺 on the Standard toolbar.

5. Click *[your initials]*2-3.ppt on the Windows taskbar to open the strategy presentation.

6. Switch to Slide Sorter view.

7. Choose Arrange All from the Window menu. Both presentations appear on the screen, each within its own window. Each window's title bar displays the name of the presentation it contains. The active presentation has the blue title bar.

8. Right-click slide 2 ("Special Menu Items") in the Fourth of July presentation, *[your initials]*2-7.ppt. This activates the presentation as it selects the slide and displays the shortcut menu.

FIGURE 2-10
Copying a slide
from one
presentation to
another

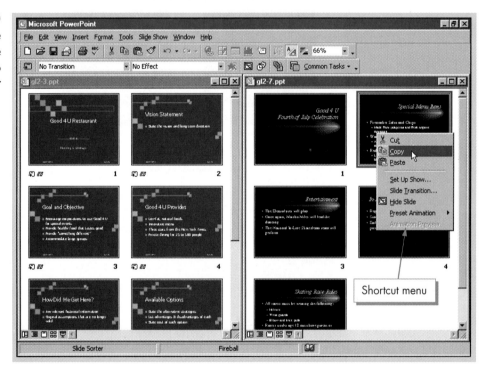

Shortcut menu

9. Choose Copy from the shortcut menu to copy the slide to the Clipboard.

TIP: You can also use the keyboard shortcuts Ctrl+X to cut, Ctrl+C to copy, and Ctrl+V to paste.

10. Scroll to display slide 5 in the strategy presentation. Right-click to the left of slide 5 and choose Paste from the shortcut menu. The slide is pasted from one presentation into the other. Notice that the pasted slide takes on the design of the presentation into which it is copied.

> **NOTE:** You can also move slides between presentations by dragging. Simply drag a slide from one window to the other, positioning the slide with the drag-and-drop pointer (and the vertical line). Using the right mouse button, drag and position the slide. A pop-up menu asks if you want to Move Here or Copy Here (or Cancel).

EXERCISE 2-10   Using the Office Clipboard to Cut, Copy, and Paste

Just as you cut, copy, and paste slides, you can cut, copy, and paste text and graphics. Additionally, you can use the Office Clipboard to collect multiple items you've copied or cut. The Office Clipboard can store up to 12 items, which you can then paste repeatedly. To use the Office Clipboard, you display the Clipboard toolbar.

Unlike the Cut command, Delete does not save items to the Clipboard.

1. Maximize the strategy presentation, *[your initials]***2-3.ppt**, by clicking the Maximize button on its title bar.

2. Switch to Outline view. Scroll so you can see slide 1 text in the outline pane.

FIGURE 2-11
Clearing the
Clipboard toolbar

3. Display the Clipboard toolbar by opening the View menu and choosing Toolbars, Clipboard. On the Clipboard toolbar, click the Clear Clipboard button , if necessary, to clear any stored material. (If the button is dimmed, nothing is stored on the Office Clipboard.)

4. Move the Clipboard toolbar into the notes pane so it doesn't hide your text.

5. On slide 3, select the text in the first bulleted item (which begins "Encourage corporations") by clicking its bullet.

6. Click the Cut button on the Standard toolbar. This deletes the text and places it on the Clipboard.

7. On slide 2, select the sample bulleted text (which begins "State the vision").

8. Point to the text item on the Clipboard. A ScreenTip identifies the item as the text you cut.

FIGURE 2-12
Cutting and
pasting text

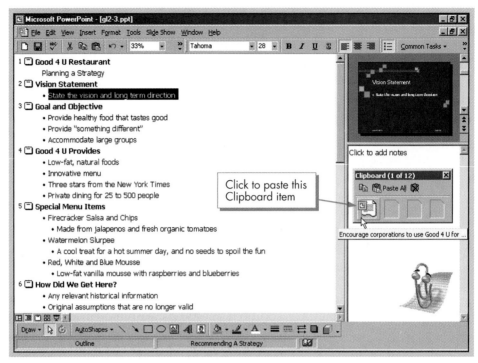

9. Click the Clipboard item to paste it. The sample text on slide 2 is replaced by the text on the Clipboard.

 NOTE: When you plan to cut and copy multiple items, it's useful to display the Clipboard toolbar so you can pick and choose the items to paste or click Paste All to paste all the stored items at once. When the Clipboard is not displayed, click the Paste button 🗎 on the Standard toolbar to paste the most recently cut or copied item.

 10. In slide 4, select the title text "Good 4 U" and click the Copy button 🗎 on the Standard toolbar or on the Clipboard toolbar. The new text item is copied to the Clipboard.

11. Position the pointer immediately before the word "Vision" in the slide 2 title. Click the second item on the Clipboard toolbar (which contains the text "Good 4 U") to paste it.

 NOTE: The Clipboard can be used to cut, copy, and paste material between Office applications. For example, you can copy slide presentation text and paste it into a Word document.

EXERCISE **2-11** **Delete Slides**

1. Change the view of the strategy presentation, *[your initials]*2-3.ppt, to Slide Sorter view.

2. Select slide 6 ("How Did We Get Here?") and press Delete.

> **TIP:** In Slide Sorter view, you can select and delete multiple slides. To select consecutive slides, click the first slide, hold down Shift, and then click the last slide. To select slides that are not consecutive, select the first slide, hold down Ctrl, and then select additional slides.

3. Right-click the last slide ("Recommendation") and choose Cut from the shortcut menu.

4. Display the new slide 5 ("Special Menu Items") in Slide view.

> **NOTE:** Notice the new addition to the Clipboard—the slide you cut in this Exercise. Point to this new item. It's identified as "Picture 1" and considered a graphic because it is an entire slide, not just text.

5. Delete slide 5 by opening the Edit menu and choosing Delete Slide.

6. Click the Undo button 🔄 to restore the slide.

7. Change the slide 5 title to **Sample Holiday Menu Items**

8. To complete this presentation, edit slide 6 ("Available Options") by changing its title to **Next Steps**. Replace the sample bulleted text with the following text:

   ■ **Develop mailing list for targeted companies**

   ■ **Develop price plan**

   ■ **Send promotional mailer to target companies**

   ■ **Prepare sales force for follow-up**

9. Clear the Clipboard contents and close the Clipboard toolbar.

10. Check spelling in the presentation and save it as *[your initials]*2-11.ppt in your Lesson 2 folder. Leave both presentations open.

Adding Headers and Footers

You can add identifying information to your presentation, such as header or footer text, the date, or a slide or page number. These elements appear in special header and footer placeholders on slides and on notes and handout pages.

TABLE 2-3   Adding Identifying Information to Presentations

INFORMATION	DESCRIPTION
Date and Time	The current date—updated automatically or fixed
Header	Descriptive text on notes and handout pages only
Page Number	Number placed in the lower right corner of notes and handout pages by default
Slide Number	Number you can place in the lower right corner of slides
Footer	Descriptive text for use on either slides or notes and handout pages

EXERCISE 2-12   Add Footers, Dates, and Page Numbers

1. Click *[your initials]***2-7.ppt** on the Windows taskbar to display the Fourth of July presentation. Switch to Normal view.

2. Choose <u>H</u>eader and Footer from the <u>V</u>iew menu. Note the tabs in the Header and Footer dialog box—one for adding information to slides and one for adding information to notes and handouts.

FIGURE 2-13
Header and Footer
dialog box,
Slide tab

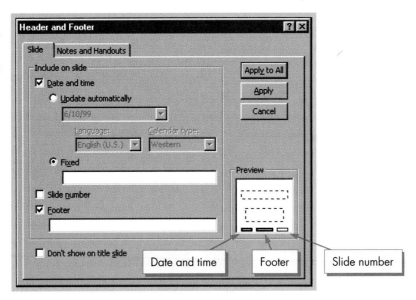

3. In the Preview box, notice the positions for the elements you can place on a slide. As you enable each element by selecting its check box, PowerPoint indicates where it will print with a bold outline in the Preview box.

4. Click the Slide Number check box to select it. Click the check box at the bottom of the dialog box so the page number does not appear on the title slide. Clear the Date and Time and the Footer check boxes.

5. Click Apply to All. The presentation now has slide numbers at the bottom right of each slide except the title slide.

6. Open the Header and Footer dialog box again and display the Notes and Handouts tab.

7. Under the Date and Time option, click Update Automatically to add today's date. Each time you print the presentation handout, it will include the current date. You can choose different date and time formats from the drop-down list.

FIGURE 2-14
Header and Footer
dialog box, Notes
and Handouts tab

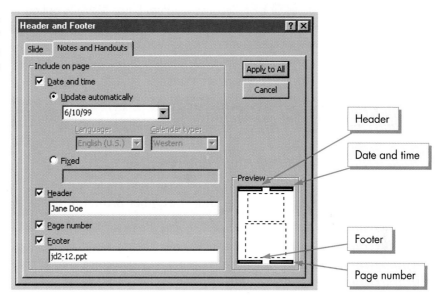

8. Check Header, if necessary. Position the insertion point in the Header text box and key your name. The header appears in the upper left corner of the page.

9. Check Page Number, if necessary. Page numbers appear at the bottom right of the page.

10. Check Footer, if necessary. Key the filename *[your initials]***2-12.ppt** in the Footer text box. Click Apply to All to add this information to all handout pages (but not to individual slides).

11. Save the presentation as *[your initials]***2-12.ppt** in your Lesson 2 folder. Leave the presentation open for printing in the next Exercise.

Choosing Print Options

As Lesson 1 demonstrated, PowerPoint provides many ways to print an entire presentation or a portion of a presentation. For example, in the Print dialog box you can select:

- Individual slides, the current slide, or a range of slides
- Slides, handouts (2, 3, 4, 6 or 9 to a page), notes, or outlines
- Multiple copies

Additionally, there are two options for printing in black and white. The Grayscale option converts the presentation colors to shades of gray. The Pure Black & White option converts all colors to either black or white, eliminating all shades of gray. In complex presentation designs, this setting is useful.

 NOTE: Because the Pure Black & White option simplifies your presentation graphics, it can sometimes speed up printing time.

EXERCISE 2-13 **Choose Print Dialog Box Options**

1. With the Fourth of July presentation displayed, choose Print from the File menu to open the Print dialog box.

2. At the top of the Print dialog box, click the down arrow in the Name box. This is where you choose another printer, if one is available.

 NOTE: The information below the Name box applies to the selected printer. For example, "Status" indicates if the printer is idle or currently printing other documents.

3. Under Print Range, click Slides and key **1,2** in the text box to print only slides 1 and 2.

TIP: To print consecutive slides, you can use a hyphen. For example, enter **2-4** to print slides 2 through 4. To print a combination of slides, you can key the range **1,3,5-9,12** to print slides 1, 3, 5 through 9, and 12.

4. Make sure the Grayscale option box is checked. This option is checked by default when you use a black and white printer, but not if you use a color printer.

5. Choose Slides from the Print <u>W</u>hat drop-down list box, if necessary, and click OK. In the printouts, notice that only slide 2 is numbered.

> **TIP:** You can create a presentation that uses overhead transparencies by printing your slides as black-and-white or color transparencies. Simply insert transparency sheets into your printer (choosing the correct type of transparencies for a laser or ink-jet printer), choose your print settings (including Slides from the Print <u>W</u>hat drop-down list), and print.

6. Open the Print dialog box again. Choose <u>A</u>ll to print all slides. From the Print <u>W</u>hat drop-down list, choose Handouts. In the Handouts box, set the Slides Pe<u>r</u> Page option to 3.

7. Make sure the <u>G</u>rayscale and Fra<u>m</u>e Slides option boxes are checked and click OK. The presentation prints on two handout sheets that include the header and footer information you added to notes and handout pages: your name, the date, the filename, and the page number.

 8. Click the Save button to save the presentation, and then close it.

9. Display *[your initials]*2-11.ppt (the strategy presentation) in Normal view. Remember that the AutoContent Wizard added a slide footer containing your name and the date.

10. Open the Print dialog box. Check the Fra<u>m</u>e Slides and P<u>u</u>re Black and White options.

11. Change the Print <u>W</u>hat setting to handouts, 6 slides per page, and change the order to <u>V</u>ertical. Click OK. The slides appear without shades of gray and in vertical order on the page. The handout prints with a footer (the presentation title), which was added automatically by the AutoContent Wizard.

12. Close the presentation. Click <u>Y</u>es when you are asked to save changes.

COMMAND SUMMARY

FEATURE	BUTTON	MENU	KEYBOARD
Spelling checker		<u>T</u>ools, <u>S</u>pelling	F7
Cut		<u>E</u>dit, Cu<u>t</u>	Ctrl + X
Copy		<u>E</u>dit, <u>C</u>opy	Ctrl + C
Paste		<u>E</u>dit, <u>P</u>aste	Ctrl + V
Find		<u>E</u>dit, <u>F</u>ind	Ctrl + F
Replace		<u>E</u>dit, R<u>e</u>place	Ctrl + H

USING HELP

PowerPoint's online Help feature is like an interactive teaching tool. One way to explore online Help is to display a list of Help topics. After you choose a topic, PowerPoint displays information or provides a demonstration.

Learn more about getting help in PowerPoint:

1. Use the <u>H</u>elp menu to display the Office Assistant, if necessary. Click the Assistant to activate it.

2. Key **print** in the text box and click <u>S</u>earch.

3. Click the topic "About printing." The About Printing Help window opens. Review the information in the Help window.

4. In the upper right corner of the Help window, click Show 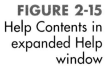 to expand the window and display the Help option tabs.

5. Click the <u>C</u>ontents tab. Scroll to review the list of Help categories, each of which is represented by a book icon ✎.

6. Click the plus sign next to the Printing Presentations category to display a list of topics, each of which is preceded by a question mark page icon ?.

FIGURE 2-15
Help Contents in expanded Help window

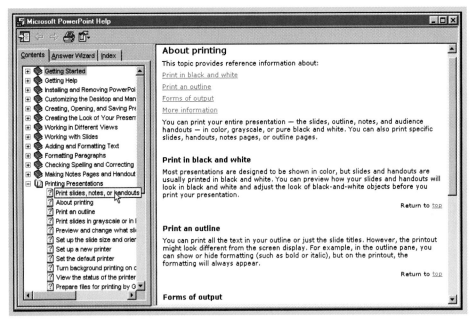

7. Click the topic "Print slides, notes, or handouts."

8. Review the information and then click another Printing topic.

9. Close the Help window when you finish. Hide the Office Assistant (right-click it and choose <u>H</u>ide from the shortcut menu).

Concepts Review

Each of the following statements is either true or false. Indicate your choice by circling **T** or **F**.

T F **1.** The AutoContent Wizard begins a presentation with the title slide.

T F **2.** The title slide in a presentation is limited to one line.

T F **3.** Before editing text in a placeholder, you must click the place-holder to activate it.

T F **4.** You can activate the spelling checker by pressing F1.

T F **5.** The Find command is located on the Edit menu.

T F **6.** The Clipboard can hold text, graphics, or entire slides.

T F **7.** To move a slide while in Slide Sorter view, you can drag it or use the Cut and Paste commands.

T F **8.** You can use either Delete or ✂ to remove a selected slide from a presentation.

Write the correct answer in the space provided.

1. When using the AutoContent Wizard, what are the two methods for moving forward to the next dialog box?

_____

2. In Slide view, what shape is the pointer when it is placed outside a text box?

_____

3. Which feature in PowerPoint, if turned on, replaces commonly misspelled words with the correct spelling as you key?

_____

4. What function does 📋 perform?

_____

5. Where can you find the Paste All command?

_____

6. When you use the Header and Footer dialog box to add slide numbers to a presentation, where do the numbers appear on the slides by default?

_____

7. How would you use the Print dialog box to print only slides 1, 3, and 5 of a presentation?

_____

8. How many items can you store on the Office Clipboard?

_____

CRITICAL THINKING

Answer these questions on a separate page. There are no right or wrong answers. Support your answers with examples from your own experience, if possible.

1. PowerPoint provides tools to help you create a uniform presentation with consistent formatting for each slide. What are the advantages and disadvantages of uniformity for the audience? For the presenter?

2. You can use headers and footers to identify your slides, handouts, and notes. What information is most important to include? Why?

Skills Review

EXERCISE 2-14

Create a new presentation using the AutoContent Wizard, change sample text in the presentation, and delete slides.

1. Use the AutoContent Wizard to create a new presentation by following these steps:

a. Start PowerPoint. In the opening dialog box, choose the AutoContent Wizard option and click OK. (If PowerPoint is already active, choose New from the File menu, click the General tab, and double-click AutoContent Wizard.)

b. In the AutoContent Wizard dialog box, click Next.

c. Click General for type of presentation and pick Generic from the list at the right of the dialog box. Click Next.

> ***d.*** Choose On-screen Presentation for type of output and click <u>N</u>ext.
>
> ***e.*** Key **Advertising Analysis** in the <u>P</u>resentation Title text box and key your name in the <u>F</u>ooter text box. Click <u>N</u>ext.
>
> ***f.*** In the last dialog box, click <u>F</u>inish.

2. Change the sample title text by following these steps:

> ***a.*** Use `PgDn` or ⬇ to go to slide 4. In the slide pane, click the title text placeholder, select the text "Topic One," and key **Newspaper Advertising**. Click outside the text box to deselect it.
>
> ***b.*** Change the title text in slide 5 to **Radio Advertising**
>
> ***c.*** Skip to slide 7 and change the title text to **Yellow Pages**

3. Change the sample body text by following these steps:

> ***a.*** In the slide pane, click the bulleted text on slide 7 to activate the placeholder.
>
> ***b.*** Drag to select all bulleted text, from "Give" through "appropriate." Press `Delete`.
>
> ***c.*** Key the following text, pressing `Enter` at the end of each new bulleted item:
>
> - **Attractive display, prominent placement**
> - **Ad appears in all metro editions**
> - **Delivers 6% of customers**

4. Change the sample body text of slide 3 to the following bulleted items:

> - **Quality**
> - **Frequency**
> - **Effectiveness**

5. Delete slides by following these steps:

> ***a.*** Switch to Slide Sorter view and select slide 2 ("Introduction").
>
> ***b.*** Hold down `Ctrl` and select slides 6 ("Topic Three") and 8 ("What This Means").
>
> ***c.*** Press `Delete` to delete all three slides.

6. Save the presentation as ***[your initials]*2-14.ppt** in your Lesson 2 folder.

7. Print the presentation as handouts, 6 slides per page, grayscale, framed. (Because this type of presentation is preset for headers and footers, the handouts will contain the date as a header and the page number and presentation title as a footer.)

8. Close the presentation.

EXERCISE 2-15

Check spelling and find and replace text.

> ***1.*** Open the file **Advert1.ppt**.

   2. Run the spelling checker by following these steps:
      a. Click the Spelling button 🔤 on the Standard toolbar.
      b. Click Change to correct the spelling of "advertising."
      c. Click Change to correct the spelling of "humorous."
      d. Click OK when the spelling check is complete, and return to slide 1.

   3. Find and replace text by following these steps:
      a. Choose Replace from the Edit menu.
      b. In the Find What text box, key **Ads**. In the Replace With text box, key **Advertising**.
      c. Check Match Case, if necessary. Click Find Next.
      d. Use the Replace button to replace "Ads" with "Advertising" in each slide title.
      e. Click OK when complete and close the dialog box.

   4. Move to slide 1, which is the only slide with an all-uppercase title. If a light bulb appears, click it. Click the first option to change text to title case. (If you don't see a light bulb, edit the text to **Advertising Analysis**.)

   5. Change "Student Name" to your name on slide 1.

   6. Save the presentation as *[your initials]***2-15.ppt** in your Lesson 2 folder.

   7. Print the presentation as handouts, 9 slides per page, grayscale, framed. (The entire presentation should fit on one page.)

   8. Close the presentation.

EXERCISE 2-16

Rearrange slides in Slide Sorter view; cut, copy, and paste slide text.

   1. Open the file **Advert2.ppt**.

   2. In slide 1, replace "Student Name" with your own name.

   3. Drag a slide to move it by following these steps:
      a. Switch to Slide Sorter view and select slide 7 ("Yellow Pages").
      b. Position the pointer within slide 7's borders, press the left mouse button, and drag the pointer to the left of slide 5. Release the mouse button.

   4. Cut and paste to move a slide by following these steps:
      a. Select slide 7 ("Mailers").
      b. Click the Cut button ✂ on the Standard toolbar to cut the slide.
      c. Click between slides 5 and 6 (make sure you see the vertical bar after you click). Click the Paste button 📋 to paste the slide.

   5. Copy a slide by following these steps:
      a. Right-click slide 1 and choose Copy from the shortcut menu.
      b. Scroll to the bottom of the presentation. Right-click the insertion point after slide 9 and choose Paste to paste the slide. (The copied slide should be slide 10.)

6. Delete slide 8, "What This Means."

7. In Normal view, edit the last slide by changing the title to **Good 4 U**. Delete the text in the placeholder below the title and key **Successful Advertising Planning for the 21st Century**

8. Work with the Clipboard toolbar by following these steps:

    a. Display the Clipboard toolbar, if necessary, by opening the View menu and choosing Toolbars, Clipboard.

    b. Clear the Clipboard, if necessary, by clicking the Clear Clipboard button 🖾 on the Clipboard toolbar.

    c. Using the outline pane in Normal view, copy the word "Advertising" from the slide 1 title to the Clipboard. Point to the copied text item on the Clipboard to verify it contains the word "Advertising."

    d. In the slide 4 title, position the pointer to the right of "Newspaper." Click the Clipboard text item you just copied to the Clipboard, making the title "Newspaper Advertising." If necessary, insert a space before "Advertising."

    e. Repeat the procedure for the slide 5 title ("Yellow Pages") and the slide 7 title ("Radio").

    f. Clear the Clipboard toolbar and close it.

9. Save the presentation as **[your initials]2-16.ppt** in your Lesson 2 folder.

10. Print the presentation as handouts, 9 slides per page, grayscale, framed.

11. Close the presentation.

EXERCISE 2-17

Add headers and footers to a presentation, delete slides, and choose print options.

1. Open the file **Advert4.ppt**.

2. In slide 1, replace "Student Name" with your name.

3. Add a footer and slide numbers by following these steps:

    a. Choose Header and Footer from the View menu.

    b. Click the Slide tab, if necessary.

    c. Check Slide Number.

    d. Check Footer and key your name as a footer.

    e. Check Don't Show on Title Slide so the footer and slide number do not print on slide 1.

    f. Click Apply to All.

4. Scroll through the presentation to check the footer and slide numbers.

5. Add a date and footer to handout pages by following these steps:

    a. Open the Header and Footer dialog box.

    b. Click the Notes and Handouts tab.

    c. Check Date and Time and Update Automatically.

      d. Check Footer and key *[your initials]*2-17.ppt in the Footer text box.

      e. Make sure Page number is checked.

      f. Click Apply to All.

6. Delete the slides with these titles: "Topics of Discussion," "Yellow Pages," and "What This Means."

7. Save the presentation as *[your initials]*2-17.ppt in your Lesson 2 folder.

8. Print slides 1 and 3 only by following these steps:

      a. Open the Print dialog box.

      b. In the Print Range box, click Slides and key **1,3** in the text box.

      c. Choose Slides from the Print What drop-down list, choose Grayscale, and click OK.

9. Print only slides 1 though 3 as handouts (change the Slides text box to **1-3**), 3 slides per page, grayscale, framed.

10. Save the file again and close it.

Lesson Applications

Create a presentation using the AutoContent Wizard, edit sample text delete slides, and check spelling.

1. Start the AutoContent Wizard to create a presentation. When choosing a presentation type, click Corporate and choose **Company Meeting** from the list at the right of the dialog box. Click Next.

2. Complete the rest of the steps in the wizard, choosing On-screen Presentation and keying **Good 4 U Power Bars** as the Presentation title and your name as the Footer. Include the slide number and date. Click Finish when you get to the last step of the wizard.

3. On slide 1, change the subtitle text to **Brainstorming Session**

4. Go to slide 2 and key the following text in the bulleted text placeholder:

   Talk about Good 4 U developing and marketing a power bar (healthy "candy" bar)

5. Delete slide 3.

6. On the new slide 3, change the title from "How Did We Do?" to **Product Development**. Replace the current body text with the following four bulleted items:

   - **Features of the product**
   - **Packaging**
   - **Naming**
   - **Promotion**

7. On slide 6, change the title from "Review of Prior Goals" to **Marketing Overview**. Change the bulleted text to:

   - **Customer profile**
   - **Market research**
   - **Advertising budget**

8. Switch to Slide Sorter view and delete slide 4 ("Organizational Overview") and slide 5 ("Top Issues Facing Company").

9. Delete the remaining slides 5 through 9. (After the title slide, there should be four slides remaining: "Agenda," "Product Development," "Marketing Overview," and "Summary.")

10. Check spelling in the presentation.

11. Save the presentation as *[your initials]*2-18.ppt in your Lesson 2 folder.

12. Run the presentation as a slide show, clicking the left mouse button to advance through the text and slides.

13. Print the presentation as handouts, 6 slides per page, grayscale, framed.

14. Close the presentation.

EXERCISE 2-19

Use the AutoContent Wizard to create a presentation, change sample text, find and replace text, check spelling and style, delete and reorder slides, add slide numbers and a footer, and choose print options.

1. Use the AutoContent Wizard to create a presentation. For the presentation type, choose Product/Services Overview from the Sales/ Marketing category. The output will be an on-screen presentation. The presentation title is **Customer Relations Training**. Do not include any footer text or the date and slide number on each slide.

2. On slide 1, change the subtitle text to your name. Select the text "Your Logo Here" and delete it.

3. Change the sample text for existing slides 2 through 5 as shown in Figure 2-16.

FIGURE 2-16

Slide 2
Overview
- How you greet and seat people is critical
- Effective handling of parties guarantees success

Slide 3
Agenda
- Receiving customers
- Handling parties

Slide 4
Parties
- Usher celebrities to their tables
- Direct reporters to their station
- Consult with event planner for details

Slide 5
Receiving Customers
- Be professional, courteous
- Guide skaters and cyclists to equipment storage area
- Practice now by role playing

 4. Delete remaining slides 6 and 7.

 5. Reverse the positions of slides 4 and 5 so "Receiving Customers" comes before "Parties."

 6. Use the Replace command to replace "parties" with "special events" (clear the Match Case check box to find both "Parties" and "parties").

 7. Correct the style inconsistency in the slide 5 title so it's consistent with the other slide titles (which are title case).

 8. Check spelling in the presentation.

 9. Add slide numbers and a slide footer that contains the text **Good 4 U** to each slide except the title slide. (This presentation will print handouts with the presentation title and the page number as a footer, automatically.)

 10. Save the presentation as *[your initials]*2-19.ppt in your Lesson 2 folder.

 11. View the presentation as a slide show.

 12. Print the presentation as handouts, 6 slides per page, pure black and white, framed.

 13. Close the presentation.

EXERCISE 2-20

Change slide text, copy a slide, copy and paste slide text, check spelling, add headers and footers, and choose print options.

 1. Open the file **Events2.ppt**.

 2. Using the Find command, find the text "21st century." Close the Find dialog box and key **21st Century** over the selected text. (The "st" should appear as superscript automatically as you key the text.)

 3. Change the subtitle text to title case (click the light bulb and choose the correct option or edit the title manually).

 4. Move slide 6 to the slide 1 position and delete slide 2 (formerly slide 1).

 5. On slide 2, create a line break before the word "Good" by pressing Shift + Enter.

 TIP: Pressing Shift + Enter creates a line break within a paragraph. Pressing Enter before the word "Good" would create a new bulleted item.

 6. Change the title of slide 2 to **Objectives** and add the following bullet point after the existing one:

 • **Increase bookings of special events from entertainment and sports industries**

7. Change the title of slide 3 to read **What Does Everyone Want?**

8. Change the third bulleted item on slide 4 to **Award-winning service and cuisine**

9. Add a new first bullet to slide 4 that reads **High-energy, high-profile atmosphere**

10. Change slide 5 ("Next Steps") to read as follows:

   Next Steps - Sports
   - **Develop list of ideas for special events**
   - **Target sports-promotion companies**
   - **Contact professional sports organizations**
   - **Ask investors to call on sports-star friends**

11. Copy slide 5. Paste it at the end of the presentation to create slide 6.

12. Change slide 6 to read as follows:

   Next Steps - Entertainment
   - **Develop list of ideas for special events**
   - **Target press agents**
   - **Target public relations firms**
   - **Ask investors to call on celebrity friends**

13. Using the outline pane, copy the word "food" in slide 3 and paste it over the word "cuisine" in slide 4. Copy the word "Contact" in slide 5 and paste it over the word "target" in slide 6, in both the second and third bullets.

14. Clear and close the Clipboard toolbar, if it is open.

15. Add slide numbers to all slides. Add a handout header that contains the completed filename, *[your initials]***2-20.ppt**. Add a handout footer that contains your name.

16. Save the presentation as *[your initials]***2-20.ppt** in your Lesson 2 folder.

17. Print the presentation as handouts, 6 slides per page in vertical order, grayscale, framed.

18. Close the presentation.

EXERCISE 2-21   *Challenge Yourself*

Use the AutoContent Wizard to create a presentation, change sample text, check spelling, find and replace text, copy and paste text, delete and reorder slides, add headers, and choose print options.

   1. Use the AutoContent Wizard to create a Generic presentation from the General category for output as a Web presentation. The presentation

title is **Premium Items**. Include the footer **Good 4 U**. Include the slide number but not the date.

2. On slide 1, change the subtitle text to your name.

3. Use the Replace command to replace each occurrence of the word "Topic" in the presentation with the word "Item." Use the Match Case and Whole Words Only options so you replace only "Topic" and not "Topics" or "topic."

4. Delete slide 2.

5. Edit the new slide 2 through slide 5 as shown in Figure 2-17. (Note the change in numeric format from "Item One" to "Item 1".)

FIGURE 2-17

Slide 2
Topics of Discussion
- Introduce new premium items to give away at special events
- All premium items will contain the Good 4 U logo

Slide 3
Item 1: Water Bottle
- Made of durable plastic
- Excellent for outdoor sports and indoor workouts

Slide 4
Item 2: Knee Pads
- Made of durable vinyl/foam
- Essential protection for skaters

Slide 5
Item 3: Visor
- Made of white cotton blend
- Adjustable, one size fits all
- Ideal for tennis, running, walking, skating

6. Delete slides 6 through 8.

7. Move the Item 3 slide before the Item 2 slide. Change the item numbers in the slide titles to be consecutive.

8. Open the file **Products.ppt**. Use the <u>W</u>indow menu to arrange both presentations, displaying them both in Slide Sorter view. (Remember, each window has its own view buttons.)

9. Copy slide 3 ("Next Steps") from the Products.ppt presentation. Paste the slide after slide 5 in your Premium Items presentation.

10. Close Products.ppt. Maximize the Premium Items presentation and display it in Normal view.

11. Display the Clipboard toolbar. Clear any items that may be stored there.

12. Copy to the Clipboard "Water Bottle" from slide 3, "Visor" from slide 4, and "Knee Pads" from slide 5.

13. Select your name in the subtitle placeholder on slide 1 and use the Paste All button on the Clipboard. Place each item on a separate line (using Shift + Enter).

14. Clear the Clipboard toolbar and close it.

15. Check spelling in the presentation.

16. Add the filename *[your initials]*2-21.htm to the handout header.

17. Save the presentation in HTML format as *[your initials]*2-21.htm in your Lesson 2 folder.

18. Print the presentation as handouts, 6 slides per page, grayscale, framed.

19. Print only slides 1 and 2 as handouts, 2 slides per page, using the pure black and white setting.

20. View the presentation in your Web browser (File, Web Page Preview), if possible, and then close the browser window.

21. Close the presentation.

Unit 1 Applications

Copy and delete slides, edit slide text, check spelling, add header and footer
information to handouts, and choose print options.

1. Open the file **Growing2.ppt**.
2. Move slide 2 after slide 7.
3. Delete the newly numbered slide 2 ("Presenting Good 4 U").
4. Move slide 3 ("Financial History") after slide 5.
5. On slide 2, add the title **Who We Are** and delete the text "Their dreams" and the subtext below it.
6. Copy slide 2 and paste it between slides 2 and 3.
7. On the new slide 3, edit the title to **What We Want**. Delete all the text in the bulleted placeholder and key these bulleted items:
   - **To encourage healthy eating**
   - **To promote participation in sports activities**
   - **To expand our market base**
8. Check spelling in the presentation.
9. Run the presentation as a slide show.
10. On the handouts, include today's date as a fixed date (remember to key today's date in the Fixed text box), add your name as the header, and add the filename *[your initials]***u1-1.ppt** as the footer.
11. Save the file as *[your initials]***u1-1.ppt** in a new folder for Unit 1 Applications.
12. Print the presentation as handouts, 4 slides per page, pure black and white, framed.
13. Close the presentation.

Copy and move slides, edit text, find and replace text, check spelling and style,
add slide numbers, and add handout headers and footers.

1. Open the file **Menu1.ppt**.
2. Copy slide 2 ("Pasta Delights") and paste it between slides 2 and 3 of the presentation.

3. Find the word "desert" and replace it with "dessert."

4. On slide 4 ("Just Sweet Enough"), delete just the sentence that begins "The striking lime flavor."

5. On slide 3 (the second "Pasta Delights" slide), change the title to **Salad Delights**.

6. Select the first bulleted paragraph with the hyphen bullet (which begins "A savory dish") and delete it. Do the same for the paragraph that begins "Delicately flavored." Edit the remaining bulleted text on slide 3 to match the text shown in Figure U1-1.

FIGURE U1-1

- Spinach Salad à la Julie

- Michelle's Cobb Salad

- Grilled Chicken Salad

- Wild Rice and Smoked Turkey Salad

- Corn, Black Bean, and Mango Salad

7. Open the file **Samples.ppt**. Arrange both presentations on the screen, displaying each in Slide Sorter view.

8. Copy slide 2 ("Appetizer Specials") from Samples.ppt. Paste it after slide 1 in Menu1.ppt. Close Samples.ppt and maximize Menu1.ppt.

9. Copy slide 1 and paste it at the end of the presentation. Change the text "New Additions to Our Menu" to **A New Experience in Dining**

10. Check spelling in the presentation. Go through each slide and check for style inconsistencies. Remove any periods that the style checker locates.

11. Add slide numbers to all slides. Add a handout header that contains your name, add a handout footer that contains the filename *[your initials]*u1-2.ppt, and add today's date as a fixed date.

12. Save the presentation as *[your initials]*u1-2.ppt in your Unit 1 Applications folder.

13. Print slide 2 of the presentation in grayscale.

14. Print the entire presentation as handouts, 6 slides per page, grayscale, framed.

15. Close the presentation.

UNIT APPLICATION 1-3

Use the AutoContent Wizard to create a new presentation, edit slide text, delete and copy slides, add handout headers and footers, and check spelling.

1. Use the AutoContent Wizard to start a new presentation. For presentation type, choose "Reporting Progress or Status" from the Projects category. The presentation will be for a Web presentation. In the last Wizard dialog box, do not include a presentation title or footer, but include the date and slide number.

2. Delete slide 1.

3. On the new slide 1, keep the title ("Status Summary"), but change the body text to the following:

   - **Currently have at least one special event scheduled per month**
   - **Some events are dependent on weather and other factors**

4. Change the title and body text of slide 2 to read as follows:

   1st Quarter Events
   - **January:**
   - **February:**
   - **March:**

5. Copy slide 2 and paste it before slide 3. Paste the same slide two additional times so four copies of the same slide appear as slides 2, 3, 4, and 5. (*Tip:* You can copy just once and paste repeatedly.)

6. Delete all slides after slide 5 except the last slide, "Goals for Next Review." (*Tip:* Use ⟦Shift⟧+click to select multiple consecutive slides.)

7. Edit slides 2 through 6 as shown in Figure U1-2.

FIGURE U1-2

1st Quarter Events

Slide 2
- January: New Year's Day power walk
- February: Westchester Girls' Gymnastics demonstration and lunch
- March: National In-line Skaters' warm-up party

2nd Quarter Events

Slide 3
- April: Health Expo brunch
- May:
- June:

continues

continued

Slide 4

3rd Quarter Events

- July: Autograph session with aerobic video star Marsha Miles
- August: Marathon runner Steve Forbo
- September:

Slide 5

4th Quarter Events

- October: Kick-boxing demonstration
- November:
- December: Holiday party for Special Olympics

Slide 6

Next Steps

- Confirm dates
- Make necessary schedule shifts
- Draft ad copy
- Post on Internet

8. Rearrange the event schedule by moving the gymnastics event from February to May and the brunch from April to June.

9. Change the first bullet in slide 1 to read **Currently have two special events scheduled per quarter**

10. Display the Clipboard toolbar. On slide 4, in the first bullet, copy "Autograph session with" and paste it before "Marathon." Change "Marathon" to lowercase.

11. On slide 6, in the second bullet, copy the word "schedule" and paste it after "ad copy" in the third bullet and after "Post" in the fourth bullet.

12. Clear the Clipboard toolbar and close it.

13. Check spelling in the presentation.

14. Check that slides have slide numbers and remove the date from the slides.

15. To the handouts, add a header that contains your name, add a footer that contains the filename *[your initials]*u1-3.htm, and add today's date as a fixed date.

16. Save the presentation as a Web page named *[your initials]*u1-3.htm in your Unit 1 Applications folder.

17. Print the presentation as handouts, 6 slides per page, grayscale, framed.

18. Preview the presentation in Web Page Preview, if possible, and then close the browser window.

19. Close the presentation.

UNIT APPLICATION 1-4

Use the AutoContent Wizard to write your own presentation, change sample text, copy and paste a slide, check spelling, work with slide and handout footers, and find and replace text.

1. Use the AutoContent Wizard to create a new Generic on-screen presentation, which you will customize to discuss launching a new Good 4 U restaurant in your hometown. Key **Good 4 U** in the Presentation title box. Exclude any slide text in the wizard dialog box except the slide number and date.

2. On slide 1, replace any subtitle text with your name. Key the name of your hometown on a new line.

3. Delete the "Introduction" slide.

4. On the "Topics of Discussion" slide, use two bulleted items: one to explain the idea of launching a Good 4 U restaurant in your hometown and the other to state the proposed street or neighborhood location.

5. On the "Topic One" slide, key **Meeting the Needs** in place of the existing title text and replace the body text with the following bullets:

   - **Neighborhood has no restaurant that supports healthy food, sports, and fitness**
   - **Health and fitness are important concerns in the community**

6. Delete the slides titled "Topic Two," "Topic Three," and "Real Life."

7. Change the title of the "What This Means" slide to **Major Benefits**. Then list three ways your town would benefit from having a restaurant that promotes healthy eating and fitness.

8. Copy the "Major Benefits" slide and paste it between slides 4 and 5. Change the title to **Major Concerns** and change the body text to the following:

   - **How will community react to a high-profile "health food" restaurant?**
   - **Can we find a large enough space for a reasonable rent?**
   - **How quickly can we locate investors?**

9. On the "Next Steps" slide, list what you think the next three steps are for launching the new restaurant (for example, finding investors and a location).

10. Find the word "Major" and replace it with **Key**

11. Add footer text to all slides except the title slide. Use the text **Prepared by** and key your name. Remove the date from all slides. On the handout, include today's date and add the filename *[your initials]***u1-4.ppt** as header text.

12. Check spelling and style in the presentation.

13. Save the presentation as *[your initials]***u1-4.ppt** in your Unit 1 Applications folder.

14. Print the presentation as handouts, 6 slides per page, pure black and white, framed.

15. Run the presentation as a slide show.

16. Close the presentation.

UNIT APPLICATION 1-5 *Making It Work for You*

Use the AutoContent Wizard to write your own presentation.

Use the AutoContent Wizard to create an on-screen presentation, using the presentation type "Communicating Bad News." The presentation can be about any real-life, fictional, or historical event. Adjust slide text and move or delete slides as needed.

In the slide footer, include the text **Prepared by** followed by your name. Include the slide number on all slides but not the date. In the handout footer, include the completed filename *[your initials]***u1-5.ppt**. In the handout header, key **Presented to** and then identify to whom you would be giving this presentation. Include in the handout the date you would be delivering the presentation. (Remember, this could be past, present, or future.)

Spell-check the presentation and save it as *[your initials]***u1-5.ppt** in your Unit 1 Applications folder. Practice delivering the presentation as a slide show, clicking to advance the slides. You might try using the pen during the presentation. Print the presentation handouts in pure black and white.

UNIT 2

Developing a Presentation

Creating a Presentation from Scratch

After completing this lesson, you will be able to:

1. **Create a new presentation.**
2. **Add new slides.**
3. **Promote and demote text.**
4. **Use the Undo and Redo commands.**
5. **Change slide layouts.**
6. **Change design templates and color schemes.**
7. **Work with speaker's notes.**

MOUS
ACTIVITIES

In this lesson:
PP2000 **1.2**
PP2000 **1.3**
PP2000 **1.8**
PP2000 **2.3**
PP2000 **2.6**
PP2000 **3.10**
PP2000 **5.2**
PP2000 **6.4**
PP2000 **E.2.3**

See Appendix F.

 Estimated Time: 1 hour

The AutoContent Wizard is a great tool for creating standard presentations, but you will soon want the freedom to design your own slides and layouts. In this Lesson you learn how to use PowerPoint's design templates and how to add colorful backgrounds to enhance your presentation design. You choose the best way to lay out text on a slide for the information you want to present. After creating the final presentation, you create speaker's notes to assist you in delivering the presentation.

Creating a New Presentation

To create a presentation from scratch, you can begin with either:

- A *design template*, which adds a uniform color and design scheme to each slide in the presentation
- A blank presentation (simple text on a plain background), to which you apply a design template later

You build each slide by choosing a slide layout and entering slide text.

EXERCISE **3-1** **Create a New Presentation by Using a Template**

1. Start PowerPoint.

2. In the opening PowerPoint dialog box, choose Design Template and click OK. The New Presentation dialog box appears with a list of templates.

FIGURE 3-1
New Presentation
dialog box

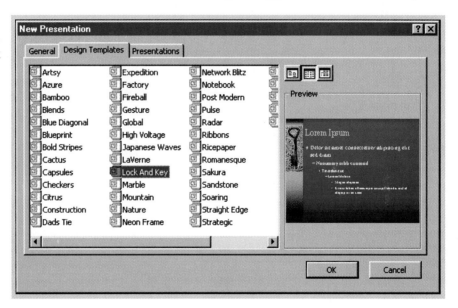

NOTE: If PowerPoint is already active, close any open presentations, choose New from the File menu, and click the Design Templates tab in the New Presentation dialog box.

3. Click a template name (make sure you don't double-click or you'll open another dialog box). The Preview box in the dialog box displays the template design.

4. Preview two or three different designs.

 NOTE: Some templates may not be installed on your computer, in which case the Preview box displays a text message instead of the template design.

5. Choose the design Lock and Key and click OK. The New Slide dialog box appears with a choice of slide layouts.

EXERCISE 3-2 Choose Slide Layouts

A slide layout, or *AutoLayout*, is determined by the slide's contents, which can consist of bulleted text, tables, charts, or simply a title for the presentation. Most presentations include at least two slide layouts: one for a title slide and one for the body of the presentation. You can choose an AutoLayout that is appropriate for the content of each slide in your presentation.

1. In the New Slide dialog box, use the scroll bar to view the different AutoLayouts.

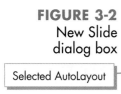

FIGURE 3-2
New Slide
dialog box

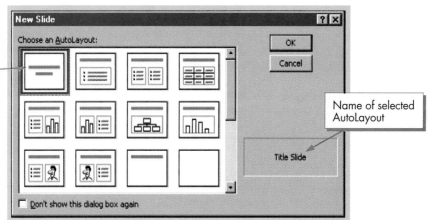

2. Click different AutoLayouts (do not double-click) to identify them by name (the name appears in the lower right corner of the dialog box).

3. Click the Title Slide (the first one) and click OK. A slide with two text placeholders appears, one for the title and one for the subtitle. The title slide is styled with the design template.

4. Close the presentation. In the next Exercise, you open a blank presentation, with no design template.

EXERCISE 3-3 Create a New Blank Presentation

Sometimes it's best to start with a blank presentation, with no suggested design or colors. You can then focus on the presentation content and decide later which template to apply.

1. Click the New button on the Standard toolbar. The New Slide dialog box appears.

NOTE: To start a blank presentation when you first start PowerPoint, choose <u>B</u>lank presentation in the opening PowerPoint dialog box and click OK. The New Slide dialog box appears with the Title Slide AutoLayout selected.

2. Choose the Title Slide layout and click OK. A title slide appears with the two text placeholders on a blank background. This blank background is the default template—notice it says "Default Design" on the status bar at the bottom of the screen.

FIGURE 3-3
Title slide

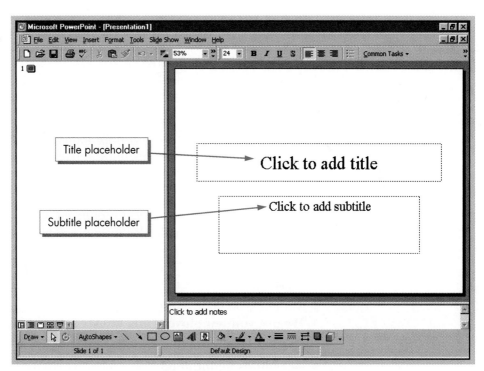

3. Click the title placeholder to activate it and key **Good 4 U Restaurant**. Notice that both the slide pane and the outline pane show the text you key.

4. Click the subtitle placeholder and key **For the Pleasure of Your Company**

> ✦ **TIP:** You can also move from the title placeholder to the subtitle placeholder by pressing `Ctrl`+`Enter`. That way you don't have to move your fingers off the keyboard.

Adding New Slides

The body of most presentations requires a different layout than the title slide. Once you begin a presentation, you can add slides with different AutoLayouts by opening the New Slide dialog box. To open this dialog box, you can:

- Click the <u>C</u>ommon Tasks button on the Formatting toolbar and choose <u>N</u>ew Slide from the submenu.
- Click the New Slide button on the Standard toolbar.
- Choose <u>N</u>ew Slide from the <u>I</u>nsert menu or press `Ctrl`+`M`.

EXERCISE 3-4 Insert New Slides

FIGURE 3-4
Bulleted List
AutoLayout icon

1. Click the New Slide button on the Standard toolbar. (You may have to click the More Buttons button » first to locate the button.) The New Slide dialog box appears with the Bulleted List AutoLayout selected. It is the default AutoLayout after a title slide.

2. Click OK.

3. Key **Excellent Service**. The text appears in the Title placeholder.

> ➢ **NOTE:** When no placeholder is activated, the text you key automatically appears in the title placeholder, so you don't have to click to activate the placeholder.

4. Press `Ctrl`+`Enter` or click the bulleted text placeholder to activate it and key the following text:

- **We put your employees and guests at ease**
- **We make your company look good**
- **Schedules maintained**
- **Professional and courteous staff**
- **Guaranteed customer satisfaction**

5. Press `Ctrl`+`Enter` to create a new bulleted list slide.

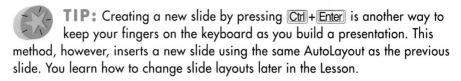

TIP: Creating a new slide by pressing Ctrl + Enter is another way to keep your fingers on the keyboard as you build a presentation. This method, however, inserts a new slide using the same AutoLayout as the previous slide. You learn how to change slide layouts later in the Lesson.

6. Key **A Delightful Menu** as the title and then key the following bulleted text:
   - **High-quality, healthy food**
   - **Variety to appeal to a broad range of tastes**

7. Click the <u>C</u>ommon Tasks button and choose <u>N</u>ew Slide. Double-click the Bulleted List icon. Another new slide appears.

FIGURE 3-5
Common Tasks menu

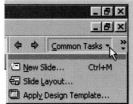

TIP: You can float the <u>C</u>ommon Tasks menu for easy access to the most frequently used tools when creating a presentation. To do this, click the <u>C</u>ommon Tasks button, point to the top of the menu, and drag the menu to another part of the screen.

8. Key **High-Energy Fun** as the title and then key the following text:
   - **Athletic decor**
   - **Sports promotions**

NOTE: Notice that AutoCorrect automatically adds the accent mark to the word "décor."

9. Press Ctrl + M to open the New Slide dialog box. Choose the Bulleted List AutoLayout.

10. Key **A Healthy Atmosphere** as the title and key the following text:
    - **Smoke-free**
    - **Alcohol optional**
    - **We sell none**
    - **We'll gladly serve your own**

11. Check spelling and then save the presentation as *[your initials]***3-4.ppt** in a new folder for Lesson 3. Leave it open for the next Exercise.

Promoting and Demoting Text

In PowerPoint you can change the level of importance assigned to bulleted items. You can show supporting ideas under main ideas, as in an outline. You can *demote* bulleted text, moving it to the next lower heading level, or *promote* bulleted text, raising it to the next higher heading level.

EXERCISE 3-5 Promote and Demote Bulleted Text

1. In slide 2, select the text "We make your company look good."

 NOTE: Remember, you can select a bulleted paragraph by clicking its bullet or dragging across the text.

 2. Click the Demote button on the Formatting toolbar. (You may need to click "More Buttons" to display this button.) The text is reduced in size and indented to the right, and the bullet shape changes.

 3. Return the text to its original size and placement by clicking the Promote button ◄. Notice the change in the outline pane as you promote and demote text.

4. Position the insertion point anywhere in the next item ("Schedules maintained") and click the Demote button ►. The item is demoted. Notice that you don't have to select the bulleted text to change its level.

5. In the next item, position the insertion point between the bullet and the word "Professional." Do not select the text. Press Tab. The bullet is demoted.

6. With the insertion point between the bullet and the text, press Shift + Tab. The bullet is promoted.

NOTE: If you press Tab when the insertion point is within the text, you insert a tab character.

7. Select the last two items by dragging over the text (avoid dragging over the bullets or you may move the bulleted text instead of selecting it).

8. Press Tab to demote both items. Slide 2 should look like Figure 3-6 (on the next page). If it doesn't, promote or demote text accordingly.

9. Switch to Slide Sorter view and move slide 5 ("A Healthy Atmosphere") to become slide 4.

10. Double-click the new slide 4 to return to Normal view. Select and demote the last two bullets, making them subtext under "Alcohol optional."

11. Click the bullet to the left of "Alcohol optional." The bulleted text and the two bullets below it are selected.

12. Press Tab or click the Demote button ►. All three lines are demoted to subtext under "Smoke-free."

13. Promote the selected text to restore the bullet levels.

FIGURE 3-6
Demoting bulleted
text

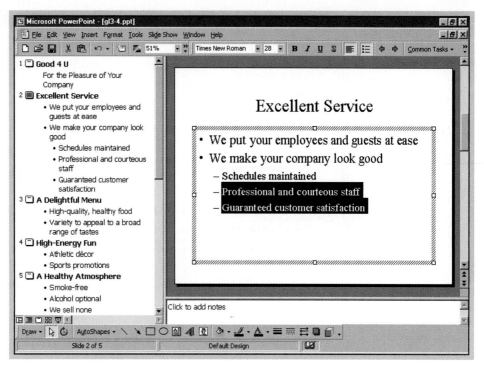

Using the Undo and Redo Commands

The Undo button ⟲ on the Standard toolbar reverses the last action you took. You can undo a series of editing actions, including keying or deleting text, promoting or demoting items, or changing formats and text attributes. You can undo multiple actions. The Redo button ⟳ reapplies editing commands in the order you undid them.

TIP: By default, PowerPoint can undo the last 20 actions. You can increase or decrease this number by choosing Tools, Options, Edit tab, and changing the Maximum number of undos. Increasing the number uses up more RAM memory on your computer.

EXERCISE 3-6   Use the Undo and Redo Commands

1. In slide 2, select the bulleted text "We make your company look good" and its three sub-bullets.
2. Click the Demote button ⇨ or press Tab three times. The items are indented and reduced in size by three levels.

FIGURE 3-7
Creating third-level
bullets

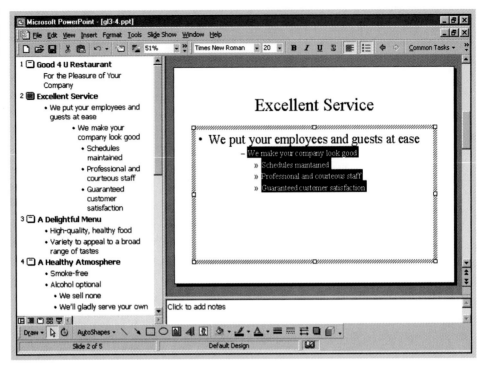

3. Choose Undo Demote from the Edit menu. The last demotion is undone.

 4. Click the Undo button [↶] (you may have to locate it by clicking More Buttons [»]). Another level of demotion is undone.

5. Press Ctrl+Z, the keyboard shortcut for Undo. The first level of demotion is undone.

6. Press Ctrl+Y, the keyboard shortcut for Redo. The most recent demotion is redone.

 7. Click the Redo button [↷]. The previous level of demotion is redone.

8. Choose Redo Demote from the expanded Edit menu. The final level of demotion is redone.

9. Undo the three demotions so the slide is restored to the levels shown in Figure 3-6 (from the previous Exercise). Deselect the selected text.

NOTE: Undo and Redo are cleared when you save a presentation. After saving, you cannot undo or redo actions performed prior to the saving.

Changing Slide Layouts

You can try out different layouts on existing slides. For example, you can change from a single-column bullet list to a two-column bullet list. If you don't like your changes, you can reverse them with the Undo option. You change the layout of the active slide with the Slide Layout dialog box. To open the dialog box:

● Choose Slide Layout from the Common Tasks menu on the Formatting toolbar.

● Choose Slide Layout from the Format menu or the shortcut menu

EXERCISE 3-7 Change a Slide Layout

1. Move to slide 5 ("High-Energy Fun"). Click the Common Tasks button and choose Slide Layout. The Slide Layout dialog box appears. (Notice its similarity to the New Slide dialog box.)

FIGURE 3-8
2 Column Text icon

2. Select the 2 Column Text layout and click Apply. The layout of the slide changes with the two existing bullets appearing in a left-column placeholder.

3. Select the second bullet ("Sports promotions") and cut it.

4. Click in the right-column placeholder (or press Ctrl+Enter) and then paste the bullet. One bullet appears in each column. Notice how each column is numbered in the outline pane.

5. Add the following item to the left column:

● **Energetic staff**

6. Add the following item to the right column:

● **Special event tie-ins**

FIGURE 3-9
Slide 5 with new
slide layout

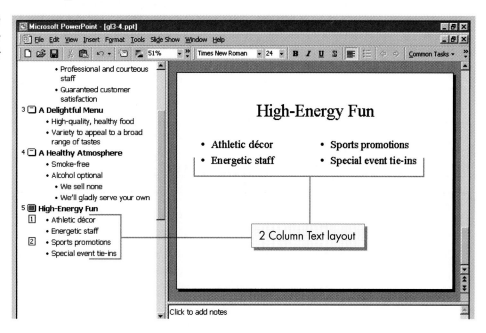

7. Press ⌈Ctrl⌉+⌈Enter⌉. A new slide appears with the 2 Column Text layout.

8. Using the arrow pointer, right-click a blank area of the slide (an area outside of a text placeholder) to display the shortcut menu. Choose Slide Layout.

9. Double-click the Bulleted List layout icon to change layouts.

10. Key the slide title **Events That Are Good 4 U** and then key the following bulleted text:
    - **High-energy meetings**
    - **Productive lunches**
    - **Company celebrations**

11. Add the footer **Good 4 U Restaurant** on every slide except the title.

12. Spell-check the presentation and save it as *[your initials]***3-7.ppt** in your Lesson 3 folder.

13. Create headers and footers for Notes and Handouts. Include the date and your name at the top of the page and the page number and filename at the bottom.

14. Print the presentation as handouts, 6 slides per page, grayscale, framed.

15. Save the presentation again and leave it open.

Applying a Design Template

Whether you began a presentation with a design template or with the Default Design template you are using now, you can change the template by using the Apply Design Template dialog box. To open the dialog box:

- Choose Apply Design Template on the Common Tasks menu.
- Choose Apply Design Template from the Format menu or the shortcut menu.
- Double-click the existing template name on the status bar.

EXERCISE **3-8** **Apply a Design Template**

1. With the presentation *[your initials]***3-7.ppt** open, click the Common Tasks button and choose Apply Design Template.

2. In the Apply Design Template dialog box, click the Views drop-down button and choose Preview, if necessary, so you can preview a template before applying it.

FIGURE 3-10
Apply Design
Template
dialog box

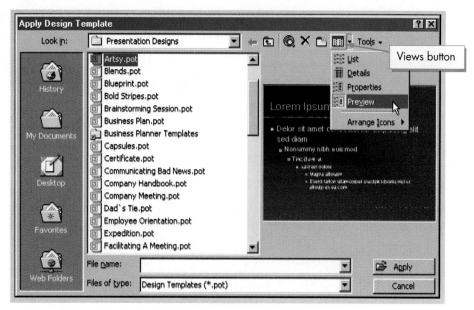

3. Scroll the list of design template filenames (which have the extension .pot) in the dialog box and choose **Marble.pot**. Click Apply. In a few seconds, your presentation is reformatted with the new design. The new template name appears on the status bar.

4. Click the Undo button 🔄 to restore the Default Design.

5. Double-click "Default Design" on the status bar to reopen the Apply Design Template dialog box, choose the **Nature.pot** design, and click Apply.

6. Review the presentation in Slide Sorter view.

7. Select slide 1 and then review the presentation in Slide Show view, using your preferred method to advance from slide to slide (such as the left mouse button or PgDn).

8. Return to Normal view.

EXERCISE   3-9   Change the Template Color Scheme

You can apply new colors to the current design template by changing the template's color scheme. Using the Color Scheme dialog box, you can choose from several standard color schemes and apply a scheme to a single slide or to all slides in a presentation. You open the Color Scheme dialog box from either the Format menu or the shortcut menu.

1. Using the arrow pointer, right-click a blank area of a slide and choose Slide Color Scheme from the shortcut menu.

2. Click the Standard tab in the Color Scheme dialog box, if necessary. Notice that for this template, there are five available color schemes and the second one is selected.

FIGURE 3-11
Color Scheme
dialog box

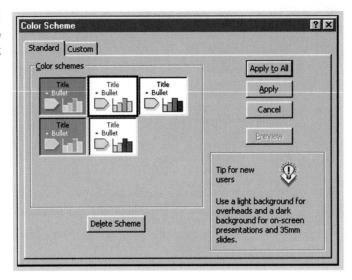

3. Select the first color scheme and click Preview.

 NOTE: You can also customize color schemes, as you'll learn in Lesson 7: "Working with Lines, Fills, and Colors."

4. Drag the dialog box out of the way so you can see the effect on the slide.
5. Click Apply to All. The color scheme of all slides in the presentation is changed.
6. Click the Undo button ⟲ to see what the previous scheme looked like.
7. Click the Redo button ⟳. The new color scheme is restored.
8. Scroll through the slides to review the color change.

EXERCISE **3-10** **Apply a Template from Another Presentation**

You may have a presentation file that uses a special template, such as one that was already customized in some way. You can apply this presentation's template to your current presentation.

1. Double-click the existing template name "Nature" on the status bar to open the Apply Design Template dialog box.
2. Open the Files of Type drop-down list and choose All PowerPoint Files.

3. Change the Look In box to the location of your student files (the ones you load, not the ones you saved with your initials).

4. Locate the file **Growing2.ppt** and click Apply. The template is applied to the current presentation. Notice that "Growing2" appears as the template name on the status bar.

5. Scroll through the presentation to see how the new template looks.

6. Because the previous template was more appropriate for the presentation content, click the Undo button 🔁 to restore it.

Working with Speaker's Notes

Speakers often use notes to guide their presentations. In PowerPoint, a notes page contains a small picture of the slide above a text section. The text can include a script, comments, or reminders. You key notes directly into the notes pane, which you can make larger, if needed.

EXERCISE 3-11 **Create and Print Speaker's Notes**

1. Display slide 2 and click the notes pane to activate it.

2. Key the following text:

> **Your choice of a meeting place says a lot about your organization. Good 4 U focuses on service for two reasons:**

3. Resize the notes pane by placing the mouse pointer on the horizontal border between the slide and notes panes. The pointer changes to a double-headed arrow. Drag the border up, enlarging the notes pane until it is approximately half the screen. (See Figure 3-12 on the next page.)

 NOTE: You can customize the size of each pane (slide, notes, and outline) by dragging the pane borders.

4. Key the following two numbered notes in the expanded notes pane:

> **1. We want you, your employees, and your guests (friends, clients, investors) to feel at ease.**
> **2. We want our professionalism to mirror yours.**

 NOTE: When you press enter after the first numbered note, PowerPoint may automatically format your text as a numbered list. If this happens, you don't have to key "2." for the next note.

5. Choose Notes Page from the View menu. When you print a notes page, this is what it looks like: slide on top and notes below it.

FIGURE 3-12
Resizing the
notes pane

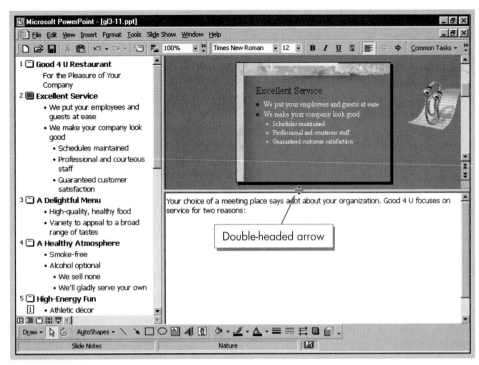

6. Scroll to slide 3 in Notes Page view.

7. Open the Zoom drop-down list box on the Standard toolbar. Choose 100%.

FIGURE 3-13
Changing the
Zoom in Notes
Page view

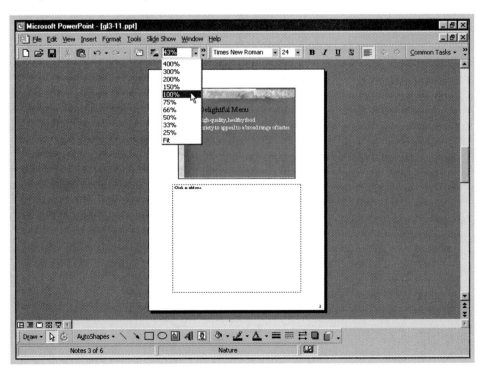

8. Scroll to the notes text placeholder, if necessary. Click the placeholder to activate it and key the following text:

Distribute menus.
Point out vegetarian and meat dishes.
Point out healthy beverages.

9. Reduce the size of the notes pane to the "Fit" setting.

10. Display slide 3 in Normal view. Reduce the height of the notes pane so you see only the three lines of note text.

11. Check spelling in the presentation.

 NOTE: The spell-checker checks for errors in note text, header and footer text, and slide text.

12. Edit the Notes and Handouts footer to reflect the filename *[your initials]* **3-11.ppt**.

13. Save the presentation as *[your initials]***3-11.ppt** in your Lesson 3 folder.

14. Print the presentation as handouts, 6 slides per page, grayscale, framed.

15. Reopen the Print dialog box. Choose Notes Pages from the Print What drop-down list.

16. Click Slides and key **2-3** in the text box to print notes pages for slides 2 and 3 only. Choose Grayscale and click OK.

17. Close the presentation.

COMMAND SUMMARY

FEATURE	BUTTON	MENU	KEYBOARD
Insert new slide		Insert, New Slide or Common Tasks, New Slide	Ctrl + M
Change slide layout		Format, Slide Layout or Common Tasks, Slide Layout	
Apply design template		Format, Apply Design Template or Common Tasks, Apply Design Template	
Demote			Tab
Promote			Shift + Tab
Undo		Edit, Undo	Ctrl + Z
Redo		Edit, Redo	Ctrl + Y

USING HELP

Your choice of color schemes can affect the tone of your presentation. Help is available to explain your options.

Exploring color schemes in Help:

1. Display the Office Assistant. Click to activate it.

2. Key **color schemes** in the text box and click <u>S</u>earch (or press Enter).

3. Click the third topic, "How color schemes work." Maximize the Help window, if necessary.

FIGURE 3-14
Using Help to understand color-scheme options

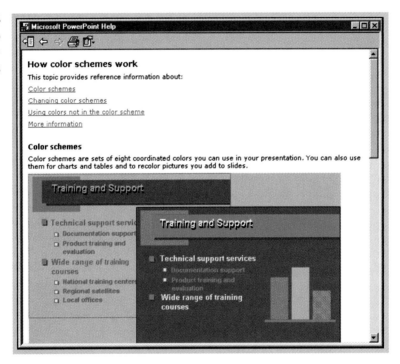

4. Scroll through the information in the Help window.

5. Close the Help window when you finish. Hide the Office Assistant.

Concepts Review

TRUE/FALSE QUESTIONS

Each of the following statements is either true or false. Indicate your choice by circling **T** or **F**.

T   F   **1.** You can start a new presentation with a blank template or a design template.

T   F   **2.** The AutoLayout dialog box shows the name of the layout that you select.

T   F   **3.** You can add a new slide by pressing Ctrl+Y.

T   F   **4.** You can use ⬅ and ➡ on the Formatting toolbar to promote and demote bullets.

T   F   **5.** The keyboard shortcut for undoing a task is Ctrl+Z.

T   F   **6.** You can change a design template in the Slide Layout dialog box.

T   F   **7.** A template color scheme is predefined and cannot be changed.

T   F   **8.** You can print speaker's notes in either grayscale or color.

SHORT ANSWER QUESTIONS

Write the correct answer in the space provided.

1. Which Common Tasks menu item can you use to change a slide from a title slide to a bulleted list slide?

_____

2. How do you add a new slide to a presentation?

_____

3. You just promoted a bullet. Name two ways you can use the mouse to return the bullet to its original size and position.

_____

4. In a blank presentation, what happens when you double-click "Default Design" on the status bar?

_____

5. If you insert a new slide while working on a title slide, what slide layout is automatically chosen for you?

_____

6. Which tab do you click in the Color Scheme dialog box to choose a predefined color scheme?

_____

7. How can you add a speaker's note without changing to Notes Page view?

_____

8. Which drop-down list in the Print dialog box contains the option to print notes pages?

_____

CRITICAL THINKING

Answer these questions on a separate page. There are no right or wrong answers. Support your answers with examples from your own experience, if possible.

1. Review PowerPoint's design templates. In what kinds of presentations might you use the different templates?
2. What are some advantages of starting with a blank presentation instead of using the AutoContent Wizard? Which method do you prefer and why?

Skills Review

EXERCISE 3-12

Create a new blank presentation and add new slides.

1. Open a new blank presentation and choose the layout for the title slide by following these steps:

   a. Start PowerPoint. Select Blank Presentation and click OK. (If PowerPoint is already running, or if the starting dialog box does not appear, click the New button 🔲 on the Standard toolbar.)

    NOTE: If the PowerPoint starting dialog box and the New Slide dialog box options are turned off, a new blank presentation will automatically appear when you start PowerPoint.

   b. In the New Slide dialog box, choose the Title Slide layout and click OK.

2. Complete the title slide by following these steps:

  a. Key **Healthy Eating** as the first line of the title (you don't have to click the text "Click to add title" to begin keying the title slide text).

  b. Press Enter to start a new title line.

  c. Key **for Young Athletes** to complete the title.

  d. Press Ctrl + Enter.

  e. Key the subtitle **A Good 4 U Seminar**

3. Add a new slide with the Bulleted List layout by following these steps:

  a. Press Ctrl + Enter.

  b. Key **Basic Food Groups** as the title.

  c. Key the following bulleted text:

    • **Fats, oils, and sweets**
    • **Dairy products**
    • **Meat, poultry, fish, eggs, beans, and nuts**
    • **Fruits and vegetables**
    • **Rice, bread, and pasta**

4. Add a third slide with the Bulleted List layout by follow these steps:

  a. Click the Common Tasks button on the Formatting toolbar.

  b. Choose New Slide from the menu.

  c. Choose the Bulleted List layout and click OK.

5. Key **Elements of a Healthy Diet** as the title of the slide.

6. Key the following bulleted text:

    • **Choose a variety of foods**
    • **Eat moderate amounts**
    • **Choose low-fat foods**
    • **Choose fresh, unprocessed foods**
    • **Avoid candy and junk foods**

7. Check spelling and style in the presentation.

8. On the handouts, include the date and your name as header and include the page number and filename *[your initials]*3-12.ppt as footer.

9. Save the presentation as *[your initials]*3-12.ppt in your Lesson 3 folder.

10. Print the presentation as handouts, 3 slides per page, grayscale, framed.

11. Close the presentation.

EXERCISE 3-13

Demote and promote bullets, use the Undo command.

1. Open the file **Pyramid1.ppt** and display the fourth slide.

2. Demote the second bullet in the left column by following these steps:
   a. Click the I-beam pointer anywhere in the second bullet ("Use sparingly").
   b. Click the Demote button ⊡ on the Formatting toolbar.

3. In the left column, demote the two bulleted items that include the text "2 to 3 servings."

4. Using the [Tab] key, demote the first bullet in the right column by following these steps:
   a. Click the bullet to the left of "Vegetables."
   b. Press [Tab].

5. Since this is not the bulleted item that should be demoted, click the Undo button ⊡ to restore the size and position of "Vegetables."

6. Demote the second, fourth, and sixth bullets in the right column (which all end in "servings").

7. Use the Demote button ⊡ to demote the last bullet in the right column ("6 to 11 servings") another level.

8. Assume that you didn't mean to demote the last bullet. Promote it by positioning the insertion point between the bullet and the number "6" and pressing [Shift]+[Tab].

9. Delete the word "and" every time it appears in slide 4 to balance the length of the bulleted text columns.

10. Check spelling in the presentation.

11. On the handouts, include the date and your name as header and include the page number and filename *[your initials]*3-13.ppt as footer.

12. Save the presentation as *[your initials]*3-13.ppt in your Lesson 3 folder.

13. Print the presentation as handouts, 4 slides per page, grayscale, framed.

14. Close the presentation.

EXERCISE 3-14

Start a new presentation using a design template, add new slides, promote and demote text, use the Undo command, and change design templates and color schemes.

1. Start a new presentation using a design template by following these steps:
   a. Choose New from the File menu.
   b. In the New Presentation dialog box, click the Design Templates tab.
   c. Choose the template Artsy and click OK.
   d. Choose the Title Slide layout for the first slide and click OK.

2. Key **Low-Fat Diet Options** for the title. Key **Good 4 U** for the subtitle.

3. Using the Common Tasks menu, add a new slide with the 2 Column Text layout.

4. Key the slide 2 title and bulleted text shown in Figure 3-15, demoting the bulleted text below "Less than" and "More than" as shown.

FIGURE 3-15

Bread, Cereal, Rice, and Pasta

Slide 2

- Less than 30% from fat
  - Bagels
  - Corn tortillas
  - Pita bread

- More than 30% from fat
  - Muffins
  - Biscuits
  - Taco shells

Vegetables

Slide 3

- Less than 30% from fat
  - Raw
  - Steamed
  - Vegetable juice

- More than 30% from fat
  - French fries
  - Hash browns
  - Onion rings

5. Add a new slide using the same layout, then key the slide 3 text shown in Figure 3-15, demoting the bulleted text as shown.

6. Apply a new design template by following these steps:
  a. Choose Apply Design Template from the Format menu (or double-click "Artsy" on the status bar).
  b. In the Apply Design Template dialog box, double-click **Blends.pot**.
  c. Scroll through the presentation to see the applied design.

7. Change the color scheme by following these steps:
  a. Choose Slide Color Scheme from the Format menu (or from the shortcut menu).
  b. In the Color Scheme dialog box, click the first choice (the black background).
  c. Click Preview and drag the Color Scheme dialog box out of the way to see the effect on the slide.
  d. Click Apply to All.
  e. Look at each slide to see the changes.

8. Click the Undo button ⟲ to compare the new color scheme with the previous. If you prefer the black background, click the Redo button ⟳ to reapply the color change.

9. Check spelling in the presentation.

10. On the handouts, include the date and your name as header and include the page number and filename *[your initials]***3-14.ppt** as footer.

11. Save the presentation as *[your initials]***3-14.ppt** in your Lesson 3 folder.

12. Print the presentation as handouts, 3 slides per page, grayscale, framed.

13. Close the presentation.

EXERCISE 3-15

Change slide layout, change the design template, and add speaker's notes.

1. Open the file **Pyramid2.ppt** and display slide 3.

2. Change the layout of slide 3 by following these steps:

    a. Click the Common Tasks button and choose Slide Layout.

    b. Select 2 Column Text and click Apply.

    c. Cut the last two bulleted items ("Eat moderately" and "Limit fats") from column 1 and paste them to column 2 (or drag and drop the items to column 2).

3. Move to slide 1 and switch to Normal view, if necessary.

4. Enlarge the notes pane by following these steps:

    a. Position the mouse pointer on the horizontal border between the slide and notes panes.

    b. Using the double-headed arrow, drag the border up to about the middle of the screen.

5. Working on slide 1, key the following text in the notes pane:

    Remind staff about Good 4 U's mission to serve healthy food.

    New menu items that balance food proportions according to FDA guidelines will be introduced next month.

6. Key the following notes for the remaining slides:

    Slide 2: **The USDA has classified foods into five basic groups.**

    Slide 3: **Emphasize whole grains and whole foods as opposed to processed foods.**

    Slide 4: **A good diet consists of foods from each of the five main groups and may contain a little fat, oil, and sweetener.**

7. Change the design template to **Notebook.pot**.

8. Resize the notes pane to its original size.

9. Check spelling in the presentation.

10. On the handouts, include the date and your name as header and include the page number and filename *[your initials]***3-15.ppt** as footer.

11. Save the presentation as *[your initials]***3-15.ppt** in your Lesson 3 folder.

12. Print the presentation as notes pages in grayscale.

13. Close the presentation.

Lesson Applications

Create a new blank presentation, add slides, apply a design template, and change the color scheme.

1. Start a blank presentation.

2. Create a title slide with the title **First in Food Safety** and the subtitle **Good 4 U Employee Training**

3. Use the Bulleted List layout to create three new slides, as shown in Figure 3-16.

FIGURE 3-16

Slide 2

Our Food Safety Programs
- Food handler training
- Management inspections
- Safety supervisors on-site
- Reports to USDA

Slide 3

Safe Food-Handling Practices
- Wear gloves, hair nets, and beard nets
- Wash hands before and after handling food
- Wear clean uniforms
- No smoking

Slide 4

Food Procurement
- Know your suppliers
- Prefer local growers
- Prefer organic food
- Insist on freshness
- Insist on cleanliness
- Test for pesticides

4. Change the slide 4 layout to two column.

5. Cut the last three bullets in column 1 and paste them into column 2.

6. Apply the design template **Ricepaper.pot** to the presentation.

7. Change the color scheme to the first one in the second row (with the white background).

8. Check spelling in the presentation.

9. View the new color scheme of the presentation in Slide Sorter view.

10. On the handouts, include the date and your name as header and include the page number and filename *[your initials]*3-16.ppt as footer.

11. Save the presentation as *[your initials]*3-16.ppt in your Lesson 3 folder.

12. Print as handouts, 4 slides per page, pure black and white, framed.

13. Close the presentation.

EXERCISE 3-17

Change slide layouts, demote bullets, add slides, and change the color scheme.

1. Open the file **Safety1.ppt**.

2. In slide 4, cut the bulleted items in column 2 and paste them at the bottom of column 1.

3. Change the layout of slide 4 to Bulleted List.

4. Change the color scheme to the first standard color scheme (with the black background) for this template.

5. Edit text in slide 4 and demote bullets as shown in Figure 3-17.

FIGURE 3-17

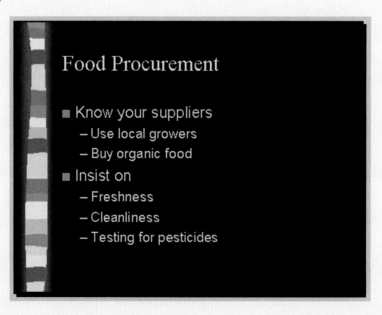

6. Add a new slide 5, using the text shown in Figure 3-18.

FIGURE 3-18

```
Inspections

☐ Training inspections

   - Scheduled

   - Cooperative

■ Internal evaluation inspections

■ USDA inspections
```

7. Without closing **Safety1.ppt**, open the file **Safety2.ppt**. Arrange both presentations on the screen in Slide Sorter view.

8. Copy slide 2 ("Should We Be Safe?") from **Safety2.ppt** to the slide 2 position in **Safety1.ppt**.

9. Close **Safety2.ppt** and maximize **Safety1.ppt**.

10. Check spelling in the presentation.

11. On the handouts, include the date and your name as header and include the page number and filename *[your initials]*3-17.ppt as footer.

12. Save the presentation as *[your initials]*3-17.ppt in your Lesson 3 folder.

13. Print the presentation as handouts, 6 slides per page, grayscale, framed.

14. Close the presentation.

EXERCISE 3-18

Start a new presentation, add slides, demote bullets, apply a template from another presentation, and change the color scheme.

1. Create a new presentation, using the text shown in Figure 3-19 (on the next page).

2. Apply the template from the file **Safety2.ppt** to the presentation.

3. Change the color scheme to the Standard scheme with the light blue background.

4. Reverse the positions of slides 2 and 3.

5. Check spelling in the presentation.

FIGURE 3-19

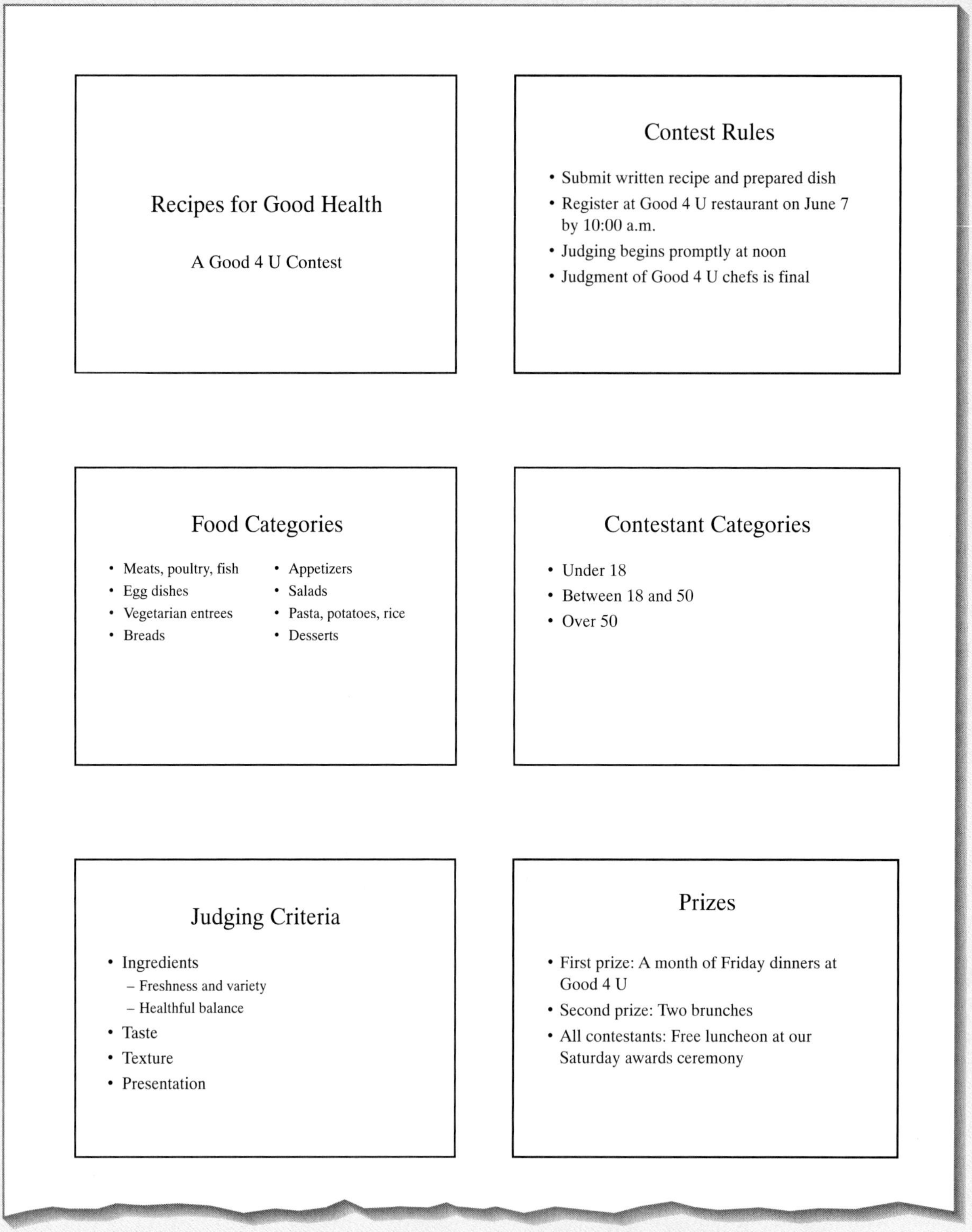

Recipes for Good Health

A Good 4 U Contest

Contest Rules

- Submit written recipe and prepared dish
- Register at Good 4 U restaurant on June 7 by 10:00 a.m.
- Judging begins promptly at noon
- Judgment of Good 4 U chefs is final

Food Categories

- Meats, poultry, fish
- Egg dishes
- Vegetarian entrees
- Breads
- Appetizers
- Salads
- Pasta, potatoes, rice
- Desserts

Contestant Categories

- Under 18
- Between 18 and 50
- Over 50

Judging Criteria

- Ingredients
  - Freshness and variety
  - Healthful balance
- Taste
- Texture
- Presentation

Prizes

- First prize: A month of Friday dinners at Good 4 U
- Second prize: Two brunches
- All contestants: Free luncheon at our Saturday awards ceremony

   6. Add slide numbers to all slides.

   7. On the handouts, include the date and your name as header and include the page number and filename *[your initials]***3-18.ppt** as footer.

   8. Save the presentation as *[your initials]***3-18.ppt** in your Lesson 3 folder.

   9. Print the presentation as handouts, 6 slides per page, grayscale, framed.

   10. Close the presentation.

EXERCISE 3-19   *Challenge Yourself*

Add a new slide, choose a slide layout, demote bullets, change design templates, and add speaker's notes.

   1. Open the file **Recipe1.ppt.**

   2. Add a new slide after the title slide, using the text shown in Figure 3-20.

FIGURE 3-20

```
Contest Rules

●  Submit an original written recipe and dish
   -  Good 4 U Restaurant, Saturday, June 7
   -  10 AM to noon
●  Judging is from noon to 2 PM
●  Judges' decisions are final
●  Anyone may enter except Good 4 U employees and their families
```

   3. Change the title of slide 3 to "Recipe Ingredients." Add **Avoid** as the new first bulleted item and demote "Corn syrup" through "MSG." Change to a two-column layout and add the following text to the second column:

   ● **Use**
      - **Rice syrup**
      - **Honey**
      - **Olive oil**
      - **Herbs**

   4. Create the last slide of the presentation as shown in Figure 3-21 (on the next page).

FIGURE 3-21

```
Awards

● Prizes
    - 1ˢᵗ place: Four Friday dinners
    - 2ⁿᵈ place: Two brunches
    - Free lunch to all entrants at awards ceremony
● Prizewinner categories
    - Under 18
    - 18 to 50
    - Over 50
```

5. On slide 1, key the subtitle **Rules, Judging, and Prizes**

6. Key a speaker's note on slide 1 stating that local businesses are sponsoring this event.

7. Key a speaker's note on slide 2 stating that three volunteer taste testers will be chosen from the entrants.

8. Reverse the position of slides 3 ("Recipe Ingredients") and 4 ("Judging Criteria").

9. Apply a design template of your choice and change the color scheme, if desired.

10. Change the slide 5 layout to two column. Move "Prizewinner categories" and its subtext to the second column.

11. If this new layout is not an improvement (for example, if the columns look unbalanced or "Prizewinner categories" wraps to two lines), undo your actions to restore slide 5's original layout.

12. Check the presentation for spelling and style.

13. Review the presentation as a slide show.

14. On the handouts, include the date and your name as header, and include the page number and filename *[your initials]***3-19.htm** as footer.

15. Save the presentation in HTML format as *[your initials]***3-19.htm** in your Lesson 3 folder.

16. Print slides 1 and 2 as notes pages in grayscale.

17. Print the entire presentation as handouts, 6 slides per page, grayscale, framed.

18. Close the presentation.

Using the Outline Pane

OBJECTIVES

MOUS ACTIVITIES

In this lesson:
PP2000 1.1
PP2000 1.5
PP2000 2.5
PP2000 3.4
PP2000 3.10
PP2000 E.1.1
PP2000 E.4.1

See Appendix F.

After completing this lesson, you will be able to:

1. Create a presentation using the outline pane.
2. Add a new slide in the outline pane.
3. Promote and demote outline entries.
4. Move bulleted items in the outline pane.
5. Move slides in the outline pane.
6. Create a summary slide.
7. Insert slides and import and export outlines.

 Estimated Time: 1½ hours

Outlining helps you organize and create a presentation by focusing on content and flow rather than appearance. Working in the outline pane, you can key text for your slides and then easily rearrange the text. You can also create a PowerPoint presentation automatically by importing a Word outline.

Creating a Presentation in the Outline Pane

You can develop a new presentation by keying all your text in the outline pane. You can work in Normal view and resize the outline pane, as needed, or switch to Outline view, where the outline pane is enlarged. The advantage of working in Outline view, which has all the same elements as Normal view, is that the enlarged outline pane allows you to focus on the text.

EXERCISE | **4-1** | **Start a New Presentation in the Outline Pane**

1. Start a new presentation using the design template **Factory.pot**.

2. Click the Outline View button ▤. Notice the enlarged outline pane and reduced slide pane. In the outline pane, the blank title slide is represented as an icon and numbered slide 1.

NOTE: Outline view resizes the three panes so you can work in the outline pane and still see the slide and note panes. Remember that you can resize the panes to your preference by dragging the pane borders.

3. Display the Outlining toolbar by clicking the <u>V</u>iew menu and choosing <u>T</u>oolbars, Outlining. (You can also right-click a toolbar and choose Outlining.)

4. Click to the right of the slide icon to place the insertion point, if necessary.

FIGURE 4-1
Creating a presentation using the outline pane

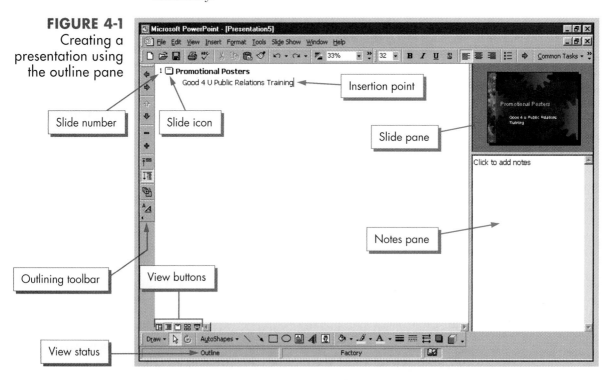

5. Key **Promotional Posters** as the slide title. The title line appears next to the slide icon. It also appears in the slide pane.

6. Press Enter. A new slide icon for slide 2 appears.

7. Press Tab. The new line is now the indented subtitle for slide 1.

 NOTE: Remember from the previous lesson that Tab demotes text, so demoting the title in slide 2 made the line into the subtitle of slide 1.

8. Key **Good 4 U Public Relations Training** as the subtitle text.

Adding a New Slide in the Outline Pane

After the title slide, when you insert a slide in the outline pane, it is automatically formatted in the Bulleted List layout. As in Normal view, you can insert a new slide, using the methods shown in the previous lesson:

- Click the Common Tasks button and choose New Slide.
- Click the New Slide button on the Standard toolbar.
- Choose New Slide from the Insert menu or press Ctrl + M.

Additionally, you can press Enter at the end of a title line to insert a new slide.

NOTE: In the outline pane, pressing Enter at the end of a line inserts a new line at the same outline level. For example, pressing Enter at the end of a title inserts a new title line (a new slide). Pressing Enter at the end of an indented line (such as a bullet line) inserts a new indented line.

EXERCISE 4-2 Add New Slides in the Outline Pane

1. While still in Outline view, place the insertion point anywhere on the indented line and press Ctrl + Enter. A second slide icon appears. Notice that the slide shown in the Slide pane is now blank, since a new blank slide is now active.

2. Key **Poster Purpose** as the title and press Ctrl + Enter. An indented bullet line appears.

NOTE: Remember, Ctrl + Enter inserts a new slide when the insertion point is in the last text box of a slide. If the insertion point is in a slide title, Ctrl + Enter creates an indented line (in this case, a bullet line).

3. Key **Inform customers** and press Enter. A second bullet appears.

4. Key **Promote our image** and press [Ctrl]+[Enter]. A new slide icon appears. Notice in the slide pane that the slide has the same layout (Bulleted List) as the previous slide.

5. Key the title **Themes**

6. Click the Common Tasks button and choose New Slide. In the New Slide dialog box, choose the 2 Column Text layout and click OK. Remember, to insert a slide with a different layout you must open the New Slide dialog box.

7. Key the title **Suggested Subjects**

8. Press [Ctrl]+[Enter] to insert the first line of bulleted text in the first column.

9. Key **Menu items** and press [Enter] to insert a new bullet line.

10. Key **Price specials** and press [Ctrl]+[Enter] to move to the first bullet in the second column.

11. Key **Holiday events**, press [Enter], and key **Sports events** as the second bullet.

12. Press [Ctrl]+[M] and insert a new slide with the Bulleted List layout. Key the title **Readability**. You should have five slides listed in the outline pane.

13. Press [Ctrl]+[Enter] and add the following bulleted items on slide 5:

   ● **Use large, simple titles**

   ● **Use color and graphics**

   ● **Limit the number of high-contrast colors**

FIGURE 4-2
Creating an outline

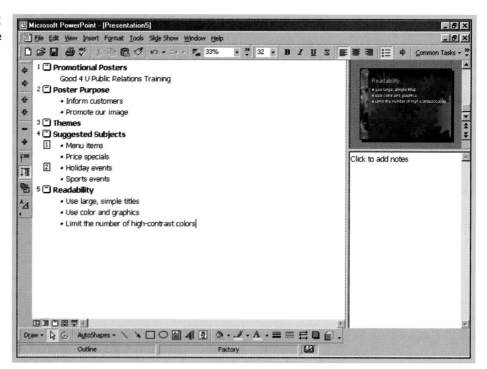

Promoting and Demoting Outline Entries

To demote slide titles and promote or demote bulleted items you can:

- Click Promote ◄ and Demote ► on the Outlining toolbar.
- Press Tab to demote an entry or Shift + Tab to promote an entry.
- Select an item and drag it left to demote it or right to promote it.

In the outline pane, you can also join or split slides by demoting or promoting entries. When a title is demoted, it becomes a bulleted item on the previous slide. When a bulleted item is promoted, it becomes the first line of a new slide.

TABLE 4-1   Outlining Toolbar Buttons

BUTTON	NAME	ACTION
◄	Promote	Raises item one level
►	Demote	Lowers item one level
▲	Move Up	Moves selection up one line
▼	Move Down	Moves selection down one line
–	Collapse	Displays titles only for selected slides
+	Expand	Displays details for selected slides
⌐	Collapse All	Displays titles only for entire outline
⌐	Expand All	Displays detail lines for entire outline
⊞	Summary Slide	Creates a new slide from titles of selected slides
A	Show Formatting	Turns display of character formatting on and off

 NOTE: At the end of this lesson, the Command Summary lists keyboard shortcuts for Outlining toolbar buttons.

EXERCISE 4-3   Promote and Demote by Using the Toolbar and Keyboard

1. Place the insertion point at the end of the last line on slide 2 (after "Promote our image"). Press Enter.
2. Add the following bulleted items to slide 2:
   - **Design suggestions**
   - **Keep it simple**
   - **Limit the number of text items**

Notice that the slide pane now displays the slide with a title and five bulleted items in miniature.

3. Position the insertion point anywhere in the line "Design suggestions" and click the Promote button 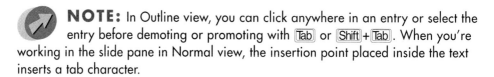 on the Outlining toolbar (or press Shift + Tab). The bullet becomes a new slide containing the next two bullets.

> **NOTE:** In Outline view, you can click anywhere in an entry or select the entry before demoting or promoting with Tab or Shift + Tab . When you're working in the slide pane in Normal view, the insertion point placed inside the text inserts a tab character.

4. Click the Demote button to rejoin the two slides.

5. Position the pointer over the slide 2 icon. Notice that the pointer changes to a four-headed arrow ✛.

6. Click the slide 2 icon. The entire slide and all its bullets are selected.

7. Position the pointer over the first bullet character on slide 2. Observe that the pointer again changes to a four-headed arrow.

8. Click the bullet. The rest of the slide contents are deselected and only the single bulleted item is selected.

> **NOTE:** Clicking a bullet always selects the bullet line and any sub-bullets below it.

9. Click the pointer anywhere in "Keep it simple" (the fourth bullet on slide 2). Press Tab to demote it under "Design suggestions."

> **NOTE:** In outline terminology, slide 2 now has three levels: the title is level 1, "Design suggestions" is level 2, and "Keep it simple" is level 3.

10. Click the "Design suggestions" bullet. Notice that this bullet and its sub-bullet are selected.

11. Select just the line "Keep it simple" and promote it by pressing Shift + Tab .

12. Promote "Design suggestions" to a new slide. Slide 3 should now be "Design suggestions" and contain two bulleted items, "Keep it simple" and "Limit number of text items."

EXERCISE 4-4   Promote and Demote by Dragging

1. Move the arrow pointer over the slide icon for "Design suggestions" until it becomes a four-headed arrow.

2. Click the slide icon. The slide title for slide 3 and its bulleted items are selected.

3. Drag the icon right. The pointer becomes a two-headed arrow and a vertical line appears.

4. Drag until the vertical line aligns with the bullets and then release. The title is demoted to a bullet and its bullets are demoted to sub-bullets.

FIGURE 4-3
Demoting by
dragging

Two-headed arrow

Vertical line

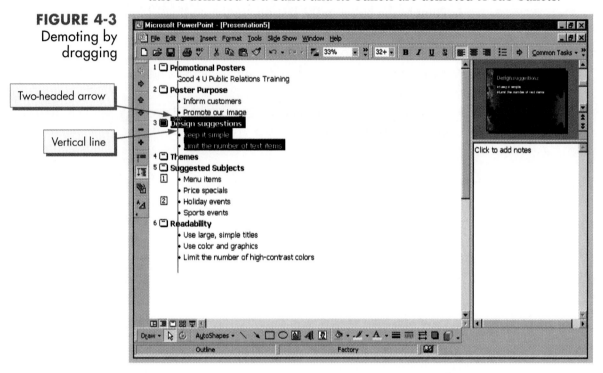

5. Position the pointer over the "Design suggestions" bullet, drag the selected material further right, and release. The items are demoted another level.

6. Drag the selected material back to the left until the vertical line aligns with the right edge of the slide icons and release. The material is promoted to a separate slide, slide 3.

> **NOTE:** If you drag selected material up or down instead of left or right, the four-headed arrow changes shape and a horizontal line appears, indicating you may be changing the order of the lines or dragging the material to a different slide.

7. At this point, change the second word in the slide 3 title to **Suggestions** (with a capital "S") to make it consistent with other slide titles.

EXERCISE 4-5 **Delete Slides and Slide Text in the Outline Pane**

To delete a slide or a line of bulleted text, you simply click the slide icon or bullet and press Delete.

1. Point to the bullet in the last line in the outline, "Limit the number of high-contrast colors."

2. Click the bullet to select the line and press Delete.

3. Assume that this was a mistake and click the Undo button ↺ to restore the text.

4. Click the slide icon for slide 4 ("Themes") and press Delete. The slide is deleted and the remaining slides are renumbered.

Moving Bulleted Items in the Outline Pane

In the outline pane, you can move selected bulleted items within slides or between slides several different ways:

- Click Move Up ⬆ or Move Down ⬇ on the Outlining toolbar.
- Drag selected bullets up or down.
- Cut and paste.

You can use ⬆ and ⬇ without selecting an item first. Only the item that contains the insertion point is moved.

EXERCISE 4-6 **Move Bulleted Items**

You can move bulleted items by using the Move Up button ⬆ and the Move Down button ⬇ on the Outlining toolbar or by dragging.

1. On slide 5, select "Use color and graphics" by clicking its bullet.

2. Click the Move Up button ⬆ on the Outlining toolbar. The selected bullet moves up one level.

3. Click ⬆ again several times until "Use color and graphics" is the last bullet on the "Design Suggestions" slide.

4. Select the second bullet on the "Design Suggestions" slide ("Limit the number of text items").

5. Click the Move Down button ⬇ several times until the selected bullet is the first bullet in slide 5, "Readability."

6. Select the last bullet on slide 5 ("Limit the number of high-contrast colors").

7. Drag the bullet up. The pointer becomes a two-headed arrow and a horizontal line appears.

8. Continue to drag up, positioning the horizontal line under "Use color and graphics" on slide 3, and then release.

FIGURE 4-4
Moving an element
by dragging

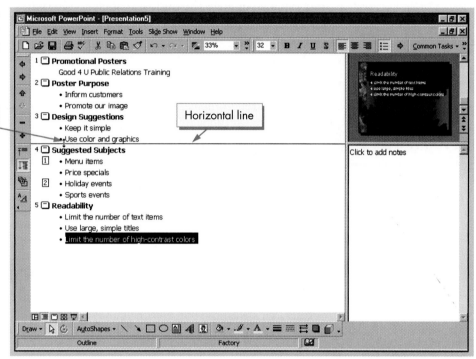

9. On slide 4, drag the I-beam pointer over the two bulleted items "Holiday events" and "Sports events." Click the Cut button ✂ to cut the text.

10. On the same slide, position the insertion point to the left of the "M" in "Menu items" and click the Paste button 📋. All four bulleted items are now in the first column.

NOTE: You can select more than one bullet or slide and drag the selection to a new position. First, drag the I-beam pointer over the text to select it. Next, move the pointer over the selection and use the white drag-and-drop arrow pointer ⧗ to drag it to a new position. An insertion point guides your placement rather than a horizontal line.

11. Use the Common Tasks button to change the slide layout of slide 4 to Bulleted List.

12. On slide 5, move "Use large, simple titles" to the first bullet position on the slide.

Moving Slides in the Outline Pane

In the outline pane, you can move entire slides the same way you move bulleted items. When you select a slide icon, you select the contents of the entire slide. You can then use the Move Up button 🔼 and the Move Down button 🔽, cut and paste, or drag and drop.

You can also change the outline display to see only slide icons and titles by clicking the Collapse All button 📄. This feature helps you see the big picture of your outline and also makes moving slides easier and safer. For example, when dragging collapsed slides, there's no danger of dropping a slide in the middle of another slide.

EXERCISE | **4-7** | **Move Slides in the Outline Pane**

1. Click the "Readability" slide icon to select the entire slide.

2. Click 🔼 five times until "Readability" becomes slide 4. The slide moves up through each line of the current slide 4. The slide number changes when "Readability" appears above "Suggested Subjects."

FIGURE 4-5
Using the
Move Up button

Click to move up
through the outline

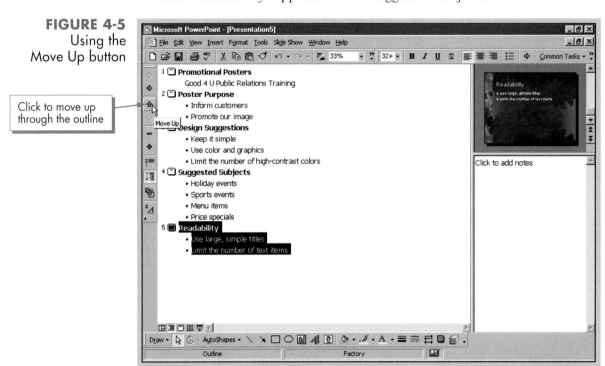

 3. Click the Collapse All button 📄 on the Outlining toolbar to display only titles for the outline.

4. Select slide 5 and drag it after slide 3. When all slides are collapsed, dragging a slide places it above or below all the text in another collapsed slide.

FIGURE 4-6
Dragging in a collapsed outline

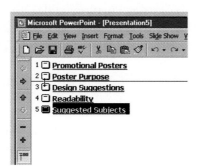

 NOTE: When you select (or move) a collapsed slide, you select (or move) all its hidden text.

5. Click the Expand button 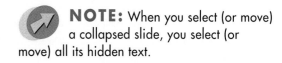 to display the hidden text of the "Suggested Subjects" slide.

6. Click the Collapse button ⊟ to display only the slide title.

7. Click in the word "Suggested" to deselect the slide.

8. Click the Move Up button ⬆ to move the slide up. Notice that the slide that contains the insertion point moves when you click the Move Up button.

⭐ **TIP:** It's easier to move slides in a long outline when only the slide titles are showing.

9. Click the Move Down button ⬇ to move "Suggested Subjects" back to its slide 4 position.

 10. Click the Expand All button ⬛ to display the entire outline.

 11. Click the Show Formatting button  to turn on the display of formatting. Notice that the outline pane content is now larger. Click the Show Formatting button again to turn it off. It is often easier to read the text of an outline when you turn off the formatting applied by the template.

Creating a Summary Slide

In a presentation, it is often a good idea to summarize the contents as either an agenda at the beginning or a wrap-up at the end. A summary slide in your presentation is based on the titles of existing slides.

The Summary Slide button 🔲 on the Outlining toolbar creates a new slide from the titles of selected slides. The summary slide creates a bulleted list from the titles of the selected slides, inserting the new slide in front of the first selected slide.

EXERCISE 4-8 **Create a Summary Slide**

1. Click within the slide 2 title, "Poster Purpose." Using the I-beam pointer, drag to the bottom of the outline to select slides 2 through 5.

2. Click the Summary Slide button on the Outlining toolbar. A summary slide is inserted above the "Poster Purpose" slide. Notice that the bulleted items on the summary slide are the titles of all the selected slides.

3. Change the default title of the summary slide to **Overview**.

FIGURE 4-7
Completed outline with summary slide

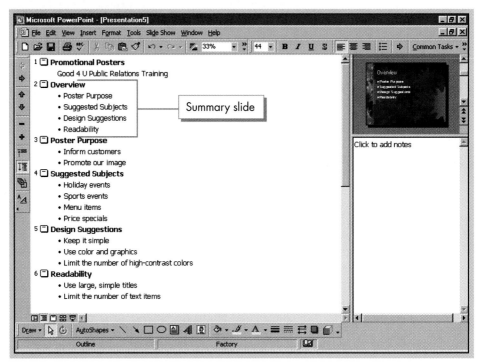

4. Check spelling and style in the presentation.

5. On the handouts, include the date and your name as a header and include the page number and filename *[your initials]*4-8.ppt as footer.

6. Save the presentation as *[your initials]*4-8.ppt in a new folder for Lesson 4.

7. Activate slide 1 and view the presentation in Slide Show view or Slide view.

8. Print the presentation outline. (In the Print dialog box, choose Outline View from the Print <u>W</u>hat drop-down list.)

TIP: You can also print a collapsed outline. First collapse the outline and then choose your Print dialog box options.

9. Print the presentation again as handouts, 6 slides per page, grayscale, framed.

10. Close the presentation.

Importing and Exporting

You can insert an outline created in another application (such as Microsoft Word or another word processor) into a new presentation or an existing one. PowerPoint will use your outline formatting (tab characters, indents, or heading styles) to create slide titles and bullets. You can also insert slides from one presentation to another without cutting or copying them.

 NOTE: Before starting the following Exercise, check with your instructor that the import feature is installed on your computer.

EXERCISE **4-9** **Import Text from Word**

You can import Word text or a Word outline into PowerPoint using the Slides from Outline command on the Insert menu.

1. Open Microsoft Word.

 NOTE: You can use another word processor.

2. Key the material shown in Figure 4-8. To create an outline, press [Tab] once or twice where indicated.

 TIP: Turn on the Show/Hide ¶ button [¶] to be sure you see tab characters. If some tab characters become indents instead, they will not translate to the correct outline level.

FIGURE 4-8

```
Poster Ideas
        [Tab]Good 4 U Public Relations Training

Restaurant Topics
        [Tab]Menu items
        [Tab]Contests
        [Tab]Ingredient profiles
        [Tab][Tab]Exotic ingredients
        [Tab][Tab]Organic ingredients
```

                                                                        continues

continued

```
Vendor Profiles
        [Tab]Local organic farmers
        [Tab]Herb farms
        [Tab]Fisheries

Special Event Announcements
        [Tab]New Health Marathon
        [Tab][Tab]Pasta party
        [Tab][Tab]Awards dinner
        [Tab]July 4th celebration
        [Tab][Tab]In-line skating race
        [Tab][Tab]Bike race
```

3. Save the outline as *[your initials]***4-9.doc** in your Lesson 4 folder.

4. Print the outline and close Word.

5. Open a new PowerPoint presentation using the **Artsy.pot** design template.

6. Choose Slides from Outline on the Insert menu. The Insert Outline dialog box appears.

7. Navigate to your Lesson 4 folder.

8. Choose *[your initials]***4-9.doc** from the list of files.

9. Click Insert. After a few seconds, PowerPoint interprets the structure of your outline, which you created using tab characters, and creates new slides from the level 1 headings and bullets from the level 2 and 3 headings.

10. If slide 1 is blank, delete it. Since all slides appear in the Bulleted List style, change the first slide to the Title Slide layout.

11. If necessary, use the outline pane to make adjustments so the outline matches Figure 4-9.

12. Change the slide color scheme to the last one (blue background).

FIGURE 4-9
Presentation with
imported outline

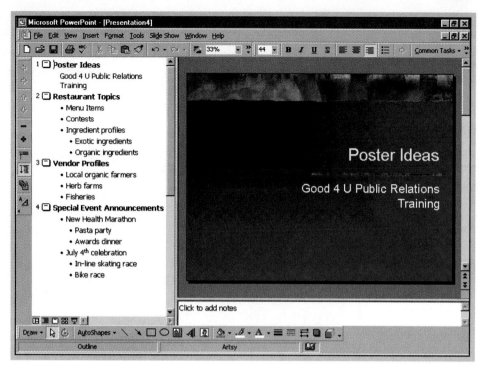

EXERCISE 4-10 Insert Slides from Another Presentation

In Lesson 2, you learned how to cut or copy a slide from one presentation to another. You can insert a slide from another presentation, without opening the presentation file, by using the Slides from Files command on the Insert menu.

1. Select slide 4. You'll insert two slides after this slide from another presentation.

 NOTE: When inserting slides, first select the slide after which you plan to insert additional slides.

2. Choose Slides from Files on the Insert menu. The Slide Finder dialog box opens.

3. Click Browse and navigate to your Lesson 4 folder. Choose *[your initials]*4-8.ppt from the list of files and click Open. The Slide Finder dialog box displays miniatures of the presentation slides.

4. Using the horizontal scroll bar below the slide miniatures, display slides 4 through 6. (See Figure 4-10 on the next page.)

5. Click slides 5 ("Design Suggestions") and 6 ("Readability") to select them. If you accidentally choose a wrong slide, click the slide again to deselect.

NOTE: You can use the two buttons in the Slide Finder dialog box, just above the slide miniatures, to change the display. The left button displays slide miniatures; the right button displays a list of slide titles with one slightly larger miniature of the selected slide.

6. Click Insert and then click Close. PowerPoint inserts the selected slides after slide 4 in your presentation.

FIGURE 4-10
Using the Slide
Finder dialog box
to insert slides

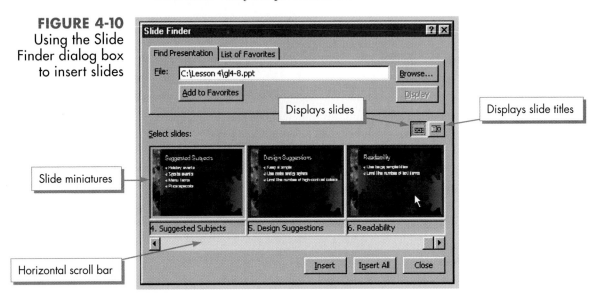

7. On the handouts, include the date and your name as header and the page number and filename *[your initials]*4-10.ppt as footer.

8. Save the presentation as *[your initials]*4-10.ppt in your Lesson 4 folder.

9. Print handouts, 6 slides per page, grayscale, framed. Leave the presentation open for the next Exercise.

EXERCISE **4-11** Exporting a PowerPoint Outline to Word

You can export a PowerPoint presentation to Word using the File, Send To command. A presentation can be exported into Word as an outline, handouts, or note pages.

1. Click File on the menu bar and choose Send To, Microsoft Word. The Write-up dialog box appears with five layout options.

2. Choose Outline Only and click OK. A copy of your presentation is now converted into a Word document.

3. Switch to Outline view in Word by clicking the Outline View button. Notice that Word converted the outline into heading styles.

4. Open the Save As dialog box in Word. Using the Save as <u>T</u>ype drop-down list, change the file type to Word Document (*.doc). (By default, Word will save the outline in another file format, Rich Text Format, which is often useful for opening a file in another application.)

5. Save the Word outline as *[your initials]***4-11.doc** in your Lesson 4 folder

6. Print the document and close Word. Close the PowerPoint presentation.

COMMAND SUMMARY

FEATURE	BUTTON	MENU	KEYBOARD
Outline View	🔲	<u>V</u>iew, <u>O</u>utline	
Promote	�		Alt + Shift + ← or Shift + Tab
Demote	▶		Alt + Shift + → or Tab
Move Up	▲		Alt + Shift + ↑
Move Down	▼		Alt + Shift + ↓
Collapse All	🔳		Alt + Shift + 1
Expand All	🔳		Alt + Shift + 1
Expand	✚		
Collapse	▬		
Show Formatting	ᴬ⁄		/ on numeric keypad (on/off)
Insert outline		<u>I</u>nsert, Slides from Ou<u>t</u>line	
Insert slides		<u>I</u>nsert, Slides from <u>F</u>iles	

USING HELP

Using the outline pane, either in Normal view or Outline view, is an excellent way to organize your thoughts and focus on presentation content. Help is available to answer questions and provide more information about developing a presentation by creating an outline.

Use Help for information about creating an outline:

1. Display and activate the Office Assistant.

2. Key **create an outline** in the text box and click Search.

3. Click the topic "Ways to organize my content in an outline."

FIGURE 4-11
Help window
about the outline
pane

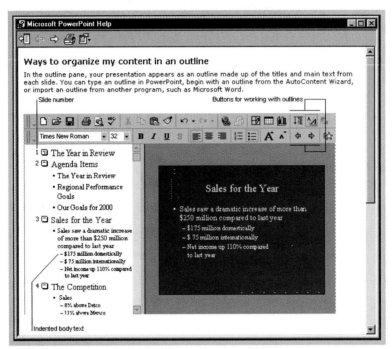

4. Review the information in the Help window. Scroll to the bottom of the window and click any of the links that interest you, such as Create a presentation from an existing outline or Keys for working in an outline. After clicking a link, press the Back button ◄ to return to the original Help window.

5. Close the Help window when you finish and hide the Office Assistant.

Concepts Review

Each of the following statements is either true or false. Indicate your choice by circling T or F.

T F **1.** The Outline command is on the View menu.

T F **2.** You can use [Ctrl]+[Enter] both to activate the next slide placeholder and to insert a new slide.

T F **3.** The Demote button on the Outlining toolbar has the same effect as the Demote button on the Formatting toolbar.

T F **4.** The Summary Slide button is on the Formatting toolbar.

T F **5.** You can drag and drop bulleted items from one slide to another.

T F **6.** You can use the Move Up button to change the positions of slides in your outline.

T F **7.** Once you create a slide, you cannot split it into two slides.

T F **8.** You use the Insert menu to insert an outline created in another application into PowerPoint.

Write the correct answer in the space provided.

1. Which key do you press to insert another bullet at the same level?

_____

2. What happens when you demote the title of slide 3 in a presentation?

_____

3. If a slide has 5 bullets (and no sub-bullets), what happens when you promote the third bullet?

_____

4. A slide has several bullets. If you select the title with the four-headed arrow in Outline view and press [Tab], what happens?

_____

5. Which two toolbars contain Demote and Promote buttons?

_____

6. Besides using the Move Up and Move Down buttons or the drag-and-drop method, how else can you move items in an outline?

   _____

7. How can you turn character formatting on and off in Outline view?

   _____

8. Which dialog box do you use to insert slides from another presentation?

   _____

CRITICAL THINKING

Answer these questions on a separate page. There are no right or wrong answers. Support your answers with examples from your own experience, if possible.

1. Do you prefer creating slides in Normal view, Slide view, or Outline view? Why?
2. When would you want to create your outline in PowerPoint? In Word? What are the advantages of developing an outline in Word?

Skills Review

EXERCISE 4-12

Start a new presentation in the outline pane, add slides, and demote outline entries.

1. Start a new presentation using the **Notebook.pot** design template. Choose Title Slide as the layout for slide 1.
2. Switch to Outline view.
3. Key **Good 4 U Restaurant** as the slide title and press Enter.
4. Press Tab. Key **Advertising Campaign**
5. Add a new slide by following these steps:
   a. Press Ctrl + Enter.
   b. Key **Types of Media**
   c. Press Ctrl + Enter.
   d. Key the following bulleted items:
      ● **Print**
      ● **Newspapers**

- **Magazines**
- **Broadcast**
- **Radio**
- **Television**

6. Add a new slide and key the title **Target Markets** and the following bulleted items:

- **Health-conscious adults**
- **Active sports enthusiasts**
- **Business professionals**

7. Add a new slide and key the title **Special Campaigns** and the following bulleted items:

- **Good Health Marathon**
- **July 4th celebration**

8. On slide 2, demote the bullets "Newspapers" and "Magazines" to sub-bullets under "Print" by following these steps:

   a. Position the insertion point anywhere in the "Newspapers" bulleted item.

   b. Click the Demote button ⊡.

   c. Position the insertion point anywhere in the "Magazines" bulleted item and press ⌜Tab⌝.

9. Using the I-beam, select the bulleted text "Radio" and "Television." Click the Demote button ⊡ to demote the text as sub-bullets under "Broadcast."

10. Check spelling in the presentation.

11. View the presentation in Slide Show view.

12. On the handouts, include the date and your name as header and the page number and filename *[your initials]*4-12.ppt as footer.

13. Save the presentation as *[your initials]*4-12.ppt in your Lesson 4 folder.

14. Print the presentation as handouts, 4 slides per page, grayscale, framed.

15. Close the presentation.

EXERCISE 4-13

Add slides and promote and demote bulleted items.

1. Open the file **Media1.ppt**. Change the design template to **Capsules.pot** using the last color scheme.

2. Switch to Outline view.

3. Using the outline pane, key three new slides as shown in Figure 4-12. (This figure displays formatting.)

FIGURE 4-12

4. Join slides 2 and 3 by following these steps:

   a. Position the insertion point in the slide 3 title. (Do not select the slide.)

   b. Press ⎣Tab⎦ (or click ➡).

5. Promote the last two bullets in slide 2 ("Additional dollar sales" and "Additional profitability") by following these steps:

   a. Click the first bullet with the four-headed arrow pointer to select it.

   b. Drag the selection to the left until the vertical line aligns with the previous bullet and then release.

   c. Repeat steps a and b for the last bullet.

6. Demote the last three bullets by following these steps:

   a. Position the insertion point anywhere within "Number of new customers."

   b. Drag the I-beam pointer down until the three lines are selected.

   c. Press ⎣Tab⎦.

7. Demote the "Production" bullet by dragging it one level to the right.

8. Demote the "Distribution" bullet by using the Demote button.

9. Demote the "Promotion" bullet by using the keyboard (⎣Alt⎦+⎣Shift⎦+➡).

10. Check spelling in the presentation.

11. On the handouts, include the date and your name as header and the page number and filename ***[your initials]*4-13.ppt** as footer.

12. Save the presentation as ***[your initials]*4-13.ppt** in your Lesson 4 folder.

13. View the presentation in Slide view.

14. Print the presentation outline. (Choose Outline View from the Print dialog box's Print <u>W</u>hat drop-down list.)

15. Print handouts, 4 slides per page, grayscale, framed.

16. Close the presentation.

EXERCISE 4-14

Move bullets and slides in the outline pane and create a summary slide.

1. Open the file **Media2.ppt**, apply the design template **Strategic.pot**, and switch to Outline view.

2. Click the Show Formatting button ▨ to turn off formatting, if necessary.

3. Move the "Newspapers" bullet from slide 3 to the end of slide 5 by following these steps:

   a. Position the insertion point in the text or click the bullet.

   b. Click the Move Down button ▣ (or press Alt + Shift + ↓) until the bullet is positioned below "Magazines" on slide 5.

4. Move the "Electronic" bullet from slide 4 to the end of slide 3 (below "Print").

5. Drag and drop the "Fliers" bullet on slide 5 to a new position on the slide by following these steps:

   a. Position the pointer over the "Fliers" bullet until the four-headed arrow appears.

   b. Drag the bullet up until the pointer becomes a two-headed vertical arrow.

   c. Position the horizontal line just under the slide 5 title, "Print Media," and then release.

6. Select the "Evaluate costs" bullet and its sub-bullets on slide 2 and move them above the "Evaluate effectiveness" bullet on the same slide.

7. Click the Collapse All button ▦ (or press Alt + Shift + 1) to display only slide titles.

8. Move slide 4 ("Electronic Media") after slide 5.

9. Move slide 2 ("Return on Investment") to the end of the presentation.

10. Click the Expand All button ▤ to display all details.

11. Create a summary slide by following these steps:

   a. Position the insertion point anywhere in the slide 2 title, "Media Categories." Drag to the bottom of the outline to select slides 2 through 5.

   b. Click the Summary Slide button ▧ on the Outlining toolbar.

   c. Change the title of slide 2, "Summary Slide," to **Discussion Topics**

   d. If necessary, remove the extra bullet at the end of slide 2.

12. Click the Show Formatting button ▨ to turn on the formatting display.

13. Check spelling in the presentation.

14. Review the presentation as a slide show.

15. On the handouts, include the date and your name as header and the page number and filename *[your initials]*4-14.ppt as footer.

16. Save the presentation as *[your initials]*4-14.ppt in your Lesson 4 folder.

17. Print the presentation outline and print handouts (6 slides per page), grayscale, framed.

18. Close the presentation.

EXERCISE 4-15

Create an outline in Word and import it into PowerPoint; export a PowerPoint outline to Word.

1. Create the outline shown in Figure 4-13 using Microsoft Word or another word processor, pressing [Tab] where indicated.

FIGURE 4-13

```
Introducing Our Honey Candies
        [Tab]Good 4 U's New Healthy Treat

Exciting Flavors
        [Tab]Exotic honey-licorice
        [Tab]Scintillating honey-cinnamon
        [Tab]Fabulous honey-fruit flavors
        [Tab][Tab]Tangy lemon
        [Tab][Tab]Robust orange
        [Tab][Tab]Apple cider

Candy Types
        [Tab]Soft-filled sweetness
        [Tab]Dramatic stick
        [Tab]Discrete drops

Availability
        [Tab]At our restaurant
        [Tab]By phone or mail order
        [Tab]In attractive gift packs
```

2. Save the file as *[your initials]*4-15a.doc in your Lesson 4 folder.

3. Print and close the document.

4. Start a new presentation in PowerPoint and cancel the New Slide dialog box (the outline pane will be blank).

5. Insert the Word outline into PowerPoint by following these steps:
   a. Choose Slides from Outline from the Insert menu.
   b. Locate the file *[your initials]*4-15a.doc and click Insert.

6. Change the first slide to Title Slide layout. Check that your presentation has a total of 4 slides.

7. Apply the design template **Nature.pot**.

8. Check spelling in the presentation.

9. Save the presentation as *[your initials]*4-15.ppt in your Lesson 4 folder.

10. Export the presentation to Word by opening the File menu and choosing Send To, Microsoft Word.

11. Choose Outline Only and click OK.

12. Save this Word outline as a Word document with the name *[your initials]*4-15b.doc in your Lesson 4 folder. Remember to change the file type to Word document (*.doc). Print the outline and close Word.

13. On the handouts of the PowerPoint presentation, include the date and your name as header and the page number and filename as footer.

14. Print the presentation as handouts, 4 slides per page, grayscale, framed.

15. Save and close the presentation.

Lesson Applications

EXERCISE 4-16

Start a new presentation in the outline pane, add slides, promote and demote text, and move bullets and slides.

1. Start a new presentation in Outline view.

2. Using the outline pane, key the title slide and the bulleted list slide shown in Figure 4-14 (which shows formatting).

FIGURE 4-14

3. Make "Food Services" and its sub-bullets a separate slide.

4. Make "Merchandise" and its sub-bullets a separate slide.

5. Add the following bullets to the "Our Products" slide:

   - **Merchandise**
   - **Food services**

6. Reverse the order of the bullets on the "Merchandise" slide ("Caps," "T-shirts," "Honey and confections").

7. Collapse the outline and move the "Merchandise" slide before the "Food Services" slide.

8. Apply the **Blends.pot** design template and change the slide color scheme to the option with the blue background.

9. Expand the outline.

10. Review the presentation in Slide view, checking styles.

11. Check spelling in the presentation.

12. On the handouts, include the date and your name as header and the page number and filename *[your initials]*4-16.ppt as footer.

13. Save the presentation as *[your initials]*4-16.ppt in your Lesson 4 folder.

14. Print the presentation as handouts, 4 slides per page, grayscale, framed.

15. Save and close the presentation.

EXERCISE 4-17

Move bullets in the outline pane and promote outline items.

1. Open the file **MktTrng.ppt** and switch to Outline view.

2. Select and delete slide 2, "Elements of Marketing."

3. Revise the bullets in the new slide 2, "Marketing Is About People," as shown in Figure 4-15.

FIGURE 4-15

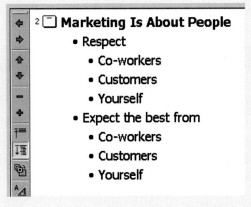

4. Promote each of the bulleted items on slide 3 ("What Are We Marketing?") to three new slides.

5. Under slide 3, "What Are We Marketing?," key the following bulleted items:

   - **Our food**
   - **Our merchandise**
   - **Our service**

6. Under the new slide 4, "Our food," key the following bulleted items:

   - **Eat in**
   - **Take out**
   - **Delivered and catered**

   7. Under slide 5, "Our merchandise," key the following bulleted items:
      - **Food products**
      - **Apparel and accessories**

   8. Move the three bulleted items under slide 7, "Marketing Our Staff," and position them under slide 6, "Our service."

   9. Delete slide 7.

   10. View the presentation in Normal view and correct heading styles to title case where necessary.

   11. Change the slide 2 layout to 2 Column Text, moving the second bullet and its sub-bullets to the right column placeholder.

   12. Check spelling in the presentation.

   13. On the handouts, include the date and your name as header and the page number and filename *[your initials]*4-17.ppt as footer.

   14. Save the presentation as *[your initials]*4-17.ppt in your Lesson 4 folder.

   15. Print the presentation outline and print handouts (6 slides per page), grayscale, framed.

   16. Save and close the presentation.

EXERCISE 4-18

Move, promote, and demote bulleted items in the outline pane; move slides; and create a summary slide.

   1. Open the file **Honeys1.ppt**.

   2. Switch to Outline view and display formatting in the outline pane.

   3. Working in the outline pane, move bullets and slides as shown in Figure 4-16 (on the next page). Correct the case of title slides as necessary.

   4. On slide 3, move and add text as follows:

      Gift Sales Services
      - **Gift-wrapping**
      - **Protective packaging**
      - **Gift certificates**
      - **Delivery**
         - **Extra charges vary with services**
         - **Express delivery required for perishables**

   5. Apply the **Sandstone.pot** design template.

   6. Create a summary slide that summarizes slides 2 through 4. Change the summary slide title to **Overview of Topics**. Make the bulleted items sentence case (only the first word starts with a capital letter).

FIGURE 4-16

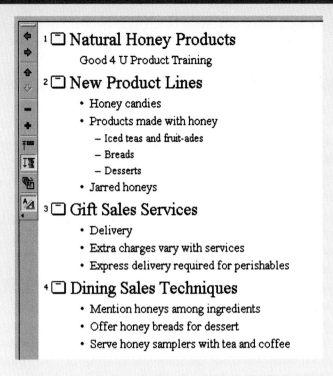

> ¹ ☐ **Natural Honey Products**
>   Good 4 U Product Training
> ² ☐ **New Product Lines**
>   • Honey candies
>   • Products made with honey
>   – Iced teas and fruit-ades
>   – Breads
>   – Desserts
>   • Jarred honeys
> ³ ☐ **Gift Sales Services**
>   • Delivery
>   • Extra charges vary with services
>   • Express delivery required for perishables
> ⁴ ☐ **Dining Sales Techniques**
>   • Mention honeys among ingredients
>   • Offer honey breads for dessert
>   • Serve honey samplers with tea and coffee

7. Check spelling in the presentation. (Leave the spelling of "fruit-ades" unchanged.)

8. View the presentation as a slide show.

9. On the handouts, include the date and your name as header and the page and filename *[your initials]***4-18.ppt** as footer.

10. Save the presentation as *[your initials]***4-18.ppt** in your Lesson 4 folder.

11. Print the presentation outline and print handouts (6 slides per page), grayscale, framed.

12. Save and close the presentation.

EXERCISE 4-19 *Challenge Yourself*

Insert a word-processed outline into a presentation, move bullets and slides, create a summary slide, insert a slide from another presentation, and export an outline to Word.

1. Open the file **Honeys2.ppt**. Apply the design template **Blends.pot** using the color scheme with the black background.

2. Switch to Outline view.

3. Using a word processor (such as Microsoft Word), open the file **Hnyprod.rtf** and save it as *[your initials]*4-19a.doc in your Lesson 4 folder. (Be sure to change the file type to Word Document.) Close it.

4. In the outline pane, select slide 2 and then insert the word-processed outline *[your initials]*4-19a.doc.

 NOTE: When inserting an outline into an existing presentation, the outline is inserted after the currently selected slide.

5. Move the slide "Breads and Desserts with Honey" so it becomes slide 4.

6. Add a new slide after slide 5 with the title **Good 4 U Honey Promotion** and the following bullets:

- **Honey-tasting contest**
- **Bread and honey samples at take-out counter**
- **Complimentary honey candies after meals**

7. Change the slide 3 layout ("Honey Beverages") to 2 Column Text, moving the second bullet and its sub-bullets to the second column placeholder. Delete any blank lines in the outline pane, if necessary.

8. In slide 7, move "Offer honey breads for dessert" so it is the last bullet on the slide.

9. After slide 7, insert slide 3 ("Gift Sales Services") from the file **Honeys1.ppt**.

10. Create a summary slide of slides 2 through 8. Change the summary slide title to **Product Training Summary**. Move this slide so it is the last slide of the presentation (slide 9.)

11. Check spelling in the presentation.

12. View the presentation in Slide view or Slide Show view.

13. On the handouts, include the date and your name as header and the page number and filename *[your initials]*4-19.ppt as footer.

14. Save the presentation as *[your initials]*4-19.ppt in your Lesson 4 folder.

15. Export the outline to Microsoft Word. Switch to Outline view in Word. Save the outline as *[your initials]*4-19b.doc in your Lesson 4 folder. Print and close the document.

16. Print the presentation handouts, 9 slides per page, grayscale, framed.

17. Save and close the presentation.

Working with Text

LESSON

5

OBJECTIVES

After completing this lesson, you will be able to:

1. Apply fonts and text attributes to text.
2. Apply text attributes to a placeholder.
3. Control presentation fonts.
4. Work with bullets.
5. Change text alignment.
6. Change the size and position of text placeholders.
7. Use master slides to format text.

MOUS
ACTIVITIES

In this lesson:
PP2000 **2.4**
PP2000 **3.2**
PP2000 **3.5**
PP2000 **4.3**
PP2000 **4.5**
PP2000 **5.1**
PP2000 **5.3**
PP2000 **E.7.1**

See Appendix F.

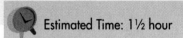 Estimated Time: 1½ hour

You can add interest to a PowerPoint presentation by varying the appearance of text—that includes changing the font, text style, bullet shape, or the position of text. You can change text appearance before or after you key it, or apply changes to the entire text in the presentation at once by using the master slide.

Applying Fonts and Text Attributes to Text

One way to change the appearance of text in your presentation is by changing the font. A *font* is a set of characters with a specific design. You can change the font face (such as Times New Roman or Arial) and the font size. Fonts are measured in *points* (there are 72 points to an inch).

Another way to change the appearance of text is by applying text attributes. For example, you can apply a text style (such as bold or italic) and effect (such as underline or shadow). You use the Formatting toolbar or the Font dialog box to change selected text.

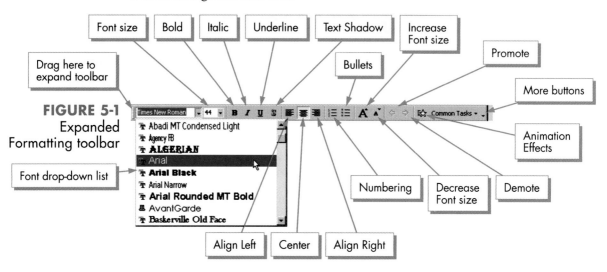

FIGURE 5-1
Expanded
Formatting toolbar

EXERCISE 5-1 Change Text Attributes with the Toolbar

1. Open the file **Heart.ppt**.

2. Expand the Formatting toolbar. To do this, place the pointer on the vertical bar at the left end of the toolbar, to the left of the Font box (the pointer changes to a four-headed arrow). Drag to the left, as far as you can go (the pointer changes to a two-headed arrow as you drag).

3. Click the title placeholder of the first slide to activate it and key **Heart**.

4. Select the word you just keyed. Click the down arrow next to the Font box on the Formatting toolbar to open the drop-down list and choose Arial. As you can see, text formatting in PowerPoint is similar to text formatting in a word processor.

FIGURE 5-2
Font Size
drop-down list

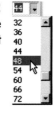

5. With "Heart" still selected, click the down arrow next to the Font Size box. Scroll down the drop-down list and choose 48. The text size increases to 48 points.

6. Click the Decrease Font Size button ▲. The font size decreases by one size. Notice the Font Size box now shows 44.

7. Click the Increase Font Size button Ａ twice. The font size increases by two sizes to 54 points.

TIP: You can select existing text and then change its attributes, or you can choose attributes and then key text, as shown in the following step.

8. Position the insertion point to the right of "Heart" and press Spacebar. Click the Bold button B and then the Italic button I to turn these attributes on. Key **Smart!** The word appears as bold italic. Notice that this word is also 54-point Arial, like the previous word.

NOTE: You can also use keyboard shortcuts to turn on/off text attributes: Ctrl+B for bold, Ctrl+I for italic, and Ctrl+U for underline.

9. Double-click the word "Heart" to select it.

10. On the Drawing toolbar at the bottom of the screen, locate the Font Color button A. Click its down arrow to open the Font Color menu.

NOTE: If you click the Font Color button and not its down arrow, the color indicated on the button is automatically applied to the selected text. You use the down arrow to choose a different color.

11. Position your pointer on the gray bar at the top of the Font Color menu and drag it to the right side of the screen. Many of PowerPoint's submenus can be converted to floating toolbars in this manner. Unlike menus, floating toolbars stay open and available until you close them.

FIGURE 5-3
Font Color menu

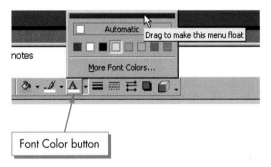

Font Color button

12. Click the red box on the Font Color floating toolbar. The selected text becomes light blue. You don't see the color you select until you deselect the text.

13. Click in the word "Smart" to deselect "Heart." "Heart" is now red.

14. Close the Font Color toolbar by clicking its Close button X. Notice that the color bar on the Font Color button is now red. If you click this button instead of the down arrow, selected text will be changed to red.

EXERCISE **5-2** **Change Text Attributes with the Font Dialog Box**

1. Select the words "Good 4 U" in the subtitle.

2. Right-click the selected text to display the shortcut menu. Choose Font to open the Font dialog box.

3. Set the Font to Arial, set the Font Style to Bold Italic, set the Size to 40, and check Underline. Notice the additional options available in this dialog box.

FIGURE 5-4
Font dialog box

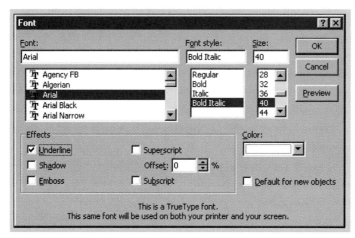

4. Click Preview and drag the Font dialog box to the side so you can see the selected text under it.

5. Drag the dialog box back to the center of the screen. Click OK to accept the formatting and close the dialog box.

6. With the text still selected, click the Underline button on the Formatting toolbar to turn off underlining. Deselect the text, which is now 40-point Arial bold italic.

7. Position the insertion point after "Good 4 U" and press Enter to create a two-line subtitle.

8. Create a slide footer for all slides. Include the date and footer text with your name and the filename *[your initials]*5-2.ppt.

9. Save the presentation as *[your initials]*5-2.ppt in a new folder for Lesson 5.

10. Print the title slide only, grayscale, framed.

NOTE: You can change text attributes in Normal view, Slide view, or Outline view by using either the toolbars or the Font dialog box.

EXERCISE 5-3 **Change the Case of Selected Text**

If you find that you keyed text in uppercase and want to change it, you don't have to rekey it. Using the Change Case command on the Format menu, you can change any text to Sentence case, lowercase, UPPERCASE, or Title Case. You can also cycle through uppercase, lowercase, and title cases by selecting text and pressing Shift + F3.

1. Move to slide 3. (The light bulb should be visible, indicating that the style checker detects a capitalization error.)

2. Select the title "Walk to good health," which has only the first word capitalized.

3. Choose Change Case from the Format menu. The Change Case dialog box appears.

FIGURE 5-5
Change Case
dialog box

4. Choose Title Case and click OK. Now every word except "to" is capitalized.

5. With the title still selected, press Shift + F3. The case changes from title case to uppercase. Press Shift + F3 again to change the text to lowercase. Press it a third time to change the text back to title case.

6. Select the first bulleted item by clicking its bullet. This text was keyed with CapsLock turned on.

7. Open the Change Case dialog box again, choose tOGGLE cASE, and click OK. This option reverses the current case, changing uppercase letters to lowercase and lowercase letters to uppercase.

8. Select the two bullets under "Walking" ("reduces…" and "lowers…") by dragging the I-beam across all the words. Open the Change Case dialog box, choose Sentence case, and click OK.

Applying Attributes to Placeholders

You can change the formatting for all text in a placeholder at one time. To do this, you select the placeholder instead of the text inside it.

For instance, suppose you want to make all the bulleted text on a slide smaller. Instead of selecting each line of text, you can select the bulleted text placeholder and then click the Decrease Font Size ■ button. You use the same formatting tools for a selected placeholder as you use for selected text.

You can select placeholders several ways:

- Click the border of an active placeholder with the arrow pointer.
- Press Esc while a placeholder is active (insertion point is in the text.)
- Press Tab to select the next placeholder on a slide (only when the insertion point is not in any text).

You can deselect placeholders several ways:

- Press Esc to deselect a placeholder or other object. (Press Esc twice if any text is selected in the placeholder.)
- Click an area of the slide where there is no object.

EXERCISE 5-4 **Select Text Placeholders**

1. Move to slide 4 and click anywhere in the title text to make the placeholder active. Notice the border is made of tiny diagonal lines and small white squares.

2. Point to any place on the border between two small squares. When you see the four-headed arrow pointer ⁺⃗⃗, click the border. Notice that the insertion point is no longer active and the border's appearance has changed slightly—it is now made of small dots instead of diagonal lines. This indicates that the placeholder is selected.

3. Press Tab. The bulleted text placeholder is selected.

 NOTE: Tab cycles through all objects on a slide, not just placeholders. If a slide contains a graphic object, Tab selects that as well.

4. Press Esc to deselect the bulleted text placeholder. Now, nothing on the slide is selected.

EXERCISE 5-5 **Apply Text Attributes to Selected Placeholders**

1. Still working on slide 4, click the title placeholder and then press Esc. This is another way to select an active placeholder.

2. Click the Decrease Font Size button ▣. The title font is decreased to 40 points and all the text now fits on one line.

 NOTE: Ignore the light bulb, which is detecting a case error in the title. Prepositions, such as "with," are usually lowercase in titles.

3. Press ⌨Tab to select the bulleted text placeholder. Notice the 20+ in the Font Size box. This indicates there is more than one font size in the placeholder and 20 points is the smallest size.

4. Click in the first bullet. Notice that its font size is 24 points. Click the first sub-bullet below it, which is 20 points. Notice that when you click text inside a placeholder, its border is no longer selected.

5. Press ⌨Esc to reselect the entire placeholder.

6. Click the Increase Font Size button A. The Font Size box now displays 24+, indicating the smallest text size in the placeholder is 24 points.

7. Click the Increase Font Size button A again so that 28+ appears in the Font Size box.

 TIP: Another way to increase or decrease font size is to press ⌨Ctrl+⌨Shift+⌨> or ⌨Ctrl+⌨Shift+⌨<.

8. Click the down arrow on the Font Color button A and choose yellow, making all bulleted text on this slide yellow.

Controlling Presentation Fonts

After you finish a presentation, you may decide that a different font will look better. You can change the font in the entire presentation easily and quickly with the Replace Font command.

If the fonts you chose for your presentation aren't available on another computer, you can embed the fonts in the presentation when you save it. This ensures that your presentation displays correctly on the other computer.

EXERCISE 5-6 Replace Fonts in a Presentation

1. Display slide 1. The slide contains the fonts Arial and Times New Roman. The rest of the presentation is in Times New Roman.

2. Choose Replace Fonts from the Format menu to display the Replace Font dialog box.

FIGURE 5-6
Replace Font
dialog box

3. Open the Replace drop-down list and choose Arial. (This list contains the fonts currently used in the presentation.)

4. Open the With drop-down list to display the available fonts. Choose Impact and click Replace.

5. Drag the dialog box out of the way to see the change on slide 1. The Arial font used in the title and subtitle is replaced with Impact.

6. Choose Times New Roman from the Replace list and choose Arial from the With list. Click Replace and close the dialog box. Notice the change in the last line of the subtitle and on the other slides, which are now in Arial instead of Times New Roman.

EXERCISE   **5-7**   # Save Embedded Fonts in a Presentation

You can save, or embed, any TrueType font included with Windows or PowerPoint in a presentation. By embedding TrueType fonts, you make sure presentations look exactly the way you designed them when viewed or printed on another computer.

1. Click to open the Font drop-down list on the Formatting toolbar. Notice that the fonts Arial and Impact are TrueType fonts, as indicated by the logo **Tr** to the left of the fonts. Notice that most of the fonts available on your computer are TrueType fonts.

 NOTE: Fonts that have the printer symbol **昆** are available only on the currently selected printer for your computer.

2. Press Esc to close the drop-down list. Choose File, Save As.

3. In the Save As dialog box, open the Tools drop-down menu and choose the option Embed TrueType Fonts.

FIGURE 5-7
Embedding
fonts in the
presentation file

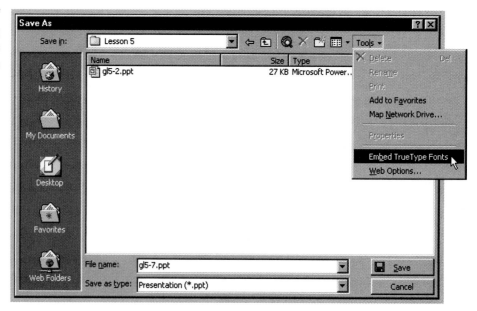

4. Save the presentation as *[your initials]*5-7.ppt in your Lesson 5 folder. The presentation is now saved with the embedded TrueType fonts Arial and Impact.

5. On the handouts, include the date and your name at the top of the page and include the page number and filename at the bottom. Eliminate the slide footer.

6. Print handouts, 6 slides per page, grayscale, framed. Save the presentation.

 TIP: If you are concerned about file size and disk space, don't embed TrueType fonts unless it's necessary. Embedded fonts increase the size of your presentation files.

Working with Bullets

When you work with bulleted text placeholders, each line automatically starts with a bullet. You can, however, turn bullets off when the slide would look better without them. You can remove bullets, add new ones, change the shape and color of bullets, and create your own bullets from pictures.

EXERCISE 5-8 Turn Bullets On and Off

1. Display slide 2. Click within the bulleted text to activate the placeholder. Press Esc to select the entire placeholder.

2. Click the Bullets button ▤ on the Formatting toolbar. This turns bullets off for the entire placeholder and moves the text to the left.

3. Click the Bullets button ▤ again to reapply the bullets.

4. Click within the first bulleted item, "Exercise regularly," and click ▤ to turn off the bullet.

5. Click ▤ again to reapply the bullet.

EXERCISE 5-9 Change the Color and Shape of a Bullet

You use the Bullet dialog box to change the color and shape of a bullet. To change the bullet shape, you can choose a character from another font. Fonts that contain potential bullet characters include Symbol, Wingdings, and Webdings.

1. With the bulleted text placeholder on slide 2 selected, right-click the placeholder border to display the shortcut menu and choose <u>B</u>ullets and Numbering.

2. In the Bullets and Numbering dialog box, click the Bulleted tab, if necessary.

FIGURE 5-8
Bullets and
Numbering
dialog box

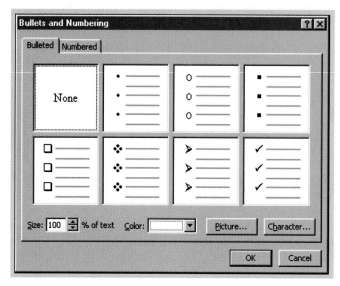

3. Choose the check mark bullet option and click OK. All bullets on slide 2 are now check marks.

4. Select the first three lines of bulleted text and choose <u>B</u>ullets and Numbering from the <u>F</u>ormat menu.

5. Click the <u>C</u>haracter button to open the Bullet dialog box.

6. Change the font by opening the <u>B</u>ullets From drop-down list and choosing the Symbol font.

7. Click the heart character in the grid. The heart is enlarged for easy viewing.

8. Open the <u>C</u>olor drop-down box and choose red.

FIGURE 5-9
Bullet dialog box

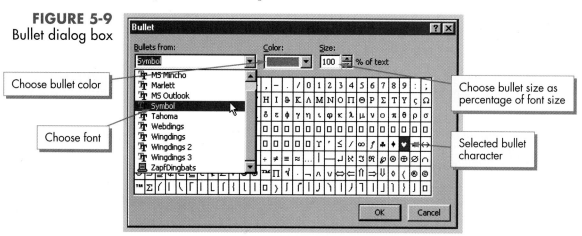

NOTE: Choose the Automatic option if you want the bullet to be the color scheme font color.

9. Click OK. The first three bullets on the slide change to red hearts.
10. Select the three lines of bulleted text with the check mark bullet. Open the Bullets and Numbering dialog box (by right-clicking the selected text or using the Format menu).
11. Change the Size to 80 percent, change the Color to yellow, and click OK. The sub-bullets on this slide are now smaller yellow check marks.

EXERCISE 5-10 Create a Bullet from a Picture

Using picture bullets allows you to truly customize a presentation—a picture bullet can be a company logo, a special occasion graphic, or anything you draw with a graphics program or scan.

1. Display slide 3 and select the bulleted text placeholder.
2. Open the Bullets and Numbering dialog box and click the Picture button. The Picture Bullet dialog box appears with a variety of bullets available in the Microsoft Clip Gallery.
3. Click the first bullet in the first row. Click the Insert Clip button 🔁 from the pop-up menu to insert the new bullet on slide 3.

FIGURE 5-10
Inserting a picture bullet

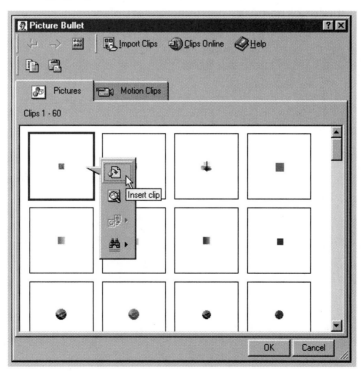

NOTE: If this picture bullet is not available on your computer, choose another one.

4. With the placeholder still selected, reopen the Picture Bullet dialog box.

5. Click Import Clips at the top of the dialog box. This will allow you to import a picture into the Clip Gallery for use as a bullet.

6. Navigate to the location of your student files and select the file **Walk.jpg**.

7. Click Import. The picture is now inserted in the Clip Gallery.

8. Click the picture and click the Insert Clip button 🖾.

9. Change the two sub-bullets on the slide (under "Walking") to yellow check marks sized at 80 percent.

TIP: When choosing a picture for a bullet, use an image with a simple design and color. Images that are reduced to the size of a bullet are not always clear and may make the presentation confusing.

EXERCISE **5-11** **Add Number Bullets and AutoNumber Bullets**

Instead of bullet characters or picture bullets, you can use numbers to order the list of items in your bulleted text placeholder. Using the Numbered tab in the Bullets and Numbering dialog box, you can apply a variety of numbering styles, including numbers, letters, and Roman numerals. You can also create a numbered list of bulleted items automatically by keying text.

1. Display slide 5 and select the bulleted text placeholder.

2. Open the Bullets and Numbering dialog box and click the Numbered tab.

3. Choose any number style and click OK. The text now has numbers as bullets.

4. Delete all the numbered text in the placeholder. Press Backspace to delete the number bullet at the beginning of the line.

5. Key **1.** and press Tab. Key **Walk with us**

6. Press Enter. The second line is automatically numbered "2."

7. Key **Eat with us** and press Enter.

8. Key **Do what's Good 4 U**. The slide now has three items, automatically numbered 1 through 3.

 TIP: You can control the numbering style that is applied automatically by keying your first item with the style you want, such as **A.** or **i.**

Changing Text Alignment

Bullets, titles, and subtitles are all considered to be paragraphs in PowerPoint. Just as in a word processor, when you press Enter, a new paragraph begins. You can align paragraphs with the left or right margin or center them between margins. You can also justify long paragraphs so both margins are squared off.

EXERCISE 5-12 **Change Text Alignment**

1. Select the three lines of numbered text on slide 5.
2. Click the Bullets button to apply regular bullets, then click the button again to turn bullets off.
3. Position the insertion point in the first line, "Walk with us."
4. Choose <u>A</u>lignment from the <u>F</u>ormat menu and choose Align <u>R</u>ight from the submenu. The paragraph aligns to the right.

> **NOTE:** Notice the keyboard shortcuts listed on the Alignment submenu for aligning paragraphs.

5. Click the Align Left button on the Formatting toolbar. The paragraph aligns to the left.

6. Select the placeholder border and click the Center button on the Formatting toolbar. All three paragraphs are centered horizontally within the placeholder.

> **NOTE:** You can apply alignment attributes to an entire placeholder just as you applied other text formatting.

Changing Size and Position of Text Placeholders

There are times when you will want to change the way text is positioned on a slide. For example, you may want to make a text placeholder narrower or wider to control how text wraps to a new line or you may want to move all the text up or down on a slide.

You can change the size and position of text placeholders several ways:

- Drag a *resize handle* to change the size and shape of a text placeholder. Resize handles are the eight small square boxes along the border of a selected text placeholder or other object.

- Drag the placeholder border to move the text to a new position.

- Change placeholder size and position settings using the Format AutoShape dialog box.

EXERCISE 5-13 Change the Size and Shape of a Placeholder by Dragging a Resize Handle

1. Display slide 5, if necessary, and select the bulleted text placeholder. Notice the small white squares around the border. These are the resize handles.

2. Position the pointer over the bottom center resize handle.

3. When the pointer changes to a double-headed arrow ↕, drag the bottom border up until it is just below "Do what's Good 4 U." As you drag, a dotted box shows the changing shape of the placeholder and the pointer turns into a small white cross. When you release the mouse, notice that the position of the text on the slide is unchanged.

FIGURE 5-11
Resizing a placeholder

4. Position the pointer over the lower left corner resize handle.

5. Drag the corner handle toward the center of the text. Using a corner resize handle changes both the height and width of the box, and the position of the text adjusts accordingly when you release the mouse button. Notice that the text size may change to fit the new box size.

6. Click the Undo button 🔄 to restore the placeholder to its previous size.

EXERCISE 5-14 **Move a Placeholder by Dragging its Border**

1. Select the bulleted text placeholder on slide 5, if necessary.

2. Position the pointer over the placeholder border anywhere except on a resize handle. The pointer changes to the four-headed arrow pointer ✛.

3. Drag the placeholder down until it appears vertically centered on the slide.

FIGURE 5-12
Moving a placeholder

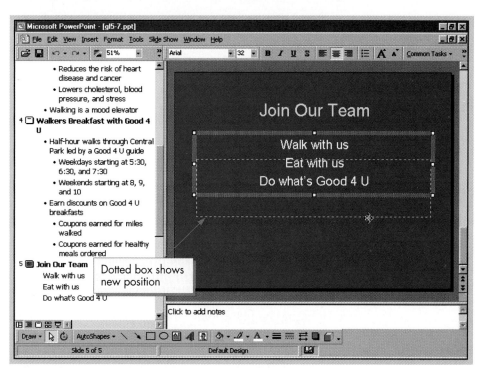

4. Deselect the placeholder. The text is now attractively placed on the slide.

EXERCISE 5-15 **Use the Format Placeholder Command**

The Format Placeholder command opens a dialog box, which offers, among other things, a way to change the size and placement of objects by using exact measurements. You'll learn more about other options in this dialog box throughout this course.

1. Move to slide 2 and select the bulleted text placeholder.

2. Right-click the placeholder border and choose Format Placeholder from the shortcut menu. The Format AutoShape dialog box appears. Notice the different tabs. (You can also open this dialog box by choosing Placeholder from the Format menu.)

FIGURE 5-13
Format AutoShape
dialog box,
Position tab

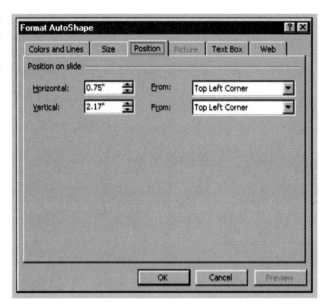

3. Click the Position tab and key **2** in the Horizontal text box. This places the placeholder two inches from the top left corner of the slide.

4. Click the Preview button and drag the dialog box to see the new position of the text. Notice that the placeholder moved to the right and its border now extends beyond the right edge of the slide.

5. Click the Size tab. Key **4** in the Height box and **6** in the Width box, making the placeholder 4 inches tall and 6 inches wide.

6. Click the Preview button to see the results, and then click OK. The placeholder is now sized appropriately for the text inside it and is attractively positioned on the slide.

7. Change the Notes and Handouts footer to reflect the filename *[your initials]*5-15.ppt and then save the presentation with this filename in your Lesson 5 folder.

8. Print as handouts, 6 slides per page, grayscale, framed.

Using Master Slides to Format Text

A *master slide* contains formatted text placeholders and background items that are designed to appear on all slides in a presentation. Changes that you make on a master slide appear on all slides in the presentation that are based on that master. There are two masters you can use for slides:

- Title master, which includes text placeholders for the title and subtitle of the title slide
- Slide master, which includes text placeholders for the title and bulleted text

In general, the slide master and the title master contain the same design elements (such as background color, graphic, and text formatting). However, the title master is arranged differently to accommodate title and subtitle text. The slide master is often less elaborate, leaving room for bulleted text and other information. You can change the formatting and design of the masters and thus set the tone for the entire presentation.

EXERCISE 5-16 **Change Font Attributes on the Slide and Title Masters**

There are two ways to display the slide and title masters:

- Use the <u>V</u>iew menu.
- Use Shift + the Slide View button .

1. Display slide 4. Notice that this is the only slide with yellow bulleted text. You'll use the masters to change all bulleted text to this color and to make some additional changes.

2. To display the slide master, open the <u>V</u>iew menu and choose <u>M</u>aster, <u>S</u>lide Master (or hold down Shift and click the Slide View button). Dotted placeholders indicate the position for title text, bulleted text, and footer information. You can change the size, shape, position, and text attributes for any of these text placeholders.

NOTE: When you press Shift and click the Slide View button ▣ to display masters, the slide master appears. If you were viewing slide 1, the title master appears.

FIGURE 5-14
Slide master

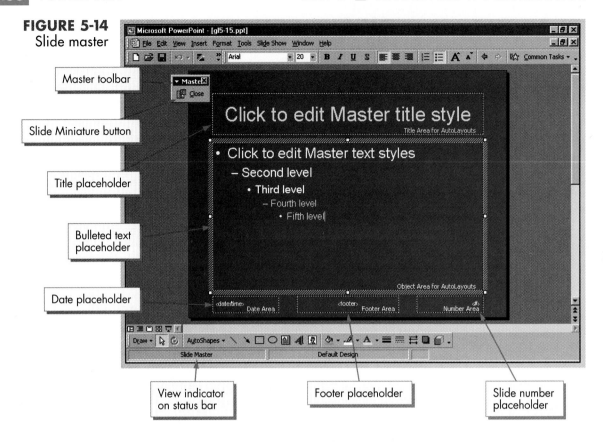

Master toolbar

Slide Miniature button

Title placeholder

Bulleted text placeholder

Date placeholder

View indicator on status bar

Footer placeholder

Slide number placeholder

 NOTE: An easy way to tell if you're viewing the slide master or title master is to check the indicator on the left side of the status bar.

3. Position the pointer over the dotted border of the title placeholder until a four-headed arrow appears and click to select the placeholder.

4. Change the font color for the title text placeholder to white, using the Font Color button **A** on the Drawing toolbar.

 5. With the title placeholder still selected, change the font size to 40 points. Click the Text Shadow button **S** on the Formatting toolbar to apply a shadow effect.

6. Select the bulleted text placeholder. Change the font color for all bulleted text to yellow.

7. Click within the first-level bullet. Format the bullet character as a red heart from the Symbol font that is 100% of the font size.

8. Format the second-level bullet as a white check mark from the Wingdings font sized at 75%.

9. Press PgDn or use the vertical scroll bar to display the title master.

TIP: You can switch between the title and slide masters by pressing `PgDn` and `PgUp`, using the vertical scroll bar, or using the <u>V</u>iew menu.

10. Review the elements on the title master. Some of the changes you made to the slide master are reflected on the title master (the title text is white, shadowed, 40 points, and the subtitle text color is yellow, like the bulleted text color). PowerPoint does this automatically to make sure your presentation is formatted consistently.

FIGURE 5-15
Title master

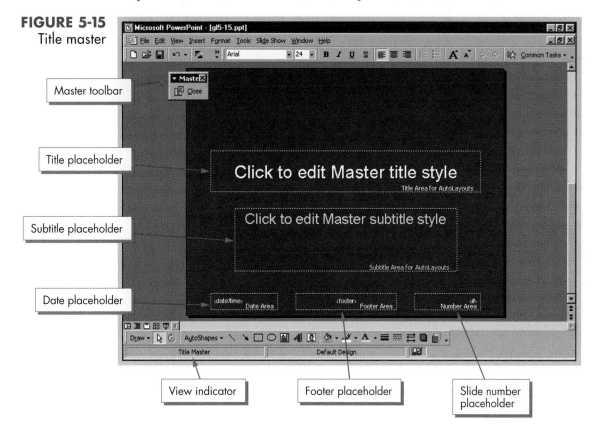

Master toolbar

Title placeholder

Subtitle placeholder

Date placeholder

View indicator

Footer placeholder

Slide number placeholder

11. Select the title placeholder. Change the font to 48-point Arial, bold, red, and keep the text shadow.

12. To return to Slide view, click <u>C</u>lose on the Master toolbar or click the Slide View button ▣. Scroll through the presentation and notice that most of the changes you made to the masters are reflected in the presentation. However, the formatting you applied to individual slides earlier in the lesson is overriding the master slide formatting. You correct this in the next Exercise.

NOTE: Unless you start a new presentation with a title slide, the presentation will not include a title master. To create one, display the slide master and choose <u>I</u>nsert, New Title Ma<u>s</u>ter or press `Ctrl`+`M`.

EXERCISE 5-17 Reapply the Slide Layout

As you've seen, changing a master does not override changes you made to individual slides. When you format individual slides and then format a slide master, you can reapply the slide layout to the individual slides to apply the master slide formatting. This ensures the entire presentation is formatted consistently.

1. Display slide 1. Click the Common Tasks button and choose Slide Layout to open the Slide Layout dialog box. With the Title Slide layout selected, click Reapply. The title master formatting replaces the title formatting applied earlier.

2. Display slide 2. This slide had its bulleted text placeholder sized and positioned and its sub-bullets changed to arrows earlier in the lesson.

3. Reapply the bulleted list layout to slide 2. The placeholder size and position change back to the default.

4. Reapply the bulleted list layout to slides 3 and 4. Leave slide 5 as is.

5. Change the notes and handouts footer to reflect the filename *[your initials]*5-17.ppt and then save the presentation with this filename in your Lesson 5 folder.

6. Print as handouts, 6 slides per page, grayscale, framed.

7. Close the presentation.

COMMAND SUMMARY

FEATURE	BUTTON	MENU	KEYBOARD
Increase Font Size	A˄		Ctrl + Shift + >
Decrease Font Size	A˅		Ctrl + Shift + <
Bold	B	Format, Font	Ctrl + B
Italic	I	Format, Font	Ctrl + I
Underline	U	Format, Font	Ctrl + U
Text Shadow	S	Format, Font	
Text Color	A	Format, Font	
Align Left	▤	Format, Alignment	Ctrl + L
Center	▤	Format, Alignment	Ctrl + E
Align Right	▤	Format, Alignment	Ctrl + R
Justify		Format, Alignment	Ctrl + J

FEATURE	BUTTON	MENU	KEYBOARD
Bullets On/Off		Format, Bullets and Numbering	
View slide master	Shift + ▢	View, Master, Slide Master	
View title master	Shift + ▢	View, Master, Title Master	
Change case		Format, Change Case	Shift + F3

USING HELP ?

Working with the slide and title masters helps you create consistent and professional-looking presentations. In later lessons you learn how to place art on a slide master so it appears throughout your presentation.

Use Help to learn more about master slides:

1. Display and activate the Office Assistant.

2. Key **slide master** in the text box and click Search.

3. Click the topic "The slide master." PowerPoint displays an overview screen about slide and title masters.

FIGURE 5-16
Slide master Help
screen

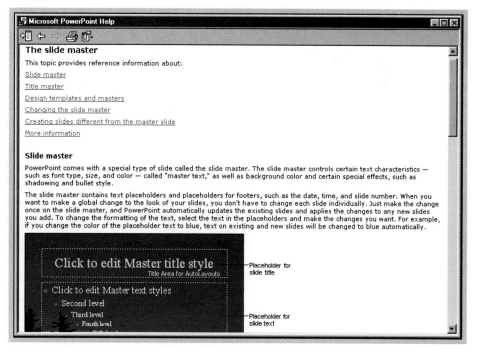

4. Review the information in the Help window by scrolling. Or, click one of the links at the top of the screen to advance to a specific section (such as <u>Design templates and masters</u>).

5. Close Help when you finish and hide the Office Assistant.

Concepts Review

Each of the following statements is either true or false. Indicate your choice by circling **T** or **F**.

T F **1.** You can change selected text from uppercase to lowercase by using the [Shift]+[F3] keyboard shortcut.

T F **2.** You can apply text attributes before you key text.

T F **3.** Sentence case capitalizes the initial letter of important words in a paragraph.

T F **4.** To search for and replace one font with another throughout a presentation, use the Replace Fonts dialog box.

T F **5.** Changes on the slide master override changes you make to individual slides.

T F **6.** The button [icon] can turn bullets on or off.

T F **7.** Placeholders for the slide number appear on both the slide master and the title master.

T F **8.** You can drag a sizing handle to reposition a placeholder.

Write the correct answer in the space provided.

1. What must you do before you can change an attribute for existing text?

2. Which dialog box do you use to change the color of text?

3. Which toolbar buttons change font size?

4. What is the quickest way to add a shadow to text?

5. Which commands do you need to choose to change bullet color?

6. How can you display the slide master without using the <u>V</u>iew menu?

_____

7. Where is the Font Color button located?

_____

8. What does the button ▤ do to selected text?

_____

CRITICAL THINKING

Answer these questions on a separate page. There are no right or wrong answers. Support your answers with examples from your own experience, if possible.

1. Explain how font faces can affect a presentation. Can you use too many fonts in a presentation? Explain your answer.

2. Adding different bullet shapes can add interest and emphasis to a presentation. How do you think a presentation would look if every slide included different bullets? If all the bullets were the same?

Skills Review

EXERCISE 5-18

Apply text attributes to selected text.

1. Open the file **Walk1.ppt**.

2. Change font size of the presentation title by following these steps:
   a. On slide 1, select the text "Power Walking" by dragging the I-beam pointer across the text.
   b. Choose 44 from the Font Size drop-down list on the Formatting toolbar.

3. Increase the font size of the title on slide 3 by following these steps:
   a. Select the title text of slide 3.
   b. Click the Increase Font Size button ▣ until 44 appears in the Font Size box.

4. Decrease the font size of the title on slide 4 to 44 points by using the Decrease Font Size button ▣.

5. Using the Font dialog box, decrease the font size of the title on slide 5 to 44 points by following these steps:

       a. Select the title text.

       b. Choose Font from the Format menu.

       c. Choose 44 from the Size list and click OK.

  6. Change the case of text on slide 5 by following these steps:

       a. Select the last bulleted item by clicking its bullet.

       b. Choose Change Case from the Format menu.

       c. Click tOGGLE cASE and click OK.

  7. Change the font size of the title of slide 6 to 44 points.

  8. Working in either Outline or Slide view, underline the title text in slide 1 by selecting the text and clicking the Underline button ⊔ on the Formatting toolbar. Do the same for the remaining slide titles.

  9. Check spelling in the presentation.

10. On the handouts, include the date and your name as header and the page number and filename *[your initials]***5-18.ppt** as footer.

11. Save the presentation as *[your initials]***5-18.ppt** in your Lesson 5 folder.

12. Print the presentation as handouts, 6 slides per page, grayscale, framed.

13. Close the presentation.

EXERCISE 5-19

Apply text attributes to text placeholders and selected text, and work with bullets.

  1. Open the file **Walk2.ppt.**

  2. Change the color of the title on slide 1 by following these steps:

       a. Press ⟦Tab⟧ until the title placeholder is selected or click the title text and then click its border.

       b. Choose Font from the Format menu.

       c. Under Font Style, choose Bold.

       d. Click the down arrow to open the Color palette and choose green.

       e. Under Effects, click the Shadow check box and then click OK.

  3. Press ⟦Tab⟧ to select the subtitle placeholder. Click the arrow on the Font Color button ⟦A⟧ on the Drawing toolbar and choose orange.

  4. Move to slide 2. Change the title to green, shadowed, and bold by following these steps:

       a. Click the title.

       b. Click the slant-line border to select the title placeholder.

       c. Change the font color to green.

       d. Click the Text Shadow button ⟦ˢ⟧ on the Formatting toolbar.

       e. Click the Bold button ⟦B⟧ on the Formatting toolbar to make the title bold.

  5. Change the titles of slides 3 and 4 to green, shadowed, and bold.

6. Select the bulleted text placeholder on slide 2 and decrease the font by one font size.

7. Change the bullets for slide 2 by following these steps:
   a. Select the bulleted text placeholder, if necessary.
   b. Choose Bullets and Numbering from the Format menu.
   c. Click the Character button.
   d. Choose Wingdings 3 from the Bullets From drop-down list.
   e. Choose a right-pointing arrow bullet and click OK.

8. Remove bullets from selected text on slide 2 by following these steps:
   a. Select the two second-level bulleted items under "When."
   b. Click the Bullets button 🔳 on the Formatting toolbar.
   c. Remove bullets from the two items under "Where."

9. Change the bullets for slides 3 and 4 by following these steps:
   a. Select the bulleted text placeholder.
   b. Click the Picture button in the Bullets and Numbering dialog box.
   c. Click a picture bullet of your choice and then click the Insert Clip button 🔳 from the pop-up menu.

10. On slide 2, add and format a word by following these steps:
    a. Change the fourth bullet to read **Free refreshments afterward**
    b. Select the word "Free."
    c. Click the Bold button 🔳.

11. On the handouts, include the date and your name as header and the page number and filename *[your initials]*5-19.ppt as footer.

12. Save the presentation as *[your initials]*5-19.ppt in your Lesson 5 folder.

13. Print the presentation as handouts, 4 slides per page, grayscale, framed.

14. Close the presentation.

EXERCISE 5-20

Apply text attributes, change text alignment, and change size and position of placeholders.

1. Open the file **Walk2.ppt** and apply the **Capsules.pot** design template.

2. On slide 1, increase the title size to 40 points.

3. Change the alignment of the title by following these steps:
   a. Click within the title text.
   b. Click the Align Left button 🔳 on the Formatting toolbar.

4. Change the subtitle text to dark green and 32 points.

5. Center-align the subtitle by using the Center button 🔳 on the Formatting toolbar.

6. Resize the subtitle placeholder by following these steps:

   a. Position the pointer over the bottom center resize handle on the border.

   b. When you see the double-headed arrow, drag the resize handle up, changing the height of the placeholder until it is just large enough to fit the text.

7. Move the subtitle placeholder to a new position by following these steps:

   a. Select the placeholder border, if necessary.

   b. Position the pointer on the border between two sizing handles.

   c. Using the four-headed arrow pointer, drag the placeholder down so it is just above the dark blue horizontal shape.

8. Center-align the title of slide 2.

9. Change the size and position of the bulleted text placeholder on slide 2 by following these steps:

   a. On the right border of the placeholder, drag the center resize handle toward the center of the text, changing the width of the placeholder to fit the text.

   NOTE: Be careful not to make the placeholder too small or PowerPoint will automatically change the font to a smaller size. If this happens, make the placeholder larger or click the Undo button and start again.

   b. Drag the bulleted text placeholder so it appears centered below the title.

10. On slides 3 and 4, center-align the titles. Resize and move the bulleted text placeholders as you did on slide 2.

11. On the handouts, include the date and your name as header and the page number and filename *[your initials]*5-20.ppt as footer.

12. Save the presentation as *[your initials]*5-20.ppt in your Lesson 5 folder.

13. Print the presentation as handouts, 4 slides per page, grayscale, framed.

14. Close the presentation.

EXERCISE 5-21

Work with the presentation master slides.

1. Open the file **Power1.ppt**.

2. Apply formatting to the title master by following these steps:

   a. Display the title master by pressing Shift and then clicking the Slide View button ⬛. If the slide master is displayed, drag the scroll bar down to display the title master (or press PgDn).

   b. Select the title placeholder by clicking its dashed border. Change the text to 54-point Arial, bold italic, shadowed.

    c. Select the subtitle placeholder and change its text attributes to 36-point Arial, bold italic, shadowed.

3. Click the Slide View button ▣ to display slide 1. Delete the line space between the two lines of text in the subtitle (press [Backspace] before "August"). View the slide titles throughout the presentation.

4. Change the formatting on the slide master by following these steps:

    a. Display the slide master by choosing <u>M</u>aster from the <u>V</u>iew menu and then choosing <u>S</u>lide Master.

    b. Select the title placeholder and change the text to 54-point Arial, bold italic, shadowed.

    c. Select the bulleted text placeholder and change the font to Arial, bold, shadowed.

    d. Change the first level bullet to a star character from the Wingdings 2 font. Size the character to 70%.

5. Format the slide number placeholder on the slide master by following these steps:

    a. Select the slide number placeholder in the lower right corner of the slide master.

    b. Set the Zoom to 75%.

    c. Change the font to 20-point italic.

    d. Position the insertion point in front of the <#> symbols.

    e. Key **Slide** and press [Spacebar].

    f. Choose Fit from the Zoom list to return to normal size.

6. Display slide 2 in Slide view. Make the bulleted text placeholder slightly wider so the "U" of "Good 4 U" fits on the first line of the first bullet. Adjust the position of the placeholder so it appears centered horizontally.

7. Using the Slide tab in the Header and Footer dialog box, apply slide numbers to all slides except the title slide.

8. On the handouts, include the date and your name as header and the page number and filename *[your initials]*5-21.ppt as footer.

9. Save the presentation as *[your initials]*5-21.ppt in your Lesson 5 folder.

10. Print the presentation as handouts, 6 slides per page, grayscale, framed.

11. Close the presentation.

Lesson Applications

Apply text attributes to selected text and placeholders, work with bullets, make changes to the slide master, resize and reposition placeholders.

1. Open the file **Walk3.ppt.**

2. On the slide master, right-align the title placeholder and make it bold.

3. Change the first-level bullet to a diamond shape from the Wingdings 2 font (third row from the bottom). Set the bullet to 75% of the text size.

4. On slide 1, change the color of the date text to dark green and make it bold. Edit the date to the current month and year.

5. Move to slide 4 and change the title to simply "Concession Products" on one line.

6. Change the layout of slide 4 to two-column. Rearrange the text as shown in Figure 5-17.

7. Increase the font size for each column by one increment (making the text 32 points). Widen the first column placeholder so "Desserts and fruit packs" appears on one line. Resize both column placeholders to fit the text they contain, and then move each one to the right, as shown.

FIGURE 5-17

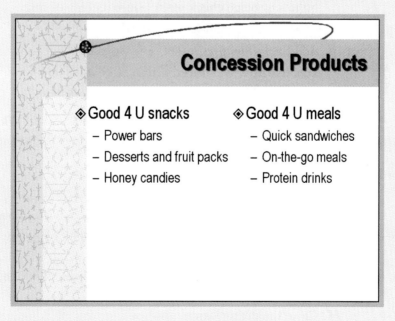

8. Check spelling in the presentation.

9. On the handouts, include the date and your name as header and the page number and filename *[your initials]*5-22.ppt as footer.

10. Save the presentation as *[your initials]*5-22.ppt in your Lesson 5 folder.

11. Print the presentation as handouts, 6 slides per page, grayscale, framed.

12. Close the presentation.

EXERCISE 5-23

Apply text attributes to selected text and text placeholders, work with bullets and the slide master, and replace fonts.

1. Open the file **Recycle1.ppt**.

2. Edit slide 1 so the title reads **Recycling Program**, and the subtitle reads **Good 4 U Management Training**. Change the font color of the subtitle to orange and make it bold.

3. In slide 2, make the words "waste," "costs," and "landfill overloads" bold.

4. In slide 3, increase the font size of the title to 48 points.

5. Use the slide master to change the titles of all slides to bold.

6. Use the slide master to change all first-level bullets to orange squares (from the Wingdings font) sized as 75% of text. Change the second-level bullets to beige check marks sized as 75% of text.

7. Change the second-level bulleted text to italic.

8. Add the following speaker notes to slide 2:

   Discuss how waste reduction is cost-effective.

9. Add the following speaker notes to slide 3:

   Mention our targeted percentages for the coming year.

10. Use the Replace Fonts command to replace Arial with Times New Roman in the presentation.

11. Check spelling in the presentation.

12. On the handouts, include the date and your name as header and the page number and filename *[your initials]*5-23.ppt as footer.

13. Save the presentation as *[your initials]*5-23.ppt in your Lesson 5 folder.

14. Print the presentation as handouts, 6 slides per page, grayscale, framed. Print notes pages for slides 2 and 3.

15. Close the presentation.

EXERCISE 5-24

Apply text attributes to selected text and text placeholders, work with bullets and the slide master, align text, and resize and reposition placeholders.

1. Start a new presentation using the **Expedition.dot** design template.

2. Import the Word outline **PowerWalk.doc**.

3. Change the layout of slide 1 to a title slide. Change the second line of the title into the subtitle.

4. On the title slide and on slides 2 and 4, format the "4 U" of "Good 4 U" as italic. Increase the font size of the "4" by one increment.

5. Replace "walking" with **biking** throughout the presentation.

6. Use the slide master to change all bullets to bicycles (using the Webdings font, the eleventh character in the third row) sized at 110% of text.

7. Use the slide master to change all text to Arial. Make all titles bold and centered.

8. On slide 2, start the text "(fitness and health participants)" on a new line by pressing [Enter] before the text. Center the new line and remove its bullet.

9. In slide 3, change the case of the bulleted text placeholder to sentence case.

10. In slide 4, resize the bulleted text placeholder to fit the text and drag it so it appears horizontally centered below the title.

11. Check spelling and style in the presentation.

12. On the handouts, include the date and your name as header and the page number and filename *[your initials]***5-24.ppt** as footer.

13. Save the presentation as *[your initials]***5-24.ppt** in your Lesson 5 folder.

14. Print the presentation as handouts, 4 slides per page, grayscale, framed.

15. Close the presentation.

EXERCISE 5-25   *Challenge Yourself*

Apply text attributes to text and text placeholders, work with bullets and the slide master, change alignment, resize and reposition placeholders, and embed the presentation font in the file.

1. Open the file **Walk4.ppt**.

2. Apply the **Dad's Tie.pot** design template and change the slide color scheme to the first standard color option in the second row.

3. On the slide master, decrease the title placeholder by one font size. Change the font of the title and bulleted text placeholders to Arial Black. On the title master, decrease the font size of the subtitle placeholder by one font size.

4. Reapply the title slide layout to slide 1.

5. Using the Format Placeholder command, change the width of the subtitle placeholder to 8.75 inches so "Good 4 U Promotional Training" fits on one line. Position the subtitle placeholder attractively on the slide.

6. At the end of the presentation, insert two new slides using the Bulleted List layout as shown in Figure 5-18.

FIGURE 5-18

```
Slide  ──→ Annual Event
title
        ●  Establish volunteer committees
        ●  Schedule year-round support events
           - Training
           - Practice walks
           - Advertising

Slide  ──→ Paths for Every Pace
title
        ●  Beginner
        ●  Intermediate
        ●  Experienced
```

7. Reapply the bulleted text slide layout to slide 2.

8. Edit the first bullet on slide 2 to read **Increase Good 4 U name recognition**

9. Insert line breaks ($\boxed{\text{Shift}}$ + $\boxed{\text{Enter}}$) before the parentheses in the second and third bullets on slide 2 and change the font to Arial for the text in parentheses.

10. Edit the second bullet on slide 3 to read **Organize training seminars**

11. On slide 4, apply bullets to the text in the bulleted text placeholder.

12. On slide 5, reapply the bullets to the lines that begin "Training walks" and "Good 4 U sports drinks."

13. Edit the bulleted items on slide 5 to read as follows:

   ● **Lectures in Good 4 U banquet room**
      - **Conducted by local marathon winners**

- **Training walks in Central Park**
  - **Free bananas and Good 4 U sports drinks**

14. Use the slide master to change the first- and second-level bullets to picture bullets of your choice.

15. Resize and reposition the bulleted text placeholders in slides 4 and 8, centering them horizontally on the slides.

16. Move the first bulleted item on slide 3 ("Advertise Power...") to the last bullet on the slide. Change this last bullet to sentence case.

17. Move slide 4 ("Advertising") to the end of the presentation so it becomes slide 8.

18. Check spelling in the presentation.

19. Add slide numbers to all but the title slide.

20. On the handouts, include the date and your name as header and the page number and filename *[your initials]***5-25.ppt** as footer.

21. Save the presentation as *[your initials]***5-25.ppt** in your Lesson 5 folder so the TrueType font (Arial Black) is embedded in the file.

22. Print the presentation as handouts, 9 slides per page, grayscale, framed.

23. Close the presentation.

Unit 2 Applications

UNIT APPLICATION 2-1

Start a new presentation using a design template, choose slide layouts, insert slides, change text attributes, work with the slide master, change alignment, and resize placeholders.

1. Begin a new presentation using the **Blueprint.pot** design template. Use the title layout for the first slide.

2. Working in either Normal view or Outline view, key the presentation shown in Figure U2-1. Use the Bulleted List layout for slides 2 through 4.

FIGURE U2-1

Slide 1
```
Power Walk and Breakfast
   Good 4 U Promotional Strategy
```

Slide 2
```
Objectives
● Encourage morning power walkers to breakfast at G4U
● Make G4U a social center for power walkers
```

Slide 3
```
Strategies
● Guided walks
● Seminars
● G4U merchandise
● Advertising
```

Slide 4
```
Cost/Benefits Analysis
● Costs
   - Walk guides' salaries
   - Seminar leaders' salaries
   - Merchandise costs
   - Advertising costs
● Benefits
   - Increase breakfasts served
   - Increase repeat business
   - Merchandise sales
   - Increase general sales
```

3. Change the slide color scheme to the first option in the first row of standard colors (the navy background).

4. Create a Good 4 U "logo" by formatting those words in the slide 1 subtitle: Format "Good 4 U" as bold, format "4 U" as italic, and increase the font size of the "4" to 36 points.

5. Use copy and paste to replace all instances of "G4U" with the logo you just created.

6. Using the slide master, center-align the slide title. Change the first-level bullet to the second option in the second row of standard bullet choices (the dotted diamond shape), sized at 100% of text.

7. On slide 3, resize the bulleted text placeholder to fit the text and drag the placeholder so it appears centered horizontally below the title.

8. Change the slide 4 layout to two-column and move the "Benefits" bullet and all its second-level bullets into the right column.

9. Turn off the bullets for "Costs" and "Benefits" and center-align these items. For the second-level bullets on this slide, change the hyphen to the same shape and color bullet you applied earlier, sized as 90% of the text.

10. Increase the font by one size for both column placeholders on slide 4.

11. Adjust the width and horizontal position of the two bulleted text placeholders so they fit attractively on the slide.

 TIP: Use the left and right arrow keys to move the placeholders without changing their vertical position.

12. Check spelling in the presentation.

13. View the presentation as a slide show.

14. On the handouts, include the date and your name as header and include the page number and filename *[your initials]***u2-1.ppt** as footer.

15. Save the presentation as *[your initials]***u2-1.ppt** in a new folder for Unit 2 Applications.

16. Print the presentation as handouts, 6 slides per page, grayscale, framed.

17. Close the presentation.

UNIT APPLICATION 2-2

Insert slides from another presentation, apply a design template, work with the slide master, change bullets, import a picture bullet, apply text attributes to selected text and placeholders, and resize and position placeholders.

1. Open the file **Seafood1.ppt** and apply the template **Whirlpool.pot**. If this template is not available, apply it from the presentation

Seafood2.ppt. (Tip: To apply a template from another presentation, open the Apply Design Template dialog box, change the file type, and locate the presentation file.)

2. After slide 2, insert slides 2 through 5 from the file **Seafood2.ppt**. (Remember to use the Insert menu so you don't have to open the file.)

3. View the additions to the presentation.

4. On slide 5 ("Shellfish"), promote all the bullet text one level to first-level bullets.

5. Use the slide master to change the title and text placeholders to Times New Roman, bold, shadowed. Increase the font size for both placeholders by two sizes.

6. Use the slide master to change the first-level bullets to the picture **Fish1.gif** sized at 175%. (Hint: You'll need to import the picture from the location of your Student Data files.)

7. Display the title master. Check that the title font is Times New Roman, bold, shadowed, and change the size to 66 points. Remove the bold from the subtitle placeholder, if necessary, and change the size to 48 points.

8. On slide 1 in the subtitle, format "Good 4 U" as a logo so "Good 4 U" is bold and shadowed, "4 U" is italic, and "4" is 54 points.

9. Left-align the subtitle text. Widen the subtitle placeholder so it appears on one line.

10. On slide 2, change the bullets to the picture **Fish2.gif** sized at 175%.

11. Change the slide 2 bulleted text to sentence case.

12. On slide 6, reduce the second-level bulleted text by one font size and change the bullets to white wavy lines ≈ (Wingdings, third row) sized at 75%.

13. Using the slide master and the Format Placeholder command, size the bulleted text placeholder to 5 inches wide and position it horizontally 2.5 inches from the top left corner of the slide.

14. Check the bulleted text position on each slide and then run the presentation as a slide show.

15. On the handouts, include the date and your name as header and include the page number and filename *[your initials]*u2-2.ppt as footer.

16. Save the presentation as *[your initials]*u2-2.ppt in your Unit 2 Applications folder.

17. Print the presentation as handouts, 6 slides per page, grayscale, framed.

18. Close the presentation.

UNIT APPLICATION 2-3

Insert an outline from a word-processing document into PowerPoint, create a summary slide, apply a design template, change a slide layout, apply text attributes, and add speaker notes.

1. Start a new presentation using the **Dad's Tie.pot** design template.

2. Insert the word-processed outline from the file **Walk5.rtf** into the presentation. Delete any blank slides, if necessary.

3. Change slide 1 to Title Slide layout.

4. On slide 2, promote the third-level bullets under "Healthy diet" to second-level bullets. Move "Customer convenience" above "Sensible exercise." Move "Healthy diet" below "Customer convenience."

5. Reverse the position of slide 4 and slide 5.

6. Create a summary slide of slides 2 through 5. (Hint: Display the Outlining toolbar, if necessary.)

7. Change the summary slide title to **Topics of Discussion**.

8. Use the slide master to format all slide titles as Arial, bold, and shadowed. Change first-level bullets to boxed check marks ☑ (Wingdings font, bottom row, second from the right) that are sized at 110% of text.

9. On slide 1, format "Good 4 U" as Times New Roman, bold, and shadowed; "4 U" as italic; and "4" as one font size larger.

10. Format the bulleted text on slides 2 and 3 as sentence case.

11. Add the following speaker note to slide 1:

    Read first paragraph from mayor's press release on power walk event.

12. Check spelling in the presentation.

13. On the handouts, include the date and your name as header and include the page number and filename *[your initials]*u2-3.ppt as footer.

14. Save the presentation as *[your initials]*u2-3.ppt in your Unit 2 Applications folder.

15. Print the presentation as handouts, 6 slides per page, grayscale, framed. Print the first slide only as a notes page.

16. Close the presentation.

UNIT APPLICATION 2-4 *Making It Work for You*

Write presentation text, format bullets, apply a design template and color scheme, change fonts, apply text attributes, create a summary slide, reposition placeholders, and change alignment.

1. Open the file **Patch1.ppt**, which contains the beginning of a presentation about a New York City community gardening project supported by Good 4 U.

2. Imagine that Good 4 U is coming to your town to set up a community gardening project. Change "New York City" in slides 1 and 2 to your city or town.

3. On slide 3, add three to five bullets describing how Good 4 U will support the community gardening effort.

4. On slide 4, add at least two bullets describing crop categories, and use sub-bullets to list specific crops. Use the two-column layout.

5. Add a fifth slide titled **How Pea-Patching Helps Good 4 U** and include at least two reasons.

6. In Outline view, create a summary slide of slides 2 through 5. Move the summary slide to the end of the presentation. Change its name to **Summary** and adjust the bulleted text to sentence case (without changing "Good 4 U").

7. Apply the design template of your choice. Change the color scheme to one of the Standard choices that prints well in grayscale view.

8. If desired, change the bullets on all the slides to a different symbol or to a picture appropriate to the theme of the presentation. Use a smaller, less obtrusive symbol for second-level bullets.

9. Use the Good 4 U logo (as created in Application 2-3, step 9) to replace the "Good 4 U" throughout the presentation.

10. Where needed, adjust the font size to create an attractive presentation. If necessary, use line breaks (Shift + Enter) to improve the appearance of long lines. Resize and reposition placeholders to create balance.

11. Add slide numbers to all slides except the title slide. Increase the slide number font size so it is at least 20 points.

12. On the handouts, include the date and your name as header and include the page number and filename *[your initials]*u2-4.ppt as footer.

13. Save the presentation as *[your initials]*u2-4.ppt in your Unit 2 Applications folder.

14. Print the presentation as handouts, 6 slides per page, grayscale, framed.

15. Close the presentation.

UNIT

3

Customizing a Presentation

Working with PowerPoint Objects

OBJECTIVES

MOUS
ACTIVITIES

In this lesson:

PP2000 **3.6**
PP2000 **4.1**
PP2000 **4.2**
PP2000 **4.3**
PP2000 **4.4**
PP2000 **4.5**
PP2000 **4.7**
PP2000 **E.2.9**

See Appendix F.

After completing this lesson, you will be able to:

1. **Use clip art.**
2. **Use WordArt for special effects.**
3. **Add floating text boxes.**
4. **Rotate text.**
5. **Work with basic drawing tools.**
6. **Use basic AutoShapes.**
7. **Place text in an AutoShape.**
8. **Work with scanned images.**

 Estimated Time: 1½ hours

An effective slide presentation uses more than text alone. While text carries most of the information, you can use several types of objects to emphasize your message and draw attention to the presentation. For example, you can add chart objects, free-floating text objects, clip art objects, and scanned images to a presentation.

You can resize, move, shade, color, and frame objects. In this lesson, you concentrate on manipulating clip art and objects created with the drawing tools.

Using Clip Art

Included with PowerPoint are expertly drawn pictures known as *clip art*. These pictures are contained in the Microsoft Clip Gallery. You can insert clip art into your presentation in one of two ways:

- Click the Insert Clip Art button on the Drawing toolbar.
- Use the Insert menu (Picture, Clip Art).

If your slide uses a layout that includes a clip art placeholder, just double-click the placeholder to insert clip art. Note that you are not limited to Microsoft Office clip art. PowerPoint supports many graphic formats from different sources.

EXERCISE **6-1** **Find Clip Art**

Clip art is grouped by category in the Microsoft Clip Gallery. You can also find appropriate clip art for your presentations by using keywords.

1. Open the file **Open1.ppt**. This one-slide presentation uses a Blank slide layout and contains graphics on the master slide. You will use the design as a background onto which you'll add your own graphic objects. (You will not use standard text placeholders.)

2. Click the Insert Clip Art button on the Drawing toolbar. The Insert ClipArt dialog box displays categories of picture, sound, and motion clips.

FIGURE 6-1
Insert ClipArt
dialog box

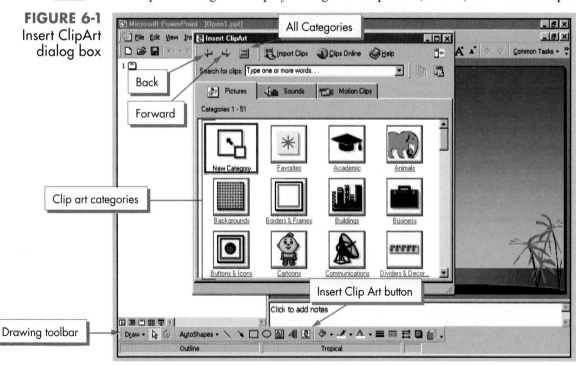

NOTE: Depending on the clip art installed on your computer, your categories may differ from those shown in Figure 6-1.

3. With the Pictures tab selected, scroll to the Business category and click it. (Click either the Business picture or category name.) The Business clip art images are displayed as *thumbnails*—miniaturized versions of the actual images.

4. Scroll the list of pictures in this category.

 5. At the end of the list, click Keep Looking, if it is available, to see more pictures in this category. Review these additional pictures and then click the Back button in the upper left corner of the dialog box.

 6. Click again to display all the categories, or click the All Categories button .

 NOTE: The Back and Forward buttons makes the dialog box act like a browser. You can always use the Back button or the All Categories button to return to the list of categories.

7. Click another category to display its pictures. Move the pointer over some of the pictures. Notice that each picture is described by one or more keywords. You can search for specific types of pictures by using keywords.

8. Click within the Search for Clips text box to select the text "Type one or more words." Key the word **success** and press Enter. All pictures that include the keyword "success" in their description are listed.

9. Click All Categories to display the categories again. Leave the dialog box open.

EXERCISE **6-2** **Insert Clip Art**

When you find a clip art image for your presentation, you can click it and use the pop-up menu to insert it. You can also drag and drop the image into your presentation, or copy it to the Clipboard and then paste it into your presentation (using the Copy and Paste buttons in the Insert ClipArt dialog box).

1. Locate a picture of a sun, either by searching the keyword "sun" or by looking in the Weather category.

2. Click a sun picture. (The picture used in this Lesson is shown in Figure 6-2 on the next page.) A pop-up menu appears with four options.

FIGURE 6-2
Clip art
pop-up menu

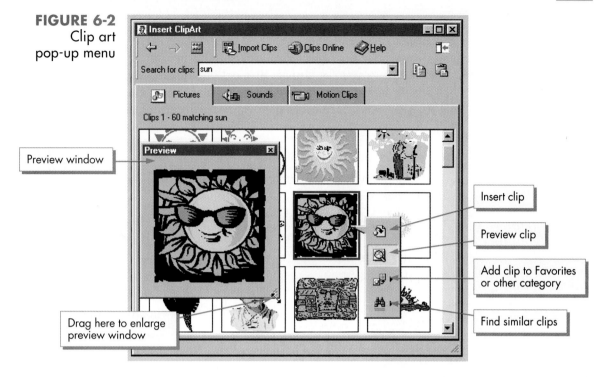

Preview window

Insert clip

Preview clip

Add clip to Favorites
or other category

Drag here to enlarge
preview window

Find similar clips

 3. Before inserting the clip, click the Preview Clip button 🔍 to view a larger version of the clip. To make the Preview window larger, you can drag the lower right corner.

4. Close the Preview window by clicking the Preview Clip button 🔍 again or by clicking the window's Close button ❌.

 5. Click the Find Similar Clips button 🔍. You can search for clip art with the same artistic style, similar colors or shapes, or specific keywords.

 6. Click the Insert Clip button 🖼. Close the Insert ClipArt dialog box. The picture is inserted on the slide and the Picture toolbar appears.

 TIP: Instead of closing the Insert ClipArt dialog box, you can minimize it like a window and then restore it when you want to add another clip.

EXERCISE 6-3 **Change the Size and Position of a Clip Art Object**

You can easily resize clip art, move it to another position on the slide, or move it to another slide. Resizing and moving clip art is similar to resizing and moving a text placeholder. First, you select the clip art by clicking it. Once selected, a clip art image displays the same small square resize handles you see on a selected placeholder.

You can make the object larger or smaller by dragging its handles. Drag a corner handle to size the clip art proportionally. *Proportional sizing* means the relationship between the height and width of the object is maintained. Dragging the side handles changes the original proportions of the clip art, creating a tall, thin image or a short, fat one.

1. On slide 1, click the sun picture to select it, if necessary.

2. Place the pointer on the top center resize handle. The pointer changes to a two-headed arrow.

3. Drag the handle up. The object becomes taller, changing the look of the image.

4. Click the Undo button 🔄 (or press Ctrl + Z).

5. With the sun still selected, place the pointer on a corner handle. The pointer changes to a diagonal two-headed arrow. Use a corner handle to resize the clip art proportionally.

FIGURE 6-3
Dragging to resize clip art proportionally

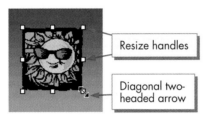
Resize handles

Diagonal two-headed arrow

6. Drag the corner handle diagonally away from the center of the picture until it is about twice its original size.

7. Click the Undo button 🔄.

8. If the Picture toolbar is not displayed when the sun is selected, right-click the sun and choose Show Picture Toolbar from the shortcut menu.

9. Click the Format Picture button on the Picture toolbar. The Format Picture dialog box appears.

> **NOTE:** You can also display the Format Picture dialog box by right-clicking the sun and choosing Format Picture from the shortcut menu.

10. Click the Size tab, if necessary.

11. Click Lock Aspect Ratio, if necessary. This locks the *aspect ratio*, which means that if the height or width of the image is changed, the corresponding dimension adjusts automatically.

12. Under Size and Rotate, set the Height to 2″ and click OK. Because the Lock Aspect Ratio is in effect, both the height and width resized proportionately.

13. Position the pointer inside the object. A four-headed arrow appears.

FIGURE 6-4
Dragging to move clip art

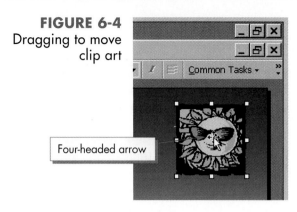

Four-headed arrow

14. Drag the picture to the upper right corner of the slide. As you drag, a dotted line shows the position the image will occupy. You can also use the arrow keys to adjust the position of the selected picture.

NOTE: Whenever you drag to move an object or text, make sure you are not dragging a resize handle by mistake. You must see the four-headed arrow pointer and not the two-headed arrow.

EXERCISE 6-4 Change Clip Art Settings

You can use the Picture toolbar to control various aspects of an image's appearance, such as size, brightness, contrast, and color.

1. Insert two new slides after slide 1, using the Blank layout.

2. On slide 3, use the Insert Clip Art button 🖼 to insert the picture of the sun.

3. Right-click the sun and choose Format Picture from the shortcut menu. Click the Size tab, if necessary.

4. Under Size and Rotate, set the Height to 4″. (Be sure Lock Aspect Ratio is selected or the picture's proportions will be distorted.)

5. Click OK to resize the picture.

6. Position the picture in the center of the slide.

7. With the picture selected, click the More Brightness button 🔆 on the Picture toolbar four times. Notice that some of the details of the image become noticeably brighter.

8. Click the Less Brightness button 🔅 twice to reduce the brightness.

FIGURE 6-5
Picture toolbar

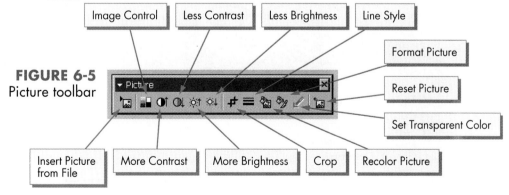

EXERCISE **6-5** **Crop a Clip Art Object**

The Picture toolbar contains a tool you can use to trim parts of a clip art image, just as you might do with a page from a magazine using a pair of scissors. This is called *cropping* the image.

1. Select the picture on slide 3, if necessary.

2. Click Crop on the Picture toolbar. The pointer changes to a cropping tool .

3. Position the cropping tool on the bottom center handle and drag the handle up slightly until the bottom edge is a straight line with no jagged edges.

   TIP: Try holding down [Alt] as you crop. This allows you to make very fine adjustments.

4. Repeat the process with the top edge, right edge, and left edge of the picture, using the center handle on each edge. Crop only slightly to create a straight black edge on all sides.

   TIP: If you crop too far, use the cropping tool to drag the handle in the opposite direction to restore that part of the picture, or click the Undo button ↺.

FIGURE 6-6
Picture after
cropping

5. Click anywhere outside the image to deactivate the cropping tool (or you can click the Crop button ⊞ on the Picture toolbar).

Using WordArt for Special Effects

WordArt can create special effects with text that are not possible with normal text-formatting tools. You can stretch or curve text and add special shading effects, dramatic 3-D effects, and much more. And because they are drawn objects, you can use drawing tools to modify and enhance WordArt text.

As you learned in previous lessons, you can change the text formatting for an entire presentation by changing the text on the slide master. Similarly, you can use the slide master to add drawing objects and clip art to every slide in a presentation. Any clip art image or WordArt text object you add to the slide master automatically appears on every slide in the presentation in the same location on the slide.

EXERCISE **6-6** **Add WordArt Text Objects to the Slide Master**

In this exercise you create a WordArt object and copy it to the slide master.

1. Display slide 1.

2. Click the Insert WordArt button ⊠ on the Drawing toolbar. The WordArt Gallery dialog box appears.

FIGURE 6-7
WordArt Gallery
dialog box

3. Choose the first style in the third row of the WordArt Gallery (the yellow-orange color) and click OK. The Edit WordArt Text dialog box appears.

4. Key **Good 4 U** and click OK. The WordArt text object is added to the slide. Notice that the object is selected and the WordArt toolbar appears.

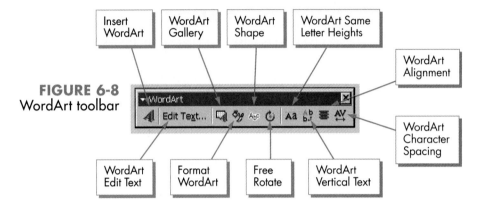

FIGURE 6-8
WordArt toolbar

5. Using a corner resize handle, make the WordArt object about twice as high and twice as wide as its original size.

 TIP: If you hold down [Shift] while dragging a corner resize handle, you resize the WordArt object proportionally.

6. With the WordArt object selected, click the WordArt Shape button [Abc] on the WordArt toolbar. A menu of text shapes appears.

FIGURE 6-9
WordArt Shape menu

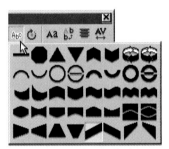

7. Choose the Slant Up shape, which is the fifth shape in the last row. The WordArt object changes to the selected shape.

8. Position the object attractively in the upper left corner of the slide. (You move WordArt objects the same way you move a clip art image—point to the center of the WordArt object and use the four-headed arrow to drag it.) With the WordArt object now formatted and positioned, you will cut and paste it onto the slide master.

9. Right-click the WordArt object and choose Cut from the shortcut menu. The WordArt object is cut from the slide and copied onto the Clipboard.

10. Display the slide master (View menu, Master, Slide Master).

11. Right-click anywhere on the slide master and choose Paste from the shortcut menu. The WordArt object is pasted into the slide master.

12. Delete the title placeholder on the slide master, because this presentation will not use titles on individual slides.

13. Adjust the position of the WordArt object, if necessary.

14. Close the slide master and switch to Slide view. Scroll through the presentation to check that the WordArt object appears on every slide in the same location.

FIGURE 6-10
WordArt text
object

![NOTE icon] **NOTE:** Text added to a presentation as a WordArt object is not checked by the spelling checker. PowerPoint treats it as an object, not text. Make sure you type and proofread WordArt text objects carefully.

Working with Floating Text Boxes

Until now, you worked with text placeholders that automatically appear when you insert a new slide. Sometimes you'll want to put text outside the text placeholders or create freeform text boxes on a blank slide.

You can add text boxes to a slide by clicking the Text Box button on the Drawing toolbar and then dragging the pointer to define the width of the text box. You can also just click the pointer and the text box adjusts its width to the size of your text. You can change the size and position of text boxes the same way you change text placeholders.

EXERCISE   **6-7**   **Create a Floating Text Object**

1. Display slide 1.

2. Click the Text Box button on the Drawing toolbar.

3. Place the pointer below the "G" in "Good 4 U" and click. A small text box containing an insertion point appears.

FIGURE 6-11
Creating a floating text box

4. Key **Here we grow again!** Notice how the text box gets wider as you key text.

 NOTE: If you accidentally drag as you click the text tool pointer, PowerPoint will think you want to restrict the width of the text box and the text you key will wrap within a tall and narrow text box. If this happens, click Undo [↶] and try again.

5. Click the text box border to select it. You select the text box the same way you select a text placeholder. Change the text to 32-point, shadowed, and choose an attractive script font like Harlow Solid Italic or Script MT Bold.

TIP: When you want to start another line in a text box, press [Enter] and continue keying. The box expands to accommodate the new line.

EXERCISE **6-8** **Create a Fixed-Width Floating Text Box**

When you drag the pointer to define the width of a text box before keying the text, the box retains that width and the text wraps within the box.

1. To create another text box, click the Text Box button [📖]. Position the pointer under the text box you created in Exercise 6-7, aligning it with the "H" in "Here." Click and hold down the left mouse button. The pointer now has a cross shape.

2. Drag diagonally to create a rectangle that is about twice as wide as the previous text box. Dragging to draw a text box automatically turns on word wrapping. Unlike the text box you created in the previous exercise, the text in this box will wrap from one line to the next.

3. In the text box, key **Welcomes you to our new restaurant in beautiful Miami Beach**

4. Click the text box border to select it. Format the text as white, 40-point Arial, bold, shadowed. The height of the box expands to fit the text. Don't worry if your text box overlaps the edges of the template design. You change that in the next steps.

5. With the text border selected, drag the center sizing handle on the right border so the text wraps on three lines, as shown in Figure 6-12.

6. Drag the text box to center it, as shown in the figure.

FIGURE 6-12
Fixed-width
text box

Rotating Text

You can rotate objects you create in PowerPoint using the Free Rotate tool on the Drawing toolbar or by changing the Rotation setting in the Format AutoShape dialog box. You can rotate text boxes, AutoShapes, freeform drawings, and in some cases, clip art. You can also control rotation of text boxes and placeholders using the Format Text Box and Format AutoShape dialog boxes.

EXERCISE 6-9 **Rotate a Text Object**

1. On slide 1, click "Here we grow again!" You will rotate the text box so it is at the same angle as the WordArt object.

2. Click the Free Rotate button on the Drawing toolbar. A circling arrow pointer appears at the top of the pointer, and four round green handles appear on the text border.

3. Place the tip of the pointer over the lower left green handle. Press and hold the mouse button. Notice that the circling arrow pointer changes to four circling arrows. Drag the rotating handle down, using Figure 6-13 (on the next page) as a guide. The dotted lines show the position of the rotation as you drag.

FIGURE 6-13
Rotating text

Dotted line shows rotated position

Pointer changes to circling arrows

 NOTE: If you hold down the Shift key as you drag the green handle, you can rotate an object in precise 15-degree increments.

4. Click again or click anywhere outside the selected object to deselect the tool.

EXERCISE 6-10 Change Rotation Settings in the Format Text Box Dialog Box

1. Select the "Here we grow again!" text box, if necessary.

2. Right-click the text box border and choose Format Text Box from the shortcut menu.

3. Click the Size tab in the Format Text Box dialog box, if necessary.

4. Key **15** in the Rotation text box to rotate the text 15 degrees clockwise. Click Preview to see the results. (Drag the dialog box to one side to see the slide, if necessary.)

5. With the dialog box still open, key **-15** in the Rotation text box. Negative numbers rotate an object in a counterclockwise direction.

6. Click OK. The text box is now on an exact 15-degree angle.

7. Use the Free Rotate tool to adjust the angle of the text box, if necessary, to match the angle of the WordArt object. You may want to move the rotated text box up so it is a little closer to the WordArt object.

Working with Basic Drawing Tools

In addition to ready-made clip art, PowerPoint provides you with a variety of drawing tools you can use to create your own drawings. In this lesson, you learn basic drawing skills. In later lessons, you learn how to enhance simple drawings and create more complex drawings.

TABLE 6-1 Drawing Toolbar

BUTTON/NAME	PURPOSE
Draw	Open the Draw menu, which contains tools for aligning, grouping, rotating, flipping, and other manipulations for drawn objects.
Select Object	Select an object. This tool is automatically in effect when no other tool is in use.
Free Rotate	Rotate an object. Any object can be rotated 360 degrees.
AutoShapes	Open the AutoShapes menu, which contains predefined shapes you can draw.
Line	Draw a straight line.
Arrow	Draw an arrow.
Rectangle	Draw a rectangle or square.
Oval	Draw an oval or circle.
Text Box	Draw a text box.
Insert WordArt	Insert a Microsoft WordArt object.
Insert Clip Art	Insert a clip art object.
Fill Color	Fill an object with colors, patterns, or textures.
Line Color	Change the color of an object's outline.
Font Color	Change the color of selected text.
Line Style	Choose a line style and thickness for the outline of a selected object.
Dash Style	Apply dotted or dashed line styles to an object.
Arrow Style	Apply arrowheads to selected lines.
Shadow	Apply shadow effects to an object. This is not the same as the Shadow tool on the Formatting toolbar, which works only on text.
3-D	Apply 3-D effects to an object.

EXERCISE 6-11 Draw Simple Lines and Shapes

In this exercise you draw a rectangle, an oval, and a line.

1. Display slide 2. Click the Rectangle ▣ tool on the Drawing toolbar. The mouse pointer changes to a cross.

2. Move the pointer to the left side of the slide, below the WordArt object.

3. Click and hold down the mouse button. Drag diagonally down and to the right. Release the mouse button. A turquoise rectangle with a white outline appears. (You learn how to change colors and line styles in the next lesson.) See Figure 6-14 for the approximate size and placement of the completed rectangle.

FIGURE 6-14
Drawn objects

NOTE: If you don't like the shape of an object, you can drag one or more of its sizing handles to change its shape, or delete the object and start again. To delete an object, select it and press Delete.

4. Click the Oval ◯ tool.

5. Move the pointer to the right of the rectangle's upper right corner.

6. Click and hold down the mouse button. Drag diagonally down and to the right. Release the mouse button. See Figure 6-14 for the approximate size and placement of the completed oval.

7. Click the Line ◥ tool.

8. Position the pointer on the left edge of the slide, just above the palm trees, for the beginning point of the line.

9. Click and hold down the mouse button. Drag the line diagonally down to the water's edge. Release the mouse button.

10. To add another line, click �diagonal again. Draw a second line using Figure 6-14 as a guide.

TIP: You can draw multiple lines by double-clicking �diagonal. Double-clicking keeps the tool activated so you can draw as many lines as you want. When you finish drawing, click �diagonal again to deactivate it. This method also works with other drawing tools, including AutoShapes.

EXERCISE 6-12 Create Squares and Circles

PowerPoint provides you with an easy method for creating a perfect square or a perfectly round circle. Simply hold down Shift as you draw. When you hold down the Shift key, you can draw a *constrained* object. This means you control the drawing or movement of the object in precise increments or proportions. When you constrain a rectangle as you draw it, the rectangle becomes a square. A constrained oval becomes a circle. Many objects can be constrained to 15-degree increments.

1. Still working on slide 2, click anywhere on the rectangle to select it. (Notice the resize handles.) Press Delete to delete the object.

2. Click Rectangle ▭.

3. Position the pointer below the first "o" in "Good."

4. Press and hold down Shift and drag diagonally down and to the right. Release the mouse button first and then release Shift. See Figure 6-15 (on the next page) for the approximate size and placement of the completed square.

NOTE: Your square may look like a rectangle on your monitor if your monitor's horizontal size and vertical size are not perfectly synchronized. Your square will print correctly even it is distorted on the screen. To check the size, open the Format Object dialog box and click the Size tab. The height and width should have the same measurement.

5. Delete the oval.

6. Click Oval ◯.

FIGURE 6-15
Square and
circle

7. Position the pointer to the upper right of the square.

8. While pressing Shift, drag diagonally down and to the right to create a circle. Move the circle to center it horizontally on the slide.

EXERCISE 6-13 Draw Constrained Lines

You can use Shift to add constrained lines to your presentation. Constrained lines can be exactly vertical, horizontal, or at a 15-, 30-, or 45-degree angle.

1. Still working on slide 2, delete the two lines you drew previously by selecting them and pressing Delete.

2. Click the Line button ▧. You're going to draw a constrained horizontal line from one side of the slide to the other.

3. Position the pointer at the left edge of the slide, below the WordArt object.

4. Hold down Shift and drag straight across the slide to the right edge. (As you drag, notice that the line remains straight if you move the mouse up or down.) Release the mouse button and then release Shift.

5. Delete the horizontal line.

6. Click ▧. Position the pointer at the bottom center edge of the circle. Hold down Shift and drag straight down to the horizon. Release the mouse button and then release Shift.

7. Click . Move the pointer to the bottom of the vertical line you just drew. Hold down `Shift` and drag up to the bottom of the square. As you drag, notice that the line jumps in 15-degree increments as you move left and right, up and down.

8. When the end of the line meets the bottom of the square, release the mouse button and then release `Shift`. See Figure 6-16 for the approximate placement of these lines. (If you have trouble getting the constrained diagonal line to meet the bottom of the square, delete the line and draw it without pressing `Shift`.)

FIGURE 6-16
Drawing
constrained lines

EXERCISE `6-14` Resize Drawn Objects

Like clip art or text objects, you can resize drawn objects randomly (without maintaining the original proportions) or proportionally. To resize a drawn object proportionally, hold down `Shift` as you drag a corner resize handle. Pressing `Shift` constrains the proportions when resizing, just as it constrains proportions when you draw circles or squares.

1. Still working on slide 2, select the circle.

2. Place the pointer on the lower right corner handle. The pointer changes to a two-headed arrow.

3. To resize the circle proportionally, hold down `Shift` and drag the handle down and to the right to make the circle larger.

4. Click .

5. Drag the same handle without holding down Shift. The circle becomes an oval.

6. Right-click the oval and choose Format AutoShape from the shortcut menu. Click the Size tab, if necessary.

7. Under Size and Rotate, key **1.5** in the Height text box and **1.5** in the Width text box and then click Preview to view the results. The object is once again a circle, because it has the same height and width. (Remember, you can move the dialog box out of the way by dragging its title bar.)

8. Click Cancel to close the dialog box without resizing the object and then click 🔄 to restore the circle to its original state.

NOTE: To make the object shrink or grow from the center rather than the side, hold down Ctrl while dragging the handle. To retain the object's proportion and make it grow from the center, hold down Shift and Ctrl while dragging the handle.

Using Basic AutoShapes

PowerPoint provides an assortment of predefined shapes called AutoShapes. You can use AutoShapes to draw perfectly shaped arrows, stars, flowchart objects, callouts, and other shapes with minimal effort.

You resize these shapes the same way you resize other objects. Some shapes include an additional yellow diamond handle to reshape the object after it is drawn.

EXERCISE | **6-15** | **Create AutoShapes**

1. Display slide 3. Move the clip art to the right of the slide.

FIGURE 6-17
Making the
AutoShape menu
float

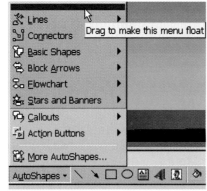

2. Click the AutoShapes button on the Drawing toolbar to display the AutoShapes menu. Expand the menu by pointing to the bottom arrows.

3. Position the pointer over the thin gray bar at the top of the AutoShapes menu. Its color changes to blue and a ScreenTip appears.

4. Drag the AutoShape menu to the upper left corner of the screen. The menu changes to a toolbar that remains on your screen until you close it. You can change its position by dragging its blue bar or close it by clicking the Close button ☒ in the upper left corner of the toolbar.

NOTE: The More AutoShapes button 🔲 on the AutoShape toolbar opens the Microsoft Clip Gallery, from which you can insert AutoShapes from various categories. For example, AutoShapes are contained in the Banners and Miscellaneous categories.

5. Click the Callouts button 🔲 on the AutoShapes toolbar.

6. Click the Rounded Rectangular Callout button 🔲, which is the second button in the first row.

7. Position the cross pointer to correspond with the upper left corner of the callout shown in Figure 6-18.

8. Drag the cross pointer diagonally down and to the right.

9. Select the callout border and place the pointer on the yellow adjustment handle. The pointer changes to a small arrowhead.

NOTE: Like other graphic objects, a selected AutoShape object is surrounded by eight resize handles. Some objects also have a small yellow diamond *adjustment handle*. You use this handle to change angles, roundness, and points of the object.

FIGURE 6-18
Creating and modifying an AutoShape

10. Drag the adjustment handle along the bottom of the callout and up the right side until it points to the sun. You add text to the AutoShape later in the lesson.

EXERCISE 6-16 Create a Constrained AutoShape

Just as you made a constrained circle and a constrained square, you can use Shift to create a symmetrical AutoShape.

1. Display slide 2. Click Stars and Banners 🌟 on the AutoShapes toolbar to display a submenu.

2. Click the 16-Point Star 🌟, which is the second button in the second row of the submenu.

3. Position the pointer to the right of the circle.

4. Hold down Shift and drag down. When the star's size is similar to the circle and the square, release the mouse and then release Shift.

5. Drag the star so it is level with the circle and square, if necessary.

6. Draw another diagonal line from the bottom of the vertical line (at the horizon) up to the star. See Figure 6-20 for approximate placement.

7. Close the AutoShapes toolbar.

> **NOTE:** As with other objects, you can use Shift as you drag a corner handle to resize an AutoShape proportionally, and you can use Ctrl to make the object shrink or grow from the center.

Placing Text in a Graphic Object

Frequently the purpose of drawing an object in a presentation is to place text in it. The object serves as an attention-getting background for the text. You can key the text directly into the object or you can cut and paste it from other locations.

In the remaining exercises, you add text to the drawn objects on slides 2 and 3.

EXERCISE 6-17 Place Text in a Graphic Object

1. Display slide 3 and select the callout object.

2. Key **Join us for the Grand Opening Celebration in November!** (The text will wrap within the callout object.)

3. Select the text (or the text box). Format the text as dark blue, 28-point Arial, bold.

 TIP: To control the way text appears in an object, you can press Enter before a word to start it on a new line.

FIGURE 6-19
Adding text to the callout object

4. Resize the callout to fit the text, if necessary.

5. Display slide 2 and select the square object.

6. Key **FUN** and format the text as dark blue, 32-point Arial, shadowed.

7. Select the circle object, key **In the**, and format the text as dark blue, 24-point Arial, shadowed.

8. Select the star object, key **Sun**, and format the text as dark blue, 32-point Arial, shadowed.

EXERCISE 6-18 Edit Text in a Rotated Object

1. Still working on slide 2, select the square.

2. Open the Format AutoShape dialog box and click Size, if necessary.

3. In the Rotation text box, key **-17** to rotate the object 17 degrees counterclockwise. Click OK. The object and the text are rotated.

4. Select the star and open the Format AutoShape dialog box again.

5. In the Rotation text box, key **17** to rotate the object 17 degrees clockwise and click OK.

6. With the star still selected, move the pointer over the text "Sun" until an I-beam appears.

7. Click the I-beam to place an insertion point. The object and text rotate to a horizontal position for easy text editing.

8. Revise the text to **SUN!**

FIGURE 6-20
Edited text in a rotated object

9. Deselect the star to return it to its rotated angle.

10. In the circle, change "In" so it starts with a lowercase "i."

11. Size and position the star, square, and circle, as desired, to make a pleasing composition.

12. Save the presentation as *[your initials]*6-18.ppt in a new folder for Lesson 6.

13. On the handouts, include the date and your name as header and include the page number and the filename *[your initials]*6-18.ppt as footer.

14. Print the presentation as handouts, 3 slides per page, grayscale, framed.

Working with Scanned Images

You can scan your own pictures and insert them into a presentation. There are two ways to work with scanned images:

• To scan an image directly into your presentation, set up the picture in the scanner (which must be attached to your computer), open the Insert menu and choose Picture, From Scanner or Camera. Choose

Web Quality (if you'll be showing your presentation onscreen) or Print Quality (if you're printing the presentation). Click Insert or Custom Insert, whichever is available. You can then use the tools on the Picture toolbar to adjust the image.

● To insert a scanned image into your presentation, open the Insert menu and choose Picture, From File. Locate the file and click Insert.

EXERCISE 6-19 Insert a Scanned Picture

In this Exercise, you insert a previously scanned picture.

1. Display slide 3 and delete the clip art picture of the sun.

2. Open the Insert menu and choose Picture, From File. Locate the file **Miami1.jpg** on your student data disk and click Insert.

3. Crop the white border from all edges. Crop the bench at the bottom of the picture and a little of the sky at the top.

4. Scale the picture to 75% of its original size. (Click the Format Picture button 🖼 on the Picture toolbar and change Height to 75%. With Lock Aspect Ratio selected, the width will also change to 75%.)

5. Move the picture to the right of the slide.

6. Select the callout AutoShape on slide 3. Change its shape by clicking Draw on the Drawing toolbar and choosing Change AutoShape. Choose the rounded rectangle from the Basic Shapes category.

7. Update the handout footer to reflect the filename *[your initials]*6-19.ppt. Add a slide footer to the current slide only, including your name, the filename, and the date.

8. Save the presentation as *[your initials]*6-19.ppt in your Lesson 6 folder.

9. Print slide 3 as grayscale, framed. Close the presentation.

COMMAND SUMMARY

FEATURE	BUTTON	MENU	KEYBOARD
Insert Clip Art	🖼	Insert, Picture, Clip Art	
Format Picture	🖼	Format, Picture	
Insert WordArt	🔲	Insert, Picture, WordArt	
Text Box	🔲	Insert, Text Box	
Rotate	🔄	Format, AutoShape, Size tab	
AutoShapes	AutoShapes	Insert, Picture, AutoShapes	

USING HELP

The Clip Gallery is an extremely useful and flexible feature in PowerPoint. Not only does it supply a wide assortment of clips, it also lets you add your own pictures or drawing objects. You can place these objects in an appropriate category and reuse them in future presentations.

Use Help to learn how to add your own images to the Clip Gallery:

1. Display and activate the Office Assistant.

2. Key **use clip gallery** and click <u>S</u>earch.

3. Click the topic "About the Clip Gallery."

 4. Review the information in the Help window and then click the Show button to display the full Microsoft PowerPoint Help window.

5. Click the <u>C</u>ontents tab, if necessary. Click the plus sign next to "Adding Clip Art and Other Pictures" to display the subtopics.

6. Click the topic "Add a drawing object of your own to the Clip Gallery." Review the information.

FIGURE 6-21
Help screen about the Clip Gallery

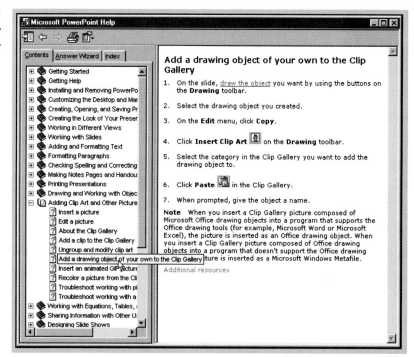

7. Click another Clip Gallery topic, such as "Insert a picture" or "Troubleshoot working with a scanner."

8. Close Help when you finish and hide the Office Assistant.

Concepts Review

TRUE/FALSE QUESTIONS

Each of the following statements is either true or false. Indicate your choice by circling **T** or **F**.

T   F   **1.** Every AutoShape includes an adjustment handle.

T   F   **2.** When you want to change the height of an object but not the width, press Shift while dragging a sizing handle.

T   F   **3.** Anything placed on a PowerPoint slide is considered to be an object.

T   F   **4.** You can type text only in an existing placeholder.

T   F   **5.** Only text objects can be rotated.

T   F   **6.** You can move and resize a scanned picture after inserting it on a slide.

T   F   **7.** Use Shift with ☐ to create a square.

T   F   **8.** To move a text box, the pointer must remain on the border and not touch a resize handle.

SHORT ANSWER QUESTIONS

Write the correct answer in the space provided.

1. How do you draw a perfect circle?

_____

2. What is the shape and color of the handle you point to when rotating an object?

_____

3. What kind of handle is the yellow diamond?

_____

4. What do you use to create floating text?

_____

5. Where do you view clip art?

_____

6. Which button on which toolbar can you use to change the angle of a drawn object?

_____

7. Where do you place the pointer when sizing objects?

_____

8. Which key do you hold to size an object proportionally?

_____

CRITICAL THINKING

Answer these questions on a separate page. There are no right or wrong answers. Support your answers with examples from your own experience, if possible.

1. Select three pieces of clip art from the Microsoft Clip Gallery and explain the type of presentation in which you might use them.

2. Comparing random and proportional sizing, which objects are better proportionally sized? When would you want to use a distorted object?

Skills Review

EXERCISE 6-20

Insert and size clip art and create WordArt text objects.

1. Open the file **Train1.ppt**.

2. Replace the title in slide 1 with a WordArt text object by following these steps:
   a. Delete the title text and the title placeholder.
   b. Click the Insert WordArt button ◀ on the Drawing toolbar.
   c. Select the third <u>W</u>ordArt style in the second row and click OK.
   d. Key **Franchise Training** and click OK.

3. Change the formatting of a WordArt text object by following these steps:
   a. Select the WordArt object, if necessary.
   b. Click the Edit Te<u>x</u>t button on the WordArt toolbar (or double-click the WordArt object).
   c. Change the font to 60-point Arial Black, bold. Click OK.

4. Change the size and position of the WordArt object by following these steps:

   a. Click the WordArt object to select it, if necessary.

   b. Point to the center of the WordArt object. Using the four-headed arrow, drag the object to position it in the title area of the slide.

   c. Drag a corner handle slightly toward the center to reduce the size of the image. Readjust the position of the object, if necessary, and then deselect the object.

> **TIP:** To resize WordArt proportionately, you must hold down the Shift key even if you're dragging a corner handle.

5. Add clip art to the slide master by following these steps:

   a. Switch to the slide master by pressing Shift while clicking ▭. Use the vertical scroll bar to move from the title master to the slide master.

   b. Click the Insert Clip Art button 🖾 on the Drawing toolbar.

   c. Click the Search For Clips text box, key **awards**, and press Enter.

   d. Locate the image of a ribbon award symbol and click it. Click the Insert Clip button 🖼 on the pop-up menu.

   e. Close the dialog box.

6. Resize and reposition the clip art by following these steps:

   a. Still working on the slide master, click the ribbon image to select it, if necessary

   b. Drag a corner handle away from the center of the image to make the ribbon slightly larger. (Remember, a corner handle sizes clip art proportionally.)

   c. Using the four-headed arrow, drag the ribbon to the lower right corner of the slide.

7. Insert the same clip art image on the title master, in the same position, making it a little larger than on the slide master.

> **TIP:** Copy the image on the slide master, paste it on the title master, and then resize it.

8. Return to Slide view and review all slides, making sure the clip art does not interfere with text.

9. On the handouts, include the date and your name as header and include the page number and the filename ***[your initials]*6-20.ppt** as footer.

10. Save the presentation as ***[your initials]*6-20.ppt** in your Lesson 6 folder.

11. Print as handouts, 4 slides per page, grayscale, framed.

12. Close the presentation.

EXERCISE 6-21

Insert clip art and floating text boxes.

1. Open the file **Train2.ppt**.
2. Insert clip art in a clip art placeholder by following these steps:
   a. Move to slide 2 and double-click the clip art placeholder to open the Microsoft Clip Gallery.
   b. Display images in the Food & Dining category. Insert the picture of the coffee cup or the purple utensils (fork, knife, and spoon).
3. Make the picture slightly smaller and position it attractively on the left side of the slide.
4. Crop clip art by following these steps:
   a. Move to slide 3. Select the picture of the waiter and click the Crop button on the Picture toolbar. (If the Picture toolbar is not showing, right-click the waiter and choose Show Picture Toolbar.)
   b. Crop the bottom of the picture, just up to the bottom of the towel that is draped over the waiter's arm.
   c. Position the picture in the bottom left corner of the slide.
5. Resize clip art by following these steps:
   a. Right-click the picture of the waiter and choose Format Picture from the shortcut menu.
   b. Click the Size tab. Set the height to 5.5 inches. Make sure Lock Aspect Ratio is checked so the picture is sized proportionally. Click OK. Reposition the clip art in the bottom left corner, if necessary.
6. Move to slide 4. Use the Clip Gallery to find and insert a picture of a computer or computer disk in a similar style to the other clip art. Resize the image appropriately and position it attractively on the left side of the slide.
7. Move to slide 6. Insert an appropriate picture from the Food & Dining category. Resize the clip art proportionally so it doesn't overlap the text.
8. Create a floating text box by following these steps:
   a. Move to slide 2. Click the Text Box button on the Drawing toolbar.
   b. Place the pointer at the bottom left of the slide, below the clip art, and click. (Be careful not to drag the mouse when you click.)
   c. Key **Ask for our list of wholesale appliance dealers**.
   d. Click the border to select the text box and then change the font to 20-point bold italic.
   e. With the text box still selected, drag it by its border—not by a resize handle—until it is positioned attractively at the bottom of the slide.

 TIP: Use the Arrow keys on your keyboard to position the text box precisely.

9. Move to slide 6. Add a text box to the bottom of the slide with the text **Please submit menu suggestions to Michelle Jenkins**. The text should appear all on one line. Format the text as 20-point bold italic.

10. Change the date on the title slide to today's date.

11. Check spelling in the presentation.

12. On the handouts, include the date and your name as header and include the page number and the filename *[your initials]6-21.ppt* as footer.

13. Save the presentation as *[your initials]6-21.ppt* in your Lesson 6 folder.

14. Print as handouts, 6 slides per page, grayscale, framed.

15. Close the presentation.

EXERCISE 6-22

Insert clip art, use drawing tools to create simple and constrained shapes, and rotate text.

1. Open the file **Train3.ppt**. Move to slide 3.

2. Use the drawing tools to create the shapes shown in Figure 6-22. First, create the wide rectangle that appears on top of the circle by following these steps:

   a. Click ▣.

   b. Position the cross pointer at the bottom left of the slide.

   c. Drag the pointer diagonally down and to the right, creating a short wide rectangle like the one shown in the figure. Release the mouse button. (Don't worry about the exact size or position. You'll size and place it in the next step.)

FIGURE 6-22

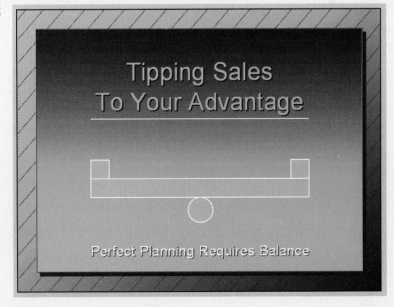

3. Precisely size and position the rectangle by following these steps:
   a. Right-click the rectangle and then choose Format AutoShape from the shortcut menu.
   b. Click the Size tab, if necessary. Key **0.5** in the Height text box and **6** in the Width text box.
   c. Click the Position tab. Key **2.0** in the Horizontal text box and **4.5** in the Vertical text box. Click OK.

4. Create the circle shown in Figure 6-22 by following these steps:
   a. Click ⬭.
   b. Position the pointer at the bottom center of the new rectangle.
   c. Hold down Shift and drag diagonally down and to the right to create a small circle. Release the mouse button first and then release Shift.
   d. Move the circle, if necessary, so it touches the bottom edge of the rectangle and is centered under the rectangle. (Remember, you can use the Arrow keys to fine-tune the position of a selected object.)

5. Draw two small squares, one sitting on each end of the rectangle. Use the Format AutoShape dialog box to make the squares exactly 0.5 inch wide and 0.5 inch high. Position the squares so they appear balanced, using Figure 6-22 as a guide for placement. (You can copy and paste the first rectangle after you size it.)

6. Create a fixed-width text box by following these steps:
   a. Click the Text Box button ▣. Position the pointer below the drawing objects and drag to create a rectangle about the same width as the one you drew previously.
   b. Key the text **Perfect Planning Requires Balance**. Format the text as 28-point Arial, shadowed.
   c. Adjust the width of the text box so the text fits on one line, if necessary. Center the text box at the bottom of the slide.

7. Create a horizontal line on slide 3 by following these steps:
   a. Click ⬂.
   b. Position the pointer below the word "To" in the title.
   c. Hold down Shift and drag to the right to underline the title. Release the mouse button first and then Shift.
   d. Adjust the position of the line, if necessary, by dragging with the four-headed arrow or using the Arrow keys.

8. Move to slide 4 and create a small floating text box in the upper left corner, keying the text **2000**. Format the text as 36-point Arial, bold.

9. Rotate the text box you created in step 8 above by following these steps:
   a. Right-click the text box border and choose Format Text Box from the shortcut menu. Click the Size tab, if necessary.
   b. Key **-25** in the Rotation text box and click OK.
   c. Reposition the text box appropriately, if necessary.

10. Delete the two clip art images on slide 4 and insert one image of your choice. (Hint: Search "money.") Size the image appropriately.

11. Check spelling in the presentation.

12. On the handouts, include the date and your name as header and include the page number and the filename *[your initials]*6-22.ppt as footer.

13. Save the presentation as *[your initials]*6-22.ppt in your Lesson 6 folder.

14. Print as handouts, 4 slides per page, grayscale, framed.

15. Close the presentation.

EXERCISE 6-23

Create AutoShapes, add text to an AutoShape, and insert a scanned image.

1. Open the file **Train4.ppt**. Replace "Date" on slide 1 with today's date.

2. Create a left arrow AutoShape by following these steps:
- **a.** Move to slide 3 and click AutoShapes on the Drawing toolbar.
- **b.** Choose Block Arrows 🔁 on the AutoShapes menu and choose the Left Arrow (the second button in the first row).
- **c.** Position the cross pointer just above the purple bar at the far right of the graph and click.

3. Rotate the arrow by following these steps:
- **a.** Click the Free Rotate button ⟳.
- **b.** Place the pointer over the upper right corner rotate handle.
- **c.** Drag the handle up until the arrow points down at about a 30-degree angle. Reposition the arrow so it points to the top of the purple bar, as shown in Figure 6-23.

FIGURE 6-23

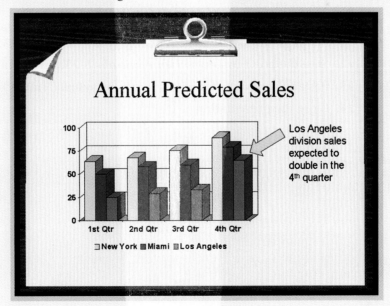

4. Draw a square text box in the space to the right of the graph. Key **Los Angeles division sales expected to double in the 4th quarter**. Change the font to 20-point Arial.

5. Adjust the position, size, and rotation of the arrow and text box so they appear as shown in Figure 6-23.

6. On slide 4, key the following bulleted items in the existing text box:

    ✓ **Our mission is to provide good healthy food and good healthy fun.**

    ✓ **Our franchise training is designed to help you meet these goals.**

7. On slide 4, insert and modify a scanned image by following these steps:
    a. Open the Insert menu and choose Picture, From File.
    b. Locate the file **Produce.jpg** on your student data disk. Select the filename and click Insert.
    c. Drag the picture into the clip art placeholder.
    d. Click to select the picture, if necessary. Crop the bottom of the picture up to the bottom of the white bowl. Crop the right slide of the picture to hide the appliance.
    e. Reposition the picture by moving it a little to the right.

8. On slide 5, use the 5-Point Star AutoShape (from the Stars and Banners submenu) to draw a constrained star in the upper right corner. Make the star approximately 2 inches wide.

9. Place text in the star by following these steps:
    a. Select the star.
    b. Key **Star**, press Enter, and key **Team**. Make the text Arial bold.
    c. Adjust the size of the star so all the text fits inside it.

10. Check spelling in the presentation.

11. On the handouts, include the date and your name as header and include the page number and the filename *[your initials]*6-23.ppt as footer.

12. Save the presentation as *[your initials]*6-23.ppt in your Lesson 6 folder.

13. Print as handouts, 6 slides per page, grayscale, framed.

14. Close the presentation.

Lesson Applications

EXERCISE 6-24

Work with clip art and WordArt.

1. Open the file **Mktg1.ppt**.

2. Find clip art using the keyword "strategy." Insert an appropriate picture on slide 1. Size and position the picture so it is centered below the slide's subtitle.

3. On slides 2 and 4 (not slide 3), insert clip art that uses the same artistic style as the clip art on slide 1. (Hint: Find the same picture in the Clip Gallery and use the Find Similar Clips ▣ button.)

4. On slide 5, insert a clip art image of money or coins. Size and position the image appropriately in the lower left corner of the slide.

5. Review the clip art you've inserted in the presentation. Look for a portion of an image that you can insert at the bottom of slide 3. (Copy the picture to slide 3 and then crop it.)

6. Return to slide 1. Delete the title text and title placeholder and replace it with a WordArt object (using the same text, "Marketing Strategy"). Choose the fourth style in the bottom row of the WordArt Gallery. Choose a different WordArt shape. Resize and position all three objects on the slide attractively.

7. In Slide Sorter view, move slide 5 before slide 4.

8. Check spelling in the presentation.

9. On the handouts, include the date and your name as header and include the page number and the filename *[your initials]*6-24.ppt as footer.

10. Save the presentation as *[your initials]*6-24.ppt in your Lesson 6 folder.

11. Print as handouts, 6 slides per page, grayscale, framed.

12. Close the presentation.

EXERCISE 6-25

Work with AutoShapes containing text and add clip art to the slide master.

1. Open the file **Cook1.ppt**.

2. Create a text box in the lower right corner of the slide with the text **Good *4* U**. Format the text as 48-point Arial bold with a text shadow. Increase the "*4*" to 60 points.

3. Rotate the "Good *4 U*" text so it slants upward in the lower right corner. Adjust the text position, if necessary.

4. Insert a new slide after slide 1 using the Bulleted List layout.

5. On slide 2, key **Good *4 U* Menu** in the title placeholder. Increase the size of the "*4*" to 48 points.

6. Key the following items in the bulleted text placeholder:

- **Good *4 U* Veggie Burger**
- **Simply Good Shrimp Salad**
- **Good Fruit Combo**
- **Andre's Lemon Dill Chicken**

7. Insert a new slide after slide 2 using the Bulleted List layout.

8. In the new slide, key **Franchise Recognition Program** in the title placeholder and then key the following bulleted text:

- **Use the finest quality ingredients**
- **Recognize creativity**
- **Encourage safety in all areas of operation**
- **Create a healthy and fun atmosphere for guests and staff**

9. Insert a new slide after slide 3 using the Title Only layout (not Title Slide layout).

10. Key **Promoting Excellence** in the title placeholder.

11. Below the title, draw a large, 16-Point Star AutoShape, placing it in the center of the slide. Key the following two lines of text in the star:

The Good *4 U*
Seal of Approval

12. Format the text as 32-point Arial bold with a text shadow. Change the size of the "*4*" to 40 points. Rotate the star so the text slants upward.

13. On the slide master, insert an image of fruit or a fruit basket (use the keyword "Fruit"). Move the image to the lower right corner and adjust its size appropriately (making it no larger than 2 inches high or wide).

14. Check spelling in the presentation.

15. On the handouts, include the date and your name as header and include the page number and the filename *[your initials]***6-25.ppt** as footer.

16. Save the presentation as *[your initials]***6-25.ppt** in your Lesson 6 folder.

17. Print as handouts, 4 slides per page, grayscale, framed.

18. Close the presentation.

EXERCISE 6-26

Insert and rotate WordArt and add clip art to the slide master.

1. Open the file **Hiring1.ppt**.

2. On the slide master, insert a clip art image of an apple. Choose a fairly simple image that will work well with the design template, such as a black-and-white illustration. Size the apple appropriately (no larger than 2.5 inches tall) and position it in the lower right corner of the slide.

3. Still working on the slide master, change the title font to Arial Black and the bullet text to Arial.

4. Copy the apple from the slide master and paste it to the title master.

5. On slide 1, insert WordArt using the text **Good 4 U**. Choose the first style from the WordArt Gallery and format the text as 36-point Arial Black, italic. Change the shape to Slant Up. Change the size to 1.25 inches high and 2.5 inches wide. Position the object in the upper left corner.

6. In the subtitle placeholder, key **New Hires**, followed by a hyphen and today's date. Move the text box to the right so it is directly below "New Employee Orientation."

7. On slide 2, break the second bulleted item into these two bulleted items:
   - **History of Company**
   - **Company Vision**

8. Insert a Bulleted List slide after slide 3 with the title **Who's Who** and the following bulleted items:
   - **Julie Wolfe and Gus Irvinelli are the co-owners of the restaurant**
   - **Michele Jenkins is the head chef**
   - **Roy Olafsen is the marketing manager**

9. Insert a line break (Shift + Enter) before "co-owners" so it starts on a new line.

10. On slide 5, key the following bulleted text:
    - **Good *4 U* is growing rapidly with our new franchising philosophy**
    - **Our healthy living message has worldwide appeal**
    - **We are relying on you, our new employees, to help us grow**

11. Check spelling in the presentation.

12. On the handouts, include the date and your name as header and include the page number and the filename *[your initials]*6-26.ppt as footer.

13. Save the presentation as *[your initials]*6-26.ppt in your Lesson 6 folder.

14. Print as handouts, 6 slides per page, grayscale, framed.

15. Close the presentation.

 EXERCISE 6-27 *Challenge Yourself*

Use drawing tools and insert a scanned image.

1. Open the file **Fund1.ppt**.

2. On slide 1, create the shapes shown in Figure 6-24. First, draw an oval and center it below the title. Then, draw a thin wide rectangle over the oval. Last, draw two vertical lines placed where the oval and rectangle intersect.

FIGURE 6-24

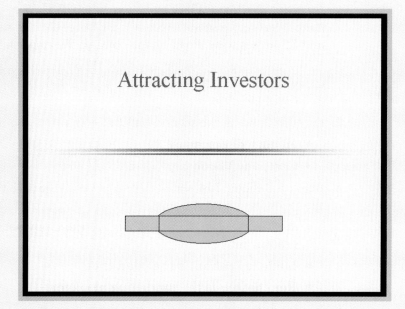

 NOTE: If you have trouble getting the parts to align correctly, hold down [Alt] while you size and drag. You can also zoom to 100% or more to place the objects more precisely.

3. Key **Good 4 U** in the rectangle. (Remember to select the rectangle first.) Change the font to 28-point Times New Roman, bold. Italicize "4 U" and change the size of the "4" to 32 points. Change the text color to the title text color.

4. Still working on slide 1, delete the title placeholder and replace it with a WordArt text object. Choose the third style in the fourth row, the style in which the color is shaded gold and the words slant together at the top. Key the text **Attracting Investors**. Choose 54-point Arial Black for the WordArt font. Change the WordArt shape to Inflate Bottom (the third shape in the fourth row). Increase the WordArt object slightly and position it attractively at the top of the slide.

5. On slide 2, change the title to **Objectives** and key the following bulleted text:

   - **Obtain investors to establish Good *4 U* as a franchise**
   - **Revisit the current business plan**
   - **Hire a marketing consulting firm**

6. In the first bullet, insert a line break (Shift + Enter) before "Good" to start it on a new line.

7. Below the bulleted list, draw an AutoShape Cube (from the Basic Shapes category) that is approximately 1.25 inches tall and 3 inches wide. Key the following two lines in the cube:

   **Investors are our
   building blocks**

8. Format the cube's text as 28-point Arial. Use the adjusting handle to reduce the thickness of the cube. Then adjust its overall width and height, if necessary, so the text fits inside.

9. On slide 3, key the following bulleted text:

   - **Organic fruit and vegetables**
   - **Fresh juices**
   - **Innovative cuisine**

10. Resize and reposition the bulleted text placeholder so it appears centered between the two pictures. Increase the brightness of the two pictures slightly.

11. On slide 4, change the title to **Investor Preferences** and key the following bulleted text:

    - **High-profile location**
      - **Hotel or storefront**
      - **City with tourism, such as Miami or New York**
    - **"Curb appeal"**

12. Change the slide 4 layout to Text & Clip Art. Insert the scanned picture **Miami2.jpg** from your student data disk. (Use the Insert menu method; do not double-click the clip art placeholder.)

13. Crop the picture on all sides to remove the white edge. Drag the picture over the object placeholder. (It will resize to fit the placeholder automatically.)

14. On slide 5, key the text shown in Figure 6-25.

FIGURE 6-25

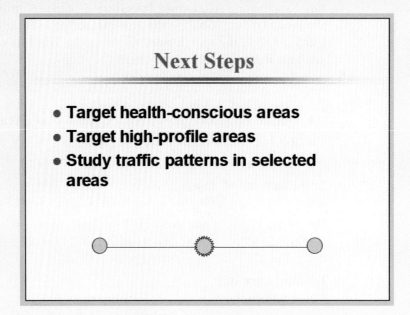

15. As shown in Figure 6-25, draw a horizontal line across the bottom of the slide below the bulleted text. Draw a small circle and position it at the left end of the horizontal line. Copy the circle, paste it, and move the copy to the right end of the line.

16. Draw a 24-Point Star AutoShape and position it in the center of the line.

17. Use the slide master to make slide titles bold.

18. Check spelling in the presentation.

19. On the handouts, include the date and your name as header and include the page number and the filename *[your initials]*6-27.htm as footer.

20. Save the presentation in HTML format as *[your initials]*6-27.htm in your Lesson 6 folder.

21. Preview the presentation in your browser (File, Web Page Preview), and then close the browser window.

22. Print as handouts, 6 slides per page, grayscale, framed.

23. Close the presentation.

Working with Lines, Fills, and Colors

LESSON
7

OBJECTIVES

MOUS
ACTIVITIES
In this lesson:
PP2000 **2.4**
PP2000 **3.9**
PP2000 **4.3**
PP2000 **4.7**
PP2000 **6.1**
PP2000 **E.1.3**
PP2000 **E.2.4**
PP2000 **E.2.6**
PP2000 **E.2.9**
PP2000 **E.3.1**

See Appendix F.

After completing this lesson, you will be able to:

1. Change the line color and style of objects.
2. Change the fill color of objects.
3. Work with fill patterns, shading, and textures.
4. Use the Format Painter tool to copy formatting.
5. Apply design elements to master slides and backgrounds to create a custom template.
6. Change the colors of clip art.
7. Change a presentation color scheme.
8. Change black and white settings for better printing.

 Estimated Time: 1½ hours

In Lesson 6, you learned how to create shapes and add clip art to your presentation. In that lesson, every shape in your presentation had the same color. This lesson shows you how to enhance your presentation by applying color, patterns, shading, and line styles to shapes you draw, text placeholders, and clip art.

Changing the Line Color and Style of Objects

To emphasize or separate text, clip art, or other objects from the rest of your slide, you can create a border using a variety of color and line options.

EXERCISE **7-1** Add a Border to a Text Placeholder and Change Its Line Style

You can add a border to a text placeholder in one of two ways:

- Click the Line Style button ▤ on the Drawing toolbar.
- Use the Format AutoShape dialog box (Colors and Lines tab).

NOTE: To open the Format AutoShape dialog box, use the Format menu or right-click the object and use the shortcut menu. You can also double-click the selected object to open the Format AutoShape dialog box.

1. Open the file **Train5.ppt**.

2. On slide 1, click anywhere on the title text to activate the placeholder, then click the placeholder border to select it.

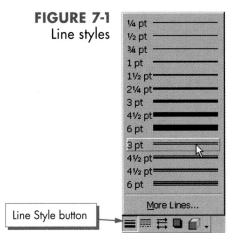

FIGURE 7-1
Line styles

Line Style button

3. Click the Line Style button ▤ on the Drawing toolbar. The line style menu appears.

4. Click to select the 3-point double line. A double line now frames the title text.

5. Deselect the text box and change the zoom to 100% to see the double lines clearly. (Remember that to change the zoom you can use the Zoom box on the Standard toolbar or the View menu.) The line color is the template's default line color. (You change the line color later in this lesson.)

6. Select the title placeholder again and apply the first 4½-point double-line style to the title text border.

7. Change the zoom setting back to Fit. Move the title text box up a little, away from the top of the bridge.

8. Move to slide 3 and select the star object.

9. Apply the 6-point single-line style. A thicker border now surrounds the object.

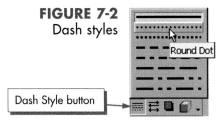

FIGURE 7-2
Dash styles

Dash Style button

10. With the star still selected, click the Dash Style button ▤ on the Drawing toolbar.

11. Apply the Round Dot style, which is the second style on the menu. A dash style line or border can produce a dramatic effect.

EXERCISE **7-2** ## Change the Line Color of an Object's Border

You can change the color of a border in one of two ways:

- Click the Line Color button 🖌 on the Drawing toolbar.
- Use the Format AutoShape dialog box (Colors and Lines tab).

1. On slide 3, select the star, if necessary.

2. Click the arrow on the Line Color button 🖌 on the Drawing toolbar to display the line color choices. The gray bar at the top of the menu indicates that the menu can be floated.

FIGURE 7-3
Line colors

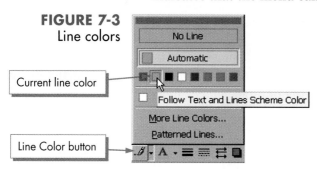

Current line color

Line Color button

3. Move the mouse pointer over each color sample without clicking and notice the ScreenTips. These tips identify the automatic colors for the PowerPoint objects that make up a presentation.

4. Click the dark pink color on the right to select it. The ScreenTip indicates this color is used as an accent color (and as a followed hyperlink if you're working on Web pages).

 NOTE: The color sample on the line color button shows the last color that you applied. If you click a color button (such as Line, Fill, or Text) without clicking its arrow, you'll apply the color shown on the button.

EXERCISE **7-3** ## Add Arrowheads to Straight Lines

You can add an arrowhead to a straight line one of two ways:

- Click the Arrow Style button 🎛 on the Drawing toolbar.
- Use the Format AutoShape dialog box (Colors and Lines tab).

1. Move to slide 4.

2. Using the Line button ◥, draw a straight diagonal line that slants down from the right, pointing toward the tallest bar on the graph.

3. With the line still selected, use the Line Style button ≡ to make the line thicker. Select the 3-point single-line style. (You can increase the zoom to see the change more clearly.)

4. Click the Arrow Style button 🎛.

FIGURE 7-4
Arrow styles

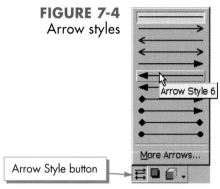

Arrow Style 6

More Arrows...

Arrow Style button

5. Select Arrow Style 6, the large left-pointing arrow.. The arrow points away from the graph.

 NOTE: The placement of the arrow is determined by where you started drawing the line. The left arrowhead appears at the beginning of the line and the right arrowhead appears at the end of the line.

6. Click the Arrow Style button ⬚ again. Select Arrow Style 5, the large right-pointing arrow.

7. Adjust the length and angle of the arrow by dragging its tail with the two-headed arrow pointer, as shown in Figure 7-5.

FIGURE 7-5
Adjusting the arrow

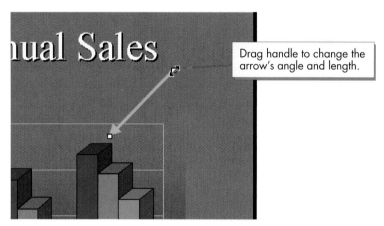

Drag handle to change the arrow's angle and length.

8. Right-click the arrow, and choose Format Aut<u>o</u>Shape from the shortcut menu.

9. Click the Colors and Lines tab, if necessary. This dialog box contains many options, making it easy to change several properties of an object at once. (See Figure 7-6 on the next page.)

10. Open the Line C<u>o</u>lor drop-down list. The first line of color samples represents the colors for the current presentation's color scheme.

11. Point to the gray color sample on the first line. The ScreenTip identifies this sample as the color scheme's background color.

12. Click the gray background color to select it.

13. Click the <u>P</u>review button and drag the dialog box out of the way to see the new color of the arrow. The arrow fades into the background.

14. Change the color to pink, the Accent scheme color. Preview the change.

15. Click OK to accept the color and close the Format AutoShape dialog box.

NOTE: You use the same technique to change the color of a line as you use to change the color of an object border.

FIGURE 7-6
Format AutoShape
dialog box, Colors
and Lines tab

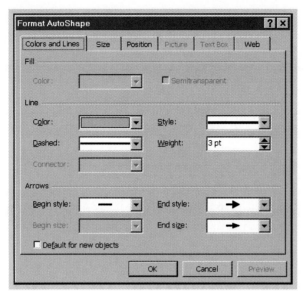

Changing the Fill Color of Objects

When you draw an object on a slide, the color of the object is determined by the presentation's color scheme. You can choose a new fill color for an object. You can also change the fill color of a text placeholder or any other PowerPoint object.

You change the fill color using one of two options:

- The Fill Color button on the Drawing toolbar
- The Format AutoShape dialog box (Colors and Lines tab)

EXERCISE **7-4** **Change the Fill Color of an Object**

1. Move to slide 3 and right-click the star. Choose Format AutoShape to open the Format Autoshape dialog box.

FIGURE 7-7
Changing an
object's fill color

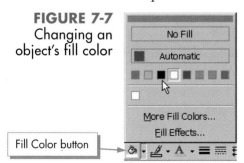

Fill Color button

2. Click the Fill Color arrow to open the fill color drop-down menu. Choose the white sample that follows the title text scheme color. Click OK.

3. With the star still selected, click the arrow next to the Fill Color button on the Drawing toolbar. Click the black sample, the shadow scheme color.

4. Click the Line Style button ≣ and choose the 4½-point line style to make the dotted border on the star thinner.

EXERCISE **7-5** **Remove Fill Colors and Lines from Objects**

1. Move to slide 5 and select the large triangle AutoShape.

2. On the Drawing toolbar, click the Fill Color button's 🔲 arrow, and choose No Fill. The color disappears, but the line remains.

3. With the triangle still selected, use the Line Color button 🔲 to choose No Line. The triangle's border disappears. Although it looks like the object disappeared, it is still there.

4. Select the circle. Remove the line from the circle so it appears as a blue dot.

Adding Patterns, Shading, and Textures

To add more interest to the objects in your slide, you can add special effects such as fill patterns, shading, and textures. PowerPoint provides many patterns, including textures that resemble wood and marble surfaces.

EXERCISE **7-6** **Apply a Shaded Fill to an Object**

In PowerPoint, applying a shaded fill means adding a *gradient fill* to an object, in which one color fades to another color. A gradient fill can use one or two colors or preset color combinations that are built into PowerPoint. You can also lighten or darken these colors and specify the direction of the gradient fill, such as horizontal or diagonal.

1. Move to slide 5, if necessary. Click the text in the invisible triangle to make its border visible. Click the border to select the entire object, just as you would select a text box.

 NOTE: If you just click the text, you will be in Edit mode. To select the entire object and all the text inside it, click its border (or press Esc).

2. Click the Fill Color button arrow 🔲 and choose Fill Effects at the bottom of the menu. The Fill Effects dialog box appears.

3. Click the Gradient tab, if necessary.

FIGURE 7-8
Fill Effects
dialog box

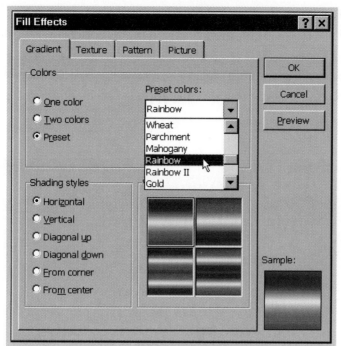

4. In the Colors options box, click Preset. The Preset Colors list box appears, containing specially created gradient fills (such as "Early Sunset"). Select some of these preset colors and then look at the display in the Variants box.

5. Choose Rainbow from the Preset Colors list box.

6. In the Shading Styles option box, choose From Corner. Notice the Sample box changes as you choose different effects.

7. Under Variants, click the option in the lower left corner. Click the Preview button and drag the dialog box out of the way so you can see the effect on the slide.

8. Click OK to accept the shading and close the dialog box.

9. Deselect the triangle. Because you changed the shading of the triangle, the text is not legible. Select the text in the triangle, change the font color to black, and apply a text shadow.

10. Select the triangle, use the Line Style button ≡ to apply a ¼-point border to the triangle, and change the line color to black.

EXERCISE 7-7   Shade a Circle to Add Dimension

1. Still working on slide 5, select the circle on top of the triangle.

2. Use the Fill Color button 🎨 to open the Fill Effects dialog box and display the Gradient tab.

3. Choose the <u>O</u>ne Color option.

4. Move the Dar<u>k</u>/Light slider to the right of center until the color samples shade from dark to light purple.

5. In the Shading styles option box, choose Fro<u>m</u> Center.

6. Choose the right Variant<u>s</u> option, which contains the light color in the center.

7. Click OK. The circle now looks like a sphere.

FIGURE 7-9
Using gradient fills

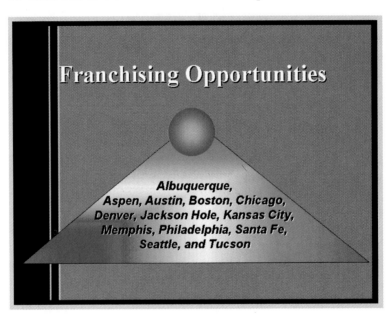

EXERCISE 7-8 **Add a Shaded Fill to a Text Placeholder**

1. Move to slide 2, and select the bulleted text placeholder.

2. Choose Colors and Lines from the Format menu to open the Format AutoShape dialog box.

3. Click the Fill <u>C</u>olor arrow and choose <u>F</u>ill Effects.

4. In the Fill Effects dialog box, choose the <u>T</u>wo Colors option.

5. Choose black for Color <u>1</u> and gray for Color <u>2</u>.

6. Choose the Hori<u>z</u>ontal shade style and the upper right variant (which is darkest at the bottom).

7. Click OK to accept the shading. Click OK again to close the Format AutoShape dialog box.

8. Move to slide 6. Apply the same shading to the text placeholder you applied on slide 2.

EXERCISE 7-9   Add a Fill Pattern to an Object

1. On slide 6, right-click the first blue diamond and choose Format AutoShape from the shortcut menu.
2. In the Format AutoShape dialog box, choose No Line from the Line Color drop-down list.
3. Choose Fill Effects from the Fill Color drop-down list box.
4. Click the Pattern tab.
5. Choose the solid diamond Pattern, which is the last pattern in the last row.

FIGURE 7-10
Adding a pattern
fill to an object

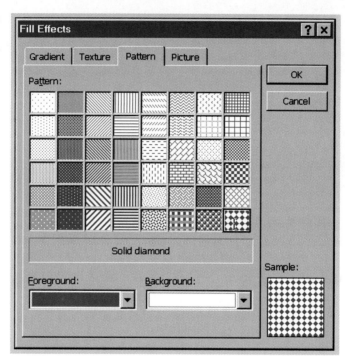

6. Change the Background color to black and click OK.
7. Click Preview to view the changes.
8. Click OK to close the Format AutoShape dialog box.

EXERCISE 7-10   Add a Textured Fill to an Object

Besides gradient color shading and patterns, you can also apply textured fill effects such as marble and wood grain.

1. On slide 6, right-click the second blue diamond and open the Format AutoShape dialog box. Click the Colors and Lines tab, if necessary.

2. Choose black for the Line Color.

3. Choose Fill Effects from the Fill Color drop-down list and click the Texture tab.

4. Click several different textures, one at a time. Notice the name of the texture and its appearance in the Sample box.

5. Click Granite, the last option in the second row.

FIGURE 7-11
Texture tab in the
Fill Effects
dialog box

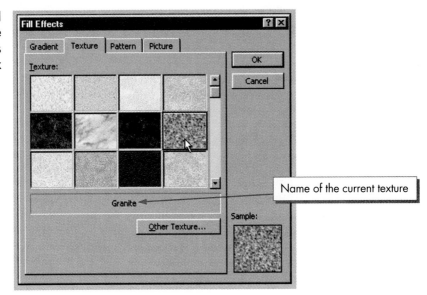

6. Click OK to accept the texture and close the Fill Effects dialog box.

7. Click OK to close the Format AutoShape dialog box.

EXERCISE 7-11 Add a Picture Fill to an Object

You can further customize your slides by using a picture file as an object fill.

1. Select the last diamond on slide 6.

2. Use the Fill Color button to open the Fill Effects dialog box and click the Picture tab.

3. Click the Select Picture button.

4. Locate your student data files and select **Produce.jpg**. Click Insert. The picture fills the diamond.

5. Remove the outline from the diamond.

6. Save the presentation as *[your initials]***7-11.ppt** in a new folder for Lesson 7.

7. View the presentation as a slide show, then return to Normal view.

Using the Format Painter Tool

If you use Word or Excel, you're probably familiar with the *Format Painter* tool. This tool makes it easy to copy the formatting from one object to another object.

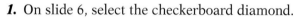 **NOTE:** Because the Format Painter copies all formatting, you may inadvertently copy unwanted formatting or lose formatting you want. For example, if you copy the formatting from a drawn object to a text placeholder, you may copy the colors and borders but lose word wrapping and centering. The Undo command comes in handy in such cases.

EXERCISE 7-12 **Copy Formatting from One Object to Another Object**

1. On slide 6, select the checkerboard diamond.

 2. Click the Format Painter button on the Standard toolbar. The checkerboard formatting is picked up by the Format Painter and the mouse pointer has a paintbrush attached to it.

3. Select within the title text. The text appears in a tiny size with a checkerboard background. Click the Undo button .

4. Select the second diamond (with the granite fill) and double-click the Format Painter button <image>. Double-clicking keeps the Format Painter active so you can copy the formatting to more than one object.

5. Click the top diamond and then click the bottom diamond. All diamonds now have the granite fill. Notice that the Format Painter button is still turned on.

6. Click again or press Esc to restore the normal mouse pointer.

 NOTE: Just as you can copy objects from one slide to another, you can copy formatting from one slide to another using Format Painter.

Applying Design Elements to Create a Custom Template

In previous lessons you learned how to change a presentation by changing text formatting and master slides elements. Now you can add the design elements you learn in this lesson—line, color, and fill effects—to create a custom template.

EXERCISE   7-13   ## Apply a Fill Effect to a Master Slide Object

1. Switch to the slide master. (Remember to use the <u>V</u>iew menu or press [Shift] while clicking the Slide View button 🔲 to display the slide master.)

2. Select the black vertical rectangle on the left slide of the slide master.

3. Use the Fill Color button 🖌 to open the Fill Effects dialog box and display the Gradient tab.

4. Choose <u>T</u>wo Colors. Choose black for color 1 and gray for color 2.

5. Choose the Hori<u>z</u>ontal shading option and the lower-right variant (the one with the darkest color in the middle). Click OK. Click OK again to close the Format AutoShape dialog box.

6. With the shaded rectangle still selected, click the Format Painter button 🖋 and switch to the title master by using the vertical scroll bar.

7. Click the black rectangle on the title master to copy the shading effect.

EXERCISE   7-14   ## Change the Color of a Master Slide Object

1. Working on the title master, deselect the rectangle, if necessary.

2. Select the left green vertical line and press [Delete] to delete it.

     NOTE: Selecting a line that's on top of another object can be tricky. Place the four-headed arrow pointer directly on top of the line and click. If you see just two sizing handles, the line is selected.

3. Select the remaining green line and change its line color to the pink sample that follows the accent scheme color.

FIGURE 7-12
Title master with fill
effects and line
color changes

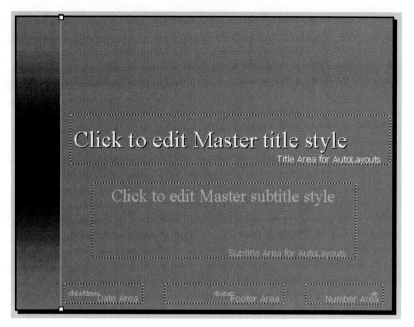

4. Switch to the slide master and make the same line changes so it matches the title master.

5. Return to Normal or Slide view and scroll through the slides to observe your changes.

EXERCISE 7-15   Create a Custom Background

One way to change a presentation's overall appearance quickly and easily is to change background effects and background colors using the Background command on the Format menu. You can change background effects for an entire presentation or for just one slide.

1. Working on any slide, choose Background from the Format menu. The Background dialog box opens.

FIGURE 7-13
Background
dialog box

2. Click the sample color box's down arrow and choose Fill Effects.

3. Click the Texture Tab, choose Granite, and click OK. Click Apply to apply the granite texture to the background of the current slide.

4. Move to another slide to verify that its background has not changed.

5. With any slide displayed, reopen the Background dialog box.

6. Open the Fill Effects dialog box and click the Gradient tab.

7. Choose the two-color option, with black for color 1 and gray for color 2.

 TIP: Notice the Picture tab in the dialog box. Just as you applied a picture as an object fill, you can also apply a picture as a background fill to an individual slide or to an entire presentation.

8. Choose the horizontal shading style, if necessary, and the first variant (with the darkest color at the top of the sample).

9. Click OK, then click Apply to All. Scroll through the presentation to verify that the shaded background appears on all slides.

EXERCISE **7-16** Remove Master Slide Graphics from a Slide

Sometimes the master slide graphics interfere with the design of one or more slides in your presentation. You can use the Background dialog box to eliminate master slide graphics on individual slides.

1. Move to slide 5, "Franchising Opportunities." Notice that the master slide graphics on the left interfere with this slide's design.

2. Open the Background dialog box.

3. Check the box in the lower left corner of the dialog box labeled "Omit background graphics from master."

4. Click Apply. The rectangle and vertical line are deleted from the slide.

NOTE: If you click Apply to All by mistake, you delete the master slide graphics from all slides. In that case, click Undo and try again.

5. Scroll through the presentation to verify that all other slides still display the master graphic elements.

6. Save the presentation as *[your initials]*7-16.ppt in your Lesson 7 folder.

EXERCISE **7-17** Save a Presentation as a Template

When you finish applying design elements to master slides, you can save a presentation as a template. You can then apply this template to other presentation files.

1. With the file *[your initials]***7-16.ppt** still open, switch to Slide Sorter view and delete all the slides. You now have a blank Slide Sorter screen.

2. Display the slide master and then the title master. This is the basic design of the template you are about to create.

 NOTE: Another way to create a new template is to start with a blank presentation, apply the formatting you want, and then save it as a design template.

3. Choose Save As from the File menu.

4. Open the Save as Type drop-down list and choose Design Template (*.pot).

5. Key your name in the File Name text box (for example, the template file will be called JaneDoe.pot).

6. Open the Save In drop-down list and locate your Lesson 7 folder.

7. Click Save. Close the template.

8. Open the file **Advert1.ppt** and apply the design template file you just created. (In the Apply Design Template dialog box, you must open the Look In drop-down list and locate your Lesson 7 folder.)

 NOTE: The template you created is used simply for its design. You can also create a content template, like those in the AutoContent Wizard. Content templates contain specific slides and slide text.

9. View the presentation in Slide Sorter view to see the effect of the new template, then switch to Normal view.

10. On slide 1, add your name in the subtitle. Leave the title uppercase.

11. Delete slide 8, and check spelling in the presentation.

12. On the handouts, include the date and your name as header and include the page number and the filename *[your initials]***7-17.ppt** as footer.

13. Save the presentation as *[your initials]***7-17.ppt** in your Lesson 7 folder.

14. Print handouts, 9 slides per page, and then close the presentation.

Changing Clip Art Colors

If you find a piece of clip art you like but the colors are not right for your presentation, you can recolor it. You can change the colors of many Clip Gallery pictures supplied with Microsoft Office. It is best to use simple drawings when recoloring.

NOTE: Pictures of certain file formats (bitmap, .jpg, .gif, .png) can only be recolored in an image editing program such as Microsoft Photo Editor.

You recolor clip art using the Recolor Picture dialog box, which can be displayed one of two ways:

- Click the Recolor Picture button 🖼️ on the Picture toolbar.
- Choose Format Picture from the shortcut menu and click Recolor on the Picture tab.

EXERCISE 7-18 Recolor a Clip Art Object

1. Open the file *[your initials]***7-16.ppt**.

2. Move to slide 2 ("Required Restaurant Equipment") and select the knife and fork picture.

 3. Click the Recolor Picture button 🖼️ on the Picture toolbar to open the Recolor Picture dialog box. Each color in the clip art object appears as an Original color. These colors include lines, backgrounds, and fills that make up the clip art object.

 NOTE: The Picture toolbar appears when a picture is selected. If the toolbar is not displayed, choose Toolbars from the View menu and click Picture.

4. In the Change box, choose Fills, if necessary.

5. Click the New drop-down list for the second color (black) and choose pink. The knife and fork are now pink.

6. Change the first color (white) to black and click OK. The picture is recolored to match the color scheme of your presentation.

7. Move to slide 1. Use the Crop button 🔲 to crop the bottom of the picture so no blue water shows. Move the picture to the bottom of the slide. Align the left side of the picture with the pink vertical line.

8. Click the Recolor Picture button 🖼️ to open the Recolor Picture dialog box. Notice that this picture contains many colors.

9. Select the Colors option in the Change box, if necessary.

10. Use the vertical scroll bar in the dialog box to scroll to the bottom of the list of color samples. The last color you see should be white. Above the white are three shades of orange and two shades of gray.

FIGURE 7-14
Recolor Picture
dialog box

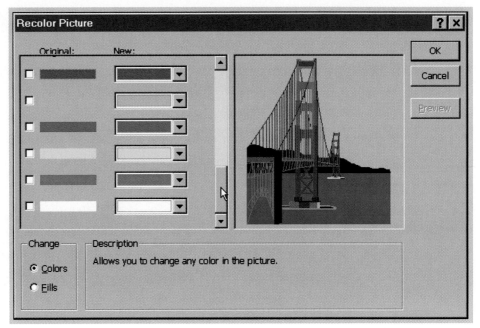

11. Change the two darker shades of orange to the dark pink, which is the last color of the color sample box. Change the lighter orange to the lighter pink in the color sample box.

12. Click Preview to view the changes. (Move the dialog box out of the way, if necessary.)

13. Click OK to accept the colors.

Changing a Presentation Color Scheme

In Lesson 3, you learned how to apply a design template to a presentation and how to modify the standard color scheme for the chosen template. Although most PowerPoint templates have different color schemes, these choices may not be suitable for your needs. If this is the case, you can change one or more colors in a scheme or create an entirely new color scheme.

EXERCISE 7-19 Make Custom Color Changes to a Color Scheme

1. Choose Slide Color Scheme from the Format menu to open the Color Scheme dialog box.

2. Click the Custom tab. The Color Scheme dialog box displays eight standard colors for the current color scheme.

FIGURE 7-15
Color Scheme
dialog box,
Custom tab

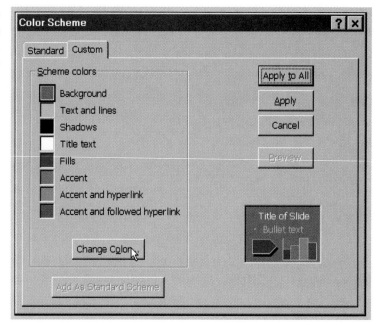

3. In the Scheme Colors box, select the gray color next to Background, if necessary, and click Change Color. The Background Color dialog box appears with a honeycomb of colors you can choose from. Note that the original gray color is selected (it has a white outline).

4. Click the next darker shade of gray, above and slightly to the right of the original color. The sample box in the lower right corner displays the new color and current color.

FIGURE 7-16
Background Color
dialog box

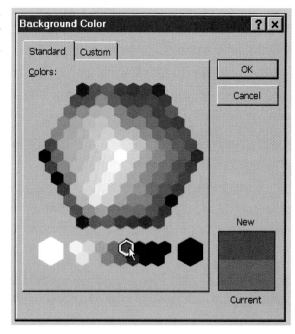

5. Click OK to accept the new background color.

6. In the Color Scheme dialog box, double-click the green Text and Lines color. The Text and Line Color dialog box opens.

7. Choose a slightly lighter shade of green. Click OK.

8. Click Apply to All to apply these subtle changes to the color scheme.

9. Scroll through all slides to view the changes.

EXERCISE 7-20 Create a New Color Scheme

1. Open the Slide Color Scheme dialog box.

2. Double-click the gray Background color to open the Background Color dialog box.

3. Choose a dark maroon and click OK.

4. Click Preview to see the color change. If you don't like the color, change it to a different shade of maroon or choose a shade of blue.

5. Click Add As Standard Scheme. Click the Standard tab. Notice that the new scheme appears as one of the choices.

6. Click Apply to All and click OK. Scroll through the presentation to observe the dramatic changes.

EXERCISE 7-21 Copy a Color Scheme from Another Presentation

You can use the Format Painter tool to copy the color scheme from a slide in one presentation to slides in another presentation.

NOTE: As you've also seen, you can apply a template from one presentation to another. This option applies all the presentation formatting in addition to the color scheme.

1. Open the file **Train1.ppt**. Choose Arrange All from the Window menu and change both presentations to Slide Sorter view.

2. Click within the **Train1.ppt** window to activate it, if necessary, and press Ctrl+A to select all slides in the presentation.

3. Select one of the slides in *[your initials]***7-16.ppt**. Click the Format Painter button to pick up the slide's color scheme.

NOTE: The Format Painter button behaves differently depending on the view you're in and what is selected in the presentation. When you're in Slide Sorter view, the Format Painter picks up a selected slide's color scheme.

4. Click one of the selected slides in **Train1.ppt**. (You'll have to click once to activate the presentation window, then click again to select the slide.) The color scheme is applied to all slides in the presentation.

5. Close **Train1.ppt** without saving. Maximize *[your initials]***7-16.ppt**.

Changing Black and White Settings

In many cases, slides look great in color, but the text becomes difficult or impossible to read when you print your presentation in black and white. To remedy this, you can adjust the black and white settings for your presentation—for an entire slide, a master slide, or individual objects on any slide or master slide. By changing the black and white settings, you can control the black and white version of your presentation without affecting the color version.

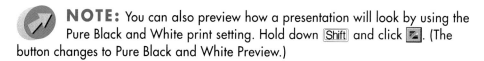

EXERCISE 7-22 **Change Black and White Settings for Printing**

Before changing the black and white settings for individual presentation slides or objects, you can use the print setting Grayscale to preview how the presentation will look.

1. With the presentation still in Slide Sorter view, click the Grayscale Preview button on the Standard toolbar. When you use this print setting, the slides will appear in black and white with shades of gray, but you won't be able to read the body text on slides 2 and 6 very well. (See Figure 7-17 on the next page.)

   NOTE: You can also preview how a presentation will look by using the Pure Black and White print setting. Hold down Shift and click . (The button changes to Pure Black and White Preview.)

2. Double-click slide 2 to display it in Slide view.

3. Right-click a blank part of the slide where there is no graphic or text object. Point to Black and White on the shortcut menu. A series of black and white options appears on a submenu.

   NOTE: The Black and White command is available only on the shortcut menu and only when slides are displayed in black and white mode.

4. Choose Light Grayscale from the submenu. The entire slide turns to gray, but this doesn't improve the appearance.

5. Click the Undo button to undo the change.

FIGURE 7-17
Previewing the
presentation in
grayscale

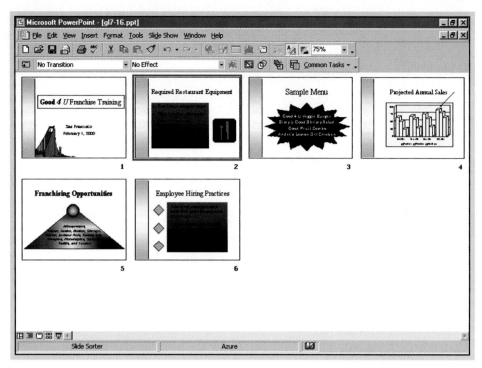

6. Right-click the bulleted text box border, point to Black and <u>W</u>hite, and choose <u>L</u>ight Grayscale from the submenu. Deselect the text box to view the effect. The text is now readable.

FIGURE 7-18
Changing black
and white settings

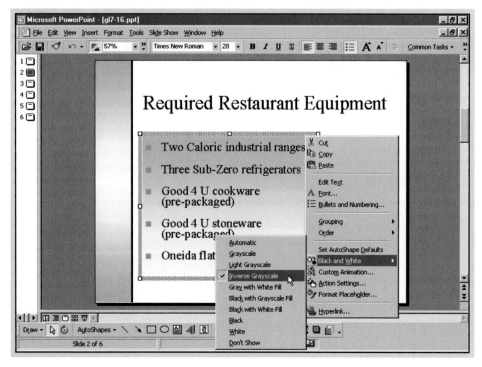

NOTE: You can also make black and white setting changes to master slide text placeholders. That way, the necessary changes will apply to all text placeholders in a presentation. You can then change individual text boxes as needed.

7. Move to slide 3. Change the star's black and white setting to Black with White Fill.

8. Change the triangle on slide 5 and the shaded text box on slide 6 to Inverse Grayscale.

9. View the presentation in Slide Sorter view.

10. Change back to Slide view. Move to slide 1 and click the Grayscale Preview button [▣] to switch back to color mode.

11. On the handouts, include the date and your name as header and include the page number and filename *[your initials]*7-22.ppt as footer.

12. Save the presentation as *[your initials]*7-22.ppt in your Lesson 7 folder.

13. Print the presentation as handouts, 6 slides per page, grayscale, framed.

14. Close the presentation.

COMMAND SUMMARY

FEATURE	BUTTON	MENU	KEYBOARD
Borders	▤	Format, Colors and Lines	
Border colors	◢	Format, Colors and Lines	
Arrowheads	⮂	Format, Colors and Lines	
Fills	◪	Format, Colors and Lines	
Grayscale Preview	▣	View, Black and White	

USING HELP

After experimenting with line styles and fills, you may decide to use a particular color, style, and fill combination throughout a presentation. Instead of reapplying the format or copying it from object to object, you can change the presentation defaults to the new format.

Using Help to learn how to change a presentation's color and line defaults:

1. Display and activate the Office Assistant.

2. Key **change defaults** and click Search.

3. Click "See more..." and then click the topic "Change the defaults for line style and fill."

4. Review the Help window instructions.

5. Close the window and hide the Office Assistant.

Concepts Review

TRUE/FALSE QUESTIONS

Each of the following statements is either true or false. Indicate your choice by circling T or F.

T F   **1.** You can use the Format Painter tool to copy formatting from one slide to another.

T F   **2.** Format Painter doesn't copy text formatting.

T F   **3.** Light grayscale is a black and white print option.

T F   **4.** When you draw an object, it appears in a color that the template chooses.

T F   **5.** Using the <u>A</u>pply button in the Color Scheme dialog box applies the color scheme to all slides in a presentation.

T F   **6.** Only one color can be used as a gradient fill.

T F   **7.** When you change the color scheme, you change only the text color.

T F   **8.** Granite and marble patterns are examples of textured fills.

SHORT ANSWER QUESTIONS

Write the correct answer in the space provided.

1. What dialog box can you use to change the colors in an AutoShape?

_____

2. What happens to the display of a presentation when you click [⬛] on the Standard toolbar?

_____

3. How do you change black and white settings for slide objects?

_____

4. Which toolbar button do you use to choose textured backgrounds?

_____

5. What do you use to view a color scheme before you commit to it?

_____

6. Which toolbar button do you use to add an outline or border to an object?

_____

7. Which button on which toolbar do you use to change the colors in clip art?

_____

8. Which button can you use to copy fills and colors to another object?

_____

CRITICAL THINKING

Answer these questions on a separate page. There are no right or wrong answers. Support your answers with examples from your own experience, if possible.

1. Think of the way you used shading to add dimension to a simple circle. What other objects could you change by using shading to add dimension?

2. Which objects in a presentation are most suited to borders? What types of border styles and colors work best against what types of backgrounds?

Skills Review

EXERCISE 7-23

Create borders, change line colors and styles, and change fill colors.

1. Open the file **Fund1.ppt**. Apply the **Bold Stripes.pot** design template.

2. On slide 1, move the title placeholder down, positioning it just above the horizontal line.

3. On slide 2, change the title to **Objectives** and key the following bulleted text:

- **Complete the business plan**
- **Complete the marketing plan**
- **Locate interested investors**
- **Investigate other funding options**

4. Create a text border by following these steps:
   a. Click the bulleted text placeholder border on slide 2.
   b. Click the Line Style button ≣ on the Drawing toolbar.
   c. Choose the 3-point line style.
   d. Resize the placeholder to frame the text. Reposition the text box in the center of the slide.

5. On slide 3, delete the two clip art images, and then key the following bulleted text:

- **Low-fat menus**
- **Non-alcoholic beverages**
- **Vegetarian meals**
- **Fresh-baked breads**

6. Resize the bulleted text placeholder to fit the text, and then delete the two clip art images.

7. Apply a 3-point line border to the bulleted text placeholder, then position it appropriately as you did with slide 2. Add one or two pieces of clip art that fit the slide content.

8. Change the border color and property of an object by following these steps:

   a. On slide 2, select the bulleted text border.
   b. Click the arrow on the Line Color button 🖉.
   c. Choose the dark blue sample that follows the title text color.
   d. On slide 3, select the bulleted text border.
   e. Click the Dash Style button ▤ and choose the Round Dot style.
   f. Increase the dotted border to 6 point.

9. Add an arrowhead to a straight line by following these steps:

   a. On slide 3, use the Line tool ◥ to draw a line that begins at the top of "fat" and ends below the first "e" in "Specialties."
   b. Using ▤, change the thickness to 6 point.
   c. Click the Arrow Style button ⇶ and choose Arrow Style 6, which is the large left-pointing arrow. (The arrowhead should be pointing down.)

10. On slide 4, key the following bulleted text:

- **Quick return of invested funds**
- **Name recognition**
- **"Healthy" image**

11. Add a 4½-point double-line border (either one) to the text placeholder. Resize and reposition the placeholder in the center of the slide.

12. Change the fill color of an object by following these steps:

   a. At the bottom center of slide 4, draw a 5-point star AutoShape. Make it exactly 1.25 inches high and wide. Adjust its position, if necessary.
   b. Click the arrow next to the Fill Color button ⬙ and choose second color from the right (the lighter blue).
   c. Set the line color to No Line.

13. Copy the star on slide 4, and paste it to slide 1. Enlarge it by 50% and add a 3-point double black border to the star. Move the star to the lower right corner of the slide.

14. Delete slide 5.

15. Check spelling in the presentation.

16. On the handouts, include the date and your name as header and include the page number and filename *[your initials]*7-23.ppt as footer.

17. Save the presentation as *[your initials]*7-23.ppt in your Lesson 7 folder.

18. Print as handouts, 4 slides per page, grayscale, framed.

19. Close the presentation.

EXERCISE 7-24

Change the fill colors and shading of objects.

1. Open the file **Cook2.ppt**.

2. Remove the fill color and lines from an object by following these steps:
  a. Move to slide 2 and select the rounded rectangle.
  b. Use the Fill Color button 🎨 to choose No Fill.
  c. With the rectangle selected, use the Line Color button 🖊 to choose No Line.
  d. Move to slide 4 and remove the outline from the circle.

3. Apply a shaded fill to an object by following these steps:
  a. Move to slide 2 and select the invisible rectangle by placing the insertion point in the rectangle text and clicking. Click the border.
  b. Click the Fill Color arrow and choose <u>F</u>ill Effects.
  c. Click the Gradient tab, if necessary.
  d. Choose <u>T</u>wo Colors (blue and white).
  e. Choose the Hori<u>z</u>ontal shade style and the bottom left Variant<u>s</u> option (with white in the middle).
  f. Click the <u>P</u>review button, drag the dialog box out of the way so you can view the results, and click OK.
  g. Change the rectangle text color to black.

4. Shade a circle to add dimension by following these steps:
  a. Move to slide 4 and select the circle.
  b. Click the Fill Color arrow, choose <u>F</u>ill Effects, and click the Gradient tab, if necessary.
  c. Click the <u>O</u>ne Color option and choose blue, if necessary.
  d. Move the Dark/Light slider to the right, just enough to see two shades of blue in the Sample box.
  e. Choose the Fro<u>m</u> Center shade style and the right Variant<u>s</u> option (which is lighter in the center).
  f. Click OK.

5. Add a shaded fill to a text placeholder by following these steps:

> ***a.*** Move to slide 3 and select the two bulleted text placeholders by pressing down the Shift key and clicking the two placeholders.
> ***b.*** Choose Colors and Lines from the Format menu.
> ***c.*** Open the Fill Color drop-down list box and choose Fill Effects.
> ***d.*** Click the Two Colors option.
> ***e.*** Choose green for Color 1 and white for Color 2.
> ***f.*** Choose the Horizontal shade style and the upper left variant (with the darkest color on the top). Click OK.
> ***g.*** Click Preview to view the changes, then click OK

6. Change the bulleted text on slide 3 to Arial bold, shadowed. Use the slide master and title master to make all titles (including the slide 1 subtitle) Arial bold.

7. On the handouts, include the date and your name as header and include the page number and filename *[your initials]*7-24.ppt as footer.

8. Save the presentation as *[your initials]*7-24.ppt in your Lesson 7 folder.

9. Print as handouts, 4 slides per page, grayscale, framed.

10. Close the presentation.

EXERCISE 7-25

Copy formatting using Format Painter, recolor a clip art object, and change the background shading.

1. Open the file **Miami1.ppt**.

2. Copy formatting from one object to another object by following these steps:
   > ***a.*** Move to slide 3 and select the center star on the bottom of the slide.
   > ***b.*** Double-click the Format Painter button ✍.
   > ***c.*** Click the left star, then click the right star.
   > ***d.*** Click ✍ again or press Esc to turn off Format Painter.

3. Move to slide 1. Insert a simple clip art picture of a palm tree that you can find using the keyword "palm." Choose a picture (not a photograph) of a single palm tree.

4. Size the picture to about 2 inches tall and place it on the left side of the slide, centered vertically.

5. Recolor the clip art object by following these steps:
   > ***a.*** With the picture selected, click the Recolor Picture button 🖼 on the Picture toolbar.

 NOTE: If you have trouble recoloring the picture, choose another one from the Clip Gallery.

b. Choose the Colors option in the Change option box.

c. Click the down arrow of the first color and choose More Colors. Click the Standard tab, if necessary. To create a silhouette effect, select a dark gray from the honeycomb of colors. Do this for each of the original colors. (Depending on the clip art you use, there may be only one color.)

6. Copy the recolored palm tree and paste it on the same slide. Make the copy very small and place it on the horizon line on the right side of the slide.

7. Change the background for the entire presentation by following these steps:

a. Working on any slide, choose Background from the Format menu.

b. Click the color sample arrow and choose Fill Effects.

c. Choose the Two Colors option. Keep the medium brown that follows the background scheme color for color 1 and choose pink for color 2.

d. Choose the horizontal shading style and the top right variant that has brown at the bottom. Click OK.

e. Click Apply to All.

8. On the slide master, change the title text size to 60 point and change its color to the brown that follows the background scheme color. Make the bulleted text bold.

9. On slide 1, select the title and click the Increase Font Size button **A** repeatedly until the font size box reads "106+". Change the title text color to turquoise (following the accent scheme color).

10. Change the background for slide 1 only by reversing the variant so the shading is brown at the top. (*Tip:* Click Apply instead of Apply to All.)

11. On the handouts, include the date and your name as header and include the page number and filename *[your initials]*7-25.ppt as footer.

12. Save the presentation as *[your initials]*7-25.ppt in your Lesson 7 folder.

13. Print as handouts, 4 slides per page, grayscale, framed.

14. Close the presentation.

EXERCISE 7-26

Add fill effects to slide master objects, change the color scheme, use Format Painter, and change black and white settings.

1. Open the file **Open2.ppt**.

2. Remove graphic elements from the slide master by following these steps:

a. Display the slide master.

    b. Point to the graphic between the title placeholder and bulleted text placeholder. Click to select it.

    c. Press Delete. Leave the graphic on the title master.

3. Create a custom color scheme by following these steps:

    a. With the slide master still displayed, choose Slide Color Scheme from the Format menu.

    b. Click the Custom tab.

    c. Double-click the Background scheme color (black) and click the Standard tab, if necessary.

    d. Choose dark blue in the upper right corner of the Standard colors.

    e. Click OK and click Apply to All.

4. Add an AutoShape object to the slide master and change its fill effects by following these steps:

    a. Use the Rectangle tool ▢ to draw a thin rectangle between the title placeholder and the bulleted text placeholder. It should be approximately the same width as the placeholders and about 0.25 inches high.

    b. Using the Line Color button ✎, select No Line.

    c. Using the Fill Color button ◈, display the Gradient tab of the Fill Effects dialog box. Click Preset and choose Early Sunset from the Preset Colors list box.

    d. Choose the Vertical shading style and the upper left variant. Click OK.

5. Select the thin rectangle and click the Draw button on the Drawing toolbar. Choose Change AutoShape, Basic Shapes, and change the shape to a rounded rectangle. Drag the yellow adjustment handle to the right as far as it goes to create rounder corners.

6. Display slide 2 and add a gradient fill to the bulleted text box. Choose the Two Colors option and use red (third color from the left) for color 1 and dark blue for color 2. Use the vertical shading style with the lower-right variant (with red in the center). Click OK.

7. Make the bulleted text bold with a text shadow.

8. Resize and reposition the text box on slide 2, centering it on the slide.

9. Apply the same fill and text effects to the text boxes on slides 3 and 4 by using the Format Painter tool. Resize and reposition the text boxes appropriately.

10. Change the background for all slides to a one-color gradient fill, horizontally shaded with dark blue in the center and black at the top and bottom.

11. Check to see if the presentation text is readable in grayscale view by clicking the Grayscale Preview button ▣ on the Standard toolbar.

12. Change black and white settings by following these steps:

> *a.* While still in grayscale mode, move to slide 2.
>
> *b.* Right-click the border of the bulleted text box. Choose Black and <u>W</u>hite from the shortcut menu and then choose <u>I</u>nverse Grayscale from the submenu.
>
> *c.* Use Format Painter to apply the same black and white setting to the text boxes on slides 3 and 4.
>
> *d.* Return to color mode by clicking ▣.

13. On slide 1, increase the title and subtitle text by one font size.

14. On the handouts, include the date and your name as header and include the page number and filename *[your initials]***7-26.ppt** as footer.

15. Save the presentation as *[your initials]***7-26.ppt** in your Lesson 7 folder.

16. Print as handouts, 4 slides per page, grayscale, framed.

17. Close the presentation.

Lesson Applications

Work with shading and fills.

1. Open the file **Hiring1.ppt**.

2. On slide 1, draw an oval above the title. Make the oval 1 inch high and 5.75 inches wide.

3. Apply a two-color gradient fill to the oval, choosing beige for color 1 and white for color 2. Choose the vertical shading style and the variant that has the lighter color on the right.

4. Apply a 2¼-point dark green outline to the oval (using the shadows scheme color).

5. Add the text **Good *4 U*** to the inside of the oval. Format the text as 36-point Arial, bold, shadowed. Make the font color gray. Format the "4 U" as italic with the "4" one font size larger. Rotate the oval –5 degrees.

6. Position the rotated oval so it overlaps the green curved line and appears to be part of that line.

7. Insert a new slide after slide 3 using the Bulleted List layout.

8. Key **Who's Who** as the title of the new slide. Key the following bulleted text:

- **Julie Wolfe, Co-Owner**
- **Gus Irvinelli, Co-Owner**
- **Michele Jenkins, Head Chef**
- **Roy Olafsen, Marketing Manager**

9. On slide 5 ("Summary"), key the following bulleted text:

- **Six-month probation period**
- **Annual salary increases**
- **Quarterly stock purchase options**
- **Annual profit sharing**

10. Draw a 16-point star that is 1.5 inches high and 2.75 inches wide.

11. Key **Substantial** in the star. Using Format Painter, copy the formatting of the oval on slide 1 to this star. Resize the text to fit the star.

12. Position the star in the bottom right corner of the slide and rotate it –5 degrees.

13. Draw a 3-point line with an arrowhead pointing from the star to the text "Annual profit sharing." Change the line color to dark green.

14. Check spelling in the presentation.

15. On the handouts, include the date and your name as header and include the page number and filename *[your initials]*7-27.ppt as footer.

16. Save the presentation as *[your initials]*7-27.ppt in your Lesson 7 folder.

17. Print as handouts, 6 slides per page, grayscale, framed.

18. Close the presentation.

EXERCISE 7-28

Change the line colors, line styles, and fill colors of objects.

1. Open the file **Franch1.ppt**. Apply the "Facilitating a Meeting" design template from the template folder labeled "1033."

2. Change the template's color scheme to the light green sample in the Color Scheme dialog box.

3. On the slide master, select and delete the large diamond object. Do not remove the diamond from the title master.

4. Delete the dollar sign clip art image on slide 2. Replace it with a clip art image of an apple that goes with the presentation color scheme. Size and position the new image so it occupies the same position on the slide as the old image.

5. On slide 3, draw a diagonal line slanting down and to the left, pointing from below the "s" in "Sales" to the tallest column on the graph.

6. Make the line 3 points wide and add an arrowhead. Change the arrow color to dark gray.

7. Add a floating text box at the tail of the arrow with the text **Estimating over $89,000** on two lines. Change the font to 20-point Arial, bold, shadowed. (Turn off the bullet that appears in the text box. This is unique to this template.)

8. Add a 3-point dark gray border to the text box. Adjust the position and size of the arrow and text box, if necessary.

9. On slide 4, delete the text placeholder. In its place, draw a floating text box. Change the fill color to dark gray.

10. Change the line style of the text box border to 6 points. Apply a pattern to the border using wide upward diagonal lines. (Hint: Click the Line Color button and choose Patterned Lines.) Choose the third pattern in the bottom row. Set the foreground color to white and the background color to dark gray.

11. Turn off bullets in the text box, and key the text **10% discount off the lunch menu, Monday through Thursday**

12. Format the text as 36-point Arial. (The text should be white.)

13. Change the text box AutoShape to a rounded rectangle from the Basic Shapes group. Resize the rectangle so the text wraps to four lines. Reposition the rectangle so it is centered with the clip art. (The effect of the rectangle should be similar to a blackboard.)

14. On slide 5, add a 4.5 point square dot border to the text placeholder and change its color to dark gray. Resize the placeholder to fit the text and center it horizontally on the slide.

15. On slide 4, change the black and white setting for the AutoShape to grayscale. Preview all the slides in grayscale view and make any necessary adjustments.

16. Check spelling in the presentation.

17. On the handouts, include the date and your name as header and include the page number and filename *[your initials]*7-28.ppt as footer.

18. Save the presentation as *[your initials]*7-28.ppt in your Lesson 7 folder.

19. Print as handouts, 6 slides per page, grayscale, framed.

20. Close the presentation.

EXERCISE 7-29

Apply textured fills, copy formatting, and recolor clip art.

1. Open the file **Train2.ppt**. Apply the design template **Notebook.pot** found in the Presentation Designs folder.

2. Change the title master's title and subtitle to a rich brown. (Choose from the honeycomb of Standard colors.) Make the title text bold.

3. On slide 1, delete the clip art object and draw a diamond AutoShape below the subtitle. Make the diamond slightly wider than the subtitle and 0.75 inch high.

4. Apply the Paper Bag texture (found on the second or third row from the bottom of the textures) to the diamond.

5. Use the slide master to change the first-level bullets in the presentation to check marks.

6. Use Format Painter to copy the formatting of the bulleted text placeholder on slide 3 to the one on slide 6. (This applies the check mark bullets to slide 6.)

7. Make the slide 6 placeholder slightly taller. Reapply the appropriate character formatting to the text "4 U" (italic, with "4" one size larger).

8. On slide 4, edit the text of the first bullet to read "Pentium III computer (network server)."

9. Make the text box wide enough to fit the first bullet on one line. Delete the line break from the last bullet line so the text appears on one line.

10. Delete the clip art placeholder on slide 4. Draw a right arrow AutoShape (on the Block Arrows menu). Make the arrow 1.5 inches wide and 0.75 inches high.

11. Use Format Painter to fill the arrow with the paper bag texture from the diamond on slide 1. Position the arrow so it points to the first bullet, which begins with the word "Pentium."

12. Delete slide 5 ("Annual Sales Per Division").

13. On slide 2, in the clip art placeholder, insert a black and white clip art image that is appropriate to the slide content. (Try searching "kitchen.") Size the image as needed.

14. On slide 3, replace the clip art with another image that uses a similar style as the clip art on slide 2. Size the image as needed.

15. On slide 5 ("Sample Menu"), insert another similar-styled clip art image, sized appropriately.

16. Recolor all three images you inserted, using one of the colors in the presentation color scheme.

17. On the handouts, include the date and your name as header and include the page number and filename *[your initials]*7-29.ppt as footer.

18. Save the presentation as *[your initials]*7-29.ppt in your Lesson 7 folder.

19. Print as handouts, 6 slides per page, grayscale, framed.

20. Close the presentation.

EXERCISE 7-30   *Challenge Yourself*

Change the presentation color scheme; work with line colors, patterns, and fills; and change black and white settings.

1. Open the file **Mktg3.ppt**.

2. Change the color scheme to the second sample on the top row of the Color Scheme dialog box.

3. Change the background for the presentation to a one-color horizontal gradient, using the medium blue color that follows the accent and hyperlink color scheme. Adjust the shading slider so it shades to a light blue. Use the horizontal shading style and the shading variant with the lightest shade in the center.

4. Change the color scheme's pale green fill color to pale purple.

5. On the title master, move the graphic object and the subtitle down about 0.5 inch.

6. On the slide master, apply a picture bullet to the first level bullet text. Choose a bullet that compliments the presentation style and color.

7. Add a text shadow to the slide master's title text.

8. On slide 1, change the subtitle font to 44-point Times New Roman, bold. Italicize "4 U" and make the "4" one font size larger. Center-align the subtitle text.

9. Delete the title placeholder on slide 1. Create a WordArt text object, using the second sample in the second row. Key **Marketing Strategy** in the Edit WordArt Text dialog box and change the font to 48-point bold, not italic. Insert the WordArt object and resize it to 1.25 inches high and 8.75 inches wide. Move the object to the title position at the top of the slide.

10. Change the WordArt's fill color to a one-color horizontal gradient, using medium blue (the accent and hyperlink color) and shading to white, with white at the top.

11. Change the slide layout of slide 2 to Clip Art & Text. Insert an appropriate clip art image. If desired, recolor the image to coordinate with the presentation colors.

12. Apply a ¼-point border to all bulleted text placeholders using the light purple color (that follows the accent scheme color).

13. Resize the slide 5 bulleted text placeholder to fit the text, then position the placeholder attractively next to the chart object.

14. Preview the presentation in grayscale mode. Change the grayscale setting for all slides so the gradient fill is visible but not too dark. Adjust the setting of the clip art image, if necessary.

15. Check spelling in the presentation.

16. On the handouts, include the date and your name as header and include the page number and filename *[your initials]*7-30.htm as footer.

17. Save the presentation in HTML format as *[your initials]*7-30.htm in your Lesson 7 folder.

18. Preview the presentation as a Web page in your browser, then close the browser window.

19. Print as handouts, 6 slides per page, grayscale, framed.

20. Close the presentation.

Manipulating PowerPoint Objects

OBJECTIVES

After completing this lesson, you will be able to:

1. Select multiple objects.
2. Align, flip, and distribute objects.
3. Group and ungroup objects.
4. Work with layers of objects.
5. Apply object shadows and 3-D effects.
6. Use the Duplicate command.
7. Work with advanced clip art editing.
8. Customize and create toolbars.

MOUS ACTIVITIES

In this lesson:

PP2000 **4.2**
PP2000 **E.2.9**
PP2000 **E.8.1**
PP2000 **E.8.2**

See Appendix F.

 Estimated Time: 1½ hours

In earlier lessons, you learned how to add clip art, scanned images, text objects, and drawings to a presentation. This lesson shows you how to move or change a group of objects, layer objects, and align objects. These are techniques to help you create more effective presentations.

Selecting Multiple Objects

When you want to treat several objects on a slide the same way, such as making them all the same color, you can select all the objects at the same time by using multiple selection techniques. There are two basic ways to select multiple objects:

- Select one object, then hold down Shift and click another object.
- Draw a selection rectangle around the objects you want to select.

You can also select all the objects on a slide by choosing Select All from the Edit menu or by pressing Ctrl+A.

EXERCISE   8-1   Select Multiple Objects

1. Open the file **Mktg2.ppt**.

2. On slide 1, click the long thin horizontal arrow at the top of the screen. Notice its sizing handles.

3. Hold down Shift and click the vertical arrow on the right side of the slide. Notice that there are sizing handles around both objects, indicating they are both selected.

4. With the two arrows selected, use the Fill Color button ![fill icon] to set the fill color to yellow. Both selected arrows turn yellow.

5. With the two yellow arrows selected, press Shift and click the bottom and left arrows. Now all four long thin arrows are selected.

FIGURE 8-1
Multiple selected objects

6. With all the arrows selected, change the fill to a two-color vertical gradient. Choose dark red, following the background scheme color, for Color 1, and choose orange, following the fills color scheme, for Color 2. Use the upper left variant (with red on the left and orange on the right).

EXERCISE 8-2 Remove an Item from a Group of Selected Objects

Sometimes you will want to change the composition of a group of selected items as you work. One way is to deselect all the objects by clicking a blank part of the slide. Another way is to hold down Shift and click the selected item to deselect it, leaving the remaining items in the group selected.

1. To deselect the arrow at the top of the slide and leave the other three selected, hold Shift and click the top arrow. The remaining three arrows are still selected.

2. Hold Shift and deselect the bottom arrow. The bottom arrow is deselected, leaving the two side arrows selected.

3. Keeping the same colors, change the shading style of the two side arrows to horizontal, using the upper left variant.

4. Deselect all the arrows by clicking a blank area of the slide, then select the arrow at the bottom of the slide. Change its gradient fill to the one with the orange on the left side.

EXERCISE 8-3 Select Objects Using the Selection Rectangle

1. Move to slide 2.

2. Position the pointer in the lower left corner of the slide.

3. Drag the mouse pointer diagonally to the right and up to draw a dotted box surrounding all four orange arrows. (It's okay if the box overlaps the slide text.) This dotted box is called a *selection rectangle*. Only objects completely enclosed in the selection rectangle are selected. (See Figure 8-2 on the next page.)

4. Release the mouse button. Resize handles surround each arrow.

5. If one of the arrows does not have a set of resizing handles, draw a new selection rectangle.

NOTE: Sometimes it is easier to add the missing object to the selection using the Shift + click method rather than drawing a new selection rectangle.

FIGURE 8-2
Selection rectangle

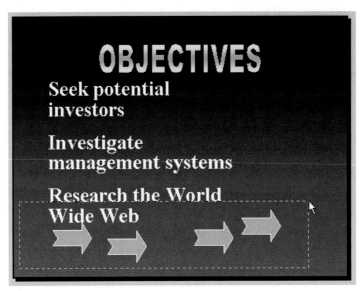

6. Change the fill of the selected arrows to a vertical two-color gradient, using the same red and orange as on the arrows on slide 1. Choose the variant that has red on the right side.

Aligning, Flipping, and Distributing Objects

PowerPoint has a number of tools that you can use to reorient objects on a slide. You can rotate and flip them, creating mirror images of the original. Objects can be aligned together, either vertically or horizontally. You can also distribute multiple objects, spacing them evenly across the slide either horizontally or vertically.

EXERCISE **8-4** ## Align Objects Horizontally and Vertically

1. Still working on slide 2, select the four arrows, if necessary. Notice that the arrows are not positioned evenly on the slide.

2. To display the Align or Distribute floating toolbar, click D<u>r</u>aw on the Drawing toolbar and point to <u>A</u>lign or Distribute. Point to the gray title bar of this submenu and drag it to a convenient place on the screen, out of the way of the selected arrows.

 NOTE: If the Drawing toolbar is not in view, choose <u>T</u>oolbars from the <u>V</u>iew menu and then choose Drawing.

TABLE 8-1   Alignment Options

CHOOSE BUTTON	TO DO THIS
▣ Align Left	Vertically align the left edges of objects
▣ Align Center	Vertically align the centers of objects
▣ Align Right	Vertically align the right edges of objects
▣ Align Top	Horizontally align the top edges of objects
▣ Align Middle	Horizontally align the center points of objects
▣ Align Bottom	Horizontally align the bottom edges of objects
▣ Distribute Horizontally	Space objects evenly in a horizontal direction
▣ Distribute Vertically	Space objects evenly in a vertical direction
Relative to Slide	A toggle button. When turned on, align or space objects relative to slide. When turned off, align objects relative to each other.

3. Notice that the first three buttons on the toolbar control vertical alignment and the next three buttons control horizontal alignment.

4. Check the Align or Distribute toolbar to be sure that Relative to Slide is not selected. If it is, click it to turn off that option.

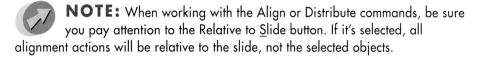 **NOTE:** When working with the Align or Distribute commands, be sure you pay attention to the Relative to Slide button. If it's selected, all alignment actions will be relative to the slide, not the selected objects.

 5. Click the Align Top button ▣. The objects line up with the top of the highest arrow.

6. Deselect the arrows, then choose Ruler from the View menu to display a horizontal and vertical ruler.

7. Drag the arrow farthest to the right up about 1 inch, using the ruler to help you position the object. Drag the arrow farthest to the left down to the bottom of the slide.

8. Select all four arrows.

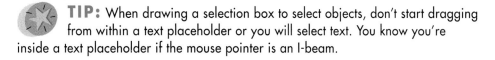 **TIP:** When drawing a selection box to select objects, don't start dragging from within a text placeholder or you will select text. You know you're inside a text placeholder if the mouse pointer is an I-beam.

 9. Click the Align Bottom button ▣. The objects align horizontally again, but this time they align with the bottom arrow.

260 POWERPOINT   UNIT 3 ■ CUSTOMIZING A PRESENTATION

10. Click the Undo button to return the arrows to their previous positions.

11. Click the Align Left button . The objects align vertically, aligning with the arrow farthest to the left, but one arrow is hidden because it is underneath another arrow.

12. Click and then click the Align Right button 🔳. The objects are arranged vertically, aligning with the arrow farthest to the right. (One arrow is still hidden behind another.)

EXERCISE 8-5 Distribute Objects Horizontally and Vertically

1. Still working on slide 2, select the four arrows, if necessary.

2. Click the Distribute Vertically button 🔳. The arrows are now evenly spaced, but they overlap.

3. Deselect the arrows, then drag the top arrow up about 1 inch.

4. Reselect the four arrows and click 🔳 again. Now the arrows are spaced farther apart.

5. With the arrows still selected, click the Distribute Horizontally button 🔳. Nothing happens because all the arrows are in the same relative horizontal position.

6. Deselect the arrows, then drag the bottom arrow about 3 inches to the left.

7. Reselect the arrows, then click 🔳 again. Now the arrows are evenly spaced horizontally, but they are not aligned.

8. Click 🔳.

EXERCISE 8-6 Align Objects Relative to the Slide

The Relative to <u>S</u>lide button makes it easy to center an object horizontally or vertically on a slide. For example, you can center a placeholder perfectly. You can also use the Relative to <u>S</u>lide setting to distribute objects evenly across a slide from edge to edge.

1. Still working on slide 2, select the bulleted text placeholder.

2. Click the Relative to <u>S</u>lide button on the Align or Distribute toolbar to turn on that option.

3. Click the Align Center button 🔳. The placeholder is centered horizontally on the slide.

4. Click the Align Middle button ▣. The placeholder is now also centered vertically on the slide.

5. With Relative to Slide still turned on, select all four arrows at the bottom of the screen.

6. Click Distribute Horizontally ▣. Now the arrows are evenly spaced across the entire width of the slide.

FIGURE 8-3
Objects
horizontally
aligned and
distributed

EXERCISE **8-7** **Flip Objects on a Slide**

Use the rotate or flip tools on a single object or a group of objects. Some of the things you can rotate or flip are drawn objects, text boxes, and WordArt.

1. To display the Rotate or Flip toolbar, click Draw on the Drawing toolbar, point to Rotate or Flip, and drag the submenu's title bar to float the toolbar.

2. Select the four arrows at the bottom of slide 2, if necessary. Click the Rotate Right button ▣. The arrows point down.

3. Click the Flip Vertical button ▣. The arrows flip vertically and point up.

4. If the arrows extend past the bottom edge of the slide, check that the Relative to Slide button is turned on, then use Align Bottom ▣ or the up arrow key on your keyboard to move the arrows up.

5. Select the WordArt title, "Objectives."

6. Click the Rotate Left button ⊿ to place the WordArt on its side.

7. With Relative to <u>S</u>lide turned on, click Align Middle ⊙, and then click Align Left ⊞. The WordArt is now centered vertically and aligned with the left edge of the slide.

8. With the WordArt still selected, use the right arrow key on your keyboard to move the WordArt to the right so it's centered between the left edge of the slide and the text placeholder.

FIGURE 8-4
Rotated and flipped objects

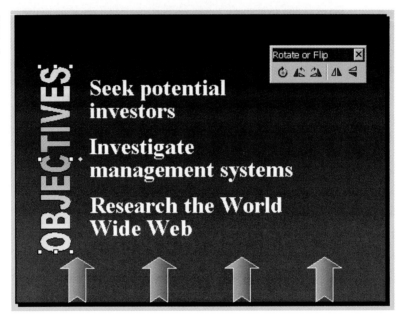

Grouping and Ungrouping Objects

You can use grouping to "glue" two or more objects together so they behave as one object. If you then move one member of a group, all the other members move with it. Grouping assures that objects meant to stay together don't accidentally get moved individually or deleted. When you need to work on an individual member of a group, you can ungroup the objects, make your changes, then regroup them.

EXERCISE 8-8 **Group Objects**

1. Still working on slide 2, delete the arrow farthest to the left, then select the three remaining arrows at the bottom of the slide. Notice the three sets of resize handles.

2. Choose <u>G</u>roup from the expanded D<u>r</u>aw menu. Now there is only one set of resize handles, indicating that all three arrows are grouped as a single object.

FIGURE 8-5
Objects after
grouping

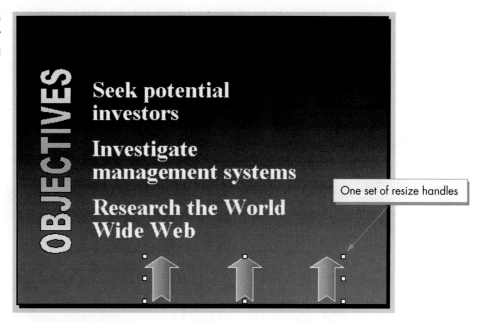

3. Deselect the object. Drag the left arrow up just below the text of the last bullet. All the arrows move up.

4. Click Rotate Left ⬛. The three arrows rotate as one unit.

5. Decrease the zoom setting so you can see all three arrows.

6. Use Align Middle ⬛ to center the arrows vertically (relative to the slide), then use Align Right ⬛ to right-align them.

7. With the group of arrows still selected, use the left arrow key to move the arrows so they are centered between the right edge of the slide and the bulleted text placeholder.

8. Increase the zoom setting to Fit.

EXERCISE   8-9   **Ungroup Objects**

You can ungroup objects to change their relative position or to change the formatting of individual members of the group.

1. Still working on slide 2, right-click the group of arrows and choose <u>G</u>rouping from the shortcut menu. Choose <u>U</u>ngroup from the submenu. Individual resize handles are displayed for each object.

2. To make sure the selected arrows are spaced vertically, turn on Relative to Slide, if necessary, and click Distribute Vertically 🔲.

3. Deselect the arrows (they are ungrouped now) and use the Format Painter tool to copy the shading from the WordArt object ("OBJECTIVES") to the middle arrow. (The remaining arrows should keep their orange-to-red shading.)

4. Select all the arrows again. Choose Group from the expanded Draw menu to group the objects again.

5. Right-click the arrows to open the Format Object dialog box. Use the Size tab to change the height of the grouped object to 4 inches. Then distribute the group again vertically relative to the slide. As you can see, grouped objects behave as a single object in many ways.

FIGURE 8-6
Completed slide 2

6. Close both floating toolbars.

Working with Layers of Objects

Although objects appear to be drawn on one surface, each of a slide's objects actually exists as a separate layer. Imagine that the objects are drawn on individual sheets of transparent plastic stacked on top of one another. When you rearrange the sheets, different objects appear on the top, sometimes hiding parts of the objects beneath them. The most recently drawn object is added to the top of the stack.

Within a stack of objects, you can move an individual object backward and forward in the following ways:

- Move an object to the bottom of the stack.
- Move an object down one layer in the stack.
- Bring an object to the top of the stack.
- Bring an object forward one layer in the stack.

EXERCISE 8-10 Create Overlapping Objects

1. Move to slide 3. Draw a large rectangle that covers the bulleted text placeholder. The rectangle fill hides the text.

2. Click D<u>r</u>aw on the Drawing toolbar, choose O<u>r</u>der from the expanded menu, and float the Order submenu.

3. Click the Send to Back button on the Order toolbar. The rectangle moves behind the text and the text is once again visible.

4. With the rectangle selected, use the D<u>r</u>aw menu to change its shape to a notched right arrow. (Click D<u>r</u>aw, <u>C</u>hange Autoshape, Block <u>A</u>rrows, and choose the second shape in the fifth row.) Resize the shape and move its adjustment handle so it looks like the arrow in Figure 8-7.

FIGURE 8-7
Overlapping text
and object

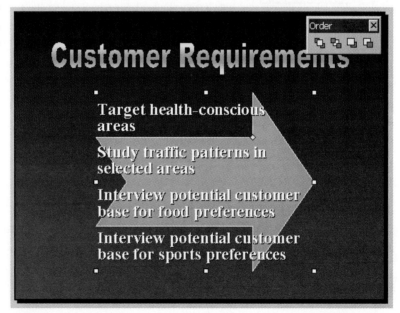

 NOTE: To manipulate an object that is located behind several other objects, you must send the top objects to the back one at a time until the desired object is on top.

Applying Object Shadows and 3-D Effects

You can add interest and depth to an object by applying shadows and 3-D effects. You apply these effects using the Shadow button ■ and 3-D button ■ on the Drawing toolbar. Each button displays a menu of 20 shadow and 3-D effects and each effect can be individually customized.

EXERCISE 8-11 Apply a Shadow Effect

FIGURE 8-8
Shadow menu

Shadow button

1. Move to slide 1 and select the quad-arrow object under the subtitle.
2. Click the Shadow button ■ on the Drawing toolbar to display a menu of shadow effects.
3. Choose Shadow Style 1, which is the first style in the first row. A strong black shadow appears.
4. Click the Shadow button ■ again and choose Shadow Style 3. This shadow style is even more dramatic. Each style orients the position and the depth of the shadow in a different way. Try several other shadow styles.
5. Change back to Shadow Style 1.

NOTE: Some of the shadow styles may change the shadow standard color from black to gray. You learn how to change the shadow color in the next exercise.

EXERCISE 8-12 Customize a Shadow

1. Select the quad-arrow object, if necessary.
2. Click the Shadow button ■ and choose Shadow Settings. The Shadow Settings toolbar is displayed. You use the buttons on this toolbar to control the angle and color of the shadow.

3. Click the Nudge Shadow Up button ■ four times. Notice that each time you click the button, the shadow moves up slightly.
4. Click the Nudge Shadow Left button ■ twice. The shadow gradually moves to the left each time you click the button.

5. Click the arrow on the Shadow Color button ■ and choose another shadow color.

6. Use the Shadow Color button to change the shadow to black.

7. Click the arrow next to the Shadow Color button 🔲 again and click Semitransparent Shadow. The shadow color is lightened.

FIGURE 8-9
Object with shadow effects applied

8. Close the Shadow Settings toolbar.

EXERCISE 8-13 Choose a 3-D Effect

1. Still working on slide 1, select the WordArt title, "Marketing Strategy."

2. Click the 3-D button 🔲 on the Drawing toolbar to display a menu of 3-D effects.

FIGURE 8-10
3-D menu

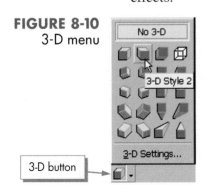

3. Choose 3-D Style 2. A dramatic 3-D effect is applied to the object.

4. Click 🔲 again and choose 3-D Style 18. Notice that some 3-D styles rotate the object and create depth. Try other styles and note the differences. Like shadows, use these effects sparingly.

5. Reapply 3-D Style 2.

EXERCISE 8-14 Customize a 3-D Effect

1. With the WordArt on slide 1 still selected, click the 3-D button  and choose 3-D Settings. You use the 3-D Settings toolbar to change the color,

FIGURE 8-11
3-D Settings
toolbar

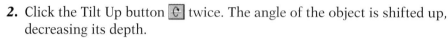
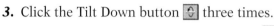
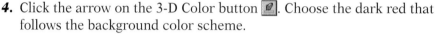
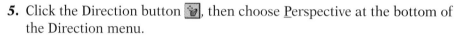

angle of rotation depth, and other features of the 3-D effect. These tools are fun to use. Try them on all types of objects, not just WordArt.

2. Click the Tilt Up button twice. The angle of the object is shifted up, decreasing its depth.

3. Click the Tilt Down button three times.

4. Click the arrow on the 3-D Color button. Choose the dark red that follows the background color scheme.

5. Click the Direction button, then choose Perspective at the bottom of the Direction menu.

6. Click the Depth button and choose Infinity.

7. Close the 3-D Settings toolbar.

8. Drag the quad arrow on top of the "Good *4 U*" subtitle.

9. Right-click the quad arrow and choose Order from the shortcut menu. Choose Send to Back, placing the quad arrow behind the text.

10. Select both the subtitle text and the quad arrow, and move them down on the slide about 1 inch.

11. With the subtitle text and quad arrow both selected, center-align them relative to the slide. Adjust the position of the WordArt title, if necessary.

FIGURE 8-12
3-D and shadow
effects on slide 1

12. Change the black and white settings for the 3-D WordArt title to inverse grayscale.

Using the Duplicate Command

The Duplicate command is an ideal tool for creating evenly spaced objects, either in a straight row or at an angle. Duplicated objects can overlap one another or be spaced apart.

To duplicate objects, choose Duplicate from the Edit menu or press Ctrl+D.

EXERCISE 8-15 **Use the Duplicate Command**

---

1. Move to slide 4. Draw a small notched right arrow to the left of "Determine methods." Using the Format Painter, copy the formatting from the WordArt "Evaluating Results" to the notched right arrow.

2. Align the middles of the arrow and the text box relative to each other. (Select both objects, turn off Relative to Slide, if necessary, and click the Align Middle button ⬗ on the Align or Distribute toolbar.)

3. Group the text box and the notched arrow.

4. Choose Duplicate from the expanded Edit menu or press Ctrl+D. A copy appears slightly offset from the original.

5. Being careful not to deselect the copy, use the arrow keys on your keyboard to move the copy down and to the right. (See Figure 8-13 on the next page for approximate positioning of the second arrow and text box.)

NOTE: The Duplicate command works only if the duplicate copy remains selected. As soon as it is deselected, the command is no longer in effect. If that happens, delete the duplicate and start again.

6. Press Ctrl+D. A second copy appears, which is offset the same amount as the first copy.

7. Press Ctrl+D again. You should now have four copies on the slide.

8. Change the text in the duplicated text boxes as shown in Figure 8-13.

9. Select all the text boxes and arrows (everything on the slide except the WordArt title).

10. Group the selection and center it horizontally relative to the slide.

FIGURE 8-13
Creating duplicates

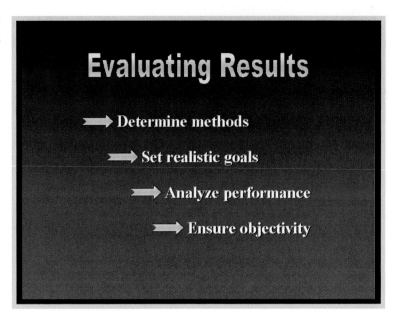

Advanced Clip Art Editing

In Lesson 6, you learned how to crop a clip art image, and in Lesson 7, you learned how to recolor an image. Many clip art images can be ungrouped, so you can treat individual parts of the image like ordinary PowerPoint objects. Once clip art is ungrouped, or disassembled, you can delete an individual part of the image or change the color of just one part.

EXERCISE   **8-16**   **Disassemble a Clip Art Image**

FIGURE 8-14
Clip art image of
meeting room

1. Move to slide 5. Open the Clip Gallery, search for pictures with the keyword "meeting room," and insert the picture shown in Figure 8-14.

2. Place the picture at the bottom of the slide.

3. Right-click the clip art image and choose <u>G</u>rouping, <u>U</u>ngroup. A dialog box asks if you want to convert this image to a Microsoft Office drawing object. When you convert a clip art image to a PowerPoint drawing, you can manipulate its components as if they are AutoShapes or freeform objects.

4. Click <u>Y</u>es. The components of the image now appear as separate objects with their own resize handles.

5. Select all the objects, if necessary, and group them.

6. Use the Format Object dialog box to rotate the image –90 degrees and increase the height to 3.5 inches. (Remember to use Lock Aspect Ratio to size the clip art proportionally.)

7. Move the text box up to make room for the resized picture.

EXERCISE 8-17 Format Parts of a Clip Art Image

1. Select the clip art image and increase the zoom for an up-close view.

2. Ungroup the image again. Deselect the image, then select one of the yellow rectangles and apply a fill effect using a paper texture (such as Parchment). Apply a different paper texture to the remaining yellow rectangles.

3. Select and delete each of the "drinks" (green circles outlined in black) on the table.

4. Select the blue table and apply the oak wood texture.

5. Select each of the purple "chairs" and fill with the red background color.

6. If desired, change the color of other objects in the picture to match the template color scheme.

7. Change the zoom back to the Fit setting. Regroup the image and center it horizontally on the slide.

8. In the middle of the table, add a floating text box with the text **Good 4 U**. Format the text as 24-point Arial, bold, with a text shadow. Increase the size of "4" to 28 points.

9. Position the text box attractively on the table. (See Figure 8-15 on the next page.)

10. Close the floating toolbars that you opened during this lesson.

11. Check spelling in the presentation.

12. Move to slide 1 and switch to grayscale preview. Change the black and white setting of the quad arrow object to black with white fill. Check the black and white settings for the balance of the presentation.

13. On the handouts, include the date and your name as header and include the page number and filename *[your initials]*8-17.ppt as footer.

14. Save the presentation as *[your initials]*8-17.ppt in a new folder for Lesson 8.

15. Print the presentation as handouts, 6 slides per page, grayscale, framed.

16. Close the presentation.

FIGURE 8-15
Completed clip art
image

Working with Toolbars

In this lesson you worked with several different toolbars, some of which you floated for easy access. PowerPoint allows you to customize toolbars. You can even create your own toolbar with the buttons you use frequently from different toolbars.

EXERCISE 8-18 Customize Toolbars

1. Right-click on any toolbar. A menu shows which toolbars are displayed. These typically are the Drawing, Standard, and Formatting toolbars. (The Standard and Formatting toolbar share one row, by default.) You can click to open any other toolbar.

2. Click Customize. The Customize dialog box allows you to customize both menus and toolbars.

3. Click the Options tab. Review the available options.

4. Under Other, click Large Icons. All icons on every toolbar enlarge for easy viewing.

5. Click Large Icons again to restore the normal icon size. Leave the dialog box open for the next exercise.

NOTE: Notice that with the Customize dialog box open, the Standard and Formatting toolbars appear on two separate rows so you can see all the buttons. You can make this a permanent setting by clearing the check box labeled "Standard and Formatting toolbars share one row."

EXERCISE 8-19 Create a Toolbar

1. Click the Toolbars tab in the Customize dialog box.
2. Click New. In the New Toolbar dialog box, key your name in the Toolbar Name text box and click OK.
3. Drag the Customize dialog box out of the way, if necessary, to see the new toolbar. You'll now add buttons to the toolbar.
4. Click the Commands tab. Commands are listed here by category.
5. In the Categories list, select Drawing. Under Commands, click Group.
6. Drag the Group command to your new toolbar. When you release the mouse button, the Group tool appears on the toolbar.
7. Drag the Ungroup command to your new toolbar.
8. Scroll the Commands list. Add three more commands that you use frequently to your new toolbar. Notice the I-beam on the toolbar as you drag tools. This helps you control the position of the tool you're adding.

FIGURE 8-16
Adding commands to a new toolbar

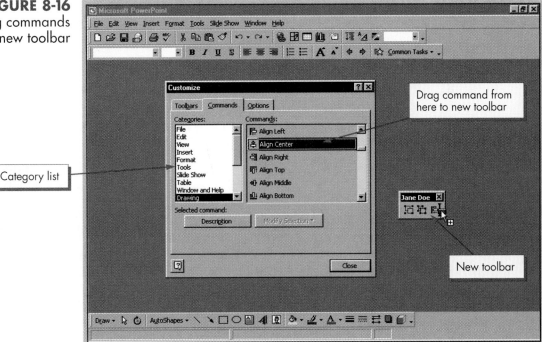

TIP: To remove a toolbar button after you add it, right-click the button and choose <u>D</u>elete from the shortcut menu.

 TIP: When adding buttons to a new toolbar, don't add commands that are plainly displayed on other open toolbars, such as Line Color or Insert WordArt. Instead, add tools that take some effort to display, such as Align or Distribute commands, or commands from other toolbars. You can display the AutoShapes category and add a specific shape you use often, such as the rounded rectangle or 16-point star.

9. Close the Customize dialog box. Right-click your new toolbar. Notice the toolbar name on the shortcut menu.

 NOTE: Ask your instructor whether you can keep the toolbar. Otherwise, perform the following three steps to delete it.

10. Click <u>C</u>ustomize on the shortcut menu and display the Tool<u>b</u>ars tab.

11. Select your toolbar from the list and click <u>D</u>elete. Click OK when asked if you're sure you want to delete the toolbar.

12. Close the dialog box.

COMMAND SUMMARY

FEATURE	BUTTON	MENU	KEYBOARD
Select all objects		<u>E</u>dit, Select A<u>ll</u>	Ctrl + A
Group objects		<u>D</u>raw, <u>G</u>roup	Ctrl + Shift + G
Ungroup objects		<u>D</u>raw, <u>U</u>ngroup	Ctrl + Shift + H
Duplicate		<u>E</u>dit, Dupli<u>c</u>ate	Ctrl + D

USING HELP

PowerPoint provides extensive help for all facets of working with objects. If you're unsure about such features as aligning, distributing, or grouping objects, use Help for clarification.

Explore Help Contents for topics on manipulating objects:

1. Display and activate the Office Assistant.

2. Key **arrange objects** in the text box and press Enter.

3. Click the topic "Arrange objects."

4. Review the Help screen, then click the topic <u>Align objects with other objects</u>.

5. Review the Help screen. Click another linked topic, such as <u>Align objects by their right edges</u>.

6. Close Help when you finish and hide the Office Assistant.

Concepts Review

Each of the following statements is either true or false. Indicate your choice by circling **T** or **F**.

T   F   **1.** You cannot use selection rectangles to select multiple objects.

T   F   **2.** The Bring Forward command brings objects forward one layer at a time.

T   F   **3.** If you continually click the Rotate Left button [icon], the object eventually returns to its original position.

T   F   **4.** To select multiple objects, press [Ctrl] while clicking each object.

T   F   **5.** The Duplicate command is available from the Insert menu.

T   F   **6.** There are 20 different 3-D effects that you can apply to an object.

T   F   **7.** You cannot change the color of object shadows.

T   F   **8.** The keyboard command to select all objects on a slide is [Ctrl]+[A].

Write the correct answer in the space provided.

1. On what layer does the most recently drawn object appear?

_____

2. What appears when you drag the mouse to select multiple objects?

_____

3. Which tool do you use to flip an object left to right?

_____

4. To select multiple objects with the mouse, which key do you press while clicking?

_____

5. Which command separates combined objects?

_____

6. Which align option do you select to horizontally align the bottom edges of multiple objects?

_____

7. Which command do you use to place an object at the top of a stack?

_____

8. What do you need to do to a clip art image before you can remove an unwanted element?

_____

CRITICAL THINKING

Answer these questions on a separate page. There are no right or wrong answers. Support your answers with examples from your own experience, if possible.

1. In this lesson you learned how to work with layers of objects. Which objects might you place on top of each other? When would you find it useful to overlap them?

2. Think of the way you used the Duplicate command to add evenly spaced objects to your slide. In what other ways could you use this feature? Which objects would you duplicate?

Skills Review

EXERCISE 8-20

Select multiple objects; and align, group, flip, and distribute objects.

1. Open the file **Cook3.ppt**.

2. Select multiple objects by following these steps:
   a. On slide 1, click one of the small green diamonds below the subtitle.
   b. Press and hold Shift while clicking the remaining two diamonds.
   c. With all diamonds selected, change the fill color to black.

3. Align and distribute the selected diamonds by following these steps:
   a. Click Draw on the Drawing toolbar and point to Align or Distribute.
   b. Float the Align or Distribute submenu by dragging its gray title bar.
   c. If necessary, turn off the Relative to Slide option by clicking it on the Align or Distribute toolbar.
   d. Click the Align Top button 🔟.
   e. Click the Distribute Horizontally button ᴼᴼᵃ.

4. Use a selection rectangle to select multiple objects by following these steps:

   a. Move the pointer to the upper right corner of slide 1.

   b. Drag the pointer diagonally down and to the left, drawing a dotted box large enough to surround the cluster of red squares in the upper right corner. (Don't include the single red square on the left side of the slide.)

   c. To add the last red square to the group, press and hold Shift while clicking the square on the left side of the slide.

   d. Change the fill color of the selected squares to black.

5. Align and distribute objects relative to the slide by following these steps:

   a. Click Relative to Slide on the Align or Distribute toolbar to turn it on.

   b. Reselect all the black squares, if necessary.

   c. Click the Align Top button ⊡.

   d. Click Distribute Horizontally ⊞. You should have a series of evenly spaced, black squares along the top edge of the slide. If not, click ↶ several times and try again.

6. With all the black squares still selected, copy and paste them. Using the four-headed arrow pointer, drag the pasted group of selected squares down and to the right to form a checkerboard pattern.

7. Deselect the squares. Copy just one square and paste it on the left end of the second row to complete the checkerboard pattern.

8. Use the selection rectangle method to select all the squares in both rows.

9. Group the squares by clicking Draw on the Drawing toolbar and choosing Group.

10. Copy and paste the grouped squares, and move the pasted copy to the bottom of the slide.

11. Flip an object by following these steps:

   a. Select the grouped squares at the bottom of the slide, if necessary.

   b. Click Draw on the Drawing toolbar. Drag the Rotate or Flip submenu's gray title bar to float the Rotate or Flip toolbar.

   c. Click the FlipVertical button ◁ to reverse the position of the two rows of squares. (The checkerboard pattern at the bottom of the slide now mirrors the pattern on the top of the slide.)

12. Copy and paste the checkerboard pattern to the top and bottom edge of the slide master so all slides in the presentation have the checkerboard pattern. (You don't need to copy the checkerboard pattern to the title master.)

13. Flip and rotate an object by following these steps:

   a. Move to slide 3. Select the red arrow below the graph.

   b. Click the Flip Horizontal button ⊿ on the Rotate or Flip toolbar to make the arrow point to the right.

      c. Click the Rotate Left button 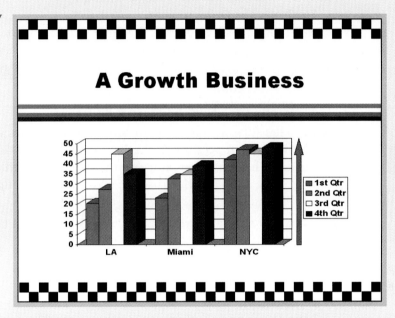 to make the arrow point up.

      d. Position the arrow on the right side of the chart between the chart and its legend. Use Figure 8-17 as a guide.

FIGURE 8-17

14. Adjust the black and white settings in the presentation, as needed.

15. Close all floating toolbars.

16. On the handouts, include the date and your name as header and include the page number and filename *[your initials]*8-20.ppt as footer.

17. Save the presentation as *[your initials]*8-20.ppt in your Lesson 8 folder.

18. Print as handouts, 4 slides per page, grayscale, framed.

19. Close the presentation.

EXERCISE 8-21

Work with layers of objects and center objects relative to the slide.

1. Open the file **Miami2.ppt**.

2. On slide 1, draw a constrained Sun AutoShape (found in the sixth row of the <u>B</u>asic Shapes menu). Position the sun on top of the subtitle text. Size the sun to 2 inches high and wide.

3. Change the sun's fill to a two-color, horizontal gradient fill, using the peach color that follows the accent and hyperlink scheme color and the pale yellow that follows the text and lines scheme color. Choose the variant with the darkest color in the middle.

4. Remove the outline from the sun.

5. Display the subtitle text in front of the sun by following these steps:

    a. Click Order on the Draw menu, then drag the submenu's gray title bar to display the Order toolbar.

    b. With the sun selected, click the Send to Back button 🔳.

6. Display the Align or Distribute toolbar. Center the sun horizontally relative to the slide by using the Align Center button 🔳. (Be sure Relative to Slide is turned on.)

7. Copy the sun from slide 1 and paste it on slide 2.

8. Reduce the sun on slide 2 proportionally to 1.5 inches wide. Move the sun so it covers the uppercase "G" in the title and send it to the back. Reposition the sun, if necessary, so the "G" is centered inside it. (Hint: To fine-tune the sun's position, use the arrow keys on your keyboard or hold down Alt and drag.)

9. Insert a new slide after slide 2 using the Bulleted List layout, with the title **What We Offer** and the following bulleted items:

    ● **Beachfront setting**

    ● **Patio juice bar**

    ● **Boardwalk**

    ● **Same great menu**

 NOTE: If you have difficulty seeing the insertion point when keying text, switch to grayscale preview.

10. Resize the text placeholder, making it just large enough for the text to fit.

11. Center the text placeholder relative to the slide by following these steps:

    a. Select the bulleted text placeholder.

    b. Turn on the Relative to Slide option, if necessary.

    c. Click the Align Center button 🔳, then click the Align Middle button 🔳.

12. Copy the sun from slide 2 and paste it on slide 3. Move it so it covers the "W" in "We," then send it to the back. Adjust its position so the "W" appears centered in the sun.

13. Close all floating toolbars.

14. Change the black and white setting for the sun to light grayscale on all slides.

15. Check spelling in the presentation.

16. On the handouts, include the date and your name as header and include the page number and filename *[your initials]*8-21.ppt as footer.

17. Save the presentation as *[your initials]*8-21.ppt in your Lesson 8 folder.

18. Print as handouts, 4 slides per page, grayscale, framed.

19. Close the presentation.

Align, group, and duplicate objects; and apply shadow and 3-D effects.

1. Open the file **Media3.ppt**.

2. Move to slide 2, then duplicate the arrow four times by following these steps:

   a. Select the arrow, then press ⌃Ctrl⌃+⌃D⌃ (or choose Dupli̲cate from the E̲dit menu).

   b. Being careful not to deselect the duplicated arrow, drag or use the arrow keys to position it as shown in Figure 8-18. (Notice that the duplicate is quite close to the first arrow.)

FIGURE 8-18

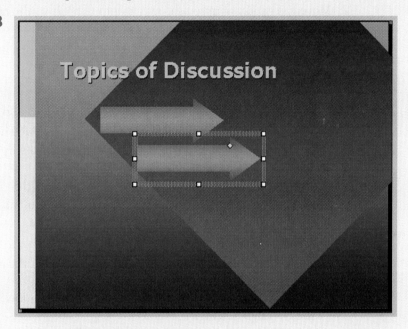

   c. Press ⌃Ctrl⌃+⌃D⌃ twice more so there are four arrows on the slide.

3. Key the following text inside the arrows:

   Arrow 1: **Quality**

   Arrow 2: **Frequency**

   Arrow 3: **Effectiveness**

   Arrow 4: **Cost**

4. Apply a 3-D effect to the arrows by following these steps:

   a. Select all four arrows.

b. Click the 3-D button ▣ on the Drawing toolbar, then choose 3-D Style 2 from the submenu.

c. Click 3-D again and click 3-D Settings.

d. On the 3-D Settings toolbar, click the Direction button ▣, and choose Perspective.

e. Click the Depth button ▣ and choose 144 pt.

5. Change the order of the arrows to reveal the hidden part of the arrowheads by following these steps:

a. If necessary, deselect all the arrows then select just the third one, which contains the text "Effectiveness."

b. Choose Order on the Draw menu, then float the Order menu.

c. Click the Bring to Front button ▣.

d. Click the arrow with the text "Frequency" and click ▣ again.

e. Click the arrow with the text "Quality" and click ▣ again.

6. Select all four arrows and group them.

7. Move the group of arrows down and to the left so the tails of the arrows extend slightly to the left of the diamond.

8. On slide 4, select the four green dots. Align their tops and distribute them evenly among themselves (not relative to the slide).

9. Group the four green dots.

10. Still working on slide 4, select the title placeholder and the green dots. Align their middles so the green dots appear to be part of the title.

11. Apply a shadow effect to the title and the green dots by following these steps:

a. If necessary, select both the green dots and the title placeholder.

b. Click the Shadow button ▣ on the Drawing toolbar.

c. Choose Shadow Style 6 (the second style on the second row).

12. Change the shadow color by following these steps:

a. With the title and green dots still selected, click the Shadow button ▣ once again.

b. Click Shadow Settings at the bottom of the Shadow menu to display the Shadow Settings toolbar.

c. Click the arrow next to Shadow Color ▣ and choose navy blue, following the background color scheme.

13. Place the text placeholder on slide 4 (which contains the three lines of text) so it's framed appropriately within the diamond.

14. Close all floating toolbars and check the slides in grayscale preview. Change the black and white setting for the arrows on slide 2 to grayscale.

15. Check spelling in the presentation.

16. On the handouts, include the date and your name as header and include the page number and filename *[your initials]*8-22.ppt as footer.

17. Save the presentation as *[your initials]*8-22.ppt in your Lesson 8 folder.

18. Print as handouts, 4 slides per page, grayscale, framed.

19. Close the presentation.

EXERCISE 8-23

Duplicate objects and disassemble clip art images.

1. Open the file **Open3.ppt**.

2. On the slide master, insert the beach umbrella clip art image shown in Figure 8-19. Make the image about 3 inches high and move it to the lower right corner.

FIGURE 8-19

3. Edit the clip art image by following these steps:

    a. Select the clip art image, if necessary, and choose Ungroup from the Draw menu.

    b. Click Yes in the dialog box that asks if you want to convert the object.

    c. Without deselecting any of the parts, group the clip art image.

    d. With the picture regrouped, display the Rotate or Flip toolbar and flip the image horizontally so the umbrella points in the opposite direction.

    e. Copy the beach umbrella image to the title master.

4. On slide 1, draw a constrained Sun AutoShape (on the Basic Shapes menu) that is 4 inches wide.

5. Change the sun's fill to a two-color gradient, shading from the center, using yellow and pale beige. Choose the variant with the yellow in the center. Remove the sun's outline.

6. Center the sun over the title and subtitle and send it to the back.

7. On slide 2, create a floating text box with the text **A health-conscious restaurant**. Format the text as 28-point Arial bold. Resize the text box if necessary so all the text fits on one line.

8. Still working on slide 2, draw a 0.75-inch constrained Sun AutoShape. Place the sun to the left of the text box. Don't change the sun's fill or outline—it should be yellow with a dark brown outline. Use Figure 8-20 (on the next page) as a guide for the sun and the text box.

9. Align the middles of the sun and the text box, then group them.

10. Copy the group to the Clipboard, then paste it three times, allowing the copies to remain where they are pasted.

11. Drag down one copy of the sun, roughly aligning it with the top of the umbrella. Drag another copy up, if necessary, so that it is approximately 1 inch below the title.

12. Select all the sun/text combinations and distribute them vertically relative to each other. If the spacing doesn't look correct, move the bottom line up or down a small amount, then vertically redistribute the combinations. Then left-align the sun/text combinations.

13. Edit lines 2 through 4 as shown in Figure 8-20.

FIGURE 8-20

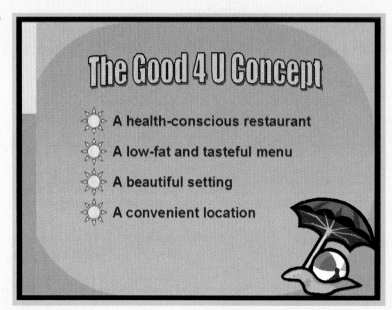

14. Group all four lines, then adjust the group's position on the slide, if necessary.

15. Copy the grouped text and paste it on slide 3. Ungroup the copied text and delete the last line. Edit the three remaining lines to show the following text:

Line 1: **Beach front**

Line 2: **Patio juice bar**

Line 3: **Boardwalk**

16. Center the slide title horizontally. Move the three lines so they are centered under the title.

17. Copy the sun AutoShape from slide 1 and paste it on slide 4. Center the text and sun relative to the slide and send the sun to the back. If needed, adjust the text position so it appears centered on top of the sun.

18. Check the slides in grayscale preview and make necessary adjustments.

19. Check spelling in the presentation.

20. On the handouts, include the date and your name as header and include the page number and filename *[your initials]***8-23.ppt** as footer.

21. Save the presentation as *[your initials]***8-23.ppt** in your Lesson 8 folder.

22. Print as handouts, 4 slides per page, grayscale, framed.

23. Close the presentation.

Lesson Applications

Select, align, and layer multiple objects, and group and ungroup objects.

1. Open the file **Franch2.ppt**.

2. On the title master, select all the tiny diamonds. Align their tops relative to each other. Then distribute them evenly relative to themselves. Group the diamonds and center the group horizontally relative to the slide.

3. Copy the group of diamonds and paste them on the slide master. Position the diamonds just below the horizontal group of stripes and wavy lines.

4. Still working on the slide master, change the first level bullet to the small diamond from the Symbol font. Make it 75% of the font size.

5. On the title master, ungroup the group of diamonds, then select one random diamond near the center of the group and change its color to light blue. Regroup the diamonds, including the light blue diamond. Change the black and white setting for the group of diamonds to light grayscale.

6. Change the presentation's background to a two-color, horizontal gradient fill, using shading that is black at the top and the dark blue that follows the background scheme color on the bottom.

7. On slide 1, position the large diamond over the subtitle and send it to the back. Center the diamond and the subtitle vertically relative to each other, then center both objects horizontally relative to the slide. Move both objects down so they're centered between the row of diamonds and the bottom of the slide.

8. On slide 2, adjust the size of the bulleted text placeholder to fit the text, then horizontally center the placeholder on the slide.

9. On slide 3, reduce the width of the bulleted text placeholder to 6.75 inches, reduce the font size to 28 points, and center the placeholder horizontally on the slide. Make the same changes to the placeholder on slide 4.

10. On slide 5, change the color of the large diamond to the lavender that follows the accent and hyperlink scheme color. Change the text in the diamond to the title text color.

11. Apply an object shadow (using the Shadow button on the Drawing toolbar) to the text in the diamond. Choose shadow style 6, make the shadow color dark blue, and adjust the nudge settings to bring the shadow closer to the text.

12. Group the text box and the diamond and center them horizontally on the slide. Center the group between the row of diamonds and the bottom of the slide.

13. Preview the presentation in grayscale and make adjustments if necessary.

14. On the handouts, include the date and your name as header and include the page number and filename *[your initials]*8-24.ppt as footer.

15. Save the presentation as *[your initials]*8-24.ppt in your Lesson 8 folder.

16. Print as handouts, 6 slides per page, grayscale, framed.

17. Save and close the presentation.

EXERCISE 8-25

Work with slide master objects, layers, shadows, and 3-D effects.

1. Open the file **Hiring2.ppt**.

2. Delete all graphic elements on the slide master as well as the title master. Only the text placeholders should remain.

3. Change the presentation's background to a two-color gradient fill that uses the From Title shading style and the colors black and gray (with gray in the center and black at the edges).

4. On the title master, draw a 0.25-inch circle, creating a small dot in the center of the slide. Make the dot the purple that follows the accent scheme color. Apply shadow style 8 to the dot. Make the shadow color black, if necessary.

5. Copy the dot you just created and duplicate it 15 times, so you have a total of 16 dots. Select all the dots, then align their tops relative to each other. Distribute the dots horizontally relative to the slide. You should now have a line of evenly spaced dots across the middle of the title master.

6. Group the dots.

7. Select the title placeholder, the group of dots, and the subtitle placeholder, and distribute them vertically relative to each other (not to the slide). This spaces the line of dots evenly between the two placeholders.

8. Copy the group of dots and paste it to the slide master, between the title placeholder and the bulleted text placeholder.

9. Move the bulleted text placeholder down 0.5 inch to add some extra space for the dots.

10. Change the bullet shape for all the bullets in the placeholder to a thick right-pointing arrow from the Wingdings3 font (use the second arrow from the right on the sixth row). Change their size to 75% and their color to bright green. (You'll have to add this color to the color scheme by choosing More Colors.)

11. Change the slide master's title text to Arial Black and apply Shadow Style 14 to the text. Make the shadow slightly more pronounced by nudging it once down and once to the right. Change the shadow color to black, if necessary.

12. On slide 1, delete the title and title placeholder. Above the row of dots, create a WordArt title with the words "New Employee Orientation." Use the fifth WordArt style on the second row (the dark blue one). Make the font 54-point Impact.

13. Change the fill color of the WordArt object to purple and the outline color to bright green. Change the WordArt shadow to Shadow Style 8 and change the shadow color to black.

14. Draw a rounded rectangle where the subtitle would appear. Make the rectangle 1 inch high and 3.5 inches wide. Apply a black, one-color horizontal gradient fill with the darkest color at the top. Adjust the shading intensity so the bottom is the same shade as the bottom of the slide's background.

15. Inside the rectangle, key **Good *4 U*** in bright green, 44-point Arial bold. Make the "4 U" italicized and make the "4" two font sizes bigger.

16. Apply the second 3-D style to the rectangle, change its direction to Perspective, change its depth to 72 point, and change its color to purple.

17. On slide 2, resize the bulleted text placeholder so it just fits the text, then center the text box vertically and horizontally on the slide.

18. On slide 3, resize the text box to 7 inches wide and center it horizontally on the slide.

19. On slide 4, key the following text in the bulleted text placeholder:

> ➔ **Reinforce our message of healthy living**
> ➔ **Describe our new franchising philosophy**
> ➔ **Encourage fresh ideas from new employees**

20. Make the bulleted text placeholder 5.5 inches wide and center it horizontally on the slide.

21. Adjust the black and white settings in the presentation, as needed.

22. Check spelling in the presentation.

23. On the handouts, include the date and your name as header and include the page number and filename *[your initials]*8-25.ppt as footer.

24. Save the presentation as *[your initials]*8-25.ppt in your Lesson 8 folder.

25. Print as handouts, 4 slides per page, grayscale, framed.

26. Close the presentation.

EXERCISE 8-26

Group and ungroup objects, align and distribute objects, work with layers, and edit clip art.

1. Open the file **Cook4.ppt**.

2. Apply the **Blends.pot** design template to the presentation. Change the template's color scheme to the standard color scheme with the black background. Customize the color scheme by changing the title text color from light gray to white. Apply the new scheme to all slides.

3. On the title master, ungroup the graphic objects and delete the red, blue, and gold rectangles. On the slide master, delete only the red and blue rectangles.

4. On slide 1, left-align the subtitle.

5. Select the carrot clip art image, then zoom to 150%. Disassemble (ungroup) the carrot, then select just the orange part and ungroup it again. Change the fill color of the light part of the carrot to a brighter shade of orange. Change the fill color of the brown part of the carrot to dark orange.

6. Select the stem part of the carrot and increase its line thickness to 1½ points. Restore the zoom to Fit, select the entire carrot, and group all its parts.

7. Increase the carrot's size proportionately, making it 3 inches tall, and rotate it to the right 60 degrees. Position the carrot in the lower right corner of the slide.

8. Make the apple slightly smaller and move it from the upper left corner to the middle of the carrot, hiding part of it.

9. Insert a clip art cluster of grapes that would work well with the other fruit images. Size the grapes appropriately and place to the left or right of the apple, whichever makes the best grouping.

10. Select the carrot and bring it forward one step. Adjust the position of the three images to create an attractive grouping.

11. Group the three images. Copy the group to the slide master. Decrease its size proportionately, making it 75% of the original size, and place in the lower right corner.

12. On slide 2, adjust the size of the bulleted text placeholder to fit the text and center it horizontally and vertically relative to the slide.

13. On slide 3 only, customize the text and lines scheme color by changing it from white to light gray. Change the black and white setting of the graph to grayscale.

14. On slide 4, reduce the bullet text by one font size and adjust the size of the placeholder to fit the text. Delete the clip art placeholder (the cup should remain).

15. Select both the bulleted text placeholder and the cup and align their middles relative to each other. Move both objects down slightly and distribute them horizontally relative to the slide to improve their spacing.

16. Change the black and white setting of the cup to inverse grayscale.

17. On the handouts, include the date and your name as header and include the page number and filename *[your initials]*8-26.ppt as footer.

18. Save the presentation as *[your initials]*8-26.ppt in your Lesson 8 folder.

19. Print as handouts, 4 slides per page, grayscale, framed.

20. Close the presentation.

EXERCISE 8-27   *Challenge Yourself*

Align and layer objects, edit clip art, and apply 3-D effects.

1. Open the file **Franch3.ppt**.

2. Customize the presentation's color scheme by changing the gray accent and followed hyperlink color to a lighter shade of gray (choose the shade to the left of the existing shade on the standard shades honeycomb).

3. Delete the black and white machinery image on the title master and replace it with an image that is appropriate to the presentation content. Make the image approximately the same size as the deleted machinery image.

4. Replace the machinery image on the slide master with a similarly-styled image as the one on the title master. Size the image to fit in the upper left corner.

5. Rotate or flip the images, if needed, to create better positioning. Recolor the images, if desired.

6. On slide 1, delete the "Good 4 U" title and its placeholder. In its place, create a WordArt image using the first choice in the first row of the WordArt Gallery. Key **Good 4 U** and format it as 60-point Arial Black. Position the WordArt appropriately and make it approximately 1 inch wider (don't change its height).

7. Apply the 3-D Style 4 (wire frame) to the WordArt. Using the Direction button on the 3-D Settings toolbar, turn on the perspective option and change the direction to the second choice in the bottom row (which

places the perspective vanishing point directly behind and slightly above the WordArt image).

8. On slide 2, resize the bulleted text placeholder to fit the text and center the placeholder horizontally and vertically on the slide.

9. Draw a constrained diamond AutoShape on slide 2. Make the shape 4.5 inches wide. Change the fill color to the lightest shade of gray (the one you customized earlier). Remove the outline. Position the diamond on top of the text and send it to the back.

10. Select both the diamond and the bulleted text placeholder and align their middles and centers relative to each other. Move both objects down on the slide about 0.5 inch.

11. Copy the diamond and paste it to slide 3. Position the diamond on top of the clip art image, then send it to the back. Change the clip art image to grayscale using the Image Control button on the Picture toolbar. Click the More Contrast button three times to sharpen the image slightly. Align the centers and middles of the clip art and diamond relative to each other, then move them slightly to the left.

12. Still working on slide 3, adjust the bulleted text placeholder to fit the text, then adjust its vertical position so it is in balance with the graphic images.

13. Format slide 5 in the same style as slide 3, then format slide 4 in the same style as slide 2.

14. Adjust the black and white settings in the presentation, as needed.

15. On the handouts, include the date and your name as header and include the page number and filename *[your initials]***8-27.htm** as footer.

16. Save the presentation in HTML format as *[your initials]***8-27.htm**.

17. Print as handouts, 6 slides per page, grayscale, framed.

18. Close the presentation.

Unit 3 Applications

UNIT APPLICATION 3-1

Create and format WordArt objects; use gradient fills; group and ungroup objects; work with clip art; and align, rotate, and flip objects.

1. Start a new blank presentation and apply the template **Dads Tie.pot** found in the Presentation Designs folder. Resize the horizontal striped graphic on the title master to 0.25 inch high, making it a thin horizontal line. Ungroup the graphic twice, then change the color of four randomly selected stripes to bright red. (You'll need to choose More Fill Colors.)

2. Regroup the horizontal stripe graphic, then copy it and paste it to the slide master. Don't change the copied position—instead, resize the bulleted text placeholder so it starts just below the horizontal stripe.

3. Delete the vertical striped graphic on the slide master, then horizontally center the title and bulleted text placeholders relative to the slide. Change the color of the bullets to bright red and change the font to dark blue Arial Black (using the blue that follows the title text scheme color).

4. Create a title slide and two bulleted text slides, as shown in Figure U3-1. Do not key any title text—you'll create WordArt titles for all slides in step 5.

FIGURE U3-1

Slide 1	Good 4 U
	Restaurant Franchise Opportunities
Slide 2	Advantages
	■ Fast-growing market
	■ Excellent income potential
	■ Expert training and support
Slide 3	Objectives
	■ Help people achieve a healthy lifestyle
	■ Help you grow a healthy business

5. Delete the title text placeholders on each slide, then Create WordArt titles using the title text in Figure U3-1. Choose the fourth WordArt style in the third row (which has multicolor characters and a shadow).

6. Using the Format WordArt dialog box, proportionally size each WordArt title to 1.3 inches high. (Remember to check the Lock Aspect Ratio box.) Set the vertical position to 0.8 inches. Center each title horizontally on the slide.

 NOTE: The first title appears larger than the others because it has no descending letters (such as "g" and "j" that extend below the text baseline).

7. On the title slide, change the WordArt fill to a vertical two-color gradient fill using the bright blue that follows the accent scheme color and the dark blue that follows the title text scheme color. Choose the variant with the lighter color in the middle. Outline the WordArt with the dark blue color. Change the WordArt shadow to Shadow Style 4.

8. Using the Format Painter, copy the WordArt formatting to the titles on slides 2 and 3.

9. On slide 1, center-align the subtitle text and center the placeholder horizontally.

10. Using the keyword "fork," locate and insert the clip art image shown in Figure U3-2. Size the image proportionally to 2.25 high. Ungroup the image, group just the fork, and delete the knife and spoon.

FIGURE U3-2 11. Apply a horizontal fill to the fork using the Silver preset and the first variant. Rotate the fork 45 degrees, duplicate it, then flip the duplicate horizontally so the forks cross each other. Align their middles, group them, and center the group below the subtitle.

12. Copy the grouped forks to the slide master. Resize and reposition the bulleted text placeholders as needed to create a pleasing composition.

13. Going back to slide 1, resize the grouped forks proportionally to 4.75 inches wide. Center the grouped forks behind the subtitle text.

14. On the handouts, include the date and your name as header and include the page number and filename *[your initials]*u3-1.ppt as footer.

15. Save the presentation as *[your initials]*u3-1.ppt in a new folder for Unit 3 Applications.

16. Print as handouts, 4 slides per page, grayscale, framed.

17. Close the presentation.

UNIT APPLICATION 3-2

Copy a color scheme; work with clip art; use drawing tools; add gradient fills, patterns, and object shadows; and group, order, align, and duplicate objects.

1. Start a new blank presentation. Apply the presentation file **Media3.ppt** as the template. (*Hint:* In the Apply Design Template dialog box, change the Files of Type to All PowerPoint Files before locating the presentation file.)

2. On the master slides, delete all the graphics. You'll use this template for its color scheme only.

3. Change the presentation background to a pattern using the diagonal pattern sample in the bottom row, third from the left. The foreground should be the dark blue that follows the background scheme and the background should be dark purple (the accent and followed hyperlink color). Apply the pattern to all slides.

4. On the title master, draw a rectangle 5.75 inches high and 8.23 inches wide. Apply a diagonal down gradient fill to it, using the same dark blue and dark purple that you used for the pattern background in step 2. Choose the variant with the lightest color in the middle.

5. Remove the outline of the rectangle and apply an object shadow using Shadow Style 14. Using the Shadow Settings toolbar, make the shadow color dark blue.

6. Draw a constrained 5-point star in the center of the rectangle. Resize the star proportionally so it is almost as high as the rectangle. Make it dark purple with no outline.

7. Center the rectangle and star vertically and horizontally relative to the slide. Group the star and rectangle, then send the objects to the back so the text placeholders are visible. Adjust the size of the title placeholder so it fits inside the rectangle, and then horizontally center both the title placeholder and the subtitle placeholder relative to the slide.

8. Change the rectangle and star's black and white setting to inverse grayscale.

9. Still working on the title master, center-align the text within the text placeholders and apply a semitransparent black object shadow to the text using Shadow Style 6.

10. Copy the rectangle and star you drew on the title master, paste it to the slide master, and send it to the back. Adjust the size and position of the title and bulleted text placeholders so they fit inside the rectangle, then apply the same object shadow and shadow color to the text placeholders that you used on the title master.

11. On the slide master, center-align the title and bulleted text. Remove the bullets

12. Create a title slide and three bulleted text slides using the text shown in Figure U3-3.

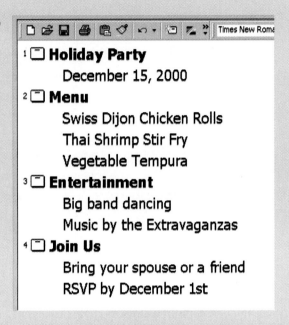

13. On slide 2, draw an AutoShape using the Up Ribbon shape (on the Stars and Banners submenu, the first shape in the third line). Make the shape large enough to cover the slide's body text and as wide as the rectangle.

14. Apply a dark blue and dark purple vertical gradient fill to the ribbon with the lightest color in the middle. Remove the ribbon's outline, then send it to the back so you can see the text. Drag the top adjusting handle to the left until the center part of the ribbon is wide enough to frame the text, then adjust the height of the ribbon. See Figure U3-4 (on the next page) for the finished result.

15. On slide 3, center-align the title. Resize the bulleted text placeholder to fit the text and center it horizontally and vertically relative to the slide.

16. Still working on slide 3, insert a simple clip art image related to music. Depending on the picture you choose, recolor it using the colors of the presentation color scheme, or change it to grayscale or black and white by using the Image Control button on the Picture toolbar. Resize the picture proportionally to 1.5 inches tall.

17. Move the picture to just inside the bottom left corner of the rectangle. Duplicate the picture enough times to fill the width of the rectangle. Arrange the pictures so they are aligned at the bottom of the rectangle and evenly distributed horizontally.

FIGURE U3-4
Slide 2

18. On slide 4, insert a clip art image of a dancing couple. Size it to 2.25 inches high and center it below the text. Use the Recolor Picture dialog box to change all the light colors to dark purple and all the dark colors to black, creating a silhouette effect.

19. Adjust the black and white settings in the presentation, as needed.

20. On the handouts, include the date and your name as header and include the page number and filename *[your initials]*u3-2.ppt as footer.

21. Save the presentation as *[your initials]*u3-2.ppt in your Unit 3 Applications folder.

22. Print as handouts, 4 slides per page, grayscale, framed.

23. Close the presentation.

UNIT APPLICATION 3-3

Work with clip art, apply fills, apply 3-D effects, group objects, apply object shadows, work with Word Art.

1. Start a new presentation using the design template **Bold Stripes.pot**. Change the slide color scheme to the one with the beige background (the last color scheme choice).

2. On the title master, resize the thin gold horizontal bar under the title so it is as wide as the title placeholder. Increase the object's thickness (height) to 0.15 inch. Apply a text shadow to the title text. Choose an object shadow for the subtitle text.

3. On the slide master, apply a text shadow to the bulleted text and an object shadow to the title text. Change the first level bullet color to gold.

4. On the title master, insert the two pictures of runners shown in Figure U3-5. (Search "runners.") Make all three runners about the same height, running in the same direction, and sized to fit the space to the left of the subtitle placeholder. They can overlap slightly.

FIGURE U3-5

5. Group the runners. Copy the runners and paste them on the slide master, in the lower right corner. Resize to about 2.5 inches high.

6. Create a title slide and three bulleted text slides using the text shown in Figure U3-6.

FIGURE U3-6

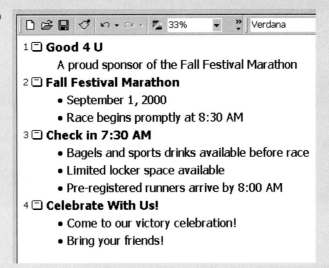

7. On slide 1, increase the title text font to 54 points and the "4" to 60 points. Make the "4 U" italic.

8. On slide 2, remove the bullets. Apply fill color to the bulleted text placeholder using the accent scheme color. Change the bulleted text placeholder to a Right Arrow AutoShape. (Hint: Select the placeholder and use Change AutoShape command on the Draw menu.)

9. Resize the arrow to frame the text, keeping the font size 32 points. Apply 3-D Style 3 to the arrow.

10. On slide 3, fill the bulleted text placeholder with the accent scheme color, but use the semitransparent setting. (Hint: Choose More Fill Colors.) Change the placeholder to the right arrow AutoShape. Resize and adjust the shape of the arrow to fit the text, keeping the font size 32 points. The arrow can overlap the runners slightly.

11. On slide 4, apply the same 3-D formatting and shape you applied on slide 2, again using no bullets and the accent scheme color as the fill color.

12. Insert a new slide after slide 4 using the blank layout. Remove the master slide elements from slide 5 only.

13. On slide 5, use the Clip Gallery to insert the fireworks picture (scanned image of black sky with reddish fireworks). Resize the image to fill the slide.

14. On slide 5, insert the gold trophy clip art. Choose the largest trophy with no background. Resize the trophy to almost the height of the slide. Tone down the brightness and contrast of the trophy so it blends more with the fireworks background. Center the trophy on the slide.

15. Create a WordArt image using the third sample in the first row of styles. Use the font 36-point Arial Black and key the following text on three lines:

    Award Ceremony
    6 PM
    Central Park

16. Change the WordArt shape to Button (Curve), which is the fourth choice in the second row. Choose an appropriate preset gradient fill for the WordArt object.

17. Position the WordArt over the top portion of the trophy. Resize the WordArt by using its sizing handles to make it rounder so it fits attractively on top of the trophy.

18. Adjust the black and white settings for the elements on slide 5 (including the background) and for the rest of the presentation, as needed.

19. On the handouts, include the date and your name as header and include the page number and filename *[your initials]*u3-3.ppt as footer.

20. Save the presentation as *[your initials]*u3-3.ppt in your Unit 3 Applications folder.

21. Print as handouts, 6 slides per page, grayscale, framed.

22. Close the presentation.

UNIT APPLICATION 3-4

Work with WordArt and clip art, apply and format 3-D effects, and group and align objects.

1. Start a new presentation using the Azure design template. Remove the graphic image from both the slide and title master. Choosing two new presentation colors, change the background to a two-color horizontal gradient, shading from navy blue at the top to purple at the bottom.

2. Change all presentation text to Arial.

3. On the title master, center the title placeholder and subtitle placeholder horizontally and move them up approximately 0.5 inch. Insert the clip art image shown in Figure U3-7 (the speaker and three people), which you can find using the keyword "speaker." Resize the image proportionally so it is 1.5 inches high, then center it horizontally approximately 1.5 inches from the bottom edge of the slide.

4. Ungroup the clip art image twice and change the fill of the speaker's lectern to the medium wood texture.

5. Group the first three people, copy them, and move the copy to the lower left corner of the slide. Resize the copy proportionally, making it 0.7 inch high. Make the fill semitransparent (by using the Format Object dialog box, Colors and Lines tab).

6. Delete the three footer placeholders at the bottom of the title slide, then copy the transparent people five times to create a total of six copies. Distribute the copies across the bottom of the slide, as shown in the figure.

FIGURE U3-7

7. Group the transparent row of people and copy the group to the slide master in the same position.

8. On the slide master, center horizontally the title and bulleted text placeholders, then insert the clip art image of the speaker giving a slide presentation, as shown in Figure U3-8. Resize the image proportionally so it is 1.75 inches high and place it at the bottom center of the bulleted text placeholder.

FIGURE U3-8

9. Recolor the clip art image on the slide master by changing the background color behind the presenter to black.

10. On slide 1, delete the title placeholder. Key **Staff Training Schedules** as the subtitle. Format the text as 36-point Arial bold.

11. Still working on slide 1, create a WordArt title using the text **Good 4 U** and the fourth choice in the second row of styles (the style with the gray and white horizontal gradient fill). Format the text as 60-point Arial Black bold.

12. Increase the width of the WordArt to 7 inches and center it above the subtitle.

13. Apply a 3-D effect to the WordArt using 3-D Style 20. Change the perspective color to purple (the background color you chose previously). Position the WordArt title so the 3-D effect touches the top edge of the slide and is centered horizontally, as shown in Figure U3-7.

14. Create three new slides using the 2-column text layout. Key the text shown in Figure U3-9 (on the next page), but don't key the titles. Right-align the text in the right-column placeholders and remove all the bullets on all three slides. Resize and arrange the placeholders attractively on each slide. Be sure to align the tops of the column placeholders.

 NOTE: You may want to create the 2-column text in slide 2 first, copy the slide twice, and then edit the copies for slides 3 and 4.

15. Create WordArt titles for slides 2, 3, and 4 using the fourth WordArt style in the second row (the same one you used for the title slide). Format the text as 54-point Arial Black. Apply the Can Up WordArt shape (the third shape in the third row). Apply 3-D Style 20 and make the 3-D effect purple. Change the depth from infinity to 288 point.

TIP: To make your job easier, first delete the title placeholders. Then, create the first WordArt title, copy and paste it to the two other slides, and edit its text by double-clicking the WordArt image.

FIGURE U3-9

```
          Training Presentation
          Managers              8:30 AM
Slide 2   Servers               10:15 AM
          Greeters              1:00 PM
          Kitchen staff         3:15 PM

          On-the-job Training
          Managers              7:30 PM
Slide 3   Servers               5:30 PM
          Greeters              8:15 PM
          Kitchen staff         4:30 PM

          Food Services Training
          Managers              January 17
Slide 4   Servers               January 18
          Greeters              January 19
          Kitchen staff         January 20
```

16. Adjust the black and white settings in the presentation as needed.

17. On the handouts, include the date and your name as header and include the page number and filename *[your initials]*u3-4.htm as footer.

18. Save the presentation in HTML format as *[your initials]*u3-4.htm in your Unit 3 Applications folder.

19. Preview the presentation as a Web page in your browser, then close the browser window.

20. Print as handouts, 4 slides per page, grayscale, framed.

21. Close the presentation.

UNIT APPLICATION 3-5 *Making It Work for You*

Write and design a presentation and work with lines, fills, colors, and objects.

1. Create a presentation of your course curriculum. Include a title slide, and at least four slides following that with four different courses. (If you don't have four courses, make up a curriculum.) Include information relevant for each course (title, time, day, instructor, and so on). Using your creativity and the skills you've learned so far, incorporate some of the following elements:

- Clip art and scanned images (customized to your specifications and used as free-floating objects, background, or fill)
- WordArt
- Drawn objects, AutoShapes and floating text boxes
- Layered objects
- Patterns, shading, and textures for object fills and backgrounds
- Custom color scheme
- Shadows and 3-D effects

2. Adjust the black and white settings in the presentation, as needed.

3. On the handouts, include the date and your name as header and include the page number and filename *[your initials]*u3-5.ppt as footer.

4. Save the presentation as *[your initials]*u3-5.ppt in your Unit 3 Applications folder.

5. Print as handouts, 6 slides per page, grayscale, framed.

6. Close the presentation.

Advanced Techniques

LESSON 9

Advanced Text Manipulation

OBJECTIVES

After completing this lesson, you will be able to:

1. Control paragraph indents by using the ruler.
2. Set tab stops and create a tabbed table.
3. Change line spacing and paragraph spacing.
4. Change text box margins and word wrap options.
5. Work with page setup options.
6. Customize handout masters and notes masters.

MOUS ACTIVITIES

In this lesson:

PP2000 **3.7**
PP2000 **E.2.1**
PP2000 **E.2.2**
PP2000 **E.5.3**

See Appendix F.

 Estimated Time: 1 hour

In earlier lessons, you learned how to add text to a slide and change text attributes such as color, font, font style, and font size. In this lesson, you learn how to change the indent settings, set tab stops and line spacing, and manipulate text in other ways.

Working with Indents

Each text placeholder has a ruler you can use to change paragraph indents and tab settings. These settings affect all text in a placeholder. To apply different settings to some of the text, you put that text in a separate placeholder.

FIGURE 9-1
Paragraph indents

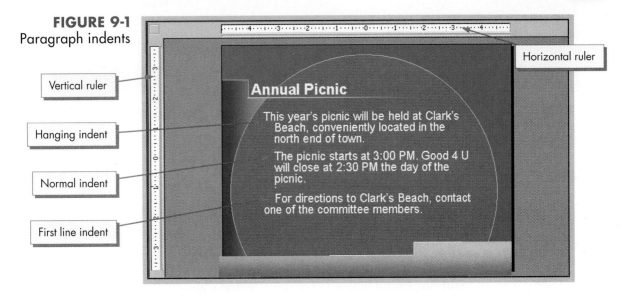

EXERCISE 9-1 Change Paragraph Indents

1. Open the file **Picnic1.ppt**.

2. Choose <u>R</u>uler from the <u>V</u>iew menu, if necessary. The vertical and horizontal rulers appear.

 NOTE: Ruler is a toggle command. Choose it once to display the rulers; choose it again to hide them.

3. Move to slide 2 and select the bulleted text placeholder. Remove the bullets. The paragraphs now have *hanging indents*.

4. Click anywhere within the placeholder as if you were planning to edit some text. Notice the *indent markers* that appear on the ruler. Also notice that the white portion of the ruler indicates the width of the text placeholder.

 NOTE: You must have an insertion point somewhere inside a text box to change settings on the ruler. The appearance of the ruler reflects whether the entire placeholder is selected or the insertion point is active within the placeholder.

5. Point to the *first-line indent* marker (the top triangle) and drag it right to the 1-inch mark on the ruler. The first line of each paragraph is now indented. Notice that each paragraph in the placeholder is indented the same way. To create different indents for different paragraphs, you must put them in separate text boxes.

FIGURE 9-2
Indent markers

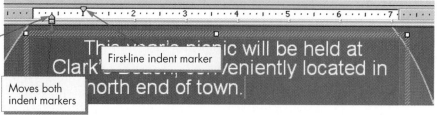

Left indent market

First-line indent marker

Moves both
indent markers

 NOTE: If a text placeholder contains more than one bullet level, you see
more than one set of indent markers on the ruler.

6. Drag the small rectangle (below the bottom triangle) to the zero mark on
the ruler (the left edge of the white portion). Notice that both triangles
move when you drag the rectangle.

7. Drag the left indent marker (bottom triangle) to the right until it aligns
with the first-line indent marker (the top triangle). Now all the lines of the
paragraphs are indented the same amount.

8. Drag the small rectangle to the zero mark on the ruler once again. Now
there are no indents set for this placeholder.

EXERCISE 9-2 Change Bullet Spacing

Sometimes you may want to change the distance between the bullets and text
in a text placeholder. You can easily do this by dragging one of the indent
markers to the left or right.

1. Move to slide 3. Click within the left bulleted text placeholder (containing
"Veggie burgers"). Notice the position of the indent markers.

2. Point to the left indent marker (the bottom triangle, not the small
rectangle) and drag it right to the 1-inch mark on the ruler. The text is
now indented 1 inch, but the bullet remains in its original position. Drag
the left indent marker left to the 0.5-inch mark.

3. Click within the right bulleted text placeholder and drag the left indent
marker right to the 0.5-inch mark.

EXERCISE 9-3 Apply Indent Settings to the Slide Master

You can also change indent settings on the slide master. Slide master changes
are automatically reflected on individual slides. However, formatting that you
apply to individual slides before you change the master is not changed by the

master slide. To make master slide changes take effect on those slides, reapply the slide layout.

1. Move to slide 4. Click inside the bulleted text placeholder and note the indent setting on the ruler. (It is at the ⅜- or 0.375-inch mark.)

2. Display the slide master.

3. Click inside the bulleted text placeholder. Note that there are five sets of indent markers, one for each bullet level.

FIGURE 9-3
Changing indents
on the slide master

4. Using the first set of indent markers for the first bullet, move the left indent marker to the left ⅛ inch (one ruler tick mark to the left), making the bullet spacing slightly smaller.

5. Switch to Slide view and move to slide 4, if necessary. Note that the text is now closer to the bullet. Click the bulleted text and look at the ruler. The left indent marker is now at the ¼- or 0.25-inch mark. The slide master automatically changed the bullet spacing.

6. Move to slide 3. The bullets were manually changed here, so the master slide changes did not take effect.

7. Choose Slide Layout from the Common Tasks toolbar and then choose Reapply. Now the bullet spacing has changed to reflect the master.

Working with Tabs

You can set tabs to create simple tables in PowerPoint. You set tabs the same way you set tabs in Word. By default, tabs are left-aligned and set at 1-inch intervals. To set your own tabs, click the Tab Type button **L** to choose the alignment style and then click the ruler at the location where you want the tab.

EXERCISE 9-4 Set Tabs in a Text Box

1. Insert a new slide after slide 2 using the Title Only layout.

2. Key the title **Picnic Committee Award Winners**

3. Draw a text box at least 7 inches wide, positioning the upper left corner about 1.5 inches below the word "Picnic."

4. Key the following, pressing Tab where indicated:
Darin Haley Tab **Sports Program** Tab **4798** Tab **112.76**
Select the text box and change the font to 20-point Arial.

5. Using the Format menu, make the width of the text box exactly 7 inches. (Select the text box and choose Format, Text Box. Click the Size tab and set the width to **7**.)

6. Click anywhere within the text box to activate the text box ruler.

7. Click the Tab Type button at the left end of the ruler. Each time you click the button, a different tab type icon appears, allowing you to cycle through the four tab type choices.

NOTE: Tabs are set when the tab type symbol appears on the ruler. It may take some practice before you are comfortable with tab type selection and tab placement.

TABLE 9-1   Types of Tabs

CHOOSE	TO DO THIS
└	Left-align text at the tab setting
┴	Center text at the tab setting
┘	Right-align text at the tab setting
┴	Align decimal points at the tab setting

FIGURE 9-4
Tab alignment

Left-aligned tab marker   Centered tab marker   Right-aligned tab marker   Decimal-aligned tab marker

Tab Type button

Left-Aligned	Centered	Right-Aligned	Decimal
Holly	Boston	Mocha	4.55
Chip	Chicago	Chocolate	3.28
Stacy	San Francisco	Raspberry	2.59
Darin	Albany	Toffee	3.49
Cindy	Washington	Vanilla	2.97

8. Click the Tab Type button until the center-aligned tab icon appears. Click the ruler at the 3-inch position. The text "Sports Program" moves so it is centered under the tab marker.

9. Set a left-aligned tab marker at the 4.75-inch position and a decimal-aligned tab marker at the 6.375-inch mark (the third tick mark after 6 inches). Note that the last number you keyed moves to align its decimal point with the tab.

TIP: Increase the zoom, if necessary, for an enlarged view of the ruler.

EXERCISE 9-5   Create a Tabbed Table

1. Working in the text box you created on slide 3, position the insertion point at the end of the line and press ⟨Enter⟩ to start a new line.

2. Key the balance of the table, shown in Figure 9-5, pressing ⟨Tab⟩ between columns and pressing ⟨Enter⟩ at the end of each line.

FIGURE 9-5
Creating a
tabbed table

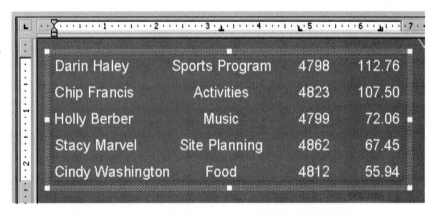

Darin Haley	Sports Program	4798	112.76
Chip Francis	Activities	4823	107.50
Holly Berber	Music	4799	72.06
Stacy Marvel	Site Planning	4862	67.45
Cindy Washington	Food	4812	55.94

NOTE: After you set tabs for a table, you can change or remove them. To change the position of a tab marker, simply drag it to a new position on the ruler. To remove a tab marker, drag it down, off the ruler.

3. Click inside the text box, if necessary, to activate the ruler. Drag the center-aligned tab marker from the 3-inch position on the ruler to 3.25 inches. The entire column moves to the right.

4. Drag the center-aligned marker down and off the ruler to remove it. The table realigns in an unattractive way.

5. Click the Undo button 🔄 to restore the table's appearance.

6. Select the entire text box by clicking its border. Adjust its height to fit the text (you may need to make the text box taller) and add a 1.5-point white outline.

7. Center the text box horizontally on the slide.

EXERCISE **9-6** **Create Column Headings for a Tabbed Table**

Because tab and indent settings in PowerPoint affect all text in a placeholder, you may need to put column headings in a separate text box to align them attractively with your table columns.

1. Still working on slide 3, create a second text box above the table, making it the same width as the table. You fine-tune the size and position later.

2. Key the following in the text box:
Name Tab **Responsibility** Tab **Extension** Tab **Points**

3. Change the font to 20-point Arial and adjust the vertical position of the text box, if necessary, so it does not overlap the table.

4. Set the following tabs in the heading text box:

Center-aligned   3.25-inch mark
Center-aligned   5.00-inch mark
Right-aligncd   6.75-inch mark

5. Add a 1.5-point white outline to the heading text box.

6. Adjust the position of the heading text box so its bottom border touches the top border of the table. Left-align the text boxes in relation to each other.

FIGURE 9-6
Completed table
with column
headings

7. Make sure the heading text box is the same width as the table text box.

8. Adjust the tab marker positions in the heading text box, if necessary, so the headings align above the table columns as shown in Figure 9-6.

9. Select both text boxes and group them. Then center them on the slide.

Controlling Line Spacing

You can control line spacing by adding more space between the lines in a paragraph or by adding more space between paragraphs. Increased line spacing can make your text layout easier to read and enhance the overall design of your slide.

EXERCISE 9-7 **Change Line Spacing Within Paragraphs**

To change spacing between lines within a paragraph, you can:

- Choose Line Spacing from the Format menu.
- Click the Increase Paragraph Spacing button 🔳 or the Decrease Paragraph Spacing button 🔳 on the Formatting toolbar. These buttons increase or decrease the space between lines within a paragraph by increments of 0.1 line.

1. Move to slide 2. Click within the first paragraph in the placeholder.

2. Choose Line Spacing from the Format menu. The Line Spacing dialog box appears.

FIGURE 9-7
Line Spacing
dialog box

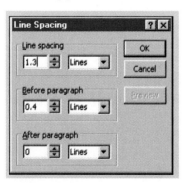

3. In the Line Spacing option box, key **1.3** or click the up arrow until 1.3 appears. Click Preview to view the changes. The line spacing of the first paragraph has increased. Click OK to accept the changes.

NOTE: The default unit of measure for line and paragraph spacing is lines. You can change the measurement to points, if you prefer, by clicking the arrow next to Lines and choosing Points.

4. Usually you will want to change the line spacing for an entire text placeholder. Select the placeholder, re-open the Line Spacing dialog box, and change the line spacing to 0.9 lines. Click OK. The text is now easier to read and more attractively placed.

 5. With the placeholder still selected, click the Decrease Paragraph Spacing button twice. The line spacing decreases.

> **NOTE:** If the Increase/Decrease Paragraph Spacing buttons do not appear on the Formatting toolbar, click More Buttons ⯈, click Add or Remove Buttons, and then click the button on the submenu. Click More Buttons ⯈ again to close the submenu.

 6. Click the Increase Paragraph Spacing button once to increase the line spacing.

> **NOTE:** The Increase/Decrease Paragraph Spacing buttons change the space between lines within a paragraph, as well as the spacing between paragraphs for all selected text. Each bullet point is a separate paragraph.

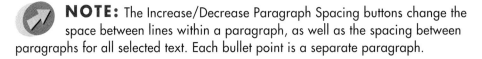

EXERCISE 9-8 **Change Spacing Between Paragraphs**

You have seen how you can change line spacing in text placeholders. You can also change the amount of space before or after a paragraph by using options in the Line Spacing dialog box.

1. Still working on slide 2, click within the second paragraph and open the Line Spacing dialog box.

2. Under Before Paragraph, change the line setting to 2 lines.

3. Click Preview to view the changes. Click OK.

4. To make all paragraph spacing uniform, select the entire text placeholder and open the Line Spacing dialog box. Change the Before Paragraph spacing to 1 line and the After Paragraph spacing to 0. (The Line spacing should remain at 0.9 lines). Click OK. The text is now evenly spaced in the placeholder.

5. Adjust the text placeholder font size to 24 points, if necessary.

> **NOTE:** If the PowerPoint feature Auto-Fit Text to Text Placeholder is turned on, the text will automatically be resized. To prevent this you can choose Options from the Tools menu, click the Edit tab, and clear the Auto-Fit Text to Text Placeholder check box.

Working with Text Box Settings

You can change the position of text within its text box or AutoShape. For example, you can place text in the upper left corner or vertically center it relative to its text box. You can also change the box margins, the text box size, and the word-wrap options. These options are found on the Text Box tab of the Format AutoShape dialog box.

TABLE 9-2   Text Box Options

CHOOSE	EFFECT
Text anchor point	Specify the position where text begins in an AutoShape.
Internal margin	Adjust the distance from the text to the Left, Right, Top, or Bottom edges of an AutoShape.
Word-wrap text in AutoShape	Make text wrap to fit within the width of an AutoShape.
Resize AutoShape to fit text	Make an object automatically adjust to the size of its text.
Rotate text within AutoShape by 90°	Turn text sideways inside an AutoShape.

EXERCISE   9-9   **Change the Text Anchor Position in an AutoShape**

The text anchor point is the position from which text begins within a placeholder or AutoShape. For example, in a bulleted text placeholder, the text begins at the top of the placeholder. When you key text in an AutoShape, it begins at the center. This point remains fixed when text shrinks and grows during editing. You can change the anchor point to Top, Middle, Bottom, Top Centered, Middle Centered, or Bottom Centered.

FIGURE 9-8
Examples of text
anchoring

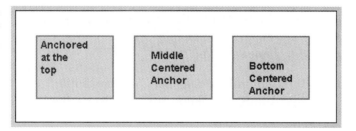

1. Move to slide 5. Select the bulleted text placeholder containing the committee members' names.

2. Apply a dark purple fill and remove the bullets. Notice that the text is positioned in the upper left corner of the box.

3. Right-click the placeholder border and choose Format Placeholder from the shortcut menu. When the Format AutoShape dialog box appears, click the Text Box tab. Drag the dialog box to the right so you can see the text box.

4. Open the Text Anchor Point list box, choose Bottom, and click Preview. The text moves to the bottom of the placeholder.

5. Choose Middle Centered and click Preview again. The text is now centered vertically and horizontally in the placeholder. Click OK.

FIGURE 9-9
Changing the
text anchor
position

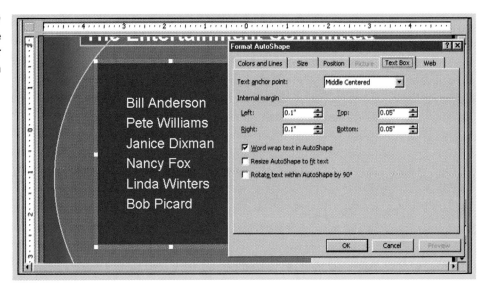

6. Change the text box AutoShape to a rounded rectangle. (Click Draw on the Drawing toolbar and choose Change AutoShape, Basic Shapes.)

EXERCISE 9-10 **Use Word Wrap and Resize AutoShape Features**

When you choose the Resize AutoShape to Fit Text option, the text box (or other AutoShape) automatically shrinks or grows as you add or delete text and when you change the font size.

1. With the committee members placeholder still selected, re-open the Format AutoShape dialog box and display the Text Box tab. Drag the dialog box to the right so you can see the placeholder.

2. Check the Resize AutoShape to <u>F</u>it Text option and click <u>P</u>review. The placeholder shrinks in height, but not in width.

3. Clear the <u>W</u>ord Wrap Text in AutoShape check box and click <u>P</u>review again. Now the placeholder shrinks in width. Word wrap changes the way the Resize option works.

4. Click OK to apply the placeholder settings.

5. Increase the committee members text by one font size. Notice that the placeholder grows.

EXERCISE **9-11** **Change Text Box Margins**

In a text box, you can change the space between the text and the border by changing the internal margin settings on the Text Box tab.

1. With the committee members placeholder still selected, re-open the Text Box tab of the Format AutoShape dialog box.

2. Under Internal Margin, change <u>L</u>eft to **0.5** and click <u>P</u>review. The left margin becomes wider.

3. Set the <u>R</u>ight margin to **0.5** inch and the <u>T</u>op and <u>B</u>ottom margins to **0.3** inch. Click OK. The size increases to accommodate the wider margins.

4. Reduce the text by one font size. The placeholder shrinks to fit the new text size.

EXERCISE **9-12** **Use Text Box Options to Change an AutoShape**

When you key text in an AutoShape, the text is automatically anchored at the middle center position, word wrap is turned off, and the Resize AutoShape feature is turned off. You can change these settings so your text fits into the AutoShape.

1. Insert a new slide after slide 5 using the blank autolayout.

2. Draw a Diamond AutoShape in the center of the slide, approximately 1 inch wide and 1 inch tall.

3. Fill the diamond with a two-color gradient, choosing dark purple (shadows scheme color) for color 1 and light purple (accent scheme color) for color 2. Choose the Fro<u>m</u> Center option and the variant with the lighter center. Remove the diamond's outline.

4. With the AutoShape selected, key **See you at the beach!** The text extends outside the diamond's border.

5. Change the text font to 48-point Arial, bold.

6. Open the Format AutoShape dialog box and click the Text Box tab. Check Resize AutoShape to <u>F</u>it Text and click OK. The text fits inside the diamond, but the diamond is too large for the slide.

7. Resize the diamond by dragging the left-center sizing handle toward the center of the slide. The text automatically word wraps even though the word wrap option was not chosen.

8. Adjust the width of the diamond so the text wraps to three lines.

9. Position the diamond in the center of the slide.

FIGURE 9-10
Text word-wrapped inside an AutoShape

10. On the handouts, include the date and your name as header and include the page number and filename *[your initials]*9-12.ppt as footer.

11. Adjust the black and white settings in the presentation, as needed.

12. Save the presentation as *[your initials]*9-12.ppt in a new folder for Lesson 9.

13. Print as handouts, 6 slides per page, grayscale, framed. Leave the presentation open for the next Exercise.

Working with Page Setup Options

You can display and print your presentation in different ways: as an on-screen show using your computer's monitor, as overhead transparencies, as 35mm slides, or as color or black and white printouts. Your printouts can be in landscape or portrait orientation. PowerPoint has built-in page size settings for each method. You use the Page Setup dialog box to choose page size settings.

NOTE: You can change the page size of your presentation at any time, but it's generally best to plan ahead and start with the one you intend to use for the finished product. Changing to a page layout with different proportions or orientation may make it necessary to change the proportions and placement of individual objects on each slide.

EXERCISE 9-13 Change Page Setup Options

So far, you've worked with slides that are sized for an on-screen presentation in landscape orientation. In this exercise, you change the page setup to a paper presentation in portrait orientation. This sort of paper presentation might be placed in a binder and distributed at a meeting when no computer is available.

1. Apply either the Citrus or the Blends template to the presentation you saved as *[your initials]***9-12.ppt**.

2. Choose Page Setup from the File menu. In the Page Setup dialog box, notice that the current presentation is sized for an on-screen presentation in landscape orientation. Notice that notes and handouts use portrait orientation.

3. Open the Slides Sized For drop-down list and notice the options. Choose Letter Paper.

FIGURE 9-11
Changing page setup options

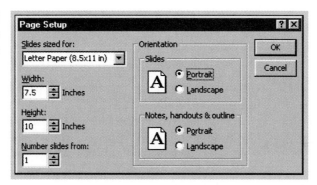

4. Under Slides, click Portrait and click OK. The slide proportions change to the new orientation.

5. Scroll through the presentation and notice the distortion in some of the graphics.

6. Make the following changes to fix the layout:

- On slide 2, make the text box 5.25 inches wide and center it horizontally. If necessary, change the font size to 28 points.
- On slide 3, make the table's font one size smaller, make both text boxes wider, and adjust the tabs to make the text align correctly. Adjust the paragraph spacing in both text boxes to make the table more attractive, and center the table horizontally on the slide.
- On slide 4, correct the proportions of the clip art by reducing its height but preserving its width. Move it to the lower right corner. Move the text in the second column to the bottom of the first column and change the slide layout to Bulleted List.
- On slide 5, remove the fill from the AutoShape text box and add a black outline. Decrease the height of the clip art image and reposition both objects attractively.
- On slide 6, remove the fill from the AutoShapes and add a black outline. Increase the width of the diamond so the text wraps to three lines. Reposition the diamond appropriately.

7. View the presentation in Slide Sorter view and then view it as a slide show.

8. Adjust the black and white settings, if necessary.

9. Update the handout footer to show the filename *[your initials]*9-13.ppt.

10. Create a slide footer for slide 3 only. Include the date, your name, and the same filename.

11. Save the presentation as *[your initials]*9-13.ppt in your Lesson 9 folder.

12. Print slide 3 as a slide, framed; then print the entire presentation as handouts, 6 slides per page, grayscale, framed.

13. Close the presentation.

Customizing Handout and Notes Masters

Just as the slide master controls the appearance of the slides in your presentation, the notes master and handout master control the overall look and formatting of notes and handouts. You can customize these masters using the same techniques you used with slide and title masters.

EXERCISE 9-14 Work with the Handout and Notes Masters

1. Reopen the file you saved as *[your initials]*9-12.ppt.

2. Open the <u>V</u>iew menu and choose <u>M</u>aster, Notes Master to display the notes master. Note the portrait orientation of the notes page. You can select any text placeholder on the notes master and move or format it. You can also insert any object on the page.

3. Open the <u>V</u>iew menu and choose <u>M</u>aster, Han<u>d</u>out Master to display the handout master. You should also see the Handout Master toolbar. (If the toolbar is not displayed, choose it from the <u>V</u>iew menu, <u>T</u>oolbars submenu.)

4. Click the first button on the Handout Master toolbar , which shows how handouts will print with two slides per page. The slides are represented by dotted outlines.

5. Click the button that shows the positioning of three slides per page; then click the button that shows a six-slide per page handout.

6. Select all four text placeholders on the handout (Header, Date, Footer, Number), using the Select All method (Ctrl+A). Change the font to 14-point Arial, bold italic.

FIGURE 9-12
The handout master with placeholders selected

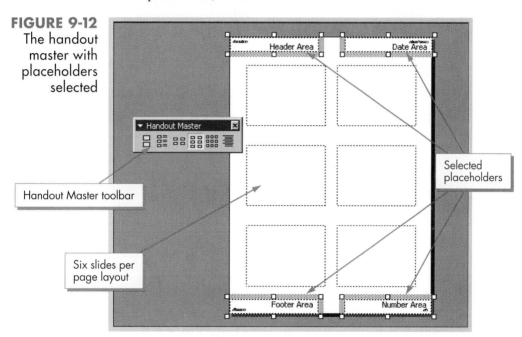

Handout Master toolbar

Selected placeholders

Six slides per page layout

7. Increase the zoom setting so you can see the placeholder formatting changes more clearly.

NOTE: Although you can work with the text placeholders on the notes or handout master, you cannot make any changes to the slides on the page.

8. Select only the Date placeholder (upper right) and delete it. Select the Header placeholder. Center-align the text in the placeholder and center the placeholder horizontally on the page.

TIP: To restore a deleted handout placeholder, you can click Handout Master Layout on the Common Tasks toolbar and check the item you want to restore.

9. Under the Header placeholder, draw a floating text box with the text **Annual Picnic Presentation**. Change the text box font to 12-point Arial, bold italic, and center the text box under the Header placeholder.

10. Return to slide view and update the handout footer to show the filename *[your initials]*9-14.ppt.

11. Save the presentation as *[your initials]*9-14.ppt in your Lesson 9 folder.

12. Print the presentation as handouts, 6 slides per page, grayscale, framed.

13. Close the presentation.

COMMAND SUMMARY

FEATURE	BUTTON	MENU	KEYBOARD
Increase paragraph spacing	📋	F<u>o</u>rmat, Line <u>S</u>pacing	
Decrease paragraph spacing	📋	F<u>o</u>rmat, Line <u>S</u>pacing	
View handout master	Shift+📋	<u>V</u>iew, <u>M</u>aster, Han<u>d</u>out Master	

USING HELP

Just like master slides and handout masters, the notes master can be customized to meet specific needs.

Use Help to find out more about the notes master:

1. Display and activate the Office Assistant.

2. Key **notes master** in the text box and click <u>S</u>earch.

3. Select the first topic, "Add, change, or delete items on the notes master." Maximize the Help window, if necessary.

4. Read about the topic. Click the Show button 🔲 to expand the Help window. Click the <u>C</u>ontents tab, if necessary.

5. Explore other topics of interest, such as Paragraph Formatting (double-click a topic or click the plus sign to the left of it to show subtopics).

6. Close the Help window when you finish. Hide the Office Assistant.

Concepts Review

Each of the following statements is either true or false. Indicate your choice by circling **T** or **F**.

T F **1.** Each paragraph in a bulleted list placeholder has its own set of tab stops.

T F **2.** The right-align tab marker aligns the last character of each entry in its column.

T F **3.** If you need to move the position of a tab marker, you must remove the marker and then set a new one.

T F **4.** The Increase Paragraph Spacing button increases only the space between paragraphs.

T F **5.** Top Centered, Middle Centered, and Bottom Centered are text anchor-point options.

T F **6.** You can remove a tab marker by dragging it off the ruler.

T F **7.** By clicking the small rectangle on the ruler, you can make the two triangular-shaped indent markers line up above it.

T F **8.** Unless you change page setup options, slides print in landscape orientation and handouts print in portrait orientation.

Write the correct answer in the space provided.

1. What do you call the position where text is attached to a placeholder?

_____

2. Which kind of tab do you use to align rows of dollars and cents?

_____

3. How do you change the distance between bullets and text?

_____

4. In which dialog box do you find the option to automatically adjust an AutoShape's size to accommodate its text?

_____

5. Where do you change indents, set tab stops, and move tab stops?

_____

6. Which function does [icon] perform?

_____

7. Assuming that the Word Wrap and Resize AutoShape to Fit Text options were applied, which settings do you change to modify the amount of space between text and the edge of an object?

_____

8. Which menu do you open to display the ruler?

_____

CRITICAL THINKING

Answer these questions on a separate page. There are no right or wrong answers. Support your answers with examples from your own experience, if possible.

1. Think of ways you might use the indent markers. When would you want lines in a block to indent at different points?

2. Comparing the difference between the different types of tab stops, when would you use centered tabs? Left-aligned tabs? Right-aligned tabs?

Skills Review

EXERCISE 9-15

Work with bullets and indents.

1. Open the file **Award.ppt**.

2. Move to slide 2. If the ruler is not in view, choose Ruler from the View menu to display it.

3. Create first-line indents by following these steps:
   a. Remove the bullets from the bulleted text.
   b. Click within the text box to activate the ruler.
   c. Drag the first line indent marker (top triangle) right to the 1-inch mark on the ruler.
   d. Drag the small rectangle left to the zero point on the ruler.

4. Move to slide 3 and change the bullet spacing by following these steps:
   a. Click within the bulleted text.

b. Drag the left indent marker (bottom triangle) right to the 0.5-inch position on the ruler.

5. On the slide master, change the first-level bullet to a star of your choice from the Wingdings font. Make the star dark blue and 100% of font size.

6. Move to slide 4 and change the bulleted text indent to 0.5 inch. Move the entire placeholder down 0.5 inch on the slide.

7. Move to slide 5 and format the text boxes to have no bullets and no indents by following these steps:
   a. Select both text boxes and remove the bullets.
   b. Make the text in both text boxes one size smaller.
   c. Click within the left text box and drag the left indent marker to the zero point. Do the same to the right text box.

8. Underline the following on slide 5: "Employee," "Hobbies," "Years of Service," and "Position."

9. On the handouts, include the date and your name as header and include the page number and filename *[your initials]*9-15.ppt as footer.

10. Adjust the black and white settings, if needed.

11. Save the presentation as *[your initials]*9-15.ppt in your Lesson 9 folder.

12. Print as handouts, 6 slides per page, grayscale, framed.

13. Close the presentation.

EXERCISE 9-16

Set tabs and create tabbed tables.

1. Open the file **Marath.ppt**.

2. Move to slide 2 and add tabs to the table by following these steps:
   a. Display the ruler if necessary and then click anywhere within the table to activate the ruler.
   b. Click the Tab Type button ⬛ until it displays a right tab ⬛.
   c. Click the ruler at the 4-inch mark.
   d. Drag the tab marker to the 4.5-inch mark on the ruler.
   e. Add another right tab at the 5.5-inch mark on the ruler.

3. Insert a new slide after slide 2 using the Title Only layout. Key **Station Assignments** in the title placeholder.

4. Create a tabbed table by following these steps:
   a. Draw a text box approximately 2 inches below the top of the slide and the same width as the title text. (The text box should be at least 7 inches wide.)
   b. Key the following table heading:
   Description Tab **Class** Tab **Station**

  c. Draw a second text box the same width directly below the table heading.
  d. Key the following, pressing ⒯ⒶⒷ between columns.

Under 18	**A**	**10**
18-39	**B**	**30**
40-54	**C**	**40**
55 and Over	**D**	**20**

5. Format the table by following these steps:
  a. Select both text box objects and align their left edges.
  b. Change the heading text to 36-point Arial, bold. Change the text color to pink and apply a text shadow.
  c. In the heading text box, set a center tab at 4 inches and a right tab at 7 inches.

 TIP: You may need to make the heading text box wider to set the 7-inch tab stop.

  d. Change the table text size to 32-point Arial, bold.
  e. In the table text box, set a left tab at 4 inches and a right tab at 6.25 inches.

6. Indent the table text 0.25 inch by following these steps:
  a. Click within the body of the table (not the heading).
  b. Drag the small rectangle on the ruler to the 0.25-inch position. Both triangles should be aligned on top of the rectangle.
  c. Adjust the table text tab markers slightly to fine-tune the alignment of the columns under the heading.

7. Use the Format Text Box dialog box to change the width of both header and table to exactly 7 inches.

8. Group the table and the table heading; then position the group so it appears centered under the slide title.

9. On the handouts, include the date and your name as header and include the page number and filename *[your initials]*9-16.ppt as footer.

10. Adjust the black and white settings, if needed.

11. Save the presentation as *[your initials]*9-16.ppt in your Lesson 9 folder.

12. Print as handouts, 3 slides per page, grayscale, framed.

13. Close the presentation.

EXERCISE 9-17

Change line spacing and paragraph spacing and customize the handout master.

1. Open the file **Lunch.ppt**.

2. Change line spacing within paragraphs by following these steps:

   a. Move to slide 2 and click within the descriptive paragraph below the bold heading "Stuffed Spinach Bread."

   b. Choose Line Spacing from the Format menu.

   c. Change the line spacing setting to 1.1 lines and click OK.

   d. Change the line spacing for each description for the remaining three appetizers to 1.1 lines. (Use the Edit, Repeat command, or press Ctrl+Y.)

3. Change spacing between paragraphs by following these steps:

   a. Move to slide 3 and select the left text placeholder.

   b. Open the Line Spacing dialog box. Under Before Paragraph, change the setting to 0.1 lines. Click OK.

   c. Apply the same paragraph spacing to the right text placeholder.

   d. Click within the bold text "Old Fashioned Cornbread."

   e. Change the Before Paragraph setting to 0.5 lines.

   f. For the remaining bold side-dish names, change the Before Paragraph settings to match.

4. Reduce the line spacing for all the text in both placeholders on the Side Dish Specials slide by following these steps:

   a. Select both text placeholders.

   b. Click the Decrease Paragraph Spacing button once.

5. Move to slide 4. For each bold heading (the lunch special names), change the before-paragraph space to 1 line and the after-paragraph space to 0 lines.

6. For each paragraph that isn't bold (the descriptions), change the before- and after-paragraph spacing to 0 lines.

7. Select both text placeholders and change the line spacing to 0.9 lines.

8. Customize the handout master by following these steps:

   a. Choose View, Master, Handout Master.

   b. Select the footer placeholder and zoom to a larger size so you can see the placeholder clearly.

   c. Delete the Number Area placeholder in the lower right corner.

   d. Position the insertion point after the text "(footer)" in the Footer placeholder.

   e. Key a comma, a space, and the text **Presentation on Lunch Specials**.

   f. Center the Footer placeholder horizontally, center-align the text within the placeholder, and make the text bold. Close the handout master.

9. On the handouts, include the date and your name as header and include the filename *[your initials]*9-17.ppt as footer.

10. Adjust the black and white settings, if needed.

11. Save the presentation as *[your initials]*9-17.ppt in your Lesson 9 folder.

12. Print as handouts, 6 slides per page, grayscale, framed.

13. Close the presentation.

Change text box settings and page setup options.

1. Open the file **Update1.ppt**. Change the color scheme to the second standard choice (magenta and orange with the white background).

2. Change the presentation to letter paper size in portrait orientation by following these steps:

    a. Choose Page Setup from the File menu.

    b. Open the Slides Sized For drop-down list and choose Letter Paper.

    c. Under Slides, click Portrait and click OK.

3. On the title master, add a 1-point orange border to the subtitle placeholder. Add the same border to the bulleted text placeholder on the slide master.

4. Change the text alignment and text anchor properties of the title slide subtitle by following these steps:

    a. On slide 1, left-align the subtitle text.

    b. With the subtitle placeholder selected, open the Format AutoShape dialog box and click the Text Box tab.

    c. Choose Middle Centered in the Text Anchor Point list box.

    d. Preview the change. Without closing the dialog box, click the Position tab.

    e. Change the vertical position to 6 inches from the top.

    f. Preview the change and click OK.

5. On slide 2, remove the bullet and hanging indent. Then change the text box resize option by following these steps:

    a. Select the text box and open the Format AutoShape dialog box.

    b. Click the Text Box tab.

    c. Check Resize AutoShape to Fit Text. If necessary, check Word Wrap Text in AutoShape.

    d. Still using the Text Box tab, change all internal margins to 0.3 inch.

    e. On the Position tab, change the Vertical setting to 4 inches. Preview the changes and click OK.

6. Using the right-center resize handle, make the text box about 1 inch narrower. Increase the text font size by one increment. With the text box selected, click the Increase Paragraph Spacing button 🔲 once to increase the space between lines. Horizontally center the text box.

7. Resize an AutoShape to fit its text by following these steps:

    a. Move to slide 3 and right-click anywhere on the slide title.

    b. Choose Format Placeholder from the shortcut menu. Click the Text Box tab in the dialog box.

    c. Check Resize AutoShape to Fit Text and click OK.

    d. Change the fill color to gold and the text color to black.

    e. Change the font size of the title text to 44 points.

8. Still working on slide 3, change the vertical position of the bulleted text box to 6 inches from the top of the slide, and change its text box setting to Resize AutoShape to Fit Text.

9. On slide 4, resize the bulleted text placeholder to fit the text and move the text box down one inch. (Tip: Add 1 inch to the vertical position setting on the Position tab.)

10. On slide 5, remove the first level bullet and the hanging indent. Increase the Before Paragraph spacing of the second level hyphen bullets to 0.5 lines. Move the text box to 3.5 inches from the top of the slide.

11. On slide 6, make the bulleted text box 4.5 inches wide and set the Format AutoShape option so the text box resizes to fit the text. Set the Before Paragraph setting for the text box to 0.5 lines. Move the clip art image (the computer) to the lower right corner of the slide. Make the clip art image shorter and wider so it is proportional and then change its outline color to black

12. On the handouts, include the date and your name as header and include the page number and filename *[your initials]*9-18.ppt as footer.

13. Adjust the black and white settings, if needed.

14. Save the presentation as *[your initials]*9-18.ppt in your Lesson 9 folder.

15. Print as handouts, 6 slides per page, grayscale, framed.

16. Close the presentation.

Lesson Applications

Work with tabbed tables, bullets, and text box options.

1. Open the file **Tucson.ppt**.

2. On the slide master, change the title text to 48-point bold with a text shadow. To the bulleted text placeholder, apply a two-color diagonal down gradient fill of pink and turquoise, using the variant with turquoise in the middle. Apply a dark green outline to the bullet placeholder.

3. On the title master, apply the same gradient fill and outline to the subtitle placeholder. Increase the font size to 36 points. Verify that the title text has the same formatting as the slide master's title text.

4. On the slide 1 subtitle placeholder, turn off the <u>W</u>ord Wrap Text in AutoShape option and turn on the Resize AutoShape to <u>F</u>it Text option. Change the left and right internal margins to 0.5 inch and the top and bottom margins to 0.3 inch.

5. On slide 2, remove the bullets and center-align the text. Change the text box margins to 0.5 inch at the top and bottom and 1 inch on the left and right. Turn off word wrap and turn on Resize AutoShape to <u>F</u>it Text.

6. Center the text box horizontally on the slide and move it down about 0.5 inch.

7. Insert a new slide after slide 2 using the Title Only layout. Key **Appetizers** as the title, and key the following in a floating text box, pressing Tab before each price:

Wild Rice Soup	**5.25**
Dill Cucumber Salad	**4.50**
Four Bean Salad	**4.25**

8. Set a decimal tab at the 5.5-inch mark to align the prices.

9. Change the line spacing to 0.9 lines, and the before-paragraph spacing to 0.2 lines.

10. Turn off word wrap, turn on Resize AutoShape to <u>F</u>it Text, set all internal margins to 0.3 inch, and change the fill and outline to match the subtitle placeholder.

11. Center the text box horizontally and make its top edge exactly 2.75 inches from the top of the slide. Change the font to 28-point Arial Narrow. (Use Arial if Arial Narrow is not available).

12. On slide 4, remove all bullets and hanging indents from the bulleted text placeholder. For the second-level text, change line spacing to 0.8 lines and the space before paragraphs to 0 lines. Change the font for the second-level text to 20-point Times New Roman, italic.

13. Set right tabs in the text box at 5 inches and 6.5 inches.

 TIP: You can use right tabs instead of decimal tabs to align numbers if all the numbers in the list have the same number of decimal places.

14. Clear the Word Wrap text box option and set the Resize AutoShape option, and set internal margins to 0.3 on all sides. Reduce the size of all the text by two increments.

15. Insert a blank line above the text "Chicken Fajitas." In the blank area above this text (within the text box), draw another text box for table headings. This text box should be the same width as the larger text box.

16. Key the following text in the heading text box, separating the words with tabs:

    Entree   Dinner   Lunch

17. Change the heading text to 24-point Arial Narrow (or Arial), bold, and change the left and right text box margins to 0.3 inch. "Entrée" should be positioned above "Chicken Fajitas."

18. Left-align the two text boxes relative to each other, and set tabs in the heading text box to center "Dinner" and "Lunch" over the price columns.

19. Position the text boxes attractively on the slide, adjusting the heading text box, if necessary, so its text is in the appropriate position.

20. On the handouts, include the date and your name as header and include the page number and filename *[your initials]*9-19.ppt as footer.

21. Adjust the black and white settings, if needed.

22. Save the presentation as *[your initials]*9-19.ppt in your Lesson 9 folder.

23. Print as handouts, 4 slides per page, grayscale, framed.

24. Close the presentation.

EXERCISE 9-20

Work with indents, tabs, and page setup options.

1. Open the file **Inventry.ppt**.

2. Working on the slide master, increase the slide title text by one font size and make it bold.

3. Still working on the slide master, increase the space between the bullet and text for the first level bullet to 0.5 inch. Change the first level bullet to the larger solid dot found on the Wingdings 2 font, and change its color to pink.

4. On slide 2, remove the bullets and the hanging indent. Reduce the line spacing for the entire text box by one increment. Make the text box approximately 6 inches wide and adjust its height to just fit the text. If necessary, increase the text size to 32 points. Center the text box horizontally and vertically.

5. On slide 3, make the text box 7.5 inches wide, adjust its height to fit the text, and reposition the text box so the bullets are aligned under the first character in the title.

6. On slide 4, remove the second-level bullets. Italicize the second-level text and make it one font size smaller. Change the text box width to 7.5 inches, and move it to the right so the bullets align with the first character in the title text.

7. On slide 5, remove the bullets from the table and insert a left-aligned tab at the 3-inch mark on the ruler. Increase the table text by one font size and center the table horizontally and vertically relative to the slide.

8. On slide 6, change the text box width to 8 inches, adjust its height to fit the text, and center the text box horizontally and vertically.

9. On the handouts, include the date and your name as header and include the page number and filename *[your initials]*9-20a.ppt as footer.

10. Adjust the black and white settings, if needed.

11. Save the presentation as *[your initials]*9-20a.ppt in your Lesson 9 folder.

12. Print as handouts, 6 slides per page, grayscale, framed.

13. Change the page setup options to resize the slides for letter paper and portrait orientation.

14. Delete the dot graphics from the title and slide masters.

15. Change the color scheme to the standard scheme with the burgundy background.

16. Review each slide, and adjust the text size, the height and width, and the position of the text boxes as needed.

17. Update the handout footer with the filename *[your initials]*9-20b.ppt.

18. Adjust the black and white settings, if needed.

19. Save the presentation as *[your initials]*9-20b.ppt in your Lesson 9 folder.

20. Print as handouts, 6 slides per page, grayscale, framed.

21. Close the presentation.

EXERCISE 9-21

Work with indents, line spacing, and text box settings.

1. Open the file **Newyr2.ppt**.

2. On slide 2, remove all the bullets and hanging indents from both text boxes. Center-align the text in the left box, change its font size to 40 points, and change its text color to gold (the title text scheme color). Format the text in the right text box as 20-point Arial, bold.

3. Resize the directions text box so its text wraps on three lines and it is just high enough for the text to fit. Position the text box at the bottom of the slide and center it horizontally.

4. Make the left text box 8 inches wide. Change the font size of the line that begins "Festivities begin" to 32 points. Change the space before paragraphs in the text box to 0 lines. Adjust the height of the text box to fit, and then center it horizontally and vertically on the slide.

5. Insert a new slide after slide 2 using the Title Only layout. Key **Evening Menu** in the title placeholder. Draw a 3-inch circle below and to the left of the title. Using Figure 9-13 as a guide, key the "Appetizers" text in the circle.

FIGURE 9-13
Slide 3

6. Make the word "Appetizers" 28-point bold, shadowed, and burgundy (the accent scheme color). Make the rest of the text 20-point, bold, shadowed, and dark pink (the fills scheme color).

7. Using the Format AutoShape dialog box, remove the outline and fill the circle with a 2-color gradient of cream (the text and lines scheme color) and gold. Choose the From Corner shading style and the variant with the darkest color in the lower right. Using the Size tab, change the size of the circle to 2.75 inches high and 3 inches wide. Change the text anchor point to Middle Centered.

8. Copy the ball and paste it three times. Use Figure 9-13 as a guide for positioning the balls in an overlapping fashion. Edit the text in the three copied balls as shown in the figure.

9. Change the shading of the Main Course ball so it shades from cream to light pink (a custom color). The Side Dishes ball should shade from cream to bright blue, and the Desserts ball from cream to bright green.

 TIP: To make the gradient fills have more color, make Color 1 cream and Color 2 the darker color.

10. On slide 4, remove all the bullets and hanging indents. Make all the first-level text bold, pink, and with a text shadow. Make the second-level text bold and change the text color to black.

11. Change the AutoShape to a rounded rectangle with a dark gold fill. Apply object shadow style 6 to the rectangle and change the shadow color to dark pink.

12. Change the text anchor point to Middle Centered and turn on the Resize AutoShape to Fit Text option. Change the line spacing for the second-level paragraphs to 0.8 lines.

13. Adjust the rectangle's width until second-level text wraps to three lines. Then adjust the vertical position and center the rectangle horizontally.

14. On the handouts, include the date and your name as header and include the page number and filename *[your initials]9-21.ppt* as footer.

15. Adjust the black and white settings, if needed.

16. Save the presentation as *[your initials]9-21.ppt* in your Lesson 9 folder.

17. Print as handouts, 6 slides per page, grayscale, framed.

18. Close the presentation.

EXERCISE 9-22 *Challenge Yourself*

Create a tabbed table, change line spacing, change box margins and anchor point settings, and customize the handout master.

1. Start a new blank presentation using the Blends template. Choose the color scheme with the black background.

2. Display the title master. Open the Clip Gallery and use the Search feature to display baseball pictures. Choose a color picture of a player swinging a bat (like the one shown in Figure 9-14, which is flipped).

3. Resize the player to 2.75 inches high and move him to the left of the subtitle text box. Copy and paste the ballplayer to the lower right corner of the slide master. If necessary, flip the player so he faces the center of the presentation. (Remember: You must ungroup and then group the clip art before you can flip it.)

4. On slide 1, key a two-line title with the text **Good *4* *U*** and **Softball Schedule**.

5. Key **Spring/Summer 2001** for the subtitle.

6. Using the Title Only layout, create slide 2 as shown in Figure 9-14. Key the table and its heading all in one text box. Use 24-point Tahoma for all the table text and make the heading bold. Set appropriate tabs. Set the line spacing for the heading to 1.5 lines and the line spacing for the body of the table to 1 line. Set the before-paragraph spacing to 0.2 lines for the whole table. Disable the Word Wrap option for the text box, enable the Resize AutoShape to <u>F</u>it Text option, and make the left and right internal margins 0.3 inch. Add a 1.5-point border to the text box and draw a 1.5-point line under the heading. Position the table appropriately on the slide.

FIGURE 9-14
Slide 2

July/August Schedule			
Date	**Opponent**	**Location**	**Time**
7/9	American Sports	Away	5:45
7/16	Jim Jones Pie Co.	Home	6:00
7/23	Smith's Shoes	Home	6:00
7/30	Ace Factory Supply	Away	5:45
8/6	American Sports	Home	6:00
8/13	Tom Jones Pie Co.	Away	6:15
8/20	Smith's Shoes	Away	6:15
8/27	Ace Factory Supply	Home	6:00

7. Using the 2 Column Text layout, create slide 3 as shown in Figure 9-15. Remove all bullets and hanging indents, center the text in each text box, and make the first line of each text box bold yellow 32-point Tahoma. Apply a one-color blue horizontal gradient fill to both text boxes, using the darkest setting with the darkest color at the bottom. Disable the Word Wrap text box option and enable the Resize AutoShape to <u>F</u>it Text option. Make all internal margins 0.4 inch. Arrange the text boxes as shown in the figure.

FIGURE 9-15
Slide 3

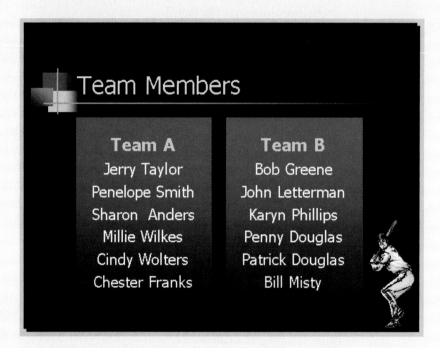

8. Using the Title Only layout, create slide 4 as shown in Figure 9-16 (on the next page), Draw a rounded rectangular callout AutoShape and key the text shown in the figure. Format the callout shape with a 2.25-point white outline and no fill. Disable the Word Wrap text box option, enable the Resize AutoShape to <u>F</u>it Text option, and change all internal margins to 0.2 inch. Drag the callout's yellow adjustment diamond to the baseball player's head.

9. On the handouts, include the date and your name as header and include the page number and filename *[your initials]***9-22.ppt** as footer.

10. Adjust the black and white settings, if needed.

11. Save the presentation as *[your initials]***9-22.ppt** in your Lesson 9 folder.

12. Print as handouts, 4 slides per page, grayscale, framed.

13. Close the presentation.

FIGURE 9-16
Slide 4

Advanced Drawing Techniques

OBJECTIVES

MOUS
ACTIVITIES
In this lesson:
PP2000 **4.2**
PP2000 **4.5**
PP2000 **E.2.9**

See Appendix F.

After completing this lesson, you will be able to:

1. **Use guides to position and measure objects.**
2. **Use zoom for precise object placement.**
3. **Explore the Snap and Nudge features.**
4. **Draw using the Freeform tool.**
5. **Edit points on a freeform drawing.**
6. **Draw using the Curve tool.**

 Estimated Time: 1½ hours

PowerPoint has some powerful tools you can use to control the position of objects to give your presentations a professional look. In Lessons 5 and 6, you learned how to control the size and position of objects by keying measurements in dialog boxes. In this lesson, you use the guides and the Snap and Nudge features to measure and place objects. You also work with advanced drawing tools to create curves and freeform objects.

Using Guides to Position and Measure Objects

You can display dotted horizontal and vertical lines on your slides to help you position text and drawing objects. You can hide these lines called *guides* when you don't need them, and display them again later. Guides do not print or appear in a slide show. When you display guides for the first time, you see one horizontal and one vertical line, each centered on the slide.

TABLE 10-1   Working with Guides

PRESS	TO DO THIS (WHILE DRAGGING A GUIDE)
Shift	Measure the distance from the guide's starting position to its new position
Ctrl	Add a new guide
Shift + Ctrl	Add a new guide at a measured distance from an existing guide

EXERCISE 10-1   Work with Guides

In this Exercise, you set up two vertical guides to help you position and size an object precisely.

1. Open the file **AdCamp.ppt** and move to slide 3 ("Newspaper Advertising").

2. To display guides, choose <u>G</u>uides from the <u>V</u>iew menu. Notice that <u>G</u>uides is a toggle command.

 NOTE: To see the guides more clearly, click the Grayscale Preview button to display the slide in black and white.

3. To prepare to move a guide, position the mouse pointer so it touches the vertical guide near the bottom of the slide, below the newspaper clip art object. Your mouse pointer should be a white arrow.

FIGURE 10-1
Working with guides in black and white view

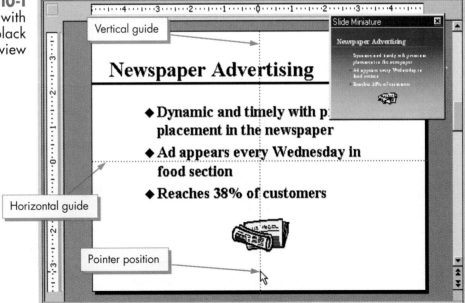

NOTE: When you drag the guide, make sure you see the white arrow pointer. If you drag the I-beam or four-headed arrow by mistake, you will move or resize an object instead of moving the guide.

4. Press and hold the mouse button. The measurement "0.00" appears in place of the pointer, indicating the guide is in the center of the slide.

5. While pressing the mouse button, move to the left until the measurement 1.25 appears, and then release the mouse. The horizontal guide moves to the left, 1.25 inches from the center of the slide. Release the mouse button.

FIGURE 10-2
Vertical guide moved 1.25 inches to the left

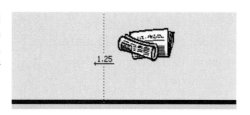

FIGURE 10-3
Adding a second vertical guide

6. To add a second vertical guide to the slide, point to the first guide and press and hold the control key Ctrl while dragging the guide to the right. The plus sign below the indicator shows that you are adding an additional guide. Drag the guide 1.25 inches to the right of center. Notice that as you drag the guide, the indicator shows "0.00" as it passes the center of the slide, then increases as you drag to the right.

7. Release the mouse button first and then release Ctrl.

 NOTE: If you release Ctrl before releasing the mouse button, the result will be moving the line, not adding a new one.

8. Enlarge the newspaper picture proportionally so it fills the space between the guides (making the picture 2.5 inches wide and centered horizontally).

9. Remove the right vertical guide by dragging it to the right, off the edge of the slide.

 NOTE: You can add up to eight horizontal and eight vertical guides. When you no longer need them, simply drag them off the slide. You can remove all but one set of guides that way. You can hide the remaining set of guides, but you cannot remove them.

10. Hide the guides by choosing Guides from the View menu. You can also press Ctrl+G to turn guides on or off.

EXERCISE 10-2 Make Measurements with Guides

You can measure the distance from a guide to an object on a slide by dragging the guide while pressing the [Shift] key.

1. Move to slide 5 ("Direct Mail") and display the guides.

2. Drag the horizontal guide to the bottom of the screen. Because there is only one horizontal guide displayed, it will not be removed by moving it to the edge of the slide.

3. While pointing to the horizontal guide (at the bottom edge of the screen), press and hold [Shift] and the mouse button. Notice the measurement "0.00."

4. While holding [Shift], drag the guide up to the top edge of the postcard clip art. Release the mouse and [Shift]. The distance from the bottom edge of the slide to the top of the postcard is 2.25 inches.

5. Without using [Shift], point to the horizontal guide and hold down the mouse button. The measurement indicates the horizontal guide is 1.5 inches below the center of the slide. Release the mouse button.

6. Using the techniques presented in steps 2–4, move the vertical guide 2 inches in from the right edge of the slide. Align the right edge of the mailbox with the guide.

7. Position the postcard 2 inches from the left edge of the slide.

8. Select the postcard, stamp, and mailbox. Click D̲raw on the Drawing toolbar and use the Distribute H̲orizontally command to space the selected objects evenly relative to each other. (Turn off the Relative to S̲lide option.)

FIGURE 10-4
Repositioned
objects

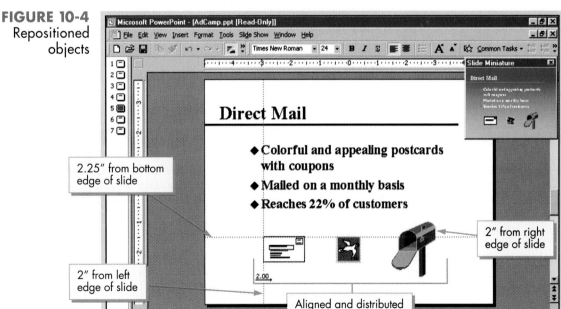

9. Center the three objects vertically relative to each other (align their middles). Turn off black and white mode now, if necessary.

Using Zoom

In previous lessons, you changed the zoom to view different parts of a slide. Zoom can be useful when you need to place objects precisely or view objects in fine detail for editing.

EXERCISE **10-3** **Use Zoom**

1. Move to slide 4 and select the radio.
2. Click the Zoom arrow on the Standard toolbar to open the Zoom drop-down list and choose 200%. The radio is magnified in the center of the screen.

   NOTE: The zoomed window displays the center of the slide if no object is selected.

3. Ungroup the radio and click a blank part of the screen to deselect the radio parts. Click the radio handle to select the radio case and change its fill color to blue.
4. Regroup the radio parts and change the zoom to Fit (the option at the bottom of the Zoom drop-down list).

   NOTE: You can also zoom to values not on the Zoom drop-down list. To do this, select the value in the Zoom text box, key another value, and press Enter.

Exploring the Snap and Nudge Features

The Snap and Nudge options offer more ways to align objects. You can set Snap so when you place an object close to another object, it "snaps" to the object as if it were magnetic, making the edges of the two objects touch. You can also set Snap so an object aligns with an imaginary grid. The grid consists of invisible horizontal and vertical lines covering your slide. When you turn on the grid, your objects automatically snap to the closest grid line. Sometimes Snap may be just what you need—at other times, it can keep you from precisely placing or drawing objects. You can use Nudge to move an object in very small increments, one tiny step at a time.

EXERCISE 10-4 **Use the Snap to Grid Option**

Like guides, the Snap to Grid option is a toggle. You click the option once to turn it on and click again to turn it off.

1. With slide 4 displayed, click Draw on the Drawing toolbar, point to Snap, and click To Grid to turn the option on, if necessary. (If the To Grid button appears to be pushed in, Snap to Grid is already in effect and clicking it will turn off the option.)

2. If necessary, turn off Snap to Shape and hide the guides if they are showing.

FIGURE 10-5
Clip art of
convertible

3. Insert clip art of the black and white convertible shown in Figure 10-5. To easily find the car, use the search word **convertible**.

4. Position the car above the radio but not touching it. With the car selected, zoom to 150%; then size the car proportionally so it is the same width as the radio.

 NOTE: You can use the Size tab on the Format Object and Format Picture dialog boxes to check the width of both the radio and the car to make them precisely the same width.

5. Try to drag the car so the bottoms of the tires exactly touch the top of the radio's handle. Notice how the car jumps from one position to the next. This is because Snap to Grid is turned on.

TIP: To temporarily disable the Snap to Grid or Snap to Guides option, press Alt while dragging an object.

6. Use the Draw menu to turn off Snap to Grid. Drag the car up and down. Notice that you can drag the car smoothly and more precisely. Position the car so that the bottoms of the tires exactly touch the top of the radio's handle. Recolor the car, changing black to red and white to black.

EXERCISE 10-5 **Use the Nudge Option**

The Nudge option gives you yet another way to precisely position an object.

1. With the car selected, change the zoom to 300%.

2. Click Draw on the Drawing toolbar and point to Nudge. Drag the gray bar at the top of the Nudge menu to float it.

FIGURE 10-6
Using the Nudge
option to precisely
position an object

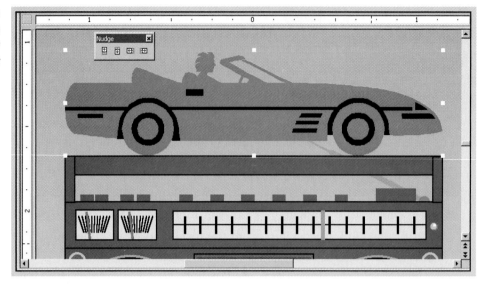

3. With the car selected, click the Nudge Up button ⊞ a few times. Then click the Nudge Down button ⊞ until the car tires are once again precisely placed on top of the radio.

NOTE: You can also nudge a selected object with the Up, Down, Left, and Right arrow keys on your keyboard. If Snap is in effect, hold down Ctrl while using the arrow keys to temporarily turn off Snap.

4. Change the zoom setting to Fit and then reactivate the Snap to Grid option.

5. Select both the car and the radio, center them horizontally (Align Center) relative to the slide, and group them.

6. Close the Nudge toolbar.

Using the Freeform Tool

Using the Freeform tool, you can draw irregular straight-sided or curved shapes. You can draw either closed objects (the end points meet) or open objects (the end points don't meet). Keep the following in mind when you draw with the Freeform tool:

- To draw connected straight lines, click at the starting point and then click at the end point of each line segment where you want a new side to start.

- To draw curved lines, drag the pointer. As you drag, the pointer changes to a pencil shape.

- You can use both straight lines and curved lines in a freeform object.
- To complete a drawing, double-click at the end point or press [Esc].

In the following Exercises, you experiment with freeform drawing on a blank slide. After you perfect your technique, you copy and paste your drawing to the appropriate slide.

EXERCISE 10-6 Practice Drawing with the Freeform Tool

1. Move to slide 7, which is a blank slide. Display the rulers if they're not already displayed.

2. Click AutoShapes on the Drawing toolbar, point to Lines, and make the Lines submenu into a floating toolbar.

FIGURE 10-7
Freeform tool on
the Lines toolbar

3. To practice drawing, you'll make an ice cream cone shape. Don't worry if your drawing is not perfect. You can delete it and try again until you get the feel of it. Click the Freeform tool 🅖 on the Lines floating toolbar.

4. Position the crosshair pointer near the center of the slide and click the left mouse button once to anchor the starting point.

FIGURE 10-8
Practice with the
Freeform tool

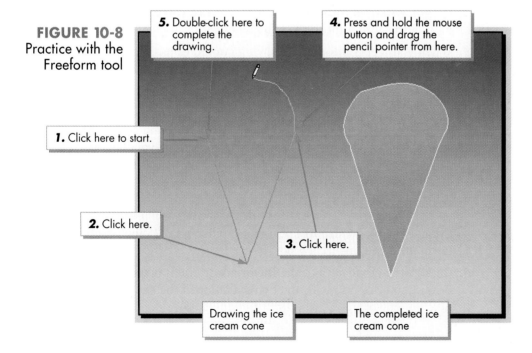

5. Click a second point diagonally down and to the right and a third point diagonally up and to the right of the second point. (See Figure 10-8.)

6. To draw the curved part of the ice cream cone, press and hold the mouse button at the third point and then drag a curved shape using Figure 10-8 as a guide. Notice that when you start dragging, the pointer changes to a pencil.

7. Make the curved shape touch the starting point. If necessary, double-click at the starting point to complete the drawing and deactivate the Freeform tool. The completed cone is filled with pink and outlined in white.

NOTE: You can also press Esc to complete a drawing and deactivate the Freeform tool. If you end precisely at the starting point, the drawing will automatically be completed, with no need to double-click or press Esc.

EXERCISE 10-7 **Create a Freeform Object with Curved Lines**

1. Delete the ice cream cone and any other practice drawings you created on slide 7.

2. Click the Freeform button ⟲. With the cursor anywhere on the slide, hold down the mouse. The pointer changes to a pencil shape. Draw a small irregular-shaped round object, making sure you complete the object by joining the end point to the starting point.

3. When you feel comfortable drawing curved objects, draw a cloud shape similar to the shape in Figure 10-9, making it about 2 inches long.

FIGURE 10-9
Freeform cloud
shape

NOTE: Don't worry if your drawing doesn't look like the figure—just do your best to make something similar. Drawing curved shapes takes some practice.

4. Change the cloud size to 1.75 inches wide and 0.75 inch high by using the Format AutoShape dialog box.

5. Change the cloud's fill to the Daybreak gradient preset, choosing the From Center option with the lightest color in the center.

6. Remove the cloud's outline.

7. Switch to Black and White view and change the cloud's black and white setting to Black with White Fill. Switch back to Normal or Slide view.

TIP: Sometimes gradient fills do not print correctly in black and white. If this happens, you can change the object's black and white setting to Black with White Fill, Black, or White.

8. Copy the cloud and paste it on slide 2. Drag the cloud to the upper right corner, copy it again, and paste it three times.

9. Arrange the clouds in the upper right corner, using Figure 10-10 as a guide.

FIGURE 10-10
Slide 2 with clouds

Advertising Media

◆ Newspaper
◆ Radio
◆ Direct mail
◆ Yellow pages

EXERCISE 10-8 Draw a Freeform Object with Straight Lines

1. Delete any drawing objects on slide 7.

2. Click the Freeform button and draw a freeform arrow using Figure 10-11 (on the next page) as a guide. Don't worry if your arrow is not perfect. You learn how to edit a freeform drawing in the next exercise. Remember, to draw straight lines, click at the end point for each side of the drawing—do not drag the pointer.

TIP: You can modify a freeform object while drawing by pressing Backspace or Delete twice to undo the last end point.

FIGURE 10-11
Drawing a
freeform arrow

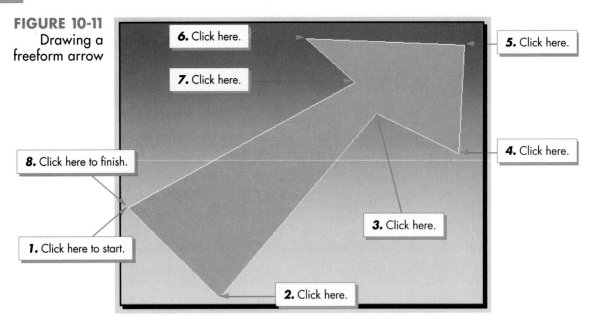

6. Click here.

7. Click here.

5. Click here.

8. Click here to finish.

4. Click here.

3. Click here.

1. Click here to start.

2. Click here.

Editing a Freeform Drawing

After you draw a freeform object, you may want to modify its shape. You make such changes by using a reshaping handle called a *vertex*. You can add, delete, and move vertexes.

TABLE 10-2   Working with Vertexes (Edit Points)

TO MAKE THIS HAPPEN	DO THIS	POINTER SHAPE
Move a vertex	Drag it to a new position.	⊹
Add a new vertex	Point to a place on a line between two vertexes and then press Ctrl while clicking the line.	┼
Delete a vertex	Press Ctrl while clicking the vertex.	✕

EXERCISE 10-9 Edit a Straight Line Freeform Object

1. On slide 7, right-click the freeform arrow you just drew and choose <u>E</u>dit Points from the shortcut menu. Small black squares—vertexes—appear at each of the line segment endpoints. When you point to a vertex, the pointer changes to a four-headed arrow you can use to alter the object's shape.

 NOTE: You can also choose Edit Points from the Draw menu to make the vertexes appear.

2. Place the pointer on the bottom-most vertex, at the bottom of the arrow. Drag the vertex to the right about 0.5 inch.

3. Place the pointer on the bottom right point of the top of the arrow. Drag the vertex slightly to the left to change the shape of the arrowhead.

4. To add a new vertex, place the pointer on the middle of the line forming the base of the arrow. Notice the crosshair pointer shape. Press and hold Ctrl and click. A new vertex appears. Drag the vertex out and away from the arrow to change its shape.

5. To delete a vertex, place the pointer on the new vertex you just added. Press and hold Ctrl. Notice the pointer shape is now an "X." While holding Ctrl, make sure the "X" pointer is visible and click. The vertex is removed and the drawing changes shape.

6. Add another vertex at the base of the arrow and drag it toward the center of the drawing.

FIGURE 10-12
The arrow after editing

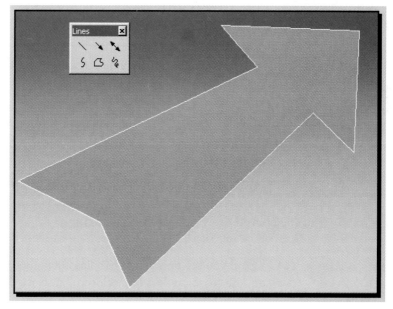

7. Continue editing points until your drawing looks similar to the one in Figure 10-12.

8. When the arrow is the shape you like, change the fill to a two-color gradient using light blue for color 1 and medium blue for color 2. Choose the diagonal down shade and the first variant (with the darker blue in the lower left corner). Remove the arrow's outline.

9. Copy and paste the arrow to slide 6 ("Yellow Pages"). Send the arrow to the back and add a text shadow to the bulleted text.

10. Change the black and white settings for the arrow to light grayscale.

11. Delete the arrow on slide 7, leaving a blank slide for more drawing.

Using the Curve Tool

Creating smooth curved lines is easy with the Curve tool. To use the Curve tool, select it from the Lines toolbar. Click on the slide where you want the curve to start, and then click wherever you want the curve to change shape or direction. To complete a curve drawing, double-click its endpoint or press Esc.

TIP: A small number of clicks spaced far apart will make a smoother curve.

EXERCISE 10-10 Use the Curve Tool

1. Move to slide 7 and delete any practice drawings on the slide.

2. Select the Curve tool [5] on the Lines toolbar, and then click a starting point anywhere on the slide. Move the crosshair diagonally down and click again. Notice the straight diagonal line that appears.

3. Move the crosshair diagonally up and click again. Notice that the line changed into a curve.

4. Make several more clicks in any position to get a feel for how this tool works.

5. End the curved drawing by double-clicking.

NOTE: If you see only resize handles but no line after completing the drawing, use [✎] to apply a line color to the selected line.

6. Practice drawing curves like the one in Figure 10-13. Keep your best attempt and delete the others.

FIGURE 10-13
Curve tool drawing

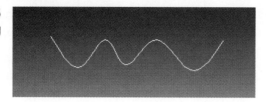

7. Display the curve drawing edit points. (Right-click the curve and choose Edit Points.) Note that a vertex appears along the curve at every place you clicked.

8. Practice adding, deleting, and dragging some vertexes to change the curve's shape. Practice drawing and editing with the Curve tool until you feel comfortable using it.

EXERCISE 10-11 Create a Finished Curve Tool Drawing

1. Move to slide 5. Draw and edit a curved line using the Curve tool ⑤ to connect the postcard, stamp, and mailbox. Use Figure 10-14 as a guide.

FIGURE 10-14
Curve drawing on slide 5

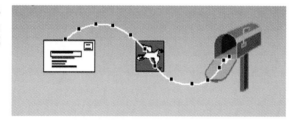

2. Select the curve by clicking it (without displaying the edit points). Change its color to red and make its line thickness 3 points. Add a solid arrowhead at the right end of the line.

3. Bring the postage stamp to the front so the red line is behind it.

FIGURE 10-15
Completed curve drawing

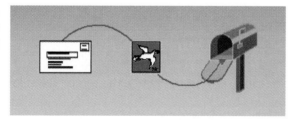

4. Group the postcard, stamp, mailbox, and curved line. Center the group horizontally on the slide.

5. Delete practice slide 7.

6. On the handouts, include the date and your name as header and include the page number and filename *[your initials]*10-11.ppt as footer.

7. Adjust the black and white settings as needed.

8. Save the presentation as *[your initials]*10-11.ppt in a new folder for Lesson 10.

9. Print as handouts, 6 slides per page, grayscale, framed.

10. Close the presentation.

COMMAND SUMMARY

FEATURE	BUTTON	MENU	KEYBOARD
Display guides		View, Guides	Ctrl + G
Nudge up	⊞	Draw, Nudge, Up	↑
Nudge down	⊞	Draw, Nudge, Down	↓
Nudge left	⊞	Draw, Nudge, Left	←
Nudge right	⊞	Draw, Nudge, Right	→
Snap		Draw, Snap, To Grid or To Shape	

USING HELP

If you have trouble with PowerPoint drawing tools, Help is available to show you how to use them.

Use Help to troubleshoot drawing objects

1. Display and activate the Office Assistant.

2. Key **draw** in the text box and click Search.

3. Click "See more..." and then click the topic "Troubleshoot drawing objects."

4. In the Help window, click a topic that interests you, such as "Freehand drawing is hard to control." Click the Back button ⇐ to return to the Troubleshoot window.

5. Close Help when you finish and hide the Office Assistant.

Concepts Review

Each of the following statements is either true or false. Indicate your choice by circling **T** or **F**.

T F   **1.** When an object is selected, pressing ⬆ is the keyboard equivalent of Nudge Up 🔲.

T F   **2.** You can use the Freeform tool to draw both straight and curved lines.

T F   **3.** If a specific percentage is not listed in the Zoom drop-down list box, you can key it in the box.

T F   **4.** You can edit points on objects drawn with the Freeform tool but not on objects drawn with the Curve tool.

T F   **5.** Press Alt while dragging a guide to measure the distance from the guide to another point on the slide.

T F   **6.** You can have more than one vertical guide on the screen at once.

T F   **7.** You can use the View menu to display an object's edit points.

T F   **8.** The Curve tool is available from the AutoShape menu, Line submenu.

Write the correct answer in the space provided.

1. What key can you press to temporarily turn off the Snap to Grid feature?

_____

2. Which menu do you open to turn the Snap to Grid option on or off?

_____

3. What shape is the pointer when you delete a vertex?

_____

4. How do you delete a point from a freeform drawing?

_____

5. How do you display and hide guides?

_____

6. How do you display a second horizontal guide?

_____

7. If you have three horizontal guides displayed, how do you remove just one of them?

_____

8. What shape is the mouse pointer when you are drawing a rounded freeform object?

_____

CRITICAL THINKING

Answer these questions on a separate page. There are no right or wrong answers. Support your answers with examples from your own experience, if possible.

1. PowerPoint gives you many ways to control the size and position of objects on a slide. In what situations do you think guides are the best tools to use?

2. Which drawing tool do you think you'd use most often in presentations? How would you use it? Which tool do you feel most comfortable with and which would you like more practice with?

Skills Review

EXERCISE 10-12

Position guides and align objects with guides.

1. Open the file **SpEvent.ppt** and display the slide master.

2. Display the guides by choosing <u>G</u>uides from the <u>V</u>iew menu (or press Ctrl + G).

3. Position the vertical guide 2 inches from the left edge of the slide master by following these steps:

    a. Point to the vertical guide near the bottom of the slide where the guide is not on top of any object.

    b. Drag the guide to the left edge of the slide.

c. Hold down Shift and drag the guide to the right until you see 2.00 on the guide indicator. Release the mouse button and then release Shift.

4. Add a second vertical guide 1 inch from the right edge of the slide by following these steps:

a. Point to the vertical guide, making sure you see the arrow pointer.

b. Press and hold Ctrl and then drag the guide to the right edge of the slide.

c. Working with the right guide, press Shift and drag the guide to the left until you see 1.00 on the guide indicator.

5. Working on the slide master, resize and reposition both the title placeholder and the bulleted text placeholder so their left edges align with the left guide and their right edges align with the right guide.

6. Position the horizontal guide 0.5 inch from the top of the slide master.

7. Add a second horizontal guide 1.5 inches below the first by following these steps:

a. Point to the horizontal guide, being sure you see an arrow pointer.

b. While pressing and holding both Ctrl and Shift, drag the guide until you see 1.50 on the indicator.

c. Release the mouse button and then release Ctrl and Shift.

8. Move the bulleted text placeholder so its top edge aligns with the second horizontal guide. Then move the title placeholder so its top edge aligns with the top guide.

9. Move the top horizontal guide so it is 2.75 inches from the top of the slide (below the second guide).

10. Add a vertical guide 0.75 inch from the left edge of the slide.

11. Draw a triangle approximately 1 inch high and 0.75 inch wide. Use the Format AutoShape dialog box to adjust the size to exactly these measurements.

12. Align the triangle's top and left points with the left vertical guide and the top horizontal guide, as shown in Figure 10-16 (on the next page).

13. Duplicate the triangle (Ctrl+D) and drag the copy directly below the first triangle so its top point aligns with the second horizontal line (and overlaps the first triangle slightly). See Figure 10-16 for placement.

14. Duplicate the triangle four more times to create a vertical line of six triangles.

15. Group the triangles. Then apply a one-color blue horizontal gradient fill, using the darkest setting, with black at the bottom, and remove the triangles' outlines.

16. Remove the bullets from the bulleted text placeholder.

17. Copy the triangles to the title master.

FIGURE 10-16
Placement of
guides and
triangles

FIGURE 10-16
Placement of
guides and
triangles

18. Hide the guides and view each slide.

19. On the handouts, include the date and your name as header and include the page number and filename *[your initials]*10-12.ppt as footer.

20. Adjust the black and white settings as needed.

21. Save the presentation as *[your initials]*10-12.ppt in your Lesson 10 folder.

22. Print as handouts, 6 slides per page, grayscale, framed.

23. Close the presentation.

EXERCISE 10-13

Use the zoom and snap options.

1. Open the file **FoodGrp.ppt**.

2. Hide the guides if they are showing.

3. Turn off the Snap to Grid option and turn on Snap to Shape by following these steps:

   a. Click D<u>r</u>aw on the Drawing toolbar.
   b. Point to <u>S</u>nap.
   c. On the Snap submenu, click To <u>G</u>rid, if necessary, to turn it off.
   d. Reopen the Snap submenu and turn on the Snap to <u>S</u>hape option.

4. Near the bottom left corner of the title slide, draw a small square. Use the Size tab of the Format AutoShape dialog box to make the square exactly 0.42 inch high and 0.42 inch wide.

5. Copy and paste the square and change the copy's fill color to reddish brown, the accent scheme color.

6. Drag the copy to the right side of the first square. It should snap to the edge of the square perfectly. Zoom to a large size to check its position, and then zoom back to a size convenient for working.

7. Make another copy of the square, this time making it bright orange, the title text scheme color. Position it next to the second square.

8. Make a dark yellow square and position it next to the orange square.

9. Copy the middle two squares and paste them to the right of the dark yellow square, creating a row of six aligned squares.

10. Group the squares. Then copy the group and position it to the right of the original squares.

11. Copy and paste the group of squares two more times, positioning them to make a strip that is as wide as the slide.

12. Turn off Snap to Shape and turn on Snap to Grid so you can precisely size the strip of squares to the width of the slide.

13. Group all the squares. Then adjust the position and width of the strip so it is exactly the width of the slide.

14. Cut the strip of squares and paste it on the title master. Position it between the title placeholder and the subtitle placeholder.

15. Copy the strip of squares to the slide master and move it to the bottom edge of the triangle.

16. Using the Colors and Lines tab of the Format Object dialog box, change the colors to semitransparent (on the slide master only).

17. View the presentation in Slide Show view. Adjust the placeholder positions where necessary to give each slide a pleasing composition.

18. On the handouts, include the date and your name as header and include the page number and filename *[your initials]*10-13.ppt as footer.

19. Adjust the black and white settings as needed.

20. Save the presentation as *[your initials]*10-13.ppt in your Lesson 10 folder.

21. Print as handouts, 4 slides per page, grayscale, framed.

22. Close the presentation.

EXERCISE 10-14

Draw and edit a freeform object.

1. Open the file **Strategy.ppt**.

2. Change the slide color scheme to the one with the green background.

3. Insert a blank slide for practice drawings.

4. Display the Lines toolbar by following these steps:

   a. Click A_utoShapes on the Drawing toolbar.

   b. Point to _Lines and then drag the top of the Lines toolbar to float it.

5. Draw a freeform object in the shape of a mountain by following these steps:

   a. On the Lines toolbar, click the Freeform button 🗋.

   b. Holding down the mouse button as you drag, draw a large irregular mountain shape on the slide. Close up the shape by making the end points meet, as shown in Figure 10-17.

FIGURE 10-17
Mountain shape

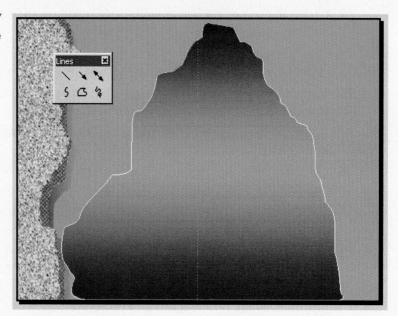

6. Apply a two-color horizontal gradient fill to the mountain using medium green (the background scheme color) and dark green (the shadows scheme color). Choose the lower right shade variant (with the light color in the middle). Remove the mountain's outline.

7. Modify the shape by following these steps:

   a. To display the drawing's vertexes, right-click the mountain and choose _Edit Points from the shortcut menu.

   b. Increase the zoom to view the vertexes more clearly.

   c. To delete a vertex, hold down [Ctrl], point to a vertex, and click the vertex when you see the x-shaped pointer.

   d. To add a new vertex, hold down [Ctrl] and click the mountain's outline at a point between two vertexes.

   e. Reposition the vertexes by dragging them.

8. Change the mountain's black and white setting to light grayscale.

9. Size the mountain to 7.5 inches high and 7.5 inches wide by using the Format AutoShape dialog box.

10. Copy and paste the mountain. Resize the copy so it becomes a smaller version of the original mountain. Move the copy to the right about 1 inch. Group the mountains.

11. Copy and paste the mountains to the title master and the slide master. On each master slide, send the mountains back one step at a time until the title placeholder, subtitle placeholder, and bulleted text placeholder are all visible.

12. Change the texture of the granite slab on the slide and title masters to dark green marble.

13. Delete the practice slide and review the presentation.

14. On the handouts, include the date and your name as header and include the page number and filename *[your initials]*10-14.ppt as footer.

15. Adjust the black and white settings as needed.

16. Save the presentation as *[your initials]*10-14.ppt in your Lesson 10 folder.

17. Print as handouts, 4 slides per page, grayscale, framed.

18. Close the presentation.

EXERCISE 10-15

Draw a curved line, using guides for precision.

1. Open the file **MiamiFun.ppt**.

2. Insert a new blank practice slide and display the guides, if they are not already displayed. (Remember, you can work in black and white view to see the guides more clearly.)

3. Set three vertical guides to the left of the center guide, spaced 1.5 inches from each other. Set up three more guides with the same spacing to the right of the center guide, making a total of seven vertical guides.

4. Move the horizontal guide 0.25 inch below the top edge of the shaded rectangle at the bottom of the slide. Set a second guide 0.5 inch above the horizontal guide. Refer to Figure 10-18 for guide placement.

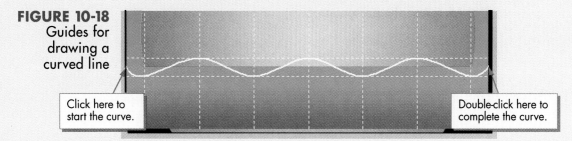

FIGURE 10-18
Guides for
drawing a
curved line

Click here to
start the curve.

Double-click here to
complete the curve.

5. Draw a curved line following these steps:

   a. Float the Lines toolbar and click the Curve button ⑤.

   b. Click the Curve tool crosshair on the left top edge of the shaded rectangle, being careful to click just inside the edge of the slide.

   c. Click again at the intersection of the leftmost vertical guide and the bottom horizontal guide.

   d. Click at the intersection of the second vertical guide and the top horizontal guide.

   e. Continue across the slide, clicking in a pattern to create the curve shown in Figure 10-18.

   f. Double-click just inside the right edge of the slide to complete the curve. Be careful when making the final point to click inside the edge of the slide.

   g. If necessary, display the curve's edit points and adjust their placement. (You can use zoom to see them more clearly.)

6. Right-click the curve and choose Format AutoShape from the shortcut menu.

7. Click the Colors and Lines tab and change the line weight to 54 points. For the line color, choose Patterned lines. Make the foreground color light green and the background blue. Choose the diamond pattern in the lower right corner of the pattern samples.

8. Format the patterned line's black and white setting as light grayscale.

9. Display the line's edit points. If necessary, drag the edit points at the ends of the line out and off the slide until the ends of the line are outside the slide.

10. Copy the patterned line and paste it on the title master and again on the slide master. Adjust the line's position so it covers the top edge of the shaded rectangle.

11. Delete the practice slide.

12. On the handouts, include the date and your name as header and include the page number and filename *[your initials]*10-15.ppt as footer.

13. Save the presentation as *[your initials]*10-15.ppt in your Lesson 10 folder.

14. Print as handouts, 4 slides per page, grayscale, framed.

15. Close the presentation.

Lesson Applications

Use guides, draw a freeform object, and edit the object.

1. Open the file **Summary.ppt**.

2. Delete the graphic shape on the title master and also on the slide master. Delete the black horizontal line on the title master.

3. Add a blank slide at the end of the presentation to use as a temporary work slide.

4. Working on the blank slide, position the horizontal guide 0.25 inch from the top of the slide. Set a second guide 2 inches below the first one. Set five more horizontal guides, starting 1 inch below the second guide and spaced 1 inch apart.

5. Position the vertical guide 0.5 inch from the left edge of the slide. Then set five more guides spaced 1 inch apart, starting 1 inch to the right of the first guide. Place one more vertical guide 0.5 inch from the right edge of the slide.

6. Working with the guides, use the Freeform tool to draw the shape shown in Figure 10-19.

FIGURE 10-19
Guides for drawing a straight-sided freeform object

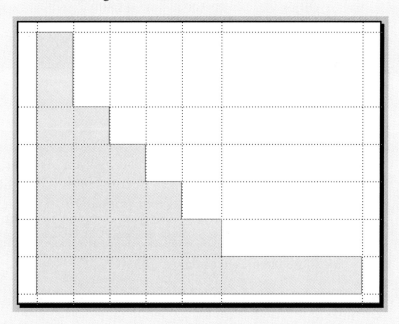

7. Hide the guides and then reposition and resize the freeform shape so its edges extend to the edges of the slide.

8. Apply a 3-point orange outline and a two-color horizontal gradient fill using light blue and pale yellow. Choose the upper left variant with blue on the top and yellow on the bottom.

9. Change the background for all slides to a horizontal two-color gradient fill using the same blue and yellow, but choose the variant that is blue in the middle and yellow on the outside.

10. Copy the freeform shape to the slide master and to the title master. Adjust its position, if necessary, and send the freeform shape to the back on both masters.

11. Delete the temporary work slide.

12. On slide 1, right-align the title and subtitle text. Create 0.5-inch right and left margins for both placeholders. Adjust the text position by moving both placeholders up enough that the text does not touch the freeform object.

13. Move and resize the bulleted text placeholders on slides 2 and 3 if they overlap the freeform object.

14. On slide 4, create a tabbed table using the following information. Use 28-point Arial bold text. Use right-aligned tabs for the "Leased" and "Bought" columns.

	Leased	Bought
Kitchen	15,450	25,350
Dining	14,400	18,650
Office	10,500	25,500
Other	15,250	16,300

15. Add 0.5 inch paragraph spacing between the column headings and the numbers. There should be no extra paragraph spacing before or after the text below the headings. Place the table attractively below the slide title, to the right of the freeform object.

16. View the presentation in Slide Show view.

17. Adjust the black and white settings as needed.

18. On the handouts, include the date and your name as header and include the page number and filename *[your initials]*10-16.ppt as footer.

19. Save the presentation as *[your initials]*10-16.ppt in your Lesson 10 folder.

20. Print as handouts, 4 slides per page, grayscale, framed.

21. Close the presentation.

EXERCISE 10-17

Use guides and draw with a variety of drawing tools.

1. Open the file **MParty.ppt**.

2. Add a new slide for practice drawing.

3. On the practice slide, create a confetti collage by drawing irregular shapes and vertical lines with the Freeform and Curve tools. (You can also try drawing lines with the Scribble tool.) Color the shapes and lines in various colors from the color scheme. Use Figure 10-20 as a guide.

FIGURE 10-20
Confetti

4. Select all the items you drew and group them. Copy the group and flip the copy horizontally and vertically.

5. Ungroup all the confetti items and randomly move, recolor, delete, and copy some of them.

6. When you are satisfied with the composition of your confetti, group it and size it so it extends from the top to the bottom of the slide and is approximately 1.5 inches wide.

7. Copy the confetti to the left edge of both the slide master and the title master.

8. On the title master, move the text placeholders to the right to make a nice composition with the confetti. Center both text placeholders relative to each other. Add a 3-point outline to the subtitle placeholder using a complementary color. Make the placeholder's internal margins 0.5 inch wide on all sides and change its text box settings to word wrap and automatic resizing.

9. On the slide master, set two vertical guides, one 3 inches to the left of center and the other 4.5 inches to the right of center. Reduce the width of both the title placeholder and the bulleted text placeholders so they fit between the guides.

10. Still working on the slide master, change the settings for the bulleted text placeholder to word wrap and resize to fit. Set the margins to 0.25 inch all around and give the placeholder a 3-point outline. For the title placeholder, increase the font size to 48 points.

11. Move to the title slide in Slide view. Increase the title text font to 66 points and change the first line of the subtitle text to 44 points. Move both placeholders up on the page until they appear centered vertically.

12. Hide the guides and delete the practice slide.

13. View the presentation in Slide Show view.

14. Adjust the black and white settings as needed.

15. On the handouts, include the date and your name as header and include the page number and filename *[your initials]*10-17.ppt as footer.

16. Save the presentation as *[your initials]*10-17.ppt in your Lesson 10 folder.

17. Print as handouts, 3 slides per page, grayscale, framed.

18. Close the presentation.

EXERCISE 10-18 *Challenge Yourself*

Use guides and draw decorative freeform shapes.

1. Open the file **Samples.ppt**.

2. Replace all the fonts for the entire presentation with Arial Black.

3. On both the slide master and the title master, ungroup the graphic elements. Then remove the pink horizontal stripe, the green vertical stripe, and the multicolor rectangle shape. Make sure the shaded background remains intact.

4. Change the second-level bulleted text to Arial with no bullet and no hanging indent. Reduce the size of all bulleted text by one font size.

5. Add a blank slide to use for drawing practice. Using the Freeform tool, draw a long, thin irregular shape like the one shown in Figure 10-21.

FIGURE 10-21
Draw this long thin shape.

6. Resize the drawing to 2.5 inches high and 0.4 inch wide. Apply a one-color gradient fill, shading from very dark green at the top to bright green at the bottom. Remove the outline.

7. Position the shape about 1 inch from the left edge of the slide, with the top of the shape slightly overlapping the top of the slide.

8. Copy and paste the shape. Resize the copy to 5.5 inches high by 0.4 inch wide. Apply a one-color horizontal fill, with bright green shading to the lightest setting. Choose the variant with green at the top and white at the bottom.

9. Position the copy so that its top slightly overlaps the original drawing's bottom. Increase the zoom to make sure the objects overlap smoothly. It's okay if the copy extends beyond the slide's bottom edge.

10. Make a copy of the longer object and rotate it 90 degrees to the left. Apply a two-color vertical gradient fill, choosing the pink that follows the accent and hyperlink scheme color and the peach that follows the shadows scheme color. Choose the variant that has pink on the left and peach on the right.

11. Use a guide to position the new object 0.5 inch from the top edge of the slide. Resize the object to extend from the left edge to the right edge of the slide.

12. Group the two green objects and bring the green group to the front. Use a guide to position it 0.5 inch from the left edge of the slide.

13. Group all the objects you drew. Then copy the group and paste it to the slide master. Adjust the position of your drawing if necessary. Bring the title placeholder to the front and move it down enough to clear the drawn objects.

14. Copy the drawing to the title master. Ungroup it and reposition the pink object so that it is centered vertically on the slide. Regroup the drawn objects.

15. Delete the practice slide and review each slide, making adjustments to placeholders as needed.

16. Adjust the black and white settings as needed.

17. On the handouts, include the date and your name as header and include the page number and filename *[your initials]*10-18.ppt as footer.

18. Save the presentation as *[your initials]*10-18.ppt in your Lesson 10 folder.

19. Print as handouts, 6 slides per page, grayscale, framed.

20. Close the presentation.

Animation and Slide Show Effects

After completing this lesson, you will be able to:

1. **Add slide transitions.**
2. **Use text animations.**
3. **Create object animations.**
4. **Add sound and motion clips.**
5. **Add animation effects to a template design.**
6. **Add hyperlinks and action buttons.**
7. **Set automatic slide timings.**

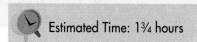

Estimated Time: 1¾ hours

MOUS
ACTIVITIES

In this lesson:
PP2000 **5.4**
PP2000 **5.5**
PP2000 **8.5**
PP2000 **E.1.2**
PP2000 **E.2.5**
PP2000 **E.2.7**
PP2000 **E.2.8**
PP2000 **E.2.10**
PP2000 **E.2.11**
PP2000 **E.2.12**
PP2000 **E.2.13**
PP2000 **E.4.4**
PP2000 **E.4.5**

See Appendix F.

Slide presentations can incorporate a variety of visual and audio effects. For example, you can control the transitions between slides and slide elements to emphasize your material. Presentations can include animated text and graphics, as well as video and audio clips, to catch your audience's attention.

Adding Slide Transitions

A *transition effect* determines the way a slide appears and disappears during a slide show. For example, a slide can appear like vertical blinds or a checkerboard, or it can dissolve from the previous slide. You can control the speed of these transition effects and enhance them with a sound effect. You can also set the time to advance to the next slide or choose to advance manually by using the mouse.

To set transitions between slides, use the Slide Transition dialog box, which you can open in the following ways:

- Choose Slide Transition from the Slide Show menu.
- In Slide Sorter view, use the Slide Transition button on the Slide Sorter toolbar.
- Right-click a slide in Slide Sorter view and choose Slide Transition from the shortcut menu.

EXERCISE 11-1 Create a Transition Effect

1. Open the file **Animate.ppt**. Display slide 2.
2. Open the Slide Show menu and choose Slide Transition. The Slide Transition dialog box opens.

FIGURE 11-1
Slide Transition
dialog box

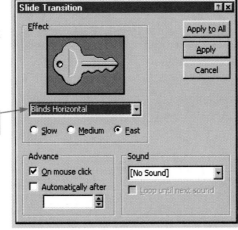

Effect drop-down list

3. Choose any effect from the Effect drop-down list. The selected effect is demonstrated as the picture of the dog changes to a picture of a key. Sample a few other effects and then choose Blinds Horizontal. Click Apply.

4. Click the Slide Show button (in the lower left corner) to display the effect. Press Esc to return to Normal view.
5. Switch to Slide Sorter view. Note that the Slide Sorter toolbar replaces the Formatting toolbar.

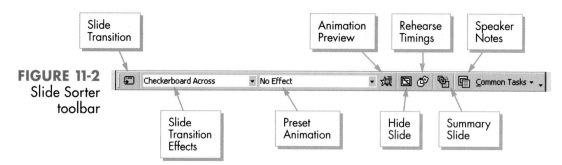

FIGURE 11-2
Slide Sorter
toolbar

6. Click slide 2, if necessary, and then click the Slide Transition button on the Slide Sorter toolbar.

7. In the Slide Transition dialog box, change the effect to Checkerboard Across. Note the effect on the dog picture.

8. Click Slow to control the speed of the transition. Under Advance, choose On Mouse Click, if necessary. This default option means you advance slides in the slide show by clicking the mouse button.

9. Choose Drum Roll from the Sound drop-down list and click Apply to apply the effect to this slide only. The Drum Roll sound will be played when the slide show moves from slide 1 to slide 2.

10. Click the transition icon under slide 2 to see a demonstration of the effect.

11. Select slide 1 and switch to Slide Show view to see your transition operate in a slide show. After slide 1 displays (you'll notice it contains a preset transition effect for the WordArt object), click the left mouse button to display slide 2. The slide appears through a slow checkerboard pattern accompanied by a drum roll.

12. Press Esc or right-click and choose End Show from the shortcut menu.

> **TIP:** Avoid using too many different transitions in a presentation. You want your audience to concentrate on your message, not on your special effects.

EXERCISE 11-2 Choose a Global Transition

You can apply the same transition to any number of selected slides.

1. Switch to Slide Sorter view, if necessary. Choose Select All from the Edit menu (or press Ctrl+A) to select all slides in the presentation.

> **TIP:** You can also select multiple slides by dragging a selection rectangle around them.

2. Open the Slide Transition Effects drop-down list (the first drop-down list on the Slide Sorter toolbar, which is now blank). Choose the Cover Left-Down effect. All slides now have a transition icon under them.

3. Click the Slide Transition button [icon] to open the Slide Transition dialog box. Note that Cover Left-Down is the selected effect.

4. Click Fast, choose Slide Projector from the Sound drop-down list, and click Apply to All.

5. With all the slides still selected, click the Animation Preview button [icon] on the Slide Show toolbar to view all the slide transitions, one after the other.

EXERCISE 11-3 Hide a Slide

Hiding selected slides is a simple way to create a short presentation from a long one. (You may also want to use this feature to hide slides that contain optional or sensitive information.) The easiest way to hide slides is to click the Hide Slide button [icon] on the Slide Sorter toolbar or use the shortcut menu.

NOTE: Hidden slides appear in Slide view but not in Slide Show view. They also print automatically unless you turn off the Print Hidden Slides option at the bottom of the Print dialog box.

1. Click between slides to deselect all slides, if necessary.

2. Right-click slide 3 to select it and choose Hide Slide from the shortcut menu. A box with a diagonal line through it marks the slide number below the slide.

FIGURE 11-3
Slide 3 marked as hidden

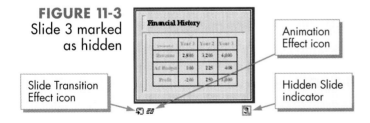

Animation Effect icon

Slide Transition Effect icon

Hidden Slide indicator

TIP: Hide Slide is a toggle command. Choose it to hide a slide and choose it again to display the slide.

3. Select slide 1 and switch to Slide Show view. Slide 1 appears with the Cover Left-Down effect and the Slide Projector sound.

4. Click the left mouse button (or press [PgDn]) to display slide 2. Click again. Slide 4, "Where We're Going," appears. Slide 3, "Financial History," was skipped.

5. Continue viewing more of the slide show or press [Esc].

6. Select slide 3 and click the Hide Slide [⬚] button on the Slide Sorter toolbar. Slide 3 is no longer hidden.

7. Hide slide 3 again.

Animating Text

You can focus attention on individual text elements by using a build effect. To *build* is to display a slide's elements one at a time. For instance, you can make a slide's bullet lines or paragraphs appear one at a time. You can also *animate* elements on a slide, which means to create special visual or sound effects for an object. You can also dim the elements that were previously displayed, so that the audience will pay more attention to the new element.

You can apply text build effects in the following ways:

- Use the Preset Animation drop-down list on the Slide Sorter toolbar.
- In Slide view or Normal view, choose Custo<u>m</u> Animation from the Sli<u>d</u>e Show menu.
- Choose an effect from the Animation Effects toolbar.

EXERCISE 11-4 Apply a Text Build

You can apply a text build to an individual slide or to a group of selected slides.

1. Select slide 4 in Slide Sorter view.

2. Open the Preset Animation drop-down list on the Slide Sorter toolbar and choose Dissolve. (You have to scroll to locate this effect.) Notice that an animation effect icon ≡✐ now appears under this slide.

3. Select slide 1, change to Slide Show view, and click through the slides until slide 4 ("Where We're Going") appears. The slide title appears, but not the bullets.

4. Click once. The first bullet dissolves onto the slide.

5. Click again to display the second bullet. Click again to display the last bullet. End the slide show.

6. In Slide Sorter view, select slides 2, 5, and 6. (Hold down [Ctrl] and click to add a slide to a selection.) You'll apply the same build effect to all three slides.

NOTE: PowerPoint applies build effects only to text objects. If you include a slide with no text object in your selection, build effects do not apply to that slide.

7. Choose Appear from the Preset Animation drop-down list.

8. View the new text build on slides 2, 5, and 6 in Slide Show view.

 TIP: If you want most slides in your presentation to have the same text build effect, apply the effect to all slides and then modify the exceptions.

EXERCISE 11-5 Use the Custom Animation Dialog Box

The Custom Animation dialog box gives you the power to control every aspect of the animation process for text and graphic objects. You can choose which slide objects to animate, which animation effects and sound effects to use, and the order in which you want objects to appear on a slide.

1. Display slide 4 in Slide view and select the bulleted text placeholder.

2. Choose Custom Animation from the Slide Show menu (or from the shortcut menu). Notice the box in the upper left corner of the dialog box listing all the elements on the slide. Also notice the slide miniature indicating that the bulleted text placeholder is selected.

3. Click the check box next to Title 1 in the list box. The slide title in the miniature is selected, and the animation effect Fly From Left is set.

4. Click the Preview button to view the animation that is in effect for this slide.

5. Uncheck the Title 1 check box to turn off the title animation effect.

FIGURE 11-4
Custom Animation dialog box

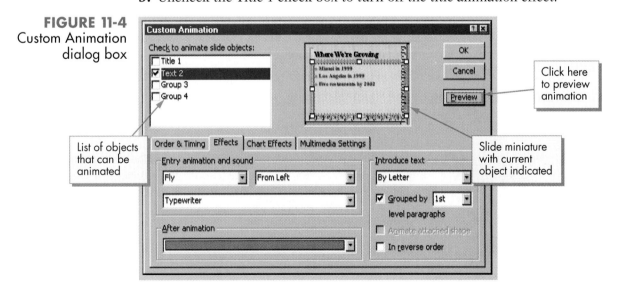

6. Preview the animation again without the title animation. Close the Custom Animation dialog box.

EXERCISE 11-6 **Animate a Text Build**

1. Still working on slide 4, reopen the Custom Animation dialog box.

2. Click the Effects tab, select Text 2 from the list box, and check it, if necessary. The Dissolve effect is already set from the text build you applied from the toolbar in Exercise 11-4 of this lesson.

3. Under Entry Animation and Sound, change Dissolve to Wipe. Change Down to Left.

4. Choose Typewriter from the Sound drop-down list.

5. Under Introduce Text, choose By Letter from the drop-down list. This setting displays each letter one at a time.

6. Choose light brown (shadows scheme color) from the After Animation drop-down list to dim a line of text before the next text build appears.

7. Click Preview to view the animation. If the Animation seems to be slow, uncheck Text 2 and then check it again. The animation should be faster now. Preview the animation again and then click OK to close the dialog box.

TIP: When you choose to dim text after animation, you should select a color on the color palette that makes the dimmed object readable but less conspicuous on the slide's background.

8. Switch to Slide Show view. Click the left mouse button to see the first paragraph appear one letter at a time from the left. Each letter is accompanied by a typewriter sound.

9. Click again. The first paragraph changes to brown as the next paragraph wipes on from the left.

10. End the slide show.

TIP: In Slide view or Normal view, you can click the Animation Effects button ⊠ on the Formatting toolbar (choose More Buttons, if necessary) to display a toolbar with frequently used animation effects. After you become more familiar with using these effects, this toolbar can help you apply settings to slide objects quickly.

Adding Object Animations and Other Effects

In a slide show, you can have objects transition one at a time on the screen, just as you did with text. (Any object, including WordArt, tables, clip art, and AutoShapes, can be animated.) You can also add sound effects and change the order in which the animations appear.

EXERCISE 11-7 Create and Animate an Object Build

1. Display slide 4 in Slide view. Use the Slide Show menu to open the Custom Animation dialog box. Click the Effects tab, if necessary.

2. Select Group 3 in the list box and verify that the ruler graphic at the bottom of the slide is selected.

3. Under Entry Animation and Sound, choose Fly and change From Bottom to From Left. Choose Whoosh for the sound effect. Click Preview.

4. Select Group 4 and verify that the vertical ruler graphic is selected. Apply the Fly From Bottom effect with the Whoosh sound. Notice that three items are checked in the Check to Animate Slide Objects box. Click Preview.

EXERCISE 11-8 Change the Order and Timing of Animation on a Slide

Use the Order & Timing tab in the Custom Animation dialog box to change the order in which animated objects appear on a slide. For example, on slide 4, you can make the rulers appear before the text build.

1. With slide 4 selected and the Custom Animation dialog box still open, click the Order & Timing tab. (See Figure 11-5 on the next page.)

2. Select Text 2, the first item in the Animation Order list box, and click the Down button twice to move the text box to the third position. Select Group 4 (the right ruler is selected in the preview box) and move it down to the second position, if necessary. This is the order in which the animation will occur. Click Preview.

3. Select Group 3 (the bottom ruler) from the list box. Under Start Animation, choose the Automatically option, 00:00 seconds after previous event.

4. Apply the same Start Animation option for Group 4 (the second ruler). Click OK.

FIGURE 11-5
Changing the
animation order
of objects

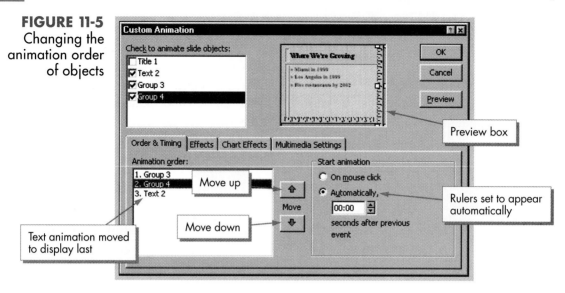

5. Switch to Slide Show view to see the object builds on slide 4. End the slide show.

NOTE: When adding sound effects for transitions or builds, you can choose Other Sound from the Sound drop-down list to apply other sound files available on your computer. Suitable sound files have a .wav extension. To preview a sound file, right-click its filename and choose Play.

Adding Sound and Motion Clips

Besides adding sound effects to slide transitions and animations, you can add sound objects that stand on their own. Sound objects can be set to play automatically, when a slide appears, or on a mouse click. Depending on how your copy of Microsoft Office 2000 was installed, you can find sound clips in the Clip Gallery or on the Office 2000 disk, or you can download them from the Internet. Sound objects can be files of many different formats, including files with the .wav and .mid extensions.

Microsoft Office also supplies many motion clips in the form of animated GIF files. A *GIF* is a picture file format that is well suited for animation. Motion clips are also available from the Clip Gallery, your Office 2000 disk, or the Internet.

EXERCISE 11-9 **Add Sound Objects**

1. Display slide 1 in Slide view.

2. Choose Mo<u>v</u>ies and Sounds from the <u>I</u>nsert menu.

3. Choose <u>S</u>ound from Gallery. The Clip Gallery opens, displaying the Sounds tab.

> **NOTE:** You can find sound files from many other sources (for example, they can be downloaded from the Internet and saved). To insert a file saved from another source, choose Sou<u>n</u>d from File and then find the location where the file was saved and open it.

4. Locate the sound clip "Conveyor Music" by using **jazz** as the search word.

5. Click the Conveyor Music icon and then click the Play Clip button 🎬 on the shortcut menu to preview the sound.

> **NOTE:** Depending on the type of media player installed on your computer, you may have to click a Play button on the player to start the clip, or click a Stop button to stop it, or close the player dialog box to continue with the Exercise.

FIGURE 11-6
Inserting a sound object from the Clip Gallery

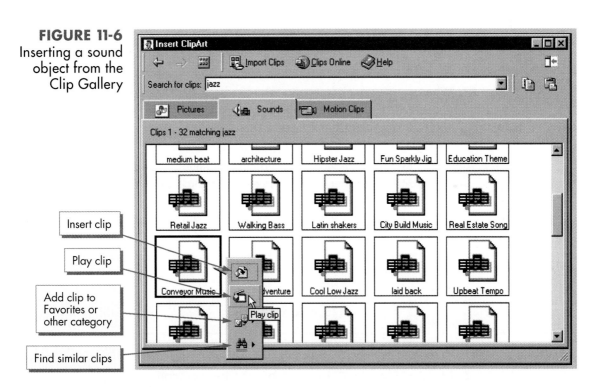

> **TIP:** To save frequently used sound files so you can find them easily in the future, click Add Clip to Favorites or Other Category and choose a convenient location. If the sound file you have found is not quite right for your purposes, click Find Similar Clips to locate related files.

6. Click the Insert Clip button at the top of the shortcut menu and then close the Clip Gallery.

7. Choose <u>Y</u>es in the dialog box that appears, to make the sound play automatically as part of your slide show. Notice the sound object, a small blue loudspeaker, in the center of the slide.

8. Move the loudspeaker to the lower right corner of the slide.

9. Move to slide 6. Click the Insert Clip Art button 🖻 on the Drawing toolbar and then click the Sounds tab.

10. Locate a group of sounds by using **hip hop** as your search words. Choose a sound clip of your choice from the Hip Hop collection.

11. Insert the sound clip and close the Clip Gallery. Choose <u>N</u>o in the dialog box that appears, so the sound will play only when you click the loudspeaker icon. Move the loudspeaker to the lower left corner of the slide, about 1 inch in from the bottom and the left side.

> **TIP:** Use sound files sparingly, to avoid distracting your audience from the message of your presentation.

12. Move to slide 1 and run the slide show. Note that the Conveyor Music sound file plays automatically.

13. When you reach slide 6, click the loudspeaker. The Hip Hop sound clip plays. While the music is playing, press the left mouse button to make the slide's text appear, one line at a time.

> **TIP:** You can make a sound play continuously until you press Esc or switch to another slide. To do this, right-click a sound object, choose Edit Sound <u>O</u>bject from the shortcut menu, and then choose <u>L</u>oop until stopped. Be careful with this option, however, because a continuously looping sound interferes with automatic slide timings.

EXERCISE 11-10 Add Animated GIFs

1. Return to slide 1 in Slide view.

2. Choose Mo<u>v</u>ies and Sounds from the <u>I</u>nsert menu.

3. Choose <u>M</u>ovie from Gallery. The Clip Gallery opens with the Motion Clips tab displayed.

4. Using **soccer** as the search word, locate the image of the soccer player shown in Figure 11-7 (on the next page). When you point to the soccer player image, the ScreenTip shows that the file type is GIF.

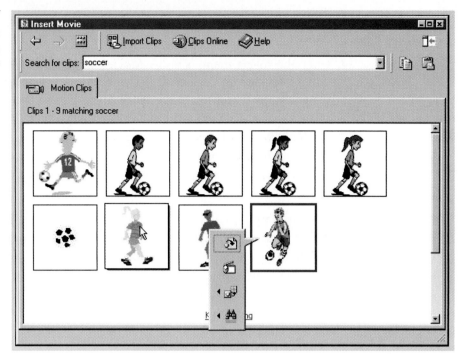

5. Click the soccer player and then click the Play Clip button to view the action.

6. Close the GIF Player window, insert the soccer clip, and then close the Clip Gallery.

7. Move the GIF to the lower right corner of the slide and then resize it to approximately 3 inches tall. Adjust the position of the sound object and the GIF so that the GIF hides the sound object.

8. Copy the GIF to the Clipboard and then paste it in the same position on slide 6.

9. Return to slide 1 and run the slide show. Note that the GIF is now animated.

NOTE: PowerPoint allows only one object on a slide to be animated at a time. This is why the GIF animation is interrupted when the WordArt object appears on slide 1 and when each block of text appears on slide 6.

EXERCISE 11-11 Add Video

If video files are available, they can also be added to a presentation. (Video files can be found in a number of sources, including commercially available

CD-ROMs and the Internet.) To add a video file to a presentation, you would use the following steps:

1. Open the Insert menu. Choose Movies and Sounds, and then choose either Movie from Gallery (if the video file you want to use has been placed in the Clip Gallery) or Movie from File (if the file has been saved somewhere else). Files with the .avi and .gif extensions work well with PowerPoint.

2. Locate the file you want to add to your presentation and click OK. The video file is inserted in the presentation as a PowerPoint object and will run either automatically or on a mouse click in Slide Show view.

NOTE: Video clips come in many different file formats, not all of which are compatible with the media tools that come with Windows. You can download additional media players from the Internet, such as QuickTime for Windows or RealPlayer, to use with video file formats that don't work with Windows media tools. These media players, if properly installed, will automatically work within PowerPoint when you choose a video with a format they recognize.

Adding Animation Effects to a Template

Just as you can animate text, objects, and charts, you can also animate elements of a template. Be aware that some template designs are more appropriate than others. Make sure animation effects add to the presentation without distracting the viewer from the message.

EXERCISE 11-12 Animate a Template Design

1. Display the slide master. Draw a right-arrow AutoShape (Block Arrows) just below the left edge of the title placeholder and color it dark red (the default fill color). Make the arrow 0.3 inch high by 0.75 inch wide.

2. Right-click the arrow and open the Custom Animation dialog box.

3. Apply the effects Fly and From Left and the Laser sound.

4. Click the Order & Timing tab. Under Start Animation, choose Automatically 00.00 seconds. Click OK.

5. Use the Duplicate command to create two more arrows on the left side of the slide just below the title. Distribute the arrows evenly, approximately 1 inch apart, aligning their bottoms just below the title placeholder. Give the second arrow a green fill and the third one a turquoise fill.

6. Right-click one arrow and then open the Custom Animation dialog box. Click the Order & Timing tab. Notice the list of arrows in the Animation

order list box. The animation settings were copied to each arrow. Click Preview.

 NOTE: Controlling the animation order can be tricky when you have animated objects on both an individual slide and a master slide. Experiment by turning master object animation on for each master element (including all text placeholders), arranging the animation order, and then turning off the elements you don't want to animate.

7. Close the dialog box.

8. Display the complete slide show, starting with slide 1, to see the effect of your slide master animation.

Adding Links

Hyperlinks are links from a particular place in your presentation to other slides, other PowerPoint presentations, other applications, and even the Internet. Hyperlinks can make your presentations more adaptable and more useful. PowerPoint also provides a set of *action buttons*—ready-made hyperlink tools that make links easier to use and easier for your audience to understand. Action buttons behave in the same way as hyperlinks, and you can use the two interchangeably, depending on how you want to format a slide.

EXERCISE **Add Links to a Summary Slide**

1. In Slide Sorter view, select slides 2, 4, 5, and 6. (Don't select slide 3).

2. Click the Summary Slide button 📄 on the Slide Sorter toolbar. A summary slide appears as new slide 2, listing the titles of each selected slide.

3. Double-click the summary slide to display it in Slide view. Change the title to **Good 4 U in a Nutshell**.

4. Select the first bullet on the summary slide, "Where We Began," and then choose Hyperlink from the Insert menu. The Insert Hyperlink dialog box opens. (See Figure 11-8 on the next page.)

5. Under Link To:, click Place in This Document (the second icon on the left side of the dialog box).

6. Under Select a Place in This Document, choose Slide Titles and then choose slide 3 ("Where We Began"). A preview of slide 3 appears. Click OK to return to slide 2. Note that "Where We Began" is now a different color and underlined, indicating that it is a hyperlink.

FIGURE 11-8
Insert Hyperlink
dialog box

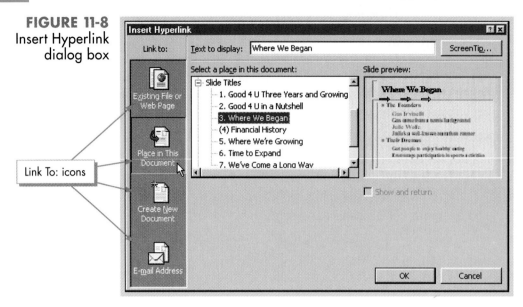

Link To: icons

7. Repeating steps 4–6, create hyperlinks for each of the remaining bullets on slide 2, linking each bullet to the slide with the matching title.

> **TIP:** You can press Ctrl+K to open the Insert Hyperlink dialog box.

8. Select the bulleted text placeholder and apply a text shadow. Remove the bullets to make the hyperlinks easier to read.

9. Switch to Slide Show view and click one of the hyperlinks. The show jumps to that slide.

10. Right-click to open the slide show shortcut menu and go back to slide 2 (Go, By Title, Slide 2). Notice that the hyperlink you visited changed color, indicating you've already been there.

11. Click another hyperlink and then end the slide show.

EXERCISE **11-14** **Add a Link to a Slide Within a Presentation**

Besides adding hyperlinks to bulleted text, you can add them to individual words or a group of words within a line.

1. Move to slide 6 ("Time to Expand").

2. Select the words "Revenue growth" under "Our Goals." Right-click the selected text and choose Hyperlink from the shortcut menu (or press Ctrl+K).

3. Under Link To:, choose Place in This Document. Then choose Slide Titles and then slide 4, "Financial History." Remember, this is the hidden slide.

4. Click the ScreenTip button in the upper right corner. Key **Financial History** in the text box that appears and click OK. When you point to the hyperlink during a slide show, the ScreenTip will appear to remind you of where the link will go. Click OK.

5. Run the slide show. Point to the hyperlink you created and notice the ScreenTip. Click the hyperlink. The presentation jumps to slide 4 (the hidden slide). End the Slide Show.

EXERCISE 11-15 Add a Presentation Within a Presentation

1. Move to slide 6.

2. Select the words "Culinary treats" under "The Plan."

3. Open the Insert Hyperlink dialog box and choose Existing File or Web Page in the Link To: section.

4. Under Browse For:, click the File button and navigate to the place where your student files are stored. Choose the file **Menu3.ppt**. Click OK to close the Link to File dialog box. Click OK again to close the Insert Hyperlink dialog box.

FIGURE 11-9
Linking to an
Existing File or
Web Page

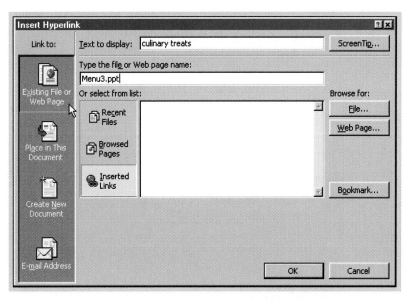

5. Display the slide in Slide Show view. Point to the "culinary treats" hyperlink. Notice that the ScreenTip shows the location of the linked file. Click the hyperlink. The linked presentation appears.

6. Click through a few slides and then end the linked presentation to return to slide 6. End the show to return to Slide view.

NOTE: When linking a presentation, make sure the file being linked is in the correct location on your hard drive, floppy disk, or CD-ROM. Always practice a presentation before delivering it. If the link doesn't work, locate the linked file, using Windows Explorer, and edit the hyperlink on the slide to point to the new location. (Right-click the link, choose Hyperlink, Edit Hyperlink, and navigate to the linked presentation's new location.)

EXERCISE 11-16 Add an Action Button

Action buttons work just like hyperlinks but have different graphics.

1. Display the slide master.

2. Open the Slide Show menu and choose Action Buttons. On the Action Buttons submenu, point to (without clicking) the various buttons and observe their names.

TIP: Use action buttons to move within a presentation, to link to other presentations and applications, to open Web pages, and to play movies and sounds. You can use the blank action button ("Custom") to define your own function for an action button.

3. Choose Action Button: Home from the Action Buttons submenu.

FIGURE 11-10
Choosing action
buttons

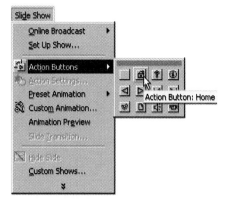

4. Click anywhere on the slide. A large red button appears, and the Action Settings dialog box opens.

TIP: You can also click and drag to draw an action button the size you prefer.

5. In the Action Setting dialog box, click the Mouse Click tab, if necessary. Open the Hyperlink To: drop-down list, choose Slide, and then choose Slide 2, "Good 4 U in a Nutshell." Click OK and click OK again to close all dialog boxes. When running a slide show, clicking the Home button will now return you to slide 2.

6. Change the action button's fill color to semitransparent beige and its outline to dark brown. Size the button to 0.5 inch high by 0.5 inch wide. You format an action button in the same way as an AutoShape.

7. Move the button to the lower left corner, just above the Date/Time placeholder and left-aligned with the placeholder.

8. Switch to Slide Show view and move to different slides in the presentation at random. On each slide, click on the action button you created and note that the presentation jumps back to slide 2.

9. End the slide show and return to the slide master.

10. Add a second action button by choosing Action Button: Return. This button is automatically set so a mouse click links to the last slide viewed. Format the Return button the same as the Home button and position it to the right of the Home button.

FIGURE 11-11
Completed action buttons on the slide master

11. Move to slide 7 ("We've Come a Long Way") and reposition the sound object (blue loudspeaker) to the right of the action buttons. Resize it to 0.5 inch by 0.5 inch.

12. Switch to Slide Show view and move to different slides in the presentation at random, using the Home button, the Return button, and the various hyperlinks.

Set Automatic Slide Timings

Instead of advancing slides manually during a presentation, you can set timings that advance slides automatically without mouse clicks. To set slide timings, enter them directly in the Slide Transition dialog box.

EXERCISE 11-17 Set Automatic Slide Timings

1. In Slide Sorter view, select slide 1 and click the Slide Transition button on the Slide Sorter toolbar.

2. Under Advance, check Automati<u>c</u>ally After and key **6** in the text box to advance automatically after 6 seconds. Note that because <u>O</u>n Mouse Click remains selected, you can still advance the slide with a mouse click.

3. Click <u>A</u>pply. The timing **:06** appears under the slide.

4. Select slides 2 through 6 and set the timing for those slides to 8 seconds.

5. Set the timing for slide 7 to 1 minute (key **1:00**).

6. Choose <u>S</u>et Up Show from the Sli<u>d</u>e Show menu to open the Set Up Show dialog box (or hold down [Shift] while clicking the Slide Show button 🖥). This dialog box allows you to display specific slides in a slide show and set advance options.

FIGURE 11-12
Set Up Show
dialog box

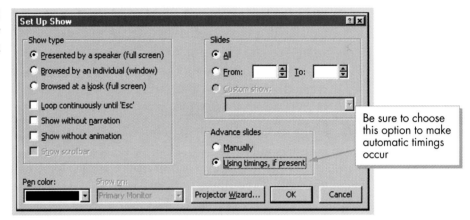

7. Under Advance slides, click <u>U</u>sing Timings, If Present and click OK.

 NOTE: If you set timings, slides do not automatically advance *unless* you activate the <u>U</u>sing Timings option in the Set Up Show dialog box.

8. Choose Slide Sho<u>w</u> from the <u>V</u>iew menu. The slide show begins and advances automatically, using the timings you set. The animations appear onscreen at evenly spaced intervals within the slide timings you set. When you get to slide 7 ("We've Come a Long Way"), click the blue loudspeaker to play the sound while the text build appears.

9. On the handouts, include the date and your name as header and include the page number and filename *[your initials]*11-17.ppt as footer.

10. Save the presentation as *[your initials]*11-17.ppt in a new folder for Lesson 11.

11. Print the presentation as handouts, 9 slides per page, grayscale, framed.

12. Close the presentation.

NOTE: For a self-running presentation accompanied by recorded speech, click Rehearse Timings on the Slide Sorter toolbar to "talk through" a presentation. Your talk is automatically timed and the slide timings are set accordingly. If proper audio equipment is connected to the computer, you can record the voice narration.

COMMAND SUMMARY

FEATURE	BUTTON	MENU	KEYBOARD
Slide Transition	🖭	Slide Show, Slide Transition	
Hide Slide	🖾	Slide Show, Hide Slide	
Custom Animation	🖾	Slide Show, Custom Animation	
Rehearse Timings	🖾	Slide Show, Rehearse Timings	
Set Up Show	Shift + 🖳	Slide Show, Set Up Show	
Hyperlink		Insert, Hyperlink	Ctrl + K

USING HELP 🔃

You learned how to create a summary slide with hyperlinks, in which a hyperlink takes you to a specific slide and another hyperlink (such as an action button) takes you back to the summary slide. A variation on this is an agenda slide. Typically used for long presentations that can be divided into sections, an agenda slide allows you to jump to each section and then automatically return to the agenda slide.

Use Help to learn how to create an agenda slide:

1. Display and activate the Office Assistant.

2. Key **agenda** in the text box and click Search.

3. Choose the topic "Create an agenda slide." (See Figure 11-13 on the next page.)

4. Read the information and then click the hyperlink to learn about creating custom shows.

5. Close the Help window when you finish and hide the Office Assistant.

FIGURE 11-13
Help topic about
agenda slides

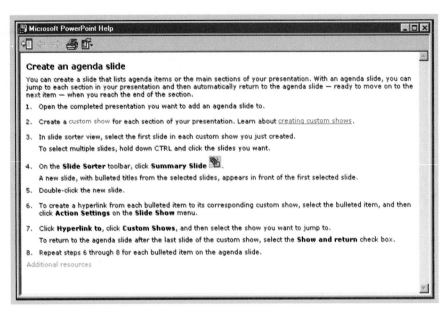

Microsoft PowerPoint Help

Create an agenda slide

You can create a slide that lists agenda items or the main sections of your presentation. With an agenda slide, you can jump to each section in your presentation and then automatically return to the agenda slide — ready to move on to the next item — when you reach the end of the section.

1. Open the completed presentation you want to add an agenda slide to.

2. Create a custom show for each section of your presentation. Learn about creating custom shows.

3. In slide sorter view, select the first slide in each custom show you just created.

    To select multiple slides, hold down CTRL and click the slides you want.

4. On the **Slide Sorter** toolbar, click **Summary Slide**.

    A new slide, with bulleted titles from the selected slides, appears in front of the first selected slide.

5. Double-click the new slide.

6. To create a hyperlink from each bulleted item to its corresponding custom show, select the bulleted item, and then click **Action Settings** on the **Slide Show** menu.

7. Click **Hyperlink to**, click **Custom Shows**, and then select the show you want to jump to.

    To return to the agenda slide after the last slide of the custom show, select the **Show and return** check box.

8. Repeat steps 6 through 8 for each bulleted item on the agenda slide.

    Additional resources

Concepts Review

TRUE/FALSE QUESTIONS

Each of the following statements is either true or false. Indicate your choice by circling **T** or **F**.

T   F   *1.* A dissolve is a transition effect.

T   F   *2.* Only one kind of slide transition can be used in a presentation.

T   F   *3.* You can preview a transition before applying it to a slide.

T   F   *4.* You can change the speed of a slide transition.

T   F   *5.* Action buttons can only be used to move within a presentation.

T   F   *6.* You can set different timings for each slide in a slide show.

T   F   *7.* Text builds can be set in the Custom Animation dialog box.

T   F   *8.* A transition is a special effect that can be used on a slide.

SHORT ANSWER QUESTIONS

Write the correct answer in the space provided.

1. What do you call an object that, when clicked, displays another slide?

_____

2. What do you do first to apply the same transition to an entire slide show?

_____

3. Which toolbar contains drop-down lists for slide transitions and text builds?

_____

4. How do you display the submenu for action buttons?

_____

5. What is the purpose of the 🔲 button?

_____

6. When working in Slide Sorter view, what can you click below a slide to preview the transition effects you applied to the slide?

_____

7. Which dialog box lets you change the animation order of slide objects?

_____

8. How do you set an animation effect to start automatically without a mouse click?

_____

CRITICAL THINKING

Answer these questions on a separate page. There are no right or wrong answers. Support your answers with examples from your own experience, if possible.

1. Which transition effects do you like best, and which ones do you think should be used in a business presentation?

2. Adding sound effects, text builds, and slide transitions to a slide show allows for a great deal of variety. How can you avoid clutter?

Skills Review

EXERCISE 11-18

Create transition effects, text builds, and an object animation; set slide timings.

1. Open the file **Hiring3.ppt**.

2. Create transition effects for slides by following these steps:

a. Working in Slide Sorter view, right-click slide 1 and choose Slide Transition from the shortcut menu.

b. Choose Box Out from the Effect drop-down list.

c. Chose Slow for the speed and click Apply.

d. Select slides 2 and 3 and click the Slide Transition button 🔲 on the Slide Sorter toolbar.

e. Choose Checkerboard Down and Medium, and click Apply.

3. Create text builds for slides 2 and 3 by following these steps:

a. Display slide 2 in Slide view and right-click within the bulleted text placeholder.

b. Choose Custom Animation from the shortcut menu. Click the Effects tab and select Text 2 in the list box, if necessary.

c. Under Entry Animation and Sound, choose the effects Fly, From Top, and Chime.

d. Choose dark gold (the fills scheme color) from the After Animation drop-down list.

      e. Click <u>P</u>review to check the results and then click OK.

      f. Apply the same text build effects to slide 3.

4. Animate a clip art drawing by following these steps:

      a. On slide 1, right-click the clip art object and choose Custo<u>m</u> Animation from the shortcut menu.

      b. Click the Effects tab, if necessary, and choose the Spiral effect.

      c. Click the Order & Timing tab and choose A<u>u</u>tomatically, 00:00 seconds. Click OK.

5. View the slide show beginning with slide 1. Click the left mouse button to change slides and to view the text builds.

6. Apply slide transitions and slide timings to all slides by following these steps:

      a. In Slide Sorter view, select all slides and click the Slide Transition button 🔲.

      b. Open the <u>E</u>ffects drop-down list and choose Fade through Black. Choose <u>S</u>low.

      c. Under Advance, key **14** in the text box to advance slides automatically after 14 seconds. Click Apply <u>t</u>o All.

      d. Open the Sli<u>d</u>e Show menu and choose <u>S</u>et Up Show. Under Advance Slides, make sure <u>U</u>sing Timings, If Present is selected. Click OK.

7. Run the slide show to review your transitions and timings.

8. For slide 1 only, reduce the slide timing to 4 seconds and run the slide show again.

9. On the handouts, include the date and your name as header and include the page number and filename *[your initials]***11-18.ppt** as footer.

10. Save the presentation as *[your initials]***11-18.ppt** in your Lesson 11 folder.

11. Print as handouts, 3 slides per page, grayscale, framed.

12. Close the presentation.

EXERCISE 11-19

Add animation effects to a template design and add action buttons.

1. Open the file **BevSales.ppt** and switch to Slide Sorter view.

2. Hide slide 3 ("Beverage Sales") by selecting the slide and clicking the Hide Slide button 🔲 on the Slide Sorter toolbar.

3. On slide 2, set up a hyperlink to slide 3 by following these steps:

      a. Display slide 2 in Slide view and choose Act<u>i</u>on Buttons from the Sli<u>d</u>e Show menu.

      b. Choose Action Button: Information 🔲 on the Action Buttons submenu.

    c. Position the cross pointer in the lower right corner of the slide and draw the button so it is sized approximately 0.75 inch square.

    d. When the Actions Settings dialog box opens, click the Mouse Click tab, if necessary, and then select the Hyperlink To: option.

    e. Open the Hyperlink To: drop-down list, choose Slide, and then choose "(3)Beverage Sales."

    f. Click OK twice to close the dialog box.

    g. Change the action button's fill color to semitransparent gray.

4. On slide 3, create an action button using the button with the return symbol 🖅. Use the Mouse Click option Hyperlink To: Last Slide Viewed. Use the same formatting and placement you used for the Information button you created on slide 2.

5. Apply animation effects to the template design by following these steps:

    a. Display the slide master. Select the dotted arrow line below the title.

    b. Using the Slide Show menu, open the Custom Animation dialog box.

    c. Choose Stretch and From Left as the entry animation.

    d. On the Order & Timing tab, set the line to start automatically (at 00:00 seconds).

    e. Click Preview and then click OK.

    f. Apply the same effect to the dotted line on the title master.

6. In Slide Sorter view, select all slides (press Ctrl + A) and apply the Wipe Down slide transition.

7. Run the slide show from slide 1, clicking to display the slides and effects. After displaying slide 2, click the Action button to display slide 3, and then continue the show.

8. On the handouts, include the date and your name as header and include the page number and filename *[your initials]*11-19.ppt as footer.

9. Save the presentation as *[your initials]*11-19.ppt in your Lesson 11 folder.

10. Print as handouts, 6 slides per page, grayscale, framed.

11. Close the presentation.

EXERCISE 11-20

Create an object build and a summary slide with hyperlinks, link to a different presentation, insert a sound object and an animated GIF.

1. Open the file **Apparel2.ppt**.

2. Create an object build by following these steps:

    a. Select the hat on slide 1 and ungroup it once.

    b. Right-click the hat and choose Custom Animation.

    c. Select Group 3 and verify that you've selected the hat, not the hat's logo.

   d. Choose the Dissolve effect for the hat.

   e. Select Group 4 and verify that the hat's logo is selected.

   f. Choose the effects Fly and From Top-Left and the Cash Register sound.

   g. Click the Order & Timing tab and select Group 3.

   h. Choose the A̲utomatically option, 00:00 seconds after previous event.

   i. For Group 4, choose the A̲utomatically option, but set the timing to 00:03 seconds after previous event. Click OK.

3. Insert a Summary slide by following these steps:

   a. Switch to Slide Sorter view and select slides 2, 3, and 4.

   b. Click the Summary Slide button 🖿.

4. Create hyperlinks on the summary slide by following these steps:

   a. Display slide 2 (the summary slide) in Normal view and change the title to **Discussion Topics**

   b. Select the first bullet ("Marketing Overview") and choose Hyperli̲nk from the I̲nsert menu (or press Ctrl + K).

   c. Under Link To:, click Pl̲ace in This Document.

   d. In the list box, choose "3. Marketing Overview" and click OK.

   e. Following steps b–d, create hyperlinks for the remaining bullet lines, linking them to the slides with the matching titles.

   f. Remove the bullets from the hyperlinks.

5. Insert a Home button on the slide master. Make the button return to slide 2, "Discussion Topics." Position the button in the lower right corner of the slide master, and format it to blend with the presentation.

6. Create a link to a different presentation by following these steps:

   a. Move to slide 5 ("Launch Strategies"), and select the word "Advertising" in the first bullet.

   b. Open the Insert Hyperlink dialog box. Under Link To:, choose E̲xisting File or Web Page.

   c. Under Browse For:, click the F̲ile button and navigate to the place where your student files are stored. Choose the file **Advert5.ppt** and click OK.

   d. Click OK again to close the Insert Hyperlink dialog box.

7. Insert a motion clip on slide 5 by following these steps:

   a. Click the Insert Clip Art button on the Drawing toolbar.

   b. Click the Motion Clips tab and locate an animated star by using the search word **Star**.

   c. Choose a clip that contains just one small star.

   d. Select the clip and click the Play Clip button 🖥 to preview the animation.

   e. Click the Insert Clip button 🖼 and close the Insert ClipArt dialog box.

   f. Position the star on the left shoulder of the blue T-shirt. Adjust the clip's size if needed.

   g. View slide 5 in Slide Show view to check the animation.

8. Insert a sound object on slide 5 by following these steps:
   a. Open the Insert ClipArt dialog box and click the Sounds tab.
   b. Use the search word **bass** to find a suitable sound clip—for example, Walking Bass.
   c. Click the sound icon and then click the Insert Clip button 🔁 and close the Insert ClipArt dialog box. Choose Yes in the dialog box that opens to make the sound play automatically in the slide show.
   d. Drag the blue loudspeaker sound icon on top of the T-shirt and then send it to the back so it's hidden under the shirt.

9. Run the slide show from slide 1, clicking the hyperlinks and Home button. When you get to slide 5 ("Launch Strategies"), be sure to click the hyperlink <u>Advertising</u> to view the linked presentation.

10. On the handouts, include the date and your name as header and include the page number and filename *[your initials]*11-20.ppt as footer.

11. Save the presentation as *[your initials]*11-20.ppt in your Lesson 11 folder.

12. Print as handouts, 6 slides per page, grayscale, framed.

13. Close the presentation.

Lesson Applications

Animate a template and create slide transitions, text and object animations, and action buttons. Add a motion clip and a sound clip.

1. Open the file **Events3.ppt**. Apply the **Blends.pot** template. Change the color scheme to the one with the royal blue background and then customize the color scheme by changing the pink Accent and Hyperlink color to red.

2. Apply a one-color horizontal gradient fill to the background, using the existing blue background color at the darkest setting. Choose the variant with black at the top.

3. On the slide master and the title master, delete all the graphic elements, leaving only text placeholders, and center the text placeholders horizontally on the masters. Center-align the text in the title master's title placeholder.

4. On the title master, draw a long, thin, right-pointing block-arrow Auto-Shape (see Figure 11-14). Make the arrow the same length as the title placeholder and position it between the title and subtitle. Use the arrow's adjustment handle to make a smaller arrowhead. Apply a vertical gradient fill to the arrow, using the Early Sunset preset. Choose the variant with the lightest color on the right. Remove the outline from the arrow.

FIGURE 11-14
Arrow shape
and placement

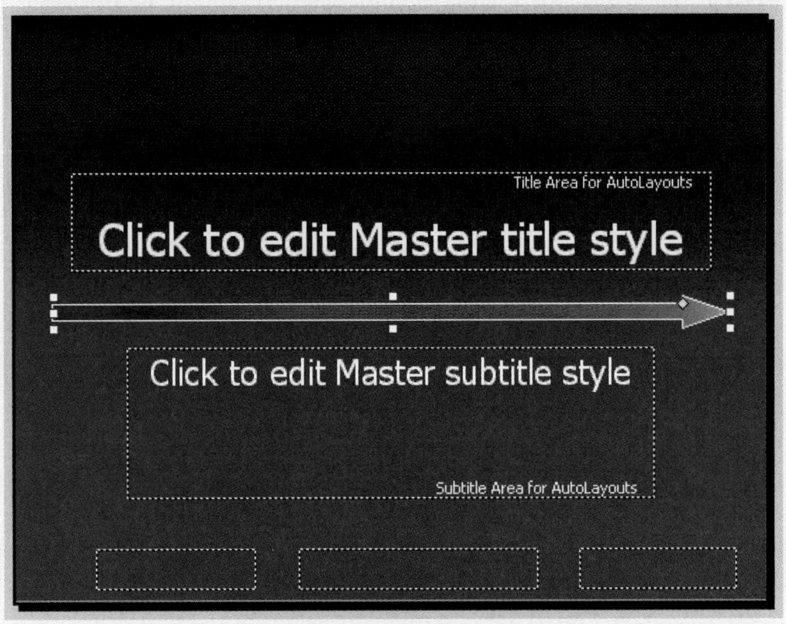

5. Apply the animation effects Stretch and From Left to the arrow, using the Drum Roll sound. Make the arrow appear automatically in zero seconds.

6. Copy the animated arrow to the slide master, and place it between the title and bullet placeholders. (Remember, for precise placement, hold down Ctrl and use the arrow keys.)

7. On slide 1, insert the motion clip of a cross-country skier that you can find with the search word **ski**. Make the skier 2 inches high by 3 inches wide. (Be sure to uncheck Lock Aspect Ratio if you use the Format Picture dialog box.)

8. Insert a sound object of your choice on slide 1. Make it play automatically, and hide it behind the skier.

9. Insert a new slide after slide 3, using the Text & Clip Art layout, titled **Promotional Ideas**. Key the following bulleted text:

- **Think globally**
  - **Multicultural themes**
  - **Environmental events**
  - **Health events**
  - **Sports events**
- **Brainstorm with staff**

10. Insert a globe clip art image of your choice using the search word **globe**. Recolor the globe to harmonize with the presentation's color scheme. Apply the Swivel animation effect to the globe and make it appear automatically. Resize the bulleted text placeholder to eliminate word wrapping, and reposition the text box and globe as needed.

11. Correct the style of the presentation titles, making them all title case.

12. On slide 2, create an Information action button that links to slide 3. Recolor it to suit your taste. Alter the button's depth by using its adjusting handle.

13. On slide 3, create a Return button that links to slide 2. Hide slide 3.

14. To the bulleted text on slides 2, 4 and 5, apply the text build Split Vertical Out, dimming to purple (accent and followed hyperlink scheme color) after the build. Introduce text all at once, grouped by second-level paragraphs. Make the text builds appear automatically, 00:03 seconds after the previous event.

15. Apply the slide transition effect Split Vertical Out to all slides, at medium speed.

16. View the presentation as a slide show. After all slide 2 text is displayed, click the action button to display slide 3. Return to slide 2 and continue viewing the slide show.

17. On the handouts, include the date and your name as header and include the page number and filename *[your initials]***11-21.ppt** as footer.

18. Save the presentation as *[your initials]***11-21.ppt** in your Lesson 11 folder.

19. Print all slides as handouts, 6 slides per page, grayscale, framed.

20. Close the presentation.

EXERCISE 11-22

Create slide transitions and text and object builds, link to another presentation, and create a template animation.

1. Open the file **Contest.ppt**. Change the color scheme to the sample with the blue background, and then change the background fill effect to a one-color blue horizontal gradient fill, moderately dark, with the lightest color in the middle. Replace the Times New Roman font with Arial Black.

2. On slide 1, ungroup the target clip art image and ungroup the three darts. Create the following object builds for the darts:
First dart: Fly From Top, laser
Second dart: Fly From Top-Right, laser
Third dart: Fly From Right, laser
Set the timing for each dart to appear automatically, one immediately after the other. Preview the animation, and adjust the order of the darts, if necessary, so they appear in clockwise order.

3. Copy the red dart and paste it on the slide master. Rotate the dart so it is horizontal, pointing to the right. Reduce the size of the dart by 50%. Move the dart just beyond the right edge of the slide (off the slide), vertically positioned between the title placeholder and the bullet text placeholder.

4. Animate the dart on the slide master with these settings:
Fly From Left, Laser sound, Hide After Animation, and start animation immediately after previous event.

5. Apply the Dissolve effect to the crowd image on slide 3 and make it appear automatically, before any text.

6. On slide 4, remove all the bullets. Apply the Dissolve effect to the food images, making the two images appear immediately, with the sandwich appearing first.

7. To slides 2 through 5, apply the Wipe Down slide transition at medium speed with no sound. Make the bulleted text fly from the top and dim to gray after building. All text animations should appear with a mouse click.

8. On slide 5, create a hyperlink from the words "Power Walking" in the second bullet. Link to the presentation file **Walk6.ppt** on your student disk. Remove the bullets on slide 5 and center the text.

9. Run the slide show to view the animations and test the link to the power walking presentation. Make any needed corrections.

10. On the handouts, include the date and your name as header and include the page number and filename *[your initials]*11-22.ppt as footer.

11. Save the presentation as *[your initials]*11-22.ppt in your Lesson 11 folder.

12. Print as handouts, 6 slides per page, grayscale, framed.

13. Close the presentation.

EXERCISE 11-23   *Challenge Yourself*

Create an object build, animate template elements, insert motion and sound objects, create a summary slide and hyperlinks.

1. Open the file **Mktg4.ppt** and apply the Artsy template.

2. On the title master, ungroup the graphic elements, and apply a Stretch From Right effect to the horizontal bar between the title and subtitle. Make the bar display automatically and immediately.

3. On the slide master, ungroup the graphic elements, and make the horizontal bar between the title and bullet text stretch automatically from the left, and make the bar on the lower right stretch automatically from the right. Make the upper left bar appear first, and make both bars appear immediately when a slide displays.

4. On slide 1, ungroup the four arrows in the lower right corner and use them to create an object build. Make the arrows fly one at a time from the corners of the slide, accompanied by the Ricochet sound, starting with the green arrow flying from the upper left and working clockwise. Make the arrows appear automatically with a 2-second delay.

5. On slide 2, insert a motion clip of a small yellow star that twinkles. You can find it by using the search word **blinking**. Place the star on top of the light bulb that is already on the slide. Use Zoom to place the star precisely.

6. Still working on slide 2, animate both images. Apply the Zoom In From Screen Center effect to the picture of the man and woman, and the Appear effect and Chime sound to the star. Make both appear automatically, with the man and woman appearing first.

7. Create a summary slide from slides 2, 3, and 4. Give the summary slide the title **Agenda**. Create a hyperlink to the appropriate slide for each bullet on the Agenda slide.

8. Still working on the agenda slide (slide 2), apply a fill pattern to the hyperlink text box, using dark gray for the foreground and black for the background. Choose the first fill pattern in the fourth row. Change the margins of the text box to 0.5 inch all around, turn off word-wrap, and turn on Resize AutoShape to Fit Text. Turn off the bullets and center the hyperlink text box both vertically and horizontally relative to the slide.

9. Insert an action button on the slide master that will display the agenda slide (slide 2) when clicked. Format the button to suit your taste.

10. On the handouts, include the date and your name as header and include the page number and filename *[your initials]*11-23.ppt as footer.

11. Save the presentation as *[your initials]*11-23.ppt in your Lesson 11 folder.

12. Print as handouts, 6 slides per page, grayscale, framed.

13. Close the presentation.

Unit 4 Applications

Work with indents, tabs, and line spacing; customize a handout master; add text animations and slide transition effects; and set automatic slide timings.

1. Open the file **JobFair2.ppt**. Change the color scheme to the one on the last row of choices, in the lower left corner. Customize the scheme by changing the background to dark blue, the text and lines color to white, and the title text color to very bright green.

2. On the slide master, increase all text in the title and bullet placeholders by one size and make all text bold. Apply the dissolve animation effect to both the title and the bulleted text.

 NOTE: Don't set automatic timing for text placeholders on the slide master. You will set slides to advance automatically later in this Exercise.

3. Still working on the slide master, change the first-level bullet to a slightly larger Wingdings 2 bullet and make it bright green. Increase the spacing between the bullet and text to 0.5 inch, and change the before paragraph spacing to 0.5 lines.

4. Still working on the slide master, select the Good 4 U logo in the lower left corner and apply an object shadow to it. Choose Shadow Style 6, and change the shadow color to semitransparent medium blue. Nudge the shadow down and to the right a few steps to make it more dramatic.

5. Apply the Fly from Bottom animation effect to the logo. Adjust the animation order, if necessary, so that the logo is the last item to appear on each slide, appearing automatically and immediately after the last event.

6. Open the Clip Gallery (Picture tab) and use the search words **network blitz** to display a group of backgrounds, borders, and buttons. Choose the first picture in the upper left corner, a deep blue pattern with a

FIGURE U4-1 bright green horizontal bar, as shown in Figure U4-1.

7. Insert the picture onto the slide master and resize it to completely fill the slide. Send the picture to the back, forming a patterned background for all the slides.

 NOTE: If this picture is unavailable, apply a background using a horizontal gradient fill, choosing the Nightfall preset with the darkest color at the top.

8. Insert a title master by choosing New Title Master on the Common Tasks toolbar. (A title master is not always automatically available.)

9. On the title master, increase the title text to 60-point bold and the subtitle text to 48-point bold. Arrange both text placeholders in the top half of the slide.

10. Resize the Good 4 U logo proportionally to 8 inches wide. Center the logo horizontally on the bottom half of the title master, above the green bar. Change the custom automation settings for the title master so that all the text appears automatically, immediately after the previous event. If necessary, arrange the animation order so that the title appears first, then the subtitle, and then the Good 4 U logo.

11. Still on the title master, insert a sound clip of your choice. (Try looking in the Entertainment or Music category of the Clip Gallery.) Make the clip play automatically.

12. Using the Custom Animation dialog box, make the speaker object appear before any other animation. Click the Multimedia Settings tab, and make sure that Play Using Animation Order is checked and the Continue Slide Show and After Current Slide options are selected. Send the speaker object to the back, hidden behind the background picture. (If you're using a gradient fill instead of a background picture, hide the speaker object behind the Good 4 U logo).

13. Insert a new slide after slide 2 using the Title Only layout. Key the title **Salary Ranges** and create a tabbed table with the following text:

Wait staff `Tab` **$** `Tab` **8.00** `Tab` **plus tips**

Assistant chefs `Tab` **$** `Tab` **12.50** `Tab` **to start**

Experienced chefs `Tab` **$** `Tab` **17.50** `Tab` **and up**

14. Format the table text as 36-point bold, insert appropriate tab stops, and size and position the text box appropriately.

15. Apply the dissolve animation effect to the table text, making it appear all at once, grouped by first level-paragraphs, and starting on a mouse click.

16. On slide 4, change the slide layout to Title Slide. Arrange the title and subtitle text so they are positioned attractively above the Good 4 U logo.

17. Using the Replace Font command, change Times New Roman to Arial Narrow throughout the presentation.

18. Apply the Wipe Left slide transition effect to all the slides in the presentation, using medium speed and no sound. Set automatic slide timings for all slides to 15 seconds.

19. Review the presentation, making adjustments to text size and text box placement as needed to make an attractive presentation. Run the slide show, and then make changes to the timing of individual slides to slow them down or speed them up.

20. Adjust the black and white settings in the presentation as needed.

21. Customize the handout master by deleting the page number placeholder and adding the text **Job Fair Presentation** to the footer placeholder (after "<footer>"). Center the footer placeholder horizontally, center-align the footer text, and increase the font one size.

22. On the handout header, include the date and your name as header. For the footer, include the filename *[your initials]***u4-1.ppt**. Clear the page number check box, if necessary.

23. Save the presentation as *[your initials]***u4-1.ppt** in a new folder for Unit 4 Applications.

24. Print as handouts, 4 slides per page, grayscale, framed.

25. Close the presentation.

UNIT APPLICATION 4-2

Change page setup options, use drawing tools, set text box options, and use tabs to create a menu.

1. Start a new blank presentation, choosing the Title Only slide layout for the first slide. Set the page orientation to Portrait with slides sized for Letter Paper.

2. Apply the **Post Modern.pot** template. Change the color scheme to the first sample on the second row, the one with shades of blue on a white background. Customize the color scheme by changing the fills color to a deep pink that harmonizes with the other colors. On the slide master, move the title placeholder up to the top of the slide so it overlaps the graphic design.

3. Working on slide 1, key **July 4th Brunch Menu** in the title placeholder. Format the text as 28-point bold, left aligned, with a text shadow.

4. Draw an oval 0.75 inch high and 2.5 inches wide. Make the fill color white and the outline deep pink. Key **Starters** in the oval. Format the text as 20-point Arial, deep pink, bold, with a text shadow. Apply Shadow Style 6 to the oval. Change the shadow color to deep pink, and then nudge the shadow down and to the right to make it a little bigger.

5. Copy and paste the oval. Format the copy as follows:

- Resize to 1.5 inches high and 3.75 inches wide.
- Set text box margins to 0.0 inch all around, turn on word wrap, and set the text box anchor point to Middle.
- Format the text as 14 point, dark gray (the text and lines scheme color). Remove the bold and text shadow.
- Left-align the text and set a decimal tab at the 2.5-inch mark.
- Make sure line spacing is set at 1 line and spacing before and after paragraphs is set to 0.

6. Change the text "Starters" in the second oval to **Red, White, and Blue**. After "Blue," insert a tab and key **3.50**. Press Enter and key **Raspberries and blueberries with a lightly sweetened vanilla yogurt topping**

7. Change the formatting of "Red, White, and Blue" to deep pink, 14 point, bold, and shadowed.

8. Copy and paste the oval three times and change the text in each oval to match the Starter menu items shown in Figure U4-2. Arrange the ovals in an overlapping pattern at the top of the screen, using the figure as a guide and changing the order of the ovals as needed. (For example, bring the "Starters" oval to the front.)

FIGURE U4-2
Slide 1

9. Select all the ovals and copy them to the bottom half of the slide. Change the deep pink text, outline, and shadow of the copied ovals to dark blue, the accent scheme color.

10. In the copied ovals, key the Bread menu items shown in Figure U4-2, and rearrange them, if necessary, so that all text is visible.

11. In Slide Sorter view, copy the slide to make a new slide 2, and then right-align the title text.

12. Select all the ovals on slide 2, group them, flip them horizontally, and then ungroup them, making a mirror image of the placement on slide 1.

13. Key the Main Dishes and Beverage menu items as shown in Figure U4-3.

FIGURE U4-3
Slide 2

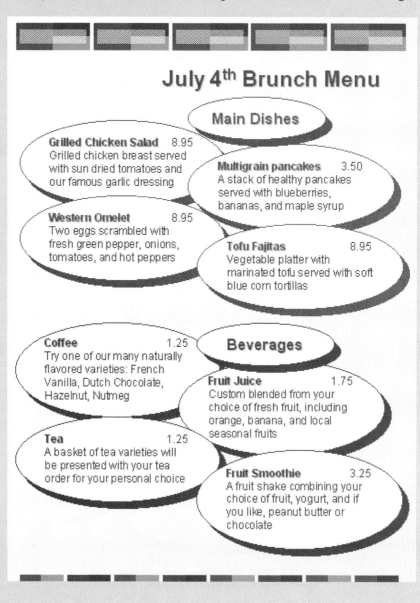

14. If necessary, adjust the height of individual ovals to accommodate the text. Change the order of the ovals on slide 2 to agree with Figure U4-3. For example, bring the "Main Dishes" oval to the front. Rearrange and reorder the ovals if needed so that no text is hidden.

15. Insert a text box in the lower right corner of slide 1 with the text *[your name]*, **Manager**. Format the text as 14-point Arial, dark gray.

16. On slide 1, apply to the background a diagonal-down gradient fill with white in the upper right corner and pale yellow in the lower left corner. On slide 2, create a mirror image of the background, using a diagonal-up gradient with white in the upper left and yellow in the lower right.

17. Check spelling in the presentation.

18. Adjust the black and white settings in the presentation as needed.

19. Save the presentation as *[your initials]***u4-2.ppt** in your Unit 4 Applications folder.

20. Print both pages of the presentation as full-size slides.

21. Close the presentation.

UNIT APPLICATION 4-3

Create a freeform drawing, work with the Snap to Shape feature, change indents, create text and object animations, apply slide transitions, and add hyperlinks.

1. Open the file **Owners.ppt**. Apply the Citrus template, delete all the graphic elements on the slide and title masters, and change the background to the Parchment texture.

2. On the slide master, adjust spacing for first- and second-level bullets so there is 0.5 inch between the bullets and the text. Resize the bulleted text placeholder to 7.5 inches wide, and center it horizontally relative to the slide. Center the title placeholder also.

3. On the slide master, create a custom animation for the title placeholder, making it fly from the left, first, automatically, immediately when the slide is displayed, and with no sound. Create another animation for the bullet text placeholder, making the text fly from the left on a mouse click with a drum roll sound.

4. Insert a new blank slide to use for practice drawing.

5. On the new slide, use the Rectangle tool to draw a 0.5-inch square. Apply a pink, horizontal one-color gradient fill using a moderately light setting, and choose the variant with the darkest color in the middle. Remove the square's outline.

6. Turn off Snap to Grid and hide guides, if they are displayed. Using the Freeform tool, draw an irregular shape that is square overall. Make it as large as is convenient for you. In the next two steps, you resize and position the shape within the square. See Figure U4-4 as a guide to the freeform shape.

FIGURE U4-4
Freeform shape
within a square

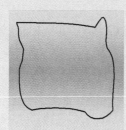

7. When you get a shape you like, size it to 0.45 inch high by 0.45 inch wide. Change the freeform drawing's fill to the stationery texture (similar to but darker than the parchment texture you used for the presentation background), and outline it in green.

8. Drag the irregular shape inside the pink square, center the objects relative to each other, and group them.

9. Turn Snap to Shape back on and move the grouped object to the left edge of the slide, roughly centered vertically. Zoom in on the grouped square object.

10. Using the Duplicate command, along with Snap to Shape and Zoom, create a continuous horizontal line composed of copies of the grouped square object. Group the entire line of objects and size it to the width of the slide, if necessary.

11. Copy the group of squares and paste it onto the title master, positioned directly below the title placeholder.

12. On the slide master, move the bulleted text placeholder down 0.5 inch and paste the group of squares directly below the title placeholder.

13. Delete your practice slide.

14. On slide 3, create a dissolve effect for the table, making it appear automatically, immediately after the previous event.

15. Insert a new slide after slide 4 using the Bulleted List layout. Key the title **The Time is Now** and the following bulleted items:

    - **Talk to other owners**
    - **Review franchise packet materials**
    - **Review financing information**
    - **Submit application**

16. Size the bulleted text placeholder to fit the text and position it attractively on the slide.

17. Using the search words **handshake, bean people**, locate the clip art

FIGURE U4-5

image shown in Figure U4-5. Size and position the clip art appropriately, and recolor it light salmon to harmonize with the slide's color scheme. Animate the image, making it zoom in from the screen center with a clapping sound, immediately after the last event.

18. Create a summary slide after slide 1, listing the titles of slides 2, 3, and 4. Change the summary slide's title to **Discussion Topics**

19. Create a hyperlink for each bulleted line on the summary slide, linking to the appropriate slide with the same title as the bulleted line. Remove all the bullets, apply a text shadow to the hyperlinks, and center-align the hyperlink text.

20. On the slide master, draw a rounded rectangle, 0.5 inch high by 1.5 inches wide. Use the rectangle's adjustment handle to make the shape as round as possible. Apply the parchment fill and Shadow Style 17, making the shape appear as a button. Key the text **Home** in the button and change the text color to gray. Move the button to the lower right corner.

21. Right-click the button and choose Action Settings to open the Action Settings dialog box. Set the mouse click options to hyperlink to slide 2 ("Discussion Topics").

22. Apply the Box Out, Medium slide transition effect to all the slides in the presentation, keeping the On Mouse Click setting.

23. Adjust the black and white settings as needed.

24. View the presentation in Slide Show view, making certain that the action button and hyperlinks you created work properly.

25. Check spelling in the presentation.

26. On the handouts, include the date and your name as header and include the page number and filename *[your initials]***u4-3.ppt** as footer.

27. Format the handout master placeholders as bold.

28. Save the presentation as *[your initials]***u4-3.ppt** in your Unit 4 Applications folder.

29. Print as handouts, 6 slides per page, grayscale, framed.

30. Close the presentation.

UNIT APPLICATION 4-4 *Making It Work for You*

Use text manipulation, drawing options, animations, and hyperlinks to present an idea.

Create a presentation to show to potential investors for a business you want to start. Choose a design template and use your creativity to customize it, or create your own template from scratch. Remember, this is for people who might invest money in your business, so it should look exciting, but don't overdo the special effects. Include the following slides:

- A title slide with the name of your new company as the title and **Business Plan** as the subtitle. Include a suitable sound clip and motion clip that will play until the next slide is displayed.

- A slide with the title **Who is *[Company Name]***. Include clip art and bulleted points describing the company.

- A slide with the title **Expansion Plans**, including appropriate bulleted points and clip art.

- A slide with the title **Why *[Company Name]* Is a Surefire Winner**. Create a series of five identical AutoShapes that contain text explaining why your company is a winning idea (for example, "Untapped market potential"). Change the text options (font, font size, line spacing) if necessary, and add shadows and other visual elements if appropriate. Arrange the AutoShapes attractively on the slide and make sure all the text is readable. Animate the AutoShapes to display one at a time, in a logical order, with a mouse click. Use an effect and sound of your choice to accompany the appearance of each AutoShape.

- A slide with the title **A Winning Team** and a table showing three to five members of your management team, with tabbed columns for each person's name, area of expertise, and experience (their last place of employment, for example). Use two separate text boxes for the headings and the body of the table, aligning the headings appropriately. Change the text and line-spacing options, if necessary, to make the table readable.

A closing slide with the text **Don't miss this opportunity to win with *[Company Name]*!** Place this text inside the same kind of AutoShape you used on slide 4, but make the shape and text larger.

Set slide transitions and text builds, and add hyperlinks you feel are appropriate. Go through the presentation to make certain all the effects work as planned and all the elements are presented clearly and attractively.

On the handouts, include the date and your name as header and include the page number and filename *[your initials]***u4-4.ppt** as footer. Adjust the black and white settings as needed. Save the presentation as *[your initials]***u4-4.ppt** and then print the presentation as handouts, 9 slides per page, grayscale, framed.

UNIT

5

Charts and Tables

LESSON 12

Creating a Chart

OBJECTIVES

After completing this lesson, you will be able to:

1. Insert a column chart.
2. Change sample data.
3. View a new chart.
4. Edit a chart.
5. Format a chart.
6. Add shapes and text objects to a chart.
7. Insert other types of charts.
8. Animate chart elements.

MOUS ACTIVITIES

In this lesson:
PP2000 **E.4.3**
PP2000 **E.10.1**
PP2000 **E.10.2**

See Appendix F.

 Estimated Time: 1½ hours

Charts, sometimes called graphs, are diagrams that display numbers in pictorial format. Charts can help you understand the significance of numeric information more easily than viewing the same information as a table or list of numbers.

Inserting a Chart

When you create a new slide, the New Slide dialog box offers three slide AutoLayouts that include a *chart placeholder*, which is the dotted box that shows the position of the chart on the slide. Two of the layouts include both chart and text placeholders; the third is for chart-only slides.

EXERCISE 12-1 Choose a Chart Slide Layout

1. Open the file **Finan1.ppt**.
2. Choose <u>N</u>ew Slide on the <u>C</u>ommon Tasks menu to open the New Slide dialog box. Notice the three chart options in the second row of AutoLayout samples.

FIGURE 12-1
Chart AutoLayout

3. Click the Chart layout (last layout on the second row) and click OK. A new slide with the chart placeholder appears.
4. Key **Sales Forecast** in the title placeholder.
5. Double-click the chart placeholder. By activating the chart placeholder, you open Microsoft Graph within PowerPoint. A sample chart and sample data appear, along with a new toolbar at the top of the screen with chart-related buttons.

Changing Sample Data

When you open Microsoft Graph, a sample datasheet appears, making it easier for you to understand how to enter your own numbers. As you enter data, you can monitor the results on the sample chart. You key new information by overwriting the sample data or by deleting it and keying your own data.

EXERCISE 12-2 Make Changes to Sample Data

The datasheet contains rows and columns of cells. You enter each number or label in a separate cell the same way you would enter information in a spreadsheet program such as Excel. The datasheet also contains gray column heads and row heads that indicate row numbers and column letters.

1. If necessary, drag the datasheet by its title bar to the upper left corner of the slide so you can see the sample chart. You can also use zoom and the scroll bars to adjust the screen so you can see everything and you can resize the datasheet to make it larger or smaller.

NOTE: When working in Microsoft Graph, be sure to click your mouse pointer only inside the datasheet, within the sample chart, or on toolbar buttons and scrollbars. If you click anywhere else, Microsoft Graph closes and you return to Normal view. If that happens, double-click the chart displayed on the slide to return to Microsoft Graph.

FIGURE 12-2
Creating a chart

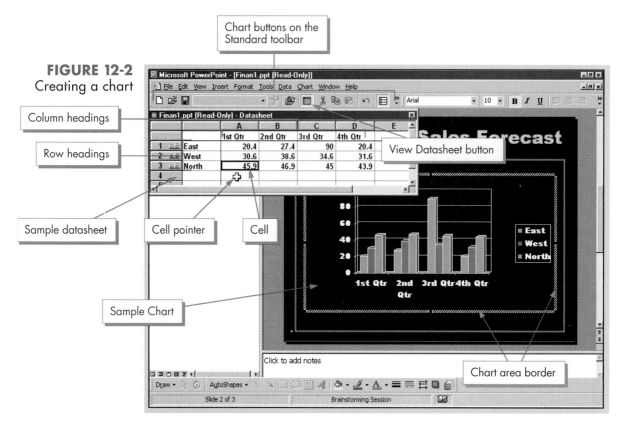

2. On the datasheet, click the word "East." A heavy black border surrounds the cell that contains "East." Notice that when you're working on the datasheet, the mouse pointer is a white cross, called a *cell pointer*.

3. Move around the datasheet by clicking on individual cells. Then try pressing [Enter], [Tab], [Shift]+[Enter], [Shift]+[Tab], and the arrow keys to get the feel for how to navigate in a datasheet.

4. Click cell A3 (the cell in column A, row 3, that contains the value 45.9).

5. Key **90** and press [Enter]. Notice on the chart that the blue column for the first quarter becomes taller automatically.

6. Click [↺] to restore the blue column to its original height.

NOTE: Although you can perform multiple undo actions elsewhere in PowerPoint and in other Microsoft Office programs, you get only one chance to undo an action when editing a chart. Be careful when making changes!

TABLE 12-1	Chart-Related Buttons on the Standard Toolbar	
	BUTTON/NAME	**FUNCTION**
	Chart Objects	Select an element of the chart.
	Format	Format the selected chart item.
	Import File	Import data from a spreadsheet or text file.
	View Datasheet	Display or hide the datasheet window.
	By Row	Display chart data by rows.
	By Column	Display chart data by columns.
	Data Table	Display the values for each data series in a grid below the chart.
	Chart Type	Change the chart type for the active chart or a selected data series.
	Category Axis Gridlines	Show or hide category axis gridlines.
	Value Axis Gridlines	Show or hide value axis gridlines.
	Legend	Add or remove a chart legend
	Drawing	Show or hide the Drawing toolbar.
	Fill Color	Change the fill color or fill effect of the selected chart object.

EXERCISE 12-3 Delete Sample Data

1. Click cell A1, the 1st quarter cell for the East region, with the value 20.4.
2. Press Delete to delete the contents of cell A1. Notice that the first green column in the chart is no longer displayed.
3. Drag the pointer from cell A2 to cell D2 to select the four numbers in row 2.
4. Press Delete. All the dark green chart columns for the West region are deleted along with their data.
5. Click the gray box in the upper left corner of the datasheet. The entire datasheet is selected.

FIGURE 12-3
Editing the datasheet

Click here to select the entire datasheet

6. Press [Delete]. The datasheet is now blank and ready for you to key new data. Notice that the chart disappears.

EXERCISE 12-4 Key New Chart Data

The Microsoft Graph datasheet contains an unnumbered row above row 1 and an unlettered column to the left of column A. This is where you key chart labels that appear below columns or in a legend.

 NOTE: If you key labels in other rows or columns or leave gaps between columns or rows as you enter data, your chart will not display correctly.

1. Click the first cell in the upper left corner. All the cells in the datasheet are deselected. Now you can enter new data.

2. Key the numbers and labels shown in Figure 12-4. Be sure to put the labels in the top row and left-most column. Notice how the chart grows as you key data.

TIP: You don't need to be concerned about number formatting in the datasheet. If you want to align decimals and add commas, however, use the Formatting toolbar, just as you would if you were working in Excel, or choose Number from the shortcut menu. You can edit the contents of a cell by double-clicking it or by selecting it and then pressing [F2].

3. Click the cell with the label "Los Angeles." Notice that the label doesn't fit in the cell.

FIGURE 12-4
Datasheet with
new data

Finan1.ppt [Read-Only] - Datasheet		A	B	C	D	E
		1999	2000	2001		
1	New York	920	1130	1450		
2	Miami	500	850	1210		
3	Los Angeles	350	760	990		
4						

Drag here to increase column width

4. Move the pointer to the right edge of the gray box at the top of the column containing Los Angeles (see Figure 12-4 for exact placement).

5. Drag the two-headed arrow pointer to the right to make the first column wide enough to display the entire label. (The chart will display properly even when datasheet columns are too narrow.)

Viewing the New Chart

After you finish entering data, you can hide the datasheet by clicking its close button ☒ or by clicking the View Datasheet button ▦ on the Standard toolbar. To redisplay the datasheet, click ▦ again (or choose <u>D</u>atasheet from the <u>V</u>iew menu).

To return to Normal view, simply click anywhere outside the datasheet and outside the chart area.

EXERCISE 12-5 **Hide the Datasheet and Return to Normal View**

---

1. Click the View Datasheet button ▦ on the Standard toolbar to hide the datasheet.
2. Click ▦ again to display the datasheet.
3. Click anywhere on the slide, outside the chart area border, to return to Normal view and close Microsoft Graph. The PowerPoint menu and toolbars reappear.

Editing a Chart

After you create a chart, you can easily edit its data, colors, and other features. When Microsoft Graph is closed, double-click a chart in Normal view to edit it.

EXERCISE 12-6 **Edit an Existing Datasheet**

---

1. In Normal view, double-click the chart on slide 2 to reactivate Microsoft Graph. If necessary, display the datasheet by clicking the View Datasheet button ▦.
2. Key **1450** in cell C3 to change the Los Angeles data for the year 2001.
3. Key **2002** in the first row of column D and press ⏎Enter. Notice that a space for new columns appears on the chart.
4. Delete the entry you just keyed. Notice that the space reserved for the new columns remains on the chart.
5. Right-click the column D head (the gray box at the top of the data column with "D" in it) to select the column and open the shortcut menu. Choose Cle<u>a</u>r Contents. Column D is no longer displayed on the chart and the extra space is removed.

TIP: Another way to display or hide a column or row on the chart is to double-click its datasheet column or row head. Double-clicking works as a toggle.

EXERCISE 12-7 Switching Rows and Columns

When you key data for a new chart, Microsoft Graph interprets each row of data as a *data series*. On a column chart, each data series is usually displayed in a distinct color. For example, using the current chart, the New York row is one data series and is displayed in light green. Miami is a second data series, displayed in dark green, and Los Angeles is a third, displayed in blue.

Sometimes it's hard to predict which will be better: arranging your data in rows or in columns. Fortunately, you can enter it either way and switch back and forth.

1. Close the datasheet, which is now complete (but keep Microsoft Graph open).

 2. Click the By Column button on the Standard toolbar (click More Buttons ⁇ if necessary). The chart columns are now grouped by city instead of by year. The city names are displayed below each group of columns.

 3. Click the By Row button ▤ to group the chart columns by year again.

4. Click the By Column button ⊞ again and click outside the chart to return to Normal view. Your chart should look like the one shown in Figure 12-5.

FIGURE 12-5
Chart with
new data

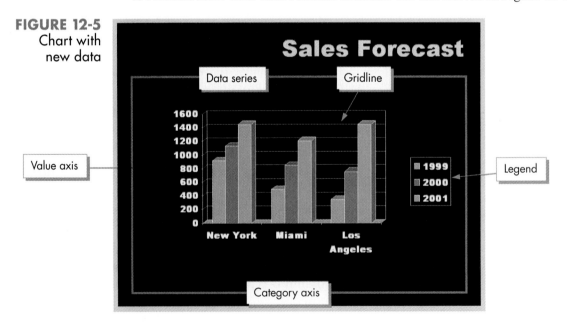

5. Create a slide footer for this slide only. Include the date, and in the footer text box, key *[your name], [your initials]*12-7.ppt.

6. Save the presentation as *[your initials]*12-7.ppt in a new folder for Lesson 12.

7. Print the current slide in full size. If you have a color printer, print it in color.

Formatting a Chart

You can apply a wide variety of format options to charts. The default chart type is a 3-D column chart, but other types include bar, area, line, pie, and surface. You can change the colors, patterns, fonts, and number formats of a chart. You can also modify the position and style of the legend. As you can see from Figure 12-5, the *legend* is the box showing the colors and patterns assigned to the data series or categories in a chart.

EXERCISE 12-8 Work with Colors, Patterns, and Line Formatting

You can change the colors of individual columns in the chart or an entire group of columns. You can even change the background color to achieve a special effect. Other special fill effects—including textures and gradient fills—can be used the same way you use them for other PowerPoint objects. You can also change the outline style of columns, bars, and other chart elements.

1. Display slide 2 in Normal or Slide view.

2. Double-click the chart to open Microsoft Graph. Hide the datasheet, if necessary.

3. Point to one of the light green columns and notice the ScreenTip that appears, identifying the data series. All parts of the chart have ScreenTips to help you select the object you want to work on.

FIGURE 12-6
Fill Color
floating menu

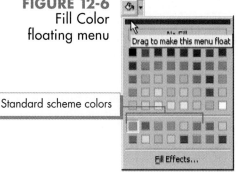

Standard scheme colors

4. Click a light green column. All the light green columns are selected.

5. Click the arrow next to the Fill Color button [icon] on the Standard toolbar to display the color menu. (Click More Buttons [icon] if necessary.) Float the menu by dragging its title bar.

6. Move the pointer across the second row from the bottom, which contains the currently selected color. ScreenTips identify some of the colors as "Standard Colors," which means they follow the presentation color scheme. Usually, the first six colors in this row are standard colors.

7. Click the gold box (the fifth color in the second row from the bottom). The selected columns in the chart become gold.

8. Click Fill Effects on the floating menu. Click the Pattern tab, if necessary. Change the Background color to red, the first color in the bottom row.

9. Choose the Wide Upward Diagonal pattern in the third column in the last row of pattern samples and click OK. The columns are now gold with diagonal red stripes.

10. Select the dark green columns and reopen the Pattern tab in the Fill Effects dialog box. Change the background to bright green (third color on the bottom row) and choose the Dark Horizontal stripes pattern in the fourth column in the bottom row. Click OK.

11. Double-click a blue column to open the Format Data Series dialog box—another place where you can change the fill color or fill effect in a chart.

12. Click the Fill Effects button on the Patterns tab, and then open the Pattern tab on the Fill Effects dialog box. Choose the Wide Downward Diagonal pattern (the third pattern in the next-to-last row), using dark blue as the background color. Click OK.

13. Still working on the Patterns tab of the Format Data Series dialog box, notice the border options on the left side of the dialog box.

14. Click the Border Color down arrow to change the column's border to dark blue. Click OK. With a dark background, the columns look better with a dark border.

15. Using the Format Data Series dialog box, change the border of the green columns to dark green and the border of the red and yellow columns to red. Close Microsoft Graph.

EXERCISE 12-9 Explore Parts of a Chart

Charts contain many different elements you can format. PowerPoint provides several tools to help you navigate around the chart and select the part of the chart on which you want to work.

1. Double-click the chart to open Microsoft Graph.

2. Move the pointer over the words "New York." The ScreenTip identifies this part of the chart as the Category Axis.

3. Using the tip of the pointer, point to a horizontal white line (gridline) within the chart. The ScreenTip identifies this as Value Axis Major Gridlines.
4. Move the pointer around other parts of the chart and try to find the Plot Area, Chart Area, and Legend.
5. On the Standard toolbar, click the down arrow to open the Chart Objects drop-down list. A list of the various chart elements is displayed.

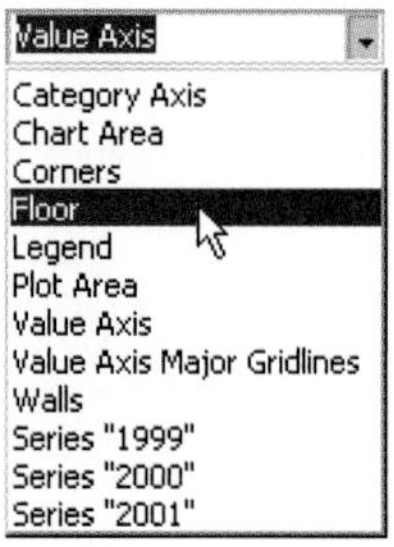

FIGURE 12-7 Chart Object drop-down list

6. Choose Floor from the list to select the chart floor. For formatting, it can be easier to select the chart's smaller elements this way instead of clicking with the pointer.
7. Open the Fill Color floating menu, if it isn't open, and choose Gold. The chart's floor color is now gold. Change the floor color to black.

EXERCISE 12-10 Format the Value Axis

In PowerPoint you can alter the appearance of your chart's axes by changing text color, size, font, and number formatting. You can also change scale and tick mark settings. The *scale* indicates the values that are displayed on the value axis and the intervals between those values. *Tick marks* are small measurement marks, similar to those found on a ruler, that can show increments on the value axis and the category axis.

1. Point to one of the numbers on the left side of the chart. Double-click when you see the Value Axis ScreenTip to open the Format Axis dialog box.

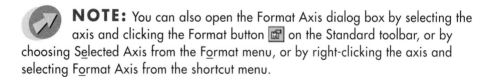

NOTE: You can also open the Format Axis dialog box by selecting the axis and clicking the Format button on the Standard toolbar, or by choosing Selected Axis from the Format menu, or by right-clicking the axis and selecting Format Axis from the shortcut menu.

2. Click the Font tab and choose Arial, Bold, 14 point.
3. Click the Number tab. In the Category box, choose Currency.
4. Click the Scale tab. Clear the Auto check boxes for Minimum, Maximum, Major Unit, and Minor Unit. Instead of using these default values, you set your own scale values in the next two steps.
5. In the Maximum text box, key **1500** to set the largest number on the value axis.

6. In the Major Unit text box, key **500** to set wider intervals between the numbers on the value axis.

7. Click OK. The chart now shows fewer horizontal gridlines, and each value is formatted with a dollar sign, a comma separating thousands, and two decimal places.

FIGURE 12-8
Formatting the
value axis

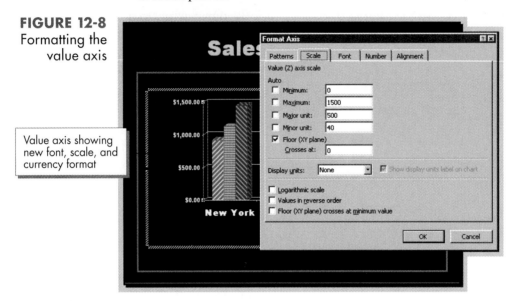

Value axis showing
new font, scale, and
currency format

8. Select the value axis, if necessary, by clicking one of the numbers.

9. Using the Formatting toolbar, click the Italic button I to change the value axis labels to italic.

10. Click the Font Size arrow [12 ▾] and choose 16.

11. Click the Decrease Decimal button twice to remove decimal places from the numbers.

NOTE: Using the Formatting toolbar to change text and number formatting is sometimes more convenient than using a dialog box. For greater convenience and to see all the buttons, drag the formatting toolbar to a new line, or float it.

EXERCISE 12-11 Format the Category Axis

1. Activate the chart, if necessary.

2. Right-click "New York" and choose Format Axis from the shortcut menu.

3. In the Format Axis dialog box, click the Font tab and choose Arial, Bold Italic, 16 point. Click OK to close the dialog box.

EXERCISE 12-12 Insert Axis Titles

1. Move the mouse pointer near the right edge of the chart until you see the Chart Area ScreenTip. Right-click inside the chart area and choose Chart Options from the shortcut menu.

2. In the Chart Options dialog box, click the Titles tab. In the Category (X) Axis text box, key **Apparel Sales**

3. In the Value (Z) Axis text box, key **(thousands)** and click OK. The new titles appear on the slide.

4. Right-click "(thousands)" and choose Format Axis Title from the shortcut menu.

5. Click the Alignment tab. Under Orientation, drag the red diamond up to 90 degrees to change the text to a vertical orientation.

FIGURE 12-9
Rotating the
axis title

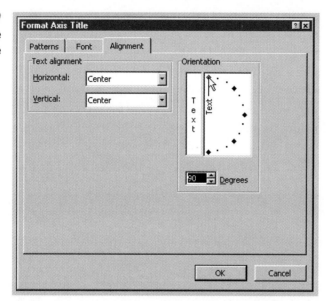

6. Click the Font tab, change the font to 14-point Arial italic, and click OK.

7. Click the Category axis title ("Apparel Sales") to select it. Use the Formatting toolbar to change the font from Arial Black to Arial.

EXERCISE 12-13 Make Changes to the Legend

You can customize the appearance of the chart *legend*, which is the box that shows the colors and patterns assigned to the data series or categories. You can change the style and appearance of the border, set background colors and patterns, and change the size and style of the fonts. You can also control the placement and overall size of the legend.

1. Right-click the legend box and choose Format Legend from the shortcut menu. The Format Legend dialog box appears with many of the same features of other formatting dialog boxes.

2. Click the Font tab and change the font to 16-point Arial, bold italic.

3. Click the Patterns tab and change the border to None.

> **TIP:** If the legend is to be the same color as the chart background, make sure the legend's Area option on the patterns tab is set to None. Choosing a fill color, even if it is the same as the background, can make it difficult to choose readable black and white settings for printing.

4. Click the Placement tab and choose Top. Click OK. The legend appears above the chart in the new font and without a surrounding border. Note that selection handles still surround the legend.

5. Using a right or left handle, resize the legend box to make it wider so there is more space between the legend items.

6. Point to the center of the legend. Using the arrow pointer, drag the legend down until it is below the top gridline and centered above the middle blue column. Adjust the width of the legend if it overlaps any columns.

7. Close Microsoft Graph to view the completed chart.

FIGURE 12-10
Completed chart

Adding Shapes and Text Objects

You can add many interesting effects to your chart. For example, you can add objects that help you make a particular point or highlight one aspect of the data. You can also annotate your charts with text—an especially useful option when your presentation contains a series of related but different charts.

EXERCISE 12-14 Use the Drawing Toolbar in the Chart Window

1. Activate Microsoft Graph, display the Drawing toolbar by clicking the Drawing button on the Standard toolbar, and hide the datasheet if necessary.

2. Click the Text Box button 📖 and then click just above the top gridline on the chart, above the New York group of columns. Key **LA may top NY in 2001** in the floating text box.

3. With the text box selected, use the Formatting toolbar to change the text to 16-point Arial, bold italic.

4. Use AutoShapes to draw a small right arrow. Make it red and rotate it as shown in Figure 12-11. Arrange the arrow and floating text box to match the figure. Close Microsoft Graph.

FIGURE 12-11
Chart with arrow and floating text

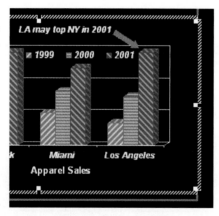

NOTE: You can also draw and add text to the chart in Normal or Slide view.

5. Working in Normal or Slide view, click the chart once to select it. Notice that it has sizing handles. Reposition and resize the chart appropriately for the slide. You can drag the chart and its handles just as you do any other object.

6. Update the filename on the slide footer for this slide only to *[your initials]*12-14.ppt.

7. Save the presentation as *[your initials]*12-14.ppt in your Lesson 12 folder.

8. Print the current slide in full size. If you have a color printer, print it in color.

Inserting Other Chart Types

Pie charts are a simple, yet highly effective presentation tool for showing numeric data as a percentage of a total. Each value in the total is displayed as a "slice" of the pie—the bigger the slice, the larger its percentage.

EXERCISE 12-15 Create a Pie Chart

In this Exercise, you create a pie chart to display the breakdown of the restaurant's sales by category.

1. Insert a new slide after slide 2 using the Title Only layout.

2. Key the title **1999 Sales Categories**

3. Click the Insert Chart button ▥ on the Standard toolbar. (You may need to click More Buttons ⁑.) The sample chart and datasheet appear.

4. Click the arrow on the Chart Type button ◪▾ on the Standard toolbar. The Chart Type drop-down list appears.

FIGURE 12-12
Chart Type
drop-down list

5. Choose Pie Chart, the first option in the fifth row. A pie chart replaces the column chart, displaying sample data.

 NOTE: By default, only the first row of data in the datasheet is plotted in a pie chart.

6. On the datasheet, click the gray box in the upper left corner to select all the sample data and then delete it.

7. Key the data shown in Figure 12-13.

FIGURE 12-13
Datasheet for
pie chart

gl12-14.PPT - Datasheet		A	B	C	D	E
		Food	Beverage	Apparel	Other	
1	1999 Sales	3339	2933	1529	906	
2						
3						
4						

8. Close the datasheet to view the chart.

EXERCISE 12-16 Add Pie Slice Labels

You can add labels to the chart's data series and edit those labels individually.

1. Double-click the chart to open Microsoft Graph, if necessary.

2. Right-click one of the pie slices and choose Format Data Series from the shortcut menu.

3. Click the Data Labels tab, choose Show Label and Percent, and click OK. Data labels appear next to the slices. The percentages represent a slice's percentage of the total. Notice that with the addition of data labels, the legend is no longer needed and the pie is now very small.

NOTE: Depending on the pie chart, sometimes parts of the data labels may be hidden by the edges of the chart placeholder. In this case, you need to resize the pie by using the Plot Area resize handles.

4. Click a data label (watch for the ScreenTip "1999 Sales" Data Labels before clicking). All the data labels are selected. Change the font for the labels to 16-point Arial, bold italic. The pie becomes a little larger.

5. Select the legend box and delete it. The pie becomes even larger.

6. Click the data label "Other 10%" once to select all labels. Click the label again to select only that label. You can now edit this label.

7. Click within the selected label's text to display an insertion point. Select the word "Other" and key in its place **Take-out**

FIGURE 12-14
Pie chart with
data labels

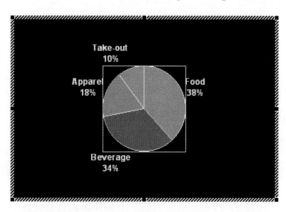

8. Click anywhere within the chart to deselect the label.

EXERCISE 12-17 Format the Pie Plot Area

1. Move the mouse pointer over a corner of the pie chart frame until the Plot Area ScreenTip appears, then right-click and choose F̲ormat Plot Area from the shortcut menu. The Format Plot Area dialog box opens. This dialog box has only one tab.

2. Under Border, click N̲one and click OK. The pie border is removed.

3. With the pie's plot area still selected, drag its lower right corner down to make the pie as big as possible, leaving room within the chart area for the "Beverage" label. Drag the upper left corner up as far as you can, leaving room for the "Take-out" label.

4. Deselect the plot area by clicking outside of it.

 NOTE: You cannot drag the plot area to center it. However, if you resize the plot area from opposing corners, you can center it within the chart area.

EXERCISE 12-18 Enhancing a Pie Chart

You can enhance the appearance of your pie chart with additional effects, such as changing the color of a slice or *exploding* a slice (dragging it out from the center of the pie) for emphasis.

1. Click the center of the pie once to select all the slices. Notice that each slice has one selection handle.

2. Click the Food slice. Six resize handles appear around the selected slice.

3. Use the Fill Color button to change the color of the Food slice to the blue that is the sixth color in the Standard Colors row. Change the Apparel slice to gold and the Take-out slice to red. Note that you can use F̲ill Effects to apply gradient fills, patterns, or textures to individual slices as well.

4. Place the pointer in the middle of the Apparel slice and drag it slightly away from the center of the pie. This is called "exploding" a slice.

5. Return to Slide view. Create a floating text box below the pie with the text **Apparel includes revenue from trademark licensing**. Format the text as 24-point Arial, bold, and center the text box horizontally on the slide.

NOTE: Although you can also insert floating text boxes in the active chart, you will sometimes want to do this in Slide view so you can place the text outside of the chart area.

6. Click the chart to display its resize handles. Make the chart slightly larger by using the corner handles. Arrange the chart so it appears centered inside the green box. Note that because of the exploded pie slice, you will want to offset the chart a little to make it appear centered.

FIGURE 12-15
Pie chart with exploded slice and floating text box

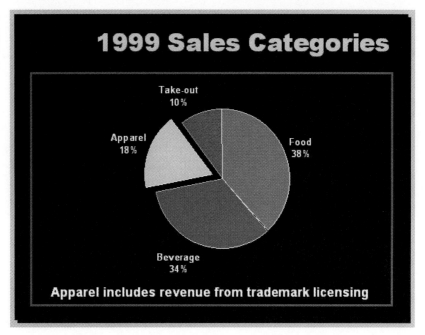

7. Create a slide footer for this slide only. Include the date, and in the footer text box key *[your name], [your initials]***12-18.ppt**

8. Save the presentation as *[your initials]***12-18.ppt** in your Lesson 12 folder.

9. Print the current slide in full size. If you have a color printer, print it in color.

EXERCISE 12-19 Importing an Excel Chart

Besides creating charts from within PowerPoint using Microsoft Graph, you can also import charts created in Excel. To insert an Excel chart, you choose Object from the Insert menu. The Insert Object dialog box gives you several choices, including creating a new Excel chart or inserting a chart from a file.

After a chart is inserted, you can make changes in Excel by double-clicking it. You can also change its colors and size using PowerPoint's Format Object dialog box.

1. Insert a new slide after slide 3 using the Title Only layout.

2. Choose <u>O</u>bject from the <u>I</u>nsert menu. Click the Create From <u>F</u>ile option.

3. Click the <u>B</u>rowse button and navigate to the folder that contains your student files. Choose the file **Apparel1.xls** and click OK. Click OK again. The outline of a small worksheet appears on the slide.

FIGURE 12-16
Inserting an
Excel chart

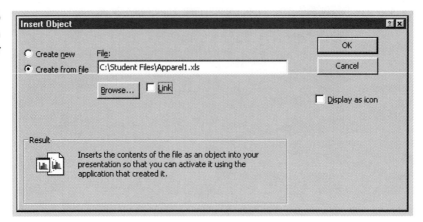

4. Make sure you're in Slide view, and increase the zoom so you can see more of the worksheet.

5. Double-click the worksheet to open Excel within PowerPoint. Notice that the toolbars and menu change to the ones used in Excel. Notice the three sheet tabs at the lower left corner named "Sheet1," "Sales Chart," and "NY Chart."

FIGURE 12-17
Working with an
Excel workbook
from within
PowerPoint

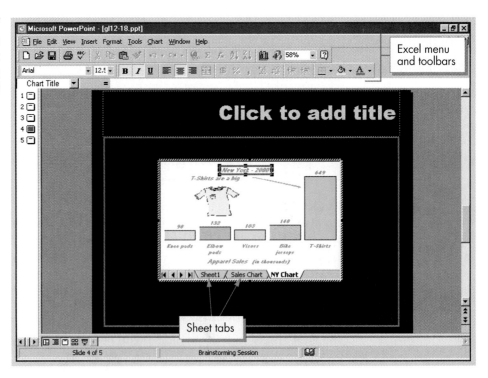

6. Click the NY Chart sheet tab to display the New York Apparel Sales chart. You can use all the tools available in Excel to edit the chart.

7. Click the chart's title, New York – 2000, and press Delete to remove it.

8. Click outside the Excel chart to return to PowerPoint. The chart is now on the PowerPoint slide, but the colors and size are wrong for this presentation.

9. Click the chart to display its resize handles. Size and position the chart until it fills the green frame on the slide.

10. With the chart selected, open the Format Object dialog box, click the Picture tab, and then click the Recolor button. Change the gray text to white, and change the colors of the columns to colors appropriate for this presentation. Use the standard colors and other bright colors. You may also want to change the color of the T-shirt.

11. In the slide's title placeholder, key **New York – 2000**

12. Change the black and white settings for the Excel chart to Inverse Grayscale.

13. Create a slide footer for this slide only. Include the date, and in the slide footer text box, key ***[your name], [your initials]*12-19.ppt**

14. Save the presentation as ***[your initials]*12-19.ppt** in your Lesson 12 folder.

15. Print the current slide in full size. If you have a color printer, print it in color.

FIGURE 12-18
Imported Excel chart

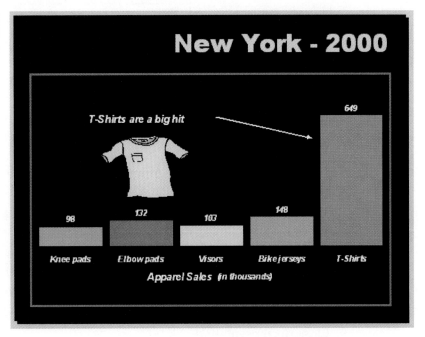

Animating Chart Elements

Just as you animated text placeholders and graphic objects, you can also animate charts to make each data series, category, or pie slice appear one at a time, automatically, or with a mouse click.

EXERCISE 12-20 **Animating a Chart**

1. Move to slide 5 ("T-shirts by Region").

2. Right-click the graph and choose Cust<u>o</u>m Animation from the shortcut menu. The Custom Animation dialog box appears.

FIGURE 12-19
Animating a chart

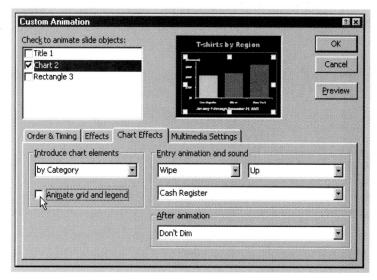

3. On the Chart Effects tab, under <u>I</u>ntroduce Chart Elements, choose By Category. Under <u>E</u>ntry animation and sound, choose Wipe, Up, and Cash Register.

4. Click <u>P</u>review and clear the Ani<u>m</u>ate Grid and Legend check box. Preview the animation again and then click OK.

5. View the presentation in Slide Show view. When you get to the animated chart, click the mouse to make each column appear, one after the other.

6. On all handout pages, include the date and your name as header and include the page number and filename *[your initials]*12-20.ppt as footer.

7. Save the presentation as *[your initials]*12-20.ppt in your Lesson 12 folder.

8. Print as handouts, 6 slides per page, grayscale, framed.

9. Close the presentation.

COMMAND
SUMMARY

FEATURE	BUTTON	MENU	KEYBOARD
Insert Chart		Insert, Chart	
Change Chart Type		Chart, Chart Type	
Insert or remove a legend		Chart, Chart Options, Legend	
View Datasheet		View, Datasheet	
By Row		Data, Series In Rows	
By Column		Data, Series in Columns	

USING HELP

When you click the Chart Type button, you see a menu with 18 chart styles from which you can choose. The Chart Type dialog box offers many preformatted varieties of these chart types.

Use Help to learn about choosing different chart types:

1. Display and activate the Office Assistant.

2. Key **chart type** in the text box and press Enter.

3. Click the topic "Select a different chart type."

FIGURE 12-20
Selecting chart
types

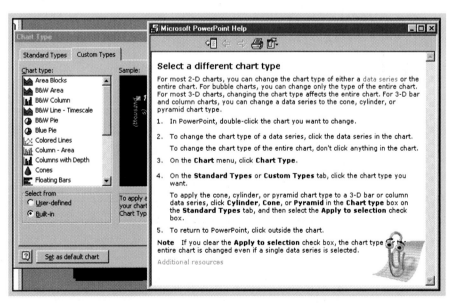

4. Read about the topic and then close Help. Hide the Office Assistant.

Concepts Review

Each of the following statements is either true or false. Indicate your choice by circling T or F.

T F **1.** PowerPoint offers three different AutoLayout choices for slides with charts.

T F **2.** The sample datasheet for a new chart is always blank.

T F **3.** You cannot see the chart while you are working on the datasheet.

T F **4.** You can change the colors and patterns of columns in a column chart to whatever you find appealing.

T F **5.** Double-clicking a pie slice or column allows you to change its size.

T F **6.** Every chart must include a legend box.

T F **7.** The scale on the value axis is set by PowerPoint and cannot be changed.

T F **8.** You can change the number formatting for chart values by using the Formatting toolbar in Microsoft Graph.

Write the correct answer in the space provided.

1. What do you do if you don't want to use the sample data in the datasheet?

_____

2. How do you change the grouping of the data series on a chart from columns to rows?

_____

3. While working on a chart, how do you display the datasheet if it is not visible?

_____

4. What type of number formatting do you apply to values to display dollar signs?

_____

5. In Microsoft Graph, what item on the Standard toolbar can you use to select different parts of a chart?

_____

6. Which button can you click to change the color of a selected pie slice?

_____

7. How can you change the font size for chart labels without opening a dialog box?

_____

8. What are the small measurement marks called that intersect a value or category axis?

_____

CRITICAL THINKING

Answer these questions on a separate page. There are no right or wrong answers. Support your answers with examples from your own experience, if possible.

1. How do you decide if a chart is needed in your presentation? Do you think a presentation can have too many charts? Explain your answer.

2. Imagine you are trying to explain to someone how you spend your waking hours during a typical day. Think of a chart that would break down your activities into different categories and show how much time you spend on each activity during the day. Describe the chart's appearance and the values you would include.

Skills Review

EXERCISE 12-21

Create a new presentation that includes a simple column chart.

1. Start a new presentation and apply the **Bold Stripes.pot** template.

2. For the first slide, choose the Title Slide AutoLayout and key **Financial Summary** as the title and **Good 4 U** as the subtitle. Increase the title text size to 60 points, the subtitle text size to 54 points, and the "4" to 66 points.

3. Insert a new slide using the Bulleted List layout. Key the title **Highlights** and the following bulleted items:

- **Earnings consistently on target**
- **Minimal seasonal fluctuations**
- **Steady increase from previous year**

4. Insert a new slide using the Chart layout. Key **2000 Quarterly Earnings** for the title. Switch to Slide view.

5. Create a chart by following these steps:

    a. Double-click in the chart placeholder on slide 3.

    b. Click the upper-left gray box on the datasheet to select all the existing data and press Delete.

    c. Key the data shown in Figure 12-21.

FIGURE 12-21
Datasheet

gl12-21.ppt - Datasheet		A	B	C	D	E
		1st Qtr	2nd Qtr	3rd Qtr	4th Qtr	
1	New York	1888	2008	2116	1543	
2	Los Angeles	1743	1799	1844	1849	
3	Miami	1634	1439	1783	1469	
4						

6. View the new chart by following these steps:

    a. Click the View Datasheet button 🔲 to hide the datasheet and preview the chart while still working in Microsoft Graph.

    b. Click outside the chart border to return to Slide view.

7. Click the chart once in Slide view to select it and then make the chart approximately 0.5 inches wider and 0.5 inches taller. Adjust the chart's position if needed.

8. On the handouts, include the date and your name as header and include the page number and filename *[your initials]***12-21.ppt** as footer.

9. Save the presentation as *[your initials]***12-21.ppt** in your Lesson 12 folder.

10. Print as handouts, 3 slides per page, grayscale, framed.

11. Close the presentation.

EXERCISE 12-22

Edit and format an existing chart.

1. Open the file **Finan2.ppt**.

2. Edit the chart on slide 4 by following these steps:

    a. Double-click the chart to open Microsoft Graph.

    b. On the datasheet, click cell A2 containing the value "-2%."

    c. Key **2%** in the selected cell to overwrite the current value. Press Enter.

    d. Click View Datasheet 🔲 to hide the datasheet.

3. Change the fill of columns to patterns by following these steps:

   a. With Microsoft Graph still open, click one of the gold columns on the chart to select the Gross Margin data series.

   b. Click the Fill Color ⬛▾ button arrow on the Standard toolbar and float the toolbar by dragging its gray title bar.

   c. Choose Fill Effects and click the Pattern tab.

   d. Change the background color to red.

   e. Choose the Wide Upward Diagonal pattern (third sample in the bottom row) and click OK.

   f. Use the same steps to change the fill pattern of the purple columns to the Wide Downward Diagonal pattern (in the second row from the bottom). Change the pattern's foreground color to light green, the third sample on the second row from the bottom. Change the background color to dark green, the fourth sample on the second row. Close the Fill Color floating menu.

4. Change the outline color of a series of columns by following these steps:

   a. Right-click one of the columns in the Gross Margin series and choose Format Data Series from the shortcut menu.

   b. On the Patterns tab, click the Color arrow in the Border option group.

   c. Choose red (the same color you used for the pattern background). Click OK.

5. Change the outline color of the columns in the Operating Margin series to the same dark green you used for the pattern's background.

6. Change the font for the category axis labels by following these steps:

   a. Click the category axis label "1998" to select the category axis.

   b. On the Formatting toolbar, choose Arial Black and remove the bold attribute.

7. Format the value axis by following these steps:

   a. Right-click a number on the value axis and choose Format Axis from the shortcut menu.

   b. Click the Scale tab.

   c. Key **25%** in the Maximum text box and key **5%** in the Major Unit text box.

   d. Click the Font tab and choose Arial Black, Regular (remove the bold attribute). Click OK.

8. Format the legend by following these steps:

   a. Right-click the legend and choose Format Legend from the shortcut menu.

   b. Click the Placement tab and choose Bottom.

   c. Click the Patterns tab, choose None for Border, and click OK.

   d. Use the Formatting toolbar to change the legend font to Arial Black, regular (not bold).

   e. Increase the width of the legend, if necessary, until it fits on one line.

9. Return to Slide view or Normal view. Resize and reposition the chart attractively on the slide.

10. On the handouts, include the date and your name as header and include the page number and filename *[your initials]*12-22.ppt as footer.

11. Save the presentation as *[your initials]*12-22.ppt in your Lesson 12 folder.

12. Print as handouts, 4 slides per page, grayscale, framed.

13. Close the presentation.

EXERCISE 12-23

Add shapes, text boxes, and animation effects to a chart.

1. Open the file **Finan3.ppt**.

2. Move to slide 4 and double-click the chart to open Microsoft Graph. Hide the datasheet.

3. Apply a different color gradient fill to each column by following these steps:

   a. Click the 1st Quarter column to select the data series. Then click the 1st Quarter column again to select just that one column.

   b. Float the Fill Color menu and choose Fill Effects.

   c. Click the Gradient tab and choose One color. For Color 1, choose purple from the sixth column. Make the shading setting moderately light, and choose the horizontal variant with the darkest color at the bottom.

   d. Click OK.

   e. Use the above steps to apply a gradient fill to each of the other columns, making the 2nd Quarter columns light gold, the 3rd Quarter columns green, and the 4th Quarter columns blue. Use colors that follow the template scheme colors.

4. Change the text formatting of the category axis by following these steps:

   a. Double-click the category axis to open the Format Axis dialog box.

   b. Click the Font tab, choose 18-point Arial Black and change the color to purple.

   c. Click the Alignment tab. Drag the red diamond up to the 30-degree setting. Click OK.

5. Change the value axis formatting by following these steps.

   a. Double-click the value axis to open the Format Axis dialog box.

   b. On the Font tab, choose 18-point Arial Black and change the color to purple.

   c. Click the Number tab and choose Currency with zero decimal places. Click OK.

6. Add a value axis title by following these steps:

    a. Move the pointer near the lower right edge of the chart border until you see the Chart Area ScreenTip.

    b. Right-click and choose Chart <u>O</u>ptions from the shortcut menu.

    c. Click the Titles tab and key **(thousands)** in the <u>V</u>alue (Z) Axis text box. Click OK.

7. Format the value axis title by following these steps:

    a. Right-click "(thousands)" and choose F<u>o</u>rmat Axis Title from the shortcut menu.

    b. On the Font tab, choose 16-point Arial, italic, and choose purple for the color. Click OK.

    c. Select the value axis title, if necessary, and drag it to the top of the value axis, positioning it so that it is centered over the "$160" label. (See Figure 12-22).

FIGURE 12-22
Completed chart

8. Add drawing objects to the chart by following these steps:

    a. Click the Drawing button 🖉 on the Standard toolbar to display the Drawing toolbar, if it isn't displayed.

    b. Click the Text Box button 🗐. Then click the pointer at the top of the chart above the 1st Quarter column and key **New Health Marathon**

    c. Change the font to 16-point Arial Black (not bold).

    d. Click the Arrow button ↘ on the Drawing toolbar. Position the pointer at the end of "Marathon" and drag it toward the top of the 4th Quarter column.

    e. Increase the arrow's weight to 2.25 point.

    f. Close Microsoft Graph by clicking outside the chart border.

9. Working in Slide view, resize and reposition the chart until it fills the space attractively.

10. Animate the chart by following these steps:

    a. Right-click the chart and choose Custo<u>m</u> Animation from the shortcut menu.

    b. If necessary, click the Chart Effects tab.

    c. Under <u>I</u>ntroduce Chart Elements, choose By Category. Clear the Ani<u>m</u>ate Grid and Legend check box.

    d. Under <u>E</u>ntry Animation and Sound, choose Wipe, Up, No Sound, and Don't Dim.

    e. On the Order & Timing tab, make sure the animation starts on a mouse click, not automatically. Click OK.

11. Run the Slide Show to test the animation.

12. On the handouts, include the date and your name as header and include the page number and filename *[your initials]*12-23.ppt as footer.

13. Save the presentation as *[your initials]*12-23.ppt in your Lesson 12 folder.

14. Print as handouts, 4 slides per page, grayscale, framed.

15. Close the presentation.

EXERCISE 12-24

Create and format a pie chart, import an Excel chart.

1. Open the file **Apparel1.ppt**.

2. Insert a new slide after slide 3 using the Chart layout. Key the title **Apparel Mix - 2000**

3. Create a pie chart by following these steps:

    a. Double-click the chart placeholder and enter the chart data shown in Figure 12-23.

    b. Click the arrow on the Chart Type button ![icon] and choose 3-D Pie Chart (the second sample in the fifth row).

FIGURE 12-23
Datasheet for pie chart

		A	B	C	D	E	
		T-shirts	Bike jerseys	Visors	Knee pads	Elbow pads	
1	Unit Sales	4208	1112	528	663	967	
2							
3							
4							

Apparel1.ppt [Read-Only] - Datasheet

4. Format a pie slice by following these steps:

    a. Hide the datasheet.

b. Click the gold pie slice (T-shirts) once to select the entire pie.

c. Click the gold slice again to select the individual slice.

d. Click the Fill Color arrow ⬛▾ and choose ice blue, the last color on the second row from the bottom.

5. Delete the pie's legend.

6. Add data labels by following these steps:

   a. Move the pointer along the outside edge of the pie until the Plot Area ScreenTip appears. Then right-click and choose Chart Options from the shortcut menu.

   b. Click the Data Labels tab and choose Show Label and Percent. Clear the Show Leader Lines check box and click OK.

7. Change the font for the data labels by following these steps:

   a. Right-click any data label and choose Format Data Labels from the shortcut menu.

   b. Change the font size to 20 points. Clear the Auto Scale check box in the lower left corner of the dialog box. Click OK.

   c. Click the "Knee pads" label to select that individual label.

   d. Change its font size to 22 points to make it larger than the other labels.

8. Resize the pie by following these steps:

   a. Select the plot area (left-click).

   b. Drag the upper-right resize handle away from the center of the pie, making the pie as large as possible without hiding "Elbow Pads."

   c. Drag the lower left corner away from the center in the same manner.

9. Format the plot area by following these steps:

   a. Right-click the pie's plot area and choose Format Plot Area from the shortcut menu.

   b. Under Border, choose None and click OK.

10. Explode a pie slice by following these steps:

    a. Select the gold "Knee pads" slice.

    b. Drag the slice away from the center of the pie.

11. Adjust the position of the data labels by following these steps:

    a. Select just the T-shirt label.

    b. Move the pointer to any part of the label border. Drag the "T-shirt" label up and to the left a little, positioning it above its slice.

    c. In the same way, adjust the position of all the data labels to make a pleasing composition.

12. Adjust the position of the chart placeholder in Slide view, if necessary.

13. Insert an Excel chart by following these steps:

    a. Insert a new slide after slide 4 using the Title Only layout. Key the title **Apparel Sales - 2000** *b.* Choose <u>O</u>bject from the <u>I</u>nsert menu to open the Insert Object dialog box.

    c. Choose Create From <u>F</u>ile, click <u>B</u>rowse, and locate the folder containing your student files. Choose the file **Apparel1.xls** and click OK.

    d. Double-click the spreadsheet image on the slide to open Excel. If necessary, use Zoom to enlarge the view of the Excel object.

    e. Click the sheet tab with the caption "Sales Chart" to display the column chart.

    f. Click the title "Apparel Sales - 2000." Press Delete to remove it.

    g. Click anywhere outside the Excel object to return to PowerPoint.

14. Format the imported chart by following these steps:

    a. Right-click the chart and choose Format <u>O</u>bject from the shortcut menu. Click the Picture tab and then click <u>R</u>ecolor.

    b. Change the gray sample to black. Change the colors of the columns to colors from the template's color scheme. Close the Format Object dialog box when the colors are completed.

    c. Resize and reposition the chart object to fit the slide.

15. On the handouts, include the date and your name as header and include the page number and filename *[your initials]*12-24.ppt as footer.

16. Save the presentation as *[your initials]*12-24.ppt in your Lesson 12 folder.

17. Print as handouts, 6 per page, grayscale, framed.

18. Close the presentation.

Lesson Applications

Create a presentation containing a column chart and format the chart.

1. Start a new presentation and apply the **Fireball.pot** template.

2. On the title slide, key the title **Three Years of Phenomenal Sales** and the subtitle **Good *4 U*.** Increase the subtitle text to 48 points and the "*4*" to two sizes larger.

3. Create a bulleted text slide with the title **Highlights** and the following bulleted text:

- **New York revenue still increasing**
- **Miami and Los Angeles meeting goals**
- **Revenues reach 120% of budget**

4. Insert a new slide after slide 2 using the Chart layout. Key the title **Sales by Region – 1998 to 2000**

5. Create a column chart using the data shown in Figure 12-24.

FIGURE 12-24
Datasheet for
chart

▦ Presentation2 - Datasheet		A	B	C	D ▲
		1998	1999	2000	
1 ▱	New York	5650	8753	11332	
2 ▱	Los Angeles	4183	5892	9852	
3 ▱	Miami	3843	6388	8487	
4					▼

6. Change the value axis scale settings to have a maximum of 12,000 and a major unit of 3,000.

7. Change the font for the value axis, category axis, and legend to 16-point Tahoma, bold. (Use Arial if your computer doesn't have Tahoma). Change the number format of the value axis to currency, no decimals.

8. Apply a one-color horizontal gradient fill to each column, shading from the column's original color at the top to dark at the bottom. Make the outline for each column black.

9. Change the floor color of the chart to black.

 TIP: Use the Chart Objects drop-down list on the Standard toolbar to select the floor.

10. Move the legend to the bottom and remove its border. Resize it, if necessary.

11. In Slide view, reposition and resize the chart to create an attractive layout.

12. On the handouts, include the date and your name as header and include the page number and filename *[your initials]*12-25.ppt as footer.

13. Save the presentation as *[your initials]*12-25.ppt in your Lesson 12 folder.

14. Print as handouts, 3 slides per page, grayscale, framed.

15. Close the presentation.

Insert a chart; change the chart type; format the chart text, data series, and legend; and add an AutoShape.

1. Open the file **Earnings1.ppt** and apply the **Construction.pot** template. On the slide master, change the first-level bullet to a bullet of your choice. Change the bullet color if you like.

2. Insert a new slide between slides 2 and 3 using the Chart layout and the title **Gross Income**

3. On the new slide, create a column chart using the following data:

	1998	1999	2000
San Francisco	1246	2033	5432
Miami	2734	4630	6325
Los Angeles	2871	4126	7235
New York	3566	5135	7555

4. Change the chart type to a one-dimensional column chart. (Click the Chart Type arrow and choose the first chart type in the third row.)

5. Change the font for the value axis, category axis, and legend to 16-point Impact. Remove the bold attribute if necessary. (Use Arial if Impact is not available,)

6. Apply a one-color horizontal gradient fill to each column, shading from the column's original color at the top to a medium dark shade at the bottom. Remove the border from each column.

7. Change the number format of the value axis to currency with no decimal places and change the scale settings so the values are displayed at intervals of 2000.

8. Add a value axis title with the text **(thousands)** and rotate it to the 90-degree position, if necessary. Format the text as 14-point Arial (not Impact), italic.

9. Move the legend to the bottom of the chart and remove its border. Resize the legend to be as wide as the chart's category axis and adjust its position, if necessary.

10. In Slide view, adjust the chart's size and position as needed.

11. Centered above the chart, create a text box containing the text **Impressive!** Change the font to 24-point Impact or Arial. Draw a small, white 5-point star and place it on the upper left corner of the San Francisco column for the year 2000. Draw a line from the text box to the star.

12. On the handouts, include the date and your name as header and include the page number and filename *[your initials]*12-26.ppt as footer.

13. Save the presentation as *[your initials]*12-26.ppt in your Lesson 12 folder.

14. Print as handouts, 4 slides per page, grayscale, framed.

15. Close the presentation.

EXERCISE 12-27 *Challenge Yourself*

Create a presentation with an animated pie chart and hyperlinks, using a customized template.

1. Open the file **Expense1.ppt**. Apply the **Fireball.pot** template.

2. Create a custom color scheme by changing the current background scheme color to medium blue (use the color that is third from the right in the top row of the Standard color honeycomb).

3. Change the presentation's background to a one-color gradient fill, using the medium blue background scheme color, the Fro<u>m</u> Title style, and darker shading at the edges.

4. On the title master, ungroup the fireball graphic and delete all graphic objects except the horizontal bar.

5. On the slide master, delete the entire fireball graphic. Center-align the title placeholder text.

6. Change the font to Arial for the entire presentation.

7. Near the top of the title master, draw a constrained five-point star that is 0.75 inch high. Apply a two-color vertical gradient fill of orange and blue with orange on the left side. Remove the star's outline.

8. Move the star to the left end of the horizontal bar and use the Duplicate command to make a string of stars across the bar, leaving some space between the stars. Adjust the position of the right-most star to cover the

right edge of the bar. Use the Align and Distribute commands to space the stars evenly and in a straight row, on top of the bar.

9. Group the stars and the horizontal bar, center the group horizontally, and copy the group to the slide master, placing it between the two text placeholders. Adjust the size of the placeholders to accommodate the stars.

10. Insert a new slide after slide 1 using the Chart layout. Key the title **Expense Breakdown**

11. On the new slide 2, create a one-dimensional pie chart using the following data:

	Food	Payroll	Depreciation	Lease
2000 Expenses	2190	1813	577	1737

12. Change the pie slices' outlines to black and add data labels to the chart, shown as percentages only. Select each percentage individually and drag it onto its pie slice.

13. Remove the pie's plot area border.

14. Increase the legend font to 22 points and remove the legend's border.

15. Resize the pie as large as it can be and still fit inside the chart border. Change the data label font size to 22 points.

16. In Slide view, adjust the position of the pie chart as needed.

17. Ungroup the pie chart and then group each data label with its pie slice. Animate each pie slice to fly from the appropriate edge of the slide, one at a time, with the cash register sound. Make the slices appear in clockwise order, starting with the gold food slice. Make them appear with a mouse click.

18. Turn each legend label into a hyperlink, linking Food to the Food & Beverages slide, Payroll to the Payroll & Benefits slide, and so on.

19. To make the hyperlink text more readable, change the presentation's Accent and Hyperlink scheme color to a lighter shade of pink.

20. On the slide master, create a home button that links to the slide with the pie chart. Format the button as you like.

21. Resize and center the bulleted text placeholders throughout the presentation.

22. On the handouts, include the date and your name as header and include the page number and filename *[your initials]*12-27.ppt as footer.

23. Save as *[your initials]*12-27.ppt in your Lesson 12 folder.

24. Print as handouts, 6 slides per page, grayscale, framed.

25. Close the presentation.

Creating a Table

OBJECTIVES

After completing this lesson, you will be able to:

1. Create a table.
2. Key text in a table.
3. Select a table, table cells, and table text.
4. Format a table.
5. Align text and numbers in a table.
6. Change the height and width of rows, columns, and tables.
7. Insert and delete rows, columns, and individual cells.
8. Insert a Microsoft Word table.

MOUS
ACTIVITIES
In this lesson:
PP2000 **4.6**
PP2000 **E.3.2**
PP2000 **E.4.2**
PP2000 **E.10.5**

See Appendix F.

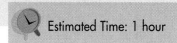 Estimated Time: 1 hour

An effective way to show information on a slide is to present it in the form of a table. A *table* displays information organized in rows and columns. This information can be numbers, text, or both. If you are familiar with using tables in Microsoft Word, you will find that working with PowerPoint tables is very similar.

Creating a Table

There are several ways to insert a new table in a presentation:

- Use the Table AutoLayout.
- Choose Ta<u>b</u>le from the <u>I</u>nsert menu.

- Click the Insert Table button  on the Standard toolbar (click More Buttons to find it).

- Click the Draw Table button  on the Tables and Borders toolbar and draw a table with the pencil pointer.

EXERCISE **13-1** **Start a Table**

When you insert a new table on a slide you are asked to define the number of columns and rows that the table will contain. It's a good idea to have a general layout planned when you start a table, but it's easy to insert or delete rows and columns later if you change your mind.

FIGURE 13-1
Table AutoLayout

1. Open the file **Manage1.ppt**. Insert a new slide after slide 2, choosing the Table AutoLayout in the first row of layout choices.

2. Key the title **Employment Levels, 2000**

3. Double-click the table placeholder to insert the new table. The Insert Table dialog box appears.

4. Change the Number of <u>C</u>olumns to **4** and the Number of <u>R</u>ows to **3**. Click OK. A blank table appears on the slide. Notice that the mouse pointer is now a pencil and the Tables and Borders toolbar appears. Drag this toolbar to the upper left corner of the screen, away from the table.

  NOTE: If the Tables and Borders toolbar is not displayed, click the Tables and Borders button on the Standard toolbar.

5. Click the Draw Table button  on the Tables and Borders toolbar to turn off the pencil pointer. (You can also turn off the pencil pointer by pressing [Esc]).

 TIP: The pencil pointer can be used to draw additional lines on the table to create more rows or columns or to split a cell into two or more cells.

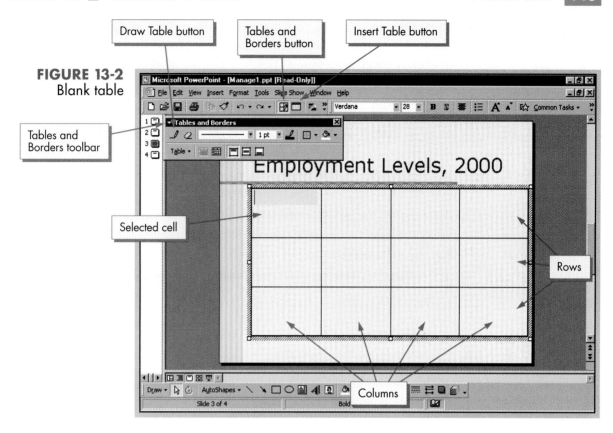

FIGURE 13-2
Blank table

Keying Text in a Table

You enter text in a new table just as you would in a spreadsheet. Each piece of information is entered in a *cell*—the box formed by the intersection of a row and a column.

EXERCISE 13-2 Practice Navigating in a Table

1. Click a cell in the second row. Notice that the blinking insertion point indicates the active cell.

2. Press Tab to move to the next cell. This is a keyboard method for moving around the table. (You can also move to a new cell by clicking the cell with your mouse).

3. Press Shift + Tab to move to the preceding cell. Press ↑ and then press ↓ to move up and down in the table. Press ← and → a few times.

4. Press Enter to go to the next line within the cell. Press Enter twice more. The row with the active cell grows. Press Backspace three times. The row returns to its original size. If you press Enter by accident, remove the extra line by pressing Backspace.

EXERCISE 13-3 Key Text in a Table

1. Move to the first cell in the second row. Key **Full-time employees**. Notice that the text wraps to three lines automatically.

2. Double-click the word "employees" to select it and then press Delete. Editing a table cell is similar to editing other PowerPoint text.

3. Key the table text shown in Figure 13-3.

FIGURE 13-3
Text in a table

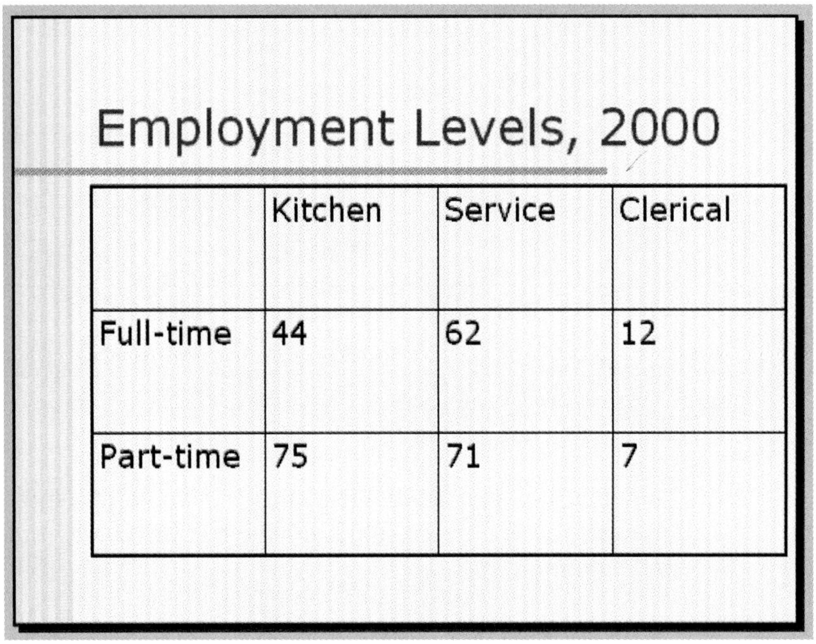

Employment Levels, 2000

	Kitchen	Service	Clerical
Full-time	44	62	12
Part-time	75	71	7

Selecting a Table, Table Cells, and Text

PowerPoint has many features you can use to enhance your table. Before you can apply special formatting to table cells, you must first select those cells. Here are some selection methods you can use:

- Select a single cell by simply clicking it.
- Select a column or row by clicking the Table button on the Tables and Borders toolbar and then choosing Select Column or Select Row from the menu.

- Select a rectangular group of cells by clicking one corner cell and dragging diagonally to the other corner.
- Click the starting cell in a selection and then press Shift and click the ending cell.

You often need to apply special formatting to the entire table. To select the table, you can do one of the following:

- Select all the cells in the table by dragging diagonally across all of them.
- Click the selected table's border.
- Right-click the table and choose Select Table from the shortcut menu.
- When the table is active, press Ctrl + A.

EXERCISE 13-4 Select Groups of Cells and Text

1. Click the cell that contains "Kitchen." The blinking insertion point indicates that the cell is active.
2. Press Tab once. "Service" is highlighted in a different color, indicating that the text "Service" is selected. Click once on the word "Service." Now there is a blinking insertion point. The cell is selected, but the text in the cell is not selected.
3. Click the "Service" cell and drag down the column to the last row. The entire column is now selected.

NOTE: Be careful when selecting a group of cells that you are dragging the I-beam and not the drag-and-drop pointer. If you accidentally drag text to a new location, use Undo to correct the error.

FIGURE 13-4
Selecting a column

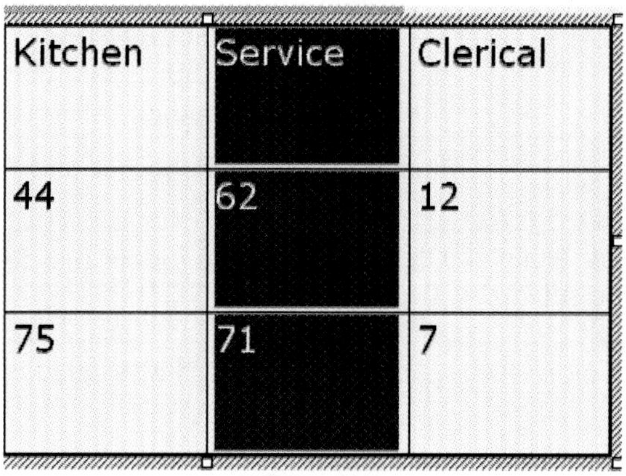

Kitchen	Service	Clerical
44	62	12
75	71	7

4. Click the cell that contains the number "44" and then press [Shift] and click the cell containing the number "7." The six cells containing numbers are now selected.

5. Use the Font Color button [A] on the Drawing toolbar to change the font color to dark blue, the title text scheme color.

EXERCISE **13-5** **Select an Entire Table**

1. Right-click any cell in the table and choose $\underline{S}$elect Table from the shortcut menu. The table's selection border changes to the same small dot pattern that other PowerPoint placeholders display when they are selected.

2. Click the Text Shadow button [s] on the Formatting toolbar to apply a shadow to all the text in the table. Click outside the table to deselect it.

3. Click the upper left cell and drag to the lower right cell to select all the cells in the table. Use the Formatting toolbar to make the selected cells bold and remove the text shadow. Change the font size to 20 points.

Formatting a Table

You can dress up a table by adding fill effects to selected cells. You can also add outlines, called *borders*, to individual cells or the entire table. A convenient way to apply formatting is to use the buttons on the Tables and Borders toolbar.

TABLE 13-1 Buttons on the Tables and Borders Toolbar

BUTTON/NAME	FUNCTION
Draw Table	Draw a table or add rows and columns by dragging the pencil pointer. Split rows, columns, or cells. Also, use it to color individual cell borders.
Eraser	Remove a table cell border and merge the two adjacent cells.
Border Style	Choose a line style for the selected cell border.
Border Width	Choose a line width for the selected cell border.
Border Color	Choose a color for the selected cell border.

continues

TABLE 13-1	Buttons on the Tables and Borders Toolbar *continued*	
BUTTON/NAME	**FUNCTION**	
▢▾ Borders	Apply the selected border color, style, and line width options to the selected cell border. This is a dynamic button, based on the selection from its submenu.	
◇▾ Fill Color	Apply a fill color or fill effect to selected cells.	
Table ▾ Table	Display a menu of commonly used table options and commands.	
▦ Merge Cells	Combine two or more selected adjacent cells and their contents into one larger cell.	
▦ Split Cell	Split a selected cell into two smaller cells.	
▤ Align Top	Align the contents of selected cells with the top of the cells.	
▤ Center Vertically	Center the contents of selected cells between the top and bottom of the cells.	
▤ Align Bottom	Align the contents of selected cells with the bottom of the cells.	

EXERCISE 13-6 Add Fill Color to Table Cells

When you first create a table, the table cells contain no fill, allowing the slide's background to show through. You can apply a fill color or other fill effects, such as a pattern or gradient effect, to one or more cells in your table. Applying fill effects is very similar to applying fills to other PowerPoint objects.

1. If necessary, click the Tables and Borders button ▦ on the Standard toolbar to display the Tables and Borders toolbar and turn off the pencil pointer.

2. Select all the cells in the top row.

3. Click the arrow on the Fill Color button ◇▾ on the Tables and Borders toolbar, and choose the gray accent scheme color.

4. Change the font color for the selected row to dark red.

TIP: You can also use the Fill Color button on the Drawing toolbar to apply fill effects to table cells.

5. Select the first column on the table and apply the same gray fill color.

6. Change the font color for the selected column to dark red.

7. Click outside the table to observe the effect.

> **NOTE:** Depending on how you first displayed the Borders and Tables toolbar, the toolbar normally disappears when the table is not active and automatically reappears the next time the table is clicked.

EXERCISE 13-7 Remove a Fill Effect from a Cell

1. Select the empty cell in the upper left corner.

2. Click the arrow on the Fill Color button ![Fill Color button] and choose No Fill. The cell now displays the slide's background.

FIGURE 13-5
Fill effects applied
to table cells

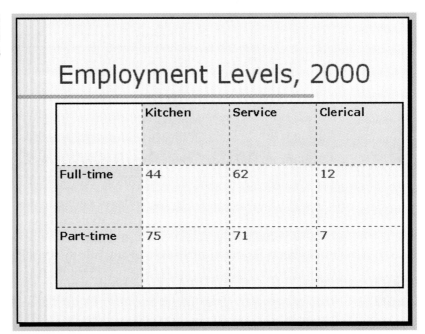

	Kitchen	Service	Clerical
Full-time	44	62	12
Part-time	75	71	7

Employment Levels, 2000

EXERCISE 13-8 Change the Color and Style of Table Borders

Changing the color and style of borders is similar to changing the outline style and color of other PowerPoint objects. First select the cells you want to change. Then use the Tables and Borders toolbar to choose the line style, line weight, and color, and apply the border effect to the appropriate border.

TIP: You can also use the Format Table dialog box to change border and fill formatting. Choose Table from the Format menu to open the dialog box (or right-click selected table cells and choose Borders and Fill from the shortcut menu).

1. Click the Table button on the Tables and Borders toolbar and choose Select Table. The dotted border surrounding the table indicates that the entire table is selected.

2. Click the arrow on the Border Style button [— ▾] on the Tables and Borders toolbar and choose the small dashed line (the third line style).

FIGURE 13-6
Border styles

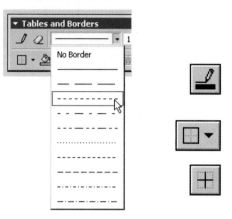

3. Click the arrow on the Border Width button [1 pt ▾] and be sure 1 point is chosen.

4. Click the Border Color button [⟋] and choose dark blue, the title text scheme color.

5. Click the arrow on the Borders button [□▾] and then click Inside Borders [+] on the menu (the third choice on the first line). The inside borders of the table are now dark blue dashed lines.

FIGURE 13-7
Applying inside borders from the Borders menu

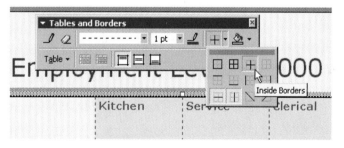

6. With the table still selected, change the options on the Tables and Borders toolbar so that the border style is a solid line, the border width is 3 points, and the border color is dark blue.

7. Click the arrow on the Borders button and choose Outside Borders [□]. The table now has a dark blue outline with dashed lines defining each cell.

TIP: You can use the pencil to change the color and style of a border. Set the border options on the Tables and Borders toolbar. Then, instead of clicking the Borders button, click the Draw Table button [⟋] and use the pencil pointer to click the borders you want to change.

Aligning Text and Numbers in a Table

In previous lessons you aligned text in drawn objects and placeholders. In a similar way, you can align text and numbers in a table cell. You can specify that text or numbers appear at the top, middle, or bottom of a cell and are left-, center-, or right-aligned.

In addition, you can use cell margin settings to refine even further the position of text and numbers in a cell.

EXERCISE 13-9 Align Text and Numbers Horizontally

1. Select the cells in the first row that contain the text "Kitchen," "Service," and "Clerical."

2. Choose <u>A</u>lignment on the <u>F</u>ormat menu and click <u>C</u>enter (or press Ctrl+E). The text is centered in each cell. You center text the same way you center other PowerPoint text.

3. Select the six cells that contain numbers and right-align them in the same way. (Remember, you can press Ctrl+R to right-align text.)

NOTE: You can also use the Alignment buttons on the Formatting toolbar.

EXERCISE 13-10 Change the Vertical Position of Text in a Cell

1. Select the cells in the first row that contain the text "Kitchen," "Service," and "Clerical."

2. Click the Align Bottom button on the Tables and Borders toolbar. The text in the selected cells is now at the bottom edge of the cells.

3. Select all the cells in the second and third rows.

4. Click the Center Vertically button . The text moves to the center of the cells.

EXERCISE **13-11** **Use Margin Settings to Adjust the Position of Text in a Cell**

Sometimes the horizontal and vertical alignment settings cannot place text precisely where you want it in a cell. You may be tempted to make adjustments by using Spacebar or Enter, but that usually doesn't work very well.

You can precisely control where to place text in a cell by using the cell's margin settings combined with horizontal and vertical alignment. For example, you can right-align a column of numbers and also have them appear centered in the column.

1. Select the six cells that contain numbers.
2. Choose Table from the Format menu. The Format Table dialog box opens.

FIGURE 13-8
Use the Format Table dialog box to set cell margins.

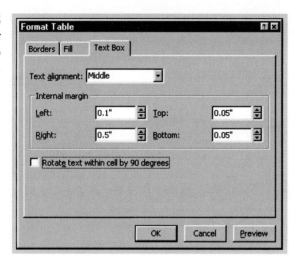

3. Click the Text Box tab. Notice that the Text Alignment setting is already set to Middle. This is equivalent to clicking the Center Vertically button on the Tables and Borders toolbar.

4. Click the Text Alignment arrow to see the other settings. Choose Middle again, if necessary.

5. Under Internal Margin, change the Right setting to **0.5** inch and click OK. The numbers are still right-aligned, but there is some space between the right cell border and the numbers.

6. Select the three cells in the first row containing the text "Kitchen," "Service," and "Clerical."

7. Right-click the selected cells and choose Borders and Fill from the short-cut menu. Click the Text box tab. Change the Bottom setting to **0.2** inch and click OK. Now there is some extra space between the text and the bottom of the cells.

8. Select all the cells in the first column (which includes "Full-time" and "Part-time") and change the left margin to 0.2 inch.

FIGURE 13-9
Table with text and
numbers aligned

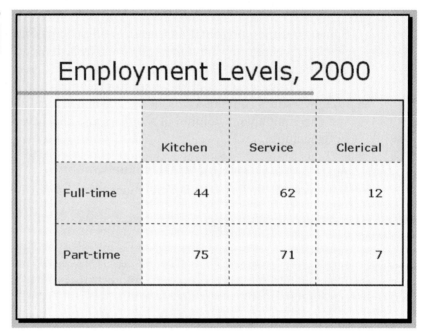

Changing the Height and Width of Rows, Columns, and Tables

When you first create a PowerPoint table, it is automatically sized to fill the available space on your slide. If you later decide to add or delete rows or columns, or to make a column wider, the table will no longer fit. You can make a table smaller or larger by dragging its handles. If you hold down Shift while dragging a corner handle, the table resizes proportionally.

You can also change the height of rows and the width of columns by dragging cell borders. Display the ruler before changing the size of columns and rows. The ruler will help you change several rows or columns to equal height or width.

EXERCISE **13-12** **Change the Width of Columns**

1. Display the rulers, if necessary, by choosing Ruler from the View menu.

2. Select the table and use Zoom to enlarge the table so it fills your screen. This will make it easier to see tick marks on the ruler for precise placement of column borders.

 NOTE: When changing column width or row height, be sure the rulers are white and not mostly gray. The ruler is gray when an insertion point is in a cell. To see the white ruler, select the entire table or click outside the table.

3. Move the mouse pointer over the right border of the first column until the pointer becomes ◂‖▸. Notice the dashed line on the ruler indicating the position of the column border.

4. Drag the column border to the 2-inch mark on the ruler. The first column width decreases.

5. Drag the right border of the "Kitchen" column to the left, to the 0.5-inch mark left of the zero center mark on the ruler.

FIGURE 13-10
Moving a
column border

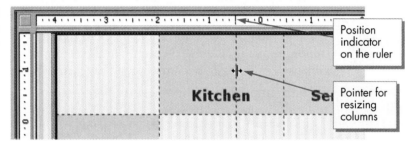

6. Move the right border of the "Service" column to the 1-inch mark (to the right of zero), and move the right border of the "Clerical" column to the 2.5-inch mark. Make sure the pointer is ◂‖▸ before you drag.

 TIP: To automatically adjust column width to fit the text, point to the column border and double-click.

EXERCISE 13-13 Change the Height of Rows

Change the height of rows in the same way as column widths: drag the row borders up or down.

1. Move the mouse pointer over the bottom border of the first row.
2. Drag the bottom border up to the 1-inch mark above the zero mark.
3. Move the bottom border of the second row to the zero mark.
4. Move the bottom border of the bottom row up to the 1-inch mark.

Inserting and Deleting Rows, Columns, and Individual Cells

When you create a table, you decide how many rows and columns the table should have. After entering some information into a table, you may discover that you have too many columns or perhaps not enough rows.

Occasionally, you may want one row or column to have more cells than the others. You can make this happen by merging a group of cells or splitting individual cells into two cells.

EXERCISE 13-14 Insert Columns in a Table

1. Change the Zoom to Fit and then select the cells in the "Kitchen" column.

2. Right-click the selected column and choose Insert Columns from the shortcut menu. A new column appears to the right of "Kitchen." It is the same size as the "Kitchen" column and has all the same formatting. The table is now wider to accommodate the extra column.

3. Click the upper left cell to select it.

 NOTE: To insert several columns at one time, select more than one column and choose the Insert Columns command.

4. Click the Table button on the Tables and Borders toolbar and choose Insert Columns to the Right. A new column appears to the right of the selected cell with the same size and format as the selected cell's column. The table now has two blank columns.

FIGURE 13-11
Inserting a column

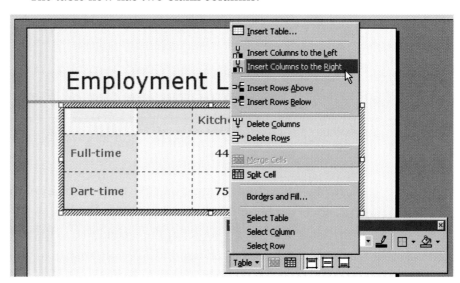

EXERCISE 13-15 Delete a Column from a Table

1. Click any cell in the second column.
2. Click the T<u>a</u>ble button on the Tables and Borders toolbar and choose Delete <u>C</u>olumns. The column that contained the selected cell is deleted. Your table should now have one blank column, to the left of the "Kitchen" column.

 NOTE: If more than one column is selected when you use the delete column command, all the selected columns will be deleted.

EXERCISE 13-16 Insert a Row in a Table

1. Click any cell in the last row of the table.
2. Click the T<u>a</u>ble button on the Tables and Borders toolbar and choose Insert Rows <u>B</u>elow. A new row is inserted at the bottom of the table, with the size and formatting preserved.

TIP: A quick way to add a new row to the bottom of a table is to move the pointer to the last cell on the right end of the bottom row and press [Tab]. This is especially helpful when you're keying information in a new table and you run out of rows.

3. Complete the table by keying the information shown in Figure 13-12 into the blank row and blank column.

FIGURE 13-12
Completed table

Employment Levels, 2000

	Mgmt	Kitchen	Service	Clerical
Full-time	2	44	62	12
Part-time		75	71	7
Temps				2

4. Select the entire table and change the font size to 24 points.

5. While holding ⎡Shift⎤, drag the lower right corner handle diagonally down to make the table larger, until there is no text-wrapping.

6. With the table selected, drag its border to adjust its position on the slide, just as you would move any other PowerPoint object.

7. Create a slide footer for this slide only. Include the date and key *[your name]*, *[your initials]***13-16.ppt** in the slide footer text box.

8. Save the presentation as *[your initials]***13-16.ppt** in a new folder for Lesson 13.

9. Print slide 2 only. If you have a color printer, print it in color.

EXERCISE 13-17 Merge Cells

You can merge two or more slides to form one cell. This is often done for the first row of a table to create a more attractive title. To merge cells, use the Merge Cells command or the Eraser tool.

1. Move to slide 4, which is titled "Employment Levels, 2001."

2. Select the first three cells in the first row.

3. Click the Merge Cells button on the Tables and Borders toolbar. The three cells are transformed into one wide cell. The text in the first cell now fits on one line.

4. Click the Eraser button on the Tables and Borders toolbar. Your mouse pointer changes into an eraser.

5. Using the eraser, click the border between the last two cells on the first row. The border disappears, and the cells are merged.

FIGURE 13-13
Using the Eraser to merge cells

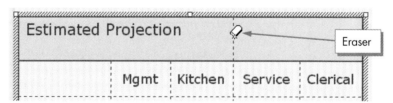

6. Click the border between the remaining cells on the first row. Now there is only one cell on the first row of the table.

7. Click the Eraser button to turn off the Eraser tool.

EXERCISE 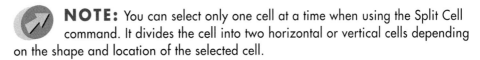 Split a Cell

You can split cells that have been merged by using the Split Cells command. Another way to split a cell is to use the pencil tool to draw a horizontal, vertical, or diagonal dividing line.

> **NOTE:** You can select only one cell at a time when using the Split Cell command. It divides the cell into two horizontal or vertical cells depending on the shape and location of the selected cell.

1. Click the cell that contains the word "Temps" to select it.

2. Click the Split Cell button ▦ on the Tables and Borders toolbar. The selected cell becomes two cells, but the border between them doesn't align with any column.

FIGURE 13-14
Splitting a cell

Full-time	2	52	
Part-time	1	82	
Temps			

3. Drag the border dividing the two cells to the right, aligning it under the left border of the "Kitchen" column.

4. Key **2** in the new cell. Right-align the number and then change its right margin to **0.5** inch.

EXERCISE 13-19 Use the Pencil to Split a Cell Diagonally

You can split a cell diagonally. For example, if you are using a PowerPoint table to create a calendar, you may want to put two dates in the same square, separated by a diagonal line if the last day of the month falls on a Sunday.

1. Place an insertion point at the end of the words "Estimated Projection" in the first row. Press ⎆Enter to start a new line in the cell. Key **Revised Figures**

2. Right-align the text on the second line.

3. If necessary, change the options on the Tables and Borders toolbar to a dashed, 1-point, dark blue line.

4. Click the Draw Table button to change the pointer into a pencil.

5. Position the pencil pointer near but not touching the lower left corner of the cell in the first row. Draw a diagonal line across the cell to the upper right corner.

> **NOTE:** Be careful where you start drawing. If you touch one of the cell borders with the pencil, the formatting of that border may change. If that happens, use Undo to restore it.

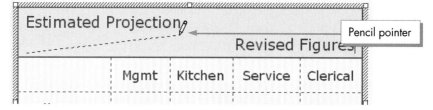

FIGURE 13-15
Using the pencil to split a cell diagonally

6. Click the Draw Table button to turn off the pencil. Note that the cell is not actually split into two cells—it's only been made to appear as two cells.

7. Deselect the table to see the results.

FIGURE 13-16
Completed table

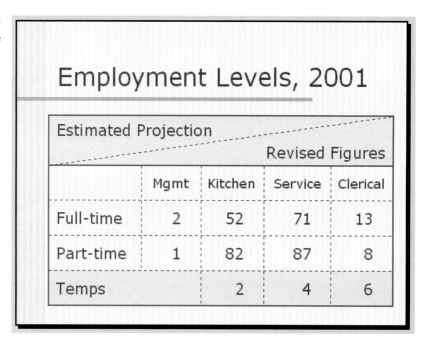

8. Create a slide footer for this slide only. Include the date and key *[your name], [your initials]*13-19.ppt in the slide footer text box.

9. Save the presentation as *[your initials]*13-19.ppt in your Lesson 13 folder.

10. Print slide 4 only. If you have a color printer, print it in color.

Inserting a Microsoft Word Table

PowerPoint provides many tools for creating interesting and attractive tables. Word, however, makes some of these tools more convenient to use and offers some additional table features. For example, you can sort data in a Word table, and setting up tabs within cells is more convenient in a Word table.

If you need the advanced table features that Word offers, create a table in Word and then copy and paste it into PowerPoint.

EXERCISE 13-20 Insert a Word Table

1. Insert a new slide after slide 4 using the Title Only layout. Key the title **Kitchen Forecast**

2. Without closing PowerPoint, start Word and open the Word document **Mgmt1.doc**, located where you store your student files.

3. Scroll to the table with the heading "2001 Estimates."

4. Move the mouse pointer within the table borders. The table move handle ⊞, a small box with a four-headed arrow in it, appears in the upper left corner of the table.

5. Click ⊞ to select the table.

6. Copy the table to the Clipboard.

7. Switch to PowerPoint and display slide 5, if necessary.

8. Choose Paste Special from the Edit menu. The Paste Special dialog box opens.

9. Choose Microsoft Word Document Object from the list of paste options and click OK. The table appears on the slide.

FIGURE 13-17
Copying a Word
table onto a
PowerPoint slide

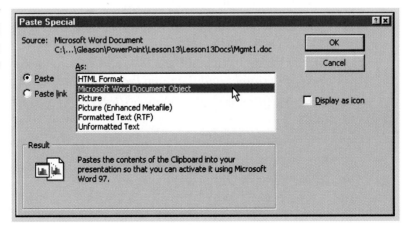

NOTE: To create Word tables from within PowerPoint, choose <u>P</u>icture from the <u>I</u>nsert menu and then choose Microsoft Word <u>T</u>able.

10. Make the table approximately 1 inch wider, and position it attractively on the slide.

11. Use the Format Object dialog box to recolor the table (R<u>e</u>color button on the Picture tab). Change all the black text to dark blue, change the royal blue lines to dark blue, change the red lines to dark red, and change the light blue fill to the gray that follows the accent scheme color.

TIP: When creating a Word table, plan in advance which PowerPoint colors you want to use. You may not be able to use the same colors in Word, but if you make each part of the table a different color, it will be easy to recolor the table in PowerPoint to suit your needs.

EXERCISE 13-21 Make Changes to a Word Table

If you need to make changes to text, numbers, or other formatting on the Word table, double-click it to open up Word within PowerPoint. You will have all the Word table tools available to work with.

1. Double-click the table on slide 5. The Word toolbars and menu appear.

2. Change the number 46 under "Clean-up" to **48**.

3. Press Ctrl + A to select the entire Word table.

4. Click the Bold button **B** on the Word Formatting toolbar.

5. Click outside the table border to return to PowerPoint. Adjust the size and position of the table to suit your taste.

6. Create a slide footer for this slide only. Include the date and key *[your name], [your initials]*13-21.ppt in the slide footer text box.

7. On the handouts, include the date and your name as header and include the page number and filename *[your initials]*13-21.ppt as footer.

8. Save the presentation as *[your initials]*13-21.ppt in your Lesson 13 folder.

9. Print slide 5 only. Then print the presentation as handouts, 6 slides per page, grayscale, framed.

10. Close the presentation.

COMMAND SUMMARY

FEATURE	BUTTON	MENU	KEYBOARD
Insert table		Insert, Table	
Select table		Table, Select Table	Ctrl + A

USING HELP [?]

This lesson shows you how to insert a PowerPoint table and how to import a Word table. There are other options for bringing a table into PowerPoint as well.

Use Help to learn more about inserting tables from other programs:

1. Display and activate the Office Assistant.
2. Key **Office programs, table** in the text box and click Search.
3. Select the topic "Office programs you can use to create a table."
4. Read the information, and then close Help and hide the Office Assistant.

Concepts Review

Each of the following statements is either true or false. Indicate your choice by circling T or F.

T F **1.** You can adjust the width of a column in a table, but cannot adjust the row heights.

T F **2.** When you define the size of a table, you must be accurate because you cannot change the size later.

T F **3.** Cell borders can be any color you want.

T F **4.** Borders are available in only one width.

T F **5.** The colors in a table should be consistent with the rest of the presentation.

T F **6.** When you insert a new column, it is always inserted to the left of the currently selected column.

T F **7.** Text can be aligned within an individual cell.

T F **8.** The Table layout includes a placeholder for a table.

Write the correct answer in the space provided.

1. What do you call a box that contains text or numbers in a table?

_____

2. To create a table with one row of headings and five rows of data, how many rows would you specify when defining the size of the table?

_____

3. What toolbar contains the Center Vertically button?

_____

4. What menu command selects the entire table?

_____

5. How do you move from one cell to another in a table?

_____

6. How do you merge cells in a table by using a toolbar?

_____

7. Which keys do you press to move to the preceding cell in a table?

_____

8. How do you insert a new column after the last column in a table?

_____

CRITICAL THINKING

Answer these questions on a separate page. There are no right or wrong answers. Support your answers with examples from your own experience, if possible.

_1._ How would you decide if a table or a chart is a better presentation tool for a particular set of numerical information? Which criteria should govern the use of one form over the other?

_2._ If you are adding a table slide to a lengthy presentation that includes a variety of slide types, what should you do to ensure that the table slide is visually consistent with the rest of the slides?

Skills Review

EXERCISE 13-22

Create a table, key text, select parts of a table, change column width, and resize the table.

_1._ Open the file **Results1.ppt**. Move to slide 4, which has the WordArt title "The Winning Fare."

_2._ Insert a new table by following these steps:

   _a._ Choose Table from the Insert menu.

   _b._ In the Insert Table dialog box, specify **2** columns and **3** rows.

   _c._ If the Tables and Borders toolbar is not showing, click the Tables and Borders button ⊞ on the Standard toolbar. Drag the toolbar out of the way.

   _d._ If the mouse pointer is a pencil, press [Esc].

_3._ Reposition and resize the table by following these steps:

   _a._ If necessary, display the rulers.

   _b._ Right-click anywhere inside the table and choose Select Table from the shortcut menu.

c. Move the pointer over the table's border until you see the four-headed arrow pointer.

d. Drag the table diagonally down and to the left. Align the left edge of the table with the 4-inch mark on the ruler.

e. Make the table wider by dragging the right-center sizing handle to the 4-inch mark on the ruler.

4. Change the width of a column by following these steps:

a. If necessary, deselect any cells so that you see the white ruler.

b. Move the mouse pointer over the border between the two columns until the pointer becomes ◂‖▸.

c. Drag the border to the left, aligning it with the 1-inch mark on the ruler. You should now have a narrower left column and a wider right column.

5. Key text in the table and change the font size by following these steps:

a. Click the upper left cell to select it. Key the underlined text **<u>Amy Grand</u>** and press Enter. On the next line, key **Hot Tomato Salsa**

b. Press Tab to move to the next cell, then key:

Tangy fresh tomato salsa with jalapenos, white corn, lots of garlic, and green and yellow peppers

c. Select the entire table and use the Formatting toolbar to change the font size to 20 points.

6. In the remaining cells, key the text shown in Figure 13-18.

FIGURE 13-18

<u>Juanita McLeod</u> Raspberry Cream Pie	Raspberry yogurt custard in a graham cracker crust that tastes like a million calories
<u>William Steinberg</u> Roasted Chicken and Vegetables	Chicken breasts marinated in garlic, herbs, and lime juice, roasted with turnips, yellow squash, and red potatoes

7. Adjust the black and white settings as needed.

8. Create a slide footer for slide 4 only. Include the date and key *[your name], [your initials]***13-22.ppt** in the slide footer text box.

9. On the handouts, include the date and your name as header and include the page number and filename *[your initials]***13-22.ppt** as footer.

10. Save the presentation as *[your initials]***13-22.ppt** in your Lesson 13 folder.

11. Print slide 4 only. Then print the entire presentation as handouts, 4 slides per page, grayscale, framed.

12. Close the presentation.

Create a table, apply border and fill options, and change cell and text alignment.

1. Open the file **Manage2.ppt**. Apply the design template **Cactus.pot** and use the color scheme with the black background.

2. Insert a new slide after slide 3 using the Table layout. Key the title **Capital Equipment, 2000**

3. Create a table on slide 4 by following these steps:

   a. Double-click the table placeholder.

   b. In the Table dialog box, specify **3** for the number of columns and **5** for the number of rows. Click OK.

   c. Click the Draw Table button 🖊 on the Tables and Borders toolbar to turn off the pencil pointer.

   d. Key the table text shown in Figure 13-19.

FIGURE 13-19

	Leased	Bought
Kitchen	9,540	24,350
Dining	14,400	18,650
Office	10,500	25,500
Other	8,252	16,300

4. Align text horizontally by following these steps:

   a. Select the first column by clicking the first cell and dragging down to the last cell.

   b. Click the Center button ≣ on the Formatting toolbar (or press Ctrl + E).

   c. Select all the cells in the first row and center that text horizontally.

   d. Select all the cells that contain numbers by dragging diagonally across the cells.

   e. Click the Align Right button ≣ on the Formatting toolbar (or press Ctrl + R) to right-align the numbers.

5. Change cell margin settings by following these steps:

   a. If necessary, reselect all the cells that contain numbers.

     b. Right-click the selected cells and choose Bord<u>e</u>rs and Fill from the shortcut menu. Click the Text Box tab.

     c. Under <u>I</u>nternal Margin, set the <u>R</u>ight text box to **0.75** inch. Click OK.

6. Change the vertical alignment of text and numbers by following these steps:

     a. Select the entire table by clicking the table's border.

     b. Click the Center Vertically button 🗄 on the Tables and Borders toolbar.

7. With the table still selected, make all the text and numbers bold.

8. Adjust column widths and row heights by following these steps:

     a. With the ruler displayed, select the entire table.

     b. Drag the right border of the first column left to the 2.5-inch mark on the ruler.

     c. Drag the right border of the second column to the 0 mark on the ruler and the right border of the third column to the 2.5-inch mark on the right side of the ruler. (Be careful not to drag the four-headed arrow or the selection handle.)

     d. Reduce the height of the first row by dragging its bottom border up.

9. Apply fill effects to table cells by following these steps:

     a. Select all the cells in the first row.

     b. Click the arrow on the Fill Color button 🎨▾ on either the Drawing toolbar or the Tables and Borders toolbar.

     c. Choose Fill Effects and click the Texture tab.

     d. Choose the second texture on the first row, named Recycled Paper. Click OK.

     e. Change the font color for the selected cells to black.

10. Select the cells in the first row that contain text, starting with "Kitchen" through "Other." Change the fill color to the warm brown accent scheme color. Change the text in the selected cells to orange.

11. Select all the cells with numbers and apply a one-color gradient fill using the warm brown accent scheme color, shading to medium dark. Use the Diagonal <u>D</u>own shading style, choosing the first variant, with the darkest part in the lower left corner. Change the text color of the selected cells to the title text color.

12. Remove all the table's borders by following these steps:

     a. Select the entire table.

     b. Click the Border Style arrow ⸻▾ and choose No Border from the drop-down list.

     c. Click the arrow on the Borders button and choose All Borders ⊞.

13. Using the four-headed arrow pointer, reposition the table diagonally down and to the right approximately 0.5 inch.

14. Drag the table's right sizing handle slightly to the right to make the table a little wider.

15. Change the table's black and white setting to Inverse Grayscale. On the slide master and the title master, change the black and white settings for the title placeholder to White.

16. Create a slide footer for slide 4 only. Include the date and key *[your name], [your initials]***13-23.ppt** in the slide footer text box.

17. On the handouts, include the date and your name as header and include the page number and filename *[your initials]***13-23.ppt** as footer.

18. Save the presentation as *[your initials]***13-23.ppt** in your Lesson 13 folder.

19. Print slide 4 only. Then print the entire presentation as handouts, 4 slides per page, grayscale, framed.

20. Close the presentation.

EXERCISE 13-24

Apply formatting to an existing table using the Tables and Borders toolbar, adjust column width, and insert a column.

1. Open the file **Reserve2.ppt.** Display the rulers, if necessary.

2. Apply the design template **Blends.pot**. Change the background to a 1-color horizontal gradient fill using white and shading to a medium gray. Choose the variant with the lightest shade in the middle.

3. Display slide 5, titled "Reservation Requests."

4. Select the table and move it diagonally until the left edge is at the 4-inch mark on the horizontal ruler and the top edge is at the 1-inch mark on the vertical ruler.

5. Reduce the text size to 24 points for the entire table and apply a text shadow. Make all the numbers red, and make all the text dark blue.

6. Insert a new row between "Weekends" and "Memorial Day" by following these steps:
   a. Right-click "Memorial Day."
   b. Choose Insert Rows from the shortcut menu.

7. Insert a new column to the left of "Brunch" by following these steps:
   a. Click anywhere in the first column.
   b. Click the Table button on the Tables and Borders toolbar.
   c. Choose Insert Columns to the Right from the Table menu.

8. Delete a column and a row by following these steps:
   a. Select the entire "Late Nite" column.
   b. Right-click the selection and choose Delete Columns from the shortcut menu.
   c. Select the "Memorial Day" row and then right-click the selection and choose Delete Rows from the shortcut menu.

9. Key the following information in the blank bottom row, pressing Tab to move to the next cell:

   Holidays   6   91   5   94

10. In the second column, key **Breakfast** for the column heading, **5** for "Weekday," and **18** for "Weekends." Make the numbers in the "Breakfast" column red. Change the "Weekday" cell to **Weekdays**

11. Make each column on the table approximately 1.75 inches wide.

> **TIP:** You may find it easier to set up a series of guides before changing column widths. Set the first guide at the 4-inch mark on the left and then use Ctrl + Shift to drag a series of guides 1.75 inches apart.

12. Drag the table's bottom-center sizing handle to lengthen the entire table until each row becomes approximately 1 inch high.

13. Center the table's column headings, right-align the numbers, and use margin settings to make the numbers appear centered under the headings. Center all the text vertically within each cell.

14. Format the table and cell borders by following these steps:
    a. Select the entire table.
    b. On the Border Style button, be sure the solid line is chosen.
    c. Click the arrow on the Border Width button on the Borders and Tables toolbar. Choose 3 pt from the drop-down menu.
    d. Click the Border Color button and choose dark blue.
    e. Click the arrow on the Borders button and choose All Borders.

15. Adjust the table's position on the slide to make a pleasing composition.

16. Create a slide footer for slide 5 only. Include the date and key *[your name], [your initials]*13-24.ppt in the slide footer text box.

17. On the handouts, include the date and your name as header and include the page number and filename *[your initials]*13-24.ppt as footer.

18. Save the presentation as *[your initials]*13-24.ppt in your Lesson 13 folder.

19. Print slide 5. Then print the entire presentation as handouts, 6 slides per page, grayscale, framed.

20. Close the presentation.

EXERCISE 13-25

Import a Microsoft Word table; merge and split cells in a PowerPoint table.

1. Open the file **Features.ppt** and move to slide 4 ("Menu Analysis").
2. Import a Microsoft Word table by following these steps:

a. Without closing PowerPoint, start Word and open the file **Menu.doc**.

b. Scroll to the table with the heading "Number of Menu Items."

c. Select the table by moving your mouse pointer onto the table. Then click the table move handle ⊞ in the upper left corner of the table.

d. Copy the table to the Clipboard and then switch to PowerPoint. Move to slide 4 if necessary.

e. In PowerPoint, choose Paste Special from the Edit menu and choose Microsoft Word Document Object from the list box. Click OK.

3. Format the imported table by following these steps:

a. Using the Format Object dialog box, recolor the table using the scheme colors that are closest to the original table colors. Make the numbers dark brown.

b. Double-click the table to open Word and edit the table's numbers as follows:

	1998	1999	2000
Meat	15	14	11
Vegetarian	9	10	13

c. Click outside the table border to return to PowerPoint.

d. Resize the peach-and-blue shaded rectangle until its edges exactly coincide with the table's borders. Use Zoom to be precise.

e. Draw a selection rectangle around both the table and the rectangle behind it. Position the two objects attractively on the slide.

 TIP: Hold down [Alt] while dragging the rectangle's edges to override Snap to Grid or Snap to Object.

4. Merge two cells by following these steps:

a. Move to slide 5, which contains a table with many rows of text.

b. Select the two cells in the first row.

c. Click the Merge Cells button ⊡ on the Tables and Borders toolbar.

d. Merge the two cells in the center column that contain the names "Susan Smith" and "Wanda Jacks."

e. In the same manner, merge the "Jan" and "Feb" cells in the first column, and merge the cell containing "No-Guilt Cherry Cheesecake" with the cell below it.

5. Split a cell into two side-by-side cells by following these steps.

a. Select the cell containing "Susan Smith" and "Wanda Jacks."

b. Click the Split Cell button ⊞ on the Tables and Borders toolbar.

c. Move "Wanda Jacks" into the new empty cell.

d. Remove any extra blank lines from the split cells by clicking on the blank line and pressing [Backspace].

6. Split a cell diagonally by following these steps:

    a. In the "Jan Feb" cell, click on the line containing "Feb" and right-align that line only (press Ctrl + R).

    b. If necessary, change the settings on the Tables and Borders toolbar to a solid 1-pt red line.

    c. Click the Draw Table button 🖉 on the Tables and Borders toolbar to turn on the pencil pointer, if necessary.

    d. Use the pencil to draw a diagonal line from the lower left corner of the cell to the upper right corner.

    e. In the same way, split the "Mar Apr" cell diagonally.

    f. Click the Draw Table button 🖉 to turn off the pencil.

7. If necessary, adjust the position of the table on the slide.

8. Create a slide footer for slide 5. Include the date and key *[your name]*, *[your initials]*13-25.ppt in the slide footer text box.

9. Create the same slide footer for slide 4.

10. On the handouts, include the date and your name as header and include the page number and filename *[your initials]*13-25.ppt as footer.

11. Save the presentation as *[your initials]*13-25.ppt in your Lesson 13 folder.

12. Print slides 4 and 5. Then print the entire presentation as handouts, 6 slides per page, grayscale, framed.

13. Close the presentation.

Lesson Applications

Create a presentation with a table slide, apply border settings, arrange and format text, insert a row, and change column widths and table size.

1. Open the file **PrintAds1.ppt.**

2. Insert a Bulleted List slide with the title **Print Advertising, 2000** and the following three bulleted items:

    - **Campaigns use a variety of print media**
    - **Each medium targets a specific market segment**
    - **Every campaign must meet specific sales objectives**

3. Insert another Bulleted List slide, with the title **Coupon Redemption** and the following bulleted items:

    - **Effective measure of return on investment**
    - **Used for promotional purposes in a variety of print media**

4. Insert a new slide after slide 3 using the Table layout, with the title **Coupons Redeemed, 1999**

5. Create a table with 4 columns and 4 rows, using the data shown in Figure 13-20. In the first row, press Enter to place the second word of each column heading on a new line.

FIGURE 13-20

Coupons Redeemed, 1999

Newspaper Magazine	Coupons Redeemed	Average Check	Cost of One Ad
NY Times	414	$31.50	$6,800
NY Magazine	476	$25.00	$2,850
NY Runner	1,063	$23.50	$975

6. Change the font for all cells to 28-point Arial, bold. Change the font color of the first row and the first column to light blue.

7. Change all right and left cell margins to 0.2 inch. Double-click each column border so that each column self-adjusts to fit the widest text in the column.

8. Change horizontal and vertical alignment settings for all text and the margin settings for the numbers to arrange the text and numbers as shown in Figure 13-20.

9. Remove all the borders from the table and then apply one horizontal border at the bottom of the first row and one vertical border on the right side of the first column, as shown in Figure 13-20. Make the borders 3 points wide, and color them bright lavender, the last sample on the right of the scheme colors.

10. Select the top row of the table, and change the space before paragraphs to 0 lines and the line spacing to 0.9 lines. Align the text in the top row with the bottoms of the cells and then reduce the height of the row.

11. Insert a new row at the bottom of the table and key the following, and then adjust the text formatting to match the rest of the table:

    NY Health Tab **125** Tab **$16.25** Tab **$650**

12. Adjust the height of the entire table by dragging its bottom-center sizing handle up until the table fits on the slide and there is some space at the bottom.

13. Review the presentation. Add decorative touches and change bullets or text arrangements on the other slides as you see fit.

14. Create a slide footer for slide 4. Include the date and key *[your name], [your initials]***13-26.ppt** in the slide footer text box.

15. On the handouts, include the date and your name as header and include the page number and filename *[your initials]***13-26.ppt** as footer.

16. Save the presentation as *[your initials]***13-26.ppt** in your Lesson 13 folder.

17. Print slide 4 Then print the entire presentation as handouts, 4 slides per page, grayscale, framed.

18. Close the presentation.

EXERCISE 13-27

Edit and format a presentation; insert a table slide; insert rows; change row height, column width, alignment, and cell margins; and create hyperlinks for table text.

1. Open the file **Advert3.ppt**. Change the background of the entire presentation to a two-color gradient fill, using medium blue and dark

blue. Choose the From Title shading style with the darkest color in the center.

2. Customize the slide color scheme as follows: change the Title Text to a darker shade of yellow, change the Accent color to bright red, change the Accent and Hyperlink color to pale blue, and change the Accent and Followed Hyperlink color to a lighter shade of gray.

3. On the slide master, make the title placeholder bold. Change the bulleted text placeholder font to Arial.

4. On slide 1, change "Student Name" to your name.

5. After slide 1, insert a Table slide with the title **Advertising Analysis**

6. Create a table using the following data:

	New Customers	Total Revenue
Newspaper	28%	30%
Radio	10%	5%
Yellow Pages	6%	12%

7. Change the table text to 28-point Arial, bold.

8. Center the text in the first row and right-align the numbers. Center all the text vertically in each cell. Use margin settings to make the numbers appear centered under the headings, and place the text in the first row 0.25 inch from the left border.

9. Adjust the column width of the first row so that "Yellow Pages" is on one line.

10. Insert a row above "Yellow Pages." Key the following in the new row:

Mailers	12%	18%

11. Make the slide attractive by adjusting the column widths, row heights, and vertical alignment of cells as necessary. Position the table in the center of the slide.

12. Fill the cells in the first row with medium blue and the remaining cells with dark blue. Change the column heading text to gold.

13. Remove all the inside borders. Then make the outline border a 3-point red solid line, and add a solid 3-point red border to the bottom of the first row.

14. Adjust the table's position on the slide.

15. Create hyperlinks from the text in each of the cells in the first column, linking the text to the appropriate slide. Insert a Return or Home button on the slide master. Format the button as you please, and make it link to slide 2, the table slide.

16. Check spelling and style in the presentation (checking for inconsistent case and end punctuation).

17. Create a slide footer for slide 2. Include the date and key *[your name]*, *[your initials]*13-27.ppt in the slide footer text box.

18. On the handouts, include the date and your name as header and include the page number and filename *[your initials]*13-27.ppt as footer.

19. Save the presentation as *[your initials]*13-27.ppt in your Lesson 13 folder.

20. Print slide 2. Then print the entire presentation as handouts, 6 slides per page, grayscale, framed.

21. Close the presentation.

EXERCISE 13-28   *Challenge Yourself*

Edit and format a table, add table data, change alignment, change table colors, and merge cells.

1. Open the file **Market1.ppt**.

2. Apply the design template **Artsy.pot** and change to the dark blue color scheme. Remove the graphics from the master slides, and change the background to solid dark blue, using the Background scheme color.

3. On the title master, draw a rectangle the width of the slide by 0.75 inches high. Remove its outline and apply a one-color horizontal gradient fill, using the same color as the background and shading to the lightest possible setting. Choose the variant with white in the middle.

4. Insert the clip art image of the horizontal string of pebbles, which you can find by using the search words **rocks, web dividers**. Resize the image proportionally to be the width of the slide. Center the image horizontally and vertically on the rectangle and then group both images.

5. Place the grouped image just below the subtitle placeholder and send it to the back.

6. Draw another rectangle 1.5 inches high and as wide as the slide. Remove the outline. Apply a one-color horizontal gradient fill, but this time shade from the background blue color to the darkest setting, with the darkest color at the bottom. Place this rectangle at the bottom of the title master and send it to the back.

7. Copy both objects and paste them on the slide master. Send the pasted objects to the back. Move the pebbles group to the top of the slide.

8. Change the grayscale settings on the master slides so that all text is black and everything else is white except the pebbles, which should be light grayscale.

9. Insert a new slide after slide 3 using the Table layout, with the title **Marketing Expenses, 2001**. Create a table using the following data:

Media	Budget	Percent
Advertising	**$295,000**	**50.4%**
Direct Mail	**$95,000**	**16.2%**
Sports Events	**$140,000**	**24.0%**

10. Insert a new row below the last row in the table. Key the following:

Promotions	**$55,000**	**9.4%**

11. Align all the text and numbers appropriately, both horizontally and vertically, and adjust the height and width of the columns and rows.

12. Fill the top and bottom rows of the table with the same color as the background, and fill the middle row with lavender (the fills scheme color). Fill the rows in between with a horizontal gradient fill that shades from the outside row's color to the inside row's color. Apply a custom color of your choice to the outside border and to the border below the headings. Apply gray to the inside borders of rows 2 through 5.

13. Change the table's black and white settings to Black with White Fill.

14. On a new slide, create a pie chart using the percentages for the 2001 estimated budget. Use a pie chart type of your choice and format it attractively to go with the rest of the presentation. Key **Estimated Budget, 2001** as the title.

 TIP: You can copy and paste the data from the table into the pie chart's data sheet.

15. Go through the presentation and add any decorative touches and changes in layout that you think would improve the overall look.

16. On the handouts, include the date and your name as header and include the page number and filename *[your initials]*13-28.ppt as footer.

17. Save the presentation as *[your initials]*13-28.ppt in your Lesson 13 folder.

18. Print as handouts, 6 slides per page, grayscale, framed.

19. Close the presentation.

Flowcharts and Organization Charts

OBJECTIVES

MOUS
ACTIVITIES
In this lesson:
PP2000 **E.10.3**
PP2000 **E.10.4**

See Appendix F.

After completing this lesson, you will be able to:

1. Draw flowchart AutoShapes.
2. Connect objects by using connector lines.
3. Create an organization chart.
4. Add boxes to organization charts.
5. Rearrange organization chart boxes
6. Format organization chart elements.

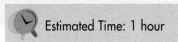 Estimated Time: 1 hour

Flowcharts are diagrams used to show a sequence of events. Flowcharts are usually associated with computer programs, but they can have many other uses.

Organization charts—or "org" charts, for short—are diagrams that are typically used by businesses or work groups to show who reports to whom, and who is responsible for what function or task. Org charts can also be useful for describing other types of relationships, such as a family tree.

Drawing Flowchart AutoShapes

PowerPoint provides special AutoShapes designed for traditional flowcharts, but you can use any AutoShape and many clip art objects in flowcharts. You can format and position flowchart shapes as you would any other AutoShape.

EXERCISE 14-1 Draw Flowchart AutoShapes

1. Open the file **Org1.ppt**. Insert a Title Only slide after slide 2 with the title **New Purchasing Procedure**.

2. Choose Flowchart from the AutoShapes menu. Float the Flowchart submenu.

3. Choose the second shape in the first row (called "Flowchart: Alternate Process"). In the upper left corner of the slide, draw a rectangle approximately 1 inch high by 2.5 inches wide.

4. Key **Get purchase pre-approval** in the rectangle. Select the rectangle and format the text as 18-point Arial, bold, black. Change the AutoShape border color to black to match the font color.

5. Using the Text Box tab in the Format AutoShape dialog box, turn on the word wrap option. (The Resize AutoShape to Fit Text option should be turned off.) Change the Text Anchor Point to Middle Centered and change the internal margins to 0.05 inch all around.

6. Adjust the AutoShape size so the text wraps to two lines, if needed.

7. Make five additional copies of the AutoShape (six boxes total) and arrange the shapes in two columns as shown in Figure 14-1. Change the text in each AutoShape to match the text in the figure.

FIGURE 14-1
Flowchart
AutoShapes

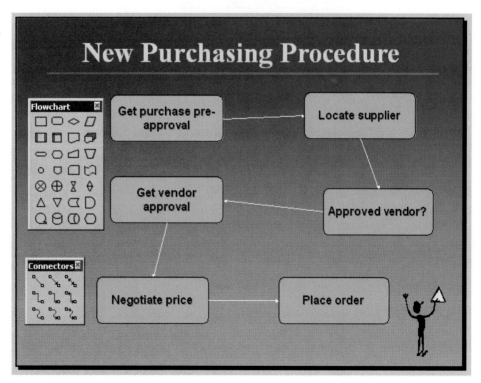

Connecting Flowchart AutoShapes

You use *connector lines* to link the shapes in a flowchart. Connector lines have endpoints that automatically attach to a shape's *connection sites*—the small blue handles that appear when you work with connector lines.

Connector lines are usually used with Flowchart AutoShapes, but they can also be used with most other AutoShapes and clip art images. When you rearrange AutoShapes on a slide, the connector lines stay attached and adjust to the new position of the AutoShapes they connect.

EXERCISE **14-2** **Add Straight Arrow Connectors**

1. Choose Connectors from the AutoShapes menu and float the Connectors submenu.

2. Choose the second connector in the top row (Straight Arrow Connector) and move the pointer over one of the green AutoShapes. Notice the blue connection sites that appear and the change in pointer shape.

FIGURE 14-2
Connection sites
and pointer

3. Click the connection pointer ⊹ on the right connection site of the first AutoShape ("Get purchase pre-approval") and move the pointer to the right. Notice the dashed line that appears.

4. Move the pointer to the second box ("Locate supplier") and click its left connection site to connect the two boxes. Notice that the endpoints of the selected connector are red.

5. Select the first box and change its position slightly. Notice that the two boxes stay connected when you move one.

6. Draw a second connector from the "Locate supplier" box to the "Approved vendor?" box. Using the same method, draw the other connectors shown earlier in Figure 14-1.

TIP: Double-click the Straight Arrow Connector button (or any other button on the Connectors submenu) to keep the connection pointer active. This will allow you to draw multiple lines without the need to click the button each time. When you're finished, click the button once to turn off the connector pointer.

EXERCISE 14-3 **Change Flowchart AutoShapes**

You can change flowchart AutoShapes just as you change other AutoShapes. In flowcharts, the diamond shape is traditionally used to signify a decision-making point, where a "Yes" takes one path and a "No" takes another path.

1. Select the "Approved vendor?" box and choose Change AutoShape from the Draw menu. Choose Flowchart and then choose the diamond in the first row (Flowchart: Decision).

2. Drag one of the diamond's side resize handles to make it slightly wider. Notice the connection lines adjust and stay connected.

3. Change the last box in the right column ("Place order") to the first shape in the third row of Flowchart shapes (Terminator). Reduce the height of this AutoShape to approximately 0.5 inch.

4. Create a small floating text box with the text **Yes**. Format it with no border and no fill. Make the text 16-point Arial, bold, center-aligned, and black. Change all its internal margins to 0.00 inch. Position the text box below the diamond shape.

5. Draw a straight connector (the first connector on the Connectors menu) from the diamond to the top of the "Yes" box.

6. Choose the Elbow Arrow Connector (fifth Connector on the menu) and draw a connector from the bottom of the "Yes" box to the top of the "Negotiate Price" box. Notice that the connector automatically bends to make a neat path between the two shapes.

7. Copy the "Yes" text box and paste it above the connector between "Get vendor approval" and "Approved vendor." Select the word "Yes" and change it to **No**.

8. Select the connector between "Get vendor approval" and "Approved vendor." Drag its right endpoint away from the diamond shape and reconnect it to the left side of the "No" box.

9. Draw a straight connector from the "Approved vendor?" diamond to the right side of the "No" box.

EXERCISE 14-4 **Align Flowchart Elements and Apply Finishing Touches**

Sometimes it's preferable to have the flowchart connectors point at odd angles, but other times you'll want them aligned horizontally or vertically.

1. Float the Align or Distribute submenu (from the Draw menu).

2. Select the three shapes in the right column and the "Yes" box. Using the <u>A</u>lign or Distribute commands, align their centers relative to each other.

3. Select the three shapes in the left column and align their centers relative to each other. Now all the vertical connectors are straight.

4. Select the top two shapes and align their middles relative to each other. Align the middles of the bottom two shapes.

5. Select the "No" box along with the two middle shapes and align their middles. Now all the connectors are straight and neat.

6. If necessary, select the bottom two shapes and move them down to create more room within the flowchart.

7. Select the first box ("Get purchase pre-approval") and change it to the Right Arrow on the Block <u>A</u>rrows AutoShape menu. Move up the arrow's adjustment handle to fit the text. Change the arrow fill color to pink.

8. Change the fill color of the diamond to red and change the last shape ("Place order") to yellow.

9. Select all the elements of the flowchart and group them.

10. Center the flowchart horizontally relative to the slide and adjust its vertical position if needed.

11. Adjust the black and white settings.

12. Create a slide footer for this slide only. Include the date and key *[your name], [your initials]*14-4.ppt in the footer text box.

FIGURE 14-3
Completed
flowchart

13. Save the presentation as *[your initials]*14-4.ppt in a new folder for Lesson 14.

14. Print the flowchart slide.

Creating an Organization Chart

The easiest way to insert an org chart in a presentation is to add a new slide with the Organization Chart AutoLayout. Org charts are created and edited in a separate program called Microsoft Organization Chart, which you activate within PowerPoint.

 NOTE: Check with your instructor that the Organization Chart feature is installed on your computer.

EXERCISE 14-5 Start the Org Chart Application

When you start a new org chart, you begin with a default chart template containing four boxes. A *chart box* is the most basic unit in an org chart. This box contains space for up to four lines of information, such as a name and a title. Each box is positioned on a *level* in the chart, which indicates its position in the hierarchy of the organization. The top box in an org chart is level 1.

FIGURE 14-4
Organization
Chart AutoLayout

1. Insert a new slide between slides 2 and 3 using the Organization Chart layout. Key the title **New Management Structure**.

2. Double-click the org chart placeholder. The Microsoft Organization Chart editing screen appears, displaying a four-box org chart. This editing screen has its own menus and toolbar. The level-1 box at the top overlaps the boxes below because it is selected. (See Figure 14-5 on the next page.)

3. Click anywhere on the blue background to deselect the org chart. The "<Comment 1>" and "<Comment 2>" lines disappear from the level-1 box and the overlap is eliminated.

4. Click inside the level-1 box. The text is highlighted.

5. Click inside the level-1 box again. The two Comment lines reappear. Each box can have as many as four lines for an individual's name, title, and two lines of comments.

6. Click the left level-2 box to highlight the text.

7. Click in the box again. The two Comment lines appear.

FIGURE 14-5
Org chart opening
layout

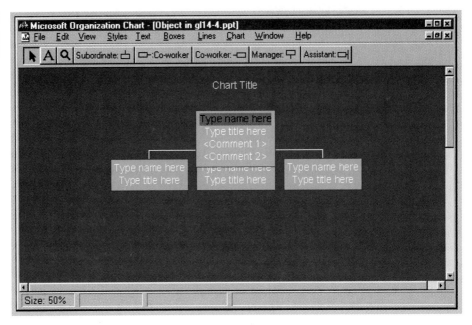

TABLE 14-1   Organization Chart Toolbar

BUTTON (NAME)	FUNCTION
�(Select)	Select and drag objects
A (Enter Text)	Create background (floating) text object
Q (Zoom)	Reduce chart so it fits in window or magnify part of chart
Subordinate:	Add subordinate box (or boxes) to a box
:Co-worker	Add co-worker box (or boxes) to left of a box
Co-worker:	Add co-worker box (or boxes) to right of a box
Manager:	Add manager box to a box
Assistant:	Add assistant box (or boxes) to a box

EXERCISE 14-6 Enter Text in an Org Chart

1. Click the level-1 box. The contents of the box are selected.

2. Key **President** and press Enter. The name is entered and the title line is now selected. Key **CEO**.

3. Click the left level-2 box. Although the box specifies "Name" and "Title," you can enter any text.

4. Key **Operations** and press Enter. The title line is selected.

5. Press Delete. Click the center level-2 box. (Notice that the title line is removed from the left box.)

6. Key **Sales & Marketing** in the center level-2 box, press Enter, and delete the title.

7. Click the right level-2 box, key **Administration**, and delete the title. Click outside the box.

> **NOTE:** The Organization Chart editing screen provides a placeholder for a chart title at the top of the chart. You can ignore or delete this placeholder if you plan to use the PowerPoint slide's title placeholder instead.

Adding Organization Chart Boxes

You can add new boxes and levels to an existing org chart by adding subordinate, assistant, or co-worker boxes.

EXERCISE 14-7 Insert Subordinate Boxes

Subordinate: ⌁

1. Click the Subordinate button. The pointer changes from an arrow to a tiny subordinate box icon.

2. Click the Administration box on level 2. A blank box appears under the Administration box.

FIGURE 14-6
Number of boxes indicated on status bar

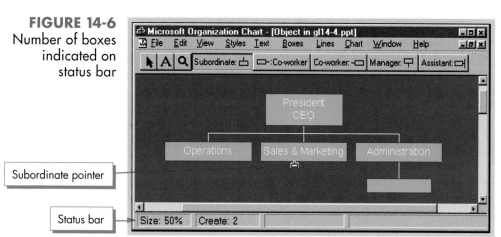

Subordinate pointer

Status bar

3. To insert two subordinate boxes at one time, click the Subordinate button twice. The status bar at the bottom of the org chart window now reads "Create: 2."

 NOTE: If you click too many times, you can press Esc to cancel the action and try again.

4. Click the Operations box. Two boxes appear under Operations.

5. Click the Subordinate button three times and then click the Sales & Marketing box. Three boxes appear under Sales & Marketing. The screen scrolls left to accommodate the increased number of boxes.

6. Maximize or resize the window to see the entire chart.

FIGURE 14-7
Org chart with
subordinate boxes
added

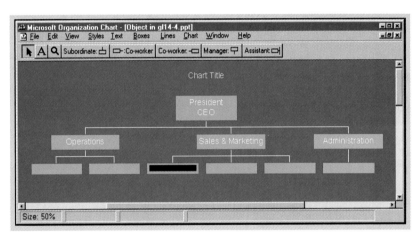

EXERCISE 14-8 Add Assistant and Co-worker Boxes

You may add assistant boxes to the org chart for positions that provide administrative assistance or other support. You may also add boxes for additional people reporting to the same manager—that is, co-worker boxes.

1. Click the Assistant button [Assistant: ☐] on the toolbar.

2. Click the level-1 box, "President." An assistant box is added just below the "President" box.

3. Click the Right Co-worker button three times [Co-worker: ☐], and then click the blank subordinate box under the Administration box. Three co-worker boxes are added to the right of the existing box for a total of four boxes now reporting to Administration.

EXERCISE 14-9   Key Text in Boxes

After you set up the structure of your org chart, you can key all the names and titles in the boxes.

1. Click the level-1 box, select the word "President," and key **Julie Wolfe**. Press Enter and key **Gus Irvinelli**, overwriting "CEO." Press Enter and key **Co-owners** in the Comment 1 field.

2. Key **Troy Scott** as the name in the assistant box. Press Enter and key **Administrative Assistant** as the title.

3. In the two boxes under Operations (on level 3), key the following employee information:

Kitchen	**Purchasing**
Eric Dennis	**Jessie Smith**
Assistant Chef	**Purchasing Mgr**

> **TIP:** You can press Ctrl + an Arrow key to move from box to box in an org chart. For example, Ctrl + Right or Left Arrow moves to a different box on the same level; Ctrl + Up or Down Arrow moves to a different level.

4. In the three boxes under Sales & Marketing, key the following employee information

Events	**Merchandise**	**Marketing**
Ian Mahoney	**Lila Nelson**	**Evan Johnson**
Sales Mgr	**Sales Mgr**	**Marketing Mgr**

5. In the four boxes under Administration, key the following (leaving the last box blank):

MIS	**Billing & Acctg**	**Human Resources**
Chuck Warden	**Sarah Conners**	**Chris Davis**
MIS Mgr	**Accounting Mgr**	**HR Mgr**

6. Add the following text to the second-level boxes:

Operations	**Sales & Marketing**	**Administration**
Michele Jenkins	**Roy Olafsen**	**Michael Peters**
Head Chef	**Marketing Mgr**	**Administration Mgr**

EXERCISE 14-10   Delete Boxes

If you have more boxes than necessary, you can delete them at any time. You can also adjust the chart size within the window to see the entire chart.

1. Use the horizontal scroll bar to display the right, empty box under Administration.

2. Click the box and press [Delete]. The box is deleted and the remaining level-3 boxes shift to the right. Even with the box deleted, it's still impossible to see the entire chart at this level of magnification.

3. Maximize the Organization Chart window, if necessary, and choose Size to Window from the View menu. The chart size is reduced so it fits within the window. Although it's difficult to read the text, you can see the overall structure of the chart.

4. Save your changes to the org chart by choosing Update [filename] from the File menu. (Notice that the filename of your PowerPoint presentation appears next to the update command.)

FIGURE 14-8
Entire org chart
sized to fit in the
window

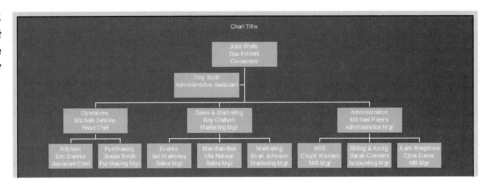

Rearranging Organization Chart Boxes

Organizations change frequently in many companies. You may need to promote, demote, or move org chart boxes as the reporting structure changes or becomes more complex.

EXERCISE 14-11 Promote and Demote Boxes

1. To enlarge the chart view again, choose 50% of Actual from the View menu (or press [F10]).

2. Use the scroll bars to locate the Events box (under Sales & Marketing). Point to the Events box and hold down the mouse button.

3. Without releasing the mouse button, drag the Events box on top of the Merchandise box and then slightly down. As you drag the box, the pointer alternates between a four-pointed arrow, a right-pointing white arrow,

and a subordinate icon. Release the mouse when you see the subordinate icon. Now Ian Mahoney reports to Lila Nelson. (If you release the mouse button when the right-pointing white arrow is displayed, Ian Mahoney becomes a co-worker of Lila Nelson on her right side.)

FIGURE 14-9
Dragging to
demote a box

NOTE: If you drop a box in the wrong location, choose <u>U</u>ndo from the <u>E</u>dit menu (or press Ctrl+Z) and try again. But remember, Microsoft Organization Chart only allows one level of Undo.

4. Edit Lila Nelson's box, changing the name to **Merchandise & Events**

5. Edit Ian Mahoney's box, deleting "Events" and changing "Sales Mgr" to **Sales Associate**

6. Click the MIS box (located under Administration) to select it and then cut the box to the Clipboard. (Choose Cu<u>t</u> from the <u>E</u>dit menu or press Ctrl+X).

7. Click the co-owners box on level 1 and paste the MIS box. (Choose <u>P</u>aste Boxes from the <u>E</u>dit menu or press Ctrl+V). The MIS box is now promoted to level 2, reporting directly to the restaurant co-owners.

8. Cut the Purchasing box (Jesse Smith) under Operations and paste it to report to Administration.

EXERCISE 14-12 Change Box Style and Arrangement

Depending on the size of your org chart, you may find it useful to rearrange a group of boxes under a manager. For example, you can arrange the boxes vertically instead of horizontally.

1. Add another subordinate box to Administration by clicking the Subordinate button and clicking the Administration Mgr box.

2. In the new box, key **Payroll & Benefits** as the name, **John Larson** as the title, and **Payroll Mgr** as Comment 1. Four boxes now report to Administration.

3. Use the arrow pointer to draw a selection rectangle around the four boxes.

 TIP: You can use shortcut keys to select boxes. Select a box and then use Ctrl+G to select a group (all the selected box's co-workers). Use Ctrl+B to select a branch (all the selected box's subordinates).

FIGURE 14-10
Style options

4. Open the Styles menu and choose the third option in the first row, which stacks the four boxes in two columns.

5. Select the three boxes reporting to Sales & Marketing. Open the Styles menu and choose the second option in the first row. The boxes in this group are now stacked in a single column.

 TIP: You can also select multiple boxes by holding down Shift and clicking the desired box. This technique is a good way to select nonadjacent boxes.

6. Choose Update *[filename]* from the File menu to update the chart.

Formatting Organization Chart Elements

After your chart is complete, you can change the color of the chart boxes, text, lines, and background; add shadows to the boxes; change the font; and alter the style of the connecting lines.

EXERCISE 14-13 Use Fill Colors, Fonts, and Shadows

1. To select all boxes in the chart, choose Select from the Edit menu and then choose All (or press Ctrl+A).

2. Choose Font from the Text menu, change the font to 18-point Arial, bold, and click OK. The boxes enlarge to accommodate the text size.

3. With all boxes selected, choose Shado<u>w</u> from the <u>B</u>oxes menu and then choose the second shadow style in the second row. Deselect the boxes to view the shadow.

4. From the <u>V</u>iew menu, choose <u>S</u>ize to Window (or press F9). Now you can see the entire chart. Select all the boxes except the level-1 co-owners box. Choose C<u>o</u>lor from the <u>B</u>oxes menu and choose medium blue. Click OK.

5. With the boxes still selected, choose Border Co<u>l</u>or from the <u>B</u>oxes menu, and change the border color to red.

6. Select the four level-2 boxes (beginning with Operations) and make them dark blue.

7. Select the co-owners box. Choose C<u>o</u>lor from the <u>T</u>ext menu and change the text color to yellow. Change the box color to red and the font size to 24 points.

EXERCISE 14-14 Format Connecting Lines

You can select lines by clicking one line at a time individually, by shift-clicking to select more than one line, or by drawing a selection box around a group of boxes and their lines. Selected lines are displayed as dashed lines.

1. Choose <u>S</u>elect from the <u>E</u>dit menu, and then choose Connecting Lines from the submenu. All the connecting lines are dashed lines, indicating they are selected.

2. Choose Co<u>l</u>or from the <u>L</u>ines menu, choose red, and click OK. Click the org chart's background to deselect the lines and see their new color.

3. Select the lines again by using the <u>E</u>dit menu or by drawing a selection box around all the boxes. Choose <u>T</u>hickness from the <u>L</u>ines menu and change the line thickness to the second line choice.

4. Click the vertical line under the level-1 co-owner's box to select it.

5. With Shift held down, click the vertical line above the level 2 Operations box. Now both lines are selected.

6. With Shift held down, continue clicking all the connecting lines above the level-2 boxes to select them (or draw a selection box wide enough to include these connecting lines).

7. Change the line color of the selected connecting lines back to white.

8. Update the chart, and then choose <u>E</u>xit and Return to *[filename]* from the <u>F</u>ile menu to return to PowerPoint.

9. In Slide view, resize the org chart proportionally by dragging corner handles to make it fill the entire slide.

NOTE: It's important to resize an org chart proportionally by dragging only its corner handles. Otherwise, the text becomes distorted.

10. Center the org chart horizontally relative to the slide.

FIGURE 14-11
Completed org
chart slide

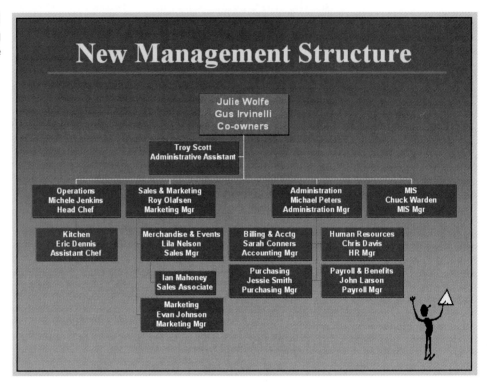

 NOTE: An org chart object is similar to a Microsoft Graph object. You edit it in a separate program from within PowerPoint. To edit an org chart, double-click it to reopen the Microsoft Organization Chart program.

11. Create a slide footer for this slide only. Include the date and key *[your name], [your initials]*14-14.ppt in the footer text box.

12. On the handouts, include the date and your name as header and include the page number and filename *[your initials]*14-14.ppt as footer.

13. Save the presentation as *[your initials]*14-14.ppt in your Lesson 14 folder.

14. Print the org chart slide. Then print the presentation as handouts, 4 slides per page, grayscale, framed.

15. Close the presentation.

COMMAND SUMMARY

FEATURE	BUTTON	MENU	KEYBOARD
Add subordinate	Subordinate:		F2
Add assistant	Assistant:		F6
Add co-worker, left	:Co-worker		F3
Add co-worker, right	Co-worker:		F4
Size to window		View, Size to Window	F9
Display at 50% of actual size		View, 50% of Actual	F10
Select all boxes		Edit, Select, All	Ctrl + A
Select a group of co-workers		Edit, Select, Group	Ctrl + G
Select a branch of subordinates		Edit, Select, Branch	Ctrl + B
Select connecting lines		Edit, Select, Connecting Lines	
Update an org chart		File, Update *[filename]*	
Return to PowerPoint window		File, Exit and Return to *[filename]*	

USING HELP

When you draw a complex diagram using AutoShapes and connector lines, you may want to simplify the drawing by changing the path the connector lines make.

Use Help to learn more about moving and rerouting connector lines:

1. Display and activate the Office Assistant.
2. Key **connector lines** and press Enter.
3. Select the topic "Move a connector line."
4. Read the topic and then select the topic "Reroute a connector line." (See Figure 14-12 on the next page.)
5. Close Help when you finish and hide the Office Assistant.

FIGURE 14-12
Help on rerouting
a connector line

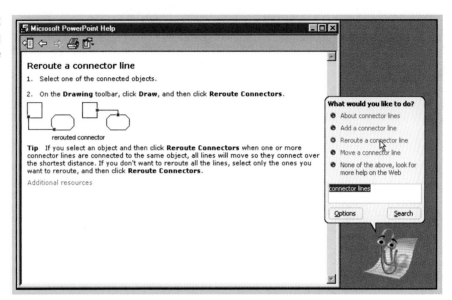

Concepts Review

TRUE/FALSE QUESTIONS

Each of the following statements is either true or false. Indicate your choice by circling **T** or **F**.

T   F   **1.** Flowcharts are always created in Microsoft Organization Chart.

T   F   **2.** You use the Organization Chart layout to insert an org chart.

T   F   **3.** You can use any shape in a flowchart.

T   F   **4.** You can move within an org chart by using ⌷Shift⌷+ Arrow keys.

T   F   **5.** If you add too many boxes to an org chart, you can always delete the extra boxes.

T   F   **6.** You can change the color of the boxes in an org chart.

T   F   **7.** An org chart is treated as a resizable object on the slide.

T   F   **8.** You can use a shape's connection sites to resize the shape.

SHORT ANSWER QUESTIONS

Write the correct answer in the space provided.

1. How do you display the connection sites of an object?

_____

2. What term refers to the top box in an org chart?

_____

3. Which shape is often used in a flowchart to show a decision point?

_____

4. How do you access the Connectors submenu?

_____

5. How do you see an entire chart if its structure exceeds the window size?

_____

6. If you have six people reporting to one manager, how do you change the six boxes so they are stacked vertically instead of lined up horizontally?

_____

7. Besides dragging, how can you rearrange boxes in an org chart?

_____

8. What type of flowchart connector has a right-angle bend?

_____

CRITICAL THINKING

Answer these questions on a separate page. There are no right or wrong answers. Support your answers with examples from your own experience, if possible.

1. Think of a task you had to explain or a job you had to describe to someone and try drawing it in a flowchart.

2. Org charts are by nature rather detail-oriented. Based on what you learned about designing presentations, how can you ensure that an org chart follows the rule of simplicity?

Skills Review

EXERCISE 14-15

Create and format a flowchart.

1. Open the file **Proc1.ppt** and move to slide 4 ("Procedures").

2. Draw flowchart AutoShapes by following these steps:
   a. Click AutoShapes on the Drawing toolbar, choose Flowchart, and float the menu.
   b. Choose Flowchart: Process (the rectangle) and draw the shape near the left edge of the slide.
   c. Key **Listen to grievance** in the AutoShape. Format the text as 18-point Arial, bold, with a text shadow.
   d. Change the AutoShape's text box properties to word wrap, set all its internal margins to 0 inches, and set the anchor point to Middle Centered. Change the fill color to dark pink and remove the outline. Apply Shadow Style 6.

3. Draw a Flowchart: Decision shape (the triangle) to the right of the first shape. Key **Employee talked to Mgr?** Format the text as 18-point Arial, bold. Use the Format Painter to apply the same text box and object formatting as the first box. Then change the fill color to bright green and the text color to black. Adjust the diamond's size to fit the text.

4. Change the shape of the pink rectangle to a right block arrow and adjust its size, if necessary.

5. Draw a connector line between the two shapes by following these steps:

   a. Choose Co<u>n</u>nectors from the A<u>u</u>toShapes menu and float the Connectors submenu.

   b. Click the Straight Arrow connector and move the pointer on top of the pink arrow to display the blue connector sites.

   c. Click the connector site at the tip of the arrow.

   d. Move the pointer to the green diamond and click the connector site on the left side of the diamond.

   e. To change the connector color, select the connector, click the Line Color arrow, and choose gray (background scheme color). Increase the line thickness of the connector to 4.5 points.

6. Add the remaining three AutoShapes shown in Figure 14-13, coloring and formatting them as shown. Key the text shown inside each AutoShape. Don't worry about aligning them yet.

FIGURE 14-13
Completed
flowchart

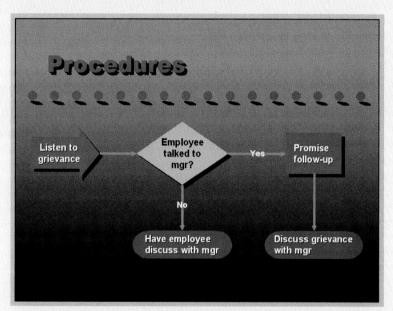

7. Insert connectors between the shapes as shown in the figure.

 TIP: Use Format Painter to format the connector lines.

8. Insert a text box between the diamond and square with the text **Yes**. Format the text as 16-point Arial, bold, white. Remove the fill and border. Size the text box appropriately and adjust its position so it rests on top of the connector.

9. Create a similar text box with the text **No**. Position it as shown in the figure.

10. Align flowchart AutoShapes by following these steps:
    a. Select the arrow, diamond, and square in the first row of shapes.
    b. Using the Align and Distribute commands, distribute them horizontally relative to themselves (not to the slide).
    c. Select the three shapes in the first row again, if necessary, and add the "Yes" box to the selection.
    d. Align the middles of the selected objects relative to themselves (not to the slide).
    e. Select the green diamond, the purple rounded rectangle below it, and the "No" text box. Align their centers relative to themselves.
    f. Align the remaining shapes similarly.

11. Adjust the black and white settings for the slide objects as needed.

12. Group all the shapes and text boxes in the flowchart, and then center the group horizontally relative to the slide. Adjust its vertical position if necessary.

13. Create a slide footer for slide 4. Include the date and key *[your name]*, *[your initials]*14-15.ppt in the footer text box.

14. On the handouts, include the date and your name as header and include the page number and filename *[your initials]*14-15.ppt as footer.

15. Save the presentation as *[your initials]*14-15.ppt in your Lesson 14 folder.

16. Print slide 4. Then print the entire presentation as handouts, 4 slides per page, grayscale, framed.

17. Close the presentation.

EXERCISE 14-16

Create a simple org chart, format boxes, and delete boxes.

1. Open the file **Kitch1.ppt**. Insert a new slide after slide 3 using the Organization Chart layout and the title **Operations**.

2. Double-click the org chart placeholder and add text to the chart by following these steps:
   a. In the level-1 box, key **Michele Jenkins** as the name, press `Enter`, and key **Head Chef & Operations Mgr** as the title.
   b. Click the left box on level 2 and key **Eric Dennis** as the name and **Asst Chef & Kitchen Mgr** as the title.
   c. Press `Ctrl`+`←` to activate the middle box on level 2. Key **Claudia Pell** as the name and **Maitre d' & Service Mgr** as the title.

3. Click the right box on level 2 to select it and press `Delete` to remove it.

4. Change the color of the org chart boxes by following these steps:

   a. Draw a selection rectangle around all three boxes. (If you miss a box, hold down [Shift] and click the box to add it to the selection.)

   b. Choose Color from the Boxes menu, chose black, and click OK.

   c. Choose Shadow from the Boxes menu and chose the second style in the third row.

5. Change the font color of the org chart boxes by following these steps:

   a. Make sure all the boxes are selected.

   b. Choose Color from the Text menu, choose cream (the second from the right on the top row), and click OK.

6. Change the font style of the org chart boxes by following these steps:

   a. Select the text "Michele Jenkins" in the top box.

   b. Choose Font from the Text menu. Choose Arial Black, italic, 18 point. Click OK.

7. Return to Slide view by clicking the Close button ☒ in the upper right corner of the window. Click Yes at the prompt to update the chart.

8. Make the org chart smaller by dragging one of its corner resize handles. Center the chart horizontally and vertically relative to the slide.

9. Adjust the black and white settings as needed.

10. Create a slide footer for slide 4. Include the date and key *[your name]*, *[your initials]***14-16.ppt** in the footer text box.

11. Save the presentation as *[your initials]***14-16.ppt** in your Lesson 14 folder.

12. Print the org chart slide. Then print the entire presentation as handouts, 4 slides per page, grayscale, framed.

13. Close the presentation.

EXERCISE 14-17

Add, promote, demote, and rearrange boxes in an existing org chart.

1. Open the file **Kitch2.ppt**. Move to slide 3 and double-click the org chart to activate it.

2. Add three subordinate boxes to the G. Robinson level-2 box by following these steps:

   a. Click the Subordinate button three times.

   b. Click the G. Robinson box.

   c. In the left box, key **Pastry** as the name and **G. Gordon** as the title.

   d. In the middle box, key **Cooks** as the name, **L. Tilson** as the title, **S. Mason** as Comment 1, and **J. Fulman** as Comment 2.

   e. In the right box, key **Banquets** as the name and **T. Domina** as the title.

3. Promote the level-3 Banquets box to level 2 by following these steps:

   a. Click outside the Banquets box to deselect it.

   b. Position the pointer over the Banquets box, hold down the mouse button, and drag the box over the level-1 box (Kitchen).

   c. When the pointer changes to a subordinate icon, release the mouse button.

4. Change the organizational style of the boxes under G. Robinson by following these steps:

   a. Select the two boxes under G. Robinson.

   b. Choose Styles from the menu and choose the second option, in which the boxes are stacked vertically.

   c. Apply the same style to the two boxes under Facilities & Maint.

5. Change the position of a box relative to its co-workers by following these steps:

   a. Move the mouse pointer over the Banquets box on the right side of level 2.

   b. Drag the box over the left box on the same level until you see a white left-pointing arrow icon.

   c. Release the mouse button.

   d. Move Facilities & Maint to the left of Sr. Cook (G. Robinson).

6. Change the color of the level-1 box (Kitchen) to yellow.

7. Increase the font size for all boxes to 18 points.

8. Update the chart and return to Slide view. Move the slide title closer to the top of the slide, and resize and position the org chart appropriately.

9. Adjust the black and white settings as needed.

10. Create a slide footer for slide 4. Include the date and key *[your name]*, *[your initials]***14-17.ppt** in the footer text box.

11. On the handouts, include the date and your name as header and include the page number and filename *[your initials]***14-17.ppt** as footer.

12. Save the presentation as *[your initials]***14-17.ppt** in your Lesson 14 folder.

13. Print the org chart slide. Then print the entire presentation as handouts, 3 slides per page, grayscale, framed.

14. Close the presentation.

EXERCISE 14-18

Format organization boxes and lines; change the arrangement style.

1. Open the file **Retail1.ppt** and move to slide 4. Double-click the org chart to make formatting changes.

2. Change the arrangement of the items in the Clothing category by following these steps:

   a. Select the four boxes below the Clothing box.

   b. To make the items appear in a vertical list with no boxes, open the Style menu and choose the second style in the second row.

   c. Apply the same style to the items in the Head Gear and Sports Gear categories.

3. Remove the fill from the remaining four boxes by following these steps:

   a. Select all the blue boxes.

   b. Choose Color from the Boxes menu, choose the color sample in the lower right corner, and click OK.

4. Change the border style and color of the boxes by following these steps:

   a. Select the four boxes and choose Border Style from the Boxes menu. Choose the last style in the last row.

   b. Choose Border Color from the Boxes menu, choose dark gray (third from the right on the top row), and click OK.

5. Format connecting lines by following these steps:

   a. Select all the level-1 and level-2 boxes.

   b. Choose Thickness from the Lines menu and then choose None to make the lines disappear.

   c. Draw a selection box that starts at the middle of the right side of the Clothing box and extends to the lower left, selecting all the lines and text below level 2.

   d. Choose Thickness from the Lines menu, and choose the third line thickness.

   e. With the lines still selected, choose Color from the Lines menu, choose dark gray, and click OK.

   f. If any of the lines below level 2 did not get formatted, select them individually by clicking them, and then format them to match.

6. Change the font for all the text to 18-point Arial Black. Increase the level-1 text to 24 points.

7. Change the text color of the level-1 text to light olive, the fourth choice on the first row, and change the level-2 text to dark gray.

8. Select the first item under each retail category ("Denim Shirts," "Bucket Hats," and "Water Bottles"). Change the text color of the selected items to medium blue, the third color on the first row.

9. Change the second item in each category to light olive, the fourth color on the first row. Continuing to use only colors on the first row, make the next item in each category dark pink and the last ones dark green.

10. Update and close Microsoft Org Chart, and return to PowerPoint.

11. Size the chart proportionally until it fills the slide. Center it horizontally and adjust its vertical position, if needed.

12. Adjust the black and white settings for all slides as needed.

13. Create a slide footer for slide 4. Include the date and key *[your name]*, *[your initials]*14-18.ppt in the footer text box.

14. On the handouts, include the date and your name as header and include the page number and filename *[your initials]*14-18.ppt as footer.

15. Save the presentation as *[your initials]*14-18.ppt in your Lesson 14 folder.

16. Print slide 4, and then print the entire presentation as handouts, 4 slides per page, grayscale, framed.

17. Close the presentation.

Lesson Applications

Create a flowchart and construct a menu using an org chart.

1. Open the file **Newyr3.ppt**. Insert a new slide 2 using the Title Only layout and key the title **New Year's Eve Reservations**

2. In the upper left corner, below the title, draw a right arrow using the Pentagon AutoShape (Block Arrows, the third item in the fifth row). Make it about 0.75 inch high and 2 inches wide. In the pentagon shape, key **Call friends**

3. Make the text 24-point Arial, bold, white, with a text shadow. Adjust the size of the AutoShape to fit the text. Make its text anchor point Middle Centered and turn on word wrap. Apply a blue fill and a black border.

4. To the right of the pentagon, insert a clip art image of a telephone (use the search word **phones**). Size the phone to approximately 1 inch square. (The image used in Figure 14-14 was a black phone, recolored with black changed to white and white changed to black).

5. Draw a curved arrow connector from the point of the pentagon to the left side of the phone. With the connector selected, change the line thickness to 4.5 points and change the line style to Round Dot.

FIGURE 14-14
Completed
flowchart

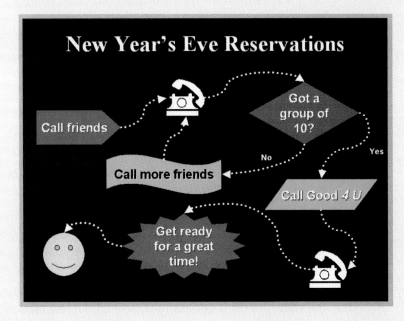

6. Using Figure 14-14 as a guide, insert the AutoShapes shown and key the appropriate text inside each shape. Format the text and the text box options to match the blue pentagon and color the shapes to match the figure (or choose other colors you like).

 TIP: Copy and paste the pentagon arrow shape four times and change the AutoShape, color, and text as needed.

7. Copy the telephone and position it as shown in the figure. Add the connectors, formatting them like the first connector you drew (use Format Painter).

8. Create the "Yes" and "No" text boxes using no fill, no border. Format the text as 16-point Arial, bold, white. Position the text boxes as shown in the figure.

9. Create a slide footer for slide 2. Include the date and key *[your name], [your initials]*14-19.ppt in the footer text box.

10. Save the presentation as *[your initials]*14-19.ppt in your Lesson 14 folder.

11. Insert a new slide after slide 2 using the Org Chart layout. Delete the title placeholder and then double-click the org chart placeholder.

12. Add an additional level-2 box, for a total of four.

13. Arrange the level-2 boxes using the third style in the first row. Make each level-2 box a different bright color, and change the border color to black.

14. Add four subordinate boxes below each level-2 box. Apply the second style in the second row (which arranges text as a list) to each subordinate box.

15. In the level-1 box, key **New Year's Eve Menu**. Key the text shown in Figure 14-15 for levels 2 and 3. (See Figure 14-15 on the next page.)

16. Format the first-level text as 36-pt Times New Roman, bold. Change the box color to none and the border to black.

17. Format the text in the second-level boxes as black, 24-point Times New Roman, italic.

18. Make the third-level text 16-point Arial, bold.

19. Select the line connecting level 1 to level 2 and all the lines connecting level-2 boxes to each other. Change their thickness to none. (Only the lines connecting level 2 to level 3 should be visible.)

20. Update the chart and return to slide view. Enlarge the chart so it fills the slide, center it horizontally, and adjust the vertical position.

21. Adjust the black and white settings in the presentation as needed.

FIGURE 14-15
Completed
org chart

22. Create a slide footer for slide 3. Include the date and key *[Your Name],
    [your initials]***14-19.ppt** in the footer text box.

23. Print slides 2 and 3, and then print handouts, 4 slides per page,
    grayscale, framed.

24. Save and close the presentation.

EXERCISE 14-20

Create, lay out, and design an Organization chart.

1. Open the file **Compute1.ppt**. Insert a new slide after slide 2 using the
   Organization Chart layout.

2. Give the new slide the title **MIS Department Organization**

3. Create an org chart using the information shown in Figure 14-16 (on
   the next page). Use whatever boxes, lines, arrangement style, fonts, and
   colors you think would look good and present the information clearly.
   Be sure to include all the information shown in the figure.

4. Adjust the black and white settings in the presentation as needed.

5. Create a slide footer for slide 3. Include the date and key *[your name],
   [your initials]***14-20.ppt** in the footer text box.

6. On the handouts, include the date and your name as header and include
   the page number and filename *[your initials]***14-20.ppt** as footer.

7. Save the presentation as *[your initials]***14-20.ppt** in your Lesson 14
   folder.

FIGURE 14-16
Org chart text

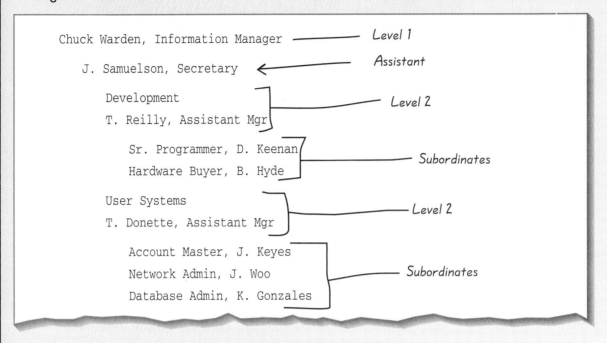

Chuck Warden, Information Manager ——————— *Level 1*

J. Samuelson, Secretary ← ———————— *Assistant*

Development
T. Reilly, Assistant Mgr ——————— *Level 2*

Sr. Programmer, D. Keenan
Hardware Buyer, B. Hyde ——————— *Subordinates*

User Systems
T. Donette, Assistant Mgr ——————— *Level 2*

Account Master, J. Keyes
Network Admin, J. Woo ——————— *Subordinates*
Database Admin, K. Gonzales

8. Print slide 3, and then print the entire presentation as handouts, 4 slides per page, grayscale, framed.

9. Close the presentation.

EXERCISE 14-21 *Challenge Yourself*

Create a 3-D org chart using AutoShapes and connector lines.

1. Start a new presentation using the Bulleted List AutoLayout for the first slide instead of the Title slide. Apply the Straight Edge design template.

2. Customize the default color scheme (the second scheme in the first row) with the following colors: change the Accent and Hyperlink color to dark purple, and change the Accent and Followed Hyperlink color to bright red.

3. Change the Times New Roman font to Arial Black for the entire presentation.

4. Apply a one-color horizontal gradient fill to the background of all slides, using the light beige shadows scheme color. Use the lightest possible shade setting, and choose the variant that has white in the middle.

5. On the slide master, reduce the bulleted text placeholder's fonts by one size. Change the placeholder's internal margins to 0.25 inch all around, turn on the Resize AutoShape to Fit Text option, and change the text anchor point to Middle. Apply a two-color Diagonal Up gradient fill, shading from red at the top to purple at the bottom. Change the text and bullet color to white with a text shadow. Change the text color of all the footer placeholders to dark blue.

6. Still working on the bulleted text placeholder, change its AutoShape to a rounded rectangle and apply 3-D Style 2.

7. On slide 1, key a two-line title with **Good *4 U*** on the first line and **Organization Structure** on the second line. Left-align the title text.

8. Key **Administration Management** in the bulleted text placeholder. Change the font size to 44 points, remove the bullet, and remove the indent. Center-align the text. Change the placeholder size to 2.25 inches high by 6.5 inches wide. Center the placeholder below the title text.

9. Insert a new slide 2 using the Bulleted Text layout. Key **Administration Management** for the title and key the following two bullets:

   Michael Peters, Administration Manager
   Responsible for business management of the restaurant

10. Reduce the width of the bulleted text placeholder to approximately 7.75 inches and center it below the title text.

11. Insert a new slide 3 using the Title Only layout. Key a two-line title with **Administration** on the first line and **Org Chart** on the second.

12. Draw a rounded rectangle 1.25 inches high by 3.5 inches wide. Format it with the same fill and 3-D effect as the text placeholder on the slide master. Position the rectangle near the top of the slide, horizontally centered. Key **Michael Peters** on the first line of the AutoShape and **Administration** on the second line. Change the rectangle's internal margins to 0.1 inch all around. Format the text as white 24-point Arial Black, with a text shadow.

13. Make a copy of the AutoShape. Resize the copy to 1 inch high by 2 inches wide. Make three copies of the resized shape. Arrange all four copies in a horizontal row below the original AutoShape. Align their bottoms relative to each other and distribute them horizontally relative to the slide.

14. Reduce the text size of the copied shapes to 16 points and key the following names and responsibilities in the shapes:

| **Jessie Smith** | **Sara Conners** | **Chris Davis** | **John Larson** |
| **Purchasing** | **Billing** | **Personnel** | **Payroll** |

15. Draw an elbow connector from the bottom of the Michael Peters box to the top of the Jessie Smith box. Change the connector line to purple

with a 3-point line weight. Draw similarly formatted elbow connectors to each of the other boxes in the second row.

16. If necessary, realign and redistribute the boxes so all the lines and boxes are perfectly aligned.

17. Group all the elements of the org chart and position it attractively on the slide.

18. Adjust the black and white settings as needed.

19. Create a slide footer for slide 3. Include the date and key *[your name], [your initials]*14-21.ppt in the footer text box.

20. On the handouts, include the date and your name as header and include the page number and filename *[your initials]*14-21.ppt as footer.

21. Save the presentation as *[your initials]*14-21.ppt in your Lesson 14 folder.

22. Print slide 3, and then print the entire presentation as handouts, 3 slides per page, grayscale, framed.

23. Close the presentation.

Unit 5 Applications

UNIT APPLICATION 5-1

Add a table, a chart, and a flowchart to a presentation.

1. Open the file **HdCount.ppt**. Apply the Blue Diagonal design template and choose the second color scheme (with the lavender background). On the title and slide masters, remove the text shadow in the bulleted text and subtitle placeholders.

2. Insert a new slide after slide 3 using the Table layout with the title **Current Breakdown**. Create a 5-column by 4-row table using the data shown in Figure U5-1.

FIGURE U5-1
Completed table

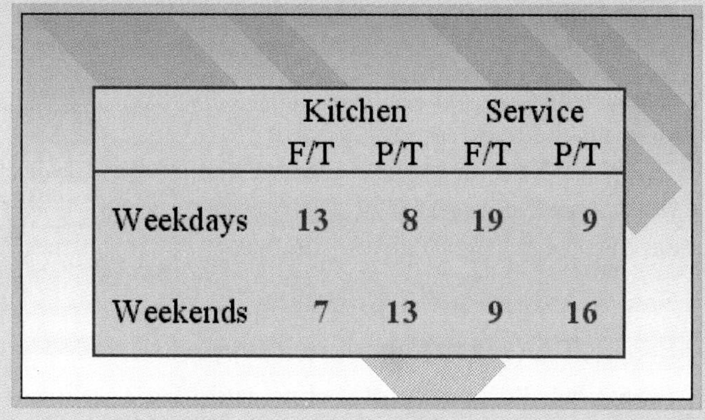

	Kitchen		Service	
	F/T	P/T	F/T	P/T
Weekdays	13	8	19	9
Weekends	7	13	9	16

3. To format the table as shown in Figure U5-1:
   - Merge two cells for "Kitchen" and two cells for "Service."
   - Adjust the column widths so the text fits attractively, and align the text to match the figure, adjusting internal margins as needed. The overall table dimensions should be approximately 6.25 inches wide by 3.25 inches tall.
   - Apply 3-pt purple borders (title text scheme color) to the table's outside border and under the headings. Apply a lavender fill (fills scheme color) to the entire table. Change the font color for the numbers to purple.

4. Adjust the table's position on the slide until it appears centered horizontally.

5. Insert a new slide after slide 4 using the Chart layout with the title **Past, Current, Projected**. Create a column chart using the data shown in Figure U5-2 (on the next page).

FIGURE U5-2

	1998	1999	2000	2001
Full-time	41	40	48	38
Part-time	30	35	46	61

6. Apply a one-color gradient fill to each column, using colors from the template's color scheme. Move the legend to the bottom, make it slightly wider, center it, and delete its border. Make other adjustments to the chart to enhance it, such as changing font size or scale.

7. In Slide view, draw a text box or AutoShape at the top of the chart with the text **Projecting 61 P/T, 38 F/T**. Draw an arrow from the text box (or shape) to the top of the 2001 columns. Format the text object and the arrow as you like.

8. Insert a new slide after slide 5 using the Title Only layout with the title **Plan for Increasing P/T Headcount**. Reduce the title font to fit the text on one line.

9. On new slide 6, create a flowchart showing the following 5 steps, placing the text for each step in a different shape (exclude the word "Step" and the number). Arrange the shapes in clockwise order and draw arrow connector lines from the first shape to the second, from the second to the third, and so on.

Step 1: **Advertise P/T positions**

Step 2: **T. Scott to schedule interviews**

Step 3: **M. Peters to interview and hire applicants**

Step 4: **J. Farla to train**

Step 5: **L. Klein to assign schedules**

10. Format the shapes, text, and connectors as you like.

11. Apply the slide transition effect Random Bars Vertical to all slides.

12. View the slide show.

13. Adjust the black and white settings as needed.

14. Create a slide footer for all slides except the title slide. Include the date and key *[your name], [your initials]*u5-1.ppt in the footer text box.

15. On the handouts, include the date and your name as header and include the page number and filename *[your initials]*u5-1.ppt as footer.

16. Save the presentation as *[your initials]*u5-1.ppt in a new folder for Unit 5 Applications.

17. Print slides 4, 5, and 6. Then print the entire presentation as handouts, 6 slides per page, grayscale, framed.

18. Close the presentation.

UNIT APPLICATION 5-2

Create a presentation with a table and a chart.

1. Start a new blank presentation. Insert a Title slide with the title **Menu Analysis** and the subtitle **Understanding Our Customers**. Apply the Artsy design template using the first color scheme on the second row (the medium blue background).

2. On the Title Master, ungroup the graphic elements. Crop the left half of the top graphic, keeping the half that has the brighter colors. Crop the image from the bottom up, leaving a brightly colored strip 0.25 inch high by 5 inches wide. Duplicate the cropped image and position the two images together so they make a strip 0.25 inch high by 10 inches wide. Align their bottoms and group them. Position the newly created graphic image near the top of the Title master, 0.25 inch down from the top edge.

3. Copy the graphic strip you just created and paste it on the Slide master, near the bottom, between the bulleted text placeholder and the footer placeholders.

4. Insert a new slide using the Bulleted List layout. Add the title **What Do We Serve?** and the following bulleted items:

- **Theme is consistently "healthy"**
- **Menu offerings designed to meet a variety of customer preferences**
- **Regular analysis eliminates less popular, labor-intensive offerings**

5. Insert another slide using the Bulleted List layout, with the title **How Do We Decide?** and the following bulleted items:

- **New menu item is first offered as a chef's special for several months**
- **If response judged acceptable, new item placed on menus for a six-month trial**

6. Insert another slide using the Bulleted List layout, with the title **Menu Analysis** and the following bulleted items:

- **Balanced between meat and vegetarian entrees**
- **Lunch more heavily weighted toward vegetarian items**
- **Dinner menu under review as customer mix changes**

7. Insert another slide, using the Table layout, with the title **Menu Offerings by Type**. Create a table using the information shown in Figure U5-3.

FIGURE U5-3

	Entrees		
	Meat	Vegetarian	Appetizers
Lunch	7	14	6
Dinner	11	9	8

8. In the first two rows, reduce the text size to 24 points. In the first column, do the same. Keep the numbers at 28 points.

9. Adjust the "Vegetarian" column to be just wide enough to fit, and then make all the other columns that contain numbers the same width as the "Vegetarian" column. (Use guides to measure). Make the first column just wide enough for its text.

10. Adjust the height of the first two rows to be just high enough to fit the text. Make the other rows 1 inch high.

11. Adjust text alignment and cell alignment to position text and numbers appropriately within the cells. Make sure numbers are right-aligned and centered under their headings.

12. Add a new column on the left side of the table with the column heading **Desserts**. Key **7** for Lunch and **8** for Dinner.

13. Adjust the horizontal position of the table, and move it up on the slide until there is approximately 1 inch between the bottom of the table and the graphic element.

14. Merge the two cells in the first row above "Appetizers" and "Desserts"; then key **Other Items** in the merged cell.

15. Make the column and row headings text yellow and the numbers cream-colored.

16. Remove all the borders, and then apply deep orange 2.25-point borders (accent and hyperlink scheme color) to just the cells containing numbers.

17. Apply a semitransparent olive green fill to the cell containing the vegetarian lunch number.

18. Add a text box under the table with the text **High appeal among female customers**. Format the text as 24-point Arial, italic, centered. Draw a cream-colored line with an arrow from the text box to the vegetarian lunches cell.

19. Create a new slide after slide 5 using the Chart layout and the title **Menu Type Comparisons**. Use the data on slide 5 to create a 3-D pie chart showing the percentages of each type of menu offering. (Add lunch and dinner numbers together for each category.) Use scheme color gradient fills for the pie slices, shading so that each slice is lightest in the center.

20. Add data labels to the pie slices, showing percent only. Move the data labels onto each slice, and change their font size to 24 points.

21. Move the legend to the bottom of the chart, remove its border, make the legend slightly wider, center it below the chart, and change its font size to 24 points.

22. In Slide view, make the pie chart a little smaller and adjust its position.

23. View the slide show.

24. Adjust the black and white settings as needed.

25. Create a slide footer for slides 5 and 6. Include the date and key *[your name], [your initials]*u5-2.ppt in the footer text box.

26. On the handouts, include the date and your name as header and include the page number and filename *[your initials]*u5-2.ppt as footer.

27. Save the presentation as *[your initials]*u5-2.ppt in your Unit 5 Applications folder.

28. Print slides 5 and 6. Then print the entire presentation as handouts, 6 slides per page, grayscale, framed.

29. Close the presentation.

APPLICATION 5-3

Create a presentation by adding an org chart and then modifying it.

1. Start a new presentation using the Neon Frame template. Create a title slide with the following two-line title:

Good *4* U
Senior Management

2. Key the subtitle **Current and Future Organization**. Change the color scheme to the second sample on the second row (the one with orange, red, and pink accents).

3. Insert a new slide after slide 1, using the Bulleted List layout with the title **Why Change What Works?** and the following bulleted items:

- **Current structure designed for a single-restaurant company**
- **Management must be positioned for a national, multi-restaurant organization**

4. Insert a new slide after slide 2, using the Organization Chart layout and the title **Current Organization**.

5. On slide 3, create an organizational chart for the Good 4 *U* restaurant using Figure U5-4. Keeping all the staff in boxes, arrange the chart boxes in an attractive and functional way.

FIGURE U5-4

```
Julie Wolfe, Gus Irvinelli, Co-owners

    Michele Jenkins, Head Chef

        Claudia Pell, Maitre d'

        Eric Dennis, Assistant Chef

    Roy Olafsen, Marketing Mgr

        Brad James, Sales

        Jane Kryler, Promotions

    Chuck Warden, Information Mgr

        Tanya Reilly, Development

        Ted Donette, User Systems

    Michael Peters, Administration Mgr

        Jessie Smith, Purchasing

        Chris Davis, Personnel

        John Larson, Payroll
```

6. Remove the fill color from the boxes. Apply a double-line border using a color of your choice. Change the connecting line color. Increase both co-owners names to 16 points and make them bold. (Leave the text "Co-owner" as is.)

7. Return to Slide view. Resize and reposition the org chart and the slide title to make an attractive composition.

8. Insert a new slide after slide 3, using the Bulleted List layout with the title **Future Structure** and the following bulleted items:

- **Reorganization planned for 2001**
- **Designed to capitalize on the individual talents of co-owners**
- **Company will be split into two functional areas**

9. Make a copy of slide 3 (the Org chart) and position the copy as slide 5 (use Slide Sorter view). Change the title of slide 5 to **Future Organization**

10. On the org chart, change level 1 so there are two boxes, one for Gus Irvinelli and one for Julie Wolfe. Give them both the title **Co-Owner**. Make Chuck Warden's and Roy Olafsen's departments report to Gus Irvinelli, and make Michele Jenkins' and Michael Peters' departments report to Julie Wolfe.

11. Insert a sound clip of your choice on slide 1, making it play automatically and keep playing until slide 2 is displayed. Center the sound icon below the subtitle, and conceal it by placing an AutoShape or clip art image (or combination) of your choice on top of it.

12. Apply a transition effect of your choice to slides 2 through 5, and animate the text on the bullet slides with an effect of your choice, making it dim to orange.

13. View the slide show.

14. Adjust the black and white settings as needed.

15. Create a slide footer for the two org chart slides. Include the date and key *[your name]*, *[your initials]***u5-3.ppt** in the footer text box.

16. On the handouts, include the date and your name as header and include the page number and filename *[your initials]***u5-3.ppt** as footer.

17. Save the presentation as *[your initials]***u5-3.ppt** in your Unit 5 Applications folder.

18. Print the two org chart slides. Then print the entire presentation as handouts, 6 slides per page, grayscale, framed.

19. Close the presentation.

UNIT APPLICATION 5-4   *Making It Work for You*

Write a presentation that includes a table, an organization chart, and a pie chart.

1. In a new presentation, create an organization chart containing at least three levels and six boxes. Use the chart to show a business, school, family, or anything that has a structure. Format the org chart attractively.

2. Create a presentation around this slide, including a title slide, at least two bulleted text slides (one of which uses a clip art and text layout), and a slide containing an attractively formatted table.

3. Create a slide containing a pie chart using the data from the table. Organize the slides in appropriate order.

4. Apply a template of your choice and customize it by changing colors, fonts, spacing, alignment, and other features.

5. Include at least one AutoShape or floating text box in the presentation. Add another drawing object, such as a freeform shape, if desired.

6. Make sure the color scheme of all slide objects matches the template colors.

7. Add at least one animation, slide transition, or sound effect.

8. Adjust black and white settings as needed.

9. On the handouts, include the date and your name as header and include the page number and filename *[your initials]*u5-4.ppt as footer.

10. Save the presentation as *[your initials]*u5-4.ppt in your Unit 5 Applications folder.

11. Print as handouts, 4 to 6 slides per page, grayscale, framed.

12. Close the presentation.

Delivering Presentations

Distributing and Presenting Your Work

After completing this lesson, you will be able to:

1. Use Meeting Minder to record notes during a presentation.
2. Distribute presentations in a variety of formats.
3. Use PowerPoint's Pack and Go feature.
4. Prepare a presentation for viewing on the Web.

 Estimated Time: 1¼ hours

MOUS
ACTIVITIES

In this lesson:
PP2000 1.10
PP2000 E.1.4
PP2000 E.5.2
PP2000 E.5.3
PP2000 E.5.4
PP2000 E.6.1
PP2000 E.6.2
PP2000 E.6.3
PP2000 E.7.2
PP2000 E.9.2

See Appendix F.

In this Lesson you learn how to use Meeting Minder to record audience feedback when presenting a slide show. You also learn how to package a presentation so it can be displayed on other computers, how to format your work for the Internet or an *intranet* (an Internet-like system that exists only within a company or organization), how to convert your work to 35mm slides, and how to print overhead transparencies.

Using Meeting Minder to Record Notes During a Presentation

When running a slide show in PowerPoint during a meeting, you can record audience feedback, slide-by-slide, by using the Meeting Minder feature. Like taking minutes at a meeting, you enter notes and list action items. The action items are recorded on a separate slide that you can display at the end of the meeting to summarize the proceedings. When the meeting is over, you can print and distribute the notes to your audience or send them via e-mail.

> **TIP:** If you're going to be holding a live meeting, slide timings are usually not appropriate because you'll want to be flexible with the amount of time spent on individual slides to encourage discussion. Slide timings are most appropriate for self-running presentations.

EXERCISE **15-1** **Use Meeting Minder During a Slide Show**

1. Open the file **Summertime.ppt**. Run the presentation as a slide show starting with slide 1. Imagine that you are presenting this at a meeting and the group is commenting and making decisions as you move from slide to slide.

2. With slide 1 displayed, right-click anywhere and choose Meeting Minder from the slide show shortcut menu.

3. In the Meeting Minder dialog box, click the Meeting Minutes tab, if necessary. Key **The Food Sample Planning Session meeting was held in New York on** *[today's date].*

FIGURE 15-1
Recording meeting minutes

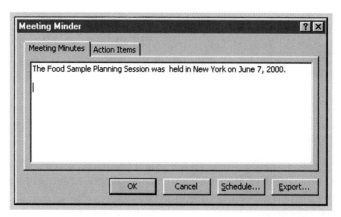

4. Press Enter twice, and then key **Roy Olafsen has agreed to take care of all convention center details, including room reservations for all attendees.** Press Enter twice to prepare for the next entry.

5. Click the Action Items tab. In the Description box, key **Confirm convention center reservations**, and then key **R. Olafsen** in the Assigned To box. In the Due Date box, key the date one week from today. Click Add, and then click OK.

FIGURE 15-2
Creating an
action item

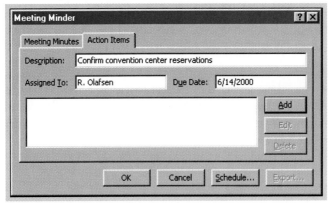

 TIP: If Microsoft Outlook is installed on your computer, you can click Schedule to enter an action item on Outlook's calendar.

6. Move to the next slide ("Appetizer Specials") and open the Meeting Minder dialog box again.

7. Press Ctrl+End to move to the end of the minutes in the text box, and then key **Michelle Jenkins and her staff will take care of all food preparation issues, including ordering food and arranging for kitchen equipment.** Press Enter twice to prepare for the next entry.

8. Click the Action Items tab and enter the following in the appropriate text boxes:
Description: **Confirm food and food prep equipment orders with all suppliers**
Assigned To: **M. Jenkins**
Due Date: *[key the date two weeks from today]*
Click Add, and then click OK.

9. Move to the next slide ("The Main Course") and add the following information in the Meeting Minder dialog box:
Meeting Minutes: **There will be only one menu item change. The Chicken and Potato Salad did not get good test reviews. It will be replaced with Black Bean Chicken Salad.**
Action Item:
Description: **Complete kitchen and taste testing for Black Bean Chicken Salad**
Assigned To: **M. Jenkins**
Due Date: *[key the date three weeks from today]*

10. Move to the next slide ("Desserts"), and then to the last slide ("Action Items"). The Action Items slide was created automatically and lists all the action items entered with Meeting Minder.

11. End the slide show. Create a slide footer for the Action Items slide only. Include the date and key *[your name], [your initials]*15-1.ppt in the slide footer text box.

12. Save the presentation as *[your initials]*15-1.ppt in a new folder for Lesson 15.

13. Print the Action Items slide and leave it open for the next Exercise.

EXERCISE 15-2 Distribute Meeting Minder Minutes

After delivering your presentation, you can distribute meeting minutes and action items in the following ways:

- Print the Action Items slide.
- Export the meeting minutes and action items to a Word document, and then print them or send them via e-mail.

1. With the file *[your initials]*15-1.ppt open, choose Meeting Minder from the Tools menu to open the Meeting Minder dialog box.

2. Click the Export button. The Meeting Minder Export dialog box opens.

 NOTE: If the Export button is dimmed, click the Action Items tab. Then select one of the action items in the list box to activate the Export button.

3. Under Export Options, select Send Meeting Minutes and Action Items to Microsoft Word. (If Post Action Items to Microsoft Outlook is checked, deselect it.)

FIGURE 15-3
Exporting meeting minutes and action items

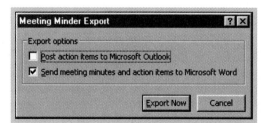

4. Click Export Now. After a brief pause, Microsoft Word displays a document listing the Meeting Minutes and Action Items. Notice that the document already has a filename. PowerPoint automatically names and saves the exported document as a Rich Text Format (.rtf) file in the Windows temp folder.

FIGURE 15-4
Meeting minutes
exported to Word

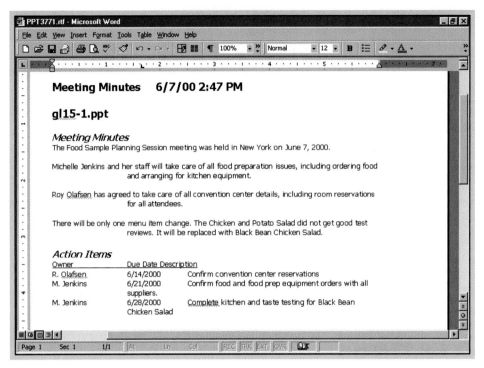

5. Key your name on the first line of the Word document. Save the document as *[your initials]***15-2.doc** in your Lesson 15 folder. Be sure to change the file type to Word Document (.doc).

6. Print the Word document. Close the file and close Word.

7. If necessary, switch to PowerPoint. Click OK to close the Meeting Minder dialog box. Close the PowerPoint presentation without saving it.

Distributing Your Work in Other Formats

Throughout this book, you view presentations on your computer screen and print them on paper. You can also print presentations on transparency film for use with an overhead projector. Or, you can send your presentation file (by disk, modem, or the Internet) to a *service bureau* where your presentation can be reproduced as 35mm slide transparencies or full-color overhead transparencies.

In Lesson 9 you used the Page Setup dialog box to change slide orientation from landscape to portrait. Using the same dialog box, you can resize presentation slides for overhead transparencies, letter paper, or 35mm slides.

TABLE 15-1   Choosing a Presentation Delivery Method

METHOD	MAXIMUM AUDIENCE	ADVANTAGE
Computer monitor	15–50, depending on monitor size	Allows last-minute changes and use of animation
Computer with a large-screen projector	200	Same as above
Slide projector	200	Quality color with high saturation
Overhead projector	200	Simple and inexpensive to create
Presentation broadcast	Any size	Can be sent via the Internet or an intranet to any number of viewers

EXERCISE   **15-3**   ## Prepare a Presentation for Use as 35mm Slide Transparencies

1. Open the file **MilSales.ppt**. Choose Page Set<u>u</u>p from the <u>F</u>ile menu to open the Page Setup dialog box. Notice that the slides have already been formatted for On-screen Show—they are 10 inches wide, 7.5 inches high, and landscape in orientation.

2. Click the <u>S</u>lides Sized For arrow to display the available choices. Notice that there are several sizes from which to choose.

FIGURE 15-5
Page Setup
dialog box

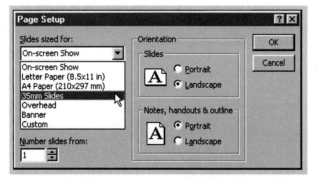

3. Choose 35mm Slides. Notice that the width has changed to 11.25 inches but the height remains the same as for On-screen Show.

> ✴ **TIP:** It is best to choose the output format of a presentation (On-screen, Overhead, 35mm slides, and so on) and the orientation (landscape or portrait) before creating the presentation. However, you may have to change the output format after the fact. In that case, review each slide and change object proportions, positions, and font sizes as needed.

4. Click OK to close the dialog box. Notice that the 35mm format is slightly wider than the On-screen format.

5. Scroll through all the slides and observe any changes in proportions to individual objects. Usually, changing from On-screen format to 35mm does not adversely affect the layout of individual slides.

6. On the handouts, include the date and your name as header and include the page number and filename *[your initials]*15-3.ppt as footer.

7. Save the presentation as *[your initials]*15-3.ppt in your Lesson 15 folder. Your presentation is now ready to be translated into 35mm slides for use with a slide projector. You can send the presentation file as an e-mail attachment to a service bureau, or you can copy the presentation to a floppy disk or zip drive and then mail or hand deliver it to a service bureau for slide transparency production.

TIP: If your presentation file is too large to fit on a floppy disk, you can use PowerPoint's Pack and Go feature (covered later in this lesson) to compress the file to fit on one or more floppy disks. Check with your service bureau first to be sure they are willing to work with Pack and Go files.

8. Print as handouts, 6 slides per page, grayscale, framed. Notice that the slide miniatures on this printout are slightly shorter and wider than slides formatted for an on-screen presentation.

NOTE: One nationwide service bureau, Genigraphics, has a strategic alliance with Microsoft. Because of this relationship, you can send files directly to Genigraphics from within PowerPoint by using the Genigraphics Wizard. To output a file to Genigraphics, choose Sen To from the File menu and follow the instructions in the Genigraphics Wizard. See Appendix G: "Advanced Presentation Delivery Options" for specific instructions.

EXERCISE 15-4 Prepare a Presentation for Use as Overhead Transparencies

You can create overhead transparencies by placing transparency film in your printer. Special transparency film is available for laser printers and for ink-jet printers. If you have a color printer, you can print color transparencies. For professional color overhead transparencies, send your presentation file to a service bureau, just as you would for 35mm slides.

1. With the file *[your initials]*15-3.ppt still open, use the Page Setup dialog box to change the Slides Sized For setting to Overhead. This changes the width to 10 inches, keeping the height at 7.5 inches, which works well for most overhead projectors.

NOTE: The proportions for an overhead transparency are the same as for an on-screen show.

2. Change the handout footer to reflect the filename *[your initials]***15-4.ppt**.

3. Save the presentation as *[your initials]***15-4.ppt** in your Lesson 15 folder.

4. Print as handouts, 6 slides per page, grayscale framed. Compare this printout to the printout from Exercise 15-3. Notice the difference in the slide proportions.

EXERCISE **15-5** **Change a Presentation's Orientation from Landscape to Portrait**

With some overhead projection systems, portrait orientation works better than landscape. If you are starting a new presentation and know you will need portrait orientation, it is best to change the page setup to portrait before creating any slides. Otherwise, you can resize slide objects after changing orientation.

1. With the file *[your initials]***15-4**.ppt still open, open the Page Setup dialog box.

2. Make sure that the <u>S</u>lides Sized For setting is for Overhead.

3. Under Orientation, change the Slides setting to <u>P</u>ortrait and click OK.

4. Scroll through the presentation and change the proportion and size of objects as needed to improve slide composition. For example, the width of bulleted text placeholders needs to be reduced and the height of the pie chart and the column chart needs to be reduced. On slides 4 and 5, delete the hyphens in the titles.

5. Change the handout footer to reflect the filename *[your initials]***15-5.ppt**.

6. Save the presentation as *[your initials]***15-5.ppt** in your Lesson 15 folder.

7. Print as handouts, 6 slides per page, grayscale, framed. Compare this printout to the printouts from Exercises 15-3 and 15-4.

8. Close the presentation.

 NOTE: Remember, any animation effects that your presentation contains will be lost when presenting as 35mm slides or overhead transparencies.

EXERCISE **15-6** **Send a Slide or Presentation as E-mail**

A convenient way to distribute a slide or a presentation is to send it as e-mail directly from PowerPoint in one of two ways:

● Send a single slide as the body of an e-mail message, in which case the slide *is* the e-mail message. The slide is sent in HTML format so recipients can view it without having PowerPoint installed on their computers.

● Send an entire presentation as an attachment to an e-mail message. To view a presentation you send as an attachment, recipients need PowerPoint 97 or later.

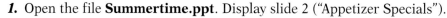 **NOTE:** To view a slide sent in HTML format as an e-mail message, recipients need Microsoft Outlook 2000 or a Web browser (such as Microsoft Internet Explorer 4 or later) that can read slides in HTML format.

1. Open the file **Summertime.ppt**. Display slide 2 ("Appetizer Specials").

2. Open the File menu and choose Send To, Mail Recipient (or click the E-mail button 🖼 on the Standard toolbar). The Office Assistant (or the E-mail dialog box) appears with your two e-mail options.

3. Click the second option, to send the current slide as the message body. An e-mail header appears in the PowerPoint window.

FIGURE 15-6
Sending a slide
as e-mail

E-mail header

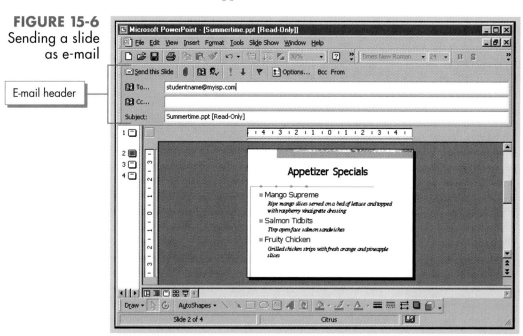

4. In the To: text box of the e-mail header, enter an e-mail address. The presentation name is already entered in the Subject line, which you can edit or replace with other text.

5. To remove the e-mail header, choose File, Send To, Mail Recipient (or click the E-mail button 🖼).

NOTE: To actually send a copy of the slide as e-mail to the specified address, you would click <u>S</u>end this Slide on the e-mail header. Check with your instructor if it's possible to send e-mail from your computer, which must be set up with Outlook 2000 or Outlook Express 5.0 as your e-mail editor.

6. Close the presentation without saving.

TABLE 15-2 Common E-mail Header Buttons

BUTTON	DESCRIPTION	FUNCTION
Send a Copy	Send	Sends a copy of the document to the e-mail address specified.
	Check Names	Checks the recipient name against the e-mail address listed in the Address Book.
	Address Book	Displays the Address Book entries added to Outlook or other address lists.
	Set Priority	Sets the importance level of the e-mail as High Priority, Normal Priority, or Low Priority.
	Attach File	Opens the Insert Attachment dialog box from which you can choose a file to attach.
Bcc	Toggle Bcc	Adds or removes a Bcc (blind carbon copy) line to the e-mail header.

Packaging Presentations for Other Computers (Pack and Go)

The presentations used in this course are small files that fit conveniently on a floppy disk. When you work in a business setting, your presentations may be much more complex and the file may be too large to fit on a single floppy disk. Although there are third-party compression programs available to solve this problem, PowerPoint has a feature called Pack and Go that conveniently compresses the file for you, creating a file that can span several disks if necessary. The packed disks also contain an installation application, making it easy for the person at the destination computer to unpack, install, and view the presentation file.

An optional feature of Pack and Go is the PowerPoint viewer. If the computer on which your presentation will be viewed does not have PowerPoint installed, you can select the PowerPoint Viewer option as part of the Pack and

Go process. When the presentation is unpacked on the destination computer, the viewer will be automatically installed.

EXERCISE **Save a Presentation for Use on Another Computer (Pack and Go)**

1. Open the file **MilSales.ppt**.
2. Insert a blank formatted disk in your floppy disk drive.

> **NOTE:** Check with your instructor that the Pack and Go feature is installed on your computer.

3. Choose Pac<u>k</u> and Go from the <u>F</u>ile menu. The Pack and Go Wizard opening dialog box appears.
4. Click <u>N</u>ext. The wizard's Pick Files to Pack dialog box appears.

FIGURE 15-7
Pack and Go
Wizard's Pick Files
to Pack dialog box

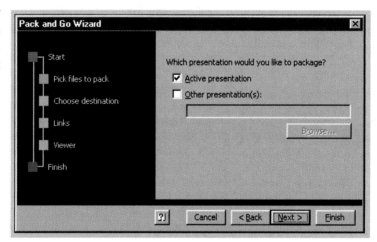

> **TIP:** If you want to pack a presentation that's not currently open, you can choose <u>O</u>ther Presentation(s) and click the B<u>r</u>owse button to locate the file on your computer or network.

5. Choose <u>A</u>ctive Presentation and click <u>N</u>ext. The wizard's Choose Destination dialog box appears.
6. Choose A:\ drive or whatever drive is appropriate. Or, click <u>C</u>hoose Destination, click the B<u>r</u>owse button, and locate the destination where your Pack and Go file should be saved. Click <u>N</u>ext.
7. In the Links dialog box, check both options (<u>I</u>nclude Linked Files and <u>E</u>mbed TrueType Fonts). Click <u>N</u>ext.

NOTE: Some third-party TrueType fonts have license restrictions and cannot be embedded. If that is the case, a message will appear to inform you that the font cannot be embedded. All TrueType fonts supplied with Microsoft software can be embedded.

8. In the Viewer dialog box, choose <u>D</u>on't Include the Viewer. Click <u>N</u>ext. The final dialog box displays the choices you made.

 NOTE: If you choose <u>V</u>iewer for Windows 95 or NT, you will need at least three blank formatted floppy disks to complete the Pack and Go process.

FIGURE 15-8
The Pack and Go
Wizard's closing
dialog box

9. Click <u>F</u>inish. The Pack and Go Status box displays the progress.

FIGURE 15-9
The Pack and Go
Status box

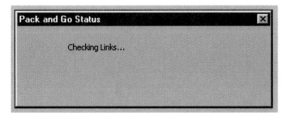

10. When the process is complete, click OK. The presentation is now compressed and saved on your floppy disk (or other destination location that you chose).

11. Close the presentation without saving it, and then remove your floppy disk and label it appropriately.

EXERCISE **15-8** **Unpack a Pack and Go Presentation File**

Unpacking a Pack and Go presentation file is easy. You locate the packed file in Windows Explorer and then double-click it.

1. Insert the floppy disk containing the packed presentation into the A:\ drive. (If you saved it to a different type of media, insert that media in the appropriate drive instead).

2. Right-click the Windows Start button and choose <u>E</u>xplore to open Windows Explorer. Click the A:\ drive (or navigate to the location where you saved the Pack and Go file).

FIGURE 15-10
Unpacking a
presentation

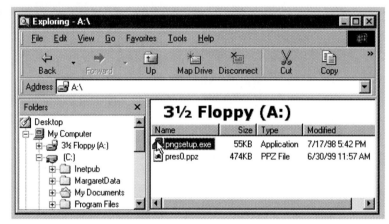

3. In the appropriate drive or file folder, double-click the file **Pngsetup.exe** to start the unpacking process. The Pack and Go Setup dialog box appears.

4. In the Destination Folder text box, key **C:\Temp** (or follow your instructor's directions on where your destination folder should be). Click OK.

FIGURE 15-11
Pack and Go Setup

5. If a message box appears informing you that the destination folder does not exist, click OK to allow Pack and Go to create it. A message box will appear informing you that the presentation was successfully installed. Click OK.

FIGURE 15-12
Click <u>Y</u>es to
run the show

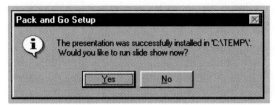

6. Click <u>Y</u>es to run the slide show.

 TIP: To run the show at a later time, locate the destination folder, right-click the presentation file, and choose Show from the shortcut menu.

7. Remove the floppy disk from the A:\ drive.

Preparing Presentations for the Web

You learned how to save a file in HTML format. Now you will explore more of the available HTML options for publishing a presentation to the Web, including changing the Web page title and targeting a specific browser.

EXERCISE 15-9 Format a Presentation for the Web

1. Open the file **MilSales.ppt**.

2. Choose Save as Web Page from the <u>F</u>ile menu. The Save As dialog box opens. It is very similar to the presentation file Save As dialog box, but there are two additional buttons: <u>P</u>ublish, and <u>C</u>hange Title. (See Figure 15-13 on the next page.)

3. Click the <u>C</u>hange Title button. In the Set Page Title dialog box, key **Good 4 U Millennium Projections** and click OK. Unless you make this change, the title text from the title slide will be the Web page title. The Web page title is the text that appears on the History list after your Web page is viewed. It is also the text that appears as a link to your presentation from another Web page or a Favorites list.

4. Click the <u>P</u>ublish button to display the Publish as Web Page dialog box. Notice that you can choose to publish the entire presentation or just some of the slides. (See Figure 15-14 on the next page.)

FIGURE 15-13
Saving a
presentation for
the Web

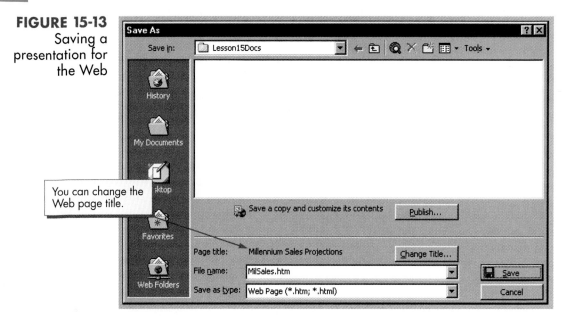

You can change the
Web page title.

FIGURE 15-14
Publish as Web
Page dialog box

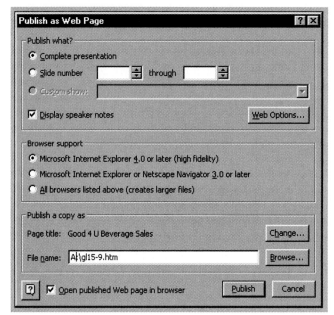

5. In the Publish What? section, choose Complete Presentation and clear the Display Speaker Notes check box.

6. In the Browser Support section, choose All Browsers Listed Above. This option will enable your Web page to be viewed on browsers compatible with either Microsoft Internet Explorer or Netscape Navigator.

NOTE: If you don't choose a Browser Support option, the first option is selected by default. This option saves the presentation in a format that is optimized for Microsoft Internet Explorer 4.0 or a later version, providing the best fidelity, fastest performance, and smallest file size. You can, however, target a specific browser. For example, if your Web presentation will be viewed by people using Netscape Navigator or Microsoft Internet Explorer 3.0, choose the second option. If you're not sure of the browser or version that will be used, choose the All Browsers option. Note that this option creates larger files.

7. Click the Browse button and navigate to your Lesson 15 folder. Key the filename *[your initials]*15-9.htm and click OK. In addition to the HTML format file (.htm), a file folder is also created with all the necessary supporting files. The folder has the name *[your initials]*15-9_files.

NOTE: This Exercise takes you through saving a presentation in HTML format so it can be viewed on the Web with a suitable browser. If you have publishing privileges at an Internet or intranet Web site, you can key the site's address (also known as its *URL*) in the File Name text box on the Publish as Web Page dialog box. See your system administrator for more information about available Web sites.

8. Select the Open Published Web Page in Browser option at the bottom of the dialog box. Click Publish to save the presentation and view it in your browser. When the save process is complete, your browser opens, displaying the presentation.

EXERCISE 15-10 View a Presentation Published for the Web

After a presentation is saved in HTML format and published to a Web site, you can view the presentation by going to the Web address and clicking the appropriate link to the presentation. The presentation will display as Web pages in your browser, as demonstrated in the following Exercise.

1. Maximize the browser window.
2. If necessary, click the Favorites button to display a list of favorites in the Explorer Bar on the left side of the screen. (See Figure 15-15 on the next page.)
3. Click the Favorites button again to turn off Favorites and close the Explorer bar. The presentation and its outline now fill the screen. Notice that the presentation's outline is displayed on the left side of the screen, listing all the slide titles.

FIGURE 15-15
Presentation
displayed in the
Internet Explorer 5
browser

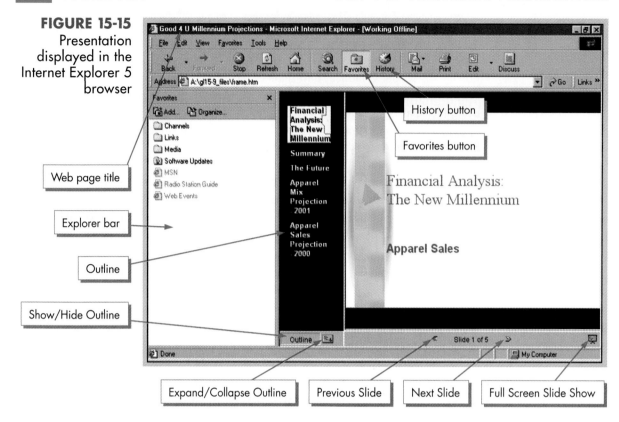

4. Point to the third title, "The Future." It changes color and the pointer changes to a hand, indicating that the title is a hyperlink to the third slide.

5. Click "The Future" in the outline. The third slide is displayed and "The Future" is highlighted on the outline.

FIGURE 15-16
Explorer bar with
History displayed

6. Click the Outline button to hide the outline.

7. Click the Next Slide button to move to slide 4. Click it again to move to slide 5.

8. Click the History button to display the Explorer bar with a list of pages you visited. Notice that the slide numbers are one number higher than the actual slide number.

9. In the Explorer bar, click "Good 4 U Millennium Projections." The first slide is displayed.

10. Try some of the other navigation buttons and hyperlinks, and then close Internet Explorer. Close the presentation MilSales.ppt.

USING HELP

Preparing a presentation for the Web can be a complex process. When you're working with different Web browsers, graphics, and Web files and links, Help is available to answer your questions.

Use Help to troubleshoot Web page options:

1. Display and activate the Office Assistant.

2. Key **web page options** and click <u>S</u>earch.

3. Select the topic "Troubleshoot Web page options."

4. Explore various Help topics, clicking the Back button ⇐ to return to the "Troubleshoot Web page options" window.

5. Close Help when you finish and hide the Office Assistant.

FIGURE 15-17
Help screen for troubleshooting Web page options.

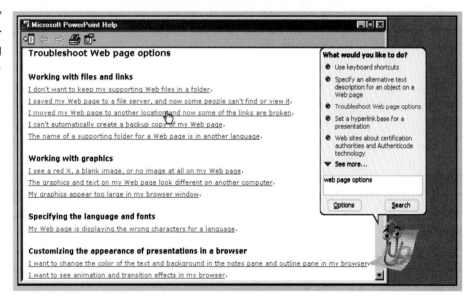

Concepts Review

Each of the following statements is either true or false. Indicate your choice by circling **T** or **F**.

T F **1.** Files can be sent to a service bureau via the Internet.

T F **2.** A presentation must be open (active) in order to be packed using Pack and Go.

T F **3.** Formatting an HTML presentation for both Internet Explorer and Netscape Navigator creates larger files that use more memory.

T F **4.** To e-mail a PowerPoint presentation, you must first open Outlook and then attach the presentation file.

T F **5.** Meeting minutes that you enter during a presentation are automatically added to a summary slide.

T F **6.** When using Meeting Minder, it is best to turn off slide timings.

T F **7.** Speaker notes appear on the summary slide of a presentation.

T F **8.** Word must be open before meeting minutes can be exported to a Word document.

Write the correct answer in the space provided.

1. How do you open Meeting Minder when in Slide Show view?

2. What file format is used for a Web presentation?

3. What is the name of the file you must locate to unpack a Pack and Go Presentation?

4. What command do you generally use to format a presentation as a Web page?

5. What must you do to your presentation after changing its orientation from landscape to portrait?

_____

6. How can you hide the outline on a presentation that is being viewed on your browser?

_____

7. What are the page dimensions of the Overhead page setting?

_____

8. When would you use the Pack and Go feature?

_____

CRITICAL THINKING

Answer these questions on a separate page. There are no right or wrong answers. Support your answers with examples from your own experience, if possible.

1. Think about when and where you might use the various presentation methods you learned about in this course. For example, which methods would be best for small groups and which would be best for large ones? How might you prepare for a presentation if you were traveling on business?

2. Discuss ways that Meeting Minder would be useful for you in another subject you are studying or when planning a social event.

Skills Review

EXERCISE 15-11

Use Meeting Minder to record meeting notes and action items.

1. Open the file **ResReqs.ppt** and start a slide show on slide 1.
2. Create meeting minutes and action items by following these steps:
   a. Right-click anywhere on the slide and choose Meeting Minder from the shortcut menu.
   b. Click the Meeting Minutes tab, if necessary. In the Meeting Minutes text box, key **Roy Olafsen, Marketing Manager, opened the meeting at 2:00 p.m. on** *[today's date]*. Click OK.
   c. Advance to slide 2. Open the Meeting Minder dialog box and click the Action Items tab.

    d. In the Description box, key **Research reservation policy studies on the Web.** In the Assigned To: box, key **Evan Johnson**. In the Due Date box, key a date three weeks from today.

    e. Click Add and then click OK to close the Meeting Minder dialog box.

3. Advance to slide 3 ("Reservations: Advantages"). Enter the following action item: **Create a chart detailing seating capacity and turnaround time for each restaurant.** Assign the action item to **Lila Nelson**, with a due date four weeks from today.

4. Advance to slide 4 ("Reservations: Disadvantages") and create the following meeting minutes entry: **A heated discussion took place concerning the advantages and disadvantages of a reservations policy. Everyone agreed to put the reservations policy on hold for six months pending further feasibility studies.**

5. Advance to slide 5 and review the action items that were recorded during the meeting.

6. Print the meeting minutes and action items by following these steps:

    a. Right-click any slide and choose Meeting Minder.

    b. If the Export button is not activated, click the Action Items tab, and then click one of the action items in the list box.

    c. Click Export. Deselect the first option (Post Action Items to Microsoft Outlook), and select the second item (Send Meeting Minutes and Action Items to Microsoft Word).

    d. Click the Export Now button.

    e. On the first line of the Word document, key **Presented by** *[your name]*

    f. Save the Word document as *[your initials]***15-11a.doc** in your Lesson 15 folder. Be sure to change the document type from Rich Text Format to Word Document format.

7. Print the Word document and close Word.

8. In PowerPoint, close the Meeting Minder dialog box and end the slide show.

9. Create a slide footer for slide 5 ("Action Items"). Include the date and key *[your name], [your initials]***15-11b.ppt** in the footer text box.

10. Save the presentation as *[your initials]***15-11b.ppt** in your Lesson 15 folder.

11. Print only the Action Items slide and then close the presentation.

EXERCISE 15-12

Reformat a presentation for 35mm slides and for overheads.

1. Open the file **Upgrade.ppt**.

2. Change the slide size and orientation by following these steps:

     a. Choose Page Setup from the File menu.

     b. In the Page Setup dialog box, choose 35mm Slides from the Slides Sized For drop-down list.

     c. Change the slide orientation to landscape. Click OK.

3. On slide 6, change the slide layout to Text & Clip Art. Drag the computer onto the clip art placeholder. Manually adjust the clip art proportions, making the computer taller.

4. Review the other slides in the presentation, making adjustments to text size and placement where needed.

5. On the handouts, include the date and your name as header and include the page number and filename *[your initials]*15-12a.ppt as footer.

6. Save the presentation as *[your initials]*15-12a.ppt in your Lesson 15 folder.

7. Print as handouts, 6 slides per page, grayscale, framed.

8. Open the Page Setup dialog box again and size the slides for overheads with landscape orientation. Review all slides, making adjustments to object proportions as needed.

9. Change the handout footer to show the filename *[your initials]*15-12b.ppt.

10. Save the presentation as *[your initials]*15-12b.ppt in your Lesson 15 folder.

11. Print as handouts, 6 slides per page, grayscale, framed.

12. Close the presentation. Compare the two printouts to see the differences in proportions between the two slide sizes.

EXERCISE 15-13

Use Pack and Go.

1. Open the file **EventRev.ppt**.

2. Pack a presentation for another computer by following these steps:

     a. Insert a blank formatted disk in your A:\ drive (or insert other storage media in the appropriate drive).

     b. Choose Pack and Go from the File menu. Click the Next button.

     c. In the Pick Files to Pack dialog box, choose Active Presentation. Deselect Other Presentation(s) if it is checked. Click Next.

     d. In the Choose Destination dialog box, choose the appropriate drive and folder where your packed files will be stored (usually the A:\ drive). Click Next

     e. In the Links dialog box, select both options and click Next.

     f. In the Viewer dialog box, select the first option: Don't Include the Viewer. Click Next.

> **g.** In the Finish dialog box, review the settings you selected. If you need to make changes, click the <u>B</u>ack button. If all the information is correct, click <u>F</u>inish.
>
> **h.** When the Pack and Go process is complete, click OK, and then close PowerPoint.

3. Remove the floppy disk from the drive and label it appropriately.

4. Unpack a presentation by following these steps:

> **a.** Insert the disk with the packed presentation into your floppy drive.
>
> **b.** Open Windows Explorer and navigate to the A:\ drive.
>
> **c.** Locate the file **Pngsetup.exe** and double-click it.
>
> **d.** In the Pack and Go Setup dialog box, key C:\Temp (or the location your instructor gives you) for the designation folder. Click OK.
>
> **e.** If a dialog box asks permission to create a new folder, click OK.
>
> **f.** When the Information box appears asking if you want to run the slide show now, click <u>Y</u>es.
>
> **g.** Close Windows Explorer and view the slide show.

5. Close the show when you finish viewing it. Don't forget to remove your floppy disk when you finish.

EXERCISE 15-14

Format a presentation for the Web and view it in a browser.

1. Open the file **BevNmbrs.ppt**.

2. Save the presentation as a Web page by following these steps:

> **a.** Choose Save as Web Page from the <u>F</u>ile menu.
>
> **b.** In the Save As dialog box, navigate to your Lesson 15 folder.
>
> **c.** Enter the filename *[your initials]*15-14.htm
>
> **d.** Click <u>P</u>ublish. The Publish as Web Page dialog box opens.
>
> **e.** Choose <u>C</u>omplete Presentation and deselect <u>D</u>isplay Speaker Notes.
>
> **f.** At the bottom of the dialog box, select <u>O</u>pen Published Web Page in Browser if it is not already checked.
>
> **g.** Click <u>P</u>ublish. The presentation is saved in HTML format, and Internet Explorer opens with the presentation displayed as a Web page.

3. Change the Web page display and navigate through the slides by following these steps:

> **a.** Maximize your browser window.
>
> **b.** If the Explorer bar is visible, open the <u>V</u>iew menu, choose <u>E</u>xplorer Bar, and click the checked item to turn it off.
>
> **c.** If the outline is not displayed on the left side, click the Show/Hide Outline button Outline in the lower left corner to turn on the outline.
>
> **d.** On the outline, click the third item, "Beverage Sales."

      e. Click the Next Slide button ⟩ at the bottom center of the screen to move to the "Healthy Drinks" slide.

      f. Navigate through all the slides by using the outline.

   4. Close your browser and close the PowerPoint presentation.

Lesson Applications

Create and print meeting notes.

1. Open the file **MktStrat.ppt**.

2. Add the following Meeting Minder minutes:

   The Marketing Strategy Meeting was called to order on Monday, July 11, 2000 at 1:15 p.m.

   It was generally agreed that there are too many areas targeted in the current marketing strategy and that items will be prioritized to create a stronger focus.

3. Add the following action items:

   Assigned to **Jane Kryler**, due **August 15, 2000**:
   Create a strategy for targeting potential customers' health-conscious interests.

   Assigned to **Eric Dennis**, due **August 8, 2000**:
   Develop a questionnaire to determine customers' food preferences. Develop a plan for doing a survey.

   Assigned to **Michael Peters**, due **September 6, 2000**:
   Investigate the high costs associated with the Miami operation. Develop a cost-containment plan for Miami.

4. Export the minutes and action items to Word. Enter your name on the first line of the Word document, and then save it in your Lesson 15 folder in Word Document format as *[your initials]***15-15a.doc**. Print the Word document and close Word.

5. Add a slide footer with the date, your name, and the filename *[your initials]***15-15b.ppt** to the Action Items slide only.

6. Save the presentation as filename *[your initials]***15-15b.ppt** in your Lesson 15 folder.

7. Print the Action Items slide and close the presentation.

Change a presentation to 35mm slide format and use Pack and Go.

1. Open the file **LunchMnu.ppt**.

2. Format the presentation for output as 35mm slides.

3. Review each slide individually, and make adjustments to font size, placeholder size, and decimal tab position so all text is uniform in size and aligned correctly.

4. On the handouts, include the date and your name as header and include the page number and filename *[your initials]* **15-16.ppt** as footer.

5. Save the presentation as *[your initials]***15-16.ppt** in your Lesson 15 folder.

6. Print as handouts, 4 slides per page, grayscale, framed.

7. Use the Pack and Go Wizard to pack the presentation on a floppy disk.

8. Unpack the presentation to the C:\Temp folder (or a location specified by your instructor) and then view the unpacked presentation.

EXERCISE 15-17

Save a presentation as a Web page

1. Open the file **InfoPak.ppt**.

2. Save the presentation as a Web page in your Lesson 15 folder using the filename *[your initials]***15-17.htm**. Change the title to **Good 4 U Franchise Information Pack** and target a browser that will let you preview the Web page.

3. Preview the Web page by using the outline and other slide navigation tools.

4. Close your browser, and then close PowerPoint.

Unit 6 Applications

Use different presentation methods to plan business strategy.

In this Application, you use your presentation skills to help plan the opening of two new restaurants. The Great Southwestern Food Company—a new division of Good 4 U—is opening two new "Tex-Mex" restaurants in Massachusetts.

1. Open the file **Southwest.ppt**.

2. Insert a new slide after slide 2 and create an organization chart using the following information:

Title	**Management Team**	
First Level:	**Sally Christopher**	**New Business Project Manager**
Second level:	**Marty Erlich**	**Manager, Boston location**
	Tawana Harris	**Manager, Framingham location**
	Mark Carmody	**Manager, Human Resources**

3. Apply a template of your choice to the entire presentation and add clip art, animations, sound clips, and slide transitions to create a Southwestern theme.

4. Using Meeting Minder (as if you were running the presentation at a strategy-planning session), enter the following action items which relate to slides 4 and 5:

Assigned to	Due Date	Description
S. Christopher	*[one week from today]*	**Prepare final budget numbers**
[your name]	*[two weeks from today]*	**Framingham market research report**
S. Christopher	*[three weeks from today]*	**Need legal opinion on property taxes**

5. Add the following Meeting Minder minutes:

There was a lengthy discussion about the high costs involved in establishing new restaurants in the Boston area. Sally Christopher will prepare final budget numbers, taking into consideration the meeting participants' budget concerns.

Tawana Harris stressed the importance of opening the Framingham restaurant well ahead of the holidays to make sure

the operation is thoroughly debugged before the busy season starts. Sally Christopher assured her that the opening would occur on schedule.

6. Review your action items slide.

7. Export your Meeting Minder minutes and action items to Microsoft Word. Insert your name on the first line of the Word document.

8. Save the Word document as *[your initials]*u6-1a.doc in a new folder for Unit 6 Applications.

9. Print the minutes, and then close the Word document.

10. On the presentation handouts, include the date and your name as header and include the page number and filename *[your initials]*u6-1b.ppt as footer.

11. Save your presentation as *[your initials]*u6-1b.ppt in your Unit 6 Applications folder.

12. Print the presentation as handouts, 6 slides per page, grayscale, framed, and then close the presentation.

13. Use the presentation as the basis for a companywide announcement that employees will view with their Web browsers. Change the presentation as follows:

   - Change the slide 1 subtitle text to read **We're opening two great new restaurants in Massachusetts!**

   - Delete slide 6 ("Action Items") and insert a new slide 6 using the Bulleted List layout. Enter the title **We're growing again...** and the body text **...and New England will never be the same!** (Remove the bullet.) Format and place the text attractively on the slide.

14. Save the presentation as a Web page with the filename *[your initials]*u6-1c.htm in your Unit 6 Applications folder. Save it as a complete presentation (assume that all company employees use Microsoft Internet Explorer 4.0) with the page title **Here We Grow Again!**

15. Preview the Web page. Consider whether the animations and other effects you added seem appropriate when viewed with a Web browser. If not, make the necessary corrections and save the presentation again, using the same filename.

16. Return to PowerPoint and use Pack and Go to save the presentation to a folder named *[your initials]*u6-1d.

17. Close PowerPoint.

UNIT APPLICATION 6-2 *Making It Work for You*

Present a personal project by using different delivery methods.

Think of an idea for a personal presentation you would like to create. It can be on any topic: for example, a business you would like to get financing for, a social event you would like to invite people to, or a school-related project. Think of the most effective way to use PowerPoint to present your idea to others. For example, if you are planning to start a business, would you want to prepare a Web page for potential investors? If you are planning to invite your classmates to a charity fundraising event, would an e-mail with an attached PowerPoint presentation file be effective?

After you decide on an idea and how to present it, create a PowerPoint presentation with at least five slides. Choose a template that is appropriate for your message and add appropriate slide transitions and animations. Then save your work in at least two of the following formats:

- A presentation file suitable for an on-screen show. (Save as *[your initials]*u6-2a.ppt.)
- A compressed (Pack and Go) presentation for use on another computer. (Save compressed files in a folder named *[your initials]*u6-2a.)
- A Web page formatted for the browser of your choice. (Save as *[your initials]*u6-2b.htm.)
- Files formatted for output as overhead transparencies in portrait orientation. (Save as *[your initials]*u6-2c.ppt.)

Print each format as handouts with appropriate handout headers and footers.

Be prepared to discuss the advantages and disadvantages of each of these presentation formats for delivering your message to your audience.

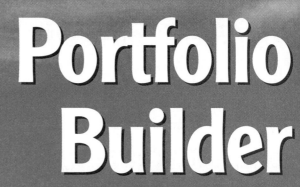

Portfolio Builder

List of Files Produced in the Portfolio Builder

Filename	Document
*[Your initials]*Res1.doc	Résumé created using a Word Résumé template
*[Your initials]*Res2.doc	Résumé created using the Word Résumé Wizard
*[Your initials]*Prospects.xls	List of prospective employers
*[Your initials]*DocList.doc	List of presentations to include in your Portfolio
*[Your initials]*CvrLtr.doc	Cover letter
*[Your initials]*AppInfo.doc	Information for use in filling out Employment Applications
10-15 additional presentations	The presentations listed in your Presentation List

Optional Documents

Thank you letter

Contract Reference Sheet

Contract Reference Card

Portfolio Builder

OBJECTIVES   By using this Portfolio Builder, you will learn how to:

1. Build a résumé.
2. Identify prospective employers.
3. Build a portfolio.
4. Target your résumé and portfolio.
5. Write a cover letter.
6. Fill out an employment application.
7. Prepare for a job interview.
8. Follow up an interview.

Finding a job is difficult—especially today in the midst of downsizing. The number of applicants often exceeds the availability of jobs. So you need to distinguish yourself from other people interested in the same job. You need to show a prospective employer what you can do.

This *Portfolio Builder* helps you build a résumé that will tell prospective employers about your work background. It also assists you in building a "representational portfolio"—a collection of your best work that you can show as evidence of your skills. The documents in your portfolio will be geared to specific employers. Finally, the *Portfolio Builder* leads you though the job-search process: including contacting prospective employers, filling out an employment application, and following up after interviews.

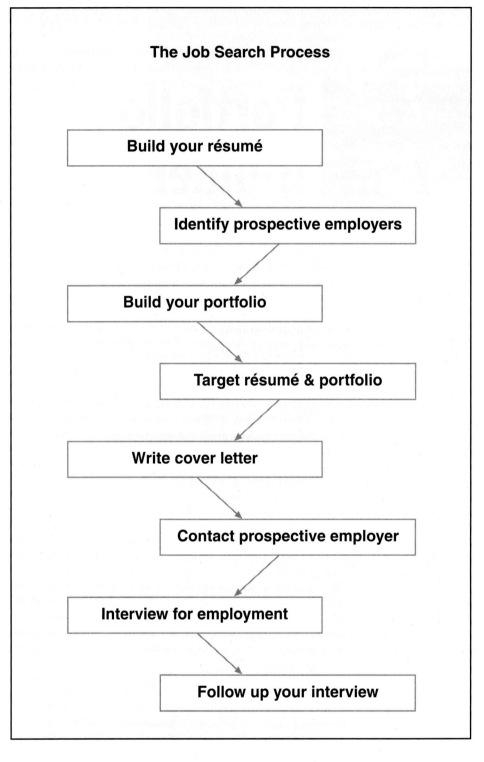

The Job Search Process

Build your résumé

Identify prospective employers

Build your portfolio

Target résumé & portfolio

Write cover letter

Contact prospective employer

Interview for employment

Follow up your interview

The *Portfolio Builder* will be helpful to you if you're planning to search for immediate employment. It is also a useful final project because it requires you to demonstrate skills you have gained from this course. Even if you're not looking for a job, it will help prepare you for an eventual job search.

Building a Résumé

A résumé is a representation of you on paper. It provides a first impression of you to a potential employer.

Building a résumé is an exercise in self-discovery. To create one, you must review your experience, identify your skills, and focus on a goal. Once you have created a résumé that states your strengths and objectives, you can begin the process of marketing yourself to prospective employers.

Although a good résumé will not guarantee a job, it is a primary tool in the job-search process.

There are three types of résumés:

- The *chronological* résumé is the traditional type of résumé. It lists your work history, starting with your most recent job. It includes a brief description of the position and your accomplishments. This is a "where you've been" type of résumé.

- The *functional* résumé highlights your skills or areas of expertise. It is a "what you can do" type of résumé.

- The *combination* résumé highlights your skill areas *and* lists the jobs you have held.

The following six pages illustrate these three kinds of résumés.

Chronological Résumé Description

Contact Information: Your name, address, and telephone number should appear at the top of the résumé. Spell out your address (do not abbreviate "Street" or "Avenue"). Include your ZIP code. Use a telephone number where you can be reached during the day or where a message can be left. Include other forms of contact, such as an e-mail address or fax number, if available. Don't use your current employer's telephone or fax number.

Job Objective: Your job objective represents the specific field or job title that you are pursuing. If you're targeting a specific job, tailor your objective to that position. Include the job type, the industry, and the geographical area in your objective (example: "Marketing position with a computer software vendor in the Chicago area"). To keep your options open, write a broader objective.

Work Experience: Describe the jobs that you have held, beginning with your most recent position. List the years of employment, company names and locations, and specific job titles. Include current and past jobs, part-time work, self-employment, volunteer work, and internships, as appropriate. The job description should focus on quantified achievements and specific skills.

Education: List the schools and training programs that you have attended. List your most recent education—school, degree or program, and date completed. Omit information about your high school if you have a college degree. Include any additional information, such as continuing education, seminars, or special course work that is related to your objective. This section can appear before **Work Experience** if you're a recent graduate, or if your education or training is your most important qualifying factor.

Additional Information: Your résumé can contain additional information that may be relevant to the job you are pursuing. For example, a section on computer proficiency can be included. You can also include **Activities**, **Professional Organizations**, or **Honors/Awards** as separate sections.

References: References are often not included on a résumé, but are provided separately if requested. Line up your references in advance, and list them on a sheet of paper. Include the name, address, telephone number, and title (if appropriate). You can ask a previous employer for a letter of recommendation, which you can then photocopy.

FIGURE P-2 Chronological résumé*

12 Juniper Drive
Any Town, State 00000
(000) 000-0000
E-mail: dmartin@xxx.xxx

Donald Martin

Objective	Seeking position as microcomputer salesperson in dynamic retail environment.

Work Experience

1996–Present   Electronics Depot   Any Town, State
Sales Associate

- Specialized in sales of computer hardware and software in busy retail outlet.
- Selected Salesperson of the Year for Midwest region.
- Established customer training program for computer sales that produced $80,000 in its first year.

1994–1996   Video Time   Any Town, State
Assistant Manager

- Managed video-rental store during most heavily-trafficked hours (evenings and weekends). Effectively handled as many as 250 customer contacts per day.
- Trained and supervised five sales assistants.
- Started "Old Time Cinema Club" that boosted sales of backlist videos by 50%.

1993–1994   Fairway Department Store   Any Town, State
Sales Assistant

- Assisted customers in busy Electronics Department.
- Handled more than $2,000 per day in cash sales.
- Completed sales training program.

Education

1997   **Fargo Technical College**   Any Town, State

- A.A., Microcomputer Systems Technology
- G.P.A. 3.93

Software/Hardware Training

- Proficiency in all Microsoft Office applications and PageMaker on both the PC and Macintosh computer.
- Can perform diagnostics on PCs and peripheral equipment, and can install/upgrade PC components such as network cards, memory chips, disk drives, and modems.

References

Available upon request.

*Created using a modified version of Word's Contemporary résumé style.

Functional Résumé Description

Contact Information: Your name, address, and telephone number should appear at the top of the résumé. Spell out your address (do not abbreviate "Street" or "Avenue"). Include your ZIP code. Use a telephone number where you can be reached during the day or where a message can be left. Include other forms of contact, such as an e-mail address or fax number, if available. Don't use your current employer's telephone or fax number.

Job Objective: Your job objective represents the specific field or job title that you are pursuing. If you're targeting a specific job, tailor your objective to that position. Include the job type, industry, and geographical area in your objective (example: "Marketing position with a computer software vendor in the Chicago area"). To keep your options open, write a broader objective.

Functional Sections: In a functional résumé, these sections provide the bulk of the information about you. Include two to four sections that describe a particular area of expertise or involvement. These areas should be directly related to the position you are pursuing. (In this résumé, the functional sections appear with the headings **Casework**, **Document Drafting**, and **Computer Skills**.) As an alternative to creating job-specific sections, create functional sections with the headings **Qualifications** and **Accomplishments**. Under these headings, list concise action statements that will catch the attention of a prospective employer.

Work Experience: A functional résumé lists your job history by date, company name and location, and title, beginning with the most recent position. Job descriptions are not included, as the résumé focuses on qualifications and skills, not work history.

Education: List the schools and training programs that you have attended. List your most recent education—school, degree or program, and date completed. Omit information about your high school if you have a college degree. Include any additional information, such as continuing education, seminars, or special course work that is related to your objective. This section can appear immediately below your **Objective** if you're a recent graduate, or if your education or training is your most important qualifying factor.

Additional Information: Your résumé can contain additional information that may be relevant to the job you are pursuing. For example, you can include sections with the following headings: **Activities**, **Professional Organizations**, **Honors/Awards**. The heading **References** may be listed at the bottom, followed by the text "Available on request" (see Chronological Résumé for more information).

FIGURE P-3   Functional résumé*

8809 Orange Terrace
Any Town, State 00000
Telephone (000) 000-0000
Fax (000) 000-0000

Lesley Brown

Objective	Paralegal position in computer or patent law

Casework
- Researched state and federal computer and patent laws. Wrote briefs for attorneys.
- Prepared preliminary arguments and pleadings in computer law.
- Obtained affidavits.

Document Drafting
- Drafted contracts under the supervision of an attorney.
- Prepared tax returns, incorporations, patent filings, and trust agreements.
- Prepared reports and schematic diagrams.
- Assisted computer law specialists in preparing hardware and software patents, contracts, applications, shareholder agreements, and packaging agreements.

Computer Skills
- Word-processing software (Word).
- Advanced use of database software (Access) and spreadsheet software (Excel).
- Researched on-line databases using Internet search engines.

Employment
1995–Present
Collimore & Hapke, Attorneys-at-Law   Any Town, State
Legal Assistant

Education
1998
York State Technical College   Any Town, State
Associate Degree, Paralegal Technology

Activities
Legal Eagles   Public Library
Volunteer coordinator of weekly youth discussion group that teaches basic law principles.

*Created using a modified version of Word's Professional résumé style.

Combination Résumé Description

Contact Information: Your name, address, and telephone number should appear at the top of the résumé. Spell out your address (do not abbreviate "Street" or "Avenue"). Include your ZIP code. Use a telephone number where you can be reached during the day or where a message can be left. Include other forms of contact, such as an e-mail address or fax number, if available. Don't use your current employer's telephone or fax number.

Job Objective: Your job objective represents the specific field or job title that you are pursuing. If you're targeting a specific job, tailor your objective to that position. Include the job type, the industry, and the geographical area in your objective (example: "Marketing position with a computer software vendor in the Chicago area"). To keep your options open, write a broader objective.

Functional Sections: Include two or three sections that describe a particular area of expertise or involvement, or that summarize your qualifications and accomplishments. Use concise statements that are easy to read.

Work Experience: As in the chronological résumé, list and describe the jobs that you have held, beginning with your most recent position. Include the years of employment, the company names and locations, and the specific job titles. You can include current and past jobs, part-time work, self-employment, volunteer work, internships, and so on, as appropriate. The job description should focus on quantified achievements and specific skills. Be careful not to repeat the same information here that you have listed in the Functional Sections.

Education: List the schools and training programs that you have attended. List your most recent education—school, degree or program, and date completed. Omit information about your high school if you have a college degree. Include any additional information that might be relevant, such as continuing education, seminars, or special course work. This section can appear above **Work Experience** if you're a recent graduate, or if your education or training is your most important qualifying factor.

Additional Information: Your résumé can contain additional information that may be relevant to the job you are pursuing. For example, you can include sections with the following headings: **Activities**, **Professional Organizations**, **Honors/Awards**. The heading **References** may be listed at the bottom, followed by the text "Available on request" (see Chronological Résumé for more information).

FIGURE P-4 Combination résumé*

ANNA LUPONE

1002 LOOKOUT POINT
ANY TOWN , STATE 00000
TELEPHONE (000) 000-0000
E-MAIL 00000@AOL.COM

OBJECTIVE

Corporate Word Processing Administrative Assistant

SUMMARY OF QUALIFICATIONS

◊ Four years experience in administrative/clerical support positions.
◊ Easily establish rapport with managers, staff, and customers.
◊ Proficient at analyzing statistics and market trends to develop accurate forecasts and effective sales presentations.
◊ Excellent problem-solving, project management, decision-making, and time management skills.
◊ Proven ability to prioritize and complete multiple tasks, independently and with little supervision.
◊ Bilingual: English/Spanish.

COMPUTER SKILLS

Operating Systems:	Microsoft Windows 98
Word Processing:	Word
Graphics:	PageMaker, PowerPoint
Database and Spreadsheets:	Access, Excel
Keyboard Speed:	85 wpm

PROFESSIONAL EXPERIENCE

1994–Present　　　COCA COLA COMPANY　　　Atlanta, Georgia
Administrative Assistant
◊ Analyze sales volume and profit.
◊ Finalize and package forecasting reports for annual sales of $100 million.
◊ Monitor monthly spending and reconciliation for $8 million budget.
◊ Manage $200,000 in advertising and promotional materials.

EDUCATION

1998　　　　　Blake Business Institute　　　　Any Town, State
A.S., Administrative Office Technology
◊ Dean's List, 4.0 GPA

REFERENCES

Available on request.

*Created using a modified version of Word's Elegant résumé style.

Choosing a Résumé Format

What type of résumé is right for you? Consider the following:

TABLE P-1

RÉSUMÉ TYPE	PREFERABLE IF:
Chronological	You have a history of steady work that reflects growth, and you are looking for a job in the same field or a related field.
Functional	You are new to the workforce, have gaps in your work history, or are changing careers.
Combination	You have some work history that is worth showcasing *and* want to highlight your marketable skills.

Choosing a Résumé Type

Be aware that the chronological résumé is the most traditional and conservative type of résumé. It is also the easiest to prepare. The functional and combination résumés, which use more innovative approaches, require greater thought, planning, and creativity.

Tips on Résumé Writing

When preparing your résumé, give yourself plenty of time, and keep in mind the following basics:

Content

- Everything in your résumé should support your job objective. Omit anything that doesn't.
- Be clear about what your skills are, both in your own mind and on paper. Your résumé should answer the question, "Why should I hire you?"
- Your résumé should convey the impression that you're focused. It should be targeted to a specific occupation or career field.
- Don't shortchange yourself. Emphasize any accomplishments, awards, and recognition you've received that supports your job objective.
- Mention promotions, raises, and bonuses, if appropriate, to prove your track record.
- Don't misrepresent yourself. Lying or exaggerating can only hurt—not help—you.
- Stress the positive—never include negative information about yourself. Your résumé should reflect what you *can* do, not what you can't.

Writing Style

- Strive for crisp, concise writing. Use short, easy-to-understand sentences.

- Use action words and phrases in your job and skill descriptions. For example, begin each description with words such as "Analyzed," "Administered," "Developed," "Initiated," "Organized," and so on.

- Use buzzwords and terminology that relate to the job you are pursuing.

- Proofread your résumé thoroughly for typographical, grammatical, or punctuation errors.

Appearance

- Your résumé should look professional. It should have an attractive layout, an easy-to-read format, and enough "white space" so that it is not too text-heavy.

- Use a good-quality printer to print your résumé. Avoid sending out photocopies, if possible.

- Limit your résumé to one page, unless you have substantial work experience that is relevant to your current job objective.

Getting Help

- Attend résumé and career workshops offered at your school or in your community.

- Read books about résumé writing to learn how to identify your skills, document your experience, and deal with special problems. Review résumé samples in such books.

- Ask someone whose judgment you trust to read your résumé before you send it out.

Résumé Templates and the Résumé Wizard

Word provides three résumé templates and a Résumé Wizard to help you create a résumé.

NOTE: Before using a résumé template or the Résumé Wizard, check the New dialog box in Word to see if they are available. If the templates have to be installed, use the Microsoft Office CD-ROM (Disk 1) to run the setup program. The Setup program location for these files is Microsoft Word for Windows, Wizards and Templates. You can also go to the Microsoft Office Web site (www.microsoft.com) and download wizards and templates.

EXERCISE **P-1** Use a Résumé Template

The résumé templates allow you to create a chronological résumé based on one of three styles: Elegant, Contemporary, and Professional.

1. Choose <u>N</u>ew from the <u>F</u>ile menu, choose the Other Documents tab, and then double-click one of the résumé template icons.

 NOTE: To preview the template before choosing it, click the résumé template icon, and then view it in the Preview box.

FIGURE P-5
Résumé templates in the New dialog box

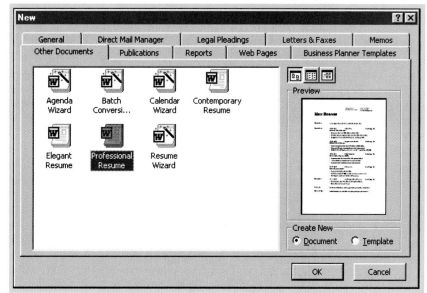

2. Replace all of the placeholder text in the document with your own information.

3. Make any formatting modifications. Save the document as *[your initials]*Res1.doc and print it.

 NOTE: Use the Résumé Wizard or résumé templates as a basis upon which to build your résumé. Modify the layout and formatting of the résumé to make it unique. Remember, you don't want your résumé to look exactly like everyone else's.

EXERCISE **P-2** Use the Résumé Wizard

The Résumé Wizard guides you through the steps needed to create a chronological or functional résumé using one of the three résumé styles.

1. Choose New from the File menu, choose the Other Documents tab, and then double-click the Résumé Wizard icon. Click Next to start.

2. In the Style dialog box, choose a résumé style. Click Next to display the next dialog box.

FIGURE P-6
Choosing a
résumé style

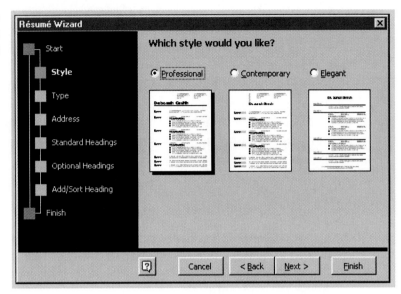

3. Choose the résumé type, and then click Next.

4. Enter your name and mailing address, and then click Next.

FIGURE P-7
Choosing headings
for your résumé

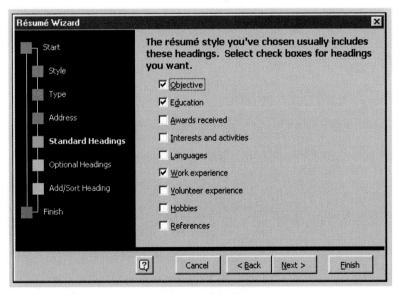

5. Choose the résumé headings you want, and then click Next.

6. Choose any optional headings you want included, and then click Next.

7. Add another heading or reorder your existing headings, and then click <u>N</u>ext.

8. Click <u>F</u>inish to view the résumé.

9. At the Office Assistant prompt, choose an option or click Cancel.

> **TIP:** You can click the Office Assistant option to create a cover letter at this point. The letter will contain sample text for you to replace with your own information. See the section "Writing a Cover Letter" in this Portfolio Builder to learn about cover-letter basics.

10. Replace the placeholder text in the résumé with your own information.

11. Make any modifications. Save the document as *[your initials]*__Res2.doc__.

Identifying Prospective Employers

Now that you've prepared a résumé, it's time to think about who will view it. Your next step is to identify the companies in your area—and the people within those companies—who may be hiring people with your skills.

Always try to identify the manager in each company or organization who heads up the division, department, or group in which you hope to work. Avoid applying through a Human Resources staff member, if at all possible. In the Human Resources Department, it's easy to become just another applicant who receives no special attention.

Help Wanted Ads

Help-wanted ads can represent a useful way to research the hiring trends of a local company. Help-wanted ads are, however, less useful as a source of real employment opportunities. They should never be used as the primary focus of your job search. In fact, some experts believe that only 10 percent of all available jobs are listed in the newspaper.

Use the back issues of your local newspapers to find out whether a company has been hiring recently, what kinds of jobs have recently been advertised, and if a particular contact person was listed in the ad.

Networking

Talk to people who are in a position to provide information about job leads and the hiring process at particular companies. They can be friends, relatives, acquaintances—anyone who can put you in touch with a job contact. Try to identify the people within a company who have the power to hire you. Get the correct spelling of each person's name, official correct job title, department, company, and, if possible, a telephone number.

Company Research

An easy way to begin your company research is with the *Yellow Pages*. Use it to locate businesses in the field in which you're interested. (You may need to use the "Business-to-Business" section for some types of businesses.)

The business section of your local library contains reference books that can give you even more information about local companies. Some of the best sources are:

- *Standard & Poor's Register of Corporations, Directors, and Executives.* McGraw-Hill. (Volume 2 lists companies by location.)
- *The National Directory of Addresses and Phone Numbers.* Gale Research, Inc.
- *Million Dollar Directory.* Dun & Bradstreet.
- *Job Seeker's Guide to Private and Public Companies.* Gale Research, Inc.
- *Job Opportunities for Business and Liberal Arts Graduates.* Peterson's Guides, Inc.
- *Job Opportunities for Engineering, Science, and Computer Graduates.* Peterson's Guides, Inc.

Some of these sources are also available in easy-to-use software versions that allow you to search for particular companies based on specific criteria. Your local librarian can often provide help in locating information about specific companies as well.

Using the Internet

Many sources of company and career information are available on the Internet. Many companies operate their own Web site or home page, and some even list their job openings there. If a prospective employer is a large company, search the Internet based on the company's name. Often, promotional materials from the company (and available in a local public library) will indicate its Internet or Web site address.

Many Web search engines (such as Lycos, Excite, or Infoseek) offer career-oriented services. Search for such general keywords as "career," "employment," or "job." A targeted search using more specific keywords may produce results that prove more immediately useful to your job search.

You can also use your Internet browser to search for locations with appropriate keywords. For example, one recent search showed 600,000 matches for the keyword "career." Obviously, the more targeted your search of the Internet, the more useful it may be.

Specialized employment search engines on the Internet may prove useful. Because these services list jobs from across the nation (and around the world), they may be less useful for a local job search. A list of places to look for jobs on the Internet follows (remember that Internet options change rapidly, so this list may need to be updated and new options may be available):

- CareerPath
  Searches classified ads in U.S. newspapers
  www.careeerpath.com

- The Career Builder Network
  www.careeerbuilder.com

- CareerMosaic
  www.careermosaic.com

- E-Span Employment Database
  www.espan.com

- HotJobs
  www.hotjobs.com

- The Monster Board
  www.monster.com

EXERCISE   P-3   Identify Prospective Employers

1. Identify at least five prospective employers. They may be located anywhere, but should represent the type of company for which you could imagine working.

2. For each prospective employer, obtain the name of a job contact. (This person would typically be a manager of the department, division, or group in which you would like to work.)

3. Key the list of prospective employers in a worksheet. Include the contact's name, department, company name, address, city, state, ZIP code, telephone number, and fax number. Save the worksheet as *[your initials]***Prospects.xls** and then print it. You'll use this list throughout this *Portfolio Builder*.

Building Your Portfolio

Your resume *describes* your experience and your skills. Your portfolio *demonstrates* your skills. It represents the best work that you can do. It also should be work with which a prospective employer can identify—that is, documents that the employer will understand.

The first step in building your portfolio is to decide what types of documents belong in it. Use the following checklist as a starting point to create a list of possible documents for your portfolio.

TABLE P-2   Possible Presentations for Portfolio

PRESENTATION	COMMENTS
Recommending a strategy	Locate information about a past strategy that was adopted. Include charts and graphics.
Products and Services overview	Use company brochures. Include charts and graphics.
Progress report	Obtain information from annual reports available at public library. Include charts and graphics.
Home page	Create a Web home page for a company. Include hyperlinks.
Business plan	Obtain information from annual reports available at the public library. Include charts and graphics. Perhaps an organization chart or flowchart is required.
Company meeting	Perhaps the agenda of the last shareholders' meeting was published in an annual report or company press release.
Organizational change	Describe a change in a company's management structure. Include an organization chart.
Financial overview	Obtain information from annual reports available at the public library. Include charts and graphics.
Marketing plan	Research the local papers, magazines that cover businesses similar to the business you are targeting, and other sources that may be recommended by a reference librarian. Include charts and graphics.

NOTE: If any of these Wizards or templates are not installed on your computer, you can install them by using the Microsoft Office CD-ROM (Disk 1) to run the setup program. You can also go to the Microsoft Office Web site (www.microsoft.com) and download wizards and templates.

EXERCISE **P-4** **Develop a List of Presentations for the Portfolio**

1. Develop a list of 15 presentations for inclusion in your portfolio. Use Table P-2 as a checklist, but also consider presentations that you may have prepared in other courses related to your field of work. If you have work experience, list actual presentations that you created. Use the following headings for your presentation list (see Figure P-8 on the next page):

Number   **Type of Presentation**   **Description**

2. Save the list as *[your initials]***DocList.doc** and print it.

3. Finalize your presentation list by reviewing it with someone who is familiar with your job search area. Adjust the list as needed. Save and print it.

EXERCISE **P-5** **Build Your Portfolio**

It isn't necessary to begin every presentation from scratch. In fact, it may not even be a good idea. Use material from your other courses, key material from brochures and newsletters that you might receive from a professional association, or recreate sample documents from people in positions similar to the one in which you are interested.

1. Create each of the presentations listed in your presentation list.

2. Adjust every presentation to give it as professional an appearance as possible. Focus on formatting. Demonstrate the skills that you learned in this course.

3. Consult the appropriate style reference for your profession to check that your formatting is acceptable.

4. Spell-check, save, and print your presentations.

5. Ask someone familiar with your future profession to review your presentations (preferably in a slide-show format) and then modify them as necessary.

FIGURE P-8 Sample presentation list for student seeking marketing position with a high technology company

No.	Type of Presentation	Description
1.	Résumé	Cover some of the details from your résumé.
2.	Progress report	Report on the progress of a marketing campaign for the company's most-recently introduced product.
3.	Business plan	Outline the company's business plan, possibly in relation to a new product or service.
4.	Financial overview	Describe the company's performance over the last three years. Use a column chart.
5.	Organizational overview	Describe the organizational structure of the company. Include an organizational chart.
6.	Company meeting	Present the agenda of the annual shareholder's meeting as published in the latest annual report.
7.	Technical report	Describe a technical aspect of the company. Use technical terms and include a flowchart.
8.	Corporate home page	Develop a Web home page for the company.
9.	Strategy recommendation	Recommend a strategy that the company recently adopted.
10.	Selling a product	Use the sales brochure about the company's products or services.

Targeting Your Résumé and Portfolio

So far you've created a résumé and a portfolio of documents that reflect something about you. Now it's time to *target* a specific company and tailor your portfolio, including your résumé, to that company.

EXERCISE | P-6 | Target Your Résumé to an Employer

1. From your list of five prospective employers, choose one as your target. Review the information you've gathered about the company. If you feel you don't have enough information, collect additional material. Ultimately, you should be very familiar with the company—and the position—you've targeted.

2. Review Table P-3.

TABLE P-3 Targeting Your Résumé

☞ TARGETING SUGGESTIONS

Objectives

☐ Change the job type to one that more closely resembles a job type available at the targeted company.

☐ Change the description of the industry or geographical area to one that more closely resembles those for the target company.

Chronological Résumé

☐ Reorder the bullets under a previous job in "Work experience" to emphasize skills that apply to the targeted position.

☐ Reorder or modify "Additional information" areas to emphasize skills that apply to the targeted position.

Functional Résumé

☐ Reorder or modify the "Functional sections" to emphasize skills that apply to the targeted position.

☐ Reorder or modify "Additional information" areas to emphasize skills that apply to the targeted position.

continues

TABLE P-3	Targeting Your Résumé *continued*

☞	**TARGETING SUGGESTIONS**

Combination Résumé

☐ Reorder or modify the "Functional sections" to emphasize skills that apply to the targeted position.

☐ Reorder the bullets under a previous job in "Work experience" to emphasize skills that apply to the targeted position.

☐ Reorder or modify "Additional information" areas to emphasize skills that apply to the targeted position.

3. Based on the checklist shown in Table P-3, modify your résumé to increase its appeal to your targeted company.

NOTE: Modifying a résumé does not mean fabricating work experience. You can, however, increase your appeal to a specific employer by highlighting certain skills. You can also minimize potential problem areas through the design and format selected for your résumé (for example, by deciding to use a functional résumé rather than a chronological one).

4. Spell-check and save your résumé.

5. Print the final copy of your résumé on appropriate paper stock.

Choosing Paper

The most commonly used résumé papers are 20-pound bond or 50-pound offset (both weigh the same) in a linen (textured) or laid (flat) finish. A 24-pound paper is thicker, has more texture, and is usually more expensive than 20-pound bond or 50-pound offset papers. You might consider using 24-pound Nekoosa, Classic Linen, or Becket Cambric for higher-level positions.

Let your résumé speak for itself. Don't go overboard in selecting a paper that will make your résumé stand out. Such a strategy could backfire. Don't use colored stock, for example. Neutral stock in different shades of white, gray, or beige is recommended.

If you're uncertain about paper choices, visit a stationery store, an office supplies store, a printer, or a local copy shop. Buy enough paper to use for your résumés, cover letters, and follow-up letters. Your envelopes should match the stationery. Your portfolio documents shouldn't be printed on the same stock as your résumé, however.

EXERCISE P-7 Target Your Portfolio to an Employer

The job contact at your targeted company is likely to respond more favorably to your portfolio if you take the time to tailor it to the company. It shows that you made an effort to learn about your prospective employer. It may also provide more conversational opportunities in a job interview.

1. Review Table P-4.

TABLE P-4 Targeting Your Portfolio

☑	TARGETING SUGGESTIONS
☐	Use the targeted company's name in worksheet titles and its address where appropriate.
☐	Modify the contents of office documents so that they apply specifically to the targeted company.
☐	Do not change a report from one of your classes (other than to make any corrections your instructor may have recommended). It's a good idea to let the targeted company know that the report was submitted as a class assignment, especially if it relates to your chosen field.

2. Based on the checklist shown in Table P-4, modify the documents in your portfolio to increase their appeal to the targeted company.

3. Spell-check and save the portfolio documents.

4. Print the final copies of your portfolio documents. Use standard printer paper.

Writing a Cover Letter

It's been said that sending a résumé without a cover letter is like giving a gift without a card. It's incomplete and confusing, and it only decreases the value of the résumé that you've spent so much time preparing and fine-tuning.

The Cover Letter Recipient A cover letter should be addressed to the job contact at a targeted company—never to Human Resources or Personnel.

First Paragraph The first paragraph should explain what job you are applying for and why you are interested in it. Be as specific as you can. Describe how you heard about the job opening. If someone told you about the company or the job opening, mention the person's name (but make sure to get his or her permission first). Describe why the work of the department or company holds particular interest for you, but don't go overboard with superlatives or hype.

Second Paragraph Describe your credentials in the second paragraph. Don't repeat your résumé. Focus, instead, on the skills, experiences, or accomplishments that are most likely to appear relevant to the employer. If you're responding to an ad, incorporate language from the ad. If you've previously read a job description or had a discussion with the employer, try to use the language the employer used in describing the position. Mention two or three key credentials.

Third Paragraph Use the third paragraph to describe what you can do for the company. You need to show that you understand the employer's needs and that you have something to offer. In this paragraph (or as a separate paragraph), you should request a personal meeting. You could then indicate the time when it's easiest to reach you, whether the employer can contact you at work, and if you'll be following up with a phone call.

General Tips

- Your cover letter should be printed on the same paper as your résumé and should be printed in the same way.

- Do not use the letterhead of your current employer.

- Use the same typeface for both your cover letter and your résumé.

- Use the standard business letter format.

- Don't send your portfolio with your résumé and cover letter. The portfolio is generally shown in an interview, but it can be sent to a prospective employer who expresses an interest in viewing it.

FIGURE P-9 Sample cover letter

Donald Martin
12 Juniper Drive
Any Town, State 00000
(000) 000-0000

January 22, 2000

Ward T. Cleaver, Manager
The Computer Warehouse, Inc.
6 Old King's Highway
Any Town, State 00000

Dear Mr. Cleaver:

I am seeking a position as a microcomputer salesperson, and read in the *Any Town News* that The Computer Warehouse was opening a new store on Old King's Highway. I have visited The Computer Warehouse in Lincoln and was impressed with the variety of hardware and software carried by the store. The store's focus on customer service was also exceptional, both through its "Trouble-Free Technical Support" program and its wide range of software training courses.

As my enclosed résumé indicates, I specialized in the sales of computer hardware and software at the Electronics Depot on Main Street. Although the sale of computers and software constitutes only a small portion of the overall sales of the Electronics Depot, computer and software sales increased by 42 percent in the past year. Part of this increase was due to the Customer Training Program that I developed. In its first year, the program produced revenues of $80,000.

Opening a new store and training a new sales staff is a difficult prospect. With my proven background in sales and customer training, I feel I would be an asset to your sales staff and would welcome the opportunity to meet with you personally to discuss your staff needs. I will contact you in the next week to schedule an appointment at your convenience. Thank you for your consideration.

Sincerely,

Donald Martin

Enclosure

EXERCISE P-8 Write a Cover Letter

Using your word-processor application, write a cover letter to accompany your résumé.

1. Using the standard business letter style (if necessary, check the *Gregg Reference Manual*), write a cover letter for your résumé. Use the three-paragraph format described earlier.

2. Ask someone familiar with your résumé and with jobs in your chosen field to review your letter. Make any necessary modifications.

3. Spell-check the cover letter and save it as *[your initials]*CvrLtr.doc.

4. Print your cover letter using the same stationery as your résumé.

5. Print an envelope for your cover letter and résumé. If possible, use the same stationery for the envelope, cover letter, and résumé.

 NOTE: Some people believe that you should use a large envelope so you don't have to fold your résumé. Others recommend a standard business envelope.

TIP: You can use Word's Letter Wizard to write a cover letter for your résumé. Choose <u>N</u>ew from the <u>F</u>ile menu, choose the Letters & Faxes tab, and double-click the Letter Wizard icon. Follow the steps to create the letter. Remember to choose the page design that matches your résumé, specify whether you're using preprinted letterhead, include "Mr." or "Ms." in the recipient's name area, and include an enclosure notation. After creating the letter, you can add, remove, or change letter elements by choosing Letter Wizard from the <u>T</u>ools menu.

Filling Out an Employment Application

Some companies require that every applicant, at every level, fill out an employment application. Other companies don't even use one. Generally, however, companies do use some form of an employment application. Whether you need to fill out such a form will depend on the company's internal personnel policies.

Often applicants are asked to fill out an employment application when they arrive at the company for an interview. To minimize stress in an already stressful situation, prepare for the employment application beforehand by creating a reference sheet that contains any information that might be included in the application and isn't found on your résumé. (Of course, you should refer to your résumé in filling out your employment application. Make sure to bring an extra copy for reference.)

Tips for Employment Applications

- Be as specific as possible when describing the position that you are seeking.
- Be careful when listing a required salary. A salary that is too high may eliminate you for some acceptable jobs, while a figure that is too low might weaken your negotiating position. Sometimes it is better to leave this line blank.
- Be prepared to list dates (month and year) for the schools you have attended. Some applications may also ask for your grade-point average and your class rank.
- Be prepared to list the following information for your previous employers: address, telephone number, name and title of supervisor, start date and end date (month and year), and a description of your duties.
- If some questions are not applicable to the job you are seeking, it is usually acceptable to write "Not Applicable" next to the question.

EXERCISE **P-9** **Create a Reference Sheet for an Employment Application**

1. Review the "Tips for Employment Applications." Note any information that isn't covered by your résumé.
2. Key all information that you will need to fill out an employment application. Use any format that makes sense to you.
3. Save the file as *[your initials]***AppInfo.doc** and then print it.

Employment Interviews

Once you have contacted a potential employer and scheduled an appointment to meet, you'll need to prepare yourself to make a good impression in person. No matter how good your résumé or credentials may be, only the interview can, ultimately, land you the job.

The more interviews you go on, the better your interviewing skills will be.

 NOTE: If possible, avoid scheduling an interview on a Monday, which is often the most hectic day in a business environment.

Preparing Yourself

- Confirm your appointment the day before, and make sure you arrive at the interview on time.
- Become as familiar with the company as possible. Read articles about the company, if they are available, or talk to people who are, or have been, employed by the company. It's always flattering to a prospective employer when an applicant appears knowledgeable about the company in an interview.
- Approach the interview with a clear mental picture of your capabilities and your job objective. Review your résumé immediately before meeting the prospective employer. Think positively.

Presenting Yourself

- Come to the interview equipped with copies of your résumé, your references, and any recommendation letters you have gathered. Have your portfolio on hand, as well as a notepad and a pen.
- Look your best. Your attire and grooming are critical to making a good impression. Dress neatly and professionally, in a manner that is appropriate to the company you are visiting. If necessary, get help in selecting an interview outfit from someone who dresses well.
- Be yourself. Act as relaxed as you possibly can, sit in a comfortable position, and focus on the interviewer.
- Ask questions. Learn what you can about the job, the company, to whom (or to how many people) you'd report, and so on. If no job is available, or the job opening is not appropriate for you, ask for recommendations about other people in the company that you might contact.
- At the end of the interview, if you want the job, express your interest in it, and be ready to explain why the company should hire you.

Frequently Asked Interview Questions

The following are frequently asked interview questions. You may want to re-hearse your answers before the interview. Never offer negative or unnecessary information to an interview question.

- Can you tell me about yourself?
- Why should I hire you?
- What are your major strengths? Weaknesses?
- What are your short-term goals? Long-term goals?
- Why do you want to leave your present job? (if employed)
- Why did you leave your previous job?
- What do you enjoy most (or least) about your current (or previous) job?
- Why do you want to work here?
- What salary do you expect to receive?

Following Up the Interview

To be successful in the interview process, you should take two important follow-up steps:

- Send a "thank you" letter.
- Keep track of your contacts.

"Thank You" Letters

Always send a "thank you" letter within 24 hours after you've interviewed with someone. It creates a positive impression, shows that you have good follow-up skills and good social skills, and reminds the person of your meeting.

The letter should be short and friendly, thanking the person for his or her time and for any information he or she may have provided. You may want to mention something that reminds the person of who you are, in case many people have interviewed for the position.

Even if you know that the interview will not lead to a specific job offer, a "thank you" letter demonstrates your professionalism.

FIGURE P-10   Sample "thank you" letter #1

Dear Ms. Jones:

Thank you for the opportunity of interviewing for the sales position. I enjoyed meeting you and appreciate the information that you shared with me.

I am very interested in the position and believe I could quickly become a productive member of your sales team.

Thanks again for the interview, and I look forward to hearing from you.

Sincerely,

FIGURE P-11   Sample "thank you" letter #2

Dear Ms. Jones:

Thank you for the interview and the information you gave me yesterday. I really appreciate your recommendation that I meet with John Doe in the Marketing Department.

I have scheduled an interview with Mr. Doe and look forward to meeting him. If this contact eventually leads to a job offer, I will be most grateful.

Thanks again for your time and help.

Sincerely,

Keeping Track of Contacts

Be organized in your job search. Keep track of everyone who has received your résumé by creating a contact log.

FIGURE P-12
Sample format for
contact log

Date Sent	Contact Name	Company	Telephone	Comments

In addition, develop a system for organizing your contacts so that you can follow up with telephone calls as appropriate. You can use a computer application of your choice or simple index cards to create the system.

If you use index cards, enter all pertinent reference information for each contact on the card. Place the cards in a box, and then sort them in the order that you want to contact the individuals. You can use tabs as date markers.

FIGURE P-13
Sample format for
contact reference
card

Company: _____

Contact Person: _____

Position:_____ Department:_____

Address:_____

Phone: _____ Fax:_____

Notes: _____

_____

_____

_____

Appendices

APPENDIX A

Lesson Applications

If you're unfamiliar with Windows, we suggest you review this Windows tutorial.

If you never used Windows before, you may need help with basic Windows actions. At appropriate points in this Tutorial, a Note will guide you to Appendix B: "Using the Mouse" or Appendix C: "Using Menus and Dialog Boxes."

Starting Windows

Individual computers may be set up differently. In most cases, however, when you turn on your computer, Windows loads and the Windows desktop appears.

The desktop contains *icons*, or symbols representing windows. If you double-click an icon, the window represented by that icon opens. Two icons are especially important:

- My Computer
  Opens a window that contains icons representing each input and output device on your printer or in your network.

- Recycle Bin
  Opens a window listing files you've deleted. Until you empty the Recycle Bin, these files can be undeleted.

 TIP: If you don't know how to use the mouse to point, click, double-click, or drag and drop, see Appendix B: "Using the Mouse."

Using the Start Menu

 The Start button on the taskbar at the bottom of the desktop is probably the most important button in Windows. Clicking ⊞Start displays the Start menu from which you can perform any Windows task.

1. Turn on the computer. Windows loads, and the Windows desktop appears.

NOTE: When you start Windows, you may be prompted to log on to Windows or, if your computer is attached to a network, to log on to the network. If you are asked to key a user name and a password, ask your instructor for help.

2. Click ⊞Start on the Windows taskbar. The Start menu appears.

TIP: If you don't know how to choose a command from a menu, see Appendix C: "Using Menus and Dialog Boxes."

FIGURE A-1
Windows desktop

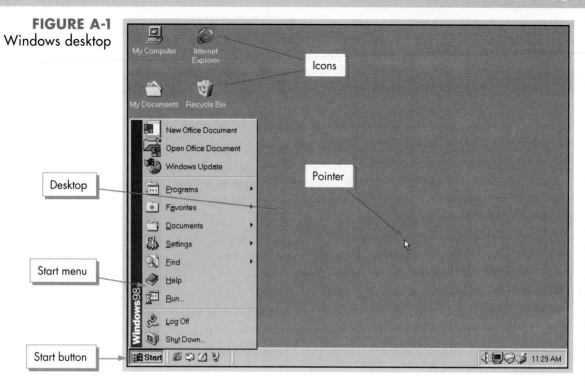

TABLE A-1   Start Menu

COMMAND	USE
New Office Document	Starts a new Office document of any type.
Open Office Document	Opens an existing Office document.
Windows Update	Connects to the Microsoft Web site for Windows updates.
Programs	Displays a list of programs you can start.
Favorites	Opens folders or connects you to Web sites that you designated as "favorites."
Documents	Displays a list of documents that you opened recently.
Settings	Displays a list of system components for which you can change settings.
Find	Helps you find a folder, a file, an address, a computer on a network; and helps you search the Internet.
Help	Starts Help. You can then use Help to find out how to perform a task in Windows.
Run	Starts a program or opens a folder when you type a command.
Log Off	Closes all programs, disconnects your computer from the network, and prepares your computer for someone else to use.
Shut Down	Shuts down or restarts your computer.

Using the Programs Command

The Programs command is the easiest way to open a program.

1. Click Start.

2. Point to Programs. The Programs submenu appears, listing the programs on your computer. Every computer has a different list of programs.

FIGURE A-2
Programs submenu

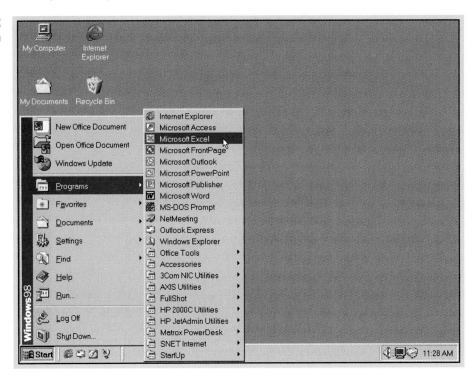

3. Point to the program you want to open and click. In a few seconds, the program loads and its first screen appears. Notice that a button for the program appears in the taskbar. Keep the program open.

NOTE: Many items on the Programs menu represent names for groups of programs. These group names have an arrow ▶ across from them on the right side of the menu. When you point to the group name, a submenu appears listing programs that you can click to select.

Using the Taskbar

A major feature of Windows is that you can work with more than one program at a time. The taskbar makes it easy to switch between open programs, and between open documents within a program.

The window in which you are working is called the *active* window. The title bar for the active window is highlighted, as is its taskbar button.

1. The program you opened in the preceding procedure should still be open. (If it's not, open a program now.) Open a second program using the <u>P</u>rogram command. Notice how the second program covers the first. The window containing the second program is now active. Its title bar is highlighted and its button on the taskbar is highlighted.

2. Click the button on the taskbar for the first program you opened. The program appears again.

3. Click the button on the taskbar for the second program to switch back to it.

4. Start a new blank document in the second program. Notice that each open document has its own taskbar button so you can easily switch between documents.

FIGURE A-3
Active window

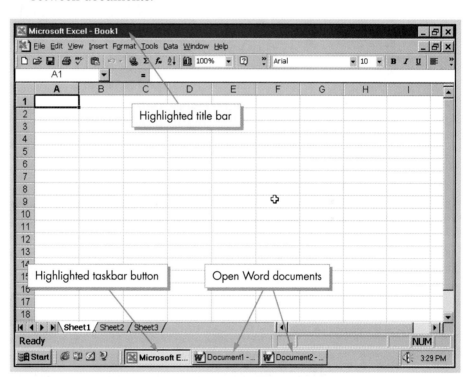

5. Practice using the taskbar to switch between program windows and document windows.

Changing the Size of Windows

In Windows it's easy to adjust the size of your windows using the pointer. You can also use the Minimize button ▬, the Maximize button ▢, and the Restore button ⬚ to adjust the size of windows.

TABLE A-2   Sizing Buttons

NAME	BUTTON	USE
Minimize button		Reduces the window to a button on the taskbar.
Maximize button		Enlarges the window to fill the desktop.
Restore button		Returns the window to its previous size. (Appears when you maximize a window.)

1. In the open window, click ⧉ at the right side of the title bar of the window. (If ☐ appears instead of ▢, the window is already reduced. In that case, go to step 2.)

2. Move the pointer to a window border. The pointer changes to a double-headed arrow ↔.

> **TIP:** Sometimes the borders of a window can move off the computer screen. If you're having trouble with one border of a window, try another border.

3. When the pointer changes shape, you can drag the border to enlarge, reduce, or change the shape of the window.

4. Make the window smaller. Notice that the other open program appears behind the currently active window.

5. Click the window that was behind the first window. It now appears in front of the first window because it has become the active window.

6. Click ▢ to minimize the active window to a button on the taskbar. The previous window becomes active.

7. Click the Close button ✕ at the top right corner of the window to close the window. The desktop should be clean.

8. Click a taskbar button for one of the other open windows. Close the window by clicking ✕. Close the remaining window. You have a clean desktop again.

> **NOTE:** When one document is open within a program, the document window contains two sets of sizing buttons and two close buttons, as shown in Figure A-4. The bottom buttons are for the document, the top buttons are for the program. When two or more documents are open within a program, each document window contains one set of sizing buttons and one close button.

Using the Documents Command

You can open an existing document using the <u>D</u>ocuments command on the Start menu. This command allows you to open one of the last 15 documents previously opened on your computer.

1. On the Start menu, point to <u>D</u>ocuments. The <u>D</u>ocuments submenu appears, showing documents that were previously opened.

2. Click a document. The document opens, along with the program in which the document was written (for example, if the document were a Word document, it would open within Word). A button for the document appears on the taskbar. You can now work on the document.

FIGURE A-4
Close buttons

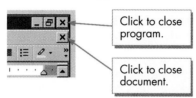

Click to close program.

Click to close document.

3. To close the document, click ☒ on the document window. Click ☒ to close the program window that contained the document.

Using the Settings Command

You can change the way Windows looks and works using the <u>S</u>ettings command. Be very careful when changing settings. Don't change them unless it's really necessary.

 NOTE: Before changing any settings, talk to your instructor.

FIGURE A-5
<u>S</u>ettings submenu

1. Open the Start menu, and point to <u>S</u>ettings. The <u>S</u>ettings submenu appears.

2. Click the option that relates to the settings you want to change. Close any open windows and clear your desktop.

TABLE A-3   **Settings Options**

OPTION	USE
<u>C</u>ontrol Panel	Displays the Control Panel, which you use to change screen colors, add or remove programs, change the date or time, and change other settings for your hardware and software.
<u>P</u>rinters	Displays the Printers window, which you use to add, remove, and modify your printer settings.
<u>T</u>askbar & Start Menu	Displays the Taskbar Properties dialog box, which you use to customize the taskbar and add and remove programs on the Start menu.
<u>F</u>older Options	Displays the Folder Options dialog box, where you choose the style for your folders (classic Windows style or Web style), and select folder and file characteristics.
<u>A</u>ctive Desktop	Displays a submenu with options to view your desktop as a Web page, customize your desktop, and update Web elements you added to your desktop.
Windows Update	Connects to the Microsoft Web site for Windows updates.

Using the Find Command

If you don't know where a document or folder is, you can use the Find command to find and open it.

1. On the Start menu, point to Find. The Find submenu appears.

FIGURE A-6
Find submenu

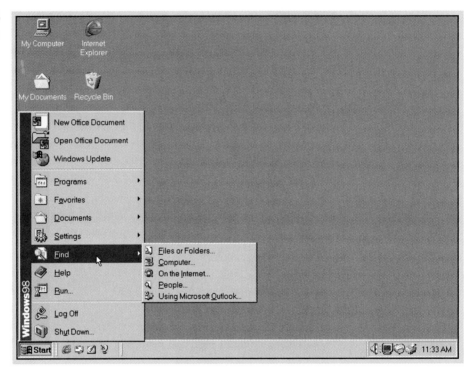

2. Click Files or Folders. The Find: All Files dialog box appears.

FIGURE A-7
Find: All Files
dialog box

3. In the Named box, key the name of the file or folder you want to find.

4. Click the arrow next to the Look In box to specify where to search. (You could also click Browse.)

TIP: To search files for specific text, use the Containing Text box. To narrow the search further, use the Date and Advanced tabs in the dialog box.

5. Click Find Now to start the search. Any matches for the file are shown at the bottom of the dialog box.

6. To open a file that was found, double-click the filename.

 TIP: If you set your Folder Options to Web style, you can single-click the filename, just like a hyperlink, to open the file.

7. When you finish viewing the file, close all open windows and clear your desktop.

Using the Run Command

If you know the name of the program you want to use, you can use the Run command to start it. This command is often employed to run a "setup" or "install" program that installs a new program on your computer.

1. On the Start menu, click Run. The Run dialog box appears.

FIGURE A-8
Run dialog box

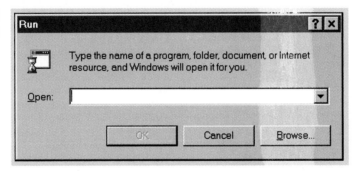

2. If you know the name of a program you want to run, key the name and click OK. The program you specified starts. Otherwise, you can click Browse to look for the program.

3. When you finish, close the program.

Displaying a Shortcut Menu

When the pointer is on an object or an area of the Windows desktop, and you click the right mouse button, a shortcut menu usually appears. This menu provides you with the commands that would be most useful in working with the object or area to which you were pointing.

FIGURE A-9
Shortcut menu for
the desktop

1. Click a blank area of the desktop with the right mouse button. A shortcut menu appears with commands that relate to the desktop, such as arranging icons, displaying properties, and so on.

2. Click outside the shortcut menu to close it.

3. Right-click the time in the bottom right corner of the taskbar. Close the shortcut menu.

4. Right-click an icon to display its shortcut menu, then close the menu.

Exiting Windows

You should always exit Windows properly before turning off your computer. You can then be sure that your work is saved and no files are damaged. To exit Windows, use the Shut Down command.

1. On the Start menu, click Shut Down. The Shut Down Windows dialog box appears.

FIGURE A-10
Shut Down
Windows
dialog box

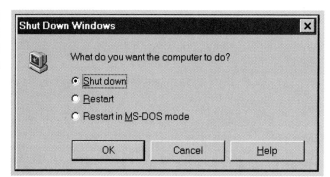

2. Choose Shut Down and click OK. Windows prompts you to save changes to any open documents. You can now turn off your computer safely.

 NOTE: Occasionally, you may need to restart your computer. One instance in which this is necessary is when you add new software.

APPENDIX B

Using the Mouse

Although you can use a keyboard with Windows, you'll probably find your-self using the mouse. Typically, you roll the mouse on a *mouse pad* (or any flat surface). A *pointer* shows your onscreen location as the mouse moves.

To select items on the computer screen using a mouse, you usually press the left mouse button. (Whenever you're told to "click" or "double-click" the mouse button, use the left mouse button. If you should use the right button, you are told to do so.)

When using a mouse, you need to become familiar with these terms.

TABLE B-1 Mouse Terms

TERM	DESCRIPTION
Point	Move the mouse until the tip of the onscreen pointer is touching an item on the computer screen.
Click	Press the mouse button and then quickly release it.
Double-click	Press and quickly release the mouse button twice.
Triple-click	Press and quickly release the mouse button three times.
Drag (or drag-and-drop)	Point to an object, hold down the mouse, and move the mouse to a new position (dragging the object to the new position). Then release the mouse button (and drop the object in the new position).

The mouse pointer changes appearance depending on where it's located and what you're doing. Table B-2 shows the most common types of pointers.

TABLE B-2 Frequently Used Mouse Pointers

POINTER NAME	POINTER	DESCRIPTION
Pointer	▹	Used to point to objects.
I-beam	I	Used when keying, inserting, and selecting text.
2-headed arrow	↖	Used to change the size of objects or windows.
4-headed arrow	✛	Used to move objects.
Hourglass	⧗	Indicates the computer is processing a command.
Hand	☝	Used in Help to display additional information.

APPENDIX C

Using Menus and Dialog Boxes

Menus

Menus throughout Windows applications use common features. To open a menu, click the menu name. An alternative method for opening a menu is to hold down [Alt] and key the underlined letter in the menu name.

Menus are adaptive—they change as you work, listing the commands you use most frequently. To see *all* the commands on a menu, expand the menu by pointing to the arrows at the bottom of the menu (or wait a few seconds and the open menu expands).

 TIP: If you open a menu by mistake, click the menu name to close it.

FIGURE C-1
Edit menu from Excel

FIGURE C-2
View menu from Word (expanded)

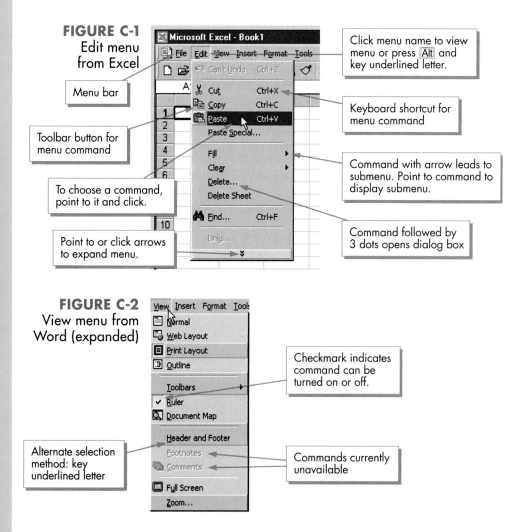

Dialog Boxes

Dialog boxes enable you to view all the current settings for a command, as well as change them. Like menus in Windows, dialog boxes share common features. The following examples show the most frequently seen features.

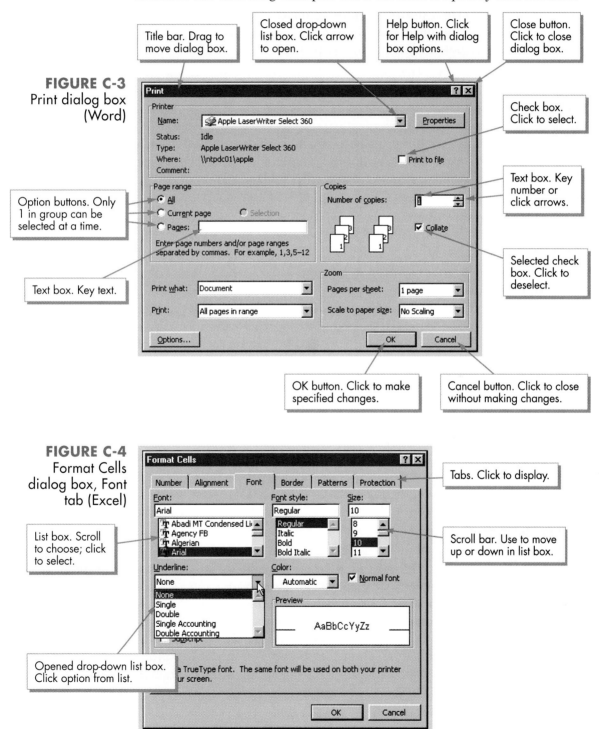

FIGURE C-3
Print dialog box (Word)

FIGURE C-4
Format Cells dialog box, Font tab (Excel)

APPENDIX D

File Management

This Appendix briefly explains how information is stored in Windows. It also introduces one of the most useful tools for managing information in Windows—the Windows Explorer.

Files, Folders, and Paths

In Windows, the basic unit of storage is a *file*. The documents you create and use are files, as are the programs you use. These files are stored in *folders*, which can also contain other folders.

Windows supports filenames that can contain up to 250 characters. A filename also has a three-letter extension, which identifies the type of file. For example, the extension "doc" identifies a file as a Word document. The extension is separated from the filename by a period. For example: "Birthdays.doc."

NOTE: In this course, we assume that your machine displays file extensions. If it doesn't, open Windows Explorer, select Folder Options from the View menu, click the View tab, and make sure that the following option is *not* selected: "Hide file extensions for known file types."

A file's *path* is its specific location on your computer or network. A file's path begins with the drive letter, followed by a colon and a backslash (example: c:\). The path then lists the folders in the order you would open them. Folders are separated by backslashes. The last item in the path is the filename.

For example: c:\My Documents\Letters\Reservations.doc

Windows Explorer

One of the most useful tools in Windows for managing files is the *Windows Explorer*, which gives you a view of your computer's components as a hierarchy, or "tree." Using Windows Explorer, you can easily see the contents of each disk drive and folder on your computer or network.

To open Windows Explorer, click the Start button [Start] with the right mouse button. Then click Explore on the Start button shortcut menu.

Table D-1 describes how to accomplish common file management tasks using Windows Explorer and shortcut menus.

FIGURE D-1
Windows Explorer

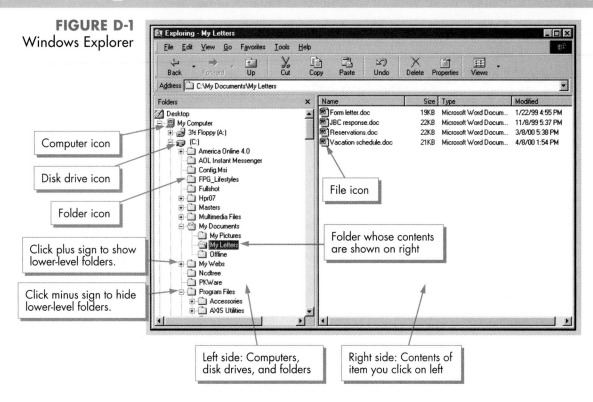

Computer icon

Disk drive icon

Folder icon

Click plus sign to show lower-level folders.

Click minus sign to hide lower-level folders.

File icon

Folder whose contents are shown on right

Left side: Computers, disk drives, and folders

Right side: Contents of item you click on left

TABLE D-1   Common File Management Tasks

TASK	HOW TO DO
Copy file or folder	Right-click file or folder to be copied and click Copy, then right-click folder in which you want to copy file and click Paste. (Alternative: Drag and drop a file from one folder to another.)
Move file or folder	Same method as above, but use Cut and Paste.
Delete a file or folder	Point to icon for file to be deleted and press Delete.
Create a new folder	Choose New from File menu, and then choose Folder. Creates new folder at current position.
Copy file to floppy disk	Point to icon for file to be copied and click right mouse button. Point to Send To and click floppy disk drive in submenu.
Edit/rename file	Point to icon for file you want to rename, press right mouse button, and click Rename.
Open file	Double-click icon for file.
Print file	Point to icon for file to be printed, click right mouse button, and click Print.

APPENDIX E

Proofreaders' Marks

PROOFREADERS' MARK		DRAFT	FINAL COPY
¶	Start a new paragraph	ridiculous! If that is so	ridiculous!
			If that is so
⌒	Delete space	to gether	together
#	Insert space	It may be	It may not be
⟲	Move as shown	it is (not) true	it is true
∩	Transpose	beleivable	believable
		(is it) so	it is so
○	Spell out	(2) years ago	two years ago
		16 Elm (St)	16 Elm Street
∧	Insert a word	How much it?	How much is it?
⟋ OR —	Delete a word	it may not be true	it may be true
∧ OR ⟋	Insert a letter	temperture	temperature
⟋ OR ⌐	Delete a letter and close up	commitment to buny	commitment to buy
⟋ OR —	Change a word	and if you won't	but if you can't
....	Stet (don't delete)	I was very glad	I was very glad
/	Make letter lowercase	Federal Government	federal government
≡	Capitalize	Janet L. greyston	Janet L. Greyston
∨	Raise above the line	in her new book*	in her new book*
∧	Drop below the line	H2SO4	H_2SO_4

PROOFREADERS' MARK		DRAFT	FINAL COPY
⊙	Insert a period	Mr⊙Henry Grenada	Mr. Henry Grenada
⋏	Insert a comma	a large⋏old house	a large, old house
⋎	Insert an apostrophe	my children⋎s car	my children's car
⋎⋎	Insert quotation marks	he wants a ⋎loan⋎	he wants a "loan"
=	Insert a hyphen	a first=rate job	a first-rate job
		ask the co=owner	ask the co-owner
⊥/M	Insert an em-dash	Here it is⊥cash!	Here it is—cash!
⊥/N	Insert an en-dash	Pages 1⊥5	Pages 1–5
___	Insert underscore	an issue of <u>Time</u>	an issue of <u>Time</u>
(ital)___	Set in italic	(ital)The New York Times	*The New York Times*
(bf)‿‿‿	Set in boldface	(bf)the Enter key	the **Enter** key
(rom)⌐	Set in roman	(rom)the *most* likely	the most likely
{ }	Insert parentheses	left today{May 3}	left today (May 3)
⌐┘	Move to the right	$38,367,000⌐┘	$38,367,000
⌐	Move to the left	⌐ Anyone can win!	Anyone can win!
ss[	Single-space	ss[I have heard he is leaving	I have heard he is leaving
ds[	Double-space	ds[When will you have a decision?	When will you have a decision?
+1l#—	Insert 1 line space	<u>Percent of Change</u> +1l# ╱ 16.25	<u>Percent of Change</u> 16.25
−1l#→	Delete (remove) 1 line space	Northeastern −1l#→ regional sales	Northeastern regional sales

APPENDIX F

MOUS Certification

This text teaches all Microsoft Office User Specialist (MOUS) Activities for PowerPoint certification at the following levels:

- MOUS Level 1 ("Core")
- MOUS Level 2 ("Expert")

This Appendix is broken down into two parts:

- Part 1: MOUS Activities Related to Lessons in the Text
- Part 2: Text Lessons Related to MOUS Activities

Part 1: MOUS Activities Related to PowerPoint Lessons

TABLE F-1   Level 1 ("Core") MOUS Activities Related to Lessons

CODE	ACTIVITY	LESSON
PP2000 1	**Creating a presentation**	
PP2000 1.1	Delete slides	2, 4
PP2000 1.2	Create a specified type of slide	3
PP2000 1.3	Create a presentation from a template and/or a Wizard	2, 3
PP2000 1.4	Navigate among different views (slide, outline, sorter, tri-pane)	1
PP2000 1.5	Create a new presentation from existing slides	4
PP2000 1.6	Copy a slide from one presentation into another	2
PP2000 1.7	Insert headers and footers	2
PP2000 1.8	Create a Blank presentation	3
PP2000 1.9	Create a presentation using the AutoContent Wizard	2
PP2000 1.10	Send a presentation via e-mail	15
PP2000 2	**Modifying a presentation**	
PP2000 2.1	Change the order of slides using Slide Sorter view	2
PP2000 2.2	Find and replace text	2
PP2000 2.3	Change the layout for one or more slides	3
PP2000 2.4	Change slide layout (Modify the Slide Master)	5, 7
PP2000 2.5	Modify slide sequence in the outline -pane	4
PP2000 2.6	Apply a design template	3
PP2000 3	**Working with text**	
PP2000 3.1	Check spelling	2
PP2000 3.2	Change and replace text fonts (individual slide and entire presentation)	5

TABLE F-1   Level 1 ("Core") MOUS Activities Related to Lessons   *continued*

CODE	ACTIVITY	LESSON
PP2000 3.3	Enter text in tri-pane view	1
PP2000 3.4	Import Text from Word	4
PP2000 3.5	Change the text alignment	5
PP2000 3.6	Create a text box for entering text	6
PP2000 3.7	Use the Wrap text in AutoShape feature	9
PP2000 3.8	Use the Office Clipboard	2
PP2000 3.9	Use the Format Painter	7
PP2000 3.10	Promote and Demote text in slide & outline panes	3, 4
PP2000 4	**Working with visual elements**	
PP2000 4.1	Add a picture from the ClipArt Gallery	6
PP2000 4.2	Add and group shapes using WordArt or the Drawing Toolbar	6, 8, 10
PP2000 4.3	Apply formatting	5, 6, 7
PP2000 4.4	Place text inside a shape using a text box	6
PP2000 4.5	Scale and size an object including ClipArt	5, 6, 10
PP2000 4.6	Create tables within PowerPoint	13
PP2000 4.7	Rotate and fill an object	6, 7
PP2000 5	**Customizing a presentation**	
PP2000 5.1	Add AutoNumber bullets	5
PP2000 5.2	Add speaker notes	3
PP2000 5.3	Add graphical bullets	5
PP2000 5.4	Add slide transitions	11
PP2000 5.5	Animate text and objects	11
PP2000	**Creating output**	
PP2000 6.1	Preview presentation in black and white	7
PP2000 6.2	Print slides in a variety of formats	2, 15
PP2000 6.3	Print audience handouts	1
PP2000 6.4	Print speaker notes in a specified format	3
PP2000	**Delivering a presentation**	
PP2000 7.1	Start a slide show on any slide	1
PP2000 7.2	Use on screen navigation tools	1
PP2000 7.3	Print a slide as an overhead transparency	2, 15
PP2000 7.4	Use the pen during a presentation	1
PP2000	**Managing iles**	
PP2000 8.1	Save changes to a presentation	1
PP2000 8.2	Save as a new presentation	1
PP2000 8.3	Publish a presentation to the Web	1
PP2000 8.4	Use Office Assistant	1
PP2000 8.5	Insert hyperlink	11

TABLE F-2   Level 2 ("Expert") MOUS Activities Related to Lessons

CODE	ACTIVITY	LESSON
PP2000 E.1	**Creating a presentation**	
PP2000 E.1.1	Automatically create a summary slide	4
PP2000 E.1.2	Automatically create slides from a summary slide	11
PP2000 E.1.3	Design a template	7
PP2000 E.1.4	Format presentations for the web	15
PP2000 E.2	**Modifying a presentation**	
PP2000 E.2.1	Change tab formatting	9
PP2000 E.2.2	Use the Wrap text in AutoShape feature	9
PP2000 E.2.3	Apply a template from another presentation	3
PP2000 E.2.4	Customize a color scheme	7
PP2000 E.2.5	Apply animation effects	11
PP2000 E.2.6	Create a custom background	7
PP2000 E.2.7	Add animated GIFs	11
PP2000 E.2.8	Add links to slides within the Presentation	11
PP2000 E.2.9	Customize clip art and other objects (resize, scale, etc.)	6, 7, 8, 10
PP2000 E.2.10	Add a presentation within a presentation	11
PP2000 E.2.11	Add an action button	11
PP2000 E.2.12	Hide Slides	11
PP2000 E.2.13	Set automatic slide timings	11
PP2000 E.3	**Working with visual elements**	
PP2000 E.3.1	Add textured backgrounds	7
PP2000 E.3.2	Apply diagonal borders	13
PP2000 E.4	**Using data from other sources**	
PP2000 E.4.1	Export an outline to Word	4
PP2000 E.4.2	Add a table (from Word)	13
PP2000 E.4.3	Insert an Excel Chart	12
PP2000 E.4.4	Add sound	11
PP2000 E.4.5	Add video	11
PP2000 E.5	**Creating output**	
PP2000 E.5.1	Save slide as a graphic	Appendix G
PP2000 E.5.2	Generate meeting notes	15
PP2000 E.5.3	Change output format (Page setup)	9,15
PP2000 E.5.4	Export to 35mm slides	15, Appendix G
PP2000 E.6	**Delivering a presentation**	
PP2000 E.6.1	Save presentation for use on another computer (Pack 'N Go)	15

TABLE F-2   Level 2 ("Expert") MOUS Activities Related to Lessons *continued*

CODE	ACTIVITY	LESSON
PP2000 E.6.2	Electronically incorporate meeting feedback	15
PP2000 E.6.3	Use Presentations on demand	Appendix G
PP2000 E.7	**Managing files**	
PP2000 E.7.1	Save embedded fonts in presentation	5
PP2000 E.7.2	Save HTML to a specific target browser	15
PP2000 E.8	**Working with PowerPoint**	
PP2000 E.8.1	Customize the toolbar	8
PP2000 E.8.2	Create a toolbar	8
PP2000 E.9	**Collaborating with workgroups**	
PP2000 E.9.1	Subscribe to a presentation	Appendix G
PP2000 E.9.2	View a presentation on the Web	15
PP2000 E.9.3	Use Net Meeting to schedule a broadcast	Appendix G
PP2000 E.9.4	Use NetShow to deliver a broadcast	Appendix G
PP2000 E.10	**Working with charts & tables**	
P2000 E.10.1	Build a chart or graph	12
P2000 E.10.2	Modify charts or graphs	12
P2000 E.10.3	Build an organization chart	14
P2000 E.10.4	Modify an organization chart	14
P2000 E.10.5	Modify PowerPoint tables	13

Part 2: PowerPoint Lessons Related to MOUS Activities

TABLE F-3

Lessons Related to MOUS Activities

LESSON	MOUS CODES
1 What Is PowerPoint?	PP2000 1.4, PP2000 3.3, PP2000 6.3, PP2000 7.1, PP2000 7.2, PP2000 7.4, PP2000 8.1, PP2000 8.2, PP2000 8.3, PP2000 8.4
2 Basic Presentation Tools	PP2000 1.1, PP2000 1.3, PP2000 1.6, PP2000 1.7, PP2000 1.9, PP2000 2.1, PP2000 2.2, PP2000 3.1, PP2000 3.8, PP2000 6.2, PP2000 7.3
3 Creating a Presentation from Scratch	PP2000 1.2, PP2000 1.3, PP2000 1.8, PP2000 2.3, PP2000 2.6, PP2000 3.10, PP2000 5.2, PP2000 6.4, PP2000 E.2.3
4 Using the Outline Pane	PP2000 1.1, PP2000 1.5, PP2000 2.5, PP2000 3.4, PP2000 3.10, PP2000 E.1.1, PP2000 E.4.1
5 Working with Text	PP2000 2.4, PP2000 3.2, PP2000 3.5, PP2000 4.3, PP2000 4.5, PP2000 5.1, PP2000 5.3, PP2000 E.7.1
6 Working with PowerPoint Objects	PP2000 3.6, PP2000 4.1, PP2000 4.2, PP2000 4.3, PP2000 4.4, PP2000 4.5, PP2000 4.7, PP2000 E.2.9
7 Working with Lines, Fills, and Colors	PP2000 2.4, PP2000 3.9, PP2000 4.3, PP2000 4.7, PP2000 6.1, PP2000 E.1.3, PP2000 E.2.4, PP2000 E.2.6, PP2000 E.2.9, PP2000 E.3.1
8 Manipulating PowerPoint Objects	PP2000 4.2, PP2000 E.2.9, PP2000 E.8.1, PP2000 E.8.2
9 Advanced Text Manipulation	PP2000 3.7, PP2000 E.2.1, PP2000 E.2.2, PP 2000E.5.3
10 Advanced Drawing Techniques	PP2000 4.2, PP2000 4.5, PP2000 E.2.9
11 Animation and Slide Show Effects	PP2000 5.4, PP2000 5.5, PP2000 8.5, PP2000 E.1.2, PP2000 E.2.5, PP2000 E.2.7, PP2000 E.2.8, PP2000 E.2.10, PP2000 E.2.11, PP2000 E.2.12, PP2000 E.2.13, PP2000 E.4.4, PP2000 E.4.5
12 Creating a Chart	PP2000 E.4.3, PP2000 E.10.1, PP2000 E.10.2
13 Creating a Table	PP2000 4.6, PP2000 E.3.2, PP2000 E.4.2, PP2000 E.10.5
14 Flowcharts and Organization Charts	PP2000 E.10.3, PP2000 E.10.4
15 Distributing and Presenting Your Work	PP2000 1.10, PP2000 E.1.4, PP2000 E.5.2, PP2000 E.5.3, PP2000 E.5.4, PP2000 E.6.1, PP2000 E.6.2, PP2000 E.6.3, PP2000 E.7.2, PP2000 E.9.2

APPENDIX G

Advanced Presentation Delivery Options

OBJECTIVES

After completing Appendix G, you will be able to:

1. **Use the Genigraphics Wizard.**
2. **Save a slide as a graphics file for use on a Web page.**
3. **Use NetShow to broadcast a presentation.**
4. **View a presentation offline.**

Estimated Time: 1½ hours

PowerPoint provides delivery tools in addition to those described in the text. These include using the Genigraphics Wizard to order slides or overhead transparencies, saving a slide as a graphics file for use on a Web page, using NetShow to broadcast a presentation, and viewing a presentation offline.

Using the Genigraphics Wizard

If you are planning to deliver your presentation in places where using a computer is inconvenient, you can make 35mm slides or full-color overhead transparencies from a presentation file. There are many service bureaus available that will do this for you.

One such service bureau is Genigraphics. The Genigraphics Wizard, included with PowerPoint, makes ordering slides, overheads, and other presentation materials an easy process. You can send files via the Internet or direct modem connection to Genigraphics at any time, and you'll typically receive your slides or overheads the next day.

To use the Genigraphics Wizard:

1. Choose Send To from the File menu and then choose Genigraph from the submenu.

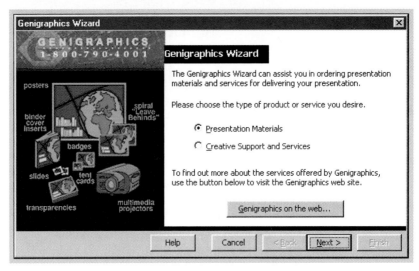

2. Click the <u>N</u>ext button. A list of options appears, allowing you to choose from a menu of slides, overheads, handouts, and other materials.

3. Choose the options you want, and then move through the screens that follow, eventually entering mailing and credit card information.

FIGURE G-2
The Genigraphics
Wizard asks you
to confirm before
placing your order

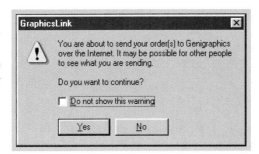

4. When you have entered all the information, click the Finish button. A dialog box asks for confirmation. If you click <u>Y</u>es, your presentation is sent via the Internet or direct modem connection to Genigraphics.

NOTE: You can choose the Send via <u>D</u>isk option. If so, you are asked for a filename and location for saving the Genigraphics file. In the GraphicsLink dialog box, you click the Print button to print an order to send with the disk.

Saving a Slide as a Graphics File for Use on a Web Page

There will be times when you want to include a PowerPoint slide as a picture in a document created by another application or as part of a Web page. You can save an individual slide as a picture, using one of the graphics formats listed in table G-1.

TABLE G-1   Graphic File Formats

FILENAME EXTENSION	GRAPHICS FORMAT
*.gif	GIF Graphics Interchange Format
*.jpg	JPEG File Interchange Format
*.png	PNG Portable Network Graphics Format
*.bmp	Device Independent Bitmap
*.wmf	Windows Metafile
*.tif	Tag Image File Format

To save a slide as a graphic:

1. Open the presentation and display the slide you want to save.
2. Choose Save As from the File menu.
3. In the Save as Type box, choose a graphics format—for example, choose GIF Graphics Interchange Format (*.gif), a good format to use for Web pages.
4. Click Save.
5. A dialog box opens, giving you the option of saving the current slide as a graphic or of saving each slide in the presentation as a separate graphic.
6. Click No to save just the current slide. If you click Yes, a folder is created containing a separate graphics file for each slide in the presentation.

Using NetShow to Broadcast a Presentation

Presentation Broadcasting is a new feature included with PowerPoint 2000. With it, a speaker can broadcast a presentation over a network in *real time*. When broadcasting in real time, a viewer sees what the presenter is doing at the actual time that it is happening. Along with the presentation's slides, the speaker can broadcast live video and audio, all at the same time. While you're broadcasting a presentation, the Microsoft NetShow encoder converts your information into *streaming data*. Streaming data is visual and audio data that is continuously broadcast to a viewer's computer as a broadcast is happening.

To use Presentation Broadcasting, it is best to have the help of a network administrator to install the software correctly. After the software is set up, you can schedule and broadcast meetings for small groups of viewers.

If you are planning a broadcast for more than 15 viewers, your network administrator needs to set up a NetShow server for you. (You can also use a special company called a NetShow service provider to broadcast your presentation over the Internet.)

Schedule a Presentation Broadcast

1. Open the presentation you want to broadcast.

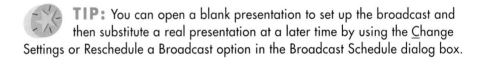 **TIP:** You can open a blank presentation to set up the broadcast and then substitute a real presentation at a later time by using the Change Settings or Reschedule a Broadcast option in the Broadcast Schedule dialog box.

2. Choose Online Broadcast from the Slide Show menu, and then choose Set Up and Schedule from the submenu.

3. In the Broadcast Schedule dialog box, choose Set Up and Schedule a New Broadcast and click OK. The Schedule a New Broadcast dialog box opens, displaying the Description tab. The information you enter on the Description tab appears on the *Lobby Page*—the opening page of your broadcast. The Lobby Page gives information about the speaker and the presentation.

FIGURE G-3
Entering Lobby
Page information

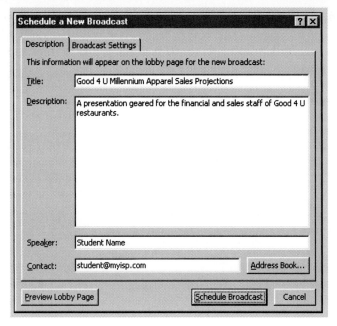

4. On the Description tab, key an appropriate title for your presentation and a detailed description (if you desire). Key the speaker's name, and in the Contact text box, key the speaker's e-mail address.

5. Click the Broadcast Settings tab. Here, you can choose from several optional settings. Under "Recording," you can enter the name of a shared folder where you can save your broadcast for viewing at a later date. (Obtain the name of an appropriate shared folder from your network administrator.)

FIGURE G-4
Choosing
Broadcast Settings
options

6. Click the Server Options button. In the Step1 section, verify that there is an address in the text box. If not, obtain a valid address from your network administrator. It is a good idea to make note of the shared address for future use.

FIGURE G-5
Get the name for a shared location from your network administrator

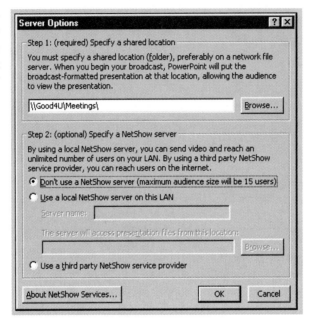

7. In the Step 2 section, there are three options. If you are broadcasting to a small audience (fewer than 15 users) you can choose the first option. This option uses the NetShow encoder built into PowerPoint's Presentation Broadcasting feature. If you anticipate a larger number of users, consult your network administrator for the correct choice and the address of an appropriate NetShow server.

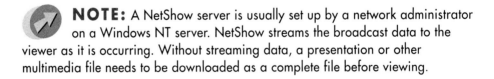 **NOTE:** A NetShow server is usually set up by a network administrator on a Windows NT server. NetShow streams the broadcast data to the viewer as it is occurring. Without streaming data, a presentation or other multimedia file needs to be downloaded as a complete file before viewing.

8. After entering all the information, close the Server Options dialog box and click Schedule Broadcast. The Meeting dialog box opens.

FIGURE G-6
Scheduling a
presentation
broadcast

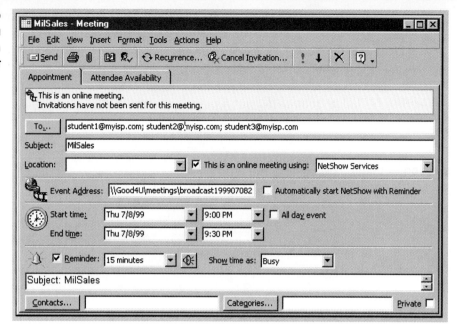

9. Enter the e-mail addresses of all the participants you want to invite. You can use the To button to select them from an address list, or enter them manually. Enter the start and end times, date, and any other information.

10. When you complete the scheduling information, click the Send button to send an e-mail to each invitee.

Run a Presentation Broadcast

Start setting up a presentation broadcast at least 30 minutes before the show is scheduled, so you can test all the components and do any fine-tuning that may be necessary. When all the preparations are in place, you click the Start button. The Microsoft NetShow encoder then converts your slides and any audio or video that accompanies them into streaming data for your audience to view in real time as the broadcast progresses.

1. Open the presentation you want to broadcast.

2. Choose Online Broadcast from the Slide Show menu and choose Begin Broadcast from the submenu. The Broadcast Presentation dialog box opens. The Microphone Check dialog box opens so you can check that the microphone, if you have one, is working correctly.

NOTE: You can use the <u>B</u>egin Broadcast command only if you have previously scheduled a broadcast for the current presentation. If the <u>B</u>egin Broadcast command is dimmed, you must first go through the steps to set up and schedule the broadcast.

3. Follow the directions on the Microphone Check dialog box, and then click OK.

FIGURE G-7
Preparing to begin a broadcast

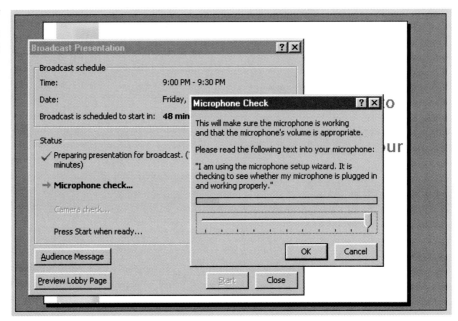

4. On the Broadcast Presentation dialog box, you can click the <u>A</u>udience Message button to add a message to the lobby page your audience views when they join the presentation. Click the <u>P</u>review Lobby Page button to see a preview of the opening page that will greet your viewers.

FIGURE G-8
Presentation
Broadcast Lobby
Page with an
audience message
displayed

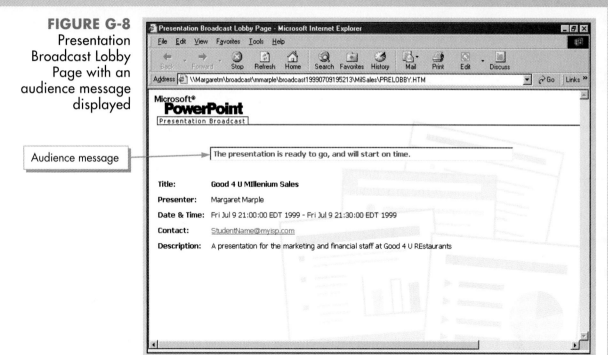

Audience message

5. Still on the Broadcast Presentation dialog box, notice the countdown indicating the time remaining until the broadcast is scheduled to start. When the countdown goes to zero, click the Start button to start the broadcast. A dialog box informs you that the NetShow encoder is starting.

Participate in a Presentation Broadcast

When a broadcast is scheduled, invitations in the form of e-mail are sent to all the participants. If you are invited to a presentation broadcast and you have Outlook installed on your computer, a reminder will open 15 minutes before the broadcast is scheduled to begin. Just click the View NetShow button to participate. Your browser opens to the broadcast's lobby page.

If you don't have Outlook, open the e-mail invitation and then click the hyperlink contained in the invitation, or open your browser and key the hyperlink address in the address box.

 NOTE: Internet Explorer 4.0 or later is required in order to view a broadcast.

Viewing a Presentation Offline (Subscribing)

If you visit a Web page that contains a PowerPoint presentation or other information, you may want to refer to it again later. You can set up your browser so you can view the presentation offline at a later time and update it periodically if changes have been made to the page.

If you were invited to a Presentation Broadcast but were unable to attend, and if the broadcast was recorded (an option that can be set when a broadcast is scheduled), you can view it offline at your convenience.

1. Contact the presenter to obtain the URL (address) of the recorded broadcast.

2. Connect to the Internet or intranet and open the appropriate Web page.

3. Choose Add to Favorites from the Favorites menu on your browser.

4. In the Add Favorite dialog box, check the Make Available Offline option.

5. If desired, click the Create In button and choose a folder in which to store the Web page. (You can make a new folder if necessary.)

6. To schedule automatic updates of the Web page—for example, if it contains information that changes often—click the Customize button and choose an option. If you do not customize, you can update manually by using the Synchronize command on the Tools menu.

Glossary

Action button
Button you can click to initiate a link or an animation action. (11)

Adjustment handle
Yellow diamond that appears in some selected AutoShape objects, used to change angles, roundness, and points of the object. (6)

Animate
To add special visual or sound effects to objects on a slide. (11)

Aspect ratio
Relationship between the height and width of an image. If the aspect ratio is locked, when you change the height or width, the corresponding dimension is automatically adjusted. (6)

AutoLayouts
24 predesigned slide layouts that contain placeholders for content, including a title, bulleted text, a chart, clip art, and so on. (3)

Axis
Line that borders one side of the chart plot area. A value axis displays a range of numbers and a category axis displays category names. (12)

Borders
In a table, lines forming the edges of cells, columns, rows, and the outline of the table. (13)

Browser
Software program, such as Microsoft Internet Explorer or Netscape Navigator, which interprets HTML documents and is used for viewing information on the World Wide Web. (1)

Build
To successively display some or all of a slide's elements one at a time. (11)

Cell pointer
Mouse pointer in the shape of a white cross used to select cells in a Microsoft Graph datasheet. (12)

Cell
Formed by the intersection of a row and column in a table or spreadsheet. (13)

Chart box
Most basic structural unit of an organization chart; a rectangular box that contains space for one or more lines of information, such as a name and a title. (14)

Chart placeholder
Box with dotted line that appears on slides using the Chart, Text & Chart, and Chart & Text layouts. Double-clicking a chart placeholder opens Microsoft Graph automatically. (12)

Chart
Diagram that displays numbers in pictorial format, such as slices of a pie or rows of columns of varying height. Charts are sometimes called graphs. (12)

Clip art
Ready-to-use graphic images that you can insert in a presentation. (6)

Clipboard
Temporary storage place for cut and copied items. (2)

Connection sites
Blue handles that appear on an AutoShape, clip art, or text box object when the connector tool is active or when a connector is selected. Connection sites indicate places where a connector can be attached to an object. (14)

Connector line
Straight, curved, or angled line with special endpoints that can lock onto connection sites on an AutoShape, clip art, or text box object. Connection line endpoints are green when unlocked and red when locked. (14)

Constrain
Control moving or drawing an object in precise increments or proportions. When you constrain a rectangle as you draw it, it becomes a square; a constrained oval becomes a circle. (6)

Crop
Trim the vertical or horizontal edges of a picture. (6)

Data series
Group of data that relate to a common object or category such as product, geographic area, or year. Often, a single chart displays more than one data series. (12)

Demote
Move selected bullet text to the next lower heading level. (3)

Design template
Custom design that you apply to a presentation to give it a uniform color scheme and a particular "look." (3)

Export
Send data to another application. (4)

Filename
Unique name given to a PowerPoint presentation file. (1)

First line indent
Paragraph indent style in which the first line is indented to the right of the body of the paragraph. (9)

Font
Set of characters of a specific design. (5)

Format Painter
Tool used to copy the characteristics of one object to another. (7)

GIF
Picture file format well-suited to animation and Web use. (11)

Gradient fill
Color of an object in which one color fades into another. (7)

Grid
Invisible matrix used to align objects automatically. If the grid is on as you draw or move objects, the objects' corners align on the nearest intersection of the grid. (10)

Guides
Dotted horizontal and vertical lines you can use to position objects on a slide. Guides can be hidden and displayed whenever you want. They do not appear in a slide show or on a printed slide. (10)

Handout
Printouts that contain 2, 3, or 6 PowerPoint slides per page. (1)

Hanging indent
Paragraph indent style in which the first line extends to the left of the body of the paragraph. This style is most often used with bullets. (9)

HTML (Hypertext Markup Language)
File format used to make a file readable in a browser, on an intranet, or on the Internet. (1)

Hyperlink
Text or graphic object you click to move to another slide, another application, or a location on the Internet. Hyperlinks are often displayed as contrasting underlined text. (11)

Import
Bring data into an application from another source. (4)

Indent markers
Two small triangles and a small rectangle that appear on the ruler when a text box is selected. The lower triangle controls the left indent setting of the text box and the top triangle controls the first-line indent setting. The rectangle moves both triangles. (9)

Internet
System of computer networks linked together to allow computers all over the world to share information with millions of users. (15)

Intranet
Network within an organization that uses Internet protocols to share information. (15)

Legend
Box showing colors and patterns assigned to the data series or categories in a chart. (12)

Level
In organization charts, position in the hierarchy of the organization being diagrammed. (14)

Lobby page
First page a viewer sees of a presentation broadcast. The lobby page contains the title, subject, presenter's name, and other information about a broadcast. (Appendix G)

Master
Slide that contains formatted placeholders and background items that appear on all slides in the presentation. (5)

Placeholder
Empty box on a slide that reserves space for a slide title, text, clip art, or another object. (1)

Point
Unit of measure for the height of characters in a font. There are 72 points to an inch. (5)

Promote
Move selected bullet text to the next higher heading level. (3)

Proportional sizing
Changing the size of an object while retaining its height and width ratio. (6)

Real time
The actual time during which events take place. (Appendix G)

Resize handle
Square that appears at each corner and along the sides of the rectangular area surrounding a selected object. Dragging a resize handle resizes the object. (5)

Scale
Specifies range of values on the value axis and interval between values. (12)

ScreenTip
Box that identifies the name of an onscreen object when you point to the object. (1)

Selection rectangle
Dotted box that you draw by dragging the mouse pointer to select objects on a slide. (8)

Service Bureau
Business that translates computer files into high-quality output in various media, such as slide transparencies, high-resolution full-color prints, and large-format prints. (15)

Streaming data
Data continuously broadcast to a viewer's computer, enabling the viewer to see a live multimedia show over the Internet or an intranet. Without streaming data, a large file must be downloaded before the multimedia show can be viewed. (Appendix G)

Table
Organized arrangement of information in rows and columns, generally used for reference purposes. (13)

Text box
Container for text in PowerPoint. (1)

Thumbnail
Miniature version of a graphic image. (6)

Tick marks
Small measurement marks, similar to marks on a ruler, that cross a value or category axis. (12)

Transition effect
Visual or sound effect that determines the manner in which a slide appears during a slide show. (11)

URL (Uniform Resource Locator)
Address to an Internet or intranet location. Examples of URLs are http://www.microsoft.com and http://www.mywebpage.edu. (15)

Vertex
Reshaping handle that is used to edit the points on a freeform, or curve drawing. (10)

Wizard
Online guide that guides you through completion of a specific task. (2)

Index

Character button, 150
Chart Type button, 420, 427
chart-related buttons, 409
Clear Clipboard button, 55
Close button, 17, 30
Collapse All button, 120
Common Tasks button, 17, 86, 91, 113
Copy button, 56
Create In button, A-32
Create New Folder button, 13, 48
Crop button, 187
Customize button, A-32
Cut button, 55
Decrease Font Size button, 145
Decrease Paragraph Spacing button, 311, 312
Delete button, 13
Demote button, 88, 116
Draw Table button, 442, 449, 458
Drawing button, 419
E-mail button, 524
e-mail header buttons, 525
Eraser button, 456
Expand All button, 121
Expand button, 121
Export button, 519
Favorites button, 531
Fill Color button, 223, 224, 413, 422
Find Similar Clips button, 183
Finish button, A-24
Font Color button, 143, 147, 446
Format button, 415
Format Painter button, 229
Format Picture button, 184
Forward button, 182
Free Rotate button, 191
Freeform button, 344, 345
Grayscale Preview button, 337
Hide Slide button, 367, 368
History button, 532
Increase Font Size button, 147
Increase Paragraph Spacing button, 311
Insert Chart button, 420
Insert Clip Art button, 181, 374
Insert Clip button, 151, 183, 374
Insert Table button, 442
Insert WordArt button, 187
Italic button, 143
Line button, 196
Line Style button, 220
Maximize button, 55
Merge Cells button, 456
More AutoShapes button, 199
More Buttons button, 17, 86, 312
Move Down button, 118
Move Up button, 118
New button, 85
New Slide button, 86, 113

Next button, 43, A-24
Next Slide button, 18, 532
Normal View button, 15
Nudge Down button, 342
Nudge Up button, 342
Organization Chart toolbar buttons, 482
Outline button, 532
Outline View button, 20, 112
Outlining toolbar buttons, 115
Paste button, 56, 119
Play Clip button, 373
Preview button, 156
Preview Clip button, 183
Previous Slide button, 18
Print button, 28, A-24
Promote button, 88, 116
Publish button, 529
Recolor Picture button, 234
Redo button, 89
Save button, 26, 61
Search the Web button, 13
Send button, A-29
Send to Back button, 265
Server Options button, A-28
Shadow button, 266
Show Formatting button, 121
Show/Hide ¶ button, 123
Slide Show button, 23, 365, 382
Slide Sorter View button, 22
Slide Transition button, 365, 366, 381
Slide View button, 21, 157, 159
Spelling button, 48
Split Cell button, 457
Start button, 11, A-31
Straight Arrow Connector button, 478
Subordinate button, 483
Summary Slide button, 121, 377
Tab Type button, 307, 308
Table button, 454
Tables and Borders toolbar buttons, 446
Text Box button, 189, 190, 419
Text Shadow button, 158, 446
To Grid button, 341
Tools button, 13
Underline button, 144
Undo button, 89, 309
Up One Level button, 13
View Datasheet button, 411
View NetShow button, A-31
Views button, 12
WordArt Shape button, 188

C

callouts, 198

case of text
  changing case, 145–146
cells (table), 443
  aligning text and numbers, 450
  borders, 446
  fill color
    adding, 447–448
    removing, 448
  merging cells, 456
  selecting
    rectangular group of cells, 445
    row or column, 444
    single cell, 444
  splitting cells, 457–458
changing
  height and width
    of rows, columns, tables, 452–453
  order and timing of animation, 371–372
  order of slides
    in outline pane, 120–121
    in Slide Sorter view, 52–57
  sample data, 407–410
  sample text, 45–48
  template color scheme, 93–94
  text alignment, 153
  text attributes
    using Font dialog box, 144
    using toolbar, 142–143
  text fonts
    entire presentations, 147–149
    individual slides, 141–147
Chart menu
  Chart Options, 427
  Chart Type, 427
charts, 84, 406–426
  adding shapes, 419
  adding text objects, 419
  animating charts, 426
  background color, 413
  category axis, 415
    formatting, 416
  chart legend, 409
  chart objects, 409
  chart placeholders, 406–407, 421
  chart slide layout, 407
  colors and patterns, 413–414
  deleting sample data, 409
  displaying chart data, 409
  editing charts, 411–413
  fill effects, 413
  fonts, 413, 415, 418, 421
  formatting charts, 413–418
  importing Excel chart, 423–425
  inserting axis titles, 417
  inserting charts, 406–407
  introduction, 406
  keying new chart data, 410
  legend, 413, 417–418

Photo Credits

Page 2: Balterman/FPG; Page 4: Lang/FPG, Luria/FPG, Taylor/FPG, Gage/
FPG; Page 9: Simpson/FPG; Page 81: Cummins/FPG; Page 179: Turner/FPG;
Page 303: Weber/FPG; Page 405: Cummins/FPG; Page 515: PhotoDisc, Inc.;
Page A-1: Hallinan/FPG

Student Files: Miami1.jpg and Miami2.jpg/P. Bayer; Produce.jpg/P. Ross